Lecture Notes in Computer Science 8028

Commenced Publication in 1973
Founding and Former Series Editors:
Gerhard Goos, Juris Hartmanis, and Jan van Leeuwen

Norbert Streitz   Constantine Stephanidis (Eds.)

Distributed, Ambient, and Pervasive Interactions

First International Conference, DAPI 2013
Held as Part of HCI International 2013
Las Vegas, NV, USA, July 21-26, 2013
Proceedings

 Springer

Volume Editors

Norbert Streitz
Smart Future Initiative
Konrad-Zuse-Str. 43
60438 Frankfurt am Main, Germany
E-mail: norbert.streitz@smart-future.net

Constantine Stephanidis
Foundation for Research and Technology - Hellas (FORTH)
Institute of Computer Science (ICS)
N. Plastira 100, Vassilika Vouton
70013 Heraklion, Crete, Greece
and
University of Crete
Department of Computer Science
70013 Heraklion, Crete, Greece
E-mail: cs@ics.forth.gr

ISSN 0302-9743   e-ISSN 1611-3349
ISBN 978-3-642-39350-1   e-ISBN 978-3-642-39351-8
DOI 10.1007/978-3-642-39351-8
Springer Heidelberg Dordrecht London New York

Library of Congress Control Number: 2013941407

CR Subject Classification (1998): H.5, H.4, J.3, H.1, K.4, H.3, J.1

LNCS Sublibrary: SL 3 – Information Systems and Application,
incl. Internet/Web and HCI

© Springer-Verlag Berlin Heidelberg 2013

Typesetting: Camera-ready by author, data conversion by Scientific Publishing Services, Chennai, India

Printed on acid-free paper

Springer is part of Springer Science+Business Media (www.springer.com)

Foreword

The 15th International Conference on Human–Computer Interaction, HCI International 2013, was held in Las Vegas, Nevada, USA, 21–26 July 2013, incorporating 12 conferences / thematic areas:

Thematic areas:

- Human–Computer Interaction
- Human Interface and the Management of Information

Affiliated conferences:

- 10th International Conference on Engineering Psychology and Cognitive Ergonomics
- 7th International Conference on Universal Access in Human–Computer Interaction
- 5th International Conference on Virtual, Augmented and Mixed Reality
- 5th International Conference on Cross-Cultural Design
- 5th International Conference on Online Communities and Social Computing
- 7th International Conference on Augmented Cognition
- 4th International Conference on Digital Human Modeling and Applications in Health, Safety, Ergonomics and Risk Management
- 2nd International Conference on Design, User Experience and Usability
- 1st International Conference on Distributed, Ambient and Pervasive Interactions
- 1st International Conference on Human Aspects of Information Security, Privacy and Trust

A total of 5210 individuals from academia, research institutes, industry and governmental agencies from 70 countries submitted contributions, and 1666 papers and 303 posters were included in the program. These papers address the latest research and development efforts and highlight the human aspects of design and use of computing systems. The papers accepted for presentation thoroughly cover the entire field of Human–Computer Interaction, addressing major advances in knowledge and effective use of computers in a variety of application areas.

This volume, edited by Norbert Streitz and Constantine Stephanidis, contains papers focusing on the thematic area of Distributed, Ambient and Pervasive Interactions, and addressing the following major topics:

- Natural Interaction
- Context-Awareness in Smart and Intelligent Environments
- Design and Evaluation of Smart and Intelligent Environments
- Smart Cities
- Multi-user, Group and Collaborative Interaction
- Smart Everyday Living and Working Environments

The remaining volumes of the HCI International 2013 proceedings are:

- Volume 1, LNCS 8004, Human–Computer Interaction: Human-Centred Design Approaches, Methods, Tools and Environments (Part I), edited by Masaaki Kurosu
- Volume 2, LNCS 8005, Human–Computer Interaction: Applications and Services (Part II), edited by Masaaki Kurosu
- Volume 3, LNCS 8006, Human–Computer Interaction: Users and Contexts of Use (Part III), edited by Masaaki Kurosu
- Volume 4, LNCS 8007, Human–Computer Interaction: Interaction Modalities and Techniques (Part IV), edited by Masaaki Kurosu
- Volume 5, LNCS 8008, Human–Computer Interaction: Towards Intelligent and Implicit Interaction (Part V), edited by Masaaki Kurosu
- Volume 6, LNCS 8009, Universal Access in Human–Computer Interaction: Design Methods, Tools and Interaction Techniques for eInclusion (Part I), edited by Constantine Stephanidis and Margherita Antona
- Volume 7, LNCS 8010, Universal Access in Human–Computer Interaction: User and Context Diversity (Part II), edited by Constantine Stephanidis and Margherita Antona
- Volume 8, LNCS 8011, Universal Access in Human–Computer Interaction: Applications and Services for Quality of Life (Part III), edited by Constantine Stephanidis and Margherita Antona
- Volume 9, LNCS 8012, Design, User Experience, and Usability: Design Philosophy, Methods and Tools (Part I), edited by Aaron Marcus
- Volume 10, LNCS 8013, Design, User Experience, and Usability: Health, Learning, Playing, Cultural, and Cross-Cultural User Experience (Part II), edited by Aaron Marcus
- Volume 11, LNCS 8014, Design, User Experience, and Usability: User Experience in Novel Technological Environments (Part III), edited by Aaron Marcus
- Volume 12, LNCS 8015, Design, User Experience, and Usability: Web, Mobile and Product Design (Part IV), edited by Aaron Marcus
- Volume 13, LNCS 8016, Human Interface and the Management of Information: Information and Interaction Design (Part I), edited by Sakae Yamamoto
- Volume 14, LNCS 8017, Human Interface and the Management of Information: Information and Interaction for Health, Safety, Mobility and Complex Environments (Part II), edited by Sakae Yamamoto
- Volume 15, LNCS 8018, Human Interface and the Management of Information: Information and Interaction for Learning, Culture, Collaboration and Business (Part III), edited by Sakae Yamamoto
- Volume 16, LNAI 8019, Engineering Psychology and Cognitive Ergonomics: Understanding Human Cognition (Part I), edited by Don Harris
- Volume 17, LNAI 8020, Engineering Psychology and Cognitive Ergonomics: Applications and Services (Part II), edited by Don Harris
- Volume 18, LNCS 8021, Virtual, Augmented and Mixed Reality: Designing and Developing Augmented and Virtual Environments (Part I), edited by Randall Shumaker

- Volume 19, LNCS 8022, Virtual, Augmented and Mixed Reality: Systems and Applications (Part II), edited by Randall Shumaker
- Volume 20, LNCS 8023, Cross-Cultural Design: Methods, Practice and Case Studies (Part I), edited by P.L. Patrick Rau
- Volume 21, LNCS 8024, Cross-Cultural Design: Cultural Differences in Everyday Life (Part II), edited by P.L. Patrick Rau
- Volume 22, LNCS 8025, Digital Human Modeling and Applications in Health, Safety, Ergonomics and Risk Management: Healthcare and Safety of the Environment and Transport (Part I), edited by Vincent G. Duffy
- Volume 23, LNCS 8026, Digital Human Modeling and Applications in Health, Safety, Ergonomics and Risk Management: Human Body Modeling and Ergonomics (Part II), edited by Vincent G. Duffy
- Volume 24, LNAI 8027, Foundations of Augmented Cognition, edited by Dylan D. Schmorrow and Cali M. Fidopiastis
- Volume 26, LNCS 8029, Online Communities and Social Computing, edited by A. Ant Ozok and Panayiotis Zaphiris
- Volume 27, LNCS 8030, Human Aspects of Information Security, Privacy and Trust, edited by Louis Marinos and Ioannis Askoxylakis
- Volume 28, CCIS 373, HCI International 2013 Posters Proceedings (Part I), edited by Constantine Stephanidis
- Volume 29, CCIS 374, HCI International 2013 Posters Proceedings (Part II), edited by Constantine Stephanidis

I would like to thank the Program Chairs and the members of the Program Boards of all affiliated conferences and thematic areas, listed below, for their contribution to the highest scientific quality and the overall success of the HCI International 2013 conference.

This conference could not have been possible without the continuous support and advice of the Founding Chair and Conference Scientific Advisor, Prof. Gavriel Salvendy, as well as the dedicated work and outstanding efforts of the Communications Chair and Editor of HCI International News, Abbas Moallem.

I would also like to thank for their contribution towards the smooth organization of the HCI International 2013 Conference the members of the Human–Computer Interaction Laboratory of ICS-FORTH, and in particular George Paparoulis, Maria Pitsoulaki, Stavroula Ntoa, Maria Bouhli and George Kapnas.

May 2013   Constantine Stephanidis
                                  General Chair, HCI International 2013

Organization

Human–Computer Interaction

Program Chair: Masaaki Kurosu, Japan

Jose Abdelnour-Nocera, UK
Sebastiano Bagnara, Italy
Simone Barbosa, Brazil
Tomas Berns, Sweden
Nigel Bevan, UK
Simone Borsci, UK
Apala Lahiri Chavan, India
Sherry Chen, Taiwan
Kevin Clark, USA
Torkil Clemmensen, Denmark
Xiaowen Fang, USA
Shin'ichi Fukuzumi, Japan
Vicki Hanson, UK
Ayako Hashizume, Japan
Anzai Hiroyuki, Italy
Sheue-Ling Hwang, Taiwan
Wonil Hwang, South Korea
Minna Isomursu, Finland
Yong Gu Ji, South Korea
Esther Jun, USA
Mitsuhiko Karashima, Japan

Kyungdoh Kim, South Korea
Heidi Krömker, Germany
Chen Ling, USA
Yan Liu, USA
Zhengjie Liu, P.R. China
Loïc Martínez Normand, Spain
Chang S. Nam, USA
Naoko Okuizumi, Japan
Noriko Osaka, Japan
Philippe Palanque, France
Hans Persson, Sweden
Ling Rothrock, USA
Naoki Sakakibara, Japan
Dominique Scapin, France
Guangfeng Song, USA
Sanjay Tripathi, India
Chui Yin Wong, Malaysia
Toshiki Yamaoka, Japan
Kazuhiko Yamazaki, Japan
Ryoji Yoshitake, Japan
Silvia Zimmermann, Switzerland

Human Interface and the Management of Information

Program Chair: Sakae Yamamoto, Japan

Hans-Jorg Bullinger, Germany
Alan Chan, Hong Kong
Gilsoo Cho, South Korea
Jon R. Gunderson, USA
Shin'ichi Fukuzumi, Japan
Michitaka Hirose, Japan
Jhilmil Jain, USA
Yasufumi Kume, Japan

Mark Lehto, USA
Hiroyuki Miki, Japan
Hirohiko Mori, Japan
Fiona Fui-Hoon Nah, USA
Shogo Nishida, Japan
Robert Proctor, USA
Youngho Rhee, South Korea
Katsunori Shimohara, Japan

Michale Smith, USA
Tsutomu Tabe, Japan
Hiroshi Tsuji, Japan

Kim-Phuong Vu, USA
Tomio Watanabe, Japan
Hidekazu Yoshikawa, Japan

Engineering Psychology and Cognitive Ergonomics

Program Chair: Don Harris, UK

Guy Andre Boy, USA
Joakim Dahlman, Sweden
Trevor Dobbins, UK
Mike Feary, USA
Shan Fu, P.R. China
Michaela Heese, Austria
Hung-Sying Jing, Taiwan
Wen-Chin Li, Taiwan
Mark A. Neerincx, The Netherlands
Jan M. Noyes, UK
Taezoon Park, Singapore

Paul Salmon, Australia
Axel Schulte, Germany
Siraj Shaikh, UK
Sarah C. Sharples, UK
Anthony Smoker, UK
Neville A. Stanton, UK
Alex Stedmon, UK
Xianghong Sun, P.R. China
Andrew Thatcher, South Africa
Matthew J.W. Thomas, Australia
Rolf Zon, The Netherlands

Universal Access in Human–Computer Interaction

Program Chairs: Constantine Stephanidis, Greece, and Margherita Antona, Greece

Julio Abascal, Spain
Ray Adams, UK
Gisela Susanne Bahr, USA
Margit Betke, USA
Christian Bühler, Germany
Stefan Carmien, Spain
Jerzy Charytonowicz, Poland
Carlos Duarte, Portugal
Pier Luigi Emiliani, Italy
Qin Gao, P.R. China
Andrina Granić, Croatia
Andreas Holzinger, Austria
Josette Jones, USA
Simeon Keates, UK

Georgios Kouroupetroglou, Greece
Patrick Langdon, UK
Seongil Lee, Korea
Ana Isabel B.B. Paraguay, Brazil
Helen Petrie, UK
Michael Pieper, Germany
Enrico Pontelli, USA
Jaime Sanchez, Chile
Anthony Savidis, Greece
Christian Stary, Austria
Hirotada Ueda, Japan
Gerhard Weber, Germany
Harald Weber, Germany

Virtual, Augmented and Mixed Reality

Program Chair: Randall Shumaker, USA

Waymon Armstrong, USA
Juan Cendan, USA
Rudy Darken, USA
Cali M. Fidopiastis, USA
Charles Hughes, USA
David Kaber, USA
Hirokazu Kato, Japan
Denis Laurendeau, Canada
Fotis Liarokapis, UK

Mark Livingston, USA
Michael Macedonia, USA
Gordon Mair, UK
Jose San Martin, Spain
Jacquelyn Morie, USA
Albert "Skip" Rizzo, USA
Kay Stanney, USA
Christopher Stapleton, USA
Gregory Welch, USA

Cross-Cultural Design

Program Chair: P.L. Patrick Rau, P.R. China

Pilsung Choe, P.R. China
Henry Been-Lirn Duh, Singapore
Vanessa Evers, The Netherlands
Paul Fu, USA
Zhiyong Fu, P.R. China
Fu Guo, P.R. China
Sung H. Han, Korea
Toshikazu Kato, Japan
Dyi-Yih Michael Lin, Taiwan
Rungtai Lin, Taiwan

Sheau-Farn Max Liang, Taiwan
Liang Ma, P.R. China
Alexander Mädche, Germany
Katsuhiko Ogawa, Japan
Tom Plocher, USA
Kerstin Röse, Germany
Supriya Singh, Australia
Hsiu-Ping Yueh, Taiwan
Liang (Leon) Zeng, USA
Chen Zhao, USA

Online Communities and Social Computing

Program Chairs: A. Ant Ozok, USA, and Panayiotis Zaphiris, Cyprus

Areej Al-Wabil, Saudi Arabia
Leonelo Almeida, Brazil
Bjørn Andersen, Norway
Chee Siang Ang, UK
Aneesha Bakharia, Australia
Ania Bobrowicz, UK
Paul Cairns, UK
Farzin Deravi, UK
Andri Ioannou, Cyprus
Slava Kisilevich, Germany

Niki Lambropoulos, Greece
Effie Law, Switzerland
Soo Ling Lim, UK
Fernando Loizides, Cyprus
Gabriele Meiselwitz, USA
Anthony Norcio, USA
Elaine Raybourn, USA
Panote Siriaraya, UK
David Stuart, UK
June Wei, USA

Augmented Cognition

Program Chairs: Dylan D. Schmorrow, USA, and Cali M. Fidopiastis, USA

Robert Arrabito, Canada
Richard Backs, USA
Chris Berka, USA
Joseph Cohn, USA
Martha E. Crosby, USA
Julie Drexler, USA
Ivy Estabrooke, USA
Chris Forsythe, USA
Wai Tat Fu, USA
Rodolphe Gentili, USA
Marc Grootjen, The Netherlands
Jefferson Grubb, USA
Ming Hou, Canada

Santosh Mathan, USA
Rob Matthews, Australia
Dennis McBride, USA
Jeff Morrison, USA
Mark A. Neerincx, The Netherlands
Denise Nicholson, USA
Banu Onaral, USA
Lee Sciarini, USA
Kay Stanney, USA
Roy Stripling, USA
Rob Taylor, UK
Karl van Orden, USA

Digital Human Modeling and Applications in Health, Safety, Ergonomics and Risk Management

Program Chair: Vincent G. Duffy, USA and Russia

Karim Abdel-Malek, USA
Giuseppe Andreoni, Italy
Daniel Carruth, USA
Eliza Yingzi Du, USA
Enda Fallon, Ireland
Afzal Godil, USA
Ravindra Goonetilleke, Hong Kong
Bo Hoege, Germany
Waldemar Karwowski, USA
Zhizhong Li, P.R. China

Kang Li, USA
Tim Marler, USA
Michelle Robertson, USA
Matthias Rötting, Germany
Peter Vink, The Netherlands
Mao-Jiun Wang, Taiwan
Xuguang Wang, France
Jingzhou (James) Yang, USA
Xiugan Yuan, P.R. China
Gülcin Yücel Hoge, Germany

Design, User Experience, and Usability

Program Chair: Aaron Marcus, USA

Sisira Adikari, Australia
Ronald Baecker, Canada
Arne Berger, Germany
Jamie Blustein, Canada

Ana Boa-Ventura, USA
Jan Brejcha, Czech Republic
Lorenzo Cantoni, Switzerland
Maximilian Eibl, Germany

Anthony Faiola, USA
Emilie Gould, USA
Zelda Harrison, USA
Rüdiger Heimgärtner, Germany
Brigitte Herrmann, Germany
Steffen Hess, Germany
Kaleem Khan, Canada

Jennifer McGinn, USA
Francisco Rebelo, Portugal
Michael Renner, Switzerland
Kerem Rızvanoğlu, Turkey
Marcelo Soares, Brazil
Christian Sturm, Germany
Michele Visciola, Italy

Distributed, Ambient and Pervasive Interactions

Program Chairs: Norbert Streitz, Germany, and Constantine Stephanidis, Greece

Emile Aarts, The Netherlands
Adnan Abu-Dayya, Qatar
Juan Carlos Augusto, UK
Boris de Ruyter, The Netherlands
Anind Dey, USA
Dimitris Grammenos, Greece
Nuno M. Guimaraes, Portugal
Shin'ichi Konomi, Japan
Carsten Magerkurth, Switzerland

Christian Müller-Tomfelde, Australia
Fabio Paternó, Italy
Gilles Privat, France
Harald Reiterer, Germany
Carsten Röcker, Germany
Reiner Wichert, Germany
Woontack Woo, South Korea
Xenophon Zabulis, Greece

Human Aspects of Information Security, Privacy and Trust

Program Chairs: Louis Marinos, ENISA EU, and Ioannis Askoxylakis, Greece

Claudio Agostino Ardagna, Italy
Zinaida Benenson, Germany
Daniele Catteddu, Italy
Raoul Chiesa, Italy
Bryan Cline, USA
Sadie Creese, UK
Jorge Cuellar, Germany
Marc Dacier, USA
Dieter Gollmann, Germany
Kirstie Hawkey, Canada
Jaap-Henk Hoepman, The Netherlands
Cagatay Karabat, Turkey
Angelos Keromytis, USA
Ayako Komatsu, Japan

Ronald Leenes, The Netherlands
Javier Lopez, Spain
Steve Marsh, Canada
Gregorio Martinez, Spain
Emilio Mordini, Italy
Yuko Murayama, Japan
Masakatsu Nishigaki, Japan
Aljosa Pasic, Spain
Milan Petković, The Netherlands
Joachim Posegga, Germany
Jean-Jacques Quisquater, Belgium
Damien Sauveron, France
George Spanoudakis, UK
Kerry-Lynn Thomson, South Africa

Julien Touzeau, France
Theo Tryfonas, UK
João Vilela, Portugal

Claire Vishik, UK
Melanie Volkamer, Germany

External Reviewers

Maysoon Abulkhair, Saudi Arabia
Ilia Adami, Greece
Vishal Barot, UK
Stephan Böhm, Germany
Vassilis Charissis, UK
Francisco Cipolla-Ficarra, Spain
Maria De Marsico, Italy
Marc Fabri, UK
David Fonseca, Spain
Linda Harley, USA
Yasushi Ikei, Japan
Wei Ji, USA
Nouf Khashman, Canada
John Killilea, USA
Iosif Klironomos, Greece
Ute Klotz, Switzerland
Maria Korozi, Greece
Kentaro Kotani, Japan

Vassilis Kouroumalis, Greece
Stephanie Lackey, USA
Janelle LaMarche, USA
Asterios Leonidis, Greece
Nickolas Macchiarella, USA
George Margetis, Greece
Matthew Marraffino, USA
Joseph Mercado, USA
Claudia Mont'Alvão, Brazil
Yoichi Motomura, Japan
Karsten Nebe, Germany
Stavroula Ntoa, Greece
Martin Osen, Austria
Stephen Prior, UK
Farid Shirazi, Canada
Jan Stelovsky, USA
Sarah Swierenga, USA

HCI International 2014

The 16th International Conference on Human–Computer Interaction, HCI International 2014, will be held jointly with the affiliated conferences in the summer of 2014. It will cover a broad spectrum of themes related to Human–Computer Interaction, including theoretical issues, methods, tools, processes and case studies in HCI design, as well as novel interaction techniques, interfaces and applications. The proceedings will be published by Springer. More information about the topics, as well as the venue and dates of the conference, will be announced through the HCI International Conference series website: http://www.hci-international.org/

General Chair
Professor Constantine Stephanidis
University of Crete and ICS-FORTH
Heraklion, Crete, Greece
Email: cs@ics.forth.gr

Table of Contents

Natural Interaction

Context-Awareness in Smart and Intelligent Environments

Design and Evaluation of Smart and Intelligent Environments

Smart Cities

Multi-user, Group and Collaborative Interaction

Smart Everyday Living and Working Environments

Part I
Natural Interaction

Comparative Evaluation among Diverse Interaction Techniques in Three Dimensional Environments

Giannis Drossis[1,2], Dimitris Grammenos[1], Maria Bouhli[1], Ilia Adami[1], and Constantine Stephanidis[1,2]

[1] Foundation for Research and Technology - Hellas (FORTH), Institute of Computer Science
N. Plastira 100, Vassilika Vouton, GR-70013, Heraklion, Crete, Greece
[2] University of Crete, Computer Science Department, Heraklion, Crete, Greece
{drossis,gramenos,bouhli,iadami,cs}@ics.forth.gr

Abstract. This paper reports on the results of a user-based evaluation that was conducted on a 3D virtual environment that supports diverse interaction techniques. More specifically, the interaction techniques that were evaluated were touch, gestures (hands and legs) and the use of a smart object. The goal of the experiment was to assess the effectiveness of each interaction modes as a means for the user to complete common tasks within the application. A comparison is attempted in order to provide an insight to the suitability of each technique and direct future research in the area.

Keywords: multimodal interaction, 3D user interfaces, gestural interaction, usability evaluation, comparative evaluation.

1   Introduction

In recent years a lot of scientific effort has been placed in the development of multimodal interaction techniques which allow users to interact with systems in non-traditional ways. Such techniques have shown promise in enhancing the user experience by allowing more natural interaction between the user and the system. The different interaction approaches often seen, apply dissimilar practices including wearable equipment such as head mounted displays, non-instrumented user tracking using cameras, tangible artifacts and desktop-based interaction.

This paper aims to assess and compare diverse modes of interaction in the demanding area of 3D environments [2], where the six degrees of freedom constitute an additional impediment as it requires extended interaction vocabulary, in order to provide an insight on the pros and cons of each approach. The means of interaction to be evaluated were selected bearing in mind the extent to which they are both affordable and natural to the users. In this direction, desktop interaction using a touch screen was chosen as a widely adopted and intuitive solution, enhanced with a tangible object (SmartBox) that complements navigation in 3D spaces. Furthermore, gestural and kinesthetic interaction is applied as a more natural expression beyond the limits of computer systems.

N. Streitz and C. Stephanidis (Eds.): DAPI/HCII 2013, LNCS 8028, pp. 3–12, 2013.

2   Background and Related Work

Jaimes et al. [6] define a multimodal system as a system that "responds to inputs in more than one modality or communication channel, such as speech, gesture, writing and others". Multimodal user interfaces support interaction techniques which may be used sequentially or concurrently, and independently or combined synergistically. According to Oviatt [11], "Multimodal interfaces process two or more combined user input modes (such as speech, pen, touch, manual gesture, gaze, and head and body movements) in a coordinated manner with multimedia system output".

Gesturing is a common approach which has been proven to be very intuitive to users and is widely used in literature [5, 8 and 17]. Gestures can be defined as a form of non-verbal communication in which visible body actions communicate particular messages. Hand gestures can be used to augment systems and allow additional interactions when combined with other means of interaction such as simple touch [14]. Gestures may not be limited to multi-touch and hands, but may be applied to feet as well: foot-based gestures are proposed by [1, 5 and 12] as an alternative interaction mechanism. Valkov et al. [16] use foot gestures to expand simple multi-touch interaction and boost navigation in dynamic and complex 3D Virtual Environments.

Body movement indicates the pose of a user's body as mentioned by Jaimes et al. [6], which can be tracked and applied for selective interaction with the environment, where the system may interpret a specific body pose in order to enable interaction in a specific manner. Papadopoulos et al. [13] use defined body poses recognition in order to allow navigation in 3d environments. According to their approach, whenever a user poses in a certain way, manipulation of a camera in a virtual 3d environment begins. Grammenos et al. [4] use the users' positions to visualize information according to the location of any user inside a room: each user can choose a topic by moving to the side and explore different information details by moving forward and backwards.

Finally, smart artifacts deliver natural, tangible interaction using predefined actions (e.g., pressure) through their embedded technology. For instance, accelerometers and magnetometers are used by [7, 15] in order to detect the orientation of items.

3   System Overview

3.1   System Design

The system the users assessed involves 3D interactive information visualization in the form of a timeline presented in two distinct views. The first view involved information visualization in the form of events placed on a two dimensional plane with time (expressed in periods) extending on the horizontal axis [Fig. 1, left]. The second view presented the same information complementarily, using the metaphor of a time tunnel, where time extends along the tunnel length. The events included multimedia information including text, images, videos and 3D models. Furthermore, the system provided the separation of events in categories as a filtration mechanism. The individual components of the timeline (such as its title and the available categories) held the same appearance in both views for consistency.

The first view of the timeline aimed to provide an overview of the events displayed and offer the perception of each event's context in a straightforward manner. Each event is hosted inside a box initially displaying its title and time of occurrence. Upon selection, the event is scaled up and brought to the center of the display, while its box is transformed to host additional information at its sides [Fig 1, right]. The item displayed inside the box for detailed examination, according to its type (e.g. a video may be played and a 3D model may be rotated). Finally, when filters are applied through categories, the events are dimmed to indicate the fact that they are not available for interaction.

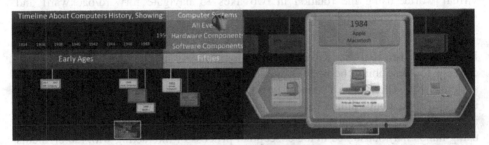

Fig. 1. The first view of the 3D timeline

The timeline's tunnel view (Fig 2) aims to provide an immersive view and focused on the sequential and exhaustive exploration of the presented information. The periods are hosted on the tunnel's roof sides while the events are placed on the floor. Aside each event the tunnel contains a "cavity" with a glass showcase, displaying a representative item that provides a visual clue. The showcase has a handle which the users may drag outwards to extend it, providing space to display additional multimedia content. The showcase may be again collapsed by dragging the hand inwards.

Fig. 2. The tunnel view

3.2 Interaction Methods

Touch Screen. Touch interaction involves the procedure of the user touching a point on the screen and the system projecting it to the virtual world. The available actions that the users may perform include clicking, dwelling upon an item and dragging.

Clicking or dwelling upon an item is translated by the system as a selection, whereas dragging serves a dual purpose: in the case where the user starts dragging an item, the action is interpreted as scrolling it in the corresponding direction, whereas if not, the system translates it as an intention to navigate in the virtual world.

Tangible Interaction. Another field of multimodal interaction is the application of tangible means using smart objects. In order to experiment with such items, a box was created, equipped with a 3-axes accelerometer which has the ability to transmit its orientation wirelessly. The smart box was employed as a joystick to navigate in the virtual world, using the rotation in two axes to navigate forward/backward and left/right. Additionally, the box was used for the rotation of the 3D models.

Kinesthetic Interaction. Kinesthetic interaction may be thought as "a unifying concept for describing the body in motion as a foundation for designing interactive systems" [3]. The types of kinesthetic interaction that this paper addresses include user's position, controlling a virtual cursor, hand and leg gesturing. Leg gesturing and moving in space cover the need for spatial navigation in the virtual 3D world, whereas using hands may subsumed in the conceptual process of interacting with the elements displayed. The users may extend their hand towards the display in order to interact with the system. The movement of the hand is tracked and the user controls the virtual cursor while the hand is raised allowing the selection of visualized elements by placing it over an item for a short duration.

Hand gesturing was also applied as an additional technique that suits better tasks such as scrolling through successive elements (e.g. the elements comprising an event's information). Furthermore, both hands are used in combination to simulate the process of pulling an item near or pushing it away in a natural and human-centric manner. The gestures may additionally involve continuous gestures that cause the system to respond while the users perform them. Such an example is the gesture for rotating the camera around the vertical axis of the virtual 3D world, which in the proposed system turns to the side while the users have their hand raised in the analogous direction (left/right). Leg gestures are applied by stepping towards any direction (right, left, up and down). Stepping is also continuous and causes the user (i.e. the virtual camera in the 3D world) to move towards the specified direction.

The interaction techniques used for the manipulation of the system should be robust and tolerant to possible user behavior that does not match the exact system specifications: the system should be able to prevent reacting in such a way that may be unexpected by the user, even at the cost of providing reduced yet sufficient functionality. Thus, the system adopts the concept of the user being able only to make a left swipe gesture with the right hand and a right swipe with the left hand.

4   Evaluation

The goal of the evaluation process was twofold. One the one hand, it aimed at assessing whether the users were more successful in using one interaction mode versus the other while trying to complete common tasks. On the other hand, it aimed at assessing the overall user experience of using each interaction mode. For the purpose of the first goal, Jakob Nielsen's User Success Rate method [10] was used. This method is good for comparison analysis and it is a simple yet effective way to estimate how successful the users were in using the system. For this method, the users were given a series of tasks to complete and each task was then marked as "Success" if the user was able to complete it in the first or second trial without asking for assistance, "Partial Success" if the user managed to complete the task after the third trial or after receiving minimum assistance by the facilitator, and as "Failure" if it took more than 3 trials to complete the task or if the user needed a lot of assistance in completing it. A simple formula was then used to calculate the Total Success Rate of the system. In order to assess the overall usability and user experience, the Think-Aloud process [9] was used during the evaluation, in which the participants were requested to express verbally their thoughts, comments, suggestions, and opinions throughout the completion of each task. In addition, at the end of the evaluation each user was asked to fill out a Likert scale based questionnaires for each interaction mode. The qualitative analysis has been presented in another paper [2]. This paper focuses more on the comparison of the user success rates of the two interaction modes.

Given that users were already familiar with touch screen technology and not so much with gestural interaction, it was expected that the touch screen interaction would show a higher user success rate than the gestures. Indeed, the quantitative results showed a slightly higher user success rate for the touch screen interaction than the gestural interaction, however, upon further examination of the qualitative data, the slight difference was found to have been caused by an interface design issue and not because of the interaction mode. These results are analyzed in more detail in the sections that follow.

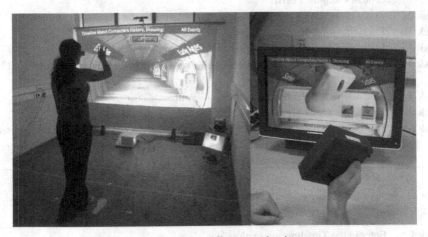

Fig. 3. The setups of the different evaluation segments

4.1 The Evaluation Process

A total of 16 volunteers participated in the evaluation, 7 females and 9 males from 20 to 40 years old. Twelve of the users (75%) had intermediate or high computer expertise whereas the other participants had limited expertise. Even though the majority of the users were familiar with computers and touch screen systems, they had very little to no experience in interacting with a system with gesturing. Two different evaluation set-ups were used (see Fig. 3 above) in the experiment. The first set-up was in a regular office room where the user would sit in front of a touch screen system and the second set-up was in a room where the application was projected on the wall and the user would stand in front of it and interact with hand and leg gestures (using Microsoft's Kinect). To eliminate bias towards either interaction method, the experiment was divided into two rounds and the users into two groups, where the first group started the interaction with the touch screen first in the office set-up and then with the kinesthetic interaction mode in the second set-up, while the second group started with the kinesthetic interaction first and then with the touch screen in the first set-up. The tasks of the second round were slightly different than the first round since the users already knew some of the answers from their first round of exposure to the application (see Tables 1 and 2).

Table 1. User Tasks performed either with the use of the touch screen or with hand and leg gestures

Task 1a	Navigate in the Timeline
Task 1b	Find how many decades are depicted in the Timeline
Task 1c	Find how many events are covered in the 1960s
Task 1d	Tell us which category of content you are currently viewing and how many other content categories exist
Task 2a	Zoom in the 1980s and find information relating to the Macintosh system
Task 2b	Find what kind of content is available for the above event
Task 3a	Find and select the photo "Another view of Apple Macintosh"
Task 3b	Open the photo and zoom in enough to read the name of the person depicted in the photo
Task 4	Find any video file, open it and play its content
Task 5	Find a file with a 3D model and explore it
Task 6	Use the SmartBox to interact with the same 3D model (the group that started with the gestures they were asked to interact with the model with hand gestures instead of the Smart Box in this particular task).

Table 2. User Tasks performed with the interaction mode that was not used in the previous round

Task 1	Enter in the Timeline and explore it
Task 2	Zoom in the 1960s and find information in relation to the first mouse device. What kind of content is available?
Task 3	Select one of the available photos and zoom in the face of the person depicted in it

Table 2. *(Continued)*

Task 4	Find a video file and play its content
Task 5	Zoom in the 1980s and find information relating to the Macintosh system
Task 6	Find what kind of content is available for the above event
Task 3a	Find and select the photo "Another view of Apple Macintosh"
Task 3b	Open the photo and zoom in enough to read the name of the person depicted in the photo
Task 4	Find any video file, open it and play its content
Task 5	Find a file with a 3D model and explore it
Task 6	Navigate to a different decade (either with the SmartBox or with leg gestures)

4.2 Result Analysis

User Success Rate. In the first round of the evaluation, the first group of users completed 11 tasks using the touch screen while the second group of users performed the same 11 tasks but with gestures. From this round of evaluation, the User Success Rate of the touch screen interaction was 89% and the User Success Rate of the gestural interaction was 82% (see fig. 4 and 5). In the second round the users from the first group performed similar tasks, but with gestures this time and the users from the second group performed these same tasks with the touch screen. This way both groups performed the same tasks using both interaction modes. The User Success Rate for the touch screen of the second round was 93,5% and the User Success Rate for the gestural interaction mode was 91% (see fig 6 and 7). As the results show both interaction modes produced higher User Success Rates in the second round of the experiment, but this was expected since the users were now more familiar with the interface and the system itself.

Combining the User Success Rates for each interaction mode from both rounds of the experiments produced a final **Total User Success Rate of 91%** for the touch screen interaction mode and a final **Total User Success Rate of 86%** for the gestural interaction mode.

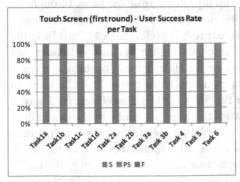
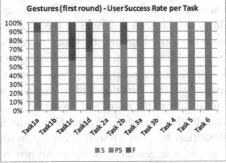

Fig. 4. Touch Screen User Success Rate per Task (first round)

Fig. 5. Gestures User Success Rate per Task (first round)

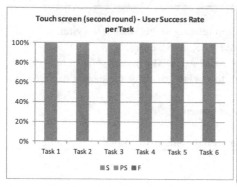
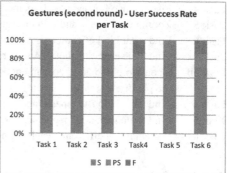

Fig. 6. Touch Screen User Success Rate per Task (second round)

Fig. 7. Gestures User Success Rate per Task (second round)

Both interaction modes received a very high user success rate, which proves that they were effective and efficient methods for interacting with the system. The high user success rates were also supported by the qualitative analysis of the observations and the Think Aloud process. From the observations during the experiment, it was shown that the majority of the users understood quickly the Timeline concept and how the information was structured in it and thus the users didn't exhibit any instances of feeling lost in the application either in the 2D representation or the 3D Tunnel representation of the Timeline.

Touchscreen Interaction and Tangible Smart Box. In the touch screen interaction mode, the users instantly knew how to perform most of the functions such as zooming in and out, dragging, scrolling, and selecting an object without receiving any particular instructions from the facilitator. The touch screen gestures used in the application seemed to fit the mental model of the users that had extensive touch screen experience. One of the main comments that came up repeatedly from the users through the evaluations was the lack of multi-touch capabilities, which a lot of the users suggested adding it as a feature. Some of the users also expressed preference of controlling the zoom level by dragging the slider instead of just pressing the (+) and (-) buttons and iterating through multimedia content by dragging the slider instead of just the content elements. The SmartBox that was used as a complimentary method for the users to navigate in the Timeline and to manipulate the 3D model in Task 6 received mixed reactions from the users and produced a few Partial Success results in the evaluation. Overall, the use of the Smart Object as a complimentary way of the touch screen interaction was not as well accepted by the users, who found that having to switch from touch screen mode to the smart box was adding unnecessary burden to the user's interaction experience. Furthermore, users commented on the need for a direct one-to-one representation of the virtual model with the Smart Box, which is not currently supported.

Kinesthetic Interaction (hand/legs Gestures). The users also didn't exhibit any serious problems in interacting with the application with hand and leg gestures even though they were much less familiar with this interaction mode than with the touch screen. The supported gestures were easy for them to use and representative of the function they supported. Additionally, the segmentation of the interaction process into two distinct categories (leg gesturing for navigation in the 3D Tunnel representation, hand gestures and the virtual cursor for interaction with the visualized elements) provided a straightforward conceptual model of how to interact with the system for them. Tasks 1c and 1d were the tasks that caused the most failures in the kinesthetic interaction mode, but that was more due to a design and display issue, than a problem of the interaction mode itself. Some of the graphics of the design did not stand out as much in the second set-up with the projection on the wall and were thus missed by the users that started the evaluation in that set-up. A few of the users suggested that the movement required for some of the gestures such as pulling or pushing items using both hands, should be shorter in order to eliminate the fatigue factor setting in after prolonged interaction with the system. Leg gesturing was almost unanimously accepted as a complimentary way of navigating through the 3D Tunnel model of the application and only one user could not navigate using his legs because Kinect failed to successfully recognize the exact placement of his legs due to the trousers the user was wearing. The combination of stepping in any direction in order to travel in space and interacting with the system elements using the hands proved a powerful method which well received by the users. This observation is more evident in the non-expert users, who supported the leg gestures even more than the expert users, as they felt more comfortable with handling the system naturally, but in a strictly defined manner. Overall, the participants found the conceptual model of moving in the space to be efficient, tireless and fascinating.

5   Conclusions

The selection of the appropriate interaction technique relies on the purpose of each system and the context in which it is designed to be used. Touch interaction proved to provide a complete and thorough set of instructions to manipulate 3D environments, suitable mainly for everyday use. Tangible artifacts received mixed reactions and their usefulness was questioned mainly due to their inability to fully handle a complex environment in terms of both navigation and object selection. Remote system handling through non-instrumented user tracking provided rich interaction vocabulary, which the users are able to successfully memorize and use in combination. The fun factor of expressing themselves by making human-like movements overruled the tiredness that appeared after extensive use, making kinematic interaction suitable for setups which involve entertainment rather than serious work.

Acknowledgements. The work reported in this paper has been conducted in the context of the AmI Programme of the Institute of Computer Science of the Foundation for Research and Technology-Hellas (FORTH).

References

1. Alexander, J., Han, T., Judd, W., Irani, P., Subramanian, S.: Putting your best foot forward: investigating real-world mappings for foot-based gestures. In: Proceedings of the 2012 ACM Annual Conference on Human Factors in Computing Systems, pp. 1229–1238. ACM (May 2012)
2. Drossis, G., Grammenos, D., Adami, I., Stephanidis, C.: To appear in INTERACT 2013. Springer (2013)
3. Fogtmann, M.H., Fritsch, J., Kortbek, K.J.: Kinesthetic interaction: revealing the bodily potential in interaction design. In: Proceedings of the 20th Australasian Conference on Computer-Human Interaction: Designing for Habitus and Habitat, pp. 89–96. ACM (December 2008)
4. Grammenos, D., Zabulis, X., Michel, D., Sarmis, T., Tzavanidis, K., Argyros, A., Stephanidis, C.: Design and Development of Four Prototype Interactive Edutainment Exhibits for Museums (2011)
5. Hilliges, O., Izadi, S., Wilson, A., Hodges, S., Mendozam, A.G., Butz, A.: Interactions in the air: adding further depth to interactive tabletop. In: Proc. UIST 2009, pp. 139–148. ACM (2009)
6. Jaimes, A., Sebe, N.: Multimodal human–computer interaction: A survey. Journal Computer Vision and Image Understanding Archive 108(1-2), 116–134 (2007)
7. Molyneaux, D., Gellersen, H.: Projected interfaces: enabling serendipitous interaction with smart tangible objects. In: Proc. TEI 2009, pp. 385–392. ACM (2009)
8. Nickel, K., Stiefelhagen, R.: Pointing Gesture Recognition based on 3D-Tracking of Face, Hands and Head Orientation. In: Proc. ICMI 2003, pp. 140–146. ACM (2003)
9. Nielsen, J.: Evaluating the thinking-aloud technique for use by computer scientists (1992)
10. Nielsen, J.: Success Rate: The Simplest Usability Metric (2001), http://www.nngroup.com/articles/success-rate-the-simplest-usability-metric/
11. Oviatt, S.L.: Advances in Robust Multimodal Interface Design (2003)
12. Pakkanen, T., Raisamo, R.: Appropriateness of foot interaction for non-accurate spatial tasks. In: CHI 2004 Extended Abstracts on Human Factors in Computing Systems, pp. 1123–1126. ACM (April 2004)
13. Papadopoulos, C., Sugarman, D., Kaufmant, A.: NuNav3D: A Touch-less, Body-driven Interface for 3D Navigation (39) (2012)
14. Sangsuriyachot, N., Mi, H., Sugimoto, M.: Novel Interaction Techniques by Combining Hand and Foot Gestures on Tabletop Environments. In: Proc. ITS 2011, pp. 268–269. ACM (2011)
15. Terrenghi, L., Kranz, M., Holleis, P., Schmidt, A.: A cube to learn: a tangible user interface for the design of a learning appliance. Journal Personal and Ubiquitous Computing Archive 10(2-3), 153–158 (2005)
16. Valkov, D., Steinicke, F., Bruder, B., Hinrichs, K.: Traveling in 3D Virtual Environments with foot gestures and a multitouch enabled World In Miniature (2010)
17. Yoo, B., Han, J.J., Choi, C., Ryu, H.S., Park, D.S., Kim, C.Y.: 3D remote interface for smart displays. In: Proceedings of the 2011 Annual Conference Extended Abstracts on Human Factors in Computing Systems, pp. 551–560. ACM (May 2011)

Understanding the Influence of Viewpoint and Image Geometry in Linear Perspective Paintings to Enhance Embodied Interaction

Franziska Hannß and Rainer Groh

Chair of Media Design, Faculty of Computer Science, Technische Universität Dresden,
Nöthnitzer Straße 46, 01062 Dresden, Germany
{franziska.hannss,rainer.groh}@tu-dresden.de

Abstract. Museums are attracted by new technologies, for example tracking systems and multitouch displays. They try to include them into their concepts, to expand the access to the artifacts. The intention of this work appears out of the image geometry of a linear perspective painting. We assume that the position of the perspective painting on the wall should depend on the observer's viewpoint. To prove this hypothesis we undertook an experiment with 20 participants and four perspective paintings. We detected a relevant connection between observer and the image geometry of the painting. Accordingly the observer, the room in front of the painting and the image itself are related together. Therefor this relation of the parameters is part of the research field of embodied interaction.

Keywords: body, movement, embodied interaction, image geometry, perspective paintings, interactive environments.

1 Introduction

Over the past years the research field of human computer interaction (HCI) has considered the role of body movement [1 - 5]. Our aim is to identify parameter for HCI research. The term observer movement is used as a synonym for walking in front of the image. We want to take an approach on integrating this movement in the social environment museum – a panel-painting exhibition. The International Council of Museums defines the term museum as "a non-profit, permanent institution in the service of society and its development, open to the public, which acquires, conserves, researches, communicates and exhibits the tangible and intangible heritage of humanity and its environment for the purposes of education, study and enjoyment" [6]. To support this task the audience has to be considered by the conception of an exhibition.

With the rediscovery of the perspective in the 15th century, the artist takes the observer in consideration [7]. The creation process includes the construction of the perspective system – the image geometry. The relation between observer and image operates in both directions. This viewpoint describes the place, where the depiction

N. Streitz and C. Stephanidis (Eds.): DAPI/HCII 2013, LNCS 8028, pp. 13–21, 2013.

seems to look coherent [11]. Therefore the observer seeks this point while viewing at the painting. This search intends to match the image geometry with the environment geometry of the observer. The image geometry is explained in the part below.

Beside an historical excursion the next section introduce contemporary research in the field of body movement in human computer interaction. Afterwards we present the experiment with the evaluated parameters. The interpretation of the collected date takes place in the followed section. The next section discusses the choice of the observer position. The conclusion and an introduction of future work complete this paper.

In 1435/36, Leon Battista Alberti wrote his "della pittura" (on painting). This treaty about "the technical principles of linear perspective" [9] summarizes the knowledge of perspective geometry of the 15th century [7]. It is the "first written account of a method of constructing pictures in correct perspective" [7]. Alberti characterizes how to draw a picture of a chequerboard floor. The conformity of this chequerboard enables the usage as a reference grid. This grid is used to proportion other items in the picture [10].

Based on the knowledge about linear perspective, optics and the observation of pictures, Alberti concludes, that its' a natural habit of the observer to seek the viewpoint while observing the picture [11] (see Fig. 1).

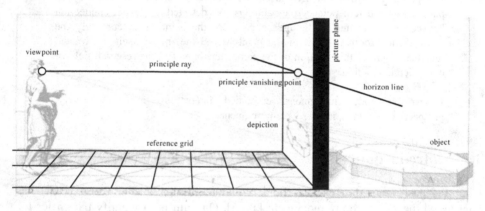

Fig. 1. Giacomo Barozzi da Vignola: Depiction out of "Two rules of practical perspective" [8] with denotations by the author

Fig. 1 describes the image geometry. The picture plane includes the principle vanishing point as the center of the construction. The horizon line and the principle ray cross in this point. Opposite of the principle vanishing point lays the viewpoint. These two points set the distance of the observer to the picture plane. The object is projected as the image on the picture plane. The outcome of this construction is the relation between observer viewpoint and image geometry.

An artist chooses the location of the principle vanishing point of a perspective construction at the beginning of his work. In contrast, the camera used by photographers always defines the location of this vanishing point in the center of the image. Due to the ubiquity of photographic images, observers are used to view images from a centered position to get the best impression [11]. Our experiment investigates if this habit can be influenced when viewing paintings with an off-centered principle vanishing point. If this is the case, the image geometry motivates the observer to move laterally in front of the image.

Contemporary research in interaction design integrates a "wide scope of systems relying on embodies interaction, body movement, tangible manipulation, and physical embodiment of date, being embedded in real space and digitally augmenting physical space" [2]. People have skills and experience to manipulate objects in the physical environment. By designing (tangible) user interfaces it is necessary to understand and translate these common skills [12]. In our case we expand Ishiis' statement out of the tangibility into the physicality of the body.

Hornecker confirms this idea by pointing out that the "physicality of our bodies is tightly linked with our experience of the physicality of our surroundings" [2]. Physicality is a parameter for interactive applications. With this parameter a new ranges of research emerge, for example "design for bodily experience [and] for the moving and feeling body" [2]. Movement and perception are linked together. In this case the design of interaction integrates the enclosed space – the spatiality [2].

Authors like Kortbek and Grønbæk, Fogtmann et al. and Fatah gen. Schieck and Moutinho discuss the role of the whole body as an interaction device [3], in interaction design [4] and for the purpose to design responsive environments [5].

2   Investigation of the Observer's Viewpoint

We want to investigate the physicality in the environment museum. This means to analyze, if the relation between observer and image geometry comes to the fore. Both elements of this relation have to be considered, first the different body height of the audience and second the representation of the artifacts. Currently it is not possible to offer everyone the opportunity to immerse in the painting. To assure a consistency of the observation, the painting has to "know" about the presence of the audience. By using tracking technology it is possible to offer an optimal view, depending on the observers viewpoint.

Due to this intention we express the hypothesis, that the image geometry of linear perspective paintings guides the observer. Furthermore it encourages the observer to move in front of the painting. We propose observer moves with the intention to find the place, which gives the best impression of the painting. We assume that this place correspond with the viewpoint.

To examine, if the perspective geometrical construction – the image geometry – really influences the observer, it is necessary to use pictures with an off-center principle vanishing point, and therefore an off-center viewpoint. The observer is forced to move towards the viewpoint and tries to adopt the image geometry of the picture to his own.

2.1   Parameter

Important parameters we want to discuss in this paper occur out of the mathematic rules of perspective, the social environment museum and the artifacts as well as the experimental installation itself. The parameters depend on the choice of the observer position – viewpoint. The parameter referring to the observer is his chosen position.

Parameter referring to the artifact – image:

- image content
- image impression
- image size
- image perspective

Parameter referring to the environment:

- experimental room
- size of the projection plane
- distance of the observer to the projection plan

2.2   Installation

To prove the hypothesis we carry out an experiment. 20 participants attended and it took place in a separate room with a rear projection plane at one side. The proportions of the experimental cube are two meter each side (see Fig. 2). A chequerboard floor in the experimental room helped identifying the position of the participant.

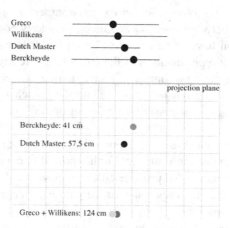

Fig. 2. Projected images, image width and principle vanishing point (top); chequerboard floor of the experimental room with the identified viewpoints, including the distance to the projection plane (bottom)

Four perspective paintings, three Renaissance and one postmodern painting, were the objects of investigation and projected in real size (see Fig. 3):

- El Greco: Christ Healing the Blind, about 1570
- Gerrit Adriaenszoon Berckheyde: Interior of St. Bavokerk at Haarlem, 1665
- Dutch Master: Holy Family in the chamber with Anna and Joachim, 15th c.
- Ben Willikens: Room 389, 20th c.

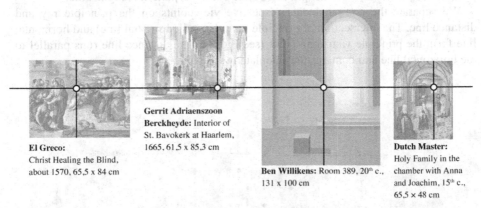

El Greco: Christ Healing the Blind, about 1570, 65,5 x 84 cm

Gerrit Adriaenszoon Berckheyde: Interior of St. Bavokerk at Haarlem, 1665, 61,5 x 85,3 cm

Ben Willikens: Room 389, 20th c., 131 x 100 cm

Dutch Master: Holy Family in the chamber with Anna and Joachim, 15th c., 65,5 × 48 cm

Fig. 3. Paintings and their image geometry: horizon line, sagittal line and principle vanishing point

All paintings have different principle vanishing points as well as different sizes. The artist integrated the auxiliary construction in the painting – the chequerboard floor. This can be used as a reference grid to relate the items of the picture to each other. To reconstruct the perspective of the picture such a reference grid is helpful. Fig. 2 shows the identified principle vanishing point in each painting. The principle vanishing point of Greco and Willikens are vertical close to the center and horizontal Greco has an off center point. The paintings of Berckheyde and the Dutch Master have off center principle vanishing points vertical as well as horizontal. Out of the image geometry it is possible to reconstruct the distance to the image plane (see Fig. 2).

The image planes of the paintings with their principle vanishing points are shown in the top area of Fig. 3. The viewpoints of all four paintings are represented in Fig. 3 bottom.

2.3   Process

Each participant entered the room. The task was to detect the ideal position, which gives the best perception of the painting. This place had to be in front of the picture plane and inside the experimental room. Afterwards they had to evaluate the referred parameter from major to minor influence. 14 of these 20 participants were male and six female. The average age was 32. 14 are computer scientists, three engineers, one architect and two business economists.

3   Outcome

The results of the experiment are multifarious. Fig. 4 shows the entire viewpoints matched according to the calculated viewpoints (point of origin) of the four perspective paintings. At first sight there is no common pattern recognizable.

We separate the compiled data respective viewpoints on the principle ray and distance line. The intersection of principle ray (also called sagittal line) and horizontal line form the principle vanishing point (see Fig. 1). The distance line runs parallel to the horizontal line and contains the calculated viewpoint.

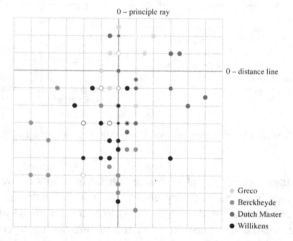

Fig. 4. Observer viewpoints corresponding to the identified viewpoints (point of origin)

In total 80 observer viewpoints have to been analyzed. We examine the positions of the observer viewpoint according to the sagittal plane (see Fig. 5 left). 27 viewpoints are located in this area. This are 33,75 %. The accumulation of the viewpoints on the principle ray is conspicuous. Therefor is a relation between observer viewpoint and geometrical system identifiable. Six up to nine viewpoints have been located on parallels of the principle ray.

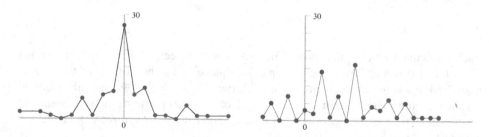

Fig. 5. Observer viewpoints according to the sagittal plane (left) Observer viewpoint according to the distance (right)

A closer examination of the viewpoints on the parallels to the distance line shows different patterns (see Fig.6). Fig. 6 splits the viewpoints referring to the painting itself. The paintings with a larger distance at 124 cm, Greco and Willikens, form one group. The detected observer viewpoints are grouped around the calculated viewpoint. The Dutch Master has a shorter distance of the calculated viewpoint. It looks like it has been moved backwards. The "main distance line" seems to be moved by three squares backward. This might be due to the projector solution. Many participants complained about the solution. The painting of Berckheyde has a very short distance of 41 cm. It shows a wide spread range of observer viewpoints. Therefore must be a more specific analysis of the raised data.

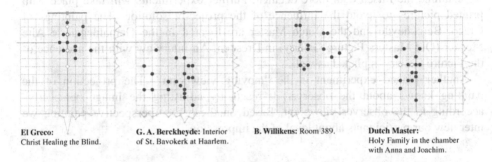

El Greco:
Christ Healing the Blind.

G. A. Berckheyde: Interior of St. Bavokerk at Haarlem.

B. Willikens: Room 389.

Dutch Master:
Holy Family in the chamber with Anna and Joachim.

Fig. 6. Observer viewpoint according to each projected image and referring to its viewpoint

Furthermore we want to discuss the relation between the observer position, the artifact – painting and the environment with the named parameter (see 3.1). We divided the parameter into two sections. Size, geometry, impression and content refer to the image. Distance to the projection plane, the size of the projection plane and the experimental room refer to the installation. Very important factors by choosing the observer position has been the image geometry, second the image impression and the image size. The content of the painting has not been named as an important parameter (see Fig. 7 left).

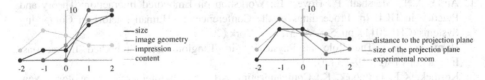

—size
—image geometry
----impression
----content

—distance to the projection plane
—size of the projection plane
—experimental room

Fig. 7. Chart of the named parameters according to the choice of the observer position image related parameter (left) and installation related parameter (right)

The parameters referring to the environment are not so important. The distance of the projection plane has no influence. The experimental room has been valued with no influence as well. Just the size of the projection plane has a negative impact on the observer.

4   Conclusion and Future Work

In this paper we discussed the influence of linear perspective paintings on the observer position. We assume, that the image geometry encourages the observer movement. Our approach takes the artifact painting as the basis of the research. We analyzed if the audience of a panel-painting exhibition is animated by the paintings and there structure. This approach is located in the contemporary interest of movement research in the field of human computer interaction.

The image geometry turned out to have an influence to the observer position. Most participants chose a position on the principle ray of the image. To expand this result we examine the raised data more detailed. Further experiments will take place with printed pictures to avoid the influence of the projector solution. The paintings of Greco, Berckheyde and the Dutch Master are located in the Gemäldegalerie Alte Meister (Old Masters Picture Gallery) in Dresden. An interview with the audience of the Picture Gallery is planed as well.

Another planed experiment is the "moving viewpoint". The projection of the painting knows about the observer. It reacts by adjusting the image perspective according to the observer viewpoint. Based on these four perspective painting we interview our participants about level of the impression.

Acknowledgement. On the part of Franziska Hannß the European Union, the European Social Fund (ESF) as well as the Free State of Saxony support parts of this work.

Gefördert aus Mitteln der Europäischen Union

Europa fördert Sachsen.
Europäischer Sozialfonds

References

1. Antle, A.N., Marshall, P., Hoven, E.: Workshop on Embodied Interaction: Theory and Practice in HCI. In: Proceedings of the Conference on Human Factors in Computing Systems (CHI 2011), pp. 5–8. ACM, New York (2011)
2. Hornecker, E.: The Role of Physicality in Tangible and Embodied Interactions. Interactions 18(2), 19–23 (2011)
3. Kortbek, K.J., Grønbæk, K.: Communicating Art through Interactive Technology: New Approaches for Interaction Design in Art Museums. In: Proceedings of the 5th Nordic Conference on Human-Computer Interaction: Building Bridges (NordiCHI 2008), pp. 229–238. ACM, New York (2008)
4. Fogtmann, M.H., Fritsch, J., Kortbek, K.J.: Kinesthetic Interaction – Revealing the Bodily Potential in Interaction Design. In: Proceedings of the 20th Australasian Conference on Computer-Human Interaction: Designing for Habitus and Habitat (OzCHI 2008), pp. 89–96. ACM, New York (2008)

5. Schieck, A.F.G., Moutinho, A.M.: ArCHI: Engaging with Museum Objects Spatially Through Whole Body Movement. In: Proceeding of the 16th International Academic MindTrek Conference (MindTrek 2012), pp. 39–45. ACM, New York (2012)
6. International Council of Museums: Statutes, Vienna (2007)
7. Field, J.V.: The invention of infinity: Mathematics and Art in the Renaissance. Oxford University Press Inc., New York (1997)
8. da Vignola, G.B.: Two rules of practical perspective, Bologna (1583)
9. Veltman, K.H.: Computers and Renaissance Perspective. Centro Ricerche Leonardiane, Brescia (1993)
10. Calter, P.: Squaring the Circle: Geometry in Art & Architecture. Wiley, Hoboken (2008)
11. Arnheim, R.: The Power of the Center: A Study of Composition in the Visual Arts. University of California Press, Berkeley (1982)
12. Ishii, H.: Tangible Bilts: Beyond Pixels. In: Proceedings of the 2nd International Conference on Tangible and Embedded Interaction (TEI 2008), pp. xv–xxv. ACM, New York (2008)

Long-Range Hand Gesture Interaction
Based on Spatio-temporal Encoding

Jaewon Kim, Gyuchull Han, Ig-Jae Kim, Hyounggon Kim, and Sang Chul Ahn

Imaging Media Research Center
Korea Institute of Science and Technology (KIST)

Abstract. We present a novel hand gesture interaction method which has a long-range working space (1m~5m) overcoming conventional approaches' limitations in cost-performance dependency. Our camera-free interaction system is composed of a pair of lighting device and an instrumented glove with photosensor markers. The lighting devices spatiotemporally encode user's interaction space via binary infrared light signals and markers' 3D position at fingertips is tracked at high speed (250 Hz) and fair accuracy (5mm at 3m working distance). Each marker consisting of a photosensor array allows a wide sensing range and minimizes fingers' self-occlusion. Experiment results demonstrate various applications where hand gestures are recognized as input commands to interact with digital information mimicking natural human hand gestures toward real objects. Our system has strengths in accuracy, speed, low price, and robustness comparing with conventional long-range interaction techniques. Ambiguity-free nature in marker recognition and little cost-performance dependency are additional advantages of our method.

1 Introduction

We present a novel hand gesture interaction method with a long-range working space (1m~5m). Such long-range hand gesture interaction is an open research area which is not practically covered by current methods or devices such as Kinect. Practical solutions for the problem imply significant influence on future TV applications like a next-generation remote controller in large space. Conventional vision-based approaches including Kinect have fundamental weakness in their performance: Interaction speed and accuracy directly depends on camera's performance and cost. Typically, vision-based approaches for long-range hand gesture interaction require expensive cameras to capture visual information at high-speed and high–resolution such as Oblong's G-Speak system. To overcome the conventional limitations, we present a camera-free hand gesture interaction method based on spatiotemporally encoded illumination.

1.1 Contributions

We present an analysis of a photosensor-based interaction system that accurately and rapidly recognize 3D position of markers through spatiotemporally encoded

N. Streitz and C. Stephanidis (Eds.): DAPI/HCII 2013, LNCS 8028, pp. 22–31, 2013.
© Springer-Verlag Berlin Heidelberg 2013

illumination. Our method proposes a practical solution for long-range hand gesture interaction with a cheap camera-free system. Included in this analysis are the following:

- performance of the hand gesture interaction method based on spatio-temporal encoding and photosensor markers,
- a unique design of a photosensor marker which consists of multiple photosensors to increase field of sensing and minimize occlusion errors,
- example applications for the hand gesture interaction, including 6 DOF manipulation of a graphic object, multi-user interaction for drawing operation, and manipulation of a deformable object.

1.2   Related Work

Vision-Based Interaction: Bare-hand interaction is earning high attention with the emergence of Kinect. Although such interaction provides the best user convenience obviating the need of wearing a device, it's been considered one of the most challenging interaction tasks. [1] presented a bare-hand interaction technique, called BiDi screen, based on a light field camera and a time-division multiplexed display. While it successfully demonstrated object manipulation by bare hands, the accuracy is not high enough to separately track each finger and the interaction speed is limited due to the time-division multiplexed operation over display frequency. Generally, bare-hand interaction techniques based on a camera vision system suffer from ambiguity problem among fingers or hands. In addition, the computational cost is high and in turn the interaction speed is slow. To overcome such limitations, [2] and [3] employed color markers and color gloves, respectively. Color information helps object ambiguity but still depth ambiguity remains in 3D interaction. So, multiple cameras, a camera-projector system, or a 3D camera have been adopted in 3D interaction domain. However, strong dependency between system cost and interaction performance appeared as an obstacle in developing practical applications. Besides, self-occlusion among fingers or hands has still remained a challenging task. To computationally tackle this matters, [4] presented an approach to jointly solve salient point association with hand pose estimation. An almost everywhere differentiable objective function was proposed to estimate hand gestures by simple local optimization taking edges, optical flow, salient points and collisions into account. [5] approached the full 3D pose estimation of a user hand with a unique wrist-worn device consisting of an IR camera-project setup and an IMU sensor. However, a fully flat or over-arching hand was still problematic in their method.

Photosensor-Based Interaction: Some researchers ([6], [7], [8]) presented interaction methods based on photosensors and an illumination device like a video projector demonstrating good augmented reality applications. While our method has a common ground in the usage of photosensors as markers, the core tracking method, spatio-temporal encoding, is completely different with their methods. The UNC's HiBall system[9] employed six photosensors and six lens to track a user's pose (location and orientation) with ceiling-mounted light-emitting diodes (LEDs). SCAAT (Single-Constraint-At-A-Time) method, recursively estimating accurate pose information from a single inaccurate measurement, was applied to the system in order to improve tracking accuracy with less latency. However, the system had a drawback in cumbersome system installation which required for mounting huge number (approximately 3000) of LEDs onto a ceiling. Contrastingly, our system requires only two lighting devices consisting of 36 LEDs for 3D position tracking. Kang[10] introduced an indoor GPS metrology system with a unique probe unit, called 3D Probe, composed of three photosensors and a ball probe tip. 3D Probe captures an object's 3D surface via scanning and 3D coordinate of a certain object point is measured by analyzing light signals transmitted from multiple light sources at known location and orientation. While the method requires measuring light sources' geometry information at a calibration stage, our method is free of such information and more accurate with less number of light sources.

Instrumented Glove-Based Interaction: Hand interaction techniques based on various sensors such as mechanical and electrical sensors have been actively commercialized. Immersion Corporation's CyberGlove[11] and Fifth Dimension Technologies' Data Glove are good examples. Generally, such products are configured into an instrumented glove assembled with a delicate sensor system. CyberGlove measures hand posture through 18 electrical sensors in long and thin strip shape which are sewn into a glove fabric. Each sensor experiences change in resistance depending on bending amount. Hand gesture is estimated by the amount of deformation at each sensor position, which is measured by electric current change. User-dependent calibration is indispensable in most sensor-based approaches since different hand size or shape affects consistent bending measurement and gesture estimation.

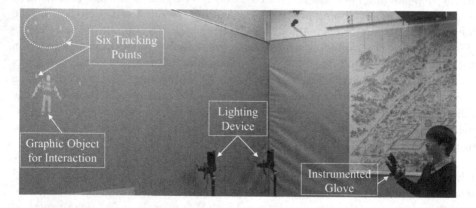

Fig. 1. A user interacts with a graphic object, Buzz, through natural hand gestures in a large space. Our interaction system consists of an instrumented glove with six photosensor markers and two lighting devices.

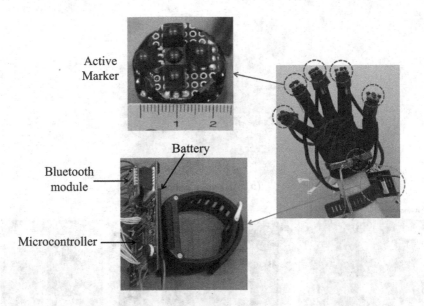

Fig. 2. Our unique glove system consisting of markers, a control unit and a battery achieves long-range hand gesture interaction at high-speed (250 Hz for 3D) and fair accuracy (5mm at 3m)

2 System Configuration

Our prototype camera-free interaction system shown in Fig.1 is composed of an instrumented glove (Fig.2) and a pair of lighting device (Fig.3). The glove is integrated with six photosensor markers, a microcontroller, a Bluetooth module, and a battery. The six markers are located at the five fingertips and the end of palm as shown in Fig.2 right. Each marker consists of multiple photosensors facing different views to cover a wide sensing range. For the photosensor, we used Vishay TSOP7000 with 455 kHz PCM (Pulse-code modulation) frequency which provides a high-speed sensing rate (1 kHz for six markers' 1D tracking). Our system's tracking speed is inversely proportional to tracking DOF (Degrees of Freedom) due to the temporal encoding nature of our method: 500 Hz and 333 Hz for 2D and 3D tracking, respectively. For 2D tracking, the lighting device (Fig.3 (a)) consisting of a pair of 1D lighting unit (Fig.3 (c)) are used to project spatiotemporally encoded light in X and Y plane. Similarly, 3D tracking requires projecting 1D lighting unit along X, Y, and Z axis, which allows 333 Hz tracking speed. However, practically such projection demands a large space so we alternatively present a stereo combination method with a pair of 2D lighting device as shown in Fig.1, which achieves 3D tracking at 250 Hz. A microcontroller (Microchip PIC18F45K20) controls all electronic devices including photosensor

(a) A lighting device

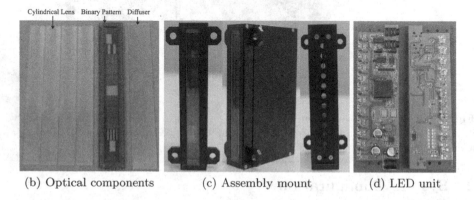

(b) Optical components   (c) Assembly mount   (d) LED unit

Fig. 3. A lighting device to project spatiotemporally encoded light. The 2D lighting device (a) is assembled with a pair of 1D lighting unit (c) positioned perpendicular to each other.

markers and a Bluetooth module in the glove. A Bluetooth module (FB755AC) transmits markers' position value to a remote server and receives event signals for haptic feedback to a user. All electronic devices in the glove are powered by a thin lithium polymer battery (3.7V/1000mA).

The 1D lighting units (Fig.3 (c)), consisting of nine IR LEDs (Vishay TSFF5210 with 180mW/sr), spatiotemporally encode user's interaction space by binary infrared light signals. Eight LEDs encodes space with 8 bit binary signals and one LED at the center of the unit sends a start signal to synchronize photosensor markers. Fig.3 (b) shows optical components including a binary pattern film, four cylindrical lens, and a diffuser. Two cylindrical lenses and a diffuser scatter LED light over a large interaction space. Other two cylindrical lenses focus LED light on the interaction space. Fig.3 (d) shows an electronic circuit board to control the nine LEDs.

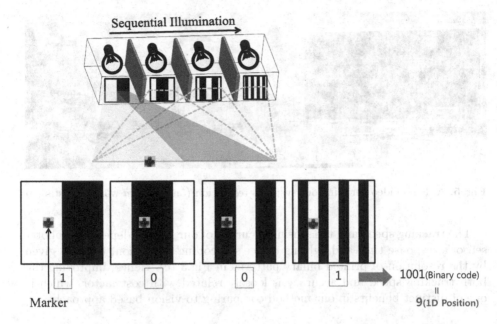

Fig. 4. When IR LEDs sequentially project binary patterns once at a time, a maker receives a unique binary code which is transformed to an 1D position value

3 Tracking Method

Our tracking method is based on spatiotemporal encoding technique [12] which temporally illuminates 8 bit binary light signals into the interaction space via the lighting device shown in Fig.3. Photosensor marker's position is simply obtained by decoding the 8 bit light signal sensed by the marker's photosensors. For example, while the lighting device sequentially illuminates 4 bit binary patterns in Fig.4, the marker receives either 0 or 1 depending on black or white light stripe region. In the figure, the marker sequentially receives 1001 which is a unique code for the position. In such a manner, 1D position is encoded by binary light codes and Cartesian coordinate position is obtained by converting a marker's received binary signal to a real, decimal value. 2D tracking is simply the two dimensionally extended case of 1D tracking with a pair of 1D lighting device which are orthogonally positioned along X and Y axis. 3D tracking can be done in the same manner with three lighting devices positioned along X, Y and Z axis. Tracking with these configurations from 1D to 3D doesn't require any calibration since a position value is directly obtained by the received light signal. However, in the case of stereo combination with a pair of 2D lighting device as shown in Fig.1, a calibration step is required to calculate 3D position from two 2D position values. We applied Miaw's calibration method ([13]) which models the relation between a 3D real position value and a 1D sensed value with seven unknown parameters.

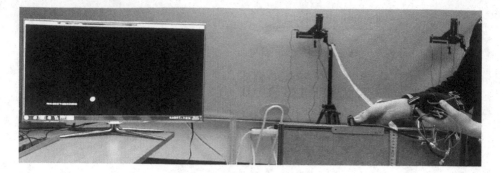

Fig. 5. A demo video verifying our system's resolution (5mm at 3m working distance)

The tracking speed and the sensing accuracy of our system depends on photosensor's response time and lighting device's encoding resolution, which is given by the resolution of printed binary patterns in Fig.3 (c). Hence, improving the both tracking speed and accuracy is loosely related with cost factor, which is one of distinct benefits in our method comparing to vision-based approaches.

4   Experimental Results

Demo video Fig.5 proves that our system's interaction resolution is 5mm at 3m distance between lighting devices and a marker. The marker's graphic representation, a white ball, moves according to actual marker's back and forth movement in 5mm interval in the video. In the supplementary videos of which still cuts are shown in Fig.6, we demonstrate hand gesture interaction where hand gestures are recognized as input commands to interact with digital information mimicking natural hand gestures for handling real objects. Fig.6 (a) shows an interaction demo with a deformable graphic object. With our system, a user can grasp the object at any point, elongate, press, and release it freely. Fig.6 (b) demonstrates interaction with a rigid object, Buzz. A user can grasp it at any point, freely manipulate it in translational and rotational movements, and change scaling. Fig.6 (c) shows multi-user interaction for a drawing operation. Two users performs drawing jobs in parallel with our system.

5   Conclusion

We presented a novel hand gesture interaction technique with a large working space (1m~5m) based on spatio-temporal encoding method. Our unique tracking system equipped with photosensor markers is optimized for hand gesture tracking with covering large sensing range and minimizing finger's self-occlusion. Demo videos verify high possibility in practical applications demonstrating natural and free hand gesture interaction at high speed and good accuracy.

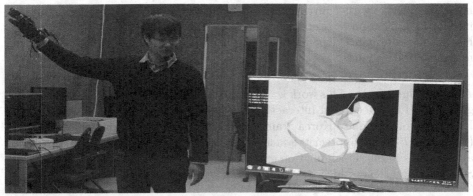

(a) Hand gesture interaction with a deformable object

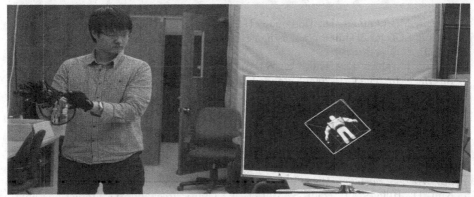

(b) 6 DOF manipulation demo for a graphic object

(c) Multiple user interaction demo for a drawing operation

Fig. 6. Our method provides natural hand gesture applications with six markers' 3D tracking at high speed (250 Hz) and fair resolution (5mm at 3m working distance)

Our system has strengths in accuracy, speed, low price, and robustness to noise comparing with conventional long-range interaction techniques. Robust marker identification, less erroneous performance for finger's self-occlusion and little cost-performance dependency are additional advantages of our photosensor marker-based system.

Ackowledgements. This work was supported by the Global Frontier R&D Program on ⟨Human-centered Interaction for Coexistence⟩ funded by the National Research Foundation of Korea grant funded by the Korean Government(MSIP) (2010-0029752). We appreciate Maciej's help on the advices regarding interesting applications in physics simulation and especially the provision of source code for Soft Body 3.0 ([14]) which was used for our demonstration in Fig.6 (a).

References

1. Hirsch, M., Lanman, D., Holtzman, H., Raskar, R.: BiDi screen: a thin, depth-sensing LCD for 3D interaction using light fields. ACM Transactions on Graphics 28 (2009)
2. Mistry, P., Maes, P., Chang, L.: WUW - Wear Ur World - A Wearable Gestural Interface. In: The CHI 2009 Extended Abstracts on Human Factors in Computing Systems (2009)
3. Wang, R., Popovic, J.: Real-time hand-tracking with a color glove. ACM SIG-GRAPH (2009)
4. Ballan, L., Taneja, A., Gall, J., Van Gool, L., Pollefeys, M.: Motion capture of hands in action using discriminative salient points. In: Fitzgibbon, A., Lazebnik, S., Perona, P., Sato, Y., Schmid, C. (eds.) ECCV 2012, Part VI. LNCS, vol. 7577, pp. 640–653. Springer, Heidelberg (2012)
5. Kim, D., Hilliges, O., Izadi, S., Butler, A.: Digits: freehand 3D interactions anywhere using a wrist-worn gloveless sensor. In: Proceedings of the 25th Annual ACM Symposium on User Interface Software and Technology (2012)
6. Nii, H., Sugimoto, M., Inami, M.: Smart Light Ultra High Speed Projector for Spatial Multiplexing Optical Transmission. In: Procams Workshop (held with IEEE CVPR) (2005)
7. Raskar, R., Beardsley, P., Van Baar, J., Wang, Y., Dietz, P., Lee, J., Leigh, D., Willwacher, T.: RFIG Lamps: Interacting with a Self-describing World via Photosensing Wireless Tags and Projectors. ACM Transactions on Graphics (SIG-GRAPH) 23 (2004)
8. Lee, J.C., Hudson, S.E., Summet, J.W., Dietz, P.H.: Moveable Interactive Projected Displays using Projector Based Tracking. In: ACM Symposium on User Interface Software and Technology (UIST), pp. 63–72 (2005)
9. Welch, G., Bishop, G.: SCAAT: Incremental Tracking with Incomplete Information. In: Proceedings of SIGGRAPH 1997, Computer Graphics Proceedings. Annual Conference Series (1997)
10. Kang, S., Tesar, D.: Indoor GPS Metrology System with 3D Probe for Precision Applications. In: Proceedings of ASME IMECE 2004 International Mechanical Engineering Congress and RD and D Expo (2004)
11. Kessler, D., Hodges, L., Walker, N.: Evaluation of the CyberGlove as a Whole-Hand Input Device. ACM Tran. on Computer-Human Interactions 2(4), 263–283 (1995)

12. Raskar, R., Nii, H., Dedecker, B., Hashimoto, Y., Summet, J., Moore, D., Zhao, Y., Westhues, J., Dietz, P., Barnwell, J., Nayar, S., Inami, M., Bekaert, P., Noland, M., Branzoi, V., Bruns, E.: Prakash: lighting aware motion capture using photo-sensing markers and multiplexed illuminators. ACM Transactions on Graphics 26, 36 (2007)
13. Miaw, D.: Second Skin: motion capture with actuated feedback for motor learning. MIT Thesis (2010)
14. Matyka, M., Ollila, M.: A pressure model for soft body simulation. In: Proc. of Sigrad (2003)

A Taxonomy-Based Approach
towards NUI Interaction Design

Florian Klompmaker[1], Volker Paelke[2], and Holger Fischer[1]

[1] University of Paderborn, C-LAB,
Fürstenallee 11, 33102 Paderborn, Germany
{florian.klompmaker,holger.fischer}@c-lab.de
[2] Leibniz Universität Hannover, Institut für Kartographie und Geoinformatik,
Appelstraße 9a, 30167 Hannover, Germany
volker.paelke@ikg.uni-hannover.de

Abstract. The rapid development in the domain of Natural User Interfaces (NUIs) and the proliferation of the hardware required to implement them places an increasing burden on interaction designers. Designers should be aware of research results relevant to their interaction problem but the increasing volume of NUI related research makes it difficult and thus hinders the development of usable real-world products. To address this problem, we have developed a decision-making tool that uses an interaction taxonomy in combination with definable application requirements. Using our tool, designers as well as HCI researchers can search for existing guidelines for a specific interaction problem fast and easily. In this paper we present the structure of the taxonomy, the decision-making process and tool as well as an evaluation and discussion of the overall approach.

Keywords: Interaction Design, Taxonomy, 3D User Interfaces, Tangible Interaction, Embodied Interaction, Geo-Visualization, Virtual Reality.

1 Introduction

Developing highly interactive and intuitive systems requires fundamental insights from the area of Human Computer Interaction (HCI) and human perception research [5]. Especially for Natural User Interfaces (NUIs) a gap exists between gathering such knowledge from research and transferring it into real-world products. This is mainly caused by the vast amount of results and publications that spread out across countless different publications and websites without a unified structure. Unfortunately, there is no simple reference tool enabling a fast look-up of NUI design guidelines for specific problems.

For the purpose of our research we restrict our definition of NUIs to systems that can be operated by gestures using body parts or the whole body. Our goal is to lower the burden of using new kinds of NUIs, especially within collaborative work settings. Therefore, we here only consider technology that requires low instrumentation, can be used ad-hoc and that does not require complicated setups or calibrations.

N. Streitz and C. Stephanidis (Eds.): DAPI/HCII 2013, LNCS 8028, pp. 32–41, 2013.
© Springer-Verlag Berlin Heidelberg 2013

NUIs can be very beneficial for group work (e.g. Computer Supported Collaborative Work - CSCW). Users interacting coactively[1] with NUIs often gain a higher degree of awareness [7], [9], [15]. However, since numerous environmental parameters have to be taken into account (e.g. group size and arrangement, display size, alignment and setup, type and dimension of the visualized data and the degrees of freedom (DOF) controlled by the input technology) coactive and co-local multi-user applications are much more challenging compared to single-user applications. Further more, input technologies can differ strongly in their suitability for coactive setups. E.g. touch-based interfaces are often a good solution because of the somatosensory feedback they provide. However, they are not applicable as soon as a large number of people interact on a large display because some areas get out of physical reach and the system cannot distinguish between different users. Because of these fundamental differences, creating easily accessible guidelines for coactive NUIs seems crucial.

To sum up, many parameters have to be taken into account when designing NUIs. For every single problem a number of alternative approaches might exist that designers have to consider. Solutions that have been proven to be good in one situation may be very poor in another. The number of research outcomes and publications is vast and not organized in an easily accessible and searchable way, hindering a seamless transfer into practice. Therefore, our goal is to make a first step to overcome this gap. In this paper we propose a structured iterative method of collecting, breaking down and evaluating NUI components considering different environmental parameters. Using this approach we have developed a database based decision-making tool that helps designers to find design guidelines for a specific interaction problem using NUIs. Further on, HCI researchers can make use of this tool as a reference database. They can also submit new findings to the database and detect gaps in it that require new interaction and usability studies.

The structure of this paper is as follows: First, we will present our taxonomy of NUI interaction techniques that adapts ideas from the area of Virtual Reality. Based on the taxonomy a decision-making process and the tool we developed are described. Finally, we present an evaluation and discussion of the process as well as of the decision-making tool.

2   A Taxonomy Based Approach

Taxonomies are a useful way to structure interaction tasks in a systematic way. Bowman et al. have developed a popular taxonomy of interaction tasks for the domain of Virtual Reality (VR) [1], [2], [3], [4]. To support the description and design of interaction techniques they have also introduced a hierarchical structure to describe how interaction techniques are composed of components to address specific

---

[1] According to [11], coactivity „*summarizes the different forms of communication, cooperation, collaboration, coordination, etc.*"

interaction tasks. While they introduced VR interaction techniques like selection, manipulation, travel and system control, we adapted their approach to the heterogeneous field of NUIs. Interaction techniques are much more diverse in this area since multiple kinds of technology offering different DOF control and multiple metaphors may be used.

Our taxonomy consists of multiple graphs, where each graph represents a single Interaction Task (ITA, see Fig. 1). A task describes an overall goal a user has to fulfill, e.g. a 2D movement of a graphical object, a rotation of a 3D graphical object or the input of text. Many ITAs are suitable for different applications but some are also very domain specific (e.g. zooming may be very different in a document management system than in geo-visualization applications). ITAs can be realized using one of the available Interaction Techniques (ITQ) as can be seen in Fig. 1. ITQs may differ in their technical realization (e.g. multitouch, tangible interaction or optical hand tracking in midair) and the metaphor they represent. ITQs can be split up into Subtasks (ST) that represent the workflow of the interaction and the order of actions (e.g. selection - manipulation - confirmation). STs therefore represent a high level view on the realized metaphor and many of them occur multiple times in the overall taxonomy. Finally, Interaction Components (IC) as the leaves in the graph represent a concrete action a user has to perform (e.g. a freehand grabbing gesture in midair or the rotation of a physical object). Since they may occur multiple times in the taxonomy STs and ICs can be realized as re-useable software components. These components can then be used for rapid prototyping and testing of new interaction techniques.

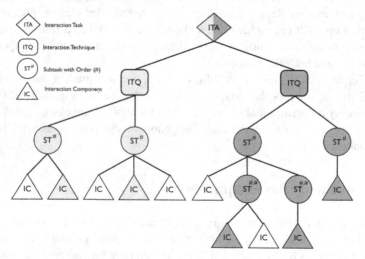

Fig. 1. Structure of an Interaction Task

Fig. 1 shows the structure of a single ITA. It shows how designers can make use of the taxonomy by choosing one of multiple available ITQs. Each ST of this ITQ has to be realized while only one of the available ICs has to be chosen. The light and dark grey shaded nodes in the graph (Fig.1) show two different possibilities for the realization of the ITA. Using the hierarchical data structure of the taxonomy decisions regarding ITQs and ICs can be automated. However, decision-making requires some kind of qualitative evaluation towards the suitability of ITQs and ICs for a specific application context. Such evaluation requires the definition of requirements that consists of ITAs, characteristics and measurable parameters.

2.1 Characteristics and Measurable Parameters

While the taxonomy in the form proposed by Bowman et al. is well suited to structure the design space of interaction techniques for VR applications, it is not quite suited as a design tool for NUIs. To enable tool support in the identification of potential interaction techniques for a task we have therefore extended the taxonomy by defining characteristics and measurable parameters. According to the idea of defining *User, Task, System and Environment Characteristics* [4] for interaction techniques, we decided to categorize characteristics for NUIs into *User, System and Application*. *User* characteristics describe the group of users and their capabilities. *System* addresses hardware characteristics while *Application* describes the software-side characteristics of the system. The categories and the definition of specific characteristics are easily extendable. We have identified some important ones that have already been addressed in research studies. Table 1 introduces some of the so far defined characteristics.

Table 1. Examples for characteristics

Group	Characteristic	Description
User	User:Cnt:2, User:Cnt:3-5, User:Cnt:5+	Describes the number of users that is coactively using the system
	User:TaskExperience:Low, User:TaskExperience:High	Describes the average experience of all users with the interaction task
System	System:DisplayAlignment:Vertical, System:DisplayAlignment:Horizontal	Describes the alignment of a single display
Application	Application:Data:2D, Application:Data:3D	Describes the dimension of the visualized data

Besides Characteristics also measurable parameters like speed, precision, intuitiveness or awareness are important for interaction designers that plan to create a specific application. These parameters can be measured within user studies either automatically (e.g. speed, precision) or using usability methods (e.g. for intuitiveness, awareness). The next section shows, how characteristics and measurable parameters are used in order to create qualified evaluations from existing user studies that address NUI interaction techniques.

2.2   Evaluating Interactions

Given the wide variety of possible interaction techniques in NUIs it would be desirable to support interaction designers with tools that allow the identification of suitable techniques and provide easy access to existing knowledge on their characteristics.

Using extendable structures like the taxonomy as well as the characteristics and measurable parameters, arbitrary application scenarios can be defined (e.g. a horizontal display setup for five users that offers precise input). After describing such a scenario using characteristics a designer or developer might further define ITAs that the application needs to offer to its users as well as a number of preferred and technically available interaction paradigms and devices. These combined descriptions are termed *requirements* (see Fig.2). Given this formalized information it becomes possible to develop a systematic procedure that is able to search for design guidelines based on the given requirements.

To enable the automated identification of suitable interaction techniques evaluation results from existing research studies must be made accessible. It is impossible to rate ITAs from the taxonomy with respect of different characteristics and measurable parameters since they represent different NUI technologies and interaction types. Therefore, the evaluation has to take place deeper in the hierarchy of the taxonomy. Evaluating ITQs and ICs on the other hand is possible and matches the choices the structure of the taxonomy offers. Therefore, we created a database-based tool that allows the evaluation of ITQs and ICs in combination with one or more characteristics and measurable parameters. All characteristics in the evaluations are described with an additional factor ranging from 1 to 3 in order to define the importance of every single characteristic. Further more, it is also possible to rate the coexistence of ICs. This is extremely useful to avoid media disruption (switching from on interaction technology to another) or to force the usage of specific ones (e.g. the use of digital pens for text input even though all other input is done without pens). Each evaluation gets a rating that can be either X (impossible to fulfill requirements), - (not recommended combination), * (good solution), ** (very good solution / best practice). The following combinations are evaluated:

- IC [1], Charakteristics [1..n] and measurable parameters [0..n] (IC eval.)
- ITQ [1], Charakteristics [1..n] and measurable parameters [0..n] (ITQ eval.)
- IC [1] and IC [1] (IC-IC eval.)

Every evaluation needs at least a reference or written defense that justifies the evaluation. Further on, technical requirements may occur for specific combinations. For example, some multitouch techniques in multi-user setups might require user identification or authentication. This is later presented to the designer along with the results. Therefore, they have also to be described while entering an evaluation using our developed tool. Fig. 4 shows some examples of evaluations that have been entered into the tool.

3   The Decision-Making Process and Tool

We have developed a decision making tool, that allows to enter and edit characteristics, measurable parameters, technical requirements, evaluation results as well as the creation of new and editing of existing ITAs. The overall decision-making process, involved roles and the input of data can be seen in figures Fig. 2 and 3. At the moment we are using an algorithm that looks up every entered evaluation for the given requirements (ITAs, characteristics, measurable parameters) and creates the best-rated overall solution for all ITAs. However, it does not simply present one solution but a number of *design alternatives* with good overall-ratings in order to present guidelines from which a designer may choose. A *design alternative* consists of a specific ITQ but only one single IC for every ST. The most interesting point here is that the resulting ITQ can be a newly created and never tested combination of ICs. Therefore, our tool creates new combinations that result in completely new NUI interaction techniques. Further more, within a design alternative, additional characteristics are given that have not been part of the requirements but are needed to design the system. Whenever needed or existing also technical requirements, annotations and existing discussions are presented within a design alternative. Our tool creates discussion threads automatically whenever conflicting evaluations are detected. Besides positive results also design alternatives with bad evaluations are presented to the user in order to give insights about bad influences to the system.

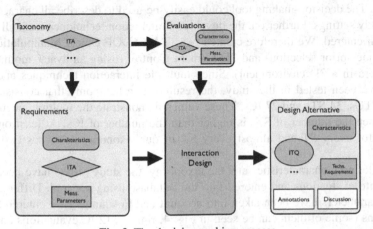

Fig. 2. The decision-making process

In summary, the tool we have created allows to enter new data and to request design guidelines based on given requirements. Guidelines consist of multiple design alternatives a designer may choose from. Designers can hence use the tool to get insights about existing knowledge about a specific interaction problem. On the other side, HCI researchers can use the tool for archiving their research results and for a fast look up of existing studies as well as for gaps in NUI research. Therefore, the tool is ideally usable in preparation of new HCI studies.

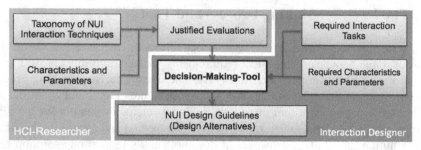

Fig. 3. Roles in the decision-making process

4   Evaluation and Discussion

In this section we present an evaluation and discussion of first tests of the developed concept and tool. The tool was implemented as a web application on an Apache web server and it uses PHP and a MySQL database.

In order to test the approach we entered data from three interaction studies that we performed in our lab into the database using the tool. Within these studies we analyzed single user 6 DOF multitouch interactions on a large tabletop display [12], 3D selection, manipulation and travel tasks using mid-air gestures in front of a large wall projection [13] and tangible interactions for 3D tasks in single and coactive user setups [14]. The decision-making tool could easily be used to describe all characteristics of the study settings. Further on, the developed interaction techniques from all studies have been entered. We therefore created two ITAs: 6DOF Object Manipulation (that also includes prior selection) and 2D Camera Control (using an avatar mounted virtual camera in a 3D environment). Since multiple interaction techniques and metaphors have been tested in the study, the result was a taxonomy that consisted of 2 ITAs, 7 ITQs, 34 STs and 27 ICs. These values demonstrate the multiple occurrences of ICs since the number of STs is higher than the number of ICs. At least one IC is required for every ST and almost every ST in our taxonomy possesses two ICs or more.

After defining characteristics and the taxonomy, the study results have been transformed into evaluations and entered into the database using our tool. Different measurable parameters have been taken into account and in summery we entered 34 ITQ evaluations (some of them can be seen in Fig. 4, right), 112 IC evaluations and 9 IC-IC evaluations.

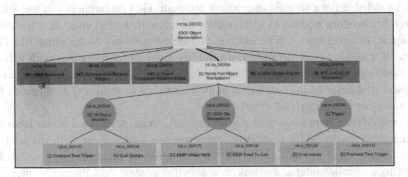

Fig. 4. Screenshot of the decision-making tool: defining requirements (left) and overview of existing ITQ evaluations (right)

Fig. 5. Screenshot of the decision-making tool: Taxonomy view

To evaluate the concept and its usage it was presented to eight researchers, mostly PhD students in the area of HCI, within two seminar lectures. All of them stated that the concept is easily understandable and allows the transformation of arbitrary NUI interaction techniques into an interaction taxonomy, the description of interactive systems using characteristics as well as entering evaluations based on study results and measurable parameters. However, at the moment it is not yet clear if designers are able to easily understand the concept. Since design alternatives consist of the description of an ITQ based on our taxonomy, they need to understand this concept.

Using the test data from the three studies we analyzed if the decision-making tool behaved the way we planned. During multiple different search queries we came to the conclusion that the programmed algorithm resulted in good as well as bad rated design alternatives as expected. Further on, also new interaction techniques have been found by combining previously untested ICs of the different STs. The test queries showed that the algorithm considered all entered evaluation data. However, it has to be investigated whether the algorithm parameters used to evaluate different combinations for the design alternatives are a good choice or whether they can be optimized in order to produce better usable results. Finally, it is still unclear, how good the results of the process are in practice since only theoretical combinations based on different user studies are combined. With our test data the algorithm needed less than two seconds to process every search query. Since we do not expect that queries with more than two ITAs will occur in practice that often, we state that the algorithm run-time is quite scalable even if the amount of data drastically increases while entering further study results.

5   Conclusion and Future Work

In this paper we presented a taxonomy-based decision-making process and tool for NUIs. This tool can be used by interaction designers in order to search for existing design knowledge for a specific interaction problem. HCI researchers can use the tool to search for existing studies, to archive their own results and to enter new Interaction Techniques. Existing ones can be extended by new taxonomy components like ITQs, STs and ICs allowing the definition of arbitrary interaction processes with different NUI technology and using different metaphors. In addition, new characteristics and parameters that describe the conditions of an interactive systems and evaluations from user studies can be defined and entered easily.

We entered data from three user studies that have been performed in our laboratory and presented results and a discussion based on our experiences with the tool. We have established that the tool allows the identification of design alternatives that are relevant to a specific interaction task in a specific context and thus aids interaction designers in making informed design decisions. We think that the combination of the taxonomy with an interactive tool is a very suitable approach of enabling a more effective transfer of NUI research results into practice.

Building on experience in collecting and hosting community portals about interaction technologies from the AMIRE project[2], as a next step we plan to make the decision-making tool available online for the NUI community. This will be done after running some usability tests and redesigning the tool in order to make it usable for designers and researchers as well. Hopefully this will result in a larger number of data from different domains. Further on, we plan to allow the community to discuss on evaluation conflicts and extensions of the overall approach. We therefore hope to get feedback and input from domain experts and HCI researches as well regarding the concept presented in this paper.

---

[2] http://www.amire.net/index.html

References

1. Bowman, D.A., Hodges, L.F.: An Evaluation of Techniques for Grabbing and Manipulating Remote Objects in Immersive Virtual Environments. In: Symposium on Interactive 3D Graphics, pp. 35–38. IEEE Press, New York (1997)
2. Bowman, D.A., Koller, D., Hodges, L.F.: Travel in Immersive Virtual Environments: An Evaluation of Viewpoint Motion Control Techniques. In: Virtual Reality Annual International Symposium, pp. 45–52. IEEE Press, New York (1997)
3. Bowman, D.A., Johnson, D.B., Hodges, L.F.: Testbed Evaluation of Virtual Environment Interaction Techniques. In: Symposium on Virtual Reality Software and Technology 1999, pp. 26–33. ACM Press (1999)
4. Bowman, D.A., Hodges, L.F.: Formalizing the Design, Evaluation, and Application of Interaction Techniques for Immersive Virtual Environments. Journal of Visual Languages and Computing 10, 37–53 (1999)
5. Few, S.: Data Visualization for Human Perception, Aarhus, Denmark (2010), http://www.interaction-design.org/encyclopedia/data_visualization_for_human_perception.html
6. Forlines, C., Lilien, R.: Adapting a Single-user, Single-display Molecular Visualization Application for Use in a Multi-user, Multi-display Environment. In: Working Conference on Advanced Visual Interfaces, pp. 367–371. ACM Press (2008)
7. Gutwin, C., Greenberg, S.: Descriptive Framework of Workspace Awareness for Real-time Groupware. Computer Supported Cooperative Work 11(3), 411–446 (2002)
8. Hancock, M., Carpendale, S.: Supporting multiple off-axis viewpoints at a tabletop display. In: Second Annual IEEE International Workshop on Horizontal Interactive Human-Computer Systems, pp. 171–178. IEEE Press, New York (2007)
9. Hornecker, E., Marshall, P., Dalton, N.S.: Collaboration and Interference: Awareness with Mice or Touch Input. In: Computer Supported Cooperative Work 2008, pp. 167–176. ACM Press (2008)
10. Jacob, R.J.K., Girouard, A., Hirshfield, L.M., Horn, M.S., Shaer, O., Solovey, E.T., Zigelbaum, J.: Reality-based Interaction: a Framework for post-WIMP Interfaces. In: ACM SIGCHI Conference on Human Factors in Computing Systems 2008, pp. 201–210. ACM Press (2008)
11. Keil, R., Selke, H.: Virtual learning spaces for co-active learning. In: International Conference on Improving University Teaching (2011)
12. Klompmaker, F., Nebe, K.: Towards 3d multitouch interaction widgets. In: Workshop on Interaction Techniques in Real and Simulated Assistive Smart Environments, Workshop at the First International Joint Conference on Ambient Intelligence (2010)
13. Klompmaker, F., Dridger, A., Nebe, K.: Evaluation of whole-body navigation and selection techniques in immersive 3d environments. In: ASME 2012 International Design Engineering Technical Conferences, Computers and Information in Engineering Conference, ASME (2012)
14. Klompmaker, F., Nebe, K., Eschenlohr, J.: Towards multimodal 3d tabletop interaction using sensor equipped mobile devices. In: Fourth International Conference on Mobile Computing, Applications and Services (2012)
15. Scott, S.D., Carpendale, M.S.T., Inkpen, K.M.: Territoriality in Collaborative Tabletop Workspaces. In: Computer Supported Collaborative Work 2004, pp. 294–303. ACM Press (2004)

Fusion of Color and Depth Video for Human Behavior Recognition in an Assistive Environment

Dimitrios I. Kosmopoulos[1], Paul Doliotis[2], Vassilis Athitsos[2], and Ilias Maglogiannis[3]

[1] TEI of Crete, Dept of Applied Informatics and Multimedia, GR-71500, Greece
[2] University of Texas at Arlington,
Dept of Computer Science and Engineering, TX-76013, USA
[3] Dept of Digital Systems, University of Piraeus, GR-18534
dkosmo@ieee.org, {doliotis,athitsos}@uta.edu, imaglo@unipi.gr

Abstract. In this paper we investigate the effects of fusing feature streams extracted from color and depth videos, aiming to monitor the actions of people in an assistive environment. The output of fused time-series classifiers is used to model and extract actions. To this end we compare the Hidden Markov model classifier and fusion methods like early, late or state fusion. Our experiments employ a public dataset, which was acquired indoors.

1 Introduction

One of the key questions in creating pervasive systems for the care of the elderly is the graceful integration with the human user [1]. Towards building such a system a highly desired property that needs to be satisfied is "non-intrusiveness". Computer vision methods can satisfy this property and are typically used in assistive environments. One of the main challenges is to transform the video stream into a useful source of information. This can be further divided in several sub-problems like how to track people in the captured video stream, how to recognize their postures and how to analyze their short term actions and long term behaviors.

Motion analysis in video, and particularly human behaviour understanding, has attracted many researchers [2], mainly because of its fundamental applications in video surveillance, video indexing, virtual reality and computer-human interfaces. The automatic modeling and recognition of human behaviour to reduce human intervention in assistive or other environments is one of the most challenging problems in computer vision. The related systems are envisaged to automatically detect, categorize and recognize human behaviors, calling for human attention only when necessary. This is expected to increase the effectiveness of 24/7 monitoring services for elderly or patients and make such services financially viable [3].

N. Streitz and C. Stephanidis (Eds.): DAPI/HCII 2013, LNCS 8028, pp. 42–51, 2013.

There are several works on human behavior recognition in assistive environments using color cameras, e.g., [4], [5]. The color information captured by conventional cameras is a very useful cue, which can be used for environment modeling and object tracking. Problems which are associated to color video tracking are the illumination changes as well as the occlusions [6]. Furthermore, since human motion is essentially three-dimensional, the information loss in the depth channel could cause degradation of the representation and discriminating capability for these feature representations. The emergence of affordable depth sensors (e.g., Microsoft Kinect) which are largely unaffected by illumination (at least indoors) has facilitated capturing in real-time not only color videos, but also depth videos with acceptable resolution (e.g., 640×480 in pixel) and accuracy (e.g., = 1cm). By employing appropriate methods we can extract three-dimensional and motion information of the monitored subjects in the scene. Therefore the depth ambiguity of the color camera could be bypassed. On the other hand such depth sensors cannot differentiate between objects of the same depth different color, which is trivial for color cameras.

Clearly the color and depth information are correlated but also complementary to a large extent, so it would be expected to have considerable benefits by fusing them appropriately together aiming at more robust pervasive behavior recognition systems. The contribution of this work is a study of the performance of fusion techniques that combine color and depth videos for human activity analysis. To this end we use the RGBD-HuDaAct dataset [7], which is publicly available. We compare fusion methods at the decision level, the feature level and the state level.

The rest of this paper is structured as follows. In the following section we briefly survey the related work regarding systems employing color and depth information. Section 3 describes the feature extraction and the fusion approaches that we employed. Section 4 describes the experimental results and finally section 5 concludes this paper.

2   Related Work

One of the earliest works on action recognition using a depth sensor was presented in [8]. In that paper the authors employ an action graph to model explicitly the dynamics of the actions and a bag of 3D points to characterize a set of salient postures that correspond to the nodes in the action graph. That method managed to halve the recognition errors comparing to the 2D silhouette based recognition. However one of the main limitations was that it completely ignored color information.

Ni et al.[7] proposed a method for human activity recognition that takes into account such color information coupled with depth information. They proposed two multimodality fusion schemes, which simply combine color and depth streams by concatenation and are developed from two state-of-the-art feature representation methods for action recognition, i.e., spatio-temporal in-terest points (STIPs) and motion history images (MHIs).

Depth and color data can also provide higher lever and more meaningfull features like skeletal joints of a person. Sung et al. [9] propose a supervised learning approach in which they collected ground-truth labeled data for training their model. Their input was color and depth images from a Kinect sensor, from which they extracted certain features (like skeletal joints) that were fed as input to a learning algorithm. They trained a two-layered maximum-entropy Markov model which captured different properties of human activities, including their hierarchical nature and the transitions between sub-activities over time.

However skeletal joint data aren't always available, especialy in scenarios, where the camera is mounted on the ceiling. Zhao et al. [10] addressed that issue and in their work they investigated performances of different ways of extracting interest points, since interest point based approaches can handle cluttered background and partial occlusions. Additionaly they proposed a local depth pattern to represent each local video volume at each interest point. They used LibSVM [11] to classify human activities in a multi-class fashion.

While Zhao et al. investigated performances of different ways of extracting interest points for activity recognition, in this paper we investigate performances of fusion techniques that fuse color and depth. In contrast to other methods we investigate fusion schemes at the state level of the popular HMM framework, which can give better results than the simple fusion schemes that rely on concatenation of the input feature streams. In this paper only region descriptors are used, however the fusion approach has no constraints regarding the type of the employed features.

3 Methodology

The proposed methodology performs initially a feature extraction step, combining the two different sources: depth videos and color videos. From the depth videos we extract two different types of feature vectors (forward and backward), as will be described next, while from the color video we calculate features describing the human blob. The features from the whole sequence are combined and given as input to a classifier, which in turn decides on the performed activity. The method is applicable on segmented actions, but can also be used for online classification, by integration with a particle filter that makes hypotheses about sequences of actions (see, e.g., [12]).

3.1 The Features

Features from Color Images. The image features that were extracted from color images were based on a variation of Motion History Images (MHIs). MHIs are among the first holistic representation methods for behavior recognition [13]. In an MHI H_τ, pixel intensity is a function of the temporal history of motion at that point. In [14], it was shown that pixel change history (PCH) images are able to capture relevant duration information with better discrimination performance.

The PCH of a pixel is defined as:

$$P_{\varsigma,\tau}(x,y,t) = \begin{cases} \min(P_{\varsigma,\tau}(x,y,t-1) + \frac{255}{\varsigma}, 255) \\ \text{if } D(x,y,t) = 1 \\ \max(P_{\varsigma,\tau}(x,y,t-1) - \frac{255}{\tau}, 0) \\ otherwise \end{cases} \tag{1}$$

where $P_{\varsigma,\tau}(x,y,t)$ is the PCH for a pixel at (x,y), $D(x,y,t)$ is the binary image indicating the foreground region, ς is an accumulation factor and τ is a decay factor. By setting appropriate values to ς and τ we are able to capture pixel-level changes over time. The result is a scalar-valued image where more recently moving pixels are brighter.

Assuming that the human blob shapes during specific actions have discriminative capabilities we use the complex Zernike moments to capture the PCH images, which provide scale invariant representations and are relatively robust to noise. The moments of order p are defined on an grayscale image f as:

$$A_{pq} = \frac{p+1}{\pi} \int_0^1 \int_{-\pi}^{\pi} R_{pq}(r) e^{-jq\theta} f(r,\theta) r dr d\theta \tag{2}$$

where $r = \sqrt{x^2+y^2}$, and $\theta = \tan^{-1}(y/x)$ and $-1 < x,y < 1$ (x,y are the image coordinates, with respect to the center, around which the integration is calculated) and:

$$R_{pq}(r) = \sum_{s=0}^{\frac{p-q}{2}} (-1)^s \frac{(p-s)!}{s!(\frac{p+q}{2}-s)!(\frac{p-q}{2}-s)!} r^{p-2s} \tag{3}$$

where $p - q = even$ and $0 \leq q \leq p$. Moments of low order hold the coarse information while the ones of higher order hold the fine details. However, the more detailed the region representation is, the more processing power will be demanded, and thus a trade-off has to be reached considering the specific application requirements.

The MHI images are represented by means of the complex Zernike coefficients A_{00}, A_{11}, A_{20}, A_{22}, A_{31}, A_{33}, A_{40}, A_{42}, A_{44}, A_{51}, A_{53}, A_{55}, A_{60}, A_{62}, A_{64}, A_{66}, for each of which the norm and the angle were included in the provided descriptors. We used a total of 31 parameters (constant elements were removed), thus providing an acceptable scene reconstruction without a computationally prohibitive dimension.

Features from Depth Images. Ni et al. [7] proposed the use of a depth sensor and they introduced the motion history along the depth changing directions. To encode the backward motion history (decrease of depth), they introduced the backward-DMHI (bDMHI):

$$H_\tau^{bD}(x,y,t) = \begin{cases} \tau, \text{if } D(x,y,t) - D(x,y,t-1) < -\delta I_{th} \\ max(0, H_\tau^{bD}(x,y,t-1) - 1), \text{otherwise.} \end{cases} \tag{4}$$

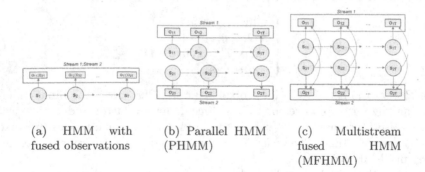

(a) HMM with fused observations

(b) Parallel HMM (PHMM)

(c) Multistream fused HMM (MFHMM)

Fig. 1. Various fusion schemes using the HMM framework for two streams. The s, o stand for the states and the observations respectively. The first index marks the stream and the second the time.

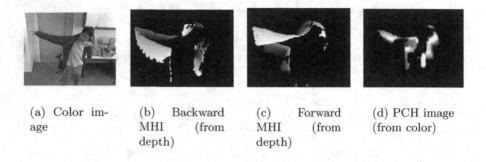

(a) Color image

(b) Backward MHI (from depth)

(c) Forward MHI (from depth)

(d) PCH image (from color)

Fig. 2. Illustration of MHI and PCH images for the *put on jacket* action

Here, H_t^{bD} denotes the backward motion history image and $D(x, y, t)$ denotes the depth sequence. δI_{th} is the threshold value for generating the mask for the region of backward motion.

Similarly, the forward history image, is defined as:

$$H_\tau^{fD}(x, y, t) = \begin{cases} \tau, \text{if } D(x, y, t) - D(x, y, t - 1) > \delta I_{th} \\ max(0, H_\tau^{fD}(x, y, t - 1) - 1), \text{otherwise.} \end{cases} \quad (5)$$

In order to calculate the depth change induced motion history images, according to the above equations, we use depth maps captured by a Kinect device. To tackle the problem of noise, we used a median filtering at the spatial domain. In the temporal domain each pixel value was replaced by the minimum of its neighbors. Similarly to the color images, each frame was represented by the 6-th order Zernike moments.

3.2 Fusion

As mentioned earlier, the depth and color images are highly complementary. Therefore, we can infer that by applying an appropriate fusion method we could achieve behavior recognition results better than the results that we could attain by using the information obtained by the individual data streams independently of each other. In the following, we shall survey the most popular fusion methods within the HMM framework and examine their applicability. The observations from this analysis will form the criterion for our selection of the most suitable HMM-based information fusion scheme to be used in the context of our system.

Existing approaches can be grouped into feature (or early) fusion and late fusion approaches. *Feature fusion* is the simplest approach; it assumes that the observation streams (sequences of feature vectors as defined in section 3.1) are synchronous. This synchronicity is a valid assumption for cameras that have overlapping fields of view and support synchronization. The related architecture *FHMM* is displayed in Fig. 1(a). Let us denote as s_t the FHMM state emitting the tth observation. Let us consider data deriving from a number of C observation streams, and denote as $\{o_{1t}, \ldots, o_{Ct}\}$ the observations at time t deriving from the available streams. Then, the full observation vector, o_t, considered by the feature fusion approach at time t, is a simple concatenation of the available individual observations:

$$o_t = \left(o'_{ct}\right)'_{c=1\ldots C} \tag{6}$$

This way, the observation emission probability of the state $s_t = i$ of the fused model, when modeled as a k-component mixture model, yields:

$$P(o_t|s_t = i) = \sum_{k=1}^{K} w_{ik} P(o_t|\theta_{ik}) \tag{7}$$

where w_{ik} denotes the weights of the mixture components, and θ_{ik} are the parameters of the kth component density of the ith model state (e.g., mean and covariance matrix of a Gaussian pdf).

The major limitations of the feature fusion approach lie in the fact that the simple concatenation of observations from different streams leads to high dimensionality and often fails to capture significant statistical dependencies between the different sources of information.

An alternative that assumes that the observation streams are independent of each other is the *parallel HMM - PHMM* [15] (see Fig. 1(b)). This HMM-type model can be applied to cameras (or other sensors) that may not be synchronized and may operate at different acquisition rates. A PHMM does also comprise a number of component *streamwise* HMMs, independently trained of one another. Similar to the synchronous case, each stream c may have its own weight r_c depending on the reliability of the source. As a consequence of this construction, the PHMM suffers from the major disadvantage of tending to neglect any dependencies on the state level between the observation streams.

The *multistream fused HMM - MFHMM* is another method recently proposed for multistream data modeling [16] (see Fig. 1(c)). The connections between the component *streamwise* HMMs of this model are chosen based on a probabilistic fusion model, which is optimal according to the maximum entropy principle and a maximum mutual information criterion for selecting dimension-reduction transforms [16]. Specifically, if we consider a set of multistream observations $O = \{o_t\}_{t=1}^{T}$, with $o_t = \{o_{ct}\}_{c=1}^{C}$, and $o^c = \{o_{ct}\}_{t=1}^{T}$, the MFHMM models this data based on the fundamental assumption

$$P(O) = \frac{1}{C} \sum_{c=1}^{C} P(o^c) \prod_{r \neq c} P(o^r | \hat{s}_c) \tag{8}$$

where $\hat{s}_c$ is the estimated hidden sequence of emitting states that corresponds to the cth stream observations, obtained by means of the Viterbi algorithm, $P(o^c)$ is the observation probability of the cth stream observed sequence, and $P(o^r | \hat{s}_c)$ is the *coupling density* of the observations from the rth stream with respect to the states of the cth stream model

$$P(o^r | \hat{s}_c) = \prod_{t=1}^{T} P(o_{rt} | \hat{s}_{ct}) \tag{9}$$

The probabilities $P(o_{rt} | \hat{s}_{ct})$ of the MFHMM can be modeled by means of mixtures of Gaussian densities, similar to the state-conditional likelihoods of the *streamwise* HMMs.

Note also that for each possible value, say i, of $\hat{s}_{ct}$, i.e. for each different state of the streamwise HMMs, a different *coupling density model* $P(o_{rt} | \hat{s}_{ct} = i)$ has to be postulated. Hence, if we consider K-state *streamwise* HMMs, there is a total of K different finite mixture models that must be trained to model the *coupling densities* $P(o_{rt} | \hat{s}_{ct})$, $\forall r, c$.

4   Experiments and Results

The employed dataset is the RGBD-HuDaAct [7], which includes twelve categories of human daily activities, motivated by the definitions provided by health-care professionals. Namely these are: (1)*make a phone call*, (2)*mop the floor*, (3)*enter the room*, (4)*exit the room*, (5)*go to bed*, (6)*get up*, (7)*eat meal*,(8)*drink water*, (9)*sit down*, (10)*stand up*, (11)*take off the jacket* and (12)*put on the jacket*. There is also a category named as background activity that contains different types of random activities. Thirty actors were involved in capturing. The actors were student volunteers, and were asked to perform each activity 2 - 4 times. Finally, approximately 46 hours of video were acquired for a total of 1189 labeled video samples. Each video sample spans about 30 - 150 seconds.

The resolutions of both color image and depth map are 640×480 pixels. The color image is of 24-bit RGB values; each depth pixel is an 16-bit integer. Both

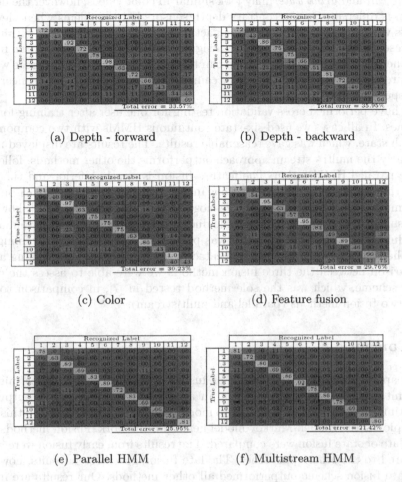

(a) Depth - forward   (b) Depth - backward

(c) Color   (d) Feature fusion

(e) Parallel HMM   (f) Multistream HMM

Fig. 3. Confusion matrices for the twelve tasks in the RGBD-HuDaAct dataset. The results are normalized based on the total number of actions, considering all cross-validation runs. The actions are: (1)*make a phone call*, (2)*mop the floor*, (3)*enter the room*, (4)*exit the room*, (5)*go to bed*, (6)*get up*, (7)*eat meal*,(8)*drink water*, (9)*sit down*, (10)*stand up*, (11)*take off the jacket* and (12)*put on the jacket*.

sequences are synchronized and the frame rates are 30 frames per second. The color and depth frames are stereo-calibrated. The horizontal and vertical distances from the camera to the scene center under capture are about two meters each and the average depth of the human subject in the scene is about three meters (i.e., which is the optimal operation range of the depth camera). This geometric setting is appropriate for home or hospital ward monitoring.

The basic observations about the dataset have to do with the complementarity of the two sources of information: color images and depth. The latter is able to differentiate between actions that take place within the human blob, e.g., *make a phone call* and *drink water* may look similar in color videos, however the depth motion is different. On the contrary depth sensors have problems when viewing objects with large discontinuities (e.g., actions *sit down, get up*, where furnitures are present); such depth maps have a significant amount of noise. After frame differencing and thresholding motion can be falsely detected even in areas where there are only still objects, while color cameras are much more robust concerning this aspect.

We have performed cross validation testing for one user after training for the rest ones. In all cases we used six-state continuous HMMs with two components for each state, which was gave reasonable results. The results are displayed in fig 3. Clearly the multi - stream approach outperforms the other methods, followed by the parallel HMM fusion. The feature fusion is clearly inferior and this is a result that agrees with the observations in [17], where a similar comparison was performed. The overall accuracies are close to the ones reported in [7], however the results are not directly comparable due to differences in the cross validation procedures. In [7] random sampling was performed to separate the training set from the test set, which was not replicated here. However, by establishing a fair comparison between the three fusion methods we were able to assess the early fusion scheme, which was the sole method tested in [7], in comparison to the other two fusion methods (parallel and multistream).

5   Conclusions

This paper investigated the effects of fusing color and depth videos, aiming to monitor the behavior of people in an assistive environment. The output of fused time-series classifiers was used to model and extract behaviors. To this end we employed the Hidden Markov model general framework. Fusion methods like early, late or state fusion were compared. The results from early fusion were weak compared to the other approaches. The late fusion gave better results, however the state fusion scheme outperformed all other methods. Our results are inline with the study in [17] for some different scenarios (industrial workflows). We expect that they can be generalized to other feature streams (e.g., spatiotemporal interest points) and we aim to investigate this hypothesis in the future.

Acknowledgment. This research has been co-financed by the European Union (European Social Fund ESF) and Greek national funds through the Operational Program "Education and Lifelong Learning" of the National Strategic Reference Framework (NSRF) - Research Funding Program: THALES. Investing in knowledge society through the European Social Fund.

References

1. Stanford, V.: Using pervasive computing to deliver elder care. IEEE Pervasive Computing 1(1), 10–13 (2002)

2. Moeslund, T.B., Hilton, A., Krüger, V.: A survey of advances in vision-based human motion capture and analysis. Comput. Vis. Image Underst. 104(2), 90–126 (2006)
3. Doukas, C., Maglogiannis, I.: Emergency fall incidents detection in assisted living environments utilizing motion, sound, and visual perceptual components. IEEE Transactions on Inf. Techn. in Biomedicine 15(2), 277–289 (2011)
4. Antonakaki, P., Kosmopoulos, D., Perantonis, S.J.: Detecting abnormal human behaviour using multiple cameras. Signal Processing 89, 1723–1738 (2009)
5. Kosmopoulos, D.: Multiview behavior monitoring for assistive environments. Universal Access in the Information Society 10, 115–123 (2011)
6. Christodoulidis, A., Delibasis, K.K., Maglogiannis, I.: Near real-time human silhouette and movement detection in indoor environments using fixed cameras. In: PETRA 2012, pp. 1:1–1:7. ACM (2012)
7. Ni, B., Wang, G., Moulin, P.: Rgbd-hudaact: A color-depth video database for human daily activity recognition. In: ICCV Workshops, pp. 1147–1153 (2011)
8. Li, W., Zhang, Z., Liu, Z.: Action recognition based on a bag of 3d points. In: CVPR4HB 2010, pp. 9–14 (2010)
9. Sung, J., Ponce, C., Selman, B., Saxena, A.: Unstructured human activity detection from rgbd images. In: Int. Conf. Robotics and Automation, pp. 842–849 (2012)
10. Zhao, Y., Liu, Z., Yang, L., Cheng, H.: Combing rgb and depth map features for human activity recognition. In: 2012 Asia-Pacific Signal Information Processing Association Annual Summit and Conference (APSIPA ASC), pp. 1–4 (December 2012)
11. Chang, C.C., Lin, C.J.: Libsvm: A library for support vector machines. ACM Trans. Intell. Syst. Technol. 2(3), 27:1–27:27 (2011)
12. Kosmopoulos, D., Doulamis, N., Voulodimos, A.: Bayesian filter based behavior recognition in workflows allowing for user feedback. Computer Vision and Image Understanding 116, 422–434 (2012)
13. Davis, J.W., Bobick, A.F.: The representation and recognition of action using temporal templates. In: Proceedings of IEEE Conference on Computer Vision and Pattern Recognition, pp. 928–934 (1997)
14. Xiang, T., Gong, S.: Beyond tracking: Modelling activity and understanding behaviour. Int. J. Comput. Vision 67(1), 21–51 (2006)
15. Chenand, C., Liang, J., Zhao, H., Hu, H., Tian, J.: Factorial HMM and parallel HMM for gait recognition. IEEE Transactions on Systems, Man, and Cybernetics, Part C: Applications and Reviews 39(1), 114–123 (2009)
16. Zeng, Z., Tu, J., Pianfetti, B., Huang, T.: Audio-visual affective expression recognition through multistream fused HMM. IEEE Transactions on Multimedia 10(4), 570–577 (2008)
17. Kosmopoulos, D., Chatzis, S.: Robust visual behavior recognition. IEEE Signal Processing Magazine 27(5), 34–45 (2010)

Subtle, Natural and Socially Acceptable Interaction Techniques for Ringterfaces — Finger-Ring Shaped User Interfaces

Mikko J. Rissanen, Samantha Vu, Owen Noel Newton Fernando,
Natalie Pang, and Schubert Foo

Centre of Social Media Innovation for Communities, Nanyang Technological University,
14 Nanyang Drive, HSS-06-15, 637332 Singapore
{mjrissanen,sgtvu,ofernando,nlspang,sfoo}@ntu.edu.sg

Abstract. This study analyzes interaction techniques in previously proposed 16 user interface concepts that utilize the form factor of a finger-ring, i.e. "ringterfaces". We categorized the ringterfaces according to their interaction capabilities and critically examined how socially acceptable, subtle and natural they are. Through this analysis we show which kind of ringterfaces are likely to become general-purpose user interfaces and what factors drive their development toward commercial applications. We highlight the need for studying context awareness in ambient intelligence environments and end-user programming in future research on ringterfaces.

Keywords: Interaction techniques, Subtle interaction, Social acceptability, Natural user interface, Finger-ring.

1 Introduction

Social acceptability and unobtrusiveness are becoming an ever higher concern in the development of ambient intelligence technology and innovative user interfaces [1, 2]. The aim in ambient intelligence technology is to make the technology 'disappear' and become socialized and part of the everyday activities of people. Jewelry has been noted as the potential medium for this purpose. Over a decade ago Miner et al. [3] envisioned digital jewelry as ambient interfaces that enable the user to see incoming email messages, check priority emails in meetings and provide affective information by using dynamically color-coded jewelry to close friends. Some of this kind of use is now enabled by smartwatches. Also finger-rings seem suitable as a universal form of ambient technology. Wide social acceptability in almost all cultures and the fact that fingers produce the highest information entropy in the human body [4] make finger-rings a good candidate for future interaction device.

Finger-ring shaped user interfaces deserve a descriptive term of their own in HCI literature — "ringterfaces". In this paper we present a literature review of 16 past ringterface concepts and an analysis of interaction techniques. We discuss the pros and cons of these ringterfaces for their input and output capabilities and critically examine

N. Streitz and C. Stephanidis (Eds.): DAPI/HCII 2013, LNCS 8028, pp. 52–61, 2013.

how socially acceptable, subtle and natural they are. We end by suggesting factors that can drive ringterfaces to become everyday digital jewelry.

This analysis focuses only on academic literature. We recognize that there are commercial products such as the gaming appliance *Ringbow*. There are also related patents pending and granted. Since none of the ringterfaces have really reached large scale commercial utilization we exclude those concepts from this analysis for now.

2   18 Years of Research — 16 Ringterface Concepts

This chapter summarizes the evolution of ringterface concepts from the first wireless keyboard prototypes in the 90's to the latest gesture ringterfaces in 2012. We then categorize the ringterfaces by the interaction techniques they support.

2.1   Ringterface Concepts and Prototypes

FingeRing in 1994 [5] and 1997 [6] was the first widely noted prototype that utilized the form factor of a finger-ring as the user interface. FingeRing was intended as a "full-time wearable interface" for inputting commands and characters by tapping a surface with fingertips which was detected by accelerometers and mapped to characters on the keyboard.

MIDS Ring [7, 8] developed by Lam et al. works as a mouse, virtual keyboard and a light pen. The system uses MEMS acceleration sensors and consisted of MIDS Ring, MIDS Watch, MIDS Interface and a computer. It was envisioned to become the interface for handwriting or playing virtual piano and assistive technology for the blind for reading Braille dot writings.

Fukumoto's HANDset [9] acts as a phone. It uses vibration conductivity of the bones in the user's hand for transmitting phone calls. The ring part of the system is used as the speaker and the wrist part as microphone. The user inserts her finger in the ear canal and speaks to her wrist. Additionally, the system supports a simple gesture such as on/off which is achieved by tapping fingertips together. Although intended primarily as a phone the device itself can be count as a ringterface since an audio-based input and output mechanism could be built on it.

Telebeads by Labrune & Mackay [10] was a concept for sharing social network mnemonics targeting teenagers. The finger-ring part of the system acted as a notification medium to e.g. vibrate when someone sent a message to the user. Telebeads also help people to remember who they are connected to and communicate with them using the ring. For simple input Telebeads included a button.

Lee et al.'s i-Throw [11] was the first ringterface to realize a wide range of hand gestures for user interaction. i-Throw was the ringterface part of a larger smart ubiquitous environment. The system recognizes gestures such as throwing (sending), ready-to-receiving, receiving and selecting virtual objects, as well as scrolling up or down, increasing or decreasing (e.g. volume), and scanning. Target devices the user wishes to interact with are chosen by pointing at them at close range.

Han et al. [12] presented the first ringterface to make use of magnetometers. Their method for handwriting input uses a magnetometer attached to the wrist and a permanent magnet worn as a finger-ring. They suggested the method could be applied for wearable computing.

Iwamoto & Shinoda [13] demonstrated a ring shaped interfaces that allows the user to press UbiButtons by tapping different parts of the index finger and use the finger as a pointing device such as mouse.

Werner et al.'s [14] United-Pulse ringterface measures and transmits the partner's pulse whenever the wearer touches the ring having the aim of for sharing intimacy.

Abracadabra by Harrison et al. [15] uses magnetometers like Han et al., but it requires a wrist display. The system supports 1D polar movement (rotation) and clicking, cursor control and 1D polar or 2D positional gestures that are done near but not directly on the display ("around device interaction").

Matsuda et al. [16] developed a Finger Braille reading system for deafblind people which consists of piezoelectric accelerometers attached to rings. Finger Braille writings are recognized when moving fingers over Braille dots.

Nenya developed by Ashbrook et al. [17] uses similar methodology as Abracadabra allowing 1D input operations. The user can twist the ring to make scrollable selections and slide it along the finger to "click". Also Nenya requires a wrist counterpart that recognizes changes in electromagnetic fields that use of the ring produces. It can be used by just one hand although two-handed use is much easier.

Bainbridge & Paradiso [18] created a ringterface based on RFID technology. Passive RFID tags are worn in each finger and a wrist piece contains an RFID reader. Five rings worn on each finger allow finger gestures such as clicking and scrolling and mouse-like operation of the cursor.

Zhang et al. [19] demonstrated a ring-shaped system and a sensing method that collects audio signals conducted by finger bones when the user slides the finger along a surface. It uses a gyroscope and an accelerometer to recognizes posture and movement of the hand. This system was intended to be used for controlling large displays such as TVs and projector systems.

Xangle by Horie et al. [20] consists of two accelerometers embedded on two different devices assuming that people can control only one axis precisely and fast by moving a body part. Xangle devices can be worn on forefingers, a forefinger and a thumb, or a forefinger and head. Pointing interaction is enabled by calculating the angle between the two devices. "Clicking" is achieved by 1-second pointing.

EyeRing by Nanayakkara et al. [21] is a ring-embedded camera that is used for taking photos of the surroundings. It was intended as an assistive technology for the blind to be used in applications such as detection of currency in bills by text recognition, recognition of colors and walking aid by recognizing space in front of the user. A small button embedded on the ring has to be pressed to initiate interaction.

Ketabdar et al. [4] developed an "around device interaction" system Pingu. It consists of built-in magnetometer, acceleration, gyro and proximity, and output capabilities via a RBG led light and a vibration transducer. Pingu recognizes small scale subtle finger gestures. Social interaction, physical activity analysis, context recognition and in-car interaction are mentioned as possible applications.

2.2 User Interaction Support in Ringterfaces

We categorized the ringterface concepts according to input and output capabilities by using the direct vs. indirect input and user task composition [22]:

- *elemental tasks* use typically one degree of freedom such as 1) text entry (e.g. typing a symbolic character), 2) making a selection (e.g. from a set of alternative), 3) indicating position (e.g. pointing on screen) and, 4) quantification (e.g. giving an exact numerical value),
- *phrasing* that utilizes muscular tension such as using a pull-down menu (press and hold mouse button, move cursor to a menu item, release button).

Table 1. Input type and user tasks supported by each ringterfaces concept

Ringterface	Fingers	Direct/ Indirect input	Elemental tasks	Phrasing tasks	Output
FingeRing	5	Indirect: keyboard	Text	N/A	N/A
MIDS Ring	2	Direct: pen Indirect: keyboard; mouse	Text, Pointing	Hand-writing	N/A
HANDset	1	Direct: voice Indirect: button	"Clicks"	N/A	Audio (voice)
Telebeads	1	Indirect: button	"Clicks"	N/A	Visual (color coding); Vibration (alert)
i-Throw	1	Indirect: gestures	N/A	Hand gestures	N/A
Han et al.	1	Direct: pen	N/A	Hand-writing	N/A
UbiButtons	1	Indirect: mouse	"Clicks", Pointing	N/A	N/A
United-Pulse	1	N/A	N/A	N/A	Vibration (pulse)
Abracadabra	1	Indirect: gestures; mouse; button	"Clicks", Pointing	Hand gestures	N/A
Matsuda et al.	3	Indirect: Finger-Braille reading	N/A	N/A	Vibration (Braille)
Nenya	1	Indirect: slider	Selection, "Clicks"	N/A	N/A
Bainbridge & Paradiso	5	Indirect: gestures; mouse; button	Pointing, Selection, "Clicks"	Hand gestures	N/A
Zhang et al.	1	Direct: touchscreen	Pointing, Selection, "Clicks"	N/A	N/A
Xangle	2	Indirect: joystick	N/A	Pointing, "Clicks"	N/A
EyeRing	1	Direct: pointing Indirect: button	"Clicks"	N/A	Audio (synthesized voice)
Pingu	1	Indirect: gestures	N/A	Hand gestures	Visual (color coding); Vibration (alert)

Compound tasks and chunking that use multiple degrees of freedom e.g. by using two hands for scrolling with keyboard and pointing with mouse are often difficult to differentiate from elemental user tasks [22]. In the case of ringterfaces, it is rather simple to differentiate between elemental and phrasing tasks, but more inconvenient to differentiate between elemental and compound tasks because the discrete motion of the finger(s). Phrasing can be taken as an input operation which requires the finger on which the ring is worn to be kept in certain position for a while, as "clicking" using Xangle. Table 1 illustrates our categorization.

Since the 90's command-line prototypes the number of rings has been reducing, the only exception being Bainbridge & Paradiso's prototype. Most of the ringterfaces (10) have adopted the indirect input paradigm. Han et al.'s and Zhang et al.'s prototypes enable direct input only. MIDS Ring, HANDset and EyeRing enable both direct and indirect input. The ringterfaces demonstrate a wide array of input methods being either button-like (5), mouse-like (4), gesture interface (4), keyboard-like (2), pen-like (2), joystick-like (1), touchscreen-like (1) or simple slider-like (1). Matsuda et al.'s Braille reading method is also indirect input. United-Pulse does not support any input.

The first two prototypes, FingeRing and MIDS Ring enable text input. Most of the ringterfaces utilizing indirect input methods enable "clicks" (7) and pointing (6) of which Zhang et al.'s prototype acts as a direct touchscreen-like input. Xangle can be taken as an indirect joystick-like method as the user has to adjust two rings to point and make selections. HANDset is a unique ringterface in a sense that it is intended as just a phone and it supports only input that is equal to pressing two buttons. 7 ringterfaces enable phrasing. Handwriting is supported by MIDS Ring and Han et al.'s prototype. i-Throw, Abracadabra, Bainbridge & Paradiso's prototype and Pingu support gesture interaction. Xangle is a unique indirect input ringterface since pointing is done by phrasing and the user has to "click" by holding the cursor still.

6 ringterfaces support output. Output is usually provided via vibro-tactile or audio feedback. Only Telebeads and Pingu demonstrate visual feedback by showing lights of various colors which meaning the user needs to interpret. HANDset was intended as just a phone. Matsuda et al.'s prototype is unique in a sense that its only function is to transfer and interpret vibration information into another person than the user.

3   Analysis of Interaction Techniques

The categorization above demonstrated that it has been technically possible to include many kinds of input methods and at least limited output into ringterfaces. In the following we analyze advantages and disadvantages of the interaction techniques. It should be noted that only limited user studies have been conducted by all the ringterface authors. We recognize the fundamental challenge of defining what subtle interaction, gestures and natural user interaction are in general, but at least we can draw approximations based on previous HCI literature on these topics.

3.1   Analysis Criteria from HCI Literature

Social Acceptability. As computer use has become a social norm, we do not question if pressing buttons, making selections, using mouse, typing on keyboard and writing with digital pens are socially acceptable input methods. On the other hand, several ringterfaces support gesture interaction. There are expressive, suspenseful, secretive and magical gestures and the observers of gesture interaction have an impact on what is socially acceptable [23]. In everyday use the effect of gestures has to be visible to the people around the user instead of looking like magic [23]. Therefore ringterfaces that use indirect non-gesture based or direct touchscreen-like interaction techniques can be expected to be socially acceptable as the effects can be observed. Gesture interaction without a touchscreen, however, appears as magical ununderstandable interaction. Secretive gestures would not be noticed at all. Lumsden & Brewster [24] questioned the social acceptance of gesture-based and speech-based interaction methods in general. Previous studies highlight two critical issues in gesture based interaction in public use. Rico et al. [25] argue that a successful gesture interfaces need to be usable and robust in addition to being socially acceptable. Gestures in general produce physical and cognitive load which has to be overcome by personalized gesture sets [26]. These challenges lead to the exclusion of all indirect gesture ringterfaces from social acceptable everyday digital jewelry. Socially acceptable ringterfaces therefore would support either: 1) conventional computer-like input or 2) secretive gestures.

Subtlety. Costanza et al. [27] studied subtle and intimate interaction using an EMG-based "motionless gesture" system worn on the upper arm under the clothes. This kind of interaction represents the most subtle and unnoticeable interaction the human body can produce using voluntary movement of muscles. Unfortunately, such interaction is difficult to incorporate into ringterfaces. The high information entropy in the finger [4] would produce lots of false positives in detecting any gesture. García-Herranz et al.'s [28] model for classification of communication consists of two axes. *Information* communicated varies from poor to rich on one axis. On the other axis communication *traffic* varies from light to heavy. Subtle communication is therefore rich in information but light in traffic, whereas the opposite is redundant communication which is poor in information but heavy in traffic. This translates to subtle interaction as minimal perceivable interaction.

Natural Interaction. Many of the ringterfaces support gesture interaction. Although a popular research topic, gestures may not be the most suitable approach for ringterfaces. Hinckley & Wigdor [22] argue that "it is a common mistake to attribute the naturalness of a product to the underlying input technology" and that "there is no inherently natural set of gestures". Rico et al. [25] summarized previous research results on naturalness of gestures indicating that natural gesture interaction may not be separated from gestures that support speech and conversations. Mouse-like and keyboard-like ringterfaces are not any more natural than the original indirect input devices which interaction they emulate. Nor are handwriting ringterfaces, except for handwriting tasks. Thinking about the finger-ring particularly as a form factor does raise a question what a natural interaction using a ringterfaces should actually be like. Mundane interactions involving ringterfaces that are already 'naturalised' would reduce the perceived level of complexity in use. Normally, rings are mere decorations and have symbolic value. Conventional rings do not have functionality. However, being part of the finger they allow a few interactions that we here take as natural: 1) Pointing with the finger the ring is worn is natural direct input, 2) playing with the ring by rolling it around, moving it along the finger or slightly fix its position which would not seem strange to most people, or 3) taking the ringterface off and putting it on which are natural and unobtrusive interactions (although potentially annoying when repeated).

3.2   Results

Fig. 1. illustrates the result of the categorization. In the following, we draw a few notions on how specific ringterfaces fit into the above-mentioned criteria.

Fig. 1. Ringterfaces categorized by analyzed three characteristics

Social Acceptability. Most of the ringterfaces allow the effect of interaction to be perceived and understood by others. Even HANDset would not differ much from a normal mobile phone headset. Mouse-like pointing would not look strange as long as the cursor can be seen. United-Pulse that does not allow input would also be socially acceptable as its output cannot be perceived by the observers. Use of Nenya, on the other hand, looks mostly like a magical gesture. All indirect gesture ringterfaces that do not relate to existing user interface devices, i.e. Bainbridge & Paradiso's, Pingu and Nenya, were judged to be socially non-acceptable based on the previous findings [24-26] discussed above. Assistive technology ringterfaces, Matsuda et al.'s Braille reading method and EyeRing, are more challenging to categorize. They are only used in situations where there are physically impaired users reading texts they do not perceive in the same way as healthy users. In that sense, if used by healthy users, these ringterfaces would be seen as strange devices.

Subtlety. Pingu and Telebeads employed somewhat similar interaction techniques and United-Pulse only uses a different modality. These ringterfaces can achieve rich information through the codification and light traffic in communication. In this sense subtle interaction can be achieved by embedding the user interaction into some ordinary and unnoticeable voluntary action that does not produce heavy communication traffic due to the use of the ringterface. MIDS Ring or Han et al.'s magnetometer-based method could therefore be used only when masqueraded as normal-looking handwriting. Nenya, on the other hand, does achieve rather light traffic, but it communicates only poor information.

Natural Interaction. Only three of the ringterfaces achieve natural interaction by providing interactivity as putting the ring on or taking it off, playing with the ring or pointing with the finger. Zhang et al.'s touchscreen-like ringterface enables the user to point and touch a surface. The only limitation in this technique is that the user usually has to point at a target device of an ambient intelligence enabled environment. The "playful" interaction is only enabled in Nenya. Mundane interactions, taking off and putting on, have not been utilized in any ringterface concept yet.

4   Discussion

The above analysis suggests that the research on ringterfaces has so far been very much technically-focused. It seems that none of the ringterfaces presented to date achieve subtle, socially acceptable and natural interaction. Social acceptability was achieved by 11 ringterfaces, subtle interaction by 3 ringterfaces and natural interaction by 3 ringterface. Only 2 ringterfaces achieve two of the three aspects. Therefore, an alternative paradigm might help us to understand how the vision of digital jewelry in the case of ringterfaces could actually be realized in terms. We suggest that that two major factors affect adoption of ringterfaces in the real world.

First, as the level of automation in our everyday technology raises due to agent technology and context-awareness, we will find less and less need for complex user interaction. Especially in the context of ambient intelligence, this becomes a key question [29]. The automation of routine tasks will release people from executing trivial tasks, and thereby give them additional time to focus on more challenging tasks. In addition, such ambient communication technologies can be considered as a platform to keep social relationships within geographically distributed people [30]. The design of ambient communication technologies will have a considerable impact on the way people communicate and interact in their daily life. The possibilities that arise from such system will not only influence communication processes, but also the way daily activities are organized. Therefore, the requirements to build ambient communication technologies that perform exactly as they are expected to do, and that protects personal data while still allowing easy access to it, are compelling.

Second, we believe end-user programming (EUP) [31] becames an essential part of future ringterfaces. Within an increasing number of domains an important emerging need is the ability for users, who have limited technical knowledge, to compose computational elements into novel configurations. EUP attempts to support naïve users to somehow find ways to control the power of computation to help with their tasks. EUP is becoming a trend in mobile communications e.g. in the form Samsung's *TecTiles*™.

Costanza et al. [27] stated that most of the personal communication through mobile devices is minimal for the most parts. For a future ringterface that enables highly automated and end-user-programmed mobile communications, even a few input commands would suffice. Our on-going work demonstrates how increasing level of automation and EUP come together as a interaction method for making real world mnemonics [32]. The concept supplements smartphones with a finger-ring shaped wearable camera that is used to take photos of the user's environment. EUP enables the user to record macros on the smartphone that are associated with a photo of a familiar scene. Taking another similar photo of the same scene triggers the macro. In this way the user is empowered to use her creativity for making the mnemonics and achieve what she wishes using EUP, yet, automation processes photo comparisons.

5   Conclusion

We analyzed 16 previous ringterface concepts in terms of interaction techniques. Especially gesture interaction seems a popular choice of interaction in the latest concepts. We argued that gesture interaction based ringterfaces will face problems in everyday commercial applications because of low social acceptance of gestures in public places. We suggested two aspects that affect the success of ringterfaces as general-purpose user interfaces. First, the ever-increasing level of automation and future advances in ambient intelligence and context-awareness will affect adoption of gesture interaction based ringterfaces negatively. Simplistic interaction techniques are most likely to prevail. Second, end-user programming is suggested to be the paradigm which is a socially acceptable and flexible step in the near future developments of ringterfaces for everyday use. We outlined our approach and on-going work on development of this kind of ringterfaces. Future research will focus on validating our suggestions and examining how they relate to other form factors of digital jewelry.

Acknowledgements. Centre of Social Media Innovations for Communities (COSMIC) is supported by the Singapore National Research Foundation under its International Research Centre @ Singapore Funding Initiative and administered by the IDM Programme Office.

References

1. Rekimoto, J.: GestureWrist and GesturePad: unobtrusive wearable interaction devices. In: Proc. ISWC, pp. 21–27 (2001)
2. Sadri, F.: Ambient intelligence: a survey. ACM Computing Surveys 43(4), Article 36 (October 2011)
3. Miner, C.S., Chan, D.M., Campbell, C.: Digital jewelry: wearable technology for everyday life. In: Proc. CHI EA 2001, 45-46 (2001)
4. Ketabdar, H., Moghadam, P., Roshandel, M.: Pingu: A new miniature wearable device for ubiquitous computing environments. In: Proc. CISIS 2012, pp. 502–506 (2012)
5. Fukumoto, M., Suenaga, Y.: "FingeRing": a full-time wearable interface. In: Proc. CHI 1994, pp. 81–82 (1994)
6. Fukumoto, M., Tonomura, Y.: "Body coupled FingerRing": wireless wearable keyboard. In: CHI 1997, pp. 147–154 (1997)
7. Lam, A.H.F., Li, W.J.: MIDS: GUI and TUI in mid-air using MEMS sensors. In: Proc. ICCA, pp. 1218–1222 (2002)
8. Lam, A., Li, W., Liu, Y., Xi, N.: MIDS: micro input devices system using MEMS sensors. In: Proc. IROS, pp. 1184–1189 (2002)
9. Fukumoto, M.: A finger-ring shaped wearable handset based on bone-conduction. In: Proc. ISWC 2005, pp. 10-13 (2005)
10. Labrune, J.-B., Mackay, W.: Telebeads: social network mnemonics for teenagers. In: Proc. IDC 2006, pp. 57–64 (2006)
11. Lee, J., Lim, S.-H., Yoo, J.-W., Park, K.-W., Choi, H.-J., Park, K.H.: A ubiquitous fashionable computer with an i-Throw device on a location-based service environment. In: Proc. AINAW 2007, pp. 59–65 (2007)

12. Han, X., Seki, H., Kamiya, Y., Hikizu, M.: Wearable handwriting input device using magnetic field. In: Proc. SICE Annual Conference, pp. 365–368 (2007)
13. Iwamoto, T., Shinoda, H.: Finger ring device for tactile sensing and human machine interface. In: Proc. SICE Annual Conference, pp. 2132–2136 (2007)
14. Werner, J., Wettach, R., Hornecker, E.: United-pulse: feeling your partner's pulse. In: Proc. MobileHCI 2008, pp. 535–538 (2008)
15. Harrison, C., Hudson, S.: Abracadabra: wireless, high precision, and unpowered finger input for very small mobile devices. In: Proc. UIST 2009, pp. 121–124 (2009)
16. Matsuda, Y., Sakuma, I., Jimbo, Y., Kobayashi, E., Arafune, T., Isomura, T.: Development of Finger Braille recognition system. JBSE 5(1), 54–65 (2010)
17. Ashbrook, D., Baudisch, P., White, S.: Nenya: subtle and eyes-free mobile input with a magnetically-tracked finger ring. In: Proc. CHI 2011, pp. 2043–2046 (2011)
18. Bainbridge, R., Paradiso, J.A.: Wireless hand gesture capture through wearable passive tag sensing. In: Proc. BSN 2011, pp. 200–204 (2011)
19. Zhang, B., Chen, Y., Qian, Y., Wang, X.: A ring-shaped interactive device for large remote display and mobile device control. In: Proc. UbiComp 2011, pp. 473–474 (2011)
20. Horie, T., Terada, T., Katayama, T., Tsukamoto, M.: A pointing method using accelerometers for graphical user interfaces. In: Proc. AH 2012, article 12 (2012)
21. Nanayakkara, S., Shilkrot, R., Maes, P.: EyeRing: a finger-worn assistant. In: Proc. CHI EA 2012, pp. 1961–1966 (2012)
22. Hinckley, K., Wigdor, D.: Input technologies and techniques. In: Jacko, J. (ed.) Human-Computer Interaction Handbook: Fundamentals, Evolving Technologies, and Emerging Applications, 3rd edn., ch. 9. CRC Press (2012)
23. Montero, C.S., Alexander, J., Marshall, M.T., Subramanian, S.: Would you do that?: understanding social acceptance of gestural interfaces. In: Proc. MobileHCI 2010, pp. 275–278 (2010)
24. Lumsden, J., Brewster, S.: A paradigm shift: alternative interaction techniques for use with mobile & wearable devices. In: Proc. CASCON 2003, pp. 197–210 (2003)
25. Rico, J., Crossan, A., Brewster, S.: Gesture-based interfaces: practical applications of gestures in real world mobile settings. In: England, D. (ed.) Whole Body Interaction. Human-Computer Interaction Series, ch. 14. Springer (2011)
26. Keates, S., Robinson, P.: The use of gestures in multimodal input. In: Proc. Assets 1998, pp. 35–42 (1998)
27. Costanza, E., Inverso, S., Allen, R., Maes, P.: Intimate interfaces in action: assessing the usability and subtlety of EMG-based motionless gestures. In: Proc. CHI 2007, pp. 819–828 (2007)
28. García-Herranz, M., Olivera, F., Haya, P., Alamán, X.: Harnessing the interaction continuum for subtle assisted living. Sensors 12(7), 9829–9846 (2012)
29. Aarts, E., Harwig, R., Schuurmans, M.: Ambient intelligence. In: Denning, P.J. (ed.) The Invisible Future: The Seamless Integration of Technology Into Everyday Life, pp. 235–250. McGraw-Hill (2001)
30. de Ruyter, B.: Social interactions in ambient intelligent environments. J. Ambient Intell. Smart Environ. 3(2), 175–177 (2011)
31. Nardi, B.A.: A small matter of programming: perspectives on end user computing. MIT Press (1993)
32. Rissanen, M.J., Fernando, O.N.N., Iroshan, H., Vu, S., Pang, N., Foo, S.: Ubiquitous shortcuts: mnemonics by just taking photos. In: Proc. CHI EA 2013 (to appear, 2013)

MTIS: A Multi-Touch Text Input System

Michael Schmidt, Anja Fibich, and Gerhard Weber

Dresden University of Technology, Institute of Applied Science,
Human-Computer Interaction, Nöthnitzer Straße 46, 01062 Dresden
{Michael.Schmidt1,Anja.Fibich,Gerhard.Weber}@tu-dresden.de

Abstract. Entering text by gesture alphabets is not one of the most efficient methods. However, there are special applications and contexts where it shows advantages. Input with little focus of attention is possible and, for short phrases, transition to other input options may be more involving. The work at hand presents a new multi-touch gesture alphabet. Multi-touch can accelerate gesture input and provides the diversity that allows to confine to single strokes that demand less attention. We analyzed the characteristics of the alphabet and compared it to a single-touch variant. Detailed investigations of text input by gestures and results of a user study are provided. The investigations revealed preferences of users and showed the need for individualization and self-definition of gestures. To meet this demands, our approach for classifying template defined letters is demonstrated.

Keywords: gesture alphabet, text input, classification, recognition, template-based, multi-touch.

1 Introduction and Motivation

Applications for controlling UI by symbolic surface gestures are browsers, air traffic control [3], accessibility of mobile [16,8] or special [20] devices or in sketching tools, directly [1,23], or to support sketch recognition [11,4]. Symbolic gestures are applied in several text entry systems, too. Gesture alphabets are, for instance, 'EdgeWrite' [22], 'Minimal Device Independent Text Input Method' (MDITIM) [7], or the 'Graffiti' alphabet realized in the Palm OS. Such methods can offer advantages over conventional text input methods. As an abstraction to handwriting, such symbols are easier to recognize by pattern matching methods. Additionally, they allow for shorthand writing and demand less attention by writing letters on top of each other. Though efficiency of these input methods is low compared to, for instance, virtual keyboards, users may still prefer them [9]. We introduce a new gesture alphabet consisting of multi-touch symbols. That allows for greater variability and similarity to Latin letters while improving writing speed. The multi-touch gesture recognizer utilized is capable of recognizing all types of symbolic surface gestures and can be trained by templates. This provides the option to compare other gesture alphabets directly. Furthermore, the classifier detects gestures invariant to rotation, scaling and speed. Therefore, it scales with users' experience in text input and is suitable for mobile devices.

N. Streitz and C. Stephanidis (Eds.): DAPI/HCII 2013, LNCS 8028, pp. 62–71, 2013.
© Springer-Verlag Berlin Heidelberg 2013

2   State of the Art

For text input in mobile environments different approaches exist. Most common is the 12-key keyboard, capable to achieve around 10 words per minute (with T9 support, approximately 20 wpm are possible) [13]. In substitution to QUERTY hardware-keyboards, less space demanding virtual keyboards are common for smartphones, too. Besides typing, other silent input systems include handwriting and entering symbols of gesture alphabets. While handwriting is natural to most users, it is still challenging for pattern recognizers. Virtual keyboard input is fast (conservative model estimation predicts at least 28 wpm [24]), but unnatural and prone to parallax errors.

Several approaches improve on pure keyboard input and diminish differences between gesturing and typing. One way is to re-arrange or group symbols to provide structures for a short way hierarchical targeting by gestural movements [17,14,15]. In [18], letters are split into a set of abstract and recurring segments to define a hierarchical structure whose navigation produces them. Other methods support gesturing on virtual keyboards to connect keys to words. Though performance gains by gesturing on virtual keyboards are possible in general, there is much room for improvements due to special layouts [19]. In [2], such input can be done even bi-manually. By interpretation of the drawn shape on the basis of a large dictionary, the approach in [10] requires no precise targeting of keys.

All these methods lack the ability of eyesfree writing. Although, methods that interpret the shape - as in [10] - demand less attention from users as they are allowed to trade accuracy for speed [13]. Overall, the precise targeting necessary for input per soft keyboards, hierarchical selection and handwriting requires focusing the input area. Eyesfree entry allows to spend more attention to supporting input techniques as word completion [12].

Pure gesturing is an alternative that uses an input area more efficiently by writing letters on top of each other. In [6], this concept was introduced as heads-up writing and it was stated being easier on the wrist for users when compared to handwriting. Another advantage of writing discrete symbols in single movements and an unrelated manner is the possibility of entering text with less attention to the screen or even without visual feedback. In [13], the term 'focus of attention' (FOA) is introduced. It indicates the level of attention a task requires from a user. For instance, blind writing of memorized text has a lower FOA than writing it with a text entry method that requires additional observation of input [13].

Gesture alphabets discretize letters by variable degrees of abstraction. The more abstract, the more robust is recognition, though users' ability to grasp them intuitively may suffer. 'EdgeWrite' [22] and MDITIM [7] facilitate robust recognition by utilizing sequences of only a few directional strokes. This enables both methods to be less dependent of input devices and input by tracking of eye movements, for instance. Little more resemblance to Latin letters can be found in 'Unistrokes' [6]. The 'Graffiti' alphabet, in contrast, mimics most Latin letters and is therefore more intuitive. Its successor 'Graffiti 2', though prone to input errors (19% at approximately 12% due to classification errors), compared to virtual keyboard is preferred by users (with word completion) because it is seen more intuitive and usable as well as less exhausting [9]. This is interesting regarding that a slow input rate (9 wpm), approximately two-thirds the input speed shown on virtual keyboard, was observed.

3   Multi-Touch Text Input

In the following, we use the same terms and taxonomy as in [21] (see Fig. 1). A gesture consists of at least one stroke, i.e., a phase during which at least one contact touches the sensing device. Each stroke can have one or multiple (partly) concurrent touches. 'Single-touch' and 'multi-touch' refers to gestures consisting of one stroke with one or multiple touches, respectively. A 'multi-stroke' is characterized by more than one subsequent but no concurrent touches. A gesture of multiple strokes containing one being multi-touch is referred to as 'sequential multi-touch'.

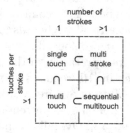

Fig. 1. The taxonomy of surface gestures from [21]. Gestures are classified by their number of strokes and the maximum number of concurrent touches within these strokes.

We present a multi-touch gesture alphabet based on the two 'Graffiti' versions. Our aim is to speed up writing by avoiding multi-stroke symbols and introducing multi-touch symbols for complex letters. The level of abstraction is low compared to 'Unistrokes' and most symbols resemble upper case Latin block letters. We balance efficiency and intuition by abstracting letters that are drawn multi-stroke when writing with a pen or that have a shape that can be produced faster using multiple touches. Variations of several letters are supported to allow for further writing speedup or individual style. In our user study, we investigated the advantages and drawbacks of this approach. For this purpose two alphabets were created, a single-stroke reference alphabet and the multi-touch text input method. Figure 2 illustrates the two alphabets. On the left side, the single-stroke reference alphabet is shown. It consists of letters from 'Graffiti' 1+2, stripped by multi-stroke symbols and enlarged by few simplified alternatives for some letters. On the right side, our multi-touch alphabet is demonstrated. We replaced selected symbols by multi-touch counterparts. The remaining single-stroke gestures are shared for the same letters between both alphabets.

To recognize both gesture alphabets of Fig. 2, the gesture classifier presented in [21] was used. It recognizes arbitrary surface gestures that were trained by

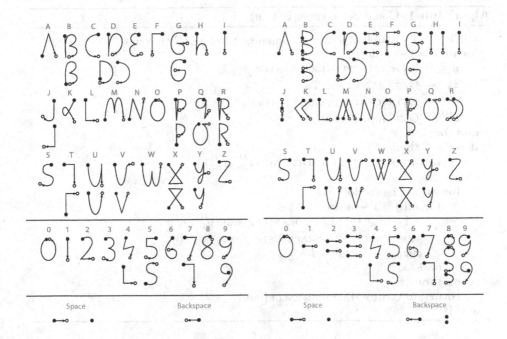

Fig. 2. Illustration of input for the single-touch (left) and the multi-touch alphabet (right). Symbols are drawn in one stroke, but may consist of up to three movements of simultaneous touches (only on the right side). A black dot depicts a touch, the arrow its movement and the blank circle the position where the contact is lost.

templates. This way a fair comparison is not hindered by different classification methods. Two gesture templates per symbol were defined in advance by the authors.

4 Gesture Recognition

Details of the applied on-line gesture recognition routine are found in [21]. The approach is based on statistical (Bayesian) classification and comprises comparisons by features of the shape and structural properties of a gesture's segments (tokens). The segmentation process splits gestures by their trajectories of touches on the sensing device. The pseudo code adapted from [21] is given in Algorithm 1. The procedure 'CompareGestures' computes the similarity of an input I and a template gesture T with the same number of tokens n.[1]

Algorithm 1 finds the best bijective matching between two sets of tokens by the negated sum of their pairwise distances of normalized structural features and their shape. Structural features of a token are its relative position, size, slope and rotation within the gesture. Shapes are compared by the Procrustes

---

[1] An input is not allowed to match a template with a different number of tokens.

Algorithm 1. CompareGestures(I, T, n)

▷ INPUT: T - template gesture; I - input gesture; n - token count
for all $i = 1 \to n$ **do**
    $\boldsymbol{y}_T^{(i)} \leftarrow$ ExtractStructuralFeatures(T,i)
    $\boldsymbol{z}_T^{(i)} \leftarrow$ GetTrajectory(T,i)
    $\boldsymbol{y}_I^{(i)} \leftarrow$ ExtractStructuralFeatures(I,i)
    $\boldsymbol{z}_I^{(i)} \leftarrow$ GetTrajectory(I,i)
end for
if $n == 1$ **then**
    return ProcrustesShapeDistance($\boldsymbol{z}_T^{(1)},\boldsymbol{z}_I^{(1)}$)
else
    for all $i = 1 \to n$ **do**
        for all $j = 1 \to n$ **do**
            md $\leftarrow$ SquaredEuclideanDistance($\boldsymbol{y}_T^{(i)},\boldsymbol{y}_I^{(j)}$)
            sd $\leftarrow$ ProcrustesShapeDistance($\boldsymbol{z}_T^{(i)},\boldsymbol{z}_I^{(j)}$)
            mm[i,j] $\leftarrow -md - sd$
        end for
    end for
    return MaximumMatchingValue(mm)
end if

---

analysis. It performs normalization of the trajectories to match them in sample rate, size and rotation[2]. A squared Euclidean distance of thus normalized 'shape signatures' is computed. The interested reader is referred to [21] for a detailed description of features and routines. Possible improvements of the classification routine concerning parameter estimation to account for feature correlations are discussed there as well. Rejection of an input is possible by defining a distance threshold that shall not be exceeded. We did not apply rejection for MTIS.

5 Evaluation

A first version of our multi-touch alphabet was evaluated with 20 users in [5]. Organized in a between group design, the multi-touch alphabet was compared to the 'Graffiti 2' alphabet by performing text-copy tasks[3]. In a questionnaire, users declared the multi-touch gesture alphabet more usable in the whole and in detail conducive to learning. Furthermore, the input of multi-touch symbols was faster in the learning phase and significant faster during tests, when averaged over the same test sentences.[4] However, 'Graffiti 2' contains few multi-stroke symbols that require a time-out for proper recognition. To gain better comparability,

---

[2] We restricted rotational invariance to 20 degrees to include gestures differing in this aspect mostly.
[3] Text-copy tasks are preferred over text-creation tasks to minimize mental workload and errors of incorrect memorization or spelling[13].
[4] In detail, letters 'E','H','M','W', for instance, proved to be significant faster.

both alphabets were modified. We restrict all symbols to single strokes in this work. Within the multi-touch alphabet, former single-touch symbols of the letters 'R' and 'K' were replaced by abstract multi-touch symbols[5].

We were interested in further insights of gesture text entry methods, more specifically, in the following questions:

- Differ the two alphabets regarding intuitivity, error rate and satisfaction?
- Compared to conservative methods, is text input per gestures perceived as useful?
- Are abstract symbols preferred, or the ones more similar to handwriting?
- Would users like to specify their own gestures?

The classifier allows for template-based specification of symbols and users can individualize their alphabets. We were keen to know if users accept such possibilities to enhance their text input system.

The second evaluation was done again with an SMS writing tool developed in [5]. This tool can be used to define and teach gesture alphabets and presents text for testing purposes. In the same between group design, each group was confronted with a different gesture alphabet and the following test schedule:

- Introduction to the alphabet, its notation and the evaluation routine.
- Training:
  1. Visual templates of symbols/variants were retraced by the user.
  2. Aiding icons were shown and symbols entered twice altogether in random order. Gestures entered correctly were automatically added as templates to make classification more robust to between user variations.[6]
  3. Symbols were entered (random) without visual aid and in the users' preferred variant.
- Test: Users were requested to enter text presented to them as quickly and accurately as possible. Corrections were done by backspace buttons or gestures only. A reminder of the gesture alphabet could be displayed on press of a help button. Altogether, 16 phrases per participant were entered by gestures.
  1. A pangram[7] was written per virtual keyboard by the user.
  2. Sentences (letters only and letters plus numbers) were entered per gestures.
  3. The pangram was entered again, this time per gestures.
- Survey per questionnaire on perceived usability and subjective preferences. A free text field gave the option to provide additional comments.

---

[5] Pretests indicated they were hard to remember, but wanted to know if abstraction or intuition is preferred.

[6] This individualization without knowledge of the users has its drawbacks. The templates did not always represent the users' style. Instructed not to play around, some users did so to test recognition. Others drew the gestures still very meticulous.

[7] Lower case version of German phrase 'Franz jagt im komplett verwahrlosten Taxi quer durch Bayern'.

As for the first evaluation [5], we used a convenience sample of participants. Of the 12 new participants (7 female, 5 male, aged 19-34), nine were students or former students of computer science. Most stated to write approximately 1-5 SMS per day. One each answered to this question with 0, 6-10, 11-20. Six participants use virtual keyboard when writing SMS, four the 12-key keyboard and two use the 'QWERTZ' hardware keyboard.

6   Results

Considering characters per minute (cpm, as defined in [13]) when writing the pangram, the multi-touch group (M=36.93, SD = 4.63, N=6) was significantly faster (two-sample t-test; t=3.1, DF = 10, p = 0.01) than the single-touch group (M = 28.13, SD = 5.19, N=6).[8] Considering overall input during the test phase, strong tendency to faster multi-touch input is shown by the same test (t = 2.08, p = 0.06).

Cumulative error rates (containing all misinterpreted input) during the third phase of training (without aid) were 13.85 for multi-touch and at 17.44 for single-touch. This difference showed no significance (two-sample t-test).

In our survey, we collected answers to questions regarding subjective sensations of error rate, temporal demand, stress and ease of memorization when writing per gestures. On a five point Likert scale (1 worst - 5 best) all items were rated slightly higher for multi-touch and in average between 3 and 4. Highest difference (3.3 versus 4) is shown in subjective error rate of gesture recognition.

The direct comparison of input by gesture alphabets to the usual text input method showed preference of the latter. In both groups, most answers to preferred technique, fun, error rate, stress and concentration got average values of 3 to 3.83 on the five point Likert scales. Increasing values describe tendencies in favor of the usual text input. Differences between the two groups are negligibly small (0.16 or less) and insignificant. One exception occurred for fun, which got a better average rating of 2 for multi-touch compared to 3 for single-touch.

All participants were confronted with a picture of both alphabets and a short explanation of the differences in the final question of the interview. Until this time, it was not communicated that a comparative evaluation took place. Asked what alphabet they would prefer, given only this choice, three (two within the multi-touch group) selected the multi-touch version and nine the single-touch alphabet.

Figure 3 displays the distribution of answers, when users were asked on preferred variants of input possibilities.

Besides evident tendencies towards specific versions of 'T', 'X' and indicated preferences for 'J', 'V', 'Y', most symbols - including commands for space and backspace - are not assigned to a generally favored gesture. This impression is affirmed by our logging data that additionally provides information for numbers. Number '8' (multi-touch) and '9' were favored in their figurative variations

---

[8] For comparison, input by virtual keyboard achieved in average 96.69 cpm.

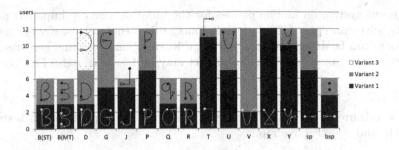

Fig. 3. Numbers of users that prefer one of the provided input methods for different symbols. Note that not all symbols are available within both alphabets.

whereas number '4' was entered in one third of the time in the abstract variant, too. For spaces and backspaces the relations were as indicated in Fig. 3.

7   Discussion and Outlook

Our results affirmed that, besides additional input options, a performance gain can be achieved when multi-touch is involved. The multi-touch alphabet itself, however, is in need of improvement. In spite of better ratings, users tend not to select it when given the choice between the single-touch and the multi-touch alphabet. Reasons for this can be found in users' comments. In three comments of multi-touch users, the awkward input for 'R' was criticized and in two that of 'K'. For both letters the help was called most often, too. Further discontents were communicated regarding the horizontal direction of the numbers 1-3 and the frequent changes in drawing directions. One participant wished for a mixture of both alphabets.

The distribution of selected input styles within the questionnaire suggest the development of gesture alphabets that allow for much more variation in users' input than it is provided in available tools. We conclude the need of individualization when offering input by gesture alphabets. This deduction is supported by answers in our questionnaire concerning whether users would rather like to specify their own gestures. All but one participant responded positively.

The instruments to evolve arbitrary gesture alphabets (see Fig. 1) by continuous modifications were presented. The template-based classification can be used for fair evaluations of different gesture alphabets under the same conditions. Rates of classification errors should be adequate for that purpose. Memorization performance and learning curves are features to be evaluated thoroughly in the future. However, a usable text input system including adaptability is still to be built. Ambiguous definitions should be prevented and aided recall created dynamically from specified templates. To be of real use, it would require sophisticated help and text correction as it is common for other input methods. Still, applications of gesture alphabets fall into a niche. Investigations of how and in which contexts this input option is of advantage are to be done. We imagine a text input system on mobile phones for the blind or visually impaired users. Possibly, with concepts of [20], a training mechanism (not necessarily per haptic sensations) can be developed that allows for learning and recalling gestures as a blind user. Input by a self defined alphabet may be fast and useful for this user group.

Acknowledgments. The authors kindly thank all participants of our tests for their help and constructive input.

References

1. Apte, A., Vo, V., Kimura, T.D.: Recognizing multistroke geometric shapes: an experimental evaluation. In: UIST 1993: Proceedings of the 6th Annual ACM Symposium on User Interface Software and Technology, pp. 121–128. ACM, New York (1993)
2. Bi, X., Chelba, C., Ouyang, T., Partridge, K., Zhai, S.: Bimanual gesture keyboard. In: Proceedings of the 25th Annual ACM Symposium on User Interface Software and Technology, UIST 2012, pp. 137–146. ACM, New York (2012)
3. Chatty, S., Lecoanet, P.: Pen computing for air traffic control. In: Proceedings of the SIGCHI Conference on Human Factors in Computing Systems: Common Ground, CHI 1996, pp. 87–94. ACM, New York (1996)
4. Coyette, A., Schimke, S., Vanderdonckt, J., Vielhauer, C.: Trainable sketch recognizer for graphical user interface design. In: Baranauskas, C., Abascal, J., Barbosa, S.D.J. (eds.) INTERACT 2007. LNCS, vol. 4662, pp. 124–135. Springer, Heidelberg (2007)
5. Fibich, A.: Evaluation von Gestenalphabeten. Diploma thesis, Dresden University of Technology (2012)
6. Goldberg, D., Richardson, C.: Touch-typing with a stylus. In: Proceedings of the INTERACT 1993 and CHI 1993 Conference on Human Factors in Computing Systems, CHI 1993, pp. 80–87. ACM, New York (1993)
7. Isokoski, P., Raisamo, R.: Device independent text input: a rationale and an example. In: Proceedings of the Working Conference on Advanced Visual Interfaces, AVI 2000, pp. 76–83. ACM, New York (2000)
8. Kane, S.K., Bigham, J.P., Wobbrock, J.O.: Slide rule: making mobile touch screens accessible to blind people using multi-touch interaction techniques. In: Proceedings of the 10th International ACM SIGACCESS Conference on Computers and Accessibility, Assets 2008, pp. 73–80. ACM, New York (2008)
9. Költringer, T., Grechenig, T.: Comparing the immediate usability of graffiti 2 and virtual keyboard. In: CHI 2004 Extended Abstracts on Human Factors in Computing Systems, CHI EA 2004, pp. 1175–1178. ACM, New York (2004)
10. Kristensson, P.-O., Zhai, S.: Shark2: a large vocabulary shorthand writing system for pen-based computers. In: Proceedings of the 17th Annual ACM Symposium on User Interface Software and Technology, UIST 2004, pp. 43–52. ACM, New York (2004)
11. Landay, J.A., Myers, B.A.: Interactive sketching for the early stages of user interface design. In: Proceedings of the SIGCHI Conference on Human Factors in Computing Systems, CHI 1995, pp. 43–50. ACM Press/Addison-Wesley Publishing Co., New York (1995)

12. Scott MacKenzie, I., Chen, J., Oniszczak, A.: Unipad: single stroke text entry with language-based acceleration. In: Proceedings of the 4th Nordic Conference on Human-Computer Interaction: Changing Roles, NordiCHI 2006, pp. 78–85. ACM, New York (2006)

13. MacKenzie, I.S., Tanaka-Ishii, K.: Text Entry Systems: Mobility, Accessibility, Universality. The Morgan Kaufmann Series in Interactive Technologies, Boston (2007)

14. Mankoff, J., Abowd, G.D.: Cirrin: a word-level unistroke keyboard for pen input. In: Proceedings of the 11th Annual ACM Symposium on User Interface Software and Technology, UIST 1998, pp. 213–214. ACM, New York (1998)

15. Martin, B.: Virhkey: a virtual hyperbolic keyboard with gesture interaction and visual feedback for mobile devices. In: Proceedings of the 7th International Conference on Human Computer Interaction with Mobile Devices & Services, MobileHCI 2005, pp. 99–106. ACM, New York (2005)

16. McGookin, D., Brewster, S., Jiang, W.: Investigating touchscreen accessibility for people with visual impairments. In: Proceedings of the 5th Nordic Conference on Human-Computer Interaction: Building Bridges, NordiCHI 2008, pp. 298–307. ACM, New York (2008)

17. Perlin, K.: Quikwriting: continuous stylus-based text entry. In: Proceedings of the 11th Annual ACM Symposium on User Interface Software and Technology, UIST 1998, pp. 215–216. ACM, New York (1998)

18. Poirier, F., Belatar, M.: Glyph 2: une saisie de texte avec deux appuis de touche par caractère - principes et comparaisons. In: Proceedings of the 18th International Conferenceof the Association Francophone d'Interaction Homme-Machine, IHM 2006, pp. 159–162. ACM, New York (2006)

19. Rick, J.: Performance optimizations of virtual keyboards for stroke-based text entry on a touch-based tabletop. In: Proceedings of the 23nd Annual ACM Symposium on User Interface Software and Technology, UIST 2010, pp. 77–86. ACM, New York (2010)

20. Schmidt, M., Weber, G.: Multitouch Haptic Interaction. In: Stephanidis, C. (ed.) UAHCI 2009, Part II. LNCS, vol. 5615, pp. 574–582. Springer, Heidelberg (2009)

21. Schmidt, M., Weber, G.: Template based classification of multi-touch gestures. Pattern Recognition (2013), doi:10.1016/j.patcog.2013.02.001

22. Wobbrock, J.O., Hudson, S.E., Mankoff, J., Simpson, R.C.: Edgewrite: A versatile design for text entry and control. Technical report (2006)

23. Yu, B., Cai, S.: A domain-independent system for sketch recognition. In: Proceedings of the 1st International Conference on Computer Graphics and Interactive Techniques in Australasia and South East Asia, GRAPHITE 2003, pp. 141–146. ACM, New York (2003)

24. Zhai, S., Hunter, M., Smith, B.A.: Performance optimization of virtual keyboards. Human-Computer Interaction, 89–129 (2002)

Enabling Interactive Surfaces by Using Mobile Device and Conductive Ink Drawing

Shu-Chuan Chiu[1,*], Chen-Wei Chiang[2], and Kiyoshi Tomimatsu[3]

[1] Graduate School of Design, Kyushu University, Fukuoka, Japan
mokochiu@gmail.com
[2] Department of Information Communication, Yuan Ze University, Taoyuan, Taiwan
chenwei@saturn.yzu.edu.tw
[3] Faculty of Design, Kyushu University, Fukuoka, Japan
tomimatu@design.kyushu-u.ac.jp

Abstract. Tangible user interfaces enable users to interact with digital information by directly interacting with physical objects. Aesthetic interaction is about triggering imagination, it is thought provoking and encourages people to think differently about the encountered interactive systems, what they do and how they might be used differently to serve differentiated goals. The aesthetic experience is one of the main elements in interaction design. We propose to combine ubiquitous computing with aesthetic interaction. In this paper, we present a new aesthetic interaction concept, a technology that enables aesthetic interaction on capacitive multi-touch devices. Our proposed a kit consists of iPhone device (Tangible device) and conductive ink sketching. We supply user draw lines or any sketches on it via conductive ink, which makes the simply interaction connection between the iPhone's capacitive touch screen. Sketching conductive ink on a paper creates an aesthetic interaction by the capacitive surfaces.

Keywords: Interaction design, Tangible device, Conductive ink drawing, Musical and Light composition.

1 Introduction

Tangible user interfaces enable users to interact with digital information by directly interacting with physical objects. Users can collaborate easily around such a space to solve problems using both hands. And then, physical objects in this type of environment can be more than just input devices: they can become embodiments of digital information. On the other hand, the aesthetics of the use experience becomes an instrumental perspective. Aesthetic interaction is about triggering imagination and it is thought provoking and encourages people to think differently about the encountered interactive systems, what they do and how they might be used differently to serve differentiated goals. [1]

As our lives are increasingly regulated by electronics and there is a drive towards the miniaturization and portability of electronics on and around the body. Moreover, our way to interact with everyday objects has been changing along with the latest advancement of technology. The idea of the human circuit will capture people's imaginations.

---

[*] Corresponding author.

N. Streitz and C. Stephanidis (Eds.): DAPI/HCII 2013, LNCS 8028, pp. 72–77, 2013.

In the cell phone industry, capacitive touchscreen displays rely on the electrical properties of the human body to detect when and where on a display the user touching. Because of this, capacitive displays can be controlled with very light touches of a finger and generally cannot be used with a mechanical stylus or a gloved hand. Examples of devices with capacitive touchscreens are the Apple iPhone.

Fig. 1. Based on the iPhone device and Conductive ink pen

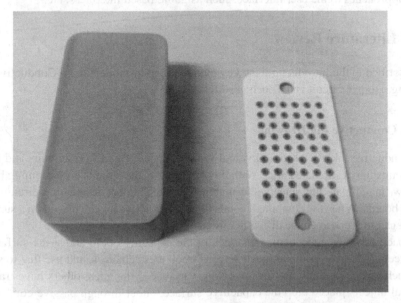

Fig. 2. Prototype testing on capacitive multi-touch panel (i.e. iPhone case)

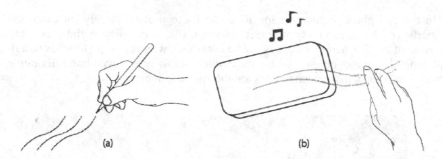

Fig. 3. The concept of our proposed kit (a) Conductive Ink Drawing (b) User Scenario: Put the iPhone device on the drawings to connect to multi-touch displays (Sensor), User touch their drawings to play based on the principle of "static electricity"

The iPhone's multi-touch display (Capacitive Touchscreen) is a new sensing board that can be applied on a piece of paper as the main medium to visualize the interaction via musical and light composition. Touching the surface of the conductive ink drawing will trigger an audio feedback in the form of musical notes and lights feedback.

We propose to combine ubiquitous computing with aesthetic interaction. The testing model of our prototype is described in Figure 1,2,3.Our goal is to design an aesthetic interaction as a better way to embody tangible devices based on daily life experiences. In addition to the description of the kit, we also discuss the concept behind the design and possible user scenarios. On the area of the interaction techniques, we plan to continue our investigation of how mobile's multi-touch display can be combined with other approaches to the user interface, such as game based interfaces, etc.

2   Literature Review

As described in the introduction, the key elements in our model kit are Conductive ink drawing, Human circuit and Touch gestures.

2.1   Conductive Ink Drawing

The conductive ink allows an individual to take a pen created from circuits and draw the circuits into a stipulated area. With this alternative, the circuits are becoming better to draw, manipulate and alter while making new techniques to creating circuits and circuit boards. When the combined metals of the conductive ink are placed on a surface, they began to work to create different circuits.

Capacitive surfaces recognize changes in the capacitive field above the surface of the screen. Modern capacitive touch screens track these changes, and use that to sense the touch of one or multiple fingers. Using variants of this idea, others have tracked physical objects placed atop the capacitive surface, either through passive conductors [2] or active electronics embedded in the physical artifact [3,4,5].

2.2   Human Circuit and Touch Gestures

To create a tangible, users draw the sketches by using the conductive ink and touching, recognizable by a capacitive screen. Using electrically conductive carbon paint, they can draw a circuit on to fabric, paper, glass and even your own skin.

Touch gestures is a very general term and can refer to a broad definition depending on the context. In this paper, we focus in a specific genre of utilizing touch gesture in tangible media that is called paper computing. Paper computing can take various forms. For example in "Paints, Paper, and Programs"[6], paper computing computational elements (sensors, actuators, and power sources) are held on paper surfaces and electrically connected by magnetic paint and magnet.

The Living Wall project explores the construction and application of interactive wallpaper [6]. The wallpaper consists of circuitry that is painted onto a sheet of paper and a set of electronic modules that are attached to it with magnets. The wallpaper can be used for a multitude of functional and fanciful applications involving lighting, environmental sensing, appliance control, and ambient information display. It explores an alternative method of conducting electricity in an interactive installation and effectively utilizes touch gestures in meaningful ways of interaction [5,7,8].

3   Design Concept and Components

The main concept is the creation of a process in which involves conductive ink drawing and touch gestures and combine them with mobile device to compose sound feedback. Users are able to contribute their idea visually, feel the result of their works with their tactile sense, and receive auditory feedbacks. On the other hand, the mobile device enables us to develop a portable installation while allowing high degree of customization. For example by customizing the software, we were able to control the pitch and tempo of the auditory feedback and even did some remix to generate interesting sound effects or LED lights interaction.
Our recognition module consists of 3 key parts, i.e.:

1. **Touching sensitivity** : To improve the touching sensitivity between the Conductive ink and the kit. The static electricity block is divided into several of regions and based on four-point, three-point, two points, one point, as the main identification way.

2. **Supporting by the mobile device** : To connect multi-touch displays (Capacitive Touchscreen as sensor), user touch their drawings to play based on the figure static electricity. Then, the main body of mobile device provides sound feedback.

3. **Interaction design of pleasurable and natural experience** : Players can drive around and explore the world of mind imaging and drawing. The mobile device case has lots of applications, such as the installation of simple dynamic reaction device or the LED light interaction changes though the conductive ink drawings.

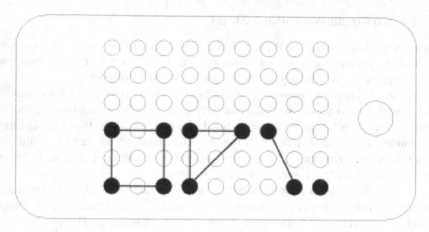

Fig. 4. The example: Static electricity block of recognition module

4   Research Method

Creating though Play: Using Conductive ink pen as a conductive surface, we identify play as one approach to capture user's attention and creativity. In accordance to unlimited possibilities of ink drawings, sketching conductive ink on a paper creates an aesthetic interaction by the capacitive surfaces, thus providing an enjoyable platform and new user experience.

Sensing: When skin makes a contact with graphite, it will generate a stable static electricity signal and electrical current can be measured directly. Thus, by sending this signal into mobile device, the quantity of the electrical current can be converted and transmitted as sound signals. The mobile device's multi-touch display (Capacitive Touchscreen) measure static electricity which is generated when a user makes a contact with the surface.

Signal Processing and Auditory Feedback: The main part of our installation is the signal processing and auditory interaction feedback. As discussed in the previous sub-section, static electrical current were measured using static electricity sensors and transmitted as sound signals in the mobile device case.

5   User Experiences

In this paper, we discussed the concept of Aesthetic Interaction currently presents theoretical considerations and will need further empirical experiments to provide more concrete guidelines for working with aesthetic interaction generally. However we see Aesthetic Interaction as a beneficial perspective when designing interactive systems.

We presented concept ideas of how we work towards aesthetic interaction in design cases. It represents a new way of interacting with music. In the prototype, we are able to record gestures with the device and relate that to playing sounds and lights.

6   Conclusion and Future Works

The playful interaction and concept envisions a pervasive computing environment, where walls, tables and floors are interactive surfaces; documents can be exchanged, moved around and arranged in a spatial setting.

In this paper, we have described an alternative interface for composing music. Our proposed kit allows users to interact in an easy way. By using mobile device and conductive ink as the sketch drawing we have succeeded in emphasizing imagination experiences in musical composition while preserving the enjoyment and quality of user experience. Furthermore, it allows the users to simultaneously experience three different modes of sensory perception, i.e.: visual, audio, and tactile.

References

1. Petersen, M.G., Iversen, O.S., Krogh, P.G., Ludvigsen, M.: Aesthetic interaction - a pragmatist's aesthetics of interactive systems. In: Proc. Conference on Designing Interactive Systems: Processes, Practices, Methods, and Techniques (2004)
2. Wiethoff, A., Schneider, H., Rohs, M., Butz, A., Greenberg, S.: Sketch-a-TUI: Low Cost Prototyping of Tangible Interactions Using Cardboard and Conductive Ink. In: Proc. of the ACM 6th International Conference on Tangible, Embedded and Embodied Interaction, TEI 2012 (2012)
3. Kratz, S., Westermann, T., Rohs, M., Essl, G.: CapWidgets: Tangible widgets versus multi-touch controls on mobile devices. In: Proc. CHI EA 2011 (2011)
4. Yu, N.-H., Chan, L.-W., Lau, S.-Y., Tsai, S.-S., Hsiao, I.-C., Tsai, D.-J., Hsiao, F.-I., Cheng, L.-P., Chen, M.Y., Huang, P., Hung, Y.-P.: TUIC: enabling tangible interaction on capacitive multi-touch displays. In: Proc. CHI 2011 (2011)
5. Chiang, C., Chiu, S.C., Dharma, A.A.G., Tomimatsu, K.: Birds on Paper: An Alternative Interface to Compose Music by Utilizing Sketch Drawing and Mobile Device. In: Proceedings of 6th International Conference on Tangible Embedded and Embodied Interaction, Kingston, Canada, pp. 201–204 (2012)
6. Buechley, L., Hendrix, S., Eisenberg, M.: Paints, paper, and programs: first steps toward the computational sketchbook. In: Proc. International Conference on Tangible and Embedded Interaction (2009)
7. Raffle, H., Vaucelle, C., Wang, R., Ishii, H.: Jabberstamp: embedding sound and voice in traditional drawings. In: Proc. International Conference on Interaction Design and Children (2007)
8. Tsandilas, T., Letondal, C., Mackay, W.E.: Musink: composing music through augmented drawing. In: Proc. International Conference on Human Factors in Computing Systems (2010)

How to Click in Mid-Air

Florian van de Camp[1,*], Alexander Schick[1,*], and Rainer Stiefelhagen[2]

[1] Fraunhofer Institute of Optronics, System Technologies and Image Exploitation,
Karlsruhe, Germany
{florian.vandecamp,alexander.schick}@iosb.fraunhofer.de
[2] Karlsruhe Institute of Technology (KIT)
rainer.stiefelhagen@kit.edu

Abstract. In this paper, we investigate interactions with distant interfaces. In particular, we focus on how to issue mouse click like commands in mid-air and we propose a taxonomy for distant one-arm clicking gestures. The gestures are divided into three main groups based on the part of the arm that is responsible for the gesture: the fingers, the hand, or the arm. We evaluated nine specific gestures in a Wizard of Oz study and asked participants to rate each gesture using a TLX questionnaire as well as to give an overall ranking. Based on the evaluation, we identified groups of gestures of varying acceptability that can serve as a reference for interface designers to select the most suitable gesture.

1 Introduction and Related Work

In this paper, we investigate interaction with distant interfaces. In particular, we focus on how to interact with distant objects that are, for example, displayed on a videowall in a control room or on a shopping window. We are interested in distant interaction because growing screen sizes require, and improved computer vision technologies allow for, interaction without actually touching the displays. We further selected the clicking gesture because it is one of the most basic forms of interaction which allows for very powerful and universal interaction designs as the computer mouse shows.

There exists a large body of literature about gestures for human-computer interaction, e.g. [6,9]. Here, we focus on clicking gestures that can be performed with one arm only. Alternatives are, e.g., two-arm clicking gestures or the use of additional devices. However, we feel that device-free one-arm clicking gestures place the least restrictions on users and allow a more general use. We also believe that they are more natural and intuitive and can more easily be related to touch.

We also focus on clicking gestures only. We do not investigate how to translate a pointing gesture to display coordinates (see [12,13] for recent examples). We also do not consider gestures that can be used as shortcuts to perform more complicated actions, e.g. [1], or on gestures for other actions, e.g. pan-and-zoom [8]. We focus on clicking because it is one of the most fundamental human-computer interactions, but at the same time one of the most useful and general ones.

---

* These authors contributed equally to this work.

N. Streitz and C. Stephanidis (Eds.): DAPI/HCII 2013, LNCS 8028, pp. 78–86, 2013.

The clicking gestures in this paper are all based on a pointing gesture to specify the area of interaction on the display. Pointing gestures have a long history in human-computer interaction, e.g. Bolt's "Put that there!" [2], Vogel and Balakrishnan [13], Schick et al. [12], to name just a few. To use pointing gestures for interaction, two main problems have to be solved: first, how is the pointing gesture translated to display coordinates, e.g. ray-casting [12,13] or relative pointing [13], and second, how is the interaction triggered, e.g. with speech [2], hand gestures [1,13], or dwell-based [12]. Here, we solely focus on how to trigger the interaction.

Even though different clicking gestures have been proposed and compared to each other, there are two drawbacks in previous work. First, the number of clicking gestures is relatively small and the selection arbitrary, thus not exploring the full design space of clicking gestures [13]. Second, they are usually implemented with a given system, e.g. based on Vicon markers [13] or video cameras [1,12]. Such systems are never absolutely perfect, e.g. due to measurement noise or physical limitations like resolution. In addition, some gestures are more difficult to recognize than others. Unfortunately, imperfections in the recognition system affect the users' perception of the gesture and, consequently, their evaluation. In this paper, we present a systematic evaluation of clicking gestures and evaluate them in a Wizard of Oz study [4], thereby eliminating the bias of an imperfect system.

There exists a large body of research on how to classify gestures in human-computer interaction and several taxonomies have been proposed [3,7,10,11,14]. A recent overview about gesture taxonomies can also be found in [14]. The proposed taxonomies usually have a relatively wide scope to capture a large range of gestures that can occur in different contexts. Even though it is possible to describe clicking gestures based on these taxonomies, almost all clicking gestures would fall into the same category. Therefore, we will introduce a new taxonomy that focuses only on one-arm clicking gestures. This allows for a more diverse categorization and a better exploration of the design space of clicking gestures.

In the remainder of this paper, we will first introduce a new taxonomy before choosing nine specific gestures that were evaluated in a Wizard of Oz study. After presenting the results of this study, we conclude with a discussion.

2 Taxonomy

In this paper, we focus on clicking gestures to interact with objects that are displayed on a distant vertical display (Figure 1). We assume that the basis of each clicking gesture is a pointing gesture to specify the object to interact with. This is very natural for humans. Pointing gestures can be split into three phases: preparation, stroke, and recovery [5]. The clicking gesture always occurs in the stroke phase.

Given established taxonomies, one-arm clicking gestures can, for example, be categorized as deictic or manipulative [10,11]. However, such a categorization is very coarse and does not capture the possible variations, as we will show now.

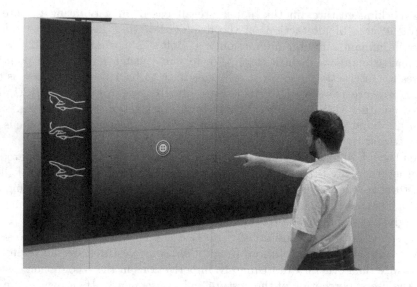

Fig. 1. The interface for the user study

A one-arm clicking gesture requires some form of movement over time. Given a pointing gesture, this can either be a movement of the arm, of the hand, or the fingers. This leads to the following categorization (see also Figure 2).

If the clicking gesture is based on arm movement, it must not affect the pointing location. This reduces possible movements to orthogonal ones (towards and away from the display) and rotation. Not moving the arm is the third option. If based on hand movement, the clicking gesture can be expressed by a bending movement, e.g. by vertically bending the hand. The most variations are possible when the clicking gesture is based on finger movements. We characterize these by the number of fingers that are part of the gesture, starting from one and up to five. We found that having three or four fingers perform a gesture are the least natural options.

In summary, the proposed taxonomy classifies one-arm clicking gestures for distant interaction based on two characteristics: first, the body part that is mainly involved, and second, the type or direction of the movement. These characteristics also influence the difficulty of implementing a system to recognize the gesture (the larger the body part, the easier it is to recognize), and how stressful it is for the body to execute the movements depending on size and how natural the movement is (e.g. push versus pull arm movements).

A clicking gesture is categorized by one single leaf node; however, even though it would increase physical and cognitive stress, it is also possible to combine leaf nodes, e.g. arm and finger movements.

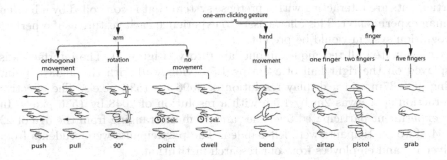

Fig. 2. Taxonomy for distant one-arm clicking and examples for each leaf node of the taxonomy. The nine representatives for clicking gestures at the bottom are the ones evaluated in the user study. Each gesture is split into three consecutive phases that are shown from top to bottom. The clicking event is triggered in the last phase.

2.1 Clicking Gestures

For our experiments, we chose for most leaf nodes of the taxonomy at least one representative. They are shown at the bottom in Figure 2 and will now be explained.

For arm movements, we chose five representatives: push and pull, 90° rotation, point, and dwell. We set the dwell time for the dwell gesture to one second. We chose this duration after experiments in our laboratory and looking at existing interfaces, e.g. Microsoft Kinect applications. The point gesture is different from dwell-based interaction, in that the clicking event is triggered as soon as the arm movement stops.

For hand movements, we chose a downward vertical bending of the hand. We found other hand movements similar, but much more stressful on the wrist.

For finger movements, we chose one, two, and five finger movements: airtap [13], pistol [13], and grab. We categorized pistol as a two-finger movement because it requires two fingers to perform the gesture. Not moving a finger is similar to the point and dwell gestures. We found three and four finger movements either similar to other gestures or as not as natural.

When comparing the gestures to mouse clicks, it is interesting to note that all gestures have phases that can be compared to hold and release (except point and dwell). Even though not required for our study, this is important for applications that require something similar to a mouse-down event. Also note that all gestures can be implemented in a real-world system; in fact, most of them are already available at our lab.

3 Experiments

Every gesture recognition is biased by the accuracy of the underlying recognition system. To overcome this problem, we used a Wizard of Oz setup [4] where participants are interacting with a pretense system that is controlled by a hidden human experimenter. This allows users to experience each gesture as if a perfect recognition system would be present.

We evaluated all techniques in our laboratory (Figure 1). The interface was displayed on the right half of a 4m by 1.5m videowall with the highest point being at 2.37m and a display resolution of 4096 by 1536 pixels. The effective interaction space was 2m by 1.5m with a resolution of 2048 by 1536 pixels. In our experiment participated 5 females and 13 males ranging from the age of 20 to 64. Two participants were left-handed. The participants were students from university and employees from our research institution.

We presented each participant with all nine clicking gestures in randomized order. The task was to click a button that was displayed on the wall (Figure 1). The size of the button was 13.6cm. Due to the Wizard of Oz setup, the size did not affect the recognition accuracy of the clicking gesture. In each run, the participants were allowed to try each gesture. Then, a succession of 25 buttons appeared that they had to click. When a button was clicked, it disappeared and the next button was displayed. The buttons were equally distributed across the screen and their order of appearance randomized.

There were two experimenters. One experimenter was present in the room and guided the participants through the study. The second, hidden experimenter was seated in a separate room and observed the participants with multiple cameras that are part of our regular system setup. By pushing a button, the hidden experimenter could trigger a clicking event. By carefully observing the scene, it was possible to only trigger clicking events when the participants were actually pointing at the button (which some did not to test the system limits). The perceived system reaction time was minimal and only affected by the latency of the cameras and the reaction time of the hidden experimenter.

After each clicking gesture, the participants were asked to rate the gesture based on a NASA TLX questionnaire. The NASA TLX questionnaire contains questions about mental, physical, and temporal demand, overall performance, frustration level, and effort. We asked participants to give their ratings for each of these categories on a 7-point Likert scale. Then, the next gesture was presented in the same fashion. After the experiment, the participants were presented with an additional questionnaire where they were asked for further comments and to select which gestures they considered generally useful. Most importantly, we asked them to rank the gestures based on how they liked them, starting from 1 for their most and ending at 9 for their least favored method.

4   Results

For presenting the results, we mainly focus on the overall ranking of the gestures because it summarizes the overall perception of the participants and we show the physical and temporal demands results from the TLX questionnaire. Table 1 shows the mean values as well as standard deviation for each gesture and the pair-wise significance comparisons. Tables 2 and 3 show results for physical and

Table 1. The gesture ranking evaluation. Each participant ranked the gestures from 1 (liked best) to 9 (liked worst). The table shows the resulting ranking from left (best) to right (worst) with mean and standard deviation in the top rows and the significance analysis results (p-values) for the pair-wise comparisons below (based on Wilcoxon rank sum test).

	airtap	point	pistol	90°	bend	grab	dwell	push	pull
μ	2.78	3.00	4.61	4.89	5.11	5.28	5.39	6.22	7.72
σ	1.93	2.13	2.16	2.26	2.38	2.28	2.31	2.15	1.19
airtap	-	0.95	< 0.01	< 0.01	≪ 0.01	≪ 0.01	≪ 0.01	≪ 0.01	≪ 0.01
point	0.95	-	0.02	0.02	0.01	< 0.01	≪ 0.01	≪ 0.01	≪ 0.01
pistol	< 0.01	0.02	-	0.62	0.54	0.41	0.30	0.03	≪ 0.01
90°	< 0.01	0.02	0.62	-	0.78	0.75	0.54	0.10	≪ 0.01
bend	≪ 0.01	0.01	0.54	0.78	-	0.94	0.72	0.18	≪ 0.01
grab	≪ 0.01	< 0.01	0.41	0.75	0.94	-	0.87	0.28	< 0.01
dwell	≪ 0.01	≪ 0.01	0.30	0.54	0.72	0.87	-	0.28	≪ 0.01
push	≪ 0.01	≪ 0.01	0.03	0.10	0.18	0.28	0.28	-	0.04
pull	≪ 0.01	≪ 0.01	≪ 0.01	≪ 0.01	≪ 0.01	< 0.01	≪ 0.01	0.04	-

temporal demands. Because the data did not always follow a normal distribution, we used the Wilcoxon rank sum test. However, a t-test showed comparable results. The significance level was 0.05. While the other categories of the TLX questionnaire are in line with the ranking, they are not as significant. This is most likely due to the fact that the TLX questions are tailored towards more complex tasks. While physical and temporal demands can be directly related and are meaningful for the simple task, the other categories like mental demand do not fit very well and might lead to inconclusive ratings.

5 Discussion

The ranking of the gestures follows a smooth descent from airtap, as the best rated gesture, to pull, as the worst. The pair-wise significance analysis (Table 1) shows that there are three groups of gestures that have similar ratings within the group but significantly differ from other groups. The results from the physical and temporal demands ratings are in line with the ranking of the gestures and support it.

The first group consists of the two highest rated gestures: airtap and point. Airtap requires minimal effort and, as several users pointed out, has a high resemblance to the use of a computer mouse thus making it very intuitive. The high rating of the point gesture is not surprising as it requires no additional effort besides pointing itself and, therefore, was perceived as very convenient and fast. It has to be pointed out, however, that a large number of users noted that they would expect a lot of errors when operating a real interface as they did not have the same level of control compared to the other gestures. Given a real interface, the pointing gesture would most likely only be useful if there is

Table 2. Physical exhaustion. How physically exhaustive was interaction with the given technique with ratings from -3 (not exhaustive at all) to +3 (very exhaustive).

	point	airtap	90°	pistol	bend	push	dwell	grab	pull
μ	-2.83	-2.28	-1.39	-1.11	-1.11	-0.89	-0.89	-0.67	0.00
σ	0.37	0.93	1.70	1.63	1.49	1.45	1.94	1.73	1.49
point	-	0.04	≪ 0.01	≪ 0.01	≪ 0.01	≪ 0.01	≪ 0.01	≪ 0.01	≪ 0.01
airtap	0.04	-	0.15	0.03	0.02	< 0.01	0.04	< 0.01	≪ 0.01
90°	≪ 0.01	0.15	-	0.55	0.47	0.31	0.48	0.22	0.02
pistol	≪ 0.01	0.03	0.55	-	0.95	0.59	0.85	0.47	0.05
bend	≪ 0.01	0.02	0.47	0.95	-	0.68	0.85	0.47	0.05
push	≪ 0.01	< 0.01	0.31	0.59	0.68	-	0.82	0.68	0.09
dwell	≪ 0.01	0.04	0.48	0.85	0.85	0.82	-	0.68	0.13
grab	≪ 0.01	< 0.01	0.22	0.47	0.47	0.68	0.68	-	0.28
pull	≪ 0.01	≪ 0.01	0.02	0.05	0.05	0.09	0.13	0.28	-

no potential for false positives. Therefore, we recommend airtap as the primary gesture for click-like commands.

The pistol, bend, 90°, grab, dwell, and push gestures make up the second group. They were rated worse than the first group but were still named when participants were asked which gestures they considered to be useful in everyday life. These gestures could be used for secondary tasks like opening a context menu.

Table 3. Temporal demand. How long did it take to execute the gesture from -3 (very short) to +3 (very long).

	point	airtap	bend	pistol	90°	grab	push	pull	dwell
μ	-2.94	-2.06	-2.00	-1.83	-1.78	-1.28	-1.22	-0.28	0.06
σ	0.23	1.22	1.00	1.30	1.23	1.59	1.69	1.56	2.12
point	-	< 0.01	≪ 0.01	< 0.01	≪ 0.01	≪ 0.01	≪ 0.01	≪ 0.01	≪ 0.01
airtap	< 0.01	-	0.67	0.61	0.47	0.14	0.20	≪ 0.01	≪ 0.01
bend	≪ 0.01	0.67	-	0.89	0.69	0.23	0.25	≪ 0.01	≪ 0.01
pistol	< 0.01	0.61	0.89	-	0.82	0.33	0.33	< 0.01	< 0.01
90°	≪ 0.01	0.47	0.69	0.82	-	0.41	0.40	< 0.01	< 0.01
grab	≪ 0.01	0.14	0.23	0.33	0.41	-	0.97	0.07	0.06
push	≪ 0.01	0.20	0.25	0.33	0.40	0.97	-	0.10	0.06
pull	≪ 0.01	≪ 0.01	≪ 0.01	< 0.01	< 0.01	0.07	0.10	-	0.68
dwell	≪ 0.01	≪ 0.01	≪ 0.01	< 0.01	< 0.01	0.06	0.06	0.68	-

The remaining gesture, pull, forms the third group. Almost no participant could imagine using the pull gesture for an actual application and in all ratings, pull was among the worst rated gestures. This seems to result from the fact that pulling the arm away from the display to click something is very counterintuitive. We advise not to use this gesture at all for clicking gestures.

As a whole, the ranking follows the general observation that a gesture with less required effort resulted in a better overall rating. While the gestures in the first group add little to no additional strain to the always required pointing gesture, the pull gesture of the third group requires movement of the complete arm which, depending on the execution of the gesture, can even include the upper body. In between are the gestures of the second group that mostly require movement of multiple fingers or the whole hand. In case of the dwell gesture, no movement is necessary but the long delay during which the arm has to remain extended is tiring.

While the point gesture and the dwell gesture are very similar, the dwell gesture performed significantly worse in the ranking. Of course, the dwell gesture has other advantages such as being easy to detect and is, therefore, robust but the delay was not well perceived by the participants. We see the dwell gesture as a good choice if robust detection of other gestures cannot be guaranteed. However, given similar robustness for any of the better rated gestures, it could be a valid design choice to consider them over the dwell gesture.

As pointed out, the ranking of the gestures shows a smooth descent which indicates that several gestures can be considered useful. This leads to the conclusion that gestures of the first group could be used for common operations, like clicking, because they were generally perceived as being faster and more efficient. Gestures of the second group would then be a good choice for less frequent but still common operations such as drag-and-drop or opening a context menu.

6 Conclusion

We presented a taxonomy specifically aimed at one-arm clicking gestures for distant interaction and evaluated nine specific gestures in a Wizard of Oz study. The rankings indicate which gestures were considered more useful over the others. Design choices based on the presented results can help to provide an improved user experience for distant interaction. As a conclusion, we recommended airtap as the primary clicking gesture and gave recommendations for secondary gestures that can be used for shortcut functions, e.g. opening a context menu.

References

1. Bader, T., Räpple, R., Beyerer, J.: Fast Invariant Contour-Based Classification of Hand Symbols for HCI. In: Jiang, X., Petkov, N. (eds.) CAIP 2009. LNCS, vol. 5702, pp. 689–696. Springer, Heidelberg (2009)
2. Bolt, R.A.: "Put-that-there": Voice and Gesture at the Graphics Interface. SIGGRAPH Computer Graphics 14(3), 262–270 (1980)
3. Grossman, T., Wigdor, D.: Going Deeper: a Taxonomy of 3D on the Tabletop. In: Proc. Horizontal Interactive Human-Computer Systems, pp. 137–144 (2007)
4. Kelley, J.F.: An Empirical Methodology for Writing User-friendly Natural Language Computer Applications. In: ACM SIGCHI Conference on Human Factors in Computing Systems, pp. 193–196 (1983)
5. Kendon, A.: Gesticulation and speech: two aspects of the process of utterance. In: Key, M.R. (ed.) The Relationship of Verbal and Nonverbal Communication, pp. 207–227 (1980)

6. Kendon, A.: Gesture: Visible Action as Utterance. Cambridge University Press (2004)
7. McNeill, D.: Hand and Mind: What Gestures Reveal about Thought. University of Chicago Press (1992)
8. Nancel, M., Wagner, J., Pietriga, E., Chapuis, O., Mackay, W.: Mid-air pan-and-zoom on wall-sized displays. In: Proc. SIGCHI Conference on Human Factors in Computing Systems, pp. 177–186 (2011)
9. Pavlovic, V.I., Sharma, R., Huang, T.S.: Visual Interpretation of Hand Gestures for Human-Computer Interaction: A Review. Pattern Analysis and Machine Intelligence 19(7), 677–695 (1997)
10. Quek, F.K.H.: Toward a Vision-Based Hand Gesture Interface. In: Proc. Virtual Reality Software and Technology, pp. 17–29 (1994)
11. Quek, F.K.H.: Eyes in the Interface. Image and Vison Computing 13(6), 511–525 (1995)
12. Schick, A., van de Camp, F., Ijsselmuiden, J., Stiefelhagen, R.: Extending Touch: Towards Interaction with Large-Scale Surfaces. In: Proc. Interactive Tabletops and Surfaces, pp. 127–134 (2009)
13. Vogel, D., Balakrishnan, R.: Distant Freehand Pointing and Clicking on Very Large, High Resolution Displays. In: ACM Symposium on User Interface Software and Technology, pp. 33–42 (2005)
14. Woobrock, J.O., Morris, M.R., Wilson, A.D.: User-Defined Gestures for Surface Computing. In: Proc. Human Factors in Computing Systems, pp. 1083–1092 (2009)

PhotoLoop: Implicit Approach for Creating Video Narration for Slideshow

Keita Watanabe[1], Koji Tsukada[2,3], and Michiaki Yasumura[4]

[1] Meiji University, Japan
[2] Future University Hakodate, Japan
[3] Japan Science and Technology Agency, Japan
[4] Keio University, Japan
watanabe@gmail.com, tsuka@acm.org, yasumura@sfc.keio.ac.jp

Abstract. People often have difficulty in browsing a massive number of pictures. To solve this problem, we focused on the activities of people who share slideshows with their friends: that is, they often talk about the each picture shown on the display. We think these activities are useful as narrations for the slideshows. Therefore, we propose a novel slideshow system, PhotoLoop, which can automatically capture people's activities while watching slideshows using video/audio recordings and integrates them (slideshows and video narrations) to create attractive contents. In this paper, first, we describe people's behavior while watching slideshows. Next, we present the PhotoLoop prototype based on our observations. Finally, we confirm the effectiveness of the system through evaluation and discussion.

Keywords: Photograph, Slideshow, Narration, Implicit creation.

1 Introduction

As digital cameras and camera equipped mobile phones became popular in recent years, people began to take more pictures than ever before. They now face the problem of managing the large number of pictures. Many researchers focused on metadata related to each picture for effective picture management. These approaches can be divided into three categories: (1) using features extracted from pictures [1], (2) using sensor information collected during the capturing process [5, 6], and (3) using metadata manually created by users [3, 4, 5, 8]. In particular, subjective metadata created by users have advantages in reflecting their judgments or intentions which are difficult to be generated by computers. However, users often experience difficulty in adding metadata continuously.

To solve this problem, we focused on the activities of people who share slideshows with their friends: that is, they often talk about the current picture shown on the display. Chalfen also reported that people usually make conversations during slideshows to avoid silences [2]. We think these activities are useful as narrations for the slideshows. Therefore, we propose a novel slideshow system, PhotoLoop, which automatically captures people's activities while watching slideshows using video/audio recordings and

N. Streitz and C. Stephanidis (Eds.): DAPI/HCII 2013, LNCS 8028, pp. 87–96, 2013.

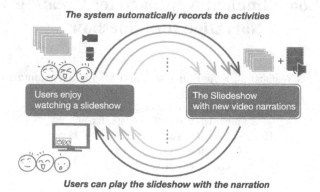

Fig. 1. The concept of PhotoLoop

integrates them (slideshows and video narrations) to create attractive content. Using PhotoLoop, users can easily add video narrations to slideshows without special efforts (Figure 1).

2   Preliminary Study

We performed a preliminary study to record people's activities while watching slideshows using video/audio recordings and analyzed their conversations and behavior. The aim of this study is to explore the number, frequency, and content of people's conversations while watching a slideshow. Moreover, we also observed their behavior during the slideshow. We explain the procedure of the study. First, we selected 16 subjects (11male and 5 female, aged between 19 and 54) who all worked at the same laboratory. We prepared 30 pictures taken at a laboratory camp. 12 of the subjects had attended the camp. We classified them into four groups. Each group includes a subject who had not attended the camp. The slideshow was manually controlled by a subject who was randomly selected in each group.

2.1   Results

We recorded the activities of the users while watching the slideshow with video/audio and wrote down all conversations. Next, we summarized the number of conversations and the length of the slideshow for each group (Figure 2). On average, the subjects spent 11:32 min watching the 30 pictures and had 367 conversations. In other words, the subjects spent 23 seconds and had 12 conversations per picture. Next, we analyzed the contents of the conversations during the slideshows to explore their features. First, we found "Questions and answers" that is, a subject asked a question such as "What is it?!", "When did it happen?", or "Who is he/she?" and other members answered to the question. For example, a subject asked "Where is this road?" while watching Figure 3 (A) and another subject answered "The road is located under the ropeway".

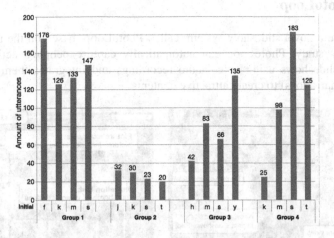

Fig. 2. Number of conversations for each group member

We also found "Recall by question": that is, a subject asked a question such as "It was a warm day, wasn't it?" to conform his/her memory. For example, a subject said "We were in the same group in the workshop, weren't we?" while watching Figure 3 (B), and another subject answered "Yes, we worked together!"

Some subjects mentioned their impression of the picture. For example, a subject mentioned "I felt fine because of the weather." while watching Figure 3 (C).

Fig. 3. Examples of pictures in preliminary study

As shown above, we observed many types of conversations related to the pictures. These conversations often contained information that was not found in the pictures themselves. Moreover, the conversations were sometimes different between groups. For this reason, we thought that the system can obtain various narrations for the slideshow by recoding conversations from multiple groups.

Furthermore, many subjects performed gestures to express their interests or emotions during conversations. For example, they often pointed at an object or a person in the picture with their fingers when talking on them.

3   PhotoLoop

We propose a novel slideshow system, called PhotoLoop, based on the results of the preliminary study. PhotoLoop can automatically capture people's activities while watching slideshows using video/audio recordings and integrates them (slideshows and video narrations) to create attractive contents.

Fig. 4. Screenshot of the main window and slideshow browser

In this section, we explain the basic features of PhotoLoop: "video narration", "overlap recording", and "pointer logging".

Video Narration. As mentioned above, PhotoLoop automatically records users' activities using a camera and a microphone while they watch slideshows. In this paper, we call these video/audio recordings as "video narration": the video includes facial expressions/ gestures and the audio includes explanations/impressions of the pictures. Figure 4 (right) shows a screenshot of the slideshow browser. The system presents thumbnails of pictures and video narrations included in the slideshow. Users can select multiple video narrations that are shown during the slideshow. When the users push the start button, the system presents the selected video narrations below the screen along with a preview of real-time video (Figure 4 (left)). Although all videos are played at the same time, the system plays only one narration (audio track) to avoid confusion. The users can easily hear another narration, just by clicking another video. When they finish watching the slideshow, the system automatically creates a new video narration and saves it to the database. Thus, PhotoLoop helps users create a video narration just by watching slideshows without any special operation.

Overlap Recording. As mentioned above, PhotoLoop can record the activities of users while they watch the slideshow with video narrations created at the previous slideshow. We call this feature "overlap recording". Using this function, the system can add various explanations and impressions to the pictures from multiple viewpoints. Moreover, some people may attach unexpected narrations while hearing previous narrations by another group. Thus, PhotoLoop can add further attractiveness to the slideshow by recording new video narrations while the users watch the slideshow with past narrations.

Pointer Logging. As mentioned in the results of the preliminary study, users performed various gestures to explain pictures while they watched the slideshow. Here, we focused on one of the most popular gesture, "pointing at a person/object in the picture", to express the main target. To record this action in a practical way, we provide the "pointer logging" function to help users add arrow cursors to the picture just by clicking the mouse button, as shown in figure 4 (left). We prepared two types of pointing device: a gyro mouse and a common mouse. While the gyro mouse was suited for casual slideshows (e.g., in a living room), we also supported a common mouse for general use. The cursors recorded in past slideshows are shown as red arrows. Figure 5 shows the basic usage of the PhotoLoop.

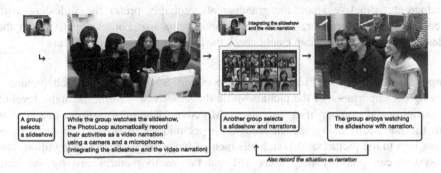

Fig. 5. Basic usage of the PhotoLoop

The PhotoLoop mainly consists of a PC (Windows XP), an LCD, a USB camera, a microphone, and a mouse, as shown in Figure 6. The system records video and audio using the USB camera and the microphone. We developed frontend software to control the above devices and play slideshows and video narrations using Adobe Air, as well as backend software to record video narrations using Adobe Flash Media Server . The resolution of the video is 320 x 240 pixels and the frame rate is 15 fps.

Fig. 6. System architecture of PhotoLoop

3.1   Scenarios

In this section, we describe three usage scenarios of the PhotoLoop.

Watching Slideshows after Trips. Most people take many pictures when they go on trips. They often watch these pictures together as a slideshow after they come home. Although this process often becomes an important part of their memories of the trip, most people do not record their activities while watching the slideshow. PhotoLoop helps users enrich their memories of trips by recording these activities without effort.

Sharing Video Narrations with Friends. When people watch slideshow after an event using the PhotoLoop, the system can generate a video narration that contains users' subjective impressions and explanations of the slideshow. We think these narrations are useful, especially for their friends/families who did not attend the event. For example, when users want to share the slideshow of their family trip with their grandparents who live apart, the grandparents probably prefer the slideshow with video narrations. Moreover, when their grandparents use PhotoLoop to watch the slideshow, the initial users can easily check the reactions of the grandparents.

Simple Annotations to Pictures. PhotoLoop can add a score to each picture – showing the importance of the picture within the slideshow – using the audio level of the narration and number of arrow cursors. Moreover, when the system extracts texts from the narrations using speech recognition techniques, these texts may work as annotations to the pictures. Although this method has a problem with recognition rate, the system can possibly help users add annotations to pictures just by watching slideshows as usual.

4   Evaluation

In this section, we verified the effectiveness of PhotoLoop through an evaluation. The main aim of this evaluation was to explore whether the video narrations can improve the attractiveness of the slideshow. We selected eight subjects (all males, aged between 19 and 27) who regularly use computers and digital cameras, and we randomly divided them into four pairs. First, the experimenter asked each pair to watch a slideshow using PhotoLoop twice. When they watched the slideshow at first, the system presented the slideshow alone. The second time, the system showed the slideshow along with the video narration that had been recorded with another pair. The second slideshows were performed after all first slideshows were finished. The slideshow included 15 pictures used in the preliminary study. After the second slideshows, the experimenter obtained subjective feedback from the subjects through questionnaires and oral interviews. Before the evaluation, the experimenter explained the basic function of PhotoLoop; that is, the system automatically records the subjects' activities during the slideshow and presents them to another pair.

In addition, we provided two wireless mice to allow both subjects in each pair to control the arrow cursor and the slideshow.

4.1   Results

To gain subjective feedback, we set two questions and scored the answers on a scale of 1 to 5 as follows: "Q.1: Did you enjoy watching the slideshow? (1: very boring – 5: very amused)" and "Q.2: Did you discover new information from the slideshow? (1: no information – 5: plenty of information". The average score of Q.1 was 4.75 (S.D.=0.46) at first slideshow and 4.25 (S.D.=0.70) at second slideshow. The average score of Q.2 was 4.25 (S.D.=0.46) at first and 4.38 (S.D.=0.51) at second.

Most participants responded favorably to Q.1 and Q.2 for both the first and second slideshows. Here we shows typical comments from the subjects as follows:

1. I was very amused just by hearing the comments from the other group.
2. I was amused by the person who said whatever he felt. The conversations between A and B were interesting.
3. The conversations between C and D reminded me of the details of the event. I preferred when the conversations occurred less frequently. I was impressed that the other group explained the picture from a different viewpoint.
4. I felt pleased to see that other people enjoyed the slideshow.
5. I was favorably impressed by C since he remembered various details of the event.
6. I was little bothered by the second slideshow since the pictures were the same.
7. I could enjoy the second slideshow because of the video narrations.
8. I enjoyed adding arrow cursors.
9. I sometimes focused on listening to the narration

4.2   Consideration

In this section, we consider the results of the evaluation in terms of "video recording", "pointer logging", and "video narration".

Video Recording. We had been concerned that users might hesitate to talk in front of the camera and microphone. However, most subjects seemed to act as usual while watching the slideshow as shown in the comment (B). Meanwhile, we observed several inappropriate conversations, such as "He looked like an awful monster!" and "His shirt was quite twisted around his neck. That looked so bad!". These "frank" comments may become attractive contents; however, we should also consider the risk that these comments may have negative influence on human relations.

Pointer Logging. In this evaluation, we observed more conversations including reference terms (e.g., "that" or "this") than those in the preliminary study. This change may have resulted from the "arrow cursor" function: that is, users often have conversations like "What's this?" when they add arrow cursors in the pictures. We found these conversations quite interesting as we had not expected the arrow cursors to affect the conversations. Meanwhile, several subjects talked about objects just by pointing to them with the cursor (without clicking). Since the current system recorded cursor positions only when the subjects clicked the mice, others could not understand the meaning of the reference terms in such cases. To solve this problem, we plan to develop another logging/display method that automatically records/visualizes the cursor movement and emphasizes the cursor when clicked. In addition, we found a unique use of the arrow cursors: some users draw pictures using arrow cursors; others attached arrow cursors archly to everywhere in the picture. These are also interesting findings for us since we had not expected these usages of the arrow cursor.

Video Narration. Some subjects informally watched the slideshow with their own narration after the evaluation. In such cases, the subjects often reacted to their own conversations in the narration: for example, they often started laughing in response to their previous laughter. Next, we observed comments from the subjects who were the friends of persons shown in the pictures as follows: "I easily understood the situation though I had not participated in the event" and "I found the arrows were useful to understand the conversations. I really like it!". Meanwhile, the number of conversations at the second slideshow was less than that at the first slideshow. These changes may arise from the fact that users were sometimes too focused on the narration and pictures and forgot to talk with each other as shown in the comment (I).

5   Related Work

There are three approaches to help users add subjective metadata: (1) supporting users to attach metadata manually [3, 4], (2) attaching metadata while capturing pictures [5, 6, 7], and (3) extracting metadata from the picture sharing process [8, 9]. Shneiderman [3] proposed a system that helps users attach labels (e.g., personal names) to pictures by drag&drop. Sigurbjörnsson [4] proposed a system that recommends tag candidates using WordNet. In contrast, WillCam [5] is a novel digital camera that can help photographers add their ideas regarding pictures via pointers. ContextCam [6] proposes a context-aware video camera that provides time, location, persons and event information using several sensors and machine learning techniques. Capturing the Invisible [7] designs real-time visual effects for digital cameras using simulated sensor data. Moreover, Aria [8] focuses on communication using pictures; that is, sending pictures by e-mail. The system can automatically create descriptions of pictures from messages written in the e-mail. Chi et al. [9] also proposed a system that supports users attaching annotations to picture sets through text chats. PhotoLoop is unique in helping users add video narrations to slideshows in a simple manner by automatically recording the users' activities (e.g., conversations and behavior) during the slideshows.

Balabanovic et al. [10] proposed a method to add narrations to a picture set efficiently. Their research is similar to PhotoLoop in that it focuses on picture narrations. However, their system aimed to record only intentional narrations: the user manually pushes the record button and starts explaining the picture. While this system is suited for creating accurate narration, it requires users' motivation and attention to create narrations. Moreover, this system cannot record new narrations while playing previous ones. PhotoLoop is unique in automatically creating video narrations of slideshows by recording the users' activities during the slideshows using a video/audio system.

There are many research projects that focused on relationship between people and photographs [14,15,16,17,18,19]. For example, David et al. [15] had pointed that some photo sharing conversations incorporate comments about the meaning and value of photos to those who took them. They have been discussing that these comments and conversations would be good to save and associate with the photos for future personal reference and consumption. Almost all works investigated how people communicate with photographs in daily life. They have not developed system yet based on the result. However, these works will be meaningful to improve PhotoLoop in the future.

There have been several projects that focused on communication by sharing video/audio data. CU-Later [11] is a communication support system that uses video messages in remote locations and different time zones. This system records users' activities while eating with a video/audio system and shares them with friends/family in remote locations. LunchCommunicator [12] supports communication between family members (the lunch-creator and the lunch-consumer) using automatic capturing/playing techniques during the preparation/consumption of the lunchbox. The EyeCatcher [13] helps photographers capture a variety of natural looking facial expressions of their subjects by keeping the eyes of the subjects focused on the camera without the stress usually associated with being photographed. PhotoLoop is unique in focusing on users' unconscious reactions while watching slideshows and utilizing them as video narrations for the slideshows.

6   Conclusion

In this paper, we propose a novel slideshow system, PhotoLoop, which automatically captures people's activities while watching slideshows using a video/audio recording system and integrates them (slideshows and video narrations) to create attractive content. We designed a prototype based on observations of subjects while watching slideshows and confirmed the effectiveness of the system through evaluation and discussion.

Acknowledgements. This work was partly supported by JST PRESTO program.

References

1. Veltkamp, R.C., Tanase, M.: Content-Based Image Retrieval Systems: A Survey. Technical Report UU-CS-2000-34, Utrecht University (2000)
2. Chalfen, R.: Snapshot versions of life. Bowling Green State University Press, Bowling Green OH (1987)

3. Shneiderman, B., Kang, H.: Direct Annotation: A Drag-and-Drop Strategy for Labeling Photos. In: Proceedings of InfoVis 2000, pp. 88–95 (2000)
4. Sigurbjörnsson, B., van Zwol, R.: Flickr tag recommendation based on collective knowledge. In: Proceeding of WWW 2008, pp. 327–336 (2008)
5. Watanabe, K., Tsukada, K., Yasumura, M.: WillCam: a digital camera visualizing users' interest. In: Extended Abstracts of ACM CHI 2007, pp. 2747–2752 (2007)
6. Patel, S.N., Abowd, G.D.: The ContextCam: Automated Point of Capture Video Annotation. In: Mynatt, E.D., Siio, I. (eds.) UbiComp 2004. LNCS, vol. 3205, pp. 301–318. Springer, Heidelberg (2004)
7. Hakansson, M., Ljungblad, S., Holmquist, L.E.: Capturing the invisible: designing context-aware photography. In: DUX 2003: Proceedings of the 2003 Conference on Designing for User Experiences, pp. 1–4 (2003)
8. Lieberman, H., Rosenzweig, E., Singh, P.: Aria: An Agent For Annotating And Retrieving Images. IEEE Computer 34(7), 57–61 (2001)
9. Chi, P.-Y., Lieberman, H.: Intelligent assistance for conversational storytelling using story patterns. In: Proceedings of ACM IUI, pp. 217–226 (2011)
10. Balabanovic, M., Chu, L.L., Wolff, G.J.: Storytelling with digital photographs. In: Proceedings of ACM CHI 2000, pp. 564–571 (2000)
11. Tsujita, H., Yarosh, S., Abowd, G.: CU-Later: A Communication System Considering Time Difference. In: Adjunct Proceedings of Ubicomp 2010, pp. 435–436 (2010)
12. Kotani, N., Tsukada, K., Watanabe, K., Siio, I.: LunchCommunicator: Communication Support System using a Lunchbox. In: Adjunct Proceedings of Pervasive 2011 pp. 9–12 (2011)
13. Tsukada, K., Oki, M.: EyeCatcher: A digital camera for capturing a variety of natural looking facial expressions in daily snapshots. In: Floréen, P., Krüger, A., Spasojevic, M. (eds.) Pervasive 2010. LNCS, vol. 6030, pp. 112–129. Springer, Heidelberg (2010)
14. Crabtree, A., Rodden, T., Mariani, J.: Collaborating around collections: informing the continued development of photoware. In: Proceedings of ACM CSCW 2004 (2004)
15. Frohlich, D., Kuchinsky, A., Pering, C., Don, A., Ariss, S.: Requirements for photoware. In: Proceedings of ACM CSCW 2002 (2002)
16. Martin, H., Gaver, B.: Beyond the snapshot from speculation to prototypes in audiophotography. In: Proceedings of the 3rd Conference on Designing Interactive Systems: Processes, Practices, Methods, and Techniques, pp. 55–65 (2000)
17. Swan, L., Taylor, A.S.: Photo displays in the home. In: Proceedings of the 7th ACM Conference on Designing Interactive Systems (DIS 2008), pp. 261–270 (2008)
18. Taylor, A.S., Swan, L., Durrant, A.: Designing family photo displays. In: Proc. ECSCW 2008, pp. 79–98. Springer, London (2008)
19. Voida, A., Mynatt, E.D.: Six themes of the communicative appropriation of photographic images. In: Proceedings of ACM CHI 2005, pp. 171–180 (2005)

Part II

Context-Awareness in Smart and Intelligent Environments

A Human-Probe System That Considers On-body Position of a Mobile Phone with Sensors

Kaori Fujinami, Yuan Xue, Satoshi Murata, and Shigeki Hosokawa

Department of Computer and Information Sciences,
Tokyo University of Agricalture and Technology
2-24-16 Naka-cho, Koganei,184-8588 Tokyo, Japan
fujinami@cc.tuat.jp

Abstract. In recent years, various sensors are embedded into a so-called smartphone. A human-probe community is paying great attention to a smartpohne as a sensing node because it allows users to participate sensing activity easily. However, on-body localization of a sensor is critical issue if we utilize a smartphone as a sensing platform for human-probe. For instance, acceleration, temperature or humidity values are affected significantly by on-body position of a terminal.

In this paper, we propose a human-probe system that considers on-body position of a sensor. A general architecture is presented, and a heatstroke alert map is implemented, which visualizes a risk of heatstroke by taking into account on-body position of a sensor. Additionally, we introduce TALESEA, which is an external environmental sensing module for an Android smartphone.

Keywords: environmental sensing, human-probe, heatstroke, smartphone, on-body positional of a device.

1 Introduction

Recent advancement of technologies such as Micro Electro Mechanical Systems (MEMS), high performance and low power computation has allowed a mobile phone to be augmented with various sensors and to extract contextual information of a user, a device and/or environment. A new sensing paradigm called human-probe (or people-centric sensing and participatory sensing) aims at realizing large scale sensing without any pre-installed infrastructure, in which a sensor-augmented mobile phone is getting great attention as a sensing node because it allows users to participate sensing activities easily [8,11].

However, the ease of carrying a "sensor node" introduces an issue. According to a study of phone carrying, 17% of people determine the position of storing a smartphone based on *contextual restrictions*, e.g. no pocket in the T-shirt, too large phone size for a pants pocket, comfort for an ongoing activity [4]. These factors vary throughout the day, and thus the users change the positions in a day. This suggests that a context, *on-body position of a sensor*, has great potentials in

N. Streitz and C. Stephanidis (Eds.): DAPI/HCII 2013, LNCS 8028, pp. 99–108, 2013.

improving the quality of sensor-dependent services. In the paradigm of human-probe, the storing position of a mobile phone terminal is considered as a key context for reliable measurement [12,16].

In this paper, we propose a human-probe system that utilizes the positional information of a sensor node (smartphone) as a meta-data for improving the quality of sensing. The rest of the paper is organized as follows. Section 2 examines related work in terms of human-probe with a smartphone. The necessity of taking into account the position of a sensor on the body is pointed out in Section 3, and a framework for a reliable human-probe system is proposed. A USB sensor module for Android-based terminal, TALESEA, is developed in Section 4. Section 5 describes a map visualization of heatstroke risk level as an application. Finally, Section 6 concludes the paper with future work.

2   Related Work

Smartphone-based environmental sensing is getting attention due to the popularity of a smartphone and the existence of communication infrastructure [8,11]. Lane et al. argued the importance of *sensor context* [11] for reliable sensing, in which the position of sensor on the body is a representative of a sensor context. NoiseTube[16] is a smartphone-based noise level sensing system, in which the possibility of conflicting the normal use of a mobile phone with the use of a noise level meter is pointed out. This means, for example, carrying a phone terminal in a trousers pocket might provide different measurement result from a terminal hanging from the neck. Furthermore, Miyaki et al. proposed a concept of *sensonomy* [13], in which environmental state of a city, e.g. CO_2 concentration, temperature, humidity and air pressure, is visualized using a data collection module attached to a smartphone; however, the visualization might contain data from inappropriate sensing conditions since the storing position of the microphone (terminal) was not taken into account. In human-probe, the positioning information on the earth, e.g. latitude, longitude and the orientation, is usually captured by GPS receiver, compass and gyroscope along with the target sensor data. Interesting findings are that even these sensors are affected by the storing position [19,2]. These facts suggest that the position of a sensor (smartphone) on the body should be taken into account in reliable human-probe system.

On-body position sensing is recently getting attention to researchers in machine learning and ubiquitous computing communities [7,10,15,18]. Vahdatpour et al. recently proposed a method to identify 6 regions on the body, e.g. head, upper arm, for health and medical monitoring systems [18]. A preliminary work by Shi et al. seeks a method of on-body positioning of a mobile device into typical *containers* such as a trousers' pocket. Inertial sensors are utilized in these work. By contrast, Miluzzo et al. proposes a framework of recognizing the position of a mobile phone on the body using multiple sensors [12]. In their initial stage, a simple placement, i.e. inside or outside pocket, is subject to detect using an embedded microphone. We have also investigated a method to identify nine typical positions on the body including bags [6] as well as an application framework [7].

3   On-body Placement-Aware Human-Probe System

We show an experiment to confirm the on-body positional dependency of an environmental status, and then a human-probe system is proposed.

3.1   Placement-Dependency of Environmental Measurement

We can imagine that the temperature and humidity sensor readings might have difference among various storing positions on our body, e.g. neck, chest pocket and trousers pocket; however, it is not clear "how" different each other. A data collection was conducted in August 2011 to understand the dependency of the temperature and humidity sensor readings on storing positions. Four positions of a sensor on our body were chosen: front/back pocket of trousers, chest pocket, and around the neck (hanging), which are popular for storing a smartphone. Note that "hanging from the neck" has a special meaning because the sensor can measure an ideal air condition and be utilized in the comparison. The data were collected from at most six participants who stored sensors in the four positions in 20-30 minutes' walking on a road paved with asphalt. Tiny data loggers (SHTDL-1/2 [17]) were utilized in the data collection.

To see the difference between an ideal measurement condition and the others, scatter plots are generated so that the horizontal axis indicates the measurement from a sensor hanging from the neck, while the measurement from the other positions are represented by the vertical axis: from a sensor in a chest pocket

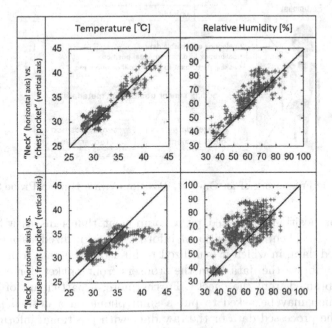

Fig. 1. The difference of measurements in storing positions. (Left: neck vs. chest pocket. Left: neck vs. front pocket of trousers.) Note that "neck" is an ideal sensing condition due to the openness to the air.

(Fig.1 top), and a front pocket of trousers (bottom). Here, the relationship between the neck and the trousers back pocket is similar to that of trousers front pocket. The plots on the diagonal line represent that the measurement from the neck and the chest pocket (or front pocket of trousers) are equal. These figures show that there is a small difference between chest pocket and neck, while the difference is large between trousers pockets and the neck. We consider that this is because the outside temperature is very high and a trousers pocket shaded the sensor from the sun's heat. By contrast, in case of the chest pocket, the heat might not be shaded since a chest pocket is nearly exposed to the air. These positional dependency may degrade the quality of data analysis based on collected data.

3.2   General Architecture

We propose a human-probe system, which consists of target sensor, on-body sensor position recognition, and position handling components on the smartphone side, while data sharing platform and applications run on the Internet side (see Figure 2).

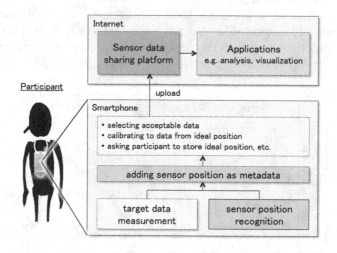

Fig. 2. Basic Framework of an On-body Position-Aware Human-Probe System

The sensor position is tracked by a component that runs as a Service of Android OS [7]. Then, the positional information is utilized as metadata of original sensed data, in which it is utilized to filter out the data from undesired position or calibrate the data from the trousers front pocket, for example, to the one as obtained from the "neck". Furthermore, a participant of a human-probe campaign may be asked to put a smartphone on a desired position if necessary. The processed data or the raw data with positional information are sent to a data sharing service on the internet such as Pachube in conjunction with global coordinates and timestamps. The shared data are further analyzed to understand the current environmental states in a particular area or predict the futuristic states. For a consumer application, heat map visualization is often utilized. In the future, a pedestrian or cyclist navigation might be provided based on collected temperature dat, in which a route is suggested to a user to avoid heatstroke or burn.

4   Sensor Module for Android-Based Smartphone Sensing

In this section, we describe the design and implementation of a sensor module for Android-based smartphone sensing.

4.1   Overview of TALESEA

A smartphone at this moment is employing a wide range of sensing modality, e.g. audio, proximity, light level, magnetic field; however, a class of environmental sensors, e.g. temperature, humidity, CO_2, ultra violet, have not yet been integrated into a smartphone. To accelerate smartphone-based environmental sensing, TALESEA (Tiny, Adjunctive and Lightweight Environmental-Sensing for Extending Andoid) was developed. TALESEA consists of a micro-controller (Arduino Pro mini (8MHz, 3.3 V)) and communicates with Android USB-API that is supported Android OS 3.1 or later. Any sensor and output element can be connected to the micro-controller; a temperature and relative humidity sensor (Sensirion Inc.'s SHT-71 [14]) is currently supported. Fig. 3-a) shows the appearance of TALESEA attached to Samsung's Galaxy NEXUS. The dimension is W48×H15×D30[mm], and the weight is 19[g].

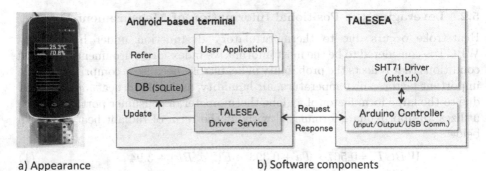

a) Appearance   b) Software components

Fig. 3. Andoid-based terminal and TALESEA: a) appearance and b) software components

4.2   Software Components

Fig. 3-b) illustrates the software components on the TALEASA's side and Android-based terminal. TALESEA Driver Service periodically sends a command to Arduino Controller running in TALESEA, which runs in the background as a Service of Android. A command includes a sensing request, an output request, e.g turning on/off on-board LED, rotating a motor by 30 degrees, and a request of referring/updating an internal state of TALESEA. The latest value from a sensor is overridden on a table of DB (SQLite) that offers asynchronous access to user applications. Here, special API is provided so that it can encapsulate Android Contents Provider API from application developers.

5   Map Visualization of Heatstroke Risk Level: An Application

Based on the framework, we implemented a map visualization system for heatstroke alert as an application.

5.1   Demands for Sharing Heatstroke Risk Level

In recent years, the number of people suffered from heatstroke is increasing, which is considered due to global high temperatures. In Japan, various consumer products for heatstroke risk alert have been available on the market, e.g. [5]. The information is, however, the level of heatstroke risk at the moment, i.e. around a user. It is difficult to find the route to the station with lowest risk, for example. On the other hand, a web application provides a current state of forecast of the level of risk at any location based on the information from a weather station; however, the spatial resolution of the information is limited to city-level. So, sharing the local measurements with global position has the potential to improve the spatial resolution and allow querying the risk level at any location.

5.2   Leveraging the Positional Information of Measurement Device

Heatstroke occurs due to thermoregulatory dysfunction under heat stress. WBGT is considered to be the most informative index for environmental thermal conditions that reflects the probability of heatstroke because it comprises of three important factors: air temperature, air humidity, and radiant heat [3]. However, due to the large form factor of a globe thermometer, a consumer portable device utilizes an approximate formula [9] without the term of radiant heat as shown below.

$$WBGT = 0.567 \times Ta + 0.393 \times E(Ta, Rh) + 3.94 \qquad (1)$$

$$E(Ta, Rh) = (Rh/100) \times 6.105 \times exp((7.27 \times Ta)/(237.7 + Ta)) \qquad (2)$$

Here, Ta and Rh represent the air temperature and relative humidity, respectively, that are easily measured in daily life.

People would not mind if the device is carried in a desirable manner. As described in Section 3.1, the temperature and relative humidity measurement might not be correct if the device is not outside or not open to the air, e.g. in the front pocket of trousers. The calculated WBGT value is also affected by the on-body positional dependency. The lower-than-actual level of the risk by an under-estimate might make a user careless. In this application, the on-body position of the device is explicitly presented to a user to facilitate the interpretation of the reliability of the calculated WBGT by him/herself.

5.3   Implementation

An uploading application on the terminal side gets latest temperature and relative humidity values from local DB, and calculate an approximate WBGT value. A global positioning information is obtained from GPS receiver on a terminal. In addition to these basic data, the level of risk of heatstroke (1 to 5) is determined based on the range of WBGT value [1], which is often utilized for a consumer heatstroke alert device as a user-friendly indicator, e.g. [5].

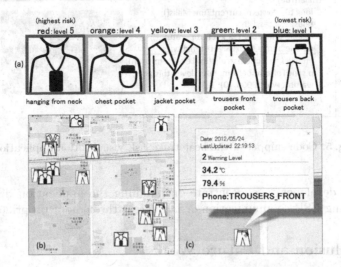

Fig. 4. Visualization of collected data on a map: (a) the icon with storing position of a sensor and the level of heatstroke risk, (b) plots on a map, and (c) detailed view

These types of information are shared and visualized on commercial web-services. The data from terminals are shared on Pachube, which is an open scaleable platform that realizes Internet of Things by connecting any device and sharing data securely. An application component on the terminal utilized *jPachube*, a Java wrapper for Pachube's API, to post the data to Pachube. The collected information is visualized using Google Map API, in which an icon and the border indicate the storing position and the level of heatstroke risk, respectively (Fig. 4-(a) and (b)). Detailed information can further be obtained by clicking an icon (Fig. 4-(c)).

Fig. 5 shows a code snippet of the uploading application. The information of a storing position is updated every time the sensor position recognition component (Fig. 2) detects a new position and set to an instance variable `pos` via `onReceive` method. In `run` method, the data are obtained from DB (line 12-14 of Fig. 5), the risk level is estimated (line 15). Then, the rawdata, the risk level and the storing position are sent to Pachube (line 16). As shown in line 8,12,13 and 14, the access to TALESEA is encapsulated by **TALESEA** class, which allows an

```
1:   private Handler handler = new PhonePosHandler() {
2:       public void onReceive(String pos, String com, double conf) {
3:           this.pos = pos;
4:       }
5:   }
6:
7:   public void run() {
8:       TALESEA talesea = new TALESEA();
9:       Pachube p = new Pachube(API_KEY);
10:      while(true) {
11:          long t0 = System. currentTimeMillis();
12:          talesea.accessDB();
13:          double tem = talesea.getTemperature();
14:          double hum = talesea.getHumidity();
15:          int level = calcHeatstrokeRiskLevel(tem, hum);
16:          p.sendToPachube(tem, hum, level, this.pos);
17:          waitInterval(10000, t0);
18:      }
19:  }
```

Implementing PhonePosHandler;
Called every update of a storing position

Instantiating TALESEA class

– Set latest temperature
  and humidity data from DB
  into instance variables
– getting temperature data
– getting humidity data

Fig. 5. Code snippet of the heatstroke risk visualization application

application developer to concentrate on handling the application data rather than handling USB communication or DB access throughout proprietary APIs.

6   Conclusion and Future Work

In this paper, we proposed a human-probe system that takes into account the position of a mobile phone terminal (with sensors) on the body. We showed a positional dependency of temperature and relative humidity sensor readings, which implies the quality of collected data by human-probe might be low unless the storing position of a sensor is not considered. A visualization system of heatstroke risk level was implemented based on a basic framework of on-body localization-aware human-probe system. A tiny sensor module for an Android-based smartphone was investigated.

Current version of the visualization system simply shows the storing position as a self-interpretive data for a user. However, another type of information can be considered, which provide a calibrated value, i.e. measured outside, and the possibility of over- or under-estimation of the measurement from a current position. In [20], we have already proposed a calibration method based on regression models that are provided for each storing position, which will be tested after refinement of the regression models based on large amount of data. We will finally investigate the appropriate way of visualization through various level of utilization of the positional information of a sensor.

Acknowledgments. This work was supported by MEXT Grants-in-Aid for Scientific Research (A) No. 23240014.

References

1. Asayama, M.: Guideline for the Prevention of Heat Disorder in Japan. Global Environmental Research 13(1), 19–25 (2009)
2. Blum, J.R., Greencorn, D.G., Cooperstock, J.R.: Smartphone sensor reliability for augmented reality applications. In: Proceedings of the 9th International Conference on Mobile and Ubiquitous Systems: Computing, Networking and Services, MobiQuitous2012 (2012)
3. Yaglou, C.P., Minard, D.: Control of heat casualties at military training centers. Arch. Ind. Hlth. 16(4), 302–305 (1957)
4. Cui, Y., Chipchase, J., Ichikawa, F.: A Cross Culture Study on Phone Carrying and Physical Personalization. In: Aykin, N. (ed.) HCII 2007. LNCS, vol. 4559, pp. 483–492. Springer, Heidelberg (2007)
5. Design Factory Inc. Thermal Stress Indicator Series, http://www.necchu-sho.com/en/index.html
6. Fujinami, K., Kouchi, S.: Recognizing a Mobile Phone's Storing Position as a Context of a Device and a User. In: Proceedings of the 9th International Conference on Mobile and Ubiquitous Systems: Computing, Networking and Services, MobiQuitous 2012 (2012)
7. Fujinami, K., Kouchi, S., Xue, Y.: Design and Implementation of an On-body Placement-Aware Smartphone. In: Proceedings of the 32nd International Conference on Distributed Computing Systems Workshops (ICDCSW), pp. 69–74 (2012)
8. Goldman, J., Shilton, K., Burke, J., Estrin, D., Hansen, M., Ramanathan, N., Reddy, S., Samanta, V., Srivastava, M., West, R.: Participatory Sensing: A citizen-powered approach to illuminating the patterns that shape our world. Foresight and Governance Project, White Paper (2009)
9. Grimmer, K., King, E., Larsen, T., Farquharson, T., Potter, A., Sharpe, P., de Wit, H.: Prevalence of hot weather conditions related to sports participation guidelines: A South Australian investigation. Journal of Science and Medicine in Sport 9(1-2), 72–80 (2006)
10. Kunze, K., Lukowicz, P., Junker, H., Tröster, G.: Where am I: Recognizing On-body Positions of Wearable Sensors. In: Strang, T., Linnhoff-Popien, C. (eds.) LoCA 2005. LNCS, vol. 3479, pp. 264–275. Springer, Heidelberg (2005)
11. Lane, N.D., Miluzzo, E., Lu, H., Peebles, D., Choudhury, T., Campbell, A.T.: A survey of mobile phone sensing. IEEE Communications Magazine 48(9), 140–150 (2010)
12. Miluzzo, E., Papandrea, M., Lane, N., Lu, H., Campbell, A.: Pocket, bag, hand, etc.-automatically detecting phone context through discovery. In: Proceedings of the First International Workshop on Sensing for App Phones, PhoneSense 2010 (2010)
13. Miyaki, T., Rekimoto, J.: Sensonomy: Envisioning folksonomic urban sensing. In: Ubicomp 2008 Workshop (2008)
14. Sensirion AG. Digital humidity and temperature sensor SHT-71, http://www.sensirion.com/en/products/humidity-temperature/humidity-sensor-sht71/
15. Shi, Y., Shi, Y., Liu, J.: A rotation based method for detecting on-body positions of mobile devices. In: Proceedings of the 13th International Conference on Ubiquitous Computing, UbiComp 2011, pp. 559–560 (2011)
16. Stevens, M., D'Hondt, E.: Crowdsourcing of Pollution Data using Smartphones. In: 1st Ubiquitous Crowdsourcing Workshop at UbiComp (2010)

17. SysCom Co. Mini Temperature and Humidity Logger SHTDL-1/2,
    `http://syscom-corp.jp/doc/product/sensor/hyg_mini-logger.html`
18. Vahdatpour, A., Amini, N., Sarrafzadeh, M.: On-body device localization for health
    and medical monitoring applications. In: Proceedings of the 2011 IEEE Interna-
    tional Conference on Pervasive Computing and Communications (PerCom 2011),
    pp. 37–44 (2011)
19. Vaitl, C., Kunze, K., Lukowicz, P.: Does on-body location of a GPS receiver matter?
    In: Proceedings of the 2010 International Workshop on Wearable and Implantable
    Body Sensor Networks (BSN 2010), pp. 219–221 (2010)
20. Xue, Y., Hosokawa, S., Murata, S., Kouchi, S., Fujinami, K.: An On-Body
    Placement-Aware Heatstroke Alert on a Smartphone. In: Proceedings of the 2012
    International Conference on Digital Contents and Applications (DCA 2012), pp.
    226–234 (2012)

Multi-person Identification and Localization
for Ambient Assistive Living

Georgios Galatas[1][2], Shahina Ferdous[1], and Fillia Makedon[1]

[1] Heracleia Human Centered Computing Lab, Computer Science and Engineering Dept.
University of Texas at Arlington, USA
[2] Institute of Informatics and Telecommunications, NCSR "Demokritos", Athens, Greece
{georgios.galatas,shahina.ferdous}@mavs.uta.edu,
makedon@uta.edu

Abstract. In this paper, we present a novel, non-intrusive system that uses RFID technology and the Kinect sensor in order to identify and track multiple people in an assistive apartment. RFID is used for both identification and location estimation while information from the Kinect sensor is used for accurate localization. Data from the various modalities is fused using two techniques. During the experiments conducted, our system exhibited high accuracy, thus proving the effectiveness of the proposed design.

Keywords: Person localization, context-awareness, multi-sensory fusion, depth information, Microsoft Kinect, RFID.

1 Introduction

Successful multi-person identification and localization is a fundamental step towards activity monitoring, emergency detection and ultimately context-awareness. The proliferation of ambient-intelligent environments has triggered research related to applications, such as monitoring Assistive Daily Living (ADL), fall detection, risk prevention and surveillance [1, 2]. Accurate person localization plays an essential role in all these applications and has been dealt with using many different approaches. Video cameras are the most commonly used devices since they are affordable and provide abundant information about people's activities and their surroundings. Nevertheless, when used domestically, they can be considered invasive, and the segmentation and tracking problems using planar video in a multi-person setting are very challenging [3, 4]. On the other hand, RFID systems are consistently used to keep track of medicine and patients in hospitals [5]. However, radio frequency signal propagation suffers from various issues such as multi-path attenuation, diffraction and reflection in an indoor environment [6] and therefore, RFID cannot be considered sufficiently accurate for localization purposes.

Therefore, in our approach, we have utilized the identification capabilities of RFID and combined that with precise 3D tracking from the Kinect to create an accurate identification and localization solution. RFID is used for both discerning between

N. Streitz and C. Stephanidis (Eds.): DAPI/HCII 2013, LNCS 8028, pp. 109–114, 2013.
© Springer-Verlag Berlin Heidelberg 2013

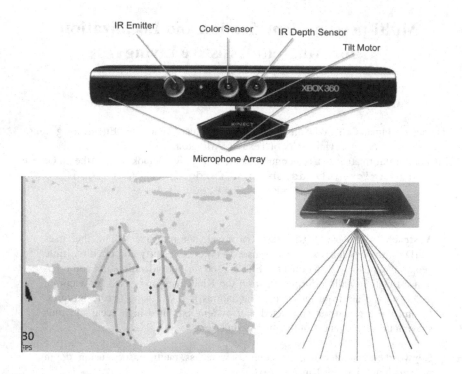

Fig. 1. The Kinect sensor (top) and examples for skeletal tracking (bottom-left) and audio localization (bottom-right)

users and providing a rough estimate of their location. Skeletal tracking is carried out using the Kinect sensor's 3D depth images and sound source localization is conducted utilizing its microphone array to deduce accurate location information. The two approaches we have used to fuse the data from all sources are classification-based and proximity-based, with the later exhibiting the highest accuracy.

In section 2 of this paper, we present the methodology used to build our system. Section 3 describes the experimental setup and results and section 4 concludes our work.

2   Methodology

The Kinect is a new device released by Microsoft that incorporates a color camera, a structured light 3D depth sensor and a microphone array (fig. 1). In our system, we utilized information captured by both the depth sensor and the microphone array. More specifically, we used skeletal tracking implemented using the MS Kinect SDK, in order to locate and track people in the field of view (FOV) of the sensor. Each detected skeleton has a unique identifier for a specific session, which is defined by the 3D space coordinates of its joints. In addition to the depth sensor, the Kinect has a microphone array comprised of 4 microphones in order to localize sounds. The information acquired using the array is the direction of the incoming sound, as well as a confidence indicator for the estimated direction. In our system, this information is utilized as a rough estimate, only if the other two sources fail to determine the exact location of the person.

The RFID system that we used was comprised of two antennas and a tag reader. Its main role was to identify the person in its field of sense (FOS), but also to provide a rough estimate of her/his location using the received signal strength indicator (RSSI) from each antenna. The mapping between the RSSI values and the actual position of the tag is accomplished through a calibration process that accounts for both the directionality of the antennas and the specific layout of the room. Multiple people are identified using their unique RFID tag and tracked as long as they remain in the FOS of the system. Skeletal tracking alone may not be able to discern between different people since a new tracking id is issued each time a person is lost from the FOV of the Kinect and then re-enters. Therefore, we improved our system's accuracy by matching the new RFID tag with the new tracking id as soon as an individual enters the room. This technique allows identification of each individual detected by the skeletal tracker. Finally, when no skeleton is detected in the FOV, but a tag is still being detected, audio localization is utilized in order to increase accuracy (e.g. triangulation when only one antenna reads the tag).

In order to combine the location information from all sources, we implemented 2 techniques: 1) proximity-based and 2) classification-based as shown in fig. 2. The proximity-based approach uses a proximity database that contains the position signature properties of: 1) the RSSI of a tag from an RFID antenna within a region, 2) the antennas that detect the particular tag and 3) the (x, y, z) coordinates range of the region, for a mesh of discrete regions in the deployment space. In the test phase, each

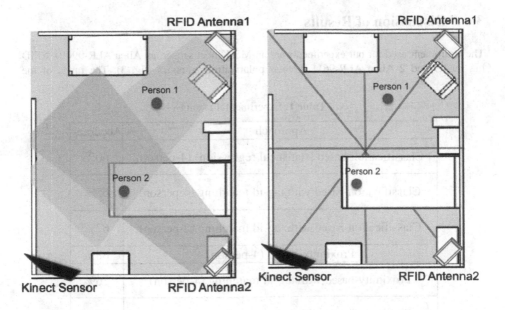

Fig. 2. Proximity-Based approach (left), Classification-Based approach (right)

detected signature vector is compared to this database and the closest match found is returned as the current position. After the region has been defined, the precise coordinates of the person within this region are estimated using the Kinect skeletal tracking. The classification approach is based on a training phase during which statistical regression is applied on pre-specified position signatures (RSSI in our case) in order to build a classifier. This classifier is then used to classify the current signature to a particular sector of the deployment space. This sector is then mapped to the location coordinates detected from the Kinect sensor. As afore-mentioned, in both approaches we use the sound from the microphone array as another modality besides skeletal tracking to resolve ambiguities in mapping.

Fig. 3. RFID system Devices

3   Discussion of Results

The equipment used for our experiments are an MS Kinect sensor, an Alien ALR-9900+ RFID tag reader and 2 Alien ALR-9611 circular polarization antennas (fig. 3). The range of the

Table 1. Experimental results

Approach	Accuracy
Classification-based (statistical regression) (4-person)	60%
Classification-based with tag-id matching (4-person)	65%
Classification-based with tag-id matching (2-person)	67%
Proximity-based (4-person)	68%
Proximity-based with tag-id matching (4-person)	76%
Proximity-based with tag-id matching (2-person)	86%

System is sufficient for a domestic environment and circular polarization ensures that tag detection is orientation-invariant. The experiments were carried out at the Heracleia assistive apartment. The antennas were placed at the 2 corners of the bedroom and the Kinect on a 3rd corner in order to maximize the FOS and FOV. Real-time tracking data is properly converted and displayed on a visualization tool (fig. 4). We conducted extensive experiments in our realistic domestic setup for 2 and 4 individuals, and the results are shown in Table 1. Accuracy denotes the percentage of correctly estimated locations for all individuals present in the room and also accounts for misidentifications and mismatches between the detected tag sector and skeletal id location. Accuracy was higher for the 2 person scenario with both methods. In

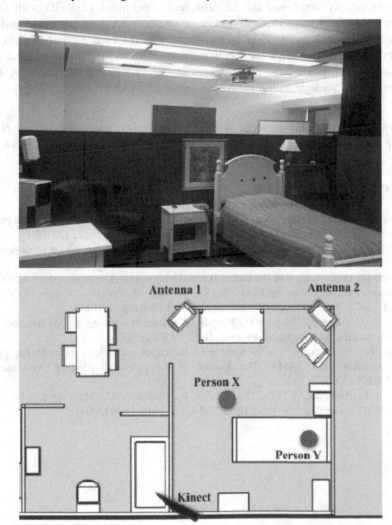

Fig. 4. The Heracleia assistive apartment (top) and the localization visualization tool (bottom)

addition, matching each RFID tag to the corresponding skeletal id resulted in a slight increase in accuracy, by minimizing false identifications. The highest accuracy was 86%, achieved using the proximity-based approach. The reason that the proximity-based approach performed better overall is that it utilizes both the RSSI and the Kinect information for sector mapping. On the other hand, the classification-based approach only uses the RSSI for mapping.

4   Conclusions

In conclusion, we combined the identification capabilities of RFID with accurate tracking from the Kinect in order to create an accurate multi-person identification and localization system for assistive environments. We used 3 types of data, RSSI, 3D depth and audio to solve the localization problem using 2 methods. The experiments conducted, proved the effectiveness of our system for this scenario. Further experiments will include additional Kinect sensors for more robust tracking.

Acknowledgments. This material is based upon work supported by the National Science Foundation under Grants No. NSF-CNS 1035913, NSF-CNS 0923494.

References

1. Teixeira, T., Jung, D., Savvides, A.: Tasking networked cctv cameras and mobile phones to identify and localize multiple people. In: Proc. Ubicomp, pp. 213–222 (2010)
2. Cucchiara, R., Fornaciari, M., Prati, A., Santinelli, P.: Mutual calibration of camera motes and RFIDs for people localization and identification. In: Proc. ICDSC (2010)
3. Mitzel, D., Horbert, E., Ess, A., Leibe, B.: Multi-person tracking with sparse detection and continuous segmentation. In: Daniilidis, K., Maragos, P., Paragios, N. (eds.) ECCV 2010, Part I. LNCS, vol. 6311, pp. 397–410. Springer, Heidelberg (2010)
4. Krumm, J., Harris, S., Meyers, B., Brumitt, B., Hale, M., Shafer, S.: Multi-camera multi-person tracking for easy living. In: Proc. IEEE IWVS (1997)
5. Ashar, B.S., Ferriter, A.: Radiofrequency identification technology in health care: benefits and potential risks. JAMA: The Journal of the American Medical Association 298, 2305–2307 (2007)
6. Hahnel, D., Burgard, W., Fox, D., Fishikin, K., Philipose, M.: Mapping and Localization with RFID Technology. In: Proc. IEEE ICRA, pp. 1015–1020 (2004)

Unobtrusive Recognition of Working Situations

Tobias Grosse-Puppendahl[1], Sebastian Benchea[1], Felix Kamieth[1],
Andreas Braun[1], and Christian Schuster[2]

[1] Fraunhofer IGD, Fraunhoferstr. 5, 64283 Darmstadt, Germany
{tobias.grosse-puppendahl,sebastian.benchea,felix.kamieth,
andreas.braun}@igd.fraunhofer.de
[2] Technische Universität Darmstadt, Hochschulstr. 10, 64289 Darmstadt, Germany
{christian.schuster}@stud.tu-darmstadt.de

Abstract. In many countries, people are obliged to remain in their jobs
for a long time. This results in an increased number of elderly people with
certain disabilities in working life. Therefore, a support with technical
assistance systems can avoid further health risks and help employees in
their everyday life. An important step for offering a suitable assistance
is the automatic recognition of working situations. In this paper we explore the unobtrusive data acquisition and classification of working situations above a tabletop surface. Therefore, a grid of capacitive sensors is
deployed directly underneath the tabletop.

Keywords: activity recognition, capacitive sensing, working situations.

1 Introduction

The demographic change in many industrialized countries and consequential
restructuring of social security systems leads to an increased number of elderly
and disabled people in working life. Considering modern societies, computer
work and activities that require a seated posture are one of the major risks for
an employees health, often resulting in a lack of exercise and stress to the spine.

These risks can be partially avoided by an ergonomic workplace that offers a
personalized technical assistance in suitable situations. For example, additional
lights can be switched on when the employee starts an activity that is related to
reading documents. Moreover, the height of the table or parameters of the chair
can be automatically adjusted to working situations. An ergonomic workplace
utilizing assistive technology can not only help people avoid developing health
issues, but can also aid people with pre-exisiting issues have a less distracting
and more productive work experience. On the following pages, we present a
method for recognition of working situations, forming the basis for realizing a
comprehensive and helpful technical assistance. We apply an array of unobtrusive capacitive sensors placed under a desk's wooden surface to enable activity
recognition. One of the benefits of the use of capacitive sensor arrays as we describe it here is the cost-effectiveness of the solution. Low power consumption
as well as low hardware costs make this a promising solution for the hardware
basis of assistive services in the office environment.

N. Streitz and C. Stephanidis (Eds.): DAPI/HCII 2013, LNCS 8028, pp. 115–121, 2013.

Based on this work, we intend to develop assistive services in the workplace to make it more ergonomic, efficient and supportive in the most relevant everyday desk work tasks. In summary, we present the following contributions:

1. We introduce a novel concept of a smart desk for recognizing working situations that is equipped with an array of capacitive proximity sensors.
2. An approach for extracting features from a grid of capacitive proximity sensors is presented. Based on this data, we introduce a concept for classifying working situations.
3. We evaluate the recognition process with different test persons that carry out a number of common office activities.

2   Related Work

Capacitive Sensing is a commonly used technology for realizing multi-touch interfaces[4]. The technology can also be employed to realize proximity sensing applications that measure the distance to objects, typically up to a distance of 50 cm [9]. Compared to camera-based solutions, capacitive proximity sensors offer the great advantage of being robust against changing lighting conditions and visual occlusion. Moreover, they can be deployed unobtrusively under any non-conductive material, such as wood, glass or plastic. Due to its low energy consumption, the sensing technique can also be employed in battery-driven or energy-harvesting applications. Given the unobtrusive nature of capacitive proximity sensors, researchers have applied the measurement technique to activity recognition in smart furniture or in wearable devices [6,11,3].

Detecting work activity has found widespread use in call centers and other fully computerized work environments to monitor productivity. However, in classical office work settings, the use of paper is still commonplace [7], making computer-only work tracking systems insufficient for widespread workplace usage.

In the area of table-top activity recognition, one can find a variety of existing approaches for detecting different activities on a desktop as well as turning the desktop itself into an interaction device. Tabletop activity recognition systems are usually built for specialized use. In recent works one can find cooking- and food-related systems like a diet-aware dining table[2], which recognizes different dishes (using RFID tags) and their weight (using a pressure-sensing surface) anm. Similarly specialized is the eLab bench, which offers support to biologists in their daily lab work [1]. Regarding office work, research has been conducted on the use of multitouch surface tabletop systems [10]. The research most related to what is described in this paper in terms of underlying technology are the work on the DiamondTouch system [4] as well as the Smart Skin large-scale surface[8]. These solutions focus on a usage similar to the multitouch surface tabletop systems.

3   Concept

The system used in this work is deployed under the surface of an ordinary desk, as illustrated in Figure 1. The grid is composed of three conductors placed horizontally and five conductors placed vertically. Using this setup, we can detect objects like hands and body parts located 10 cm above the desk, with a sensor update rate of approximately 50 Hz. This setup is the basis for subsequent feature extraction and classification. In this work, we employed loading-mode sensing, which measures the capacitance between an electrode and its surrounding environment [9]. However, there are other sensing methods, that can be used to perform those measurements, such as shunt-mode and transmit-mode sensing [9]. We chose loading-mode sensing due to its simplicity, as it is only based on a single electrode and very easy to implement.

Fig. 1. The smart desk is equipped with a 3 by 5 grid of capacitive proximity sensors. The sensors measure the proximity to a user's body parts, for example the knees placed below the table, or the hands placed upon the table.

In this work, we used the OpenCapSense evaluation toolkit, which is suitable for rapidly prototyping capacitive proximity sensing applications [5]. Therefore, we placed eight loading-mode sensors under the tabletop surface and connected them to the wires under the desk's surface. The loading mode sensors were then attached to the OpenCapSense board by using standard USB cables. We used OpenCapSense's measurement and evaluation application Sensekit to record activities for later evaluation with the WEKA machine learning framework[1].

As a first processing step for recognizing working situations, we extracted time-windows of five second length from the eight proximity sensors. We then calculated the mean and standard deviation for each sensor window. Moreover, we extracted the center of mean and the center of standard deviation from all sensors. This can be achieved by weighting the sensors' x- or y-positions

---

[1] http://www.cs.waikato.ac.nz/ml/weka/

with the corresponding mean or standard deviation. These features acted as an input vector for later classification of the performed activity. The sensors were configured with a high update rate of 50 Hz enabling us to capture fast movements. Using the features extracted from the time-window, we applied RBF Networks for classification.

4   Experiment

4.1   Setup and Scenario

In our experiment, we were able to show that our approach is a promising concept for classifying working situations among different users. We also investigated if the classification approach can be generalized for all users, enabling cross-user classification without separately annotating training data for each person. However, we expected that the working situations are often carried out very differently, highly depending on the specific person and habits. Figure 2 shows an exemplary measurement result from a working situation. We can see that the sensor values reflect the placement of the user's hands and the proximity to his knees.

Fig. 2. Exemplary visualization of sensor values, depending on an activity. High sensor values are marked in red, low sensor values are marked in green.

Fig. 3. The office chair's positions were split into five discrete classes: (a) outer right, (b) middle right, (c) middle left, (d) outer left and no person

We identified the following classes that are typical for the presented office scenario: typing on a computer (employing only the keyboard), mousework (employing only the mouse), reading a book, phoning, pause, hand-writing and no person. Figure 4 shows two exemplary activities, that were carried out in our evaluation. In addition to these common working activities, we aimed to recognize the office chair's position, illustrated in Figure 3. This position was classified separately employing five classes: outer right, middle right, middle left, outer left and no person. Even though the person might not always place the hands close to the table, it is possible to detect the proximity of the knees to make inferrations about the office chair's position.

Fig. 4. Two exemplary activities, carried out above the smart desk: phoning and writing. The position of both hands is very different and can be exploited to distinguish between the two activities.

Our test set consists of the activities of 12 persons who carried out each activity for approximately two minutes. The activities were always interrupted by non-related activities, such as moving away from the table or walking. In order to evaluate scenarios like reading or typing, we placed several office-related items like keyboards, mice and books on the table. These items have a very low impact on the sensor values, as they are not grounded and only slightly influence the measurements with their permittivity.

4.2   Evaluation Results

The main goal of the evaluation was to identify working situations on the given data basis. Furthermore, we aimed to find out if a single training set can be shared among all participants and if the working situations of unknown participants can be reliably classified. In order to evaluate the possiblity of having a shared data set, we performed a 4-fold cross validation on the recorded and annotated data of all participants.

With the RBF network classifier, we achieved an overall accuracy of 93.2 % for the four different desk chair positions. Splitting the test set into six participants for training and six participants for testing, we achieved an overall accuracy of 70.5 %. The reason for this lack of precision can be assumed to lie in the great variety of sitting postures and the different ways of placing one's arms on a desk's surface. Regarding the confusion matrix, it is obvious that office chair positions are often misclassified in their neighboring ones, such that misclassifications will not have a very negative effect on later applications using this data.

Considering the seven different working situations, we achieved an overall accuracy of 81.8 % for a 4-fold cross-validation. As the hand positions are very similar for reading and writing activities, these classes were often confused. With an accuracy of 93.7%, the class *mousework* showed the best performance for the given test set. The *pause* activity was classified with a very poor accuracy of

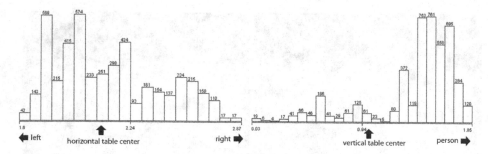

Fig. 5. The two center-of-mean features in x- (horizontal) and y-direction (vertical). The number above the bars represent the number of instances in the data set.

59.9 %. Regarding this activity, there were many variations in the body posture (for example leaning back) and the type of activity (e.g. eating chocalate).

When splitting the data set into a dedicated test and training set of six participants each, the classifier could achieve an overall accuracy of 49.8 %. Therefore, we must conclude that office activities are highly individual and must be trained in advance with each person. Moreover, the placement of the electrodes is not optimal, as Figure 5 shows. The plot for the y-axis center-of-mean shows that most activity was performed in the first half of the table, the area which is close to the person. Thus, it would be reasonable to deploy more electrodes in this area to achieve a higher resolution. The x-axis center-of-mean reveals that the placement of tools, such as a phone, and the user's characteristics, such as being right-handed, leads to a very unbalanced usage of the two tabletop halfs.

5   Summary

On the last few pages we have presented an approach to recognize working situations using a grid of capacitive sensors that is unobtrusively placed below the surface. Using self-capacitance measurements from various electrodes we were able to gather information about the working situation using a minimal amount of required hardware. We have created a prototype system based on the Open-CapSense rapid prototyping toolkit [5] and performed an evaluation with 12 users. We tried to differentiate six different working situations associated to a typical office employment (typing, mouse-work, reading, hand-writing, pausing and talking on the phone). The results have shown that theses tasks are varying strongly between the different persons and it is difficult to correlate training data from one user to measurements of another. We can therefore conclude that a single array of sensors is not sufficient to reliably detect working situations. However they form a solid base for this approach and can be easily combined with other systems. In the future we intend to create heterogenous sensing systems that will enable a more reliable detection of working situations. For example, we are planning to integrate further capacitive sensors into the office chair, which will give us additional data particularly concerning the position of the back that is correlated to the current working situation. Additionally we plan to extend the system with vibration or shock sensors, e.g. based on accelerometers or piezo technology. They also can be applied unobtrusively and be hidden below the office desk. We expect the vibration of the desk to correlate with typing and handwriting tasks. It may even be possible to extract mouse click features. Additionally, we need to gather more training data with a larger variety of users. Finally we want to investigate a more generic approach that will allow us to transfer our method to other working desks or additional working situations.

Acknowledgments. We would like to thank the evaluation participants from Fraunhofer IGD.

References

1. Tabard, A., Hincapié-Ramos, J.-D., Esbensen, M., Bardram, J.E.: The eLabBench: an interactive tabletop system for the biology laboratory. In: ITS 2011, pp. 202–211 (2011)
2. Chang, K.H., Liu, S.Y., Chu, H.H., Hsu, J.J., Chen, C., Lin, T.Y., Chen, C.Y., Huang, P.: The diet-aware dining table: Observing dietary behaviors over a tabletop surface. In: Fishkin, K.P., Schiele, B., Nixon, P., Quigley, A. (eds.) PERVASIVE 2006. LNCS, vol. 3968, pp. 366–382. Springer, Heidelberg (2006)
3. Cheng, J., Amft, O., Lukowicz, P.: Active capacitive sensing: Exploring a new wearable sensing modality for activity recognition. In: PerCom 2010, pp. 319–336 (2010)
4. Dietz, P., Leigh, D.: DiamondTouch: A Multi-User Touch Technology. In: UIST 2001, pp. 219–226 (2001)
5. Grosse-Puppendahl, T., Berghoefer, Y., Braun, A., Wimmer, R., Kuijper, A.: OpenCapSense: A Rapid Prototyping Toolkit for Pervasive Interaction Using Capacitive Sensing. In: PerCom 2013 (2013)
6. Grosse-Puppendahl, T., Marinc, A., Braun, A.: Classification of User Postures with Capacitive Proximity Sensors in AAL-Environments. In: Keyson, D.V., et al. (eds.) AmI 2011. LNCS, vol. 7040, pp. 314–323. Springer, Heidelberg (2011)
7. Seong, J., Lee, W., Lim, Y.-K.: Why we cannot work without paper even in a computerized work environment. In: CHI 2009 EA, pp. 4105–4110 (2009)
8. Rekimoto, J.: SmartSkin: an infrastructure for freehand manipulation on interactive surfaces. In: CHI 2002, pp. 113–120 (2002)
9. Smith, J.R., Gershenfeld, N., Benton, S.A.: Electric Field Imaging. PhD Thesis (1999)
10. Steimle, J., Khalilbeigi, M., Mühlhäuser, M., Hollan, J.D.: Physical and digital media usage patterns on interactive tabletop surfaces. In: ITS 2010, pp. 167–176 (2010)
11. Wimmer, R., Kranz, M., Boring, S., Schmidt, A.: A Capacitive Sensing Toolkit for Pervasive Activity Detection and Recognition. In: PerCom 2007 pp. 171–180 (2007)

Blog Based Personal LBS

Hideki Kaji and Masatoshi Arikawa

Center for Spatial Information Science, The University of Tokyo
5-1-5, Kashiwanoha, Kashiwa, Chiba 277-8568, Japan
{kaji,arikawa}@csis.u-tokyo.ac.jp

Abstract. One of the problems in the current commercial LBS (Location-based Service) is weak functionality for users to use their own generated content on the LBS. This paper proposes a new framework of *Personal LBS* which solves the problem by using blog as both a description language for the extension and a simple CMS (Content Management System). A blog entry is a kind of story. Better a story is, more easily and efficiently readers can understand it. One of the most important LBS applications is a location-based guided tour which can be created as geotagged stories on a blog. The framework allows the geotagged stories to be moved from a blog to a local software application on mobile devices as story packages for publishing, reproducing and exchanging on LBS. We also discuss the capability and importance of personal LBS for location-based communication among ourselves, families, friends, groups and all users beyond time.

Keywords: Blog, Geotag, Location-based service, Story-based LBS package, User generated content, private content, sustainability.

1   Introduction

The advent of smartphone has made it possible for many people to use various location-based services (LBS) easily in their daily lives. The GPS integrated mobile phones allow users to find their positions, search points of interest (POI), generate itineraries of their trips using complex time tables of public transportation, and navigate in the real world [1]. Furthermore, location based social networking services (SNS) such as Foursquare [3] and Facebook Places [4] become popular where users can checks in venues with using their current locations acquired by GPS. Then, users can communicate one another on same venues. They also have chances to get some good things like coupons for venues if they often visit there. There has been kinds of location-based personal content recorders and managers using GPS such as Garmin Connect [5]. They can provide users with their personal content about their movement and result of training for outdoor sports. Users appreciate the personal historical content of GPS data for their movements as well as other information such as heart rate, speed and other sensors' captured data for analyzing their exercise and planning future training. This paper focuses on user generated content for personal LBS rather than the sensor generated one. Most of current commercial LBSs provide users with their generated content as a collection of only unstructured geotagged objects such as

N. Streitz and C. Stephanidis (Eds.): DAPI/HCII 2013, LNCS 8028, pp. 122–127, 2013.

POIs like geotagged photos and lines with less meaning for route planning and trajectory. Storylines could be more important to make a collection of geotagged objects more attractive and valuable for future LBS applications, but current commercial LBS does not explicitly support the function of the storyline depending on locations.

Current commercial LBSs are considered to be designed for everyone and the present time now. Users cannot appreciate their owned and created private content on the commercial LBS. For example, users cannot appreciate push services of their photos and blog entries when they are located near the locations of the photos and blog entries unless all content become in public on the Web or LBS. Also, users cannot find Web mappings showing past places, e.g., map of three years ago, because Web mappings of only the present time are available. Even if users have their old generated content on Web mappings, users can use only the latest maps, but cannot obtain old background maps unless they bought the background maps when they created the old content, but most people do not imagine such a bad situation happens and buy snapshots of the Web mappings. It is not reasonable for map providers to enable users to move to any temporal point for browsing old maps on the Web from the financial viewpoint, thus no map provider realizes the time machine service for Web mappings. Even if a user has his/her own maps or bought maps of certain times, there is almost no way to use it on current LBS. Most of users usually never think about time aspects of maps when they use only Web mappings and live only now. It is bad not to give users chances to think and learn real world in terms of time aspects using maps. Many of stories are created by creating relations with real places with historical relations. We have researched on personal LBS based on our developing place-enhanced blog. It provides an environment for creating and managing story-based LBS packages to solve the above problems and provides users with more meaningful experiences in the real world.

2   Basic Concepts

2.1   Place-Enhanced Blog

Many people record and publish their day-to-day occurrences on various online media like blogs, SNS and other content management system (CMS). One of the reasons why people keep recording on blogs is not only informing other users about author's opinions, but also retrieving them as needed [2]. Most of the records, however, might never be accessed in their lives. If a blog system has a function for geotagging blog entries, users could be pleased to meet their old blog entries when they are located near the places of entries.

2.2   Personal LBS

The definition of personal LBS is not decided, but they are designed for personal use and functionality for user generated content for users, groups and public. The followings are main functions of personal LBS.

1. Place-based memory refresher: It is a push service to present some content and information such as old photos and things to buy if they are located near the places of the content and information. For example, an old photo of a father is displayed when I am walking near the place of the photo. It can be interpreted as spatial alarm.
2. LBS enabler of private content: Users can appreciate private content such as maps, art, music, and books as LBS. For example, a user can use an old map as a background map for LBS, and make spatial links of music and books.
3. Location-based guided tour: Users can create content of guided tours synchronized with routes on maps, photos, videos, voices, texts and so on depending on a user's location.

2.3   Story and Package

If a *story* is poor, it may be difficult for users to understand, enjoy and memorize it. Good stories on personal LBS allow users to easily acquire and organize knowledge from the real world. A collection of user generated content on a blog is also a set of stories, but the stories are not often designed well. If users want to present some descriptions of a blog entry to others, they must consider the background of the others and design stories well for them to understand easily and enjoy well with removing useless parts and adding more context of connecting other knowledge such as events and land marks on maps and timelines as well as personal memory such as place and time of birth. We introduce a concept of story package as story with related content information which allows users to understand even if they do not know the background of the authors. The story package includes most of all information of the story, but each description of a user's blog entry may be difficult for new users to understand and often makes them not to be boring and interested in. The concept is also good for exchanging among multiple platforms and becomes independent and sustainable even if its services and platforms change and disappear.

3   Story-Based LBS Package

A story is composed of events. Figure 1 shows conceptual examples of nesting stories with three levels of a hierarchy. The levels can be chosen for use depending on levels of users such as beginners and advanced users. Our developed system adopts this structure for story-based content, called *story-based LBS package* in our developed system. The followings explain about it.

— Smallest unit is a point object. A point can include a text, a photo and an audio.
— A polyline object is a totally ordered list of point objects and vertexes they only have a coordinate.
— A package is structured as ordered lists composed of LBS objects, that is, point and line objects, and other packages.
— The package is also a unit to be read in mobile application software. It can work even if network connection is not available. Also, user's log and generated content can be both included as components of the package.

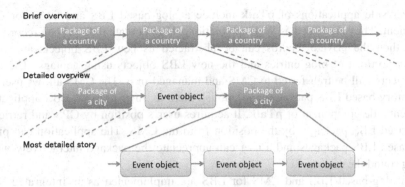

Fig. 1. Conceptual image of nested story-based LBS packages. Examples of stories about travels around the world with three levels of detail.

4   Development of Personal LBS

We are developing a networked IT service **pTalk**, which is a software family to realize our proposed framework of personal LBS. **pTalk** is composed of the following three software components. (1) Blog-based LBS: A blog system with functions of dealing with spatial information. (2) CMS (Content Management System) for LBS: It manages personal LBS objects and packages in our developed blog, and LBS objects imported from other LBS. It also communicates with LBS applications for providing and recording data through Internet. (3) LBS Application: It is a front end software running on a mobile device to realize personal LBS by interaction with users.

pTalk is a whole system composed of family software applications. Figure 2 shows a concept of the architecture of **pTalk** which is designed as an open platform to realize personal LBS based on protocols of Internet.

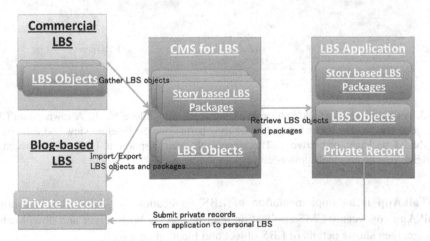

Fig. 2. Architecture of our developed system **pTalk**

Server side applications of **pTalk** include a blog-based LBS and CMS for LBS component. They are coded as Web applications. Users create their private records on a blog then the private records can be abstracted as new LBS objects and links between portions of blog entries and the new LBS objects using geotags. The new LBS objects will be transferred to CMS and managed in it. The CMS allows users to create story-based LBS packages and publish them to other users. A LBS application is a client side component of **pTalk**. It acquires user's position by GPS and retrieves story-based LBS packages by the position from the CMS. The application can plays story-based LBS packages and a user can appreciate the package interactively while moving round the real world.

Both blog-based LBS and CMS for LBS are implemented as an integrated Web application. Server scripts are processed on the Web server and the blog's user interface is constructed Adobe Flash and Google Maps API for Flash.

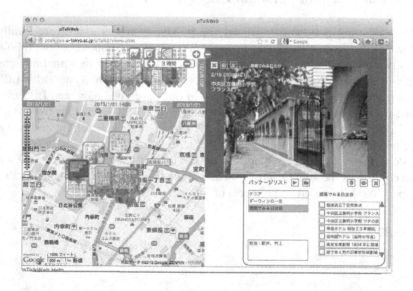

Fig. 3. An Example of **pTalkWeb** on Web browsers with Adobe Flash. A town guide LBS package in Hibiya. The upper-left and lower-right parts show the timeline view and a dialog of story-based package, respectively. The upper-right part displays a LBS object which is highlighted on the map in the lower-left part of the screen.

pTalkApp is an implementation of LBS application for Apple Inc.'s iPhone. **pTalkApp** connects to CMS application interface on the Web server and downloads a package, then shows details of LBS object and location on a map.

Fig. 4. Examples of **pTalkApp** on Apple Inc.'s iPhone. A town guide LBS package in Ginza. The screen shot at the left shows the information about the main building of a famous bread company 木村屋(Kimuraya) with the user's current location, the location of the building and its photo. The screen shot at the right shows photos of Japanese style sweet breads on the upper part and playing the audio for explaining the breads at the bottom.

5   Conclusion

The current fashion of LBS is the style of disposable digital content. Freshness of the content is more important than quality and depth. Our proposed framework of personal LBS may enables users to consider value of their own old content and to realize significance of long-term for appreciating change of places and their life. The framework also make user generated and private content become more sustainable, and gives users more chances to refresh their old memory at right places. More users use the content, longer they survive because our memory continues beyond generations. It is also possible for personal historical content to be developed to family and more general history ones.

Reference

1. Arikawa, M., Konomi, S., Ohnishi, K.: NAVITIME: Supporting Pedestrian Navigation in the Real World. IEEE Pervasive Computing, Special Issue on Urban Computing 6(3), 21–29 (2007)
2. Nardi, B.A., Schiano, D.J., Gumbrecht, M., Swartz, L.: Why We Blog. Communications of the ACM 47(9), 41–46 (2004)
3. Foursquare, http://foursquare.com/
4. Facebook, http://www.facebook.com/
5. Garmin Connect, http://connect.garmin.com/

Detecting Emotion from Dialogs and Creating Personal Ambient in a Context Aware System

Lun-Wei Ku[1] and Cheng-Wei Sun[2]

[1] Institute of Information Science, Academia Sinica, Taipei, Taiwan
lwku@iis.sinica.edu.tw
[2] Department of Information Science and Engineering, National Yunlin University of Science and Technology, Yunlin, Taiwan
chengwei.kenny.sun@gmail.com

Abstract. This paper presents a personal ambient creation systme, IlluMe, which detects users' emotion from their chatting context in instant messages and then analyze them to recommend suitable lighting and music to create a personal ambient. The system includes a mechanism for recording users' feedback of the provided ambient to learn their preference. The aim of the proposed system is to link human language and emotion with the computer created environment seemlessly. To achieve this, we propose four apporaches to calculate emotion scores of words: Topical Approach, Emotional Approach, Retrieval Approach and Lexicon Approach. Natural language processing techniques such as normalization, part of speech tagging, word bigram utilization, and sentiment dictionaries lookup are incorporated to enhance system performance. Experiments results are shown and discussed, from which we find the system satisfactory and several future research directions are inspired.

Keywords: emotion detection, blog articles, instant messages, ambient creation, context aware system.

1 Introduction

Language is one of the major tools used by users to interact with computer interfaces, which includes texts, speech, facial expressions and body languages. To provide a satisfactory usage experience, context aware systems have tried to detect users' emotion when receiving commands [3], [8] and considered it in the proceeding process. To find the users' emotion, real time information like the facial expression or the speech utterance was gathered [2]. However, additional cameras and microphones became necessary. Some researchers used sensors to watch the heart beat and the body temperature of residents to know their current emotion for further respondence, but then users had to wear sensors and it was inconvenient. Instead of watching body signals, we postulate that the communication among people is one of the important factors to influence their emotions and from the content we can find hints over a certain period of time. Therefore, we hope to watch users' conversations and then detect their emotion.

N. Streitz and C. Stephanidis (Eds.): DAPI/HCII 2013, LNCS 8028, pp. 128–137, 2013.

In the natural language processing research community, emotion analysis has drawn a lot attention and the development of fundamental approaches as well as applications has been proposed [4], [9], [12]. In this research, clues from users' textual conversations were mined by these approaches to detect their psychological emotion state. Then the ambient of their personal working or living space will be changed as a feedback of the designed system. As a start, music and lightings were utilized. The design of the proposed system could be easily integrated into or applied to personal emotion management, self-care, wellness management, or any other human-machine interfaces which intend to consider users' emotion.

There are many ways to categorize emotions. Different emotion states were used for experiments in previous research [1]. To find suitable categories of emotions, we adopted the three-layered emotion hierarchy proposed by Parrott shown in Table 1 [7]. Six emotions are in the first layer, including love, joy, surprise, anger, sadness and fear. The second layer includes 25 emotions, and the third layer includes 135 emotions. Using this hierarchical classification enables the system the ability to categorize emotions from rough to fine granularities and degrade to the upper level when the experimental materials are insufficient. In addition, mapping categories in other researches to ours becomes easier with the hierarchy, and more information is provided to annotators when marking their current emotion.

We hope to find emotion from authors' aspect instead of readers' aspect from texts to fulfill our purpose. In this research, users' conversations were collected from the log of instant message software Yahoo! Messenger. To automatically learn the accompanied emotion from a large dataset, texts containing emoticons in Yahoo! blog articles were utilized. Then statistical approaches were adopted and compared. As to relations of emotions and the music, most researchers looked for the emotions in songs or rhythms [10-11]. They classified music into different emotional categories and developed the system to tell what emotion a song might bring to a listener, which was from readers' aspect. However, if the aim is to create a comfortable ambient, what songs a person in a certain emotional state wants to listen to becomes the question. A happy user does not always enjoy happy songs, and vice versa, which makes the technology developed in the previous work not applicable. Learning and adapting to the personal preference become the aim in this research. This is also true for the lightings. To further help the system perform better, collecting users' feedback was realized by using smart phones as the personal controller.

Table 1. Emotion Categories (Tertiary Emotion Not Listed)

Primary Emotion	Secondary Emotion
Love	Affection, Lust, Longing
Joy	Cheerfulness, Zest, Contentment, Pride, Optimism, Enthrallment, Relief
Surprise	Surprise
Anger	Irritation, Exasperation, Rage, Disgust, Envy, Torment
Sadness	Suffering, Sadness, Disappointment, Shame, Neglect, Sympathy
Fear	Horror, Nervousness

In this paper, we described the interfaces and functions of the context aware system IlluMe but focused more on its core technology, the emotional analysis. We hope the proposed techniques can help to develop future systems considering users' emotions.

2   System Description

The potential working area for IlluMe is home or a small space. The system was designed to fit in with the modern people's life style: programs are installed in users' personal computer and smart phone. The smart phone functions as the remote control and the music player, while all setting signals are sent out from the personal computer. The smart phone and the personal computer communicate through the wireless network. The only additional hardware requirement is the lighting set. Now many smart phones are functioned with instant messages. In that case, the personal computer is not necessary and the system is obviously more convenient.

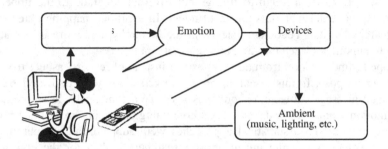

Fig. 1. System Illustration of IlluMe

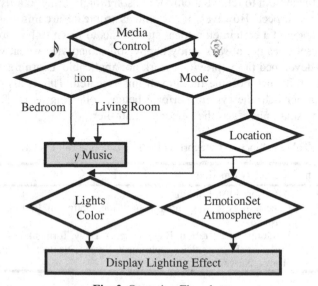

Fig. 2. Operation Flowchart

Figure 1 demonstrates the proposed system IlluMe designed for a small space personal environment. Detailed system framework can be found in Ku's research [6]. We expect that this system could interactively respond to users' personal status by providing a feeling of the companion. We view the IlluMe system as a realization of detecting emotions from users' textual conversations and then responding the best ambient accordingly. System features include an *Emotion Detection Switch* which detects users' current emotion according to messenger logs once a preset time period; an *Auto Ambient Setting* which sets the current ambient by a specific combination of a song and a light group which corresponds to the emotion or represents a special atmosphere; a *Manual Ambient Adjustment* which provides a user interface to change the settings of music and lightings from smart phones; a *Personal Preference Learning Mechanism* which records the new settings, learns the preference and then performs the user adaptation; the *Unlimited Melodies and Rich Light Colors* where songs are added by users and 65,536 lighting colors are provided; *Instant State Update* which watches the users' input from messenger when the software is on and changes the music and lighting according to the detected emotion to make users feel like the environment is interacting with them. Figure 2 shows the operational flow of the user interface.

We adopted the concept of collaborative filtering to design the function of personal ambient learning. In the early stage of using IlluMe, it proposes the most frequently selected settings, that is, the choice of a group of people in the specific emotional state. If the user is connected to the Internet, the user experience will be transferred back to the servers to help suggest a better ambient to other users.

The user experience can be optimized because of design of using smart phones. As the users update the settings, the system knows their preference. In the later stage, the learning function is able to consider the preference of both the individual and the group to create a unique ambient for each user.

3   Emotion Analysis

The emotion analysis that IlluMe performed is to find the emotions that texts in messenger logs bear in order to create a comfort ambient by sound and lighting accordingly. To achieve this, the system needs to understand the Internet language first, and then detect emotions and categorize them. The system works on the Chinese chatting environment and analyzes Chinese texts to detect emotions. Two dictionaries, the Chinese sentiment dictionary NTUSD [14] and the Chinese emotion dictionary [13], were adopted for detecting emotions. The former categorized sentiment words into positive and negative, while the latter into eight emotion types: awesome, heartwarming, surprising, sad, useful, happy, boring, and angry. Notice that these eight emotion types appeared in Yahoo! News Taiwan in the year 2008 and not all of them were general emotion states. Therefore, we tried to align Lin's emotion categories with those in Parrott's emotion hierarchy before using his dictionary.

Messenger logs were used as the source to detect emotions. We collected texts from Yahoo! Messenger and MSN Messenger logs of 8 annotators. When the installed collecting program in their computers was on, it ran as a service and continuously logged their messages. Whenever there was at least one new message, once an hour the collecting program would pop up the menu and ask them to annotate the current emotion together with the preferred settings of the music and lighting. There were 3,290 songs, 15 emotional lighting colors and 6 atmospheres for selection. A total of 150 records are annotated for experiments.

Before the sentiment analysis, some preprocessing steps were performed. In addition to the segmentation and part of speech tagging [16], which are the common preprocessing steps when utilizing Chinese texts, messenger logs and sentiment dictionaries were first transformed into zhuyin [15], a Chinese phonetic symbol set, before looking for emotions to avoid the mismatch caused by this popular type of creative use of writing systems.

3.1   Learning Emotional Scores of Words

The emoticon sentences, i.e., there is at least one emoticon in these sentences, were treated as the learning materials and from them the emotional score of each word was calculated. The learned emotional scores of the words in the messenger log were accumulated to determine the emotion class of the log. Four approaches were proposed: *Topical Approach*, *Emotional Approach*, *Retrieval Approach* and *Lexicon Approach* [5]. *Topical Approach* utilized the concept of *tf* • *idf* score (term frequency multiplied by inversed document frequency) and distributed it to 40 emoticon classes by the probability of observing the emoticon sentences in each emoticon class over all emoticon sentences; In *Emotional Approach* the emoticon sentences of the same emoticon class were concatenated into one document and scores of words were calculated as in *Topical Approach* (the mapping is shown in Table 2); *Retrieval Approach* took the current sentence for judgment as a query and found the most similar 10 sentences (P@10, precision at ten) to determine the emotion it bore; *Lexicon Approach* looked up words from the Chinese emotion dictionary [13] and calculates their emotional scores [14]. *Topical Approach* and *Retrieval Approach* consider the importance of words in the query sentence and the emoticon sentences, while *Emotional Approach* calculates the "emoticonal" tendency of the words in the query sentence.

Table 2. The Mapping of the Emotion Class and Emoticon Classes

Emotion	Emoticon
Love	7(love), 8(shy), 10(kiss)
Joy	1(smile), 4(happy), 13(smug), 18(laugh)
Surprise	11(surprise)
Angry	12(angry)
Sadness	17(cry), 37(sign)
Fear	15(worried)

3.2   Experimental Results and Discussions

To evaluate the performance of the emotion detection in messenger logs, 10-fold experiments were performed. The results of four approaches for emotion detection were listed in Table 3. The best result of emotion detection among four approaches was generated by *Topical Approach*, while *Emotional Approach* performed the worst. After looking over the emotional scores, we found that the unsatisfactory performance of *Emotional Approach* was caused by the concatenation of the emoticon sentences of the same class. This process made forty very large documents so that term frequency became the dominate factor and deteriorated the performance.

Retrieval Approach was better than *Emotional Approach* but worse than *Topical Approach*. Instead of distributed the *tf • idf* score to 40 emotion classes like *Topical Approach*, *Retrieval Approach* utilized it to rank sentences for voting on the emotion class. As a result, we can say that considering the composite important words to find the emotion class performs better than letting similar sentences to determine.

Lexicon Approach was different from the other three in that it did not calculate scores based on emoticon sentences. Its performance was the second among all. The advantage of using lexicons was that we could find words not appearing in the emoticon sentences and hence would still be able to know the emoticon class of sentences, even though there were no previously seen words in them. However, having fixed lexicon set was also its disadvantage. When there were many emoticon sentences so that scores of various words were learned in *Topical Approach*, *Lexicon Approach* suffered from the limited lexicons.

Table 3 shows that all approaches tended to perform unsatisfactory for emotion class Love, Angry and Fear. For Angry and Fear, the insufficiency of emoticon sentences was one causing factor of the low performance. Moreover, these two emotion classes were seldom selected by annotators. Logs of these classes might be related to specific events represented by special word compositions instead of a certain subjective words.

Generally for all approaches, we found several causes of mis-categorization. First, some infrequent words (i.e. less than 10 times) had unreasonably high scores. Second, the polarity of a sequence of words might be different from that of its composite words. Third, positive words in negative sentences (and vice versa) caused noise when determining the polarity. We hence proposed corresponding enhancement approaches in the next section.

Table 3. Performance of Emotion Detection in Message Logs

Approach→ Metric↓	Topical	Emotional	Retrieval	Lexicon
Love	0.000	0.000	0.000	0.000
Joy	0.850	0.238	0.438	0.325
Surprise	0.000	0.000	0.000	1.000
Angry	0.000	0.000	0.000	0.000
Sadness	0.103	0.000	0.103	0.026
Fear	0.000	0.000	0.000	0.000
Macro-Avg	0.159	0.040	0.090	0.225
Micro-Avg	0.480	0.127	0.260	0.187

3.3   Performance Enhancement Approaches

According to the observations mentioned in section 3.2, we tried several approaches to improve the performance. Three of them made some progress and are listed below.

Accumulated Probabilistic (*AcuProb*). As mentioned, *Topical Approach* considers the inversed document frequency (*idf*) in emoticon classes to give the same word different score in each class, but the numbers of documents in these classes vary a lot. Emoticon class *laugh* (☺) contains 131,148 emoticon sentences, which is the largest quantity, while the smallest class *secret* (☺) contains only 5,855 sentences. This causes infrequent words to obtain unreasonable high scores. Therefore, we removed the *idf* part in the calculation process but added a normalization factor to it to make the new score more like a normalized probabilistic one. Scores of words were summed up (accumulated) to generate the final score for the sentence for judgment.

Word Bigram with Specific Parts of Speech (*BiPos*, *NBiPos*). From the previous experiments, we found that very often only a set of words, a two-word set (bigram) is the most commonly seen, can express a complete emotional concept. Therefore, we extracted four word bigram classes which bear emotion most often according to their parts of speech and treated them as one word when calculating emotional scores (*Bi-Pos*). These word bigrams are

— *Vt + Vi.* A transitive verb is followed by an intransitive verb, such as 喜歡 (like to) 飛行 (fly) and 不利 (harm) 辦事 (work);
— *ADV + V.* An adverb is followed by a verb, such as 很 (very) 偷懶 (be lazy) and 更 (more) 用力 (use power);
— *N + Vi.* A noun is followed by an intransitive verb, such as 壽命 (lifetime) 增加 (increase);
— *Vt + N.* A transitive verb is followed by a noun, such as 打擊 (fight) 犯罪 (crime).

An extension which incorporatee the negation, such as no, not, but, cannot, etc., with the word bigram was also tested (*NBiPos*).

Noise Elimination by Sentiment (*EliNoise*). As we have sentiment and emotion dictionaries, their entries were utilized to eliminate noise. Forty emoticon classes were put on the arousal-valence sentiment plane [13] according to the emotions they bear as shown in Figure 3. Words whose polarities were different from that of the classes were treated as noise. Therefore, those words found in positive dictionaries were eliminated in the sentences of negative emoticon classes before calculating scores, and vice versa.

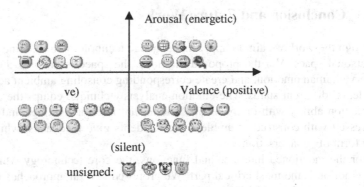

Fig. 3. Emoticons on the Sentiment Plane

To treat each emoticon class as of equal importance, we evaluated the performance by the Macro Average metric here. We compared the performance of the enhancement approaches on *Topical Approach*. Experiment results are shown in Table 4.

Table 4. Performance of enhancement approaches

Approach	Topical	AcuProb	BiPos	NBiPos	EliNoise
Macro-Avg	0.159	0.136	0.158	0.164	0.159
t-test ($\alpha=0.05; dof=39$)	N/A	passed	Passed	passed	Failed

From *Macro Average*, we found that the enhancement was not obvious as we had a total of 1,540,163 emoticon sentences. Among all improvement approaches, only the *Macro Average* of *NBiPos* was increased. We further performed a t-test on the "emoticonal analysis" over 40 emoticon classes. The t-test showed that when we compared the performance before the enhancement (*Topical Approach*) with that after the enhancement, *AcuProb*, *BiPos*, and *NBiPos* all significantly improved the system. After taking a detail look at the *EliNoise* approach, we found that though it did not improve the performance as a whole, it did significantly improve the performance for 28 categories (and decreased the others). In other words, sentences of some emoticon classes are more controversial than others so that there is more noise in these sentences. Therefore, we can say that selecting enhancement approaches depends on the emotions we want to deal with for that *AcuProb* and *BiPos* improve the performance of most categories. Moreover, *NBiPos* improves the performance from both macro and micro perspectives.

Bellegarda reported that his best f-measure was 0.340 also for 6 categories. Notice that his work analyzed from the reader's perspective, while our work analyzed from the author's perspective. The emotion analysis from author's perspective was generally considered more difficult than from the reader's perspective as what a user felt might not be consistent with what he/she wrote in instant messages. Therefore, though Bellegarda's experiments and experiments in this paper were done on different datasets and evaluated by different metrics, we believe the performance reported by this paper was comparable.

4   Conclusion and Future Work

Through the work we aim to apply the language technology to redefine the concept of a personal space. Via the proposed interface, the space is enabled the capability to observe human emotion, and create corresponding consoling ambient according to the residents' different status. The emotion analysis technique equips the space with the interaction ability with the residents. The instant interior lightings and music change expressed with constructed ambient and residents give feedbacks, which complete a new form of "conversation".

For the mentioned interface and functions, the core technology which detects users' emotion is the most critical part. We proposed several approaches to enhance the performance of the system, and showed satisfactory results. Along with the developed technology, a good communication between computer controlled devices and users is feasible. Moreover, several further applications utilizing system components become easier to implement.

Continuing collecting annotated materials and user feedbacks for learning, and then performing a long term experiment to develop good learning approaches is the future plan. Conversations from the Internet, such as Facebook, blog feedbacks, or line could be sources to gather various materials for advanced emotion detection. Making the system components real products like the home lighting system, the intelligent table lamp, or the music album promoter will be the next research direction.

Ackowledgements. Research of this paper was partially supported by National Science Council, Taiwan, under the contract NSC101-2628-E-224-001-MY3.

References

1. Bellegarda, J.R.: Emotion Analysis Using Latent Affective Folding and Embedding. In: Proceedings of the NAACL HLT 2010 Workshop on Computational Approaches to Analysis and Generation of Emotion in Text, Los Angeles, pp. 1–9 (2010)
2. Busso, C., Deng, Z., Yildirim, S., Bulut, M., Lee, C.M., Kazemzadeh, A., Lee, S., Neumann, U., Narayanan, S.: Analysis of Emotion Recognition using Facial Expressions, Speech and Multimodal Information. In: Proceedings of ACM 6th International Conference on Multimodal Interfaces (ICMI 2004), State College, PA (2004)
3. Conti, N., Jennett, C., Celdran, J., Sasse, A.: When Did My Mobile Turn Into A 'Sellphone'? A Study of Consumer responses to Tailored Smartphone Ads. In: Proceedings of the 26th Annual BCS Interaction Specialist Group Conference on People and Computers (HCI 2012), pp. 215–220 (2012)
4. Das, D.: Analysis and Tracking of Emotions in English and Bengali Texts: A Computational Approach. In: Proceedings of the International World Wide Web Conference (WWW 2011), Ph. D. Symposium, pp. 343–347 (2011)
5. Ku, L.-W., Sun, C.-W.: Calculating Emotional Score of Words for User Emotion Detection in Messenger Logs. In: Proceedings of the 2012 IEEE 13th International Conference on Information Reuse and Integration (IEEE IRI 2012), EMRITE Workshop, pp. 138–143 (2012)

6. Ku, L.-W., Sun, C.-W., Hsueh, Y.-H.: Demonstration of IlluMe: Creating Ambient According to Instant Message Logs. In: Proceedings of the 50th Annual Meeting of the Association for Computational Linguistics (ACL 2012), pp. 97–102 (2012)
7. Parrott, W.: Emotions in Social Psychology. Psychology Press, Philadelphia (2001)
8. Roast, C., Zhang, X.: Exploring the Motivations Involved in Context Aware Services. In: Proceedings of the 26th Annual BCS Interaction Specialist Group Conference on People and Computers (HCI 2012), pp. 274–279 (2012)
9. Sarwar, B., Karypis, G., Konstan, J., Riedl, J.: Item Based Collaborative Filtering Recommendation Algorithms. In: Proceedings of the International World Wide Web Conference (WWW 2001), pp. 285–295 (2001)
10. Yang, Y.-H., Chen, H.H.: Ranking-Based Emotion Recognition for Music Organization and Retrieval. IEEE Transactions on Audio, Speech, and Language Processing 19(4) (2011)
11. Zbikowski, L.M.: Music, Emotion, Analysis. Music Analysis. Blackwell Publishing Ltd., Oxford (2011)
12. Zheng, V.W., Cao, B., Zheng, Y., Xie, X., Yang, Q.: Collaborative Filtering Meets Mobile Recommendation: A User-centered Approach. In: Proceedings of Twenty-Fourth National Conference on Artificial Intelligence, AAAI 2010 (2010)
13. Lin, K.H.-Y., Yang, C., Chen, H.-H.: Emotion Classification of Online News Articles from the Reader's Perspective. In: Proceedings of the 2008 IEEE/WIC/ACM International Conference on Web Intelligence, pp. 220–226 (2008)
14. Ku, L.-W., Chen, H.-H.: Mining Opinions from the Web: Beyond Relevance Retrieval. Journal of American Society for Information Science and Technology. Special Issue on Mining Web Resources for Enhancing Information Retrieval 58(12), 1838–1850 (2007)
15. Su, H.-Y.: The Multilingual and Multi-Orthographic Taiwan-Based Internet: Creative Uses of Writing Systems on College-Affiliated BBSs. Journal of Computer-Mediated Communication 9(1) (2003), http://jcmc.indiana.edu/vol9/issue1/su.html
16. CKIP (Chinese Knowledge Information Processing Group): The Content and Illustration of Academica Sinica Corpus. (Technical Report no 95-02/98-04). Taipei: Academia Sinica (1995/1998)

Creating Rule Sets for Smart Environments through Behavior Recording

Alexander Marinc, Tim Dutz, Felix Kamieth, Maxim Djakow, and Pia Weiss

Fraunhofer Institute for Computer Graphics Research IGD, Darmstadt, Germany
{alexander.marinc,tim.dutz,felix.kamieth,maxim.djakow,
pia.weiss}@igd.fraunhofer.de

Abstract. In recent years, there has been a steady rise in the installation of smart environment systems. These systems can consist of a wide range of sensors and actuators and as such can become very complex, which brings the average user to the limits of her technical understanding. Consequently, innovative methods are required to simplify the interaction with such systems. This paper describes an approach for recording events triggered by a user and for linking those to actuator effects. Through this, even those end-users who are inexperienced with modern day technology can create custom rule sets for smart environment systems.

Keywords: Smart Environments, User Interaction, Behavior Recording.

1 Introduction

Over the last few decades, the amount of technical devices that populate our homes and work places has increased significantly. However, as of today, the majority of those devices are not capable of communicating with one another (just think of your TV and your fridge). Researchers envision that in the not-too-far future, all technical devices distributed in our surroundings will work together and form device ensembles with which we will be able to interact in a natural manner.

A multitude of challenges need to be overcome before this vision can become reality and in recent years, many research and development projects have been aimed at creating a software platform to support smart environments (e.g., [2], [3], and [4]). However, many of these research projects focus on solving the problem of interoperability, that is, on developing the means for integrating heterogeneous devices into a single system and thus enabling them to communicate with one another. And while this is obviously a key aspect of making smart environments a reality, we have noticed that oftentimes the question of how the user is supposed to control these complex systems once they have been established falls a bit short.

From the perspective of smart environments, the technical devices that they are based on can be grouped into two categories. While devices from the first category, sensors, are used by the system to perceive the state of its environment, devices from the second category, actuators, are used to influence the environment's state.

N. Streitz and C. Stephanidis (Eds.): DAPI/HCII 2013, LNCS 8028, pp. 138–143, 2013.

Frequently, the differentiation between these two categories is not clear and many devices are both, sensors and actuators (e.g., a smartphone). Usually, smart environment systems will rely on sets of control rules for the purpose of logically linking the sensor input to the actions performed by its actuators [1], meaning that in a specific situation S (as perceived by the system's sensors), a system will instruct its actuators to perform a certain set of actions A. In our work, we are proposing a new approach on how to enable users to define control rules through "demonstrating" the desired behavior to the system. The underlying principle is not entirely new, and our main contribution lies in its adaptation to the area of smart environments.

2   Related Work

Our approach was largely inspired by the Visual Basic recorder that comes with the Microsoft Office software suite. This application allows users to record his or her activities while using one of the products from the Office suite, for example Microsoft Word. Users are capable of saving these behavior patterns to shortcuts for the purpose of evoking them at a later time – a single button click will then start and automatically "replay" the whole process.

Research on the acceptance of such features goes back to Rosson's work in 1984 [7], which evaluated the advances people make when learning to work with a text-editor software. Similar macro-recording features have been used in more recent work where repetitive browsing tasks have been automated using voice-enabled macros [8]. This shows that the use of recordable macros withstood the test of time as an intuitive and user-friendly means of end-user programming.

The use of end-user programming in the context of smart environments has been suggested as a new research perspective in the field in [6]. This suggestion was then built upon in the detailed description of a concept for end-user configuration of smart environments in [1]. This concept takes into account different levels of technical expertise among end-users and presents solutions for the description as well as the recording and definition of system configurations based on multimodal user input.

3   Concept

For this work, we have developed a simple application (dubbed "the macro recorder") that provides a very similar functionality as the Visual Basic recorder described in section 2 for a smart environment system (Figure 1 shows a screenshot of the application's prototypical user interface). In a nutshell, the macro recorder application works like this: If a user wants to add a specific behavior pattern to the system, she will start the application, press the "record" button and then trigger the individual events and effects which are supposed to be part of the desired pattern. Our application, which must have access to the communication channels of the system, will then display all sensor events (e.g., movement registered by a movement sensor) and actuator actions (e.g., the activation of the kitchen lights) in order of their occurrence (more specifically: in the order of their processing by the system). Once all relevant events and actions have been recorded and the user has stopped the recording, a first version of the new control rule is automatically generated.

This preliminary rule requires the appearance of the exact same pattern of sensor events in order to trigger the same series of actuator actions. However, this may not lead to the desired effect, as it may include additional, unlooked for events and actions. As an example, imagine that the user has entered the living room (an event captured by a movement sensor) while the ambient temperature is 75.2 degrees Fahrenheit (an event captured by a temperature sensor). These two events will then comprise the event part of the new rule, and the occurrence of these events will initiate the rule's action part, for example, an activation of the ceiling lights in the living room. Obviously, in most cases one will not to want to be dependent on the ambient temperature from the rule, though, as otherwise the rule will only apply in those rare cases in which the exact same temperature is measured. For this reason, we have also provided the means for editing rules, i.e., for manually removing (and adding) sensor events and actuator actions from (and to) a given rule.

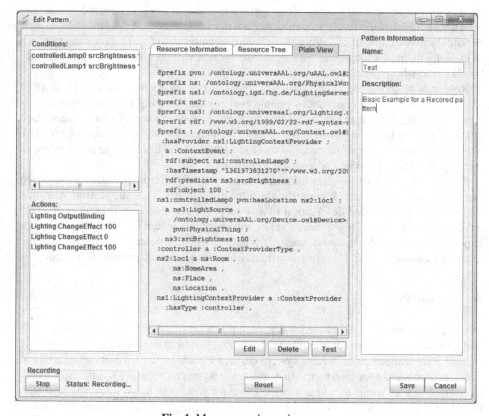

Fig. 1. Macro recorder main screen

Figure 1 shows a screenshot of the macro recorder's main screen. On the left side of the screenshot, one can see two lists, one for the occurred conditions (sensor events) and another one for the occurred actions (actuator effects). The central view shows the information stream as processed by the underlying platform, from which

.the conditions and actions are being extracted. The text boxes on the right enable the user to name and describe the current "pattern" (practically the rule currently created). Once the recording is stopped by the user, the new pattern (rule) is automatically added to the platform's rule database, but flagged as being created by the macro recorder software. This allows an easy identification of the same and its later adaptation. Figure 2 has a screenshot of the frame that shows an overview of all patterns created during this session (on the screenshot, there is only a single pattern called "Test").

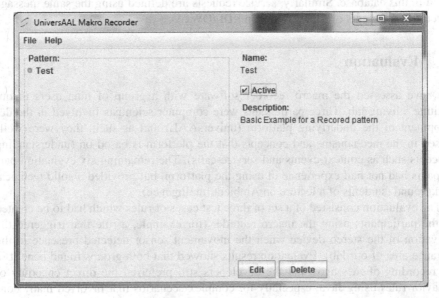

Fig. 2. Pattern overview

By selecting one of the patterns and clicking the "Edit"-button, the users is capable of editing both the "Conditions" (sensor events) and the "Actions" (actuator events) of this specific pattern. This includes the removal of specific entries, and also the possibility of moving certain events and actions upwards and downwards in the lists.

The smart environment system for which our macro recorder was developed is based on the universAAL platform [4]. This software platform allows the connection of heterogeneous devices to one another and uses multiple communication channels for the purpose of transferring information and service calls between them. The two main channels which we have been making use of are the so-called "Context Bus" for sharing contextual information between the components of the system (so-called "context events"), and the "Service Bus", whose job is the delivery of service calls ("service requests") between devices and applications.

Context events sent via the Context Bus of the universAAL platform are modeled based on the RDF/OWL format. According to this standardized format, statements are described as triples of a subject, a predicate and an object to convey information about the environment's current state. As a simple example, consider the statement "Lamp hasBrightness 100". It consists of three parts, the subject "Lamp", the predicate "hasBrightness" and the object value "100". This triple describes the state of a lamp which has a brightness value of 100 percent (indicating that the lamp is "on"). Such a triple is sent through the system via the Context Bus and conveys the information that the respective lamp has been turned on (via a light switch, for example). To allow for later access, all of these context events are also saved in a central database. The reason for this is that system components which enter the system (as it is an open system facilitating dynamic interoperability between system components) can then be informed about the current state of the system by referring to past context events saved in this database. Similarly, service requests are defined using the same message structure (statements of triples based on RDF/OWL).

4   Evaluation

We have assessed the macro recorder software with a group of nine users in our institute's living lab. Three participants were computer scientists involved in the development of the underlying platform (universAAL) and as such, they were well-versed in the mechanisms and concepts that the platform is based on (understanding concepts such as context-events and service-calls). The remaining six evaluation participants had not had experience in using the platform, but provided a solid technical background (students of a lecture on Ambient Intelligence). ·

The evaluation consisted of a set of three test cases of rules which had to be created by the participants using the macro recorder (for example, a rule that triggered the activation of the stereo device when the movement sensor detected presence in the entrance area of our lab). Evaluation results showed that both groups found benefit in the recording of messages, but the developers still preferred the direct encoding of behavior rules using Java, especially for complex scenarios that involved many context events and service calls. However, they confirmed the hypothesis that they might consider using the recorder for the encoding of simple rules once they would have gotten used to it.

The second group of users, the students, reported positively on the fact that they were able to "program" the system, something which they had considered beyond their capabilities before the test. However, some aspects of the system were considered confusing and irritating by this group, especially the statements in the RDF/OWL format. The users explained that they would have actually preferred a different user interface which hid the exact technical details and rather only shows simple abstractions of the underlying information (such as "A light was activated in the living room").

4.1   Conclusion and Future Work

In this work, we have described our approach for creating rule sets for smart environments by recording the behavior of a user. We were able to successfully implement and test the concept with a group of nine test users, who were able to "program" the system, even if they had no further experience in working with it. However, the evaluation showed some areas of improvement for the software. While developers of the underlying platform were comfortable with the user interface, the other users found some aspects of it too technical and offered various suggestions for its improvement.

The main point of criticism was the overall complexity and too many references to the technical concepts of the underlying platform. As such, as a future work we intend to create a more advanced version of our macro recorder software which will be capable of hiding many of the technical details. It may even be possible to provide an entirely graphical user interfaces based on graphical representations of the sensors and actuators only, which should make "programming" of the system possible for a much larger group of users.

Furthermore, as the macro recorder is currently only covering implicit interaction events (such as movement and occupation of certain areas), we intend to extend it to also handle explicit user interaction, such as voice and gesture commands. This would allow for the realization of even more complex rule patterns.

Acknowledgements. We would like to thank all evaluation participants from Fraunhofer IGD and the Technische Universitaet Darmstadt. The research leading to these results has received funding from the European Community's Seventh Framework Programme (FP7/2007-2013) under grant agreement no 247950, project *universAAL*.

References

1. Marinc, A., Stocklöw, C., Braun, A., Limberger, C., Hofmann, C., Kuijper, A.: Interactive personalization of Ambient Assisted Living environments. In: Smith, M.J., Salvendy, G. (eds.) HCII 2011, Part I. LNCS, vol. 6771, pp. 567–576. Springer, Heidelberg (2011)
2. Georgantas, N., Mokhtar, S., Bromberg, Y., Issarny, V., Kalaoja, J., Kantarovitch, J., Gerodolle, A., Mevissen, R.: The Amigo service architecture for the open networked home environment. In: Proceedings of the 5th Working IEEE/IFIP Conference on Software Architecture. IEEE Computer Society, Washington DC (2005)
3. Fides-Valero, Á., Freddi, M., Furfari, F., Tazari, M.-R.: The PERSONA framework for supporting context-awareness in open distributed systems. In: Aarts, E., Crowley, J.L., de Ruyter, B., Gerhäuser, H., Pflaum, A., Schmidt, J., Wichert, R. (eds.) AmI 2008. LNCS, vol. 5355, pp. 91–108. Springer, Heidelberg (2008)
4. universAAL - universal open platform and reference specification for Ambient Assisted Living, http://www.universaal.org (accessed February 28, 2013)
5. Aarts, E., de Ruyter, B.: New research perspectives on Ambient Intelligence. Journal of Ambient Intelligence and Smart Environments 1 (2009)
6. Rosson, M.: Effects of Experience on Learning, Using, and Evaluating a Text Editor. Human Factors: The Journal of the Human Factors and Ergonomics Society 26 (1984)
7. Borodin, Y.: Automation of repetitive web browsing tasks with voice-enabled macros. In: Proceedings of the 10th International ACM SIGACCESS Conference on Computers and Accessibility. ACM, New York (2011)

The Mobile Context Framework: Providing Context to Mobile Applications

Luís Oliveira, António Nestor Ribeiro, and José Creissac Campos

Departamento de Informática/Universidade do Minho & HASLab/INESC TEC
Braga, Portugal
anr@di.uminho.pt

Abstract. The spread of mobile devices in modern societies has forced the industry to create software paradigms to meet the new challenges it faces. Some of these challenges are the huge heterogeneity of devices or the quick changes of users' context. In this scenario, context becomes a key element, enabling mobile applications to be user centric and adapt to user requirements. The Mobile Context Framework, proposed in this paper, is a contribution to solve some of these challenges. Using Web servers running on the devices, context data can be provided to web applications. Besides the framework's architecture, a prototype is presented as proof of concept of the platform's potential.

Keywords: Context, mobile devices, mobile web servers, RIA, Web 2.0.

1 Introduction

Many authors have already defined the concept of context. Dey et al. say that context is any information that can be used to characterize the situation of an entity [1]. An entity is a person, place, or object that is considered relevant to the interaction between a user and an application, including the user and application themselves. The same authors state that a system is context-aware if it uses context to provide relevant information and/or services to the user where relevancy depends on the user's task.

Mobile computing constitutes an excellent area where these definitions can be properly applied. In fact, as mobile devices become very common in modern societies, and with the significant improvements of their capabilities (in terms of software and hardware), these devices may store an important percentage of user context data. Besides, as the users carry the mobile devices with them, the context is always updated. The main problem is figuring out an efficient way to allow mobile applications to access and use this information. This paper proposes the Mobile Contextual Framework (MCF) as a solution to this problem.

2 Development of Mobile Applications

There are different approaches when considering the development of applications to mobile devices (see Figure 1). A first approach is developing applications that run

N. Streitz and C. Stephanidis (Eds.): DAPI/HCII 2013, LNCS 8028, pp. 144–153, 2013.

natively in a selected platform. The advantage of this approach is that we can access the APIs of mobile operating systems and optimize the user experience for the target platform. However, one drawback of this approach is the tight coupling between applications and mobile platforms, resulting in high costs to maintain the same application for different operating systems.

A different approach is using web technologies (HTML5, CSS and JavaScript) to build a site/application that is accessed using a mobile browser. This results in applications that are generic – platform independent – and provide a good user experience with reduced effort both for developers and for final users. This approach has been gaining popularity mainly due to the fast improvement of mobile browsers and the currently numerous community of web developers.

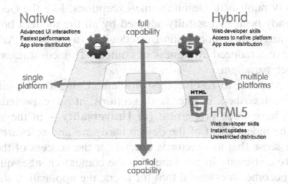

Fig. 1. Mobile development approaches (from [2])

A third approach – known as **hybrid** - results from the mix of native and web paradigms. In this paradigm, which we will adopt, the code is built using web technologies and is wrapped in a generic container, which is, in fact, a native application. This wrapper also exposes some of native APIs through a JavaScript (or similar) abstract layer allowing the developer to take advantage of some of features of mobile device. The main drawback of this approach is the, sometimes, poor performance of mobile applications and the lack of available frameworks. The most popular is Apache Cordova[1].

3   Contextual Information in Mobile Devices

Applying the definition of context referenced above to the mobile computing world, we can consider context to encompass both static and dynamic properties. The **static** ones are the properties that do not change throughout time. Mainly, device characteristics such as model, capabilities, supported formats, among others. In fact, static properties represent only a part of the contextual data (not the most important). We should also be concerned with **dynamic** properties such as location, temperature, who's near, user PIM, user calendar, mood, financial status, etc.

---

[1] http://cordova.apache.org/ (last accessed: 28/02/2013).

Recently, the World Wide Web Consortium (W3C) created groups to work on integration of web applications with mobile devices such as **a) Device APIs WG** [3] which main goal is to create client-side APIs that enable the development of Web Applications that interact with device hardware, services and applications such as the camera, microphone, system sensors, native address books, calendars and native messaging applications; **b) Geolocation WG** [4] which mission is to define a secure and privacy-sensitive interface for using client-side location information in location-aware Web applications and **c) Web Applications WG** [5] that is chartered to develop specifications for web applications, including standard APIs for client-side development, and a packaging format for installable web applications. This group is also responsible to specify the APIs to deal with devices file systems. The main problem of these groups is the lack of implementation by industry on the specifications already published. Despite some exceptions, like the Geolocation API [6], which was already been successfully adopted by all the modern browsers[2], there is no standard way to get this information from devices (using local APIs) so current web applications have a reduced awareness of context. This constitutes an important drawback for the web paradigm.

This paper is a proposal to resolve this problem. Using the Mobile Contextual Framework (MCF), described in the next sections, it is expected that mobile applications should have three properties: (a) **Universality** – in the sense that the application should be independent of the device hardware and software; (b) **Context awareness** – in the sense that this factor is crucial for the success of the solution (in fact, today, users are constantly in movement so the context changes quickly, and, as the mobile phones become an essential tool for users, the application should know in detail one of these context in order to assist the users in an effective way), (c) **Low Cost** – in the sense that the effort to design, implement and maintain the solution should be small.

The solution implemented by the Mobile Context Framework – MCF (see Fig. 2) – is based on Web standards like HTTP and JSON. Instead of adding new capabilities to browsers, MCF uses local web servers. In order to get contextual data, the web pages need only to make local HTTP requests and process the JSON responses.

4   Mobile Web Servers

Mobile Web Servers are HTTP servers – like Apache or IIS – that run in mobile platforms. One of first versions was designed to run on top of .NET Compact Framework [7]. Later, Nokia launched a port of Apache – Raccoon[3] – targeted to Symbian devices. Other implementations are available for iOS[4] and Android[5]. Use-cases scenarios for the Mobile Web Servers, can be found in [8] and include sharing personal contents with others (e.g., contacts, calendar events, photos, videos, etc.);

---

[2] http://caniuse.com/geolocation (last accessed 28/02/2103).

[3] http://sourceforge.net/projects/raccoon/ (last accessed 28/02/2013).

[4] https://github.com/robbiehanson/CocoaHTTPServer
  (last accessed 8/02/2013).

[5] http://code.google.com/p/i-jetty/ (last accessed 28/02/2013).

remote use via a web user interface (e.g., to locate the device); or the creation of context dependent content (e.g. obtaining information from people nearby).One of the issues when using mobile web servers in real scenarios is related to mobile operator's security policies. In fact, mobile operators networks are configured only to allow IP traffic originated from mobile devices. This means that an HTTP request done by an Internet host will not reach the target due to lack of **connectivity**. Additionally, it is not common that mobile devices connected to the Internet have fixed IP address. This brings another problem – **addressability.** Both issues can be solved using a gateway, outside the mobile operator network, in order to maintain HTTP connections from each device. These connections will be used whenever someone on the Internet makes a request to a certain device. Besides, this gateway guarantees the correct name resolution for mobile devices. This gateway-based solution is better explained in [9].

Upon the mobile web servers, developers are able to deploy web applications (like in other web servers). In order to allow running of web applications and dynamic pages, Raccoon implements a Python module - Python S60[6] – as well as the Personal Apache MySQL PHP module – PAMP[7]. Both modules provide APIs to guarantee direct access to operation system calls and, using this strategy, to get information about user PIM data or interact with GPS, camera, etc.

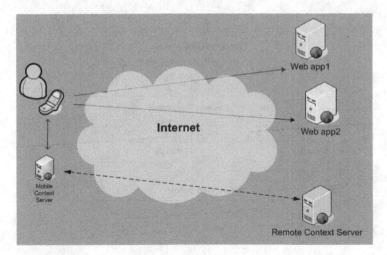

Fig. 2. MCF solution

5   MCF Architecture

The Mobile Context Framework (MCF) architecture encompasses two main components (see Figure 2):

1. **MCS** – Mobile Context Server
2. **RCS** – Remote Context Server

---

[6] http://sourceforge.net/projects/pys60/ (last accessed 28/02/2013).
[7] http://sourceforge.net/projects/pamp/ (last accessed 28/02/2013).

MCS runs on the mobile device as an application of the mobile web server. This component does not implement any logic dependent of a specific web application. It acts like a lightweight device API accepting HTTP requests and sending back responses in the JSON format.

In this way, the web application can access the device API, and gather contextual information just doing some more HTTP requests (to the localhost interface). From a user point of view, this solution is transparent since it does not require any additional device configuration or software installation in order to work properly (assuming that the mobile web server is installed by default in mobile devices). From a technical perspective, this solution joins both remote HTTP requests, in order to retrieve content from a remote web application, as well as local HTTP requests, to allow access to user context.

The MCS reference implementation was developed on top of the Raccoon server and using the Python module. The API is divided into two scripts: a main script – API-MCS.py - to manage metadata and textual responses (PIM, location) and an auxiliary script to fetch multimedia files such as images or videos in a streaming mode (Figure 3).

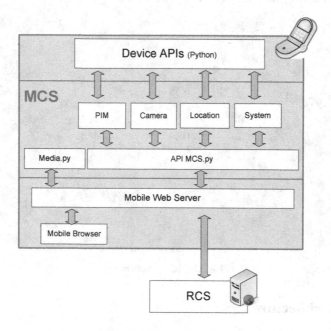

Fig. 3. MCS architecture

The contextual data, stored in mobile devices, is grouped in 4 categories: PIM, Camera, Location and System. Each of these categories has a correspondent class to manage, which acts like a bridge to device APIs. These APIs allow developers not only to grant access to context data but also to update it explicitly (e.g. to create a new calendar event). In what concerns to MCS API invocation, it is done asynchronously using callbacks to get the results.

As an example, let us consider a cinema tickets application, which contains a page listing the rooms near the user. To get the user current location (assuming that the user has a GPS device), the developer would need to add a script element which source URL should be http://localhost/mcs/api-mcs.py?op=getDeviceLocation. Besides that, it is required to implement the **mcf_callback** function in order to get the corresponding response (in this particular case, the location). In this example, the coordinates returned by MCF are used to make an Ajax request to a cinema service in order to get the rooms nearby. The full example code is listed in Figure 4.

```
<html>
<head>
<title>Location Test</title>
<script type="text/javascript">
var lat, longit;
function mcf_callback(obj) {
   lat = obj.location.lat;
   longit = obj.location.longit;
}
function updateRoomsDiv() { ... }
</script>
<script type='text/javascript'
         src='http://127.0.0.1/mcs/api-mcs.py?op=getDeviceLocation'>
</script>
</head>
<body>
  <h1>Location Test</h1>
  <div id="result" style="display: none">
     <span id="status">Searching cinemas...</span>
     <img src="ajax-loader.gif">
  </div>
<script type="text/javascript">updateRoomsDiv();</script>
</body></html>
```

Fig. 4. MCS invocation example

Figure 5 depicts a sequence diagram of the interactions expected to occur in this example. First, the device browser performs a request to the cinemas web site hosted in the Internet. The response includes a reference to a localhost resource, which makes the browser perform an HTTP request to this local URL. This request is afterwards received by the mobile web server. Internally, the request is processed by MCS, which will perform a call to the operating system in order to get the device location. Once the result is obtained, it is sent back to the device browser. At the same time, the browser makes an Ajax request to get the cinema's set of rooms giving the location as parameter. When the final result is sent back to the browser, it is dynamically included in the page. All these steps are done transparently for the user.

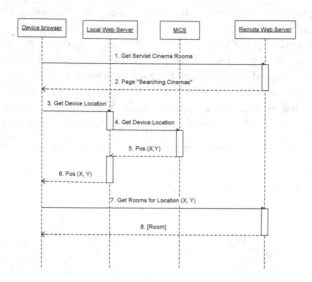

Fig. 5. Sequence diagram of a MCS invocation

The second component – RCS – is also a web application, and runs on a remote host. It includes an **Utils** sub-component, which helps MCS in more complex tasks. Consider, for instance, the processing of a 2D code. When a web page requests the MCS to read a 2D code, the component captures a photograph using the camera device API (assuming that user is pointing the device to a 2D code). Then, instead of doing the image processing in the mobile device it makes a request to the RCS. Besides this sub-component, the RCS also includes a **Trigger** sub-component, implementing rule based user notifications. For instance, if the user has a meeting in location X and, some minutes before the scheduled meeting time, he is far from it, the RCS would notify the user.

Internally, the trigger has a list of rules configured for each user. If the requirements of a rule occur, the corresponding event (in most cases, a notification to the user) is fired. In order to check the rules requirements, the RCS component makes periodical requests to the MCS, in order to get updated context information (for each user who subscribes some RCS rule). The mechanism that manages how rules are run is generic, independent of each specific rule.

While the MCS component has a **passive** behavior (it just responds to requests that are made when user is browsing in context aware web applications), the RCS component has an **active** behavior, mainly the trigger. This constitutes a great advantage when compared to solutions designed to work only in a passive mode. In the case of MCF, the MCS API is remotely called by the trigger component.

Regarding security and data privacy, the solution can run in a **local only** mode in order to guarantee that there's no remote requests performed to device web server. In this mode, the trigger component of RCS is disabled since it cannot communicate with MCS.

6   An Example

To illustrate the potential of MCF, a prototype was implemented. The prototype was based on the use case described next.

Mary is a university student in London and a cinema fan. One day, while waiting for the bus, she sees an advertising spot about a new movie. Curious about it, Mary picks her phone, opens her operator mobile portal page and points the phone to the 2D code next to the advertisement. The phone camera captures the code and the data stored in it is sent to the RCS in order to be processed.

Next, Mary is presented a page with the movie details, including an option to see a trailer (Figure 6-a). After watching the trailer, she decides to buy two tickets, one for her and another for her boyfriend.

(a) Movie details page   (b) Sessions list screen

Fig. 6. Choosing a session

In the screen to choose the date and session of the movie, Mary notices that some sessions are unavailable for selection (Figure 6-b). She then understands that those sessions are in conflict with events in her agenda. Mary chooses the Saturday night session.

After Mary has bought the second ticket, the application asks her for whom the second ticket is. Mary chooses her boyfriend contact from the phone contact list (Figure 7-a). Next, since this cinema chain has rooms in many cities in the UK, the application asks Mary to choose the room's location. John realizes that the default cinema room is already in London (but other options are also available). In fact, the application has made a location request to the device and it has chosen the nearest room as the default one. Then, Mary finalizes the tickets purchase (Figure 7-b) and, immediately, the application adds an event in Mary's agenda.

Some days later, Mary has forgotten about the tickets she bought and is travelling to Manchester that weekend. One hour before the movie starts, the application realized that Mary is far away from the room's location. Thus, it sends a short message to her, suggesting a change of movie location to Manchester since there are rooms from the cinema company there.

(a) Select friends screen   (b) Confirmation screen

Fig. 7. Inviting friends

When considering the implementation of this use case, we could think that the cinema company implemented a native mobile application and that shared it to the customers. However, the company directors did not agree on paying a high quantity to develop and maintain versions of this application for the 4 main mobile platforms.

An application supporting the use case was implemented using MCF to provide context adaptation. The screenshots in Figures 6 and 7 are taken from the application. The application is provided as a Web application written in PHP. The code snippets presented throughout the paper, to illustrate MCF's usage, are taken from this particular application.

As illustrated by the use case description, the application is capable of accessing the device's camera and contact list, change the agenda, and request services from the server, in order to provide a contectualised usage experience to its users.

7   Conclusions

Enabling applications to access contextual information, allows for services with greater added value, and an improved usage experience. The mobile web is gaining an increased relevance in the information society age. It is foreseeable that in a few years mobile devices will be the primary means of accessing the web [10, 11]. At the same time, Web programming technologies evolution means that it is now possible to build complex applications that are largely device independent, and that can be made immediately available to anyone with a web enabled device. Finally, mobile web servers make it possible for those applications to have access to the user's context, without the need to install special purpose plug-ins in the browser.

This paper put forward MCF – the Mobile Context Framework – as a generic mechanism to enable mobile Web applications to interact with the mobile devices they will be *running* on. The proposed solution is invisible to users, assuming that devices will be delivered pre-installed with a mobile Web server, as argued for by Wikman et al. [9]. Besides the MCF framework, the paper presents a prototype application: Cinema Mobile Tickets. This application is a context sensitive application, built on top of MCF. The application is open source and demonstrates the feasibility of using the framework in a real life scenario.

Acknowledgments. The authors acknowledge funding by the ERDF through Programme COMPETE and by the Portuguese Government through FCT - Foundation for Science and Technology, within project ref. FCOMP-01-0124-FEDER-015095.

References

1. Dey, A., Abowd, G.: Towards a Better Understanding of Context and Context-Awareness. In: Proceedings of the CHI 2000 Workshop on the What, Who, Where, When, and How of Context-Awareness, Netherlands (April 2000)
2. Korf, M., Oksman, E.: Native, HTML5, or Hybrid: Understanding Your Mobile Application Development Options. Developerforce Technical Library (May 2012)
3. Hazael-Massieux, D. (ed.): W3C Device APIs Working Group Charter. W3C (2011), http://www.w3.org/2011/07/DeviceAPICharter.html
4. Womer, M.: W3C Geolocation Working Group Charter. W3C (2010), http://www.w3.org/2008/geolocation/
5. Schepers, D., Barstow, A., McCathieNevile, C.: W3C Web Applications (WebApps) Working Group Charter, W3C (2012), http://www.w3.org/2008/webapps/
6. W3C, Geolocation API Specification (2012)
7. Pratistha, I., Nicoloudis, N., Cuce, S.: A Micro-Services Framework on Mobile Devices. In: Proceedings of the International Conference on Web Services, ICWS 2003, pp. 320–325. CSREA Press (2003)
8. Wikman, J., Dosa, F.: Personal Website on a Mobile Phone, Nokia Research Center (May 2006)
9. Wikman, J., Dosa, F.: Providing HTTP Access to Web Servers Running on Mobile Phones, Nokia Research Center (May 2006)
10. Huynh, S.: Mobile Internet Users Will Soon Surpass PC Internet Users Globally. Forrester Blogs (February 21, 2012)
11. Lee, M., Wong, J.: Web access via mobile phone trumps PC in China: report. Reuters, Shanghai (July 19, 2012)

Web Based Me-Centric Resource Management System for Pervasive Environment

Daeil Seo[1], Sang Chul Ahn[1], and Heedong Ko[1,2]

[1] Department of HCI and Robotics, University of Science and Technology
Daejeon, South Korea
[2] Imaging Media Research Center, Korea Institute of Science and Technology
Seoul, South Korea
{xdesktop,prime,ko}@imrc.kist.re.kr

Abstract. This paper presents a design and implementation of a web-based scalable me-centric resource management platform to support pervasive applications. The proposed system, LinkMe, builds me-centric overlay network, a private network of resources, for managing devices located in the user's situated environment, as permitted resources. A resource may be atomic or a set of fine-grained resources. By this resource hierarchy, pervasive applications can choose a variety of resources combinations based tasks situated in the physical environment. Using web, resources are identified by URI and can be manipulated using HTTP verbs. Pervasive application can access resources using a set of RESTful APIs. To reduce technical barrier, developers can choose proper resources using URI and build a pervasive application easily based on web technologies such as HTML5, CSS and JavaScript.

Keywords: Me-centric, Resource management system, Pervasive, Resource decomposition, Web technology, URI, HTML5, CSS, JavaScript.

1   Introduction

Recently, embedded devices are in wide spread use in our environment and most people use a smartphone with sensors, and other wearable smart devices. These devices can collect information about our situated environment to help pervasive systems for understanding user context more efficiently. A device has a lot of features and can perform a variety of roles depending on situation.

However, these smart devices can provide their own predefined services but they are hard to interoperate among themselves and even harder to compose their functionalities. If a pervasive system provides a simple way to access features in the device and to compose them from various devices, we can use available resources in situated environment more efficiently. For example, we bind volume buttons of the smartphone to control a HVAC system for increasing and decreasing temperature in the accustomed way. For this reason, we need a more sophisticated resource management system and their interaction model.

N. Streitz and C. Stephanidis (Eds.): DAPI/HCII 2013, LNCS 8028, pp. 154–162, 2013.

Another problem is that typical pervasive systems do not scale well for different situation because these systems provide many different communication approach including RMI, CORBA, and SOA, making pervasive applications difficult and time consuming for developers to implement.

The Web is raising alternative methodology. R. Fielding [1] proposed REST architectural style, developed as an abstract model of the Web. The Web provides uniform interface and loosely coupled architecture, we can benefit scalable and load balancing, and searching. Web of Things [2] proposed REST based approach for integrating real-world devices to the Web. Using the Web, developers make a pervasive application likes a web application and even a web page.

We developed the LinkMe as web based me-centric resources management system. By linking between resources and me, LinkMe provides me-centric overlay network, a private network of resources that the user can access. Also, the system supports granularity for fine-grained resource addressability. The user can decompose a resource or combine any physical and virtual resources to declare a new virtual resource. The declaration of the new virtual resource is described by HTML or JSON. A resource is identified by URI and addressed by URL. LinkMe follows REST architecture that provides an interface for accessing many resources of the device in a uniform way. The proposed system adopts a resources-oriented architecture and supports a set of RESTful APIs. Developers also write pervasive applications as web applications using familiar languages such as HTML5, CSS and JavaScript.

The rest of this paper is structured as follows. Next, we present related work in Section 2. In Section 3, we introduce system design and the next section we shows our prototype implementation. Finally, we conclude with a summary and outlook on future work in Section 5.

2   Related Work

This section gives an overview of related projects and technologies. The HP Cooltown [3] project aimed to provide an infrastructure for nomadic computing and focused on extending web technology. In this project, devices, people, and things have a web-presence identified by a URI. Gaia [4] is aiming for providing user-centric, resource-aware, multi-device, context-sensitive mobile services in active spaces. The Context File System in Gaia project builds a virtual directory structure based on context predicates and manages storages infrastructure's view. Service oriented architectures (SOA) [5] can be used as base in order to realize suitable frameworks to develop pervasive applications. Web of Things [2] integrates real-world devices to the Web and applies REST principles to embedded devices. Previous pervasive system considers only the environment around user except user already owned and permitted resources. Also, these systems except Web of Things used CORBA [4] or SOAP for management and communication.

There are many web-based approach for accessing devices. They define a set of APIs using JavaScript and write application using HTML5, JavaScript, and CSS.

Webinos [6] is a cross-device distributed middleware for web applications and widgets. It provides APIs for accessing device features and communication with others. Webinos is based the concept of personal zones, the set of all their devices. LG Open webOS [7] is web-centric platforms and applications can be written using either the Mojo or Enyo framework. PhoneGap [8] is platform-independent framework with a runtime providing standard APIs. The W3C Device APIs Working Group [9] is currently developing client-side device APIs. These approaches allow non-expert users to create or modify a web application using device feature easily. However, they concern only local resource.

To manage all the resources that are available to the user, the proposed system builds me-centric resource overlay for user's point of view and manages web-enabled resources using HTTP method and URI. This system treats a resource as an atomic resource or as a set of the atomic resources and provides declaration methodology for giving resource granularity using web technologies.

3   System Design

In this section, we introduce our system design and a prototype implementation.

3.1   Architecture and Concept

In this section, we introduce our system design and a prototype implementation. We developed the LinkMe as a me-centric resources management system for pervasive environment based on web technologies. The proposed system builds me-centric overlay network and offers the Single Sign-On (SSO) service for communication among resources. LinkMe Server is a primary component and is responsible for managing resources that the user has an authority to access them even if they are connected different networks. It manages user information that contains a profile and accounts of services. Also, it considers social relations of the user and devices that are owned and shared to the user depending on user context. The proposed system deals with resources such as user information, social relations and devices; however, in this paper, we focus on management of device resources.

Fig.1 depicts an example of pervasive environment around the user and resource trees of LinkMe. The resource tree shows available resources and their hierarchal relations. Fig.1 (b) shows resources in the office. All the resources in the office are registered on the LinkMe and the system is in charged of managing resources in the place and permission that who has an authority to access a resource. In Fig.1 (c) depicts resources on user's perspective. The LinkMe of the user performs role management of owned and shared resources. A user's smartphone connected telephone network and a printer are shared devices for family members. A computer is located near the user in pervasive environment and connected to a local network. Resources are shown in resource tree because the user can access them.

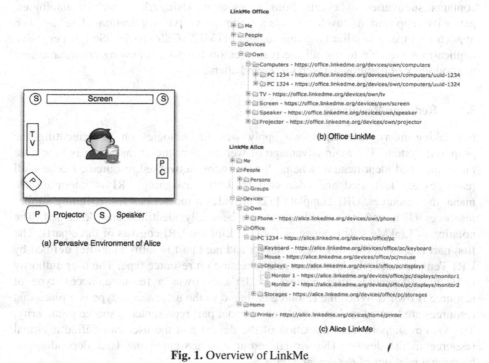

Fig. 1. Overview of LinkMe

For interacting with the resources, we first find resources and register them to the system. Discovery is a procedure for retrieving information of resources. Local discovery technologies such as UPnP, Multicast DNS are good solution because a lot of devices already implement these protocols and provides interaction method for services; however, interoperation among protocols is a big problem. We only use these protocols for discovery, and hide communication between LinkMe Server and resources. The user only uses http protocol to request and response a message from resources. LinkMe Server acts like traditional web server and addressed by URI. URIs are identifiers of all the resources in LinkMe. When a web browser visits a URI of a resource, LinkMe responses status information of the resource using web page. For this interaction, we choose REST architecture, resource-oriented architecture, because HTTP protocol correctly used following the principles. REST supports the set of operations for the web services using HTTP methods.

It is important to collect and understand user and environment context from resource status. To receive event notification and feed from resources, we choose two kinds of method such as Server-Sent Events (SSE) [10] and Atom [11]. SSE is an API for opening an HTTP connection for receiving push notifications from a server in the form of DOM events, and is useful for sending message updates or continuous data streams to a browser. The role of SSE on LinkMe is processing events occurred frequently, for example, button press events. Atom Syndication Format is an XML language used for web feeds. Atom feeds can be based on simple GET operations and contains summaries of events from a resource. Using these web technologies, pervasive application developers also write pervasive applications like as web applications using familiar language such as HTML5, CSS and JavaScript. Pervasive applications are able to use all the resources on the web following communication methodology of traditional a web server and client.

3.2   Redesign Resource

For taking many advantages, we apply web technologies on implementing the proposed system. The main advantage of web architecture is that there is now a de facto universal identification scheme for accessing networked resources. Because all resources are identified and addressed by URIs, assigning URI is important for managing resources. URI Template [12] provides a mechanism for assigning similar resources URIs and its variable parts can be easily identified and described. The notation of LinkMe URI is given in Table 1. LinkMe URI consists of three parts. The first part is an identifier of LinkMe Server and next part is entity identifier defined by URI Template and which notation rule is related on resource type. The user authority is decided depending user context. If the user owns a resource, access-type of resource is owned. When the resource is shared to the user, access-type is a place that resources are located in. Last is only an optional part represented resource granularity. The system supports decomposition of the device and the user can define a virtual resource in the device. The virtual resource is assigning the URI depending on hierarchal relations of the parent device.

Table 1. LinkMe URI Notation

Resource	URI Notation	Example URI
Me	/me	http://alice.linkedme.org/me
Device	/devices/{access-type}/{resource-type}/{resource-id}	http://alice.linkedme.org/devices/own/pc/uuid-1234
Person	/people/person/{person-id}	http://alice.linkedme.org/people/persons/bob
Group	/people/groups/{group-id}/{person-id}	http://alice.linkedme.org/people/groups/friends/bob

To declare granularity of a resource, we apply web technology. In the Web, browsers and servers do content negotiation, a mechanism to serve different representation of a resource at the same URI. HTML and JSON are typical representation of resources in the Web. HTML document is rendering resources on the web page and JSON is lightweight data-interchange format. We use HTML and JSON for declaring hierarchical relation on a device. Fig. 2 depicts an example that declares a television that is decomposed into four resources. HTML body is consists of three sections and the section is defined by HTML div tag and CSS class. The HTML document has a CSS link that is describing the presentation semantics for section. First is general information of a resource such as name, description. Next is resource granularity that the user declares a resource hierarchy and a new virtual resource. URI of new resources are assigning based on a physical resource. The anchor tag defines a hyperlink, which is used to link from one page to another, and indicates the link's destination. Rel attribute of anchor tag can specify the relationship between the current document and the linked document. For resource composition, we use a rel attribute to point an origin URI of the resource. We can add a usage to the anchor tag for hierarchical relation using this notation. As a result, a resource has a self-description through web page. HTTP method for interaction with the resource is followed. The resources on the LinkMe are RESTful and can be manipulated using HTTP verbs such as OPTION, PUT, GET, POST and DELETE. Fig. 2 (b) shows JSON example that is another representation of the resource. Attributes of the resource are key-value notation, and decomposed resources and available methods are list-value.

```html
<html>
    <head>
        <title>Television</title>
        <link rel="stylesheet" type="text/css"
              href="http://linkedme.org/resource.css">
    </head>
    <body>
        <p>Information</p>
        <div class="information">
            <ul>
                <li><span>Name</span> : Television</li>
                <li><span>Description</span> : Smart tv</li>
            </ul>
        </div>
        <p>Resource</p>
        <div class="resource">
            <ul>
                <li><a href="display">Display</a> : </li>
                <li><a href="volume">Volume</a> : Volume controller</li>
                <li><a href="channel">Channel</a> : </li>
                <li><a href="source">Input Source</a> : </li>
            </ul>
        </div>
        <p>Method</p>
        <div class="method">
            <ul>
                <li><span>OPTION</span> : GET</li>
                <li><span>GET</span> : Description of tv</li>
            </ul>
        </div>
    </body>
</html>
```

```json
{
    Name: "Television",
    Description: "Smart tv",
    Resource: [
        {
            Display: {
                URL: "display"
            }
        },
        {
            Volume: {
                URL: "volume",
                Description: "Volume controller"
            }
        },
        {
            Channel: {
                URL: "cahnnel"
            }
        },
        {
            Input Source: {
                URL: "source"
            }
        }
    ],
    Method: [
        {
            OPTION: "GET"
        },
        {
            GET: "Description of tv"
        }
    ]
}
```

(a) Resource Declaration by HTML   (b) Resource Declaration by JSON

Fig. 2. Declaration of Hierarchical Relation

4   Prototype Implementation

To demonstrate the feasibility of our proposed system, we develop a pervasive application using the LinkMe. We use JavaScript for a programming logic and build a UI of application with HTML5 and CSS.

First scenario is a tour application. The user has a smartphone and takes a picture with it; however, its storage is limited and does not support sharing method. To overcome this problem, the user uses social services that serve cloud storages. Nevertheless, these services are also limited storage and need a payment. If the user has storage and it is linked to LinkMe, the smartphone is able to connect to the storage by LinkMe. The user is able to full capacity of the storage and does not need any cost to use. The application assigns storage URI for storing a picture and the smartphone sends a picture to the URI using HTTP method. If the application subscribes an event, LinkMe acts like as proxy and relays an event to resource. Atom gives summaries of uploading photos to the storage from the smartphone.

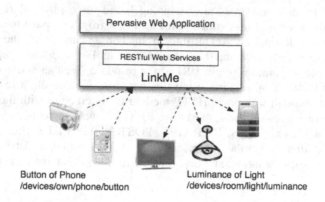

Fig. 3. Overview of Prototype Application

Second scenario shows resource granularity. The application receives a key press event from a variety of inputs and sends the event to the connected outputs. All the appliances are permitted to the user and LinkMe assigned URIs to resources. Now, the application can identify resources by given URIs and interact among them using HTTP methods. The application gets resource presence to request a given URI. The user of the application selects a resource to affect a key press event from inputs. The event is interpreted by the resource that receive the event. When the user pressed an up button and a volume of television is a target, the volume is increased. If a target is luminance of a light, the luminance is increased. The affect of the event is depending on the target resource. The application delivers the event from inputs to the target resource. Fig. 3 depicts overview of application design. It is detailed description of communication between the LinkMe and resources. LinkMe Server receives a HTTP request from the application and sends a message, predefined by the resource such as UPnP, JSON-RPC, to the resource. The resource processes a request message and responses the result to LinkMe Server. LinkMe Server sends a HTTP response to the application. For pushing event from resources to application such as key press event, we choose SSE that pushes events to the application.

Other application is a virtual movie player that is an example of resource composition. In Fig.1, we already depict an example of pervasive environment. A screen, television and monitor of a computer can display a movie. Speakers beside the screen, television, and speakers of a computer are able to output sound of the movie. The user chooses an input source to play and watches it using the best resources that are allowed to the user. To satisfy these requirements, we design a new resource, a movie player. This virtual resource is configurable and is able to provide fine-grained addressability. We choose a resource for display, sound player, and input source. The movie player has candidate set of available resources and the application chooses a resource among a set of resources depending on user and environment context. The user is able to choose an input sources such as a file in the storage of a computer or the television. If the user is alone in the place, the application chooses the screen, speaker, and projector because there are the best playing the movie. When the user uses a computer and other persons exist in the same place, the application selects proper resources as component of the computer for playing movie not to disturb others. Fig.4 depicts components of a virtual movie player and resource declaration. URIs also identifies a virtual resource and components of it. The resources in the new one have another URI because they are already registered and assigned URIs on the system. The application interacts to the virtual resource likes as physical resource using HTTP method. When the application sends a request to the URI of components in the virtual resource, the system send a message to the origin URI and return the response to the application.

```
{
    Name: "Virtual Movie Player",
    Description: "Resource composition for playing movies",
  - Resource: [
      - {
          - Display: {
              URL: "display",
              - Origin: [
                  http://office.linkedme.org/devices/own/screen,
                  http://office.linkedme.org/devices/own/computers/uuid-1234/monitor,
                  http://office.linkedme.org/devices/own/tv/display
              ]
          }
      },
      - {
          - Volume: {
              URL: "volume",
              - Origin: [
                  http://office.linkedme.org/devices/own/speaker,
                  http://office.linkedme.org/devices/own//computers/uuid-1234/speaker,
                  http://office.linkedme.org/devices/own/tv/speaker
              ]
          }
      },
      - {
          - Input Source: {
              URL: "source",
              - Origin: [
                  http://office.linkedme.org/devices/own/projector,
                  http://office.linkedme.org/devices/own/computers/uuid-1234,
                  http://office.linkedme.org/devices/own/tv
              ]
          }
      },
      - Method: [
          - {
              OPTION: "GET"
          },
          - {
              GET: "Description of Movie Player"
          }
      ]
}
```

Fig. 4. Virtual Resource Declaration Example

Using web architecture, the application uses unified interface. When resources are increased in the environment, we just add a declarative description of resources. Changing of environment does not influence the application. By example, we clarify that our proposed system is useful in pervasive environment, and provides scalability and simple interface for interacting resources.

5   Conclusion

In this paper, we proposed the LinkMe, web based me-centric resource management system for pervasive environment. We apply web technologies on implementing the proposed system because the web is now a de facto universal identification scheme for accessing networked resources. URIs are identified and addressed web-enabled resources. Pervasive application developers write applications using familiar language such as HTML5, CSS and JavaScript. Also, the system provides a method for declaring granularity of a resource. The user is able to fine-grained control to the resources. We give example applications for testing feasibility of our system.

We only focus on the device resources in the paper. As next step the system will consider social relation and social services that are tightly connected the user. We will be able to get more context and useful information from linked resources.

Acknowledgments. This research is supported by Ministry of Culture, Sports and Tourism(MCST) and Korea Creative Content Agency(KOCCA) in the Culture Technology(CT) Research & Developement Program 2012.

References

1. Fielding, R., Taylor, R.: Principled Design of the Modern Web Architecture. ACM Trans. Internet Technology 2(2), 115–150 (2002)
2. Guinard, D., Trifa, V.: Towards the web of things: Web mashups for embedded devices. In: Workshop on Mashups, Enterprise Mashups and Lightweight Composition on the Web (MEM 2009), Proceedings of WWW (International World Wide Web Conferences), Madrid, Spain (2009)
3. Barton, J., Kindberg, T.: The challenges and opportunities of integrating the physical world and networked systems. HPL Technical Report 2001-18 (2001)
4. Roman, M., Hess, C., Cerqueira, R., Ranganathan, A., Campbell, R.H., Nahrstedt, K.: A middleware infrastructure for active spaces. IEEE Pervasive Computing 1(4), 74–83 (2002)
5. Tigli, J.Y., Lavirotte, S., Rey, G., Hourdin, V., Riveill, M.: Lightweight Service Oriented Architecture for Pervasive Computing. International Journal of Computer Science Issues (IJCSI) 4, 1–9 (2009)
6. Lyle, J., Faily, S., Fléchais, I., Paul, A., Göker, A., Myrhaug, H., Desruelle, H., Martin, A.: On the design and development of *webinos*: A distributed mobile application middleware. In: Göschka, K.M., Haridi, S. (eds.) DAIS 2012. LNCS, vol. 7272, pp. 140–147. Springer, Heidelberg (2012)
7. Open WebOS Project, http://www.openwebosproject.org
8. PhoneGap, http://www.phonegap.com
9. W3C Device APIs Working Group, http://www.w3.org/2009/dap
10. Server-Sent Events, http://dev.w3.org/html5/eventsource
11. RFC 5023 - The Atom Publishing Protocol, http://tools.ietf.org/html/rfc5023
12. RFC 6750 - URI Template, http://tools.ietf.org/html/rfc6570

SemanticRadar: AR-Based Pervasive Interaction Support via Semantic Communications

Heesuk Son, Byoungoh Kim, Taehun Kim, Dongman Lee, and Soon Joo Hyun

Computer Science Department, Korea Advanced Institute of Science and Technology,
Guseong-dong, Yuseong-gu, Daejeon, Korea
{heesuk.son,cmossetup,kingmbc,dlee,sjhyun}@kaist.ac.kr

Abstract. Augmented Reality (AR) overlays relevant virtual information onto a real world view and allows the user to interact and virtually manipulate surroundings. Since virtual information resides not only in a virtual space, but also in a physical space, users can be spontaneously given a number of opportunities for enriched interactions with their environments. In this paper, we propose an AR-based pervasive interaction support, SemanticRadar, which allows a user to spontaneously interact with smart objects through semantic communications, leveraging the placeness of a user's current location.

1 Introduction

Augmented Reality (AR) [1] allows the user to interact and virtually manipulate surroundings by overlaying relevant virtual objects onto a real world view. A recent advent of light weight AR devices like Google glass [2] has made it possible to the daily lives of normal users. As Mark Weiser envisioned embodied virtuality [3], the advancement of information technology is turning daily objects into smart objects with storages, processors, and networking capability, making them seamlessly embodied into our environments. Due to this paradigm shift, virtual information resides not only in a virtual space, but also in a physical space. Since this embodied virtuality is able to provide additional services and information, users can be spontaneously given a number of opportunities for enriched interactions with their environments.

There have been several research efforts to understand users' contexts and provide personalized information through an AR interface [4–7]. Sentient Visor [5, 6] visualizes context information of each object based on user preference. SmartReality [4] augments related information about the objects crawled from Linked Open Data (LOD) cloud and web service repositories by leveraging user profiles and GPS data. Ajanki et al. [7] provide relevant annotations that the user is interested in by capturing user face, speech, location, and time. However, existing works do not find which interactions are suitable with objects since a space can have multiple meanings perceived by people over time based on the social activities performed in it. In other words, they do not consider varying interaction dynamics with target objects perceived by the user according to the given context. For example, a projector in a

N. Streitz and C. Stephanidis (Eds.): DAPI/HCII 2013, LNCS 8028, pp. 163–172, 2013.

seminar room should augment information about a presentation assistant service when a user is having a presentation, while information about a video player service should be given when a group of users is watching a movie. For this, we need to consider the varying semantics that each place may have for different users, so-called *placeness* [8]. According to this perception difference, it is required to augment different information for suitable interactions.

In this paper, we propose a pervasive interaction framework, SemanticRadar, which enables a user AR device to spontaneously interact with smart objects through semantic communications, leveraging the placeness of a user's current location. It finds out relevant interaction semantics for target smart objects by discovering the user perceptions on the current location and exchanging contextual information with smart objects. We assume that there exists a cloud (hereafter called placeness cloud) which infers placeness by mining the interaction history of the people and other context information accumulated in the location. From this, as a user gets into a target location, SemanticRadar on a user device (hereafter called a user device) extracts the placeness that similar users have on the current location using an ontology including locations and the type of possible interactions. When a user gazes at a target smart object, the user device asks possible interactions for the given placeness and the user profile toward SemanticRadar on a target object (hereafter called a target object). Assuming the target object accumulates its interaction history, it infers and replies possible interaction types for the given user. Then, if the user selects one of the possible types, the user device requests the target object a suitable interface for the interaction type. As a result, the target object returns the visualization information to use the result interface which is to be augmented through the user's view. We call this stepwise communication procedure as semantic communications. We implement SemanticRadar on top of smartphones running Android 4.2 and smart objects (e.g. projector, curtain, LED light, and door powered by Beagle board-xM) running Ubuntu Linux.

The rest of this paper is organized as followed. Section 2 introduces related works on context-aware service provisioning which encourages user interactions with ubiquitous virtual reality. In section 3, we describe our design considerations which are necessary to resolve our challenges. In section 4, we present how our proposed scheme can release current limitations, and in section 5, we conclude this paper with our future works.

2   Related Works

Sentient Visor [5, 6] visualizes context information of each object based on user preference. In this work, they design a framework, UbiSOA, in which objects are abstracted as a virtual web service implemented with RESTful interface. On top of it, they propose an IoT browser, Sentient Visor, which is an AR-based mediator to discover nearby objects and support user-to-environment interactions. Considering the heterogeneity of smart objects and the data they exchange, to make each object understand the semantics and enable semantic interactions between them, they put ontology prefixes as semantic tags for each data into the exchanged messages. To process this semantic information and provide personalized information derived from current contexts, they deploy a web service which is responsible of hosting knowledge base and processing semantic queries from Sentient Visor. Once Sentient Visor receives what should be displayed in which format, the result about the object is augmented in user's AR interface. However, this framework just focuses on static semantics of what the target object is and how they can be understood in user's perspective in a given context, while overlooking the fact that those semantics can vary according to the user's perception on the current place. Without considering this dynamics, the likelihood that suggested interactions can satisfy the user may not be high enough, especially in a public place.

SmartReality [4] augments related information about the objects crawled from Linked Open Data (LOD) cloud and web service repositories by leveraging user profiles and GPS data. Once a user device recognizes an object, the object is linked to Things-of-Interst (ToI) description stored in ToI store in a server. Then, the server loads related data and services from Linked Open Data (LOD) cloud and web service repository according to a set of Linked Data crawling rules with collected context sources. These loaded entities are packed together and delivered to the user in a meaningful and useful manner through the AR interface. This work not just tries to suggest personalized interactions based on user contexts, but also expand the data retrieval range by including LOD as their information source. However, like Sentient Visor, this work also overlooks the dynamics of semantics that each place has. Because of that, the system doesn't know which interactions are likely to satisfy current user's need which could change along with the place semantics, resulting in wrong service and data hosting.

Ajanki et al [7] provide relevant annotations that the user is interested in by capturing user face, speech, location, and time. By recognizing objects in AR view, the user's location, face, speech, and finger pointing, this framework infers in which object the user is interested and what the user wants to do with it. Once they are figured out, relevant annotations which are likely to be interesting for the user are loaded from the back-end server and shown through the AR user interface. In this work, since the most of contextual cues are given as a real-time streaming, a dedicated back-end server to process the stream data in real time has been installed. While this framework tries to enrich user interactions with the environments by means of analyzing user actions as critical contextual cues, it also overlooks the dynamic semantics of each place and its possible relationships to the users or embodied smart objects.

3   Design Considerations

3.1   Extracting User Perceptions on Interaction Semantics of Current Location

In [8], a space can have multiple meanings perceived by people over time based on the social activities performed in it. We call these diverse user perceptions on the interaction semantics of a space as "placeness". In order to extract placeness associated with a location, we need to capture what type of activities people repeatedly perform there. For this, we need to collect user information such as profiles including age, role, and gender, and experiences at different places on top of social relations data among users. This information is then utilized to find appropriate interactions for a user. However, it is highly challenging to formalize a person's conceptualization of a place into a computational method. Several existing approaches to the mining of user experiences with a place can generally be put into two categories in terms of the knowledge source. These are the online cyber world and the offline physical world. In the former, some studies analyze the geospatial contents from travelogues and social media [9–12]. Although we can summarize the features of a place as a topic-based word cloud, as done by Abdelmoty et al. [13] and KUSCO [14, 15], it is difficult for their approaches precisely to extract social interaction information, including members, activities, and times from the coarse-grained tag clouds. This makes the results of dynamic interaction opportunity discovery inaccurate. In the second approach, one branch of research has considered the mining of user experience from user behavior logs in the real world [16–18]. As these works have aimed to discover important places from GPS traces, they have not supported recommendations of feasible interactions in those places. Therefore, on top of the approaches in these studies, we consider a method to extract placeness from virtual and physical worlds and exploit it to find appropriate interactions.

3.2   Augmenting Relevant Interaction Semantics via Semantic Communications

Even if the placeness is extracted, since a user has no prior knowledge about a target object in the current location, it is hard to figure out which interactions are possible with it. To do that, we need a communication procedure through which they get to know each other and eventually find relevant interaction semantics. Juba [19] introduces semantic communications which is a sequential procedure through which intelligent individuals without a common language build a shared knowledge and achieve a common goal such as solving a complex problem. Supposing that there are two intelligent agents A and B who are not sharing any common language, to communicate each other and achieve a common goal, they need to try everything they can do to understand who the other is and what he can do. If they can make even a small but common understanding, one can start asking more questions to get more hints to enlarge their shared knowledge pool. As repeating asking and replying, they can eventually reach an understanding of a common goal and start thinking of how they can solve the given problem by going through the same steps they have performed.

Considering the absence of the prior knowledge between a user and a target object, it is worth applying this Juba's semantic communication model to our problem to figure out relevant interaction semantics to be augmented. For that, we need to tune its computational model into our context. First, we need to define three main components, an intelligent individual with local knowledge base, a common goal to solve together, and communication procedures. Next thing to do is setting up assumptions which may help us take the first step. In our context, SemanticRadar in a user device or a target smart object is an intelligent individual with its local knowledge. In this definition, in order to focus on the communication steps, we assume our intelligent individuals are sharing a common language, which means they can at least communicate each other. The common goal to solve in our work is providing users with personalized interactions with a target object. For the communication procedures, since we assume the existence of common language between individuals, we can only focus on how they can leverage their local knowledge to decide what to ask and its answer.

4   Proposed Scheme

4.1   Overview

SemanticRadar has three components to extract placeness and find personalized interaction semantics as shown in Fig. 1. Placeness cloud, accumulates user interaction history at different locations in its Knowledge Base (KB). Then, the core service module, Placeness Inference Service, infers how people perceive that place and which interactions they usually do by leveraging the history data through a mediator module, Context Manager (CM) which loads and manages the stored history data. SemanticRadar on a user device is a personal mobile device with AR user interface. It captures every user interaction with a smart object and reports that interaction log to the cloud with the user profile such as age, gender in Context Manager (CM), and location information. When the user wants to interact with a target object, SemanticRadar extracts the placeness from the cloud and goes through the semantic communications with the target object to find personalized interaction semantics. During the semantic communications, the network sessions and stepwise procedures are managed by Semantic Communication Manager (SCM). SemanticRadar on a smart object provides users with interaction services. It accumulates which interaction and interface it served for each user profile and placeness before in its KB. By means of this knowledge base which is managed by Context Manager (CM), it infers which interaction interface should be given for a user by going through semantic communications

4.2   Extracting Placeness: Mining User Activity Context

When a user enters a certain location, he requests the placeness of the current location with his user profile to Placeness Cloud. Then, the cloud extracts the placeness from the collected experience data set. For this, we exploit the experiences of people who have been to the place and share similar profiles with a target user. This is based on the finding of Magnusson and Ekehammar such that people behave similarly in similar situations [20]. Thus, Placeness Cloud continuously logs experience data consisting of user profiles, interactions, other contexts, and location information with keywords extracted from the Internet as shown in Table 1. Since the placeness is diachronic and generalized for common users, Placeness Cloud select users in the cloud and co-located users, whose profiles are similar to a given user based on k-nearest neighbors algorithm [21], and analyze how they perceive the given location based on what interactions are frequently performed by them. For example, from Table 1, the cloud extracts 'workspace' as placeness from interaction experiences such as 'presentation' and 'system checking'. More detailed explanation can be found in [22].

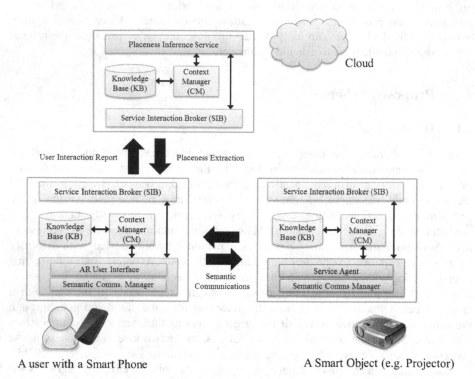

A user with a Smart Phone   A Smart Object (e.g. Projector)

Fig. 1. An Overall Architecture of SemanticRadar Framework and Participants

Table 1. Examples of User Interaction History Data

User			Interaction		Location
Age	Gender	Role	Interaction Type	Time	Place Characteristics
...	...	...	...	...	...
28	Male	Student	Presentation	2012.11.30 14:24 PM	Seminar Room = {seminar, presentation, smart environment, ...}
...	...	...	...	...	...
44	Male	Admin	System Checking	2012.12.17 9:14 AM	Seminar Room = {seminar, presentation, smart environment, ...}
53	Male	Student	Movie Watching	2013.1.4 10:15 PM	Seminar Room = {seminar, presentation, smart environment, ...}
...	...	...	...	...	...

4.3   Finding Personalized Interaction Semantics: Semantic Communication with a Target Object

When the user device gazes at a target object, it starts semantic communications with the target object to find a personalized interaction interface for the user's profile. Fig.2 describes messages exchanged in semantic communications between the user device and the target object through an example. In the example, a student enters a seminar room and extracts the placeness, 'Workspace' and 'Entertainment'. Out of various smart objects installed in the seminar room, as the user gazes at a projector with his smartphone, it starts semantic communication session with the target projector by sending a query about the possible interactions under the given placeness and its user profile. Then, based on the local interaction history, the projector infers interaction types, *Presentation*, *System Checking*, *Movie Watching*, etc., that similar users performed. When the user chooses an interaction, the user device requests the projector the interaction interface which is suitable for the received user profile. As the result, the information on how to visualize the interaction interface is replied and the user can start presenting a slide with the personalized projector interface.

5   Prototype Implementation

We implement SemanticRadar on top of smartphones running Android 4.2 and smart objects running Ubuntu Linux. We use Protégé 4.2 beta to design our ontology and Jena framework to host ontologies and handle SPARQL queries. For the user smartphone, we leverages androJena framework to handle semantics. To verify

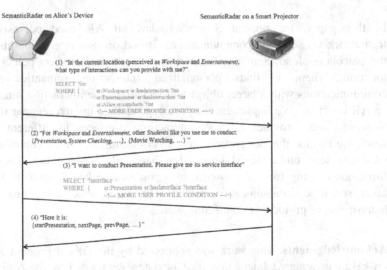

Fig. 2. Semantic Communications to Find Interaction Interfaces along with an Ontology Path

placeness-based personalized interaction support via semantic communications, we build a testbed [23] and install smart objects such as a smart projector, a smart curtain, LED lights, etc. powered by Beagle board-Xm. Fig. 3 depicts how SemanticRadar differentiates interaction interfaces of a target object, projector. The left side is the projector interface augmented for a Lecturer who wants to start a presentation, while the right side interface is for a Student who wants to watch a movie with the projector in the testbed. As shown in the picture, the presentation slide and projector controller interface is given for the Lecturer, while the video controller interface is given for the Student who wants to watch a movie. This final interface comes through the placeness extraction and the semantic communications. Fig. 4 shows how long it takes from the start of semantic communications to interface visualizations.

Fig. 3. Personalized Interaction Interfaces on User's AR device

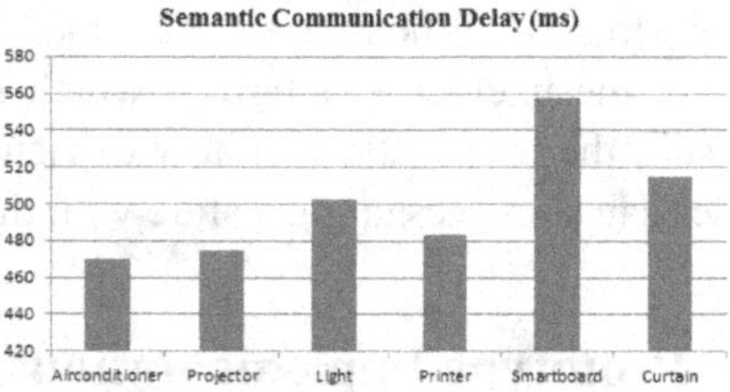

Fig. 4. Semantic Communications Delay (ms)

6   Conclusions and Future Work

In this paper, we present SemanticRadar, an AR-based pervasive interaction framework via semantic communications. Based on user interaction history mined in the placeness cloud, SemanticRadar extracts how similar users perceive the current location. Then, it finds personalized interaction semantics via semantic communications with a target object and visualizes the interaction semantics through an AR interface. We implement the prototype testbed upon a seminar room and show SemanticRadar provides different interaction interfaces to different users. In this work, we assume that our participants can communicate with a common protocol and they can lean on a shared knowledge base, placeness cloud. To overcome the limitation coming from the absence of a common protocol, we will design a cross-layer semantic communication protocol to incorporate with smart objects with heterogeneous protocols as our future work.

Acknowledgments. This work was supported by the Global Frontier R&D Program on <Human-centered Interaction for Coexistence> funded by the National Research Foundation of Korea grant funded by the Korean Government (MEST).

References

1. Feiner, S., MacIntyre, B., Seligmann, D.: Annotating the real world with knowledge-based graphics on a see-through head-mounted displa. In: Proceedings of the Conference on Graphics Interface 1992, pp. 78–85 (1992)
2. Google Glass, http://www.google.com/glass/start/
3. Weiser, M.: The computer for the 21st century. Scientific American 265, 94–104 (1991)
4. Nixon, L., And, B.N., And, J.G., And, G.R., Scicluna, J.: SmartReality: Integrating the Web into Augmented Reality. Proceedings of the I-SEMANTICS 2012, pp. 48–54 (2012)
5. Avilés-López, E., García-Macías, J.A.: Mashing up the Internet of Things: a framework for smart environments. EURASIP Journal on Wireless Communications and Networking 79 (2012)
6. García Macías, J.A., Alvarez-Lozano, J., Estrada, P., Aviles Lopez, E.: Browsing the Internet of Things with Sentient Visors. Computer 44, 46–52 (2011)
7. Ajanki, A., Billinghurst, M., Gamper, H., Järvenpää, T., Kandemir, M., Kaski, S., Koskela, M., Kurimo, M., Laaksonen, J., Puolamäki, K., Ruokolainen, T., Tossavainen, T.: An augmented reality interface to contextual information. Virtual Reality 15, 161–173 (2010)
8. Harrison, S., Dourish, P.: Re-place-ing space. In: Proceedings of the 1996 ACM Conference on Computer Supported Cooperative Work, CSCW 1996, pp. 67–76. ACM Press, New York (1996)
9. Hao, Q., Cai, R., Wang, C., Xiao, R., Yang, J.-M., Pang, Y., Zhang, L.: Equip tourists with knowledge mined from travelogues. In: Proceedings of the 19th International Conference on World Wide Web, WWW 2010, New York, USA, p. 401. ACM Press, New York (2010)
10. Adams, B., McKenzie, G.: Inferring Thematic Places from Spatially Referenced Natural Language Descriptions. In: Sui, D., Elwood, S., Goodchild, M. (eds.) Crowdsourcing Geographic Knowledge, pp. 201–221. Springer, Netherlands (2013)
11. Lee, R., Wakamiya, S., Sumiya, K.: Urban area characterization based on crowd behavioral lifelogs over Twitter. Personal and Ubiquitous Computing (2012)
12. Fukazawa, Y., Ota, J.: Automatic modeling of user's real world activities from the web for semantic IR. In: Proceedings of the 3rd International Semantic Search Workshop on SEMSEARCH 2010, pp. 1–9. ACM Press, New York (2010)
13. Abdelmoty, A.I., Smart, P., Jones, C.B.: Building place ontologies for the semantic web. In: Proceedings of the 4th ACM Workshop on Geographical Information Retrieval, GIR 2007, p. 7. ACM Press, New York (2007)
14. Antunes, B., Alves, A., Pereira, F.C.: Semantics of place: Ontology enrichment. In: Geffner, H., Prada, R., Machado Alexandre, I., David, N. (eds.) IBERAMIA 2008. LNCS (LNAI), vol. 5290, pp. 342–351. Springer, Heidelberg (2008)
15. Pereira, F.C., Alves, A., Oliveirinha, J., Biderman, A.: Perspectives on Semantics of the Place from Online Resources. In: 2009 IEEE International Conference on Semantic Computing, pp. 215–220. IEEE (2009)
16. Zheng, Y., Zhang, L., Xie, X., Ma, W.-Y.: Mining interesting locations and travel sequences from GPS trajectories. In: Proceedings of the 18th International Conference on World Wide Web, WWW 2009, p. 791. ACM Press, New York (2009)
17. Kirmse, A., Udeshi, T., Bellver, P., Shuma, J.: Extracting patterns from location history. In: Proceedings of the 19th ACM SIGSPATIAL International Conference on Advances in Geographic Information Systems, GIS 2011, p. 397. ACM Press, New York (2011)

18. Chon, Y., Lane, N.D., Li, F., Cha, H., Zhao, F.: Automatically characterizing places with opportunistic crowdsensing using smartphones. In: Proceedings of the 2012 ACM Conference on Ubiquitous Computing, UbiComp 2012, p. 481. ACM Press, New York (2012)
19. Juba, B., Sudan, M.: Universal semantic communication I. In: Proceedings of the Fourtieth Annual ACM Symposium on Theory of Computing, STOC 2008, p. 123. ACM Press, New York (2008)
20. Magnusson, D., Ekehammar, B.: Similar situations—Similar behaviors? Journal of Research in Personality 12, 41–48 (1978)
21. Cover, T., Hart, P.: Nearest neighbor pattern classification. IEEE Transactions on Information Theory 13, 21–27 (1967)
22. Kim, B., Kim, T., Lee, D., Hyun, S.J.: SpinRadar: A Spontaneous Service Provision Middleware for Place-aware Social Interactions. Personal and Ubiquitous Computing, 1–14 (2013)
23. Kim, B., Kim, T., Ko, H.-G., Lee, D., Hyun, S.J., Ko, I.-Y.: Personal Genie: A Distributed Framework for Spontaneous Interaction Support with Smart Objects in a Place. In: Proceeding of International Conference on Ubiquitous Information Management and Communication 2013, pp. 1–10 (2013)

Architecture for Organizing Context-Aware Data in Smart Home for Activity Recognition System

Konlakorn Wongpatikaseree, Junsoo Kim, Yoshiki Makino,
Azman Osman Lim, and Yasuo Tan

School of Information Science
Japan Advanced Institute of Science and Technology, Ishikawa, Japan 923-1211
{w.konlakorn,junsoo,m-yoshi,aolim,ytan}@jaist.ac.jp

Abstract. Knowing human activity in each day is relevant information
in several purposes. However, existing activity recognition systems have
limitation to identify the human activity because they cannot get the
appropriate information for recognition. To address this limitation, we
present three relevant components in Context-aware Activity Recognition Engine (CARE) architecture for organizing context-aware information in home. First, we introduce Context Sensor Network (CSN). The
CSN provides the raw environment information from the diversity of
sensors. Second, data manager component is proposed to process the
pre-processing in the raw data from the CSN. The data must be normalized and transformed in order to make the system more efficient. The last
component is system repository that composes of three essential tasks
for controlling the information in the system. In this paper, the ontology
based activity recognition (OBAR) system is used to evaluate the data
from proposed components. The high accuracy of results can refer to the
well organization of proposed components.

Keywords: Human activity, context-aware activity recognition engine,
ontology based activity recognition.

1 Introduction

Recently, the high technologies play vital roles to built a variety of the healthcare
system, especially in smart home. For example, home health care (HHC) system
[1] proposed to help the people gain the better health in the home. Nevertheless,
only home user's health condition might not enough for analysing and treatment
the disease because sometime home user might perform something that leads to
the disease, but home user does not know by himself or herself.

In that sense, human activity recognition system has been proposed to capture the human activity in each day. The physician or healthcare system can
utilize the results from the activity recognition system for diagnosis, treatment
or prevention the disease. However, to observe the human activity is not an easy
task because there is several environment information in home that we have to
consider such as home environment or human information. For sensing data in

N. Streitz and C. Stephanidis (Eds.): DAPI/HCII 2013, LNCS 8028, pp. 173–182, 2013.

the home, most of the researches have implemented the system that obtains the context information based on only single concept: body sensor network (BSN) or home sensor network (HSN). The system might get the imperfect data [2] if only one concept is developed. It can lead to occur the "Ambiguous activity problem". In this paper, we aim to improve the ability of activity recognition by proposing three relevant components in the Context-aware Activity Recognition Engine (CARE) architecture that can organize and provide the appropriate information for recognition the human activity.

The rest of paper is organized as follows: in section 2, we briefly describe related works on activity recognition area, especially in sensing data process. Then, we introduce the overview of CARE system architecture in section 3. Section 4, CSN proposes for collecting the environment information in home. After that, we present the way to normalize the data in section 5. In section 6, System repository component shows the process for controlling the information in the system. Next, in section 7, we demonstrate the experiment and results in this research. Finally, conclusion and future work are in section 8.

2   Background and Related Worked

Among of existing researches in activity recognition area, they have proposed several ways to identify the daily physical activity. Not only the classification process plays a vital role for recognition the human activity, but sensing data process is also relevant to collect the appropriate information. Thus, in this section, we will describe the existing techniques that used for sensing data in activity recognition system. Currently, there are three main sensing data techniques.

First, visual sensing technique has been proposed in the computer vision area. To perceive the information in this technique, high-resolution camera is mainly used for collecting the image or video files. Normally, there are two ways to perceive data: single viewpoint-based surveillance and multi viewpoint-based surveillance. In the single viewpoint-based surveillance, it is not difficult to design the system architecture because data from only one camera is used to recognize the human activity [3], but in the multi viewpoint-based surveillance method [4], it has the heavy task to perform the camera network for synchronisation the information between cameras. The information from distributed camera network can be used to identify the human in several purposes such as human action, human location, or travel time in each room. However, the privacy problem is the crucial problem for classification the human activity.

The rest two techniques for sensing data are BSN and HSN. The concept of BSN [5] is that attach the sensor on the human body for capturing the motion of human. Thus, system will perceive only the information from the human sensor. Nevertheless, only information from the human sensor might not enough to recognize some specific activities such as "Watching TV", or "Working on computer". The HSN has been proposed for solving in this problem. Diversity of sensors is embedded in the home facility for detecting the interaction between human and object. The system recognizes the human activities by monitoring,

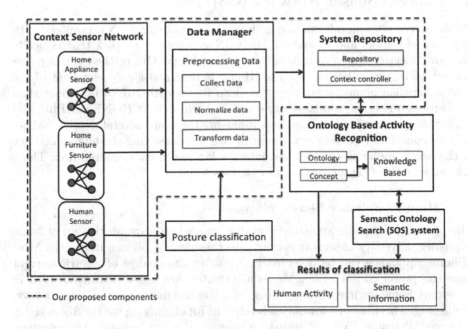

Fig. 1. CARE Architecture

which home facility is being used and how long user spends time on that facility [6]. However, the drawback of this technique is when several objects are activated in the same time. It leads the system classify several possible resultant activities.

3 CARE Architecture Overview

Until now, homes in 21st have embedded the ubiquitous system for different purposes. Sensing, managing, controlling the amount of data in smart home are a challenging task for organizing proper data before processing the activity recognition. According to the dis/advantage of sensing data techniques in section 2, designing the architecture is effected to the results of activity recognition system. In this section, we briefly describe the system architecture that used for organization the home information and human information for activity recognition. Figure. 1 presents a high-level of CARE architecture. In our proposed, there are tree main components for obtaining, managing, and controlling the data in CARE architecture. First, Context Sensor Network (CSN) observes the surrounding information in smart home, including human information (Section 4). Second, data manager normalizes the raw data from the CSN (Section 5). Last, system repository takes a responsibility to control the flow of data in the system (Section 6).

4   Context Sensor Network (CSN)

To obtain the relevant information in the real environment, CSN is proposed with diversity of sensors and protocols. The CSN is a sensor network that typically uses for collecting the context data in the smart home. Our testbed of this paper is establishing in an iHouse [7]. The iHouse is designed for development of the next-generation home network system. Two floors with 107.76 m^2, more than 250 sensors and home appliance are connected through ECHONET, UPnP, and Zigbee. Considering in the home environment, there are several details that we have to consider. Two of relevant information for classifying the human activity in the home are home environment information and human information. There are three kinds of sensor networks in CSN as followed:

4.1   Home Appliance Sensor Network

The main task of home appliance sensor network is to capture the use of home appliance. Diversity of sensors is built into the home appliance in iHouse. Most of home appliance can be detected by measure the change of electric current from the power consumption. Meanwhile, water-flow sensors are embedded in the smart home for monitoring the use of water appliance such as sink, shower, or flushing. This kind of information is relevant for classifying the specific activity such as "Watching TV", "Working on computer" or "Cooking". For example, we can know the user might performing the "Cooking" activity when the system recognize "Electric stove" is being used, or the system classify the activity as "Taking a bath" if the water-flow sensor detects the flow of water from the "Shower" object.

In our research, to transfer the data in home appliance sensor network, there are two protocols for sending the requested command to each sensor: ECHONET [8] and UPnP [9]. The ECHONET is an international home network protocol standard that is used to control, monitor, and gather information from equipment, and sensor. UPnP is used to make the requested command for monitoring the sensor status. An interval time is set to five seconds for sending the requested command.

4.2   Home Furniture Sensor Network

Apart from the home appliances, we still need to consider other home environment, such as "Sofa", "Bed", or "Broom" object. Normally, the object in this sensor network can be divided into two cases. First is the direct purpose object. That means the object can infer to only one activity. For example, "Broom" object can be used only for "Sweeping the floor" activity. Second is the multi-purpose object. There is some home furniture in home that the user uses in several purposes. For example, home user uses "Sofa" object for sitting and watching TV, or lying down on the "Sofa" for relaxing.

This kind of home furniture information can compose with the home appliance information for performing the specific activity. For example, if "Computer" object is turned on, it does not means that user performing "Working on computer"

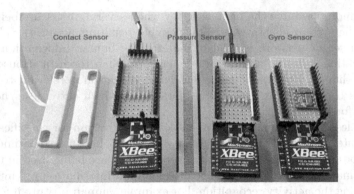

Fig. 2. Arduino Fio with external board and sensor

activity. Normally, user tends to sit on the "Chair" for "Working on computer". In this paper, pressure sensor, gyro sensor, and magnetic sensor are deployed and attached on the home furniture. For example, pressure sensors are attached on the "Bed" object to detect the "Bed" is being used or not. Gyro sensor is attached on the home furniture that has movement such as "Broom", "Mop", or "Coffee bottle". Magnetic sensor is used for the item that has open-close property such as "Cupboard".

Nevertheless, we cannot utilize the ECHONET protocol for transmission the data same as home appliance sensor network because most of the home furnitures are not in the international home network protocol standard. In this sensor network, we select the Arudino board [10] for sensing the home furniture data. There are two basic module in this sensor network: sensor node and coordinator. For the sensor node, we have selected the Arudino Fio as a microcontroller board based on the ATmega328P. Arduino Fio is connected with pressure sensor, gyro sensor, and magnetic sensor via external board, shown in Fig. 2. Arduino Fio also allows the developer to program it wirelessly, over a pair of XBee radio. Therefore, we emulated the Zigbee protocol for transmission the data between home furniture sensor and server. For the coordinator side, Arduino Ethernet is developed belonging to Xbee shield. The Xbee shield allows an Arduino board to communicate wirelessly using Zigbee. At this stage, the coordinator node will collect data from sensor node via Zigbee protocol and transmit to server via Ethernet cable. Each coordinator node will be placed on the conner of each room. Therefore, system will perceive where the data is come from based on the "Coordinator id" and "Sensor id".

4.3   Human Sensor Network

Normally, only the home environment data might not enough to conform the user's context for classifying the human activity. It can lead to the "Ambiguous activity problem" when using only home environment data. For example, if we consider only object activation to perform the activity recognition system, the system cannot guarantee the high accuracy when several object are being used. It makes the system generated several possible resultant activities. Therefore, the human sensor network is used to monitor the human information such as human location. Infrared sensors are deployed in each room in iHouse for detecting the human location. The current human location is relevant to activity recognition because it can give useful hints about which activities s/he can or cannot perform.

Nonetheless, using human location and object activation for classification are still encountering the "Ambiguous activity problem" because sometime human location does not hint any activities if several objects are being used in the same current human location. Recently, the other human information are introduced for improving the activity recognition. For example, human posture information is utilized with the common user's context (object activation and human location) [11]. It shows the advantage to reduce the "Ambiguous activity problem" when using human posture. To obtain human posture in CARE architecture, range-based algorithm [12] is proposed to classify the human posture based on a range between body parts. The devices that are capable to measure the distance between sensors are used in this architecture.

5   Data Manager

According to the CSN, there are several environment data in home that the system have to obtain because several objects in the home can infer to the human activity. Not only the amount of data in smart home is effect to the system, but also the perfect of data. Although the system can obtain the data from the diversity of sensor, it still suffers with missing data or noise from the sensor. There are particular problems in data when due with hardware. Therefore, data manager component aim to normalize data before send to the system repository.

There are two techniques to normalize the raw data from the CSN. Firstly, supply missing data function is developed for solving the missing data problem. The supply missing data function will find and add the suitable data for making the user's context perfectly. For example, the system cannot perceive the human location from the infrared sensor if the user has little movement. In this case, the supply missing data function will retrieve the last human location instead the current human location for making the completed user's context. Second, eliminate data function is the relevant function to cut the unexpected data or noise from the sensor. The unexpected data problem can make the result of recognition changed easily. In this paper, we apply the threshold technique in eliminate data function. The lower bound is set for filtering the noise in some circumstances. For example, normally, although we turn off the TV but plugging, the sensor still detect a little electric current from TV. It can make the system decide that TV is being used. The result might be changed easily if there is this kind of noise.

6   System Repository

To control the data in the CARE architecture, the system repository play an important role to control data flow between system repository and OBAR, illustrated in Fig. 3. The system repository can be divided into two modules. First, repository is the module that takes a responsibility to keep the normalized data from the data manager, and also store the temporal reasoning from the OBAR. Second, context controller module has a duty to control all of data in the system. There are three main tasks in context controller:

- **Mapping Data:** Based on CARE architecture, ontology concept is used to explicit the huge information from the variety of sensors. In this research, the ontology concept is described in the abstract level. The ontology application management framework [13] is adopted to map between the properties concept in ontology and the data in the repository. However, we cannot use a relational database through this step directly. We need to transform the relational database to resource description framework (RDF) for interchange the data on the web.
- **Composition Data:** The necessary information in the repository will be conform to the user's context. In one user's context, system can know various kind of semantic information such as object activation, human location, time or human posture. The user's context will be served as the input data in OBAR. Every one minute, system will conform the user's context for classifying the human activity.
- **Reprocessing Data:** According to the original idea of ontology concept, it does not support the temporal reasoning. In this task, we implement the external java program to keep tracking the temporal reasoning. Then the temporal reasoning will be collected in the repository, and it is sent to the inference method for the next classification. This information is vital useful when system lacks data to classify the human activity.

7   Experiment and Results

7.1   Ontology Based Activity Recognition (OBAR)

To evaluate the organization's performance of the three proposed components, we implemented the OBAR [11] for inference the human activity based on data from proposed components. In this section, we will describe the workflow of OBAR briefly. There are two parts of OBAR: ontology modeling and recognition engine. For modeling the human activity, the ontology concept is used to explicit the semantic information in smart home. There are two main ontologies models. First, the context-aware infrastructure ontology is designed for definition the surrounding information in smart home. Second, the activity log ontology is used to identify the historical information. As describe in section 6, these two ontologies will be mapped with the repository by context controller.

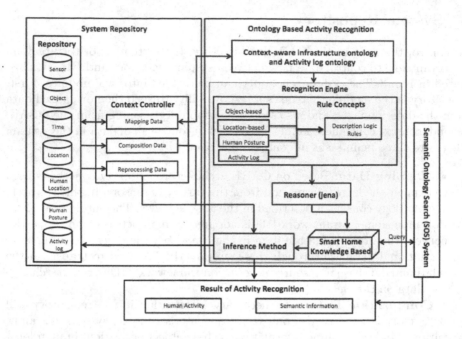

Fig. 3. Data flow between system repository and OBAR

Recognition engine is the core of OBAR to classify the human activity. Normally, the ontology concept does not have the ability to classify the human activity. Description logic (DL) rules are established for supporting inference and reasoning. To create the DL rules, object activation, human location, human posture, and activity log are used to create the DL rules. The example below indicates the DL rule for "Washing dishes" activity.

$Wash\ dishes \sqsubseteq Functional\ Activity$
$\sqsubseteq Kitchen\ Activity$
$\sqcap\ use(Object.Furniture(Sink))$
$\sqcap\ Object.Human.Current\_location(kitchen)$
$\sqcap\ HumanPosture(Stand)$
$\sqcap\ LastActivity.Kitchen\ Activity(Eating\ or\ drinking)$

After that, the built-in reasoner is implemented for computing the DL rules for the new knowledge and collect into the smart home knowledge based. Inference method has a responsibility to check the data from the composition data that consistent with the knowledge in smart home knowledge based or not. The system will give the results if user's context is consistent with the rule in smart home knowledge based. After that, the system will keep the results of classification into the repository for processing in the next classification.

Table 1. Recognition accuracy of OBAR

Activity	Accuracy	Other possible resultant activities
A_1 = Working on computer	92.25 %	A_2 (6.90 %), A_7 (0.42 %), A_{14} (0.43 %)
A_2 = Watching TV	97.94 %	A_{14} (2.06 %)
A_3 = Reading a book	100 %	-
A_4 = Scrubbing the floor	93.75 %	A_{14} (6.25 %)
A_5 = Sweeping the floor	96.67 %	A_{14} (3.33 %)
A_6 = Sitting on the toilet	93.75 %	A_1 (2.08), A_{14} (4.17 %)
A_7 = Taking a bath	100 %	-
A_8 = Lying down & relaxing	100 %	-
A_9 = Sleeping	91.86 %	A_3 (3.49 %), A_{14} (4.65 %)
A_{10} = Making coffee	100 %	-
A_{11} = Cooking	86.21 %	A_{14} (13.79 %)
A_{12} = Eating or drinking	100 %	-
A_{13} = Washing dishes	100 %	-
A_{14} = Idle	100 %	-

7.2 Results and Discussion

Table 1 illustrates the recognition accuracy in 14 activities. The recognition accuracy of OBAR exhibits the organization's performance of proposed components. Although OBAR can achieve the high accuracy with 96.6 %, it still has problems that make the OBAR classify incorrect results.

The delay of sensor in CSN and the interval time for composition data in system repository (composition data task) are not synchronized. The strange result ("Taking a bath" activity) in the "Working on computer" is the outstanding example that shows the asynchronous problem. Since when sensor is activated, it will be delayed one minute for sensing the next status while the context controller will compose the user's context every one minute. Consequently, it is possible that the user already changes the activity, but the system still using the old information for classification. To address these shortcoming, in the future work, the interval time for composition data should have to have the adaptive function to adjust the interval time for composition the data for recognition the human activity.

8 Conclusion

In this paper, we proposed the three components in CARE architecture that use for organizing context-aware data in smart home. First, we introduced the CSN that used to observe the surrounding information in the smart home. Three kinds of sensor networks are proposed for collecting the object activation and human information via diversity of sensors and protocols. Second, data manager component is presented for normalizing the data. This component is helpful for the system to make the complete data. Supplying missing data function and eliminate noisy data function are implemented for providing the appropriate data to the system repository. Last, system repository is exhibited the vital role to control the huge of data in the system. Based on the real data from these three components, the OBAR can achieve the high recognition accuracy with 96.60 %. Even though the results cannot exactly conclude that proposed components make the high recognition accuracy, it demonstrates that proposed components can provide the appropriate information for the classification.

References

[1] Takahashi, S., Maeda, S., Tsuruta, N., Morimoto, T.: A home health care system for elderly people. In: Proceedings of the 7th Korea-Russia International Symposium on Science and Technology, KORUS 2003, Pohang, vol. 2, pp. 97–102 (July 2003)

[2] Henricksen, K., Indulska, J.: Modelling and using imperfect context information. In: Proceedings of the Second IEEE Annual Conference on Pervasive Computing and Communications Workshops, Washhington, DC, pp. 33–37 (March 2004)

[3] Ben-Arie, J., Wang, Z., Pandit, P., Rajaram, S.: Human activity recognition using multidimensional indexing. IEEE Transactions on Pattern Analysis and Machine Intelligence 24(8), 1091–1104 (2002)

[4] Fiore, L., Fehr, D., Bodor, R., Drenner, A., Somasundaram, G., Papanikolopoulos, N.: Multi-camera human activity monitoring. Journal of Intelligent and Robotic System 52(1), 5–43 (2008)

[5] Maurer, U., Smailagic, A., Siewiorek, D., Deisher, M.: Activity recognition and monitoring using multiple sensors on different body positions. In: International Workshop on Wearable and Implantable Body Sensor Networks, Boston, pp. 113–116 (April 2006)

[6] Zhang, S.S., McClean, Scotney, B., Chaurasia, P., Nugent, C.: Using duration to learn activities of daily living in a smart home environment. In: 4th International Conference on Pervasive Computing Technologies for Healthcare (PervasiveHealth), Munich, pp. 1–8 (March 2010)

[7] Tan, Y.: Home Network Technologies for Smart Houses. Impress R&D (2011) (in Japanese)

[8] Matsumoto, S.: Echonet: A home network standard. IEEE Pervasive Computing 9(3), 88–92 (2010)

[9] Kim, K.S., Park, C., Seo, K.S., Chung, I.Y., Lee, J.: Zigbee and the upnp expansion for home network electrical appliance control on the internet. In: The 9th International Conference on Advanced Communication Technology, Gangwon-Do, vol. 3, pp. 1857–1860 (February 2007)

[10] Arduino, http://www.arduino.cc (accessed: February 18, 2013)

[11] Wongpatikaseree, K., Ikeda, M., Buranarach, M., Supnithi, T., Lim, A., Tan, Y.: Activity recognition using context-aware infrastructure ontology in smart home domain. In: Seventh International Conference on Knowledge, Information and Creativity Support Systems (KICSS), Melbourne, pp. 50–57 (November 2012)

[12] Wongpatikaseree, K., Lim, A., Tan, Y., Kanai, H.: Range-based algorithm for posture classification and fall-down detection in smart homecare system. In: IEEE 1st Global Conference on Consumer Electronics (GCCE), Tokyo, pp. 243–247 (October 2012)

[13] Buranarach, M., Thein, Y., Supnithi, T.: A community-driven approach to development of an ontology-based application management framework. In: The 2nd Joint International Semantic Technology Conference (JIST), Nara (December 2012)

A Context-Aware Middleware for Interaction Device Deployment in AmI

Tao Xu, Huiliang Jin, Bertrand David, René Chalon, and Yun Zhou

Université de Lyon, CNRS,
Ecole Centrale de Lyon, LIRIS, UMR5205
{tao.xu,huiling.jin,bertrand.david,rene.chalon,
yun.zhou}@ec-lyon.fr

Abstract. Miniaturization of smart devices and sensors, as well as widespread use of new interaction modalities make Ambient Intelligence (AmI) not a prospect for the future but an impending reality of existence. This requires methods for solving the issues on how to integrate interaction devices into a context-aware environment. We thus designed a middleware to provide a promising approach. Our middleware adopts a two-layer structure. The low layer is the enterprise service bus, which is in charge of integrating context sensors and interaction devices, and of discovering context. The high layer is the versatile context interpreter, which is responsible for context inference, expressive query, and persistent storage. Finally, we implemented the prototype of this middleware on the street and store marketing scenario.

Keywords: Middleware, Context Awareness, Ambient Intelligence, Human Computer Interaction.

1 Introduction

20 years ago, Marc Weiser formulated the prospect of computers in the 21st century, and proposed the pioneering notion of ubiquitous computing. Many aspects of his visions have already become reality in the past two decades. Furthermore, one of his primary ideas has recently evolved to a more general paradigm known as Ambient Intelligence (AmI). This defines an interaction between users and a context-aware environment, which adapts its behaviors intelligently to users' preferences and habits so as to facilitate and enhance users' life [2]. Going one step further, the AmI focus augments ubiquitous computing with additional requirements for natural interaction and context-awareness [2].

Human-Computer interaction (HCI), and context awareness, as two standalone core concepts of AmI, play important roles in this research area respectively. Context awareness suggests that systems could adapt their functionality to a user's activity and situation in the environment [3]. Context-aware systems, on the other hand, are concerned with acquisition of context, abstraction and understanding of context, and application behaviors based on the recognized context [16].

N. Streitz and C. Stephanidis (Eds.): DAPI/HCII 2013, LNCS 8028, pp. 183–192, 2013.
© Springer-Verlag Berlin Heidelberg 2013

HCI involves the study, planning, and design of interaction between people (users) and computers. The emergence of proxemic interaction provides a possibility for fusion of two technologies (HCI and Context Awareness), which takes spatial relationships into consideration and extends the traditional interaction from the binary relationship (computer and human) to the context-aware environment [4]. More and more researchers are taking into account the intersection part of HCI and Context awareness to enable users to interact more naturally in pervasive environments. Our team has been working on the user interface related to augmented reality in HCI for many years and has proposed three innovative user interfaces [7]. One of these is the in-environment interface (IEI) [21] [22], meaning that the environment provides all interaction support including input and output devices, as well as environment dependent information. Furthermore, more issues and challenges face researchers than ever before. Programmers need an enhanced platform integrating various sensors and actuators and interaction technologies in order to propose an appropriate and up-to-date HCI according to observed environment behavior. We propose a context-aware middleware for interaction device deployment (CMID) in AmI, based on MOCOCO principles (MObility, COntextualization and COoperation) [6]. CMID takes into account multi-modal interaction technologies (hand gestures, marks, large-scale body movements, etc.) in relation with users' AmI environment context.

In the remainder of this paper, an AmI situation scenario is presented allowing contextualizing following a technical explanation. Then, several aspects of our middleware are explained starting with a low layer based on an ESB (Enterprise Service Bus), in charge of communicating in standard manner with in-environment sensors and actuators and of managing their dynamic discovery. The next step is a description of a high layer called the VCI (Versatile Context Interpreter), providing higher and semantic data interpretations. The general structure and main components of the VCI are described and related to our scenario. Finally, the paper ends with the conclusion and future work.

2   Street and Store Marketing Scenario (SSM)

Up-to-date ubiquitous computing with in-environment distributed sensors, actuators and user interface devices are able to create an Ambient Intelligence environment in a shopping area. The main goal is to detect potential shoppers and propose them appropriate goods, i.e. goods in relation with their shopping profiles and identified present needs. To allow this, we need first to capture potential consumer presence by appropriate sensor(s), then to study his/ her profile and determine what kind of information it seems appropriate to present him/ her with in order to intercept his/ her attention. The first stage in this capture process occurs in the street. Data collected by the sensors provide the system with information about the potential consumer, data that can be more or less precise: a young man or woman at least, or a store regular client, etc. In relation with this profile, the system could display in the shop window an appropriate advertisement. In the shop window display, it seems important to display advertising information not only for one passer-by and potential client but for several. Display strategy can be organized by applying the proxemic user interface policy i.e. give more information to shop windows near located client(s) and less to distant ones. It may prove interesting to take two additional behaviors into account: in-shop continuation of consumer tracking, in order to provide more precise information in relation to his/ her movement in the store and also in-the-street movement, in-the-street walking and shop window watching. In the first case, increasingly detailed information can be given to the potential consumer in relation with his/ her location in the store (suit, shirt, pants department, or kitchen furniture department) with detailed knowledge of his situation (just married, etc.). The system can collect, store and use the information collected from previous purchases in the store or elsewhere (his/ her Facebook profile). In the second situation (in-the-street walking) it could be interesting to propagate the discovered profile of the potential consumer to other stores to allow them to use this information to provide him/ her with increasingly detailed and appropriate advertising.

3   CMID

Context-aware applications are becoming increasingly prevalent and can be found in the areas of wearable computing, intelligent environments, context-sensitive interfaces, etc. [10]. A now generally accepted definition of context is given by Dey and Abowd [1]: "Any information that can be used to characterize the situation of an entity. An entity is a person, place, or object that is considered relevant to the interaction between a user and an application, including the user and application themselves". The context-aware system is defined as the system that uses context to provide relevant information and/or services to the user, where relevancy depends on the user's task.

Development of context-aware applications is inherently complex. These applications adapt to change context information: physical context, computational context, and user context/tasks [4]. To reach this aim, it needs to integrate all sensors, actuators, communication objects and computing devices into the system. Low-level mechanisms and drivers are necessary. Then, either we have to create only one standalone application within which high-level context reasoning takes place, or we propose a set of applications or a system and propose to create an application-independent common high-level of contextualization making it possible to collect, process, interpret and propagate information with the context model and reasoning mechanisms [20].

To implement this more in-depth approach of context-aware services in AmI, we designed a context-aware middleware, organized in two layers: the low layer is an Enterprise Service Bus, which provides a solution to integrate sensors and actuators with a standardized data representation and unified standard interface to achieve the core functions of service interaction: service registry, service discovery and service consumption.

The versatile context interpreter is our high layer, which is in charge of context inferences, expressive query, and persistent storage. Detailed information will be provided in the following sections.

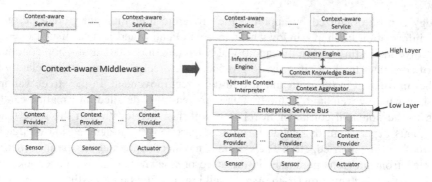

Fig. 1. Two context-aware architectures

3.1   Enterprise Service Bus

An enterprise service bus is a software architecture model used for designing and implementing interaction and communication between mutually interacting software applications in a service-oriented architecture (SOA). ESB allows services to be easily plugged in and out of the network without impact on other components and without the need to restart the system or even stop running applications. It is centered on a bus which provides a common backbone through which services can interoperate with a standardized format of data representation. In our paper, the context provider is the service used to obtain context from sensors, the web or other sources, and dispatch commands to actuators. ESB provides a unified standard interface to achieve the core functions of service interaction: service registry, dynamic service discovery, and service consumption. ESB also integrates interaction devices and a set of APIs for different interaction modalities to support development of interaction approaches.

3.2   Versatile Context Interpreter

The versatile context interpreter (VCI) is a high layer of context-aware middleware, as shown in Fig.1, made up of four parts: Context Aggregator, Inference Engine, Context Knowledge Base, and Query Engine. It leverages ESB basic services results to deliver and manage context-aware views and interpretations in order to deliver high-level information to the application. It adopts an ontology-based approach for context modeling and interpretation. Before detailing the description of other parts of the versatile context interpreter, the context model is introduced.

Ontology-Based Context Model

A context model, as a fundamental part of the context-aware system, aims at defining and storing context data in a machine processing form [3]. To develop a flexible and useable context model that covers the wide range of possible contexts is a challenging task [18]. We adopt the ontology-based context model to construct our context-aware middleware. For us, ontology is a reference model for components and behaviors of context [19]. The ontology-based model has a large number of good features for developing the context-aware system, such as knowledge sharing, knowledge reuse, logic inference, etc. In particular logic inference enables the application using directly the deduced high-level context information.

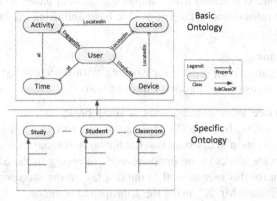

Fig. 2. Context expression ontology

We employ a hierarchical structure to describe the user's situation and circumstance based on Web Ontology Language (OWL) [9], which is an ontology markup language adopted by W3C as standard for semantic web. The structure is shown in Fig.2. The basic model defines generic conceptions and relationships in AmI, which come up with a basic context structure. It has five interrelated basic classes: user, location, time, activity, and device, which represent who, where, when, what activities, and devices; seven properties (relationships) between classes are identified. General context-aware ontology can be completed and upgraded by more precise information related to a particular application or application area. In our case, the general context-aware model for AmI context-aware systems is considered as the basic model. For a new application area such as the "Street and store marketing" application (SSM application), we propose a more precise and specific context-aware model. According to our build methodology, Fig.3, the general context-aware model is developed as the whole system by CMID designers and developers. The "Street and store marketing" application is developed in the scope of the CMID system by application developers. Most recent adaptation options can be implemented directly and dynamically during the application by the system (and its reasoning on collected data) or by the users (experienced users).

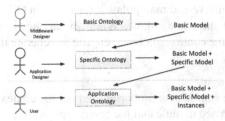

Fig. 3. Different contributors in the context-aware system

According to different context sources, we divide context into two categories: the low-level context and the high-level context. Context that can be extracted directly from sensors and devices such as location, time etc. is considered as low-level context. High-level context is issued from inference treatment based on low-level context data and semantic rules stored in the knowledge base and using the inference engine.

Context Aggregator

The context aggregator is responsible for working with basic contextual data collected by ESB to carry out fusion and fission of information:

1. The fusion service aims at integrating several basic data to discover high-level semantic information. In our SSM application, we can group the current date and the user's identification to discover that his birthday is today.
2. The fission service works in the opposite way, allowing in the SSM application a special discount for this user as well as the display on the shop window of the message "Happy birthday Mr. X", using the appropriate actuator.

Context Knowledge Base

The context knowledge base provides persistent storage for context through the use of relational databases, as well as supplying a set of library procedures for other components to query and modify context knowledge. We adopted the aforementioned ontology-based context model to build the environment and the user model. The ontology-based context model paves the way for the inference engine. The entire context is stored as the triple pattern.

In relation with different sources, the context is divided into three categories: pre-defined context, detected context and inferred context. Pre-defined context refers to context expressed in the application context model elaborated by application designers, such as user's profile context and specific environment context. Detected context is obtained from sensors as well as low-level context Inferred context is determined from collected data and knowledge rules by inference engine, and is considered as high-level context.

Context Query Engine

The context query engine has two main tasks:

1. Handle queries from the application: it supports SPARQL, which is an RDF query language, able to retrieve and manipulate data stored in OWL.
2. Invoke the context inference engine. When the application needs high-level context, it will invoke the context inference engine to generate the inferred context.

Context Inference Engine

The context inference engine is an important part of the context-aware system. It consists of the basic inference module and the predictive module.

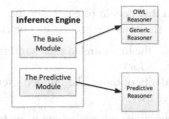

Fig. 4. Different inference engines and their use

The basic inference module is made up of Web Ontology language (OWL) Reasoner and Generic Reasoner. It focuses on checking context consistency and determining high-level context from low-level context. Consistency checking of the context model is an important action, activated by the CMID developer when he modifies the context-aware basic model. Generic Reasoner is activated by high-level middleware at each transaction between ESB and the context aggregator

OWL has a built-in reasoner based on the description logic. The reasoner can fulfill the essence of logical requirements, which comprises concept satisfiability, class subsumption, class consistency, and instance checking.

Generic Reasoner offers a more flexible alternative. It adopts first order logic, which is more powerful than description logic. The application developer can freely define the rules for the specific situation. It is interpreted by an example in Fig. 5. Generic Reasoner is used to infer high-level context. Once the basic inference module is invoked, the knowledge base should be updated accordingly.

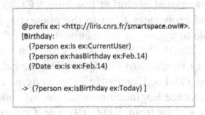

```
@prefix ex: <http://liris.cnrs.fr/smartspace.owl#>.
[Birthday:
    (?person ex:is ex:CurrentUser)
    (?person ex:hasBirthday ex:Feb.14)
    (?Date  ex:is ex:Feb.14)

-> (?person ex:isBirthday ex:Today) ]
```

Fig. 5. An example of a rule

Predictive Reasoner comes up with the available recommended information for the application according to analyzed users' previous activity. It has two main tasks: one is to provide users' recommended information based on users' previous behavior, while the other is to provide the proper interaction modality based on other users' selections.

We employ the classic decision tree algorithm (C4.5) to provide a recommended choice based on the training data set of users' activities [12]. This algorithm offers a fast and powerful method for different cases. In SSM, it can recommend the favorite style of clothes for clients approaching the shop window by analyzing this client's previous purchases.

We adopt the collaborative filtering algorithm to provide the proper interaction modality based on other users' previous selection. The motivation for collaborative filtering is based on the idea that people often obtain the best recommendation from someone with similar tastes. The common process can be reduced to two steps:

1. Look for users who share the like-minded user's information with the active user (the user whom the prediction is for).

2. Use the interaction modality of those like-minded users found in step 1 to give a recommendation for the active user.

In SSM, this provides the appropriate interaction input modality (hand gesture) by user situation (distance between user and screen, number of users in front of the screen).

CMID Behavior Workflow

To summarize our proposal of a user-centric context-ware middleware for interaction device deployment (CMID system), we comment on the global workflow as shown in Fig.8: in the overall architecture we have 3 main components: an application layer with high level context-aware services related to the application, a high level middleware called VCI (Versatile Context Interpreter), and a low level middleware based on an ESB (Enterprise Service Bus). As stated earlier, two levels of behavior and their modeling are supported: a basic level related to general problems of AmI and context modeling, and a more specific level related to an application area. In particular, the application layer informs the VCI layer of the application area to take into account, while the ESB layer is mainly application area independent. With this in mind, the overall workflow functions as follows: (1) The application must inform the VCI of the context (specific model) to use. This model will be used by the Inference Engine, Query Engine, Context KB, and Context Aggregator. (2) Application Context Aware Services ask to receive contextual evolution from the VCI. (3) ESB collects the data from different sensors and propagates them to the context aggregator. (4) When the Context Aggregator is able to aggregate the received data, it does so, and places them in KDZ (Knowledge Data Zone). (5) Arrival of new data in KDZ generates the notification to the Context Query Engine. (6) The Query Engine calls on Context Inference to apply context inference. (7) The Context Inference engine introduces inferred data to KDZ. (8) When the Inference Engine terminates the inference process, the Context Query Engine collects new data from KDZ. (9) The Context Query Engine sends these data to the application. (10) The application context-aware services can also decide to update actuator states. They send new data to the Context aggregator which, using the Fission service, propagates the data to the appropriate actuator using ESB.

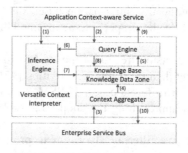

Fig. 6. CMID behavior workflow

4   Related Works

A large number of context-aware middleware has been proposed in the literature. Gaia [12] provides a distributed middleware infrastructure that coordinates software entities and heterogeneous networked devices contained in a physical space. Aura [17] comes up with services for managing tasks, and contexts for ubiquitous computing applications. SOCAM [8] has used an ontology-based model to represent the real environment, which provides efficient support for acquiring, discovering, interpreting and accessing various contexts to build context-aware services. MiddleWhere [13] is a distributed middleware infrastructure for location that separates applications from location detection technologies, utilizes probabilistic reasoning techniques to resolve conflicts, and determines the location of people given different sensor data. While these context-ware middleware provide several promising solutions for context awareness, they have not taken interaction modalities into account.

5   Conclusion and Future works

We have designed and implemented CMID, a user-centric context-ware middleware for interaction device deployment in AmI. This provides a platform associated with service discovery, mobility, environmental changes, and context retrieval. Besides the aforementioned features, it also integrates multi-modal interaction technologies (hand gestures, marks, large-scale body movements, etc.) and takes the user's context into consideration for extending the physical interactive environment to AmI. However, our context-aware middleware does not take into account the problem of users' privacy. When interacting in ubiquitous environments, protection of user's privacy is also a major problem. We will try to improve our middleware on this field to make it both intelligent and safe.

References

1. Abowd, G.D., et al.: Towards a Better Understanding of Context and Context-Awareness. In: Proceedings of the 1st International Symposium on Handheld and Ubiquitous Computing, pp. 304–307. Springer, London (1999)
2. Athanasopoulos, D., et al.: CoWSAMI: Interface-aware context gathering in ambient intelligence environments. Pervasive Mob. Comput. 4(3), 360–389 (2008)
3. Baldauf, M., et al.: A survey on context-aware systems. Int. J. Ad Hoc Ubiquitous Comput. 2(4), 263–277 (2007)
4. Ballendat, T., et al.: Proxemic interaction: designing for a proximity and orientation-aware environment. In: ACM International Conference on Interactive Tabletops and Surfaces, pp. 121–130. ACM, New York (2010)
5. Bettini, C., et al.: A survey of context modelling and reasoning techniques. Pervasive and Mobile Computing 6(2), 161–180 (2010)

6. David, B.T., Chalon, R.: IMERA: Experimentation Platform for Computer Augmented Environment for Mobile Actors. In: IEEE International Conference on Wireless and Mobile Computing, Networking and Communication, p. 51. IEEE Computer Society, Los Alamitos (2007)

7. López De Ipiña, D., et al.: EMI 2 lets: A Reflective Framework for Enabling AmI. J. UCS (2008)

8. Gu, T., et al.: A middleware for building context-aware mobile services. In: 2004 IEEE 59th Vehicular Technology Conference, VTC 2004, vol. 5, pp. 2656–2660 (Spring 2004)

9. Gu, T., et al.: Toward an OSGi-Based Infrastructure for Context-Aware Applications. IEEE Pervasive Computing 3(4), 66–74 (2004)

10. Krumm, J. (ed.): Ubiquitous Computing Fundamentals. Chapman and Hall/CRC (2009)

11. Lukowicz, P., et al.: From Context Awareness to Socially Aware Computing. IEEE Pervasive Computing 11(1), 32–41 (2012)

12. Quinlan, J.R.: C4.5: programs for machine learning. Morgan Kaufmann Publishers Inc., San Francisco (1993)

13. Ranganathan, A., et al.: MiddleWhere: a middleware for location awareness in ubiquitous computing applications. In: Proceedings of the 5th ACM/IFIP/USENIX International Conference on Middleware, pp. 397–416. Springer-Verlag New York, Inc., New York (2004)

14. Román, M., et al.: Gaia: A Middleware Infrastructure to Enable Active Spaces. IEEE Pervasive Computing 1, 74–83 (2002)

15. Schilit, B., Theimer, M.: Disseminating Active Map Information to Mobile Hosts. IEEE Network 8, 22–32 (1994)

16. Schmidt, A., et al.: There is more to Context than Location. Computers and Graphics 23, 893–901 (1998)

17. Sousa, J.P., et al.: Aura: an architectural framework for user mobility in ubiquitous computing environments. In: Proceedings of the 3rd Working IEEE/IFIP Conference on Software Architecture, pp. 29–43. Kluwer Academic Publishers (2002)

18. Stojanovic, D.: Context-Aware Mobile and Ubiquitous Computing for Enhanced Usability: Adaptive Technologies and Applications (Premier Reference Source). Information Science Reference (2009)

19. Wang, X.H., et al.: Ontology Based Context Modeling and Reasoning using OWL. In: Proceedings of the Second IEEE Annual Conference on Pervasive Computing and Communications Workshops, pp. 18–23. IEEE Computer Society Press, Washington, DC (2004)

20. Xu, T., et al.: A context-aware middleware for ambient intelligence. In: Proceedings of the Workshop on Posters and Demos Track, pp. 10:1–10:2. ACM, New York (2011)

21. Zhou, Y., David, B., Chalon, R.: Innovative user interfaces for wearable computers in real augmented environment. In: Jacko, J.A., et al. (eds.) Human-Computer Interaction, Part II, HCII 2011. LNCS, vol. 6762, pp. 500–509. Springer, Heidelberg (2011)

22. Zhou, Y., et al.: PlayAllAround: Wearable One-hand Gesture Input and Scalable Projected Interfaces. Presented at the ERGO-IHM 2012, Biarritz (2012)

Part III

Design and Evaluation of Smart and Intelligent Environments

How Does User Feedback to Video Prototypes Compare to that Obtained in a Home Simulation Laboratory?

Prina Bajracharya, Thelxi Mamagkaki, Alexandra Pozdnyakova,
Mariana Viera da Fonseca Serras Pereira, Tetiana Zavialova, Tin de Zeeuw,
Pavan Dadlani, and Panos Markopoulos

Eindhoven University of Technology, Department of Industrial Design,
5600 MB Eindhoven, The Netherlands
{prina.bajracharya,thelxi,tanya.zavyalova,mserraspereira,
t.dezeeuw}@gmail.com, alexpozdnyakova@yandex.ru,
pavan.dadlani@philips.com, p.markopoulos@tue.nl

Abstract. This paper compares the user feedback obtained from viewing a video prototype of a domestic Ambient Intelligence application called MatchMaker to that obtained by evaluating the user experience in a home simulation laboratory. The video was reverse engineered, from the final application to ensure that it provides a valid representation of the system tested in the lab. The comparison indicates that video prototypes give results consistent with the laboratory evaluation. It seems to be harder to uncover issues of appropriation of the technology as only a narrow and typically normative use of it is shown on a video prototype. Given the ease with which feedback from many people can be collected, video prototyping seems better able to identify variety of contextual factors that may influence acceptance and use of the intended system.

1 Introduction

Video scenarios alias video prototypes are a very commonly used technique for representing design concepts during early phases of interaction design. Video prototypes are created using a range of simple or more complex techniques like stop motion animation, video editing, narrative voice-overs, computer animations, etc. These common techniques for the video medium help create audio-visual narratives illustrating a design concept, placing it in context, and conveying an impression of the intended interaction and user experience. The video can be shared with stakeholders in a design process to inspire developments but also, very importantly, to obtain feedback regarding their attitudes and expectations regarding the design concept shown.

Video prototyping was adopted by the HCI community during the eighties as a way of obtaining early feedback from users during a user centered design process, though it was discussed explicitly as a method for interaction design slightly later, see for example [12]. The method was originally used for the standard design problems of the era, e.g., prototyping graphical and multimodal interfaces, for which software prototypes were at the time expensive and time consuming to create, thus not lending themselves as well for iterative user centered design. While over the years software

N. Streitz and C. Stephanidis (Eds.): DAPI/HCII 2013, LNCS 8028, pp. 195–204, 2013.
© Springer-Verlag Berlin Heidelberg 2013

prototyping techniques have become more efficient, video prototyping still remains attractive especially for systems that are harder to implement, such as ambient intelligence / ubicomp applications. For such cases video prototypes are particularly appropriate as they make it easy to embed the envisioned interaction in different living and working contexts, to show dynamic aspects of interaction, to bridge time spans, and explain with narration or video effects the workings behind the scenes (e.g., adaptation, profiling, and communication).

For some time now, a range of well known vision videos capitalized on the ability of the technique to illustrate futuristic technologies, e.g., see the STARFIRE video by Sun Microsystems [11], or the seminal Knowledge Navigator video by Apple [8], which have managed to visualize interactive technologies that are now part of current technological habitat long before they were feasible to build. Over time the research field has become very much accustomed to such videos and there is quite some expertise available as to how best to use video as a medium, see for example [13].

Much of the knowledge on video prototyping reported in related literature is best described as anecdotal or craft knowledge. There has been little attempt to provide empirical evidence for the advice given and to consider the applicability, validity and generalisability of related methodology. This study is part of an investigation that attempts to address this omission.

In earlier work, we have examined the impact of fidelity in representations used in video prototypes. The generally perceived wisdom that low fidelity prototypes lead test participants to be more critical and to focus on higher level detail was not confirmed in the case of video prototypes [3]. Different filming techniques were compared, e.g., one using actors and one using cut-out animations, showing that the added realism of context and of the protagonists also did not result in different feedback to be obtained by viewers. [6].

Batalas et al [1] examine how video prototyping impacts the overall design process, focusing on the domain of ambient intelligence. Note that video is particularly attractive as a prototyping technique in this domain as it makes it easier to prototype and solicit user feedback, liberating non technology savvy designers from implementation concerns and even democratizing the design process enabling user participation and feedback. The embedding of a video on the design process is interesting for several reasons. A concise and vivid video representation can have communicative and persuasive uses towards managers, a development team, but also, can serve as a common ground within a design team. On the other hand, as [1] found it might draw attention to issues captured well with the medium, while ignoring other important aspects that simply do not lend themselves for filming. Further they argue how a slick presentation may conceal serious usability and user experience limitations of the envisioned design.

2   Aims of This Study

In the last 15 years, the field of human computer interaction has been paying increasing attention to the importance of context for the emerging user experience. Field testing of fully functional prototypes is often considered the golden standard for evaluating with users. Evaluating user experiences in a realistic physical and social context is accepted as a key aspect of iterative interaction design and user oriented research. Still for many systems that are experimental and at early phases of development, field testing may be too expensive or even infeasible, and the logistics of observation and experimentation in the field may be prohibitive. For these reasons, several research institutes around the world have established what we could call *context simulation laboratories* with the aim to create in a lab context much of the appearance and experiential aspects of real life contexts like homes, schools, hospitals, or even restaurants. Context simulation laboratories serve for the implementation of experimental technologies, the facilitation of observation and data collection. A typical example is the home simulation laboratory used in the present research study.

Given the considerations above which point towards functional prototypes and real world deployments, one should question how valid is the feedback obtained during early design phases from representative users viewing video prototypes. Can we consider their attitudes regarding a system, the design of the interaction and their expectations regarding the user experience intended by the designer as representative of what would be found by evaluating actual use?

This paper aims to address this issue by comparing feedback obtained from video prototypes to that obtained by evaluating a working system in a home simulation laboratory. We describe a case study concerning MatchMaker, an ambient intelligence application that notifies people in different households that a connected other is engaging in a similar activity at that very moment. To evaluate how feedback obtained from a video prototype evaluation compares to that obtained from testing, we reverse engineered a video prototype to represent the exact same concept. The original system had been evaluated in a home simulation environment with 46 participants spread over the role of the parent and the child. For this study we showed the video prototype to 11 participants fitting the demographics of the initial experiment. Qualitative interviews were conducted, gauging the value this system could bring for participants and issues relating to acceptance. Interviews were analyzed qualitatively using an inductive approach and the results were compared to the findings of the experimental evaluation. In the following sections, we report the study and its results in more detail.

3   The MatchMaker System

MatchMaker is an experimental ambient intelligence system that was designed to support peripheral awareness between inhabitants in two connected households so as to increase connectedness between elderly parents and their adult children living remotely. The system provides cues of when the connected individuals are engaging in a similar activity assuming that awareness of this similarity would enhance feelings of closeness and connectedness. MatchMaker was developed in an iterative design process and a feasibility prototype was installed in a home simulation laboratory. The design, implementation, and evaluation of MatchMaker are reported elsewhere [5].

Experimental context sensing technology was developed to a) identify moments when connected parties are engaged in similar activities, and b) do so only for selected types of activity that do not compromise the autonomy and privacy of the connected parties. Two Internet connected picture frames at each location light up when the system detects matching activities, e.g., both parties cooking, both watching television, tidying up, etc. The activity recognition technology enabling this function is still experimental which makes the home simulation laboratory particularly suitable for supporting experimental evaluations.

Fig. 1. Snapshots from the evaluation of MatchMaker in a home simulation laboratory, showing two participants tidying up after dinner at different locations, with their frame indicating the similarity of the activities identified by the system.

The potential affective benefits of similarity awareness were evaluated in a laboratory experiment involving 23 pairs of a parent and a child; this experiment reported in [5] shows that similarity awareness can significantly enhance social connectedness. During the evaluation each participant was given a set of tasks that they should carry out, e.g., tidying up, preparing dinner, etc. As they were carrying out these tasks the frame would indicate to them whether their relation who was present at a different location in the same campus, was engaging in the same activity at that same time. That experiment (described in [5]) is outside the scope of this paper; suffice it to say that the quantitative analysis confirmed the overall concept while a wealth of comments and reactions were recorded regarding the system, its potential to enhance connectedness, concerns regarding privacy, expectations regarding its value, etc. For the purposes of the present study, we compare related findings to those obtained by interviewing people who viewed the video prototype of Match Maker discussed below.

In creating the video prototype of MatchMaker we did not seek a persuasive and promotional video but one that would be a reasonable and low cost representation of the design concept, such as those used during early phases of interaction (see [12]).

The first step of creating the video prototype was a storyboard based on the core use cases of the MatchMaker. The scenario consists of two stories taking place in

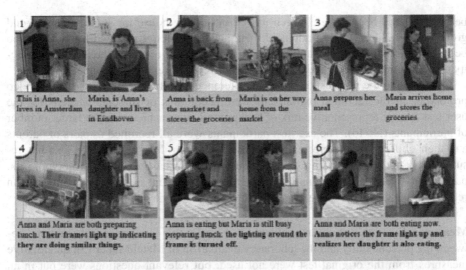

Fig. 2. Snapshots from the reverse engineered video prototype of the MatchMaker concept

different settings. The first scenario narrates the story of a mother, an empty nester, coming back home after groceries and then preparing a meal, having dinner, doing the dishes, having a drink and then vacuum cleaning. The second is about the daughter, who now lives on her own and does some of the same activities in her own place.

The video was shot at two different locations, a house and a student studio, to achieve more realism. The photo frame was placed on the counter in the kitchen at the mother's house and on a table at the daughter's studio, and it remained visible during the whole video. The activities that are synchronized (matched) in the video are: the preparation of the meal, having dinner, vacuum cleaning and having a drink. The frame lights up when there is a match between the activities that mother and daughter do. At appropriate times the scene is split in two parts to emphasize that mother and daughter are doing the same activity. Narration is used to provide some context to the story and call attention for the moment where the frame was lighting up.

4   Evaluating the MatchMaker Video Prototype

A different set of participants was recruited to view and comment on the video prototype. During the recruiting they were briefed that the study was about communication between parents and children. Participants were invited for the interview that was held at the Eindhoven University of Technology. They were first shown the video after which, they were interviewed regarding the concept as a whole, and more specifically regarding its potential to support feelings of social connectedness.

Participants. Two groups of participants took part. The first group was made up of empty nesters, parents (2 men, age 54 and 58 respectively and 3 women, aged between 50 and 58) whose children moved out of the house for studies. The second group were children (young adults; 3 men, aged between 20-21 and 3 women, aged between 23-25) that left the family house to live on their own. All the recruited participants were employees or students from Eindhoven University of Technology.

Compared to the user test of [5] some differences can be noted. In case of the video prototype, all the recruited participants were academics or students whereas for the user test a more representative mix of backgrounds was achieved and a larger number of participants (N=46). The user test participants were all recruited as pairs of parents and their children who were really connected through their parentage. This has resulted in better understanding of their bond, while in case of video prototyping the participants were recruited apart and could only comment on their own situation in relation to the child that moved out or their parents that they had left.

Measures. Since this study only aimed for a qualitative comparison of reactions between the present study and the laboratory evaluation of MatchMaker [5], quantitative measures from the original test were not used, but relevant questions were put in an interview format.

The resulting interview consisted of questions about social connectedness [2] and Social Presence [10]. Measuring social connectedness and social presence with questionnaires when showing a video prototype would retrieve only hypothetical results, since participants did not experience a real and direct interaction with the MatchMaker. In addition, a short questionnaire concerning demographics and background, motivation, and feelings of intimacy was used for each participant. This questionnaire was the same used on the original research [5].

The script of the semi-structured interview was similar to that of the laboratory evaluation and had three parts. In the first part, the questions regarded the MatchMaker concept and were the same as in the original research. The second part of the interview was designed to gather information on social connectedness loosely based on the Social Connectedness Questionnaire (SCQ). Finally, the third part was based on the Social Presence Questionnaire [10] to gather information concerning differences in feelings of social presence.

5   Comparing the Evaluation of Matchmaker in Lab and from Video Prototype Viewings

Interview sessions were recorded, transcribed, and open coded to identify inductively different categories of responses that characterize the reaction of viewers of the video. These are discussed below comparing them directly to the results of the user test.

Closeness and Social Connectedness. Viewers thought that closeness would be enhanced by using MatchMaker and that using the photo frame would evoke feelings of belonging, being more in touch and together - "feeling that you're not doing it alone but together with your parents in different places". Some negative aspects of the closeness that the frame creates were also expressed in the present research - "might feel a bit like as if parents are present, that's the part I might not like" - while they were not mentioned in the user test, where participants did not actually experience such feelings in the short and inevitably de-contextualized usage they had in the laboratory. Regarding connectedness, the feedback from viewers suggests that the quality of the relationship will not change because of the photo frame, in particular it will not help to understand more what the other thinks and feels, neither will help to talk about difficult topics. However, potential positive changes were also mentioned, such as feeling more connected to each other or that it might trigger more contact.

These results are congruent with the results of the MatchMaker user study [5].

About Similarity Matching. In general the concept was perceived as a new and indirect way of communication and easily comprehended by viewers of the video prototype. However, for some it was difficult to predict if using this system in daily life would be enjoyable. Several concerns about the frame were expressed; parents and children with different schedules and routines wondered how frequently and when the system would match an activity – "the probability that my eating happens at the same time as my son's eating is not that big". The same problem was referred when considering that the two parties live in different countries with different time zones. Similar results were not found in the user test of [5].

Tricking the System. Considering the synchronization and matching of activities, users expressed sometimes that they would try to trick the system to find out what the other party is doing at a specific moment, by trying different activities. This is consistent with the user test where participants suggested that at home they would try different activities until the frame would lights up in order to find what the other party is doing.

Triggering Communication. Matching activities was considered to trigger contact in most of the cases – "Could be an occasion to establish contact" – but the possibility of having automatic calls when there is a match was not appreciated and was rejected as an option by the majority of viewers – "If a phone line opens automatically it will be privacy invading". Moreover, it was stated that they would use the information that the frame offers to know when the other party is busy or not so that they do not disturb with a call.

Although the system triggers contact, worries about the obligations and expectations that the system might create were also expressed. Especially children were worried that their parents would expect a phone call when there is a match and in case they did not call they would feel guilty. It was also suggested that if activities never match, this could also bring disappointment. Moreover, children are worried that they may have to give explanations about what they were doing at a specific moment – "Bossy parents would say you are not doing your work properly".

These comments are fully in line with the reactions of participants in the user test.

Privacy. Privacy concerns were one of the main topics discussed during the interviews. In general the concept was not considered as privacy invading as long as the activities matching were between parents and children and were regular daily activities (cooking, having dinner, watching TV etc.) – "It's your parents, it's not like a stranger" (sic). Nevertheless, users were clear about the privacy matters that they worried about. Personal and intimate moments should not be taken into account when matching activities – "When my son invites his girlfriend perhaps he doesn't want me to interfere in his love life" (sic). Another worry concerned the feeling of being watched and controlled through the frame – "I moved out for a reason" (sic).

The users of the MatchMaker system expressed analogous opinions concerning these privacy matters.

Control System and Preferences. Users want to have control over the system, which means being able to switch off the device when they want. As a consequence of having control over the system, a need for different settings and preferences emerges. Participants would want to be able to choose which activities match and to have control settings for the color and intensity of the light. The possibility to have additional communication channels, such as videoconference, calls, chat or messages would also be appreciated. A need for messages that illustrate the user's mood and feelings was also suggested. The same results regarding the system's control and preferences were also found in the MatchMaker user studies.

On Matching Activities vs. Matching Location. One question that concerned the evaluation was whether activity recognition as such is useful: could it be replaced by the technologically simpler matching of location within the house? E.g., lighting up the frame in the kitchen, when the remote party is in the kitchen too. When asked about matching location instead of matching activities, users were not as positive. They thought that matching activities would be more meaningful while matching locations would not add more value. In addition matching location can be a problem when one party lives in a small apartment, studio or shared apartment and the other party lives in a house with several rooms. A consequence of this problem would be the frame lighting up permanently, which would make the device lose its spontaneity and meaning.

Relaxation or individual chores were also suggested by viewers of the video as good options for matching, such as reading or doing the dishes. Although similar consensus regarding the preference of matching activities was found in both studies, the concern about the size of each party's house and its consequences was not mentioned by the MatchMaker user test participants, perhaps because the whole experience and the interview were very much focused on the actual usage in the test session.

6   Conclusion

User feedback obtained from viewers of a video prototype was very comparable to the findings from testing in a context simulation laboratory, particularly with respect to the main questions of the study regarding closeness and social connectedness, privacy issues, control and preference settings, tricking the system and triggering communication.

However, some differences were remarked that were unexpected. Viewers of the video prototype were more forthcoming regarding practical considerations and fitting the application in their lives and context than participants in the test. For example, the difficulty of using the system over different time zone was missed by participants in the laboratory test who arrived together at the laboratory and live in nearby locations. Also, remarks concerning the configuration of the participants' own home did not arise in the home simulation laboratory that is bigger than the apartment of some of the participants. Conversely, video viewers did not envision explorative and playful usage of the system that was observed in the MatchMaker test and their responses were more normative and aligned with the designer's intent than was the case in the test. So the two methods are complimentary and by their nature will shed light to different aspects of the user experience.

This study is encouraging regarding the validity of feedback obtained by video prototyping, but also regarding its efficacy. As one would expect video prototyping appears to be blind to issues of appropriation, but it did trigger the imagination of viewers who could compare the proposed usage and user experience to their own lives and contexts. Given that it is easier to involve larger number of users, it appears that it helps bring into consideration a large variety of contextual factors relevant to viewers, that would be practically difficult to capture in a user test: one can only test in a limited number of locations and contexts, and when one is testing in an experience laboratory (e.g., home simulation), many of these contextual factors become contrived.

References

1. Batalas, N., Bruikman, H., Van Drunen, A., Huang, H., Turzynska, D., Vakili, V., Voynarovskaya, N., Markopoulos, P.: On the Use of Video Prototyping in Designing Ambient User Experiences. In: Paternò, F., de Ruyter, B., Markopoulos, P., Santoro, C., van Loenen, E., Luyten, K. (eds.) AmI 2012. LNCS, vol. 7683, pp. 403–408. Springer, Heidelberg (2012)
2. Van Bel, D.T., Ijsselsteijn, W.A., de Kort, Y.A.W.: Interpersonal Connectedness: Conceptualization and Directions for a Measurement Instrument. In: CHI 2008 Extended Abstracts, 3129–3134. ACM (2008)
3. Bojic, M., Goulati, A., Szostak, D., Markopoulos, P.: On the effect of visual refinement upon user feedback in the context of video prototyping. In: SIGDOC 2011, pp. 115–118. ACM, New York (2011)
4. Buxton, B.: Sketching User Experiences: getting the design right and the right design. Morgan Kaufmann (2007)
5. Dadlani, P., Markopoulos, P.: Similarity awareness: using context sensing to support connectedness in intra-family communication (submitted for publication, 2013)

6. Dhillon, B., Banach, P., Kocielnik, R., Emparanza, J.P., Politis, I., Pączewska, A., Marko-poulos, P.: Visual fidelity of video prototypes and user feedback: a case study. In: BCS-HCI 2011 British Computer Society, Swinton, UK, pp. 139–144 (2011)
7. Dow, S., Saponas, T.S., Li, Y., Landay, J.A.: External representations in ubiquitous compu-ting design and the implications for design tools. In: DIS 2006, p. 241 (2006)
8. Dubberly, H., Mitch, D.: The Knowledge Navigator. Apple Computer, Inc., video (1987)
9. Markopoulos, P., Romero, N., van Baren, J., IJsselsteijn, W., de Ruyter, B.: Keeping in touch with the family: home and away with the ASTRA awareness system. In: CHI Extended Abstracts, pp. 1351–1354. ACM (2004)
10. Short, J., Williams, E., Christie, B.: The social psychology of telecommunication. John Wiley & Sons, London (1976)
11. Tognazzini, B.: The "Starfire" video prototype project: a case history. In: Proceedings CHI 1994, pp. 99–105. ACM, New York (1994)
12. Vertelney, L.: Using video to prototype user interfaces. SIGCHI Bulletin (1989)
13. Ylirisku, S., Buur, J.: Designing with Video: Focusing the user-centred design process. Springer (2007)

Experience the World with Archetypal Symbols: A New Form of Aesthetics

Huang-Ming Chang[1,2], Leonid Ivonin[1,2], Marta Diaz[1], Andreu Catala[1],
Wei Chen[2], and Matthias Rauterberg[2]

[1] CETpD Research Center, Universitat Politècnica de Catalunya, Barcelona, Spain
{marta.diaz,andreu.catala}@upc.edu
[2] Dept. Industrial Design, Eindhoven University of Technology, The Netherlands
{h.m.chang,l.ivonin,w.chen,g.w.m.rauterberg}@tue.nl

Abstract. According to the theories of symbolic interactionism, phenomenology of perception and archetypes, we argue that symbols play the key role in translating the information from the physical world to the human experience, and archetypes are the universal knowledge of cognition that generates the background of human experience (the life-world). Therefore, we propose a conceptual framework that depicts how people experience the world with symbols, and how archetypes relate the deepest level of human experience. This framework indicates a new direction of research on memory and emotion, and also suggests that archetypal symbolism can be a new resource of aesthetic experience design.

Keywords: Human Experience, Symbols, Phenomenology, Archetypes.

1   Introduction

Interaction involves a series of expression and interpretation between us as human beings and the world around us. Speaking of aesthetics in interaction, what intrigues us more is the very moment when meaning emerges while human beings are experiencing the world. Through experiencing the world, human beings then know how to appreciate the beauty of interaction. *Symbolic Interactionism* [1] is a sociological theory that aims at analyzing the patterns of communication, interpretation and adjustment between people. This theory provides a framework for understanding how people interact with each other through the meanings of symbols. A fundamental premise is that people do not directly react to the ontological-existing reality, but respond to their *understanding* of this reality. Contrary to the traditional view of human in the machine paradigm, humans act toward things on the basis of the meanings that they ascribe to these things [2]. People interact with each other by interpreting each other's actions instead of merely reacting to each other's actions. Their response is not made directly to the actions of one another, but instead is based on the meaning that they attach to such actions. That is, each action, object, or event has its own symbolic meaning to be revealed. It is symbols that bridge the gap between the physical

N. Streitz and C. Stephanidis (Eds.): DAPI/HCII 2013, LNCS 8028, pp. 205–214, 2013.

reality and what humans perceive, feel, and understand as a reality. While the hypothesis is made, a further question is raised: how are symbols created? Symbolic interactionism assumes that symbolic meaning emerges while interaction is happening between people within the same social context. On the other hand, symbolic meaning is in turn given by the social context where the interaction is situated. This forms a reciprocal causation relationship between the symbolic meaning and the interaction.

The hypothesis of symbolic interactionism shared similarity with some discussions about human experience in cognitive science [3]. Human experience has been a tough topic for researchers. The tradition of behavioral science sees the physical world as the true reality, and even to the extreme, argues that psychological phenomena are just illusions [4]. Therefore it only takes into account how human bodies function in response to external stimuli, and rejects the existence of human mind. Nevertheless, while some researchers try to describe the physical world as an independent body of knowledge, phenomenologist Husserl [5] argues that human can never rid themselves of the world and observe it objectively. The world, as a phenomenon, only emerges while we are *living* within it. Therefore, he proposes the concept of 'life-world', saying that the world is a grand theater of objects variously arranged in space and time relative to perceiving subjects. The life-world is already and always there, and can be thought of as the background for all human experiences. All our personal experiences can thus be built upon this background through living within it. In this sense, the world we are talking about is never ontologically-objective, but always ontologically-subjective to the life-world we all share. It is argued that this life-world is considered as the *real* reality that researchers should focus. What we need to further understand is how personal subjective experience is built upon this consensual reality.

It seems that behaviorism and phenomenology hold completely opposite positions on their understanding about human experience. Fortunately, this dilemma was resolved when 'phenomenology of perception' was proposed [6]. Inherited from Husserl's concept of 'life-world,' Merleau-Ponty also believes that the physical world and what we experience as the world are different but inseparable realities. However, different from the above dualistic point of view, he further claims that the perception (or the sensation) is the channel that communicates the physical world and the experienced world. That is, he acknowledges that both physical world and the life-world exist as realities. For example, when you open your eyes, your perception is actively automated to senses the red color or any other attributes of the physical world. When you shut your eyes, you can still *embody* the redness or any other qualities—as part of the lived-world—in your mind. In this sense, psychology and physiology are no longer two paralleled science, but two accounts of human experience [6]. Based on this argument, a further question to answer is that: what are the media that transmit the information between the physical world and the life-world?

This question has been long annoying researchers since they tried to define psychological phenomena. Since we have acknowledged that these psychological phenomena are real, what we need to answer is that how these phenomena *become* real [4]? Psychology thus comes into play. Some cognitive scientists hold a similar opinion with symbolic interactionists. They argue that symbols, as the media that bear meaning, flow through the channel of perception between the ontologically-objective world and ontologically-subjective human experience [3].

2   Experience the World with Symbols

What are symbols? Do symbols equal to signs? A Sign is a representation of one concrete concept that implies a direct connection between itself and the concept it refers to. What it means 'direct connection' is that this connection to the extreme leads to a causal relationship. For example, thunders are usually known as the sign of a storm due to the fact that thunders always come with storms. In contrast, symbols are used to signify things without rational correlations, such as a flag is a symbol of a country. It is further argued that sign can only be used to refer to the known things, whereas symbols indicate something that is still unknown, or ideas that cannot be precisely depicted [7], e.g. peace, love, and culture. In essence, symbols itself are ontologically objective, and bear no psychological meaning. Their meanings emerge only when one's life-world is being lived. By saying this means that the meaning of symbols is ontologically subjective to human knowledge. Therefore, symbols can be in any kind of forms or values of anything in the physical world depending on how we approach the physical world to reveal our life-world [8]. In other words, the meaning of symbols would vary based on which layers of knowledge are adopted to support the experiencing procedure. Opposite to explicit knowledge that needs to be acquired by conscious learning and repetitive remembering, Sperber [9] argues that symbolism is a kind of tacit knowledge, an autonomous cognitive mechanism that, alongside the perceptual and conceptual mechanisms, participates in the construction of knowledge and in the functioning of memory. However, different from semiology, symbolic interpretation is not a matter of decoding, but an improvisation that rests on an implicit knowledge and obeys unconscious rules. He further propose a hypothesis that the basic principles of the symbolic mechanism are not induced from experience but are, on the contrary, part of the innate mental equipment that makes experience possible.

In the traditional psychological concept, especially behaviorism, humans are usually understood with a "stimulus-response" process. However, a gap emerges between the physical matters and psychological states. In research of emotion, appraisal theories [10] provides an fine argument to bridge this gap. While one is being chased by a tiger, it is not the 'physical' tiger that causes the fear, but the appraisal of this situation—being chased by a tiger—triggers this emotion of fear. This theory thus calls into the question: what provides the reference for the process of appraisal? Barrett [4] claims that humans share a kind of 'category knowledge' in their cognition process to interpret the ontologically-subjective meaning of ontologically-objective events. This knowledge enables the psychological phenomena to link the body to the world to create meanings. She further argues that the society can be the source of the knowledge. The society, by the definition of symbolic interactionism [1], is a reality that is embodied through interaction among the people within it. On the other hand, the society in turn provides the symbolic meaning of everything within its social context. Symbolic meaning is seen as a dynamic phenomenon, being constructed while interaction occurs, and in turn, grounding the basic understanding among people within it. It could also be understood as a *pre-understanding* of the physical world. Extended from this pre-understanding by *living* within it, humans create their new *understanding*, which in turn becomes the pre-understanding of the society. This loop is so-called hermeneutic circle [11]. Interestingly, not only symbolic interactionists but also some psychologist support the same idea that the society should be one of the sources of symbolic meaning [4]. It is obvious that people in the same society to some extent share the same languages, value system, and even ways of thinking. This knowledge is not always explicitly given through education, but more often is gained implicitly through living within it.

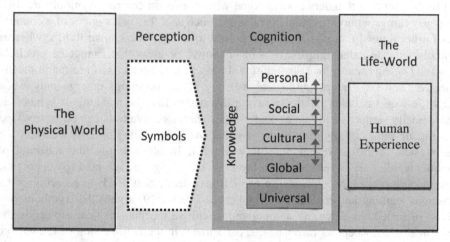

Fig. 1. The framework of how human experience is built with symbols

Beyond the society, we argue that there are many levels of knowledge that supports our building process of the life-world (see figure 1). These five levels of knowledge are personal, social, cultural, global, and universal. These first four levels of knowledge are neither static nor independent, but in a dynamic circulation. Information flows through different levels, influencing their next level of knowledge simultaneously. Top four levels of knowledge change differently with time [12] while the deepest level of knowledge remains consistent across time and space, as we call it universal knowledge of symbols.

3   Archetypal Symbolism

Psychologist Jung [7] reveals insights about unconsciousness in a wider sense throughout analyzing myths and fairytales from numerous cultures. He proposed the concept of 'collective unconsciousness' [13], arguing that besides the personal psyche (includes both conscious and unconscious minds), there exists a deeper level of unconscious mind, which contains some contents and modes of behavior that are identical in all individuals over time and space. The collective unconsciousness thus constitutes a common psychic substrate of a universal nature which is present in every one of us. This theory shares a similar idea with the Hindu view of reality [14] (see Figure 2). Egos of people are like separated islands above the water, as people see each other as independent individuals in the physical world. Our conscious thinking makes us believe that we are separate entities who are floating freely above the water. However, people can hardly notice the unconscious part of their mind under the surface of water. Furthermore, people are unaware that they are connected to each other by means of the ocean floor beneath the water. This is what Jung claimed that our personal unconsciousness rests upon a deeper layer, the collective unconsciousness, which is not a personal acquisition but is inborn as the foundation of the psyche [13].

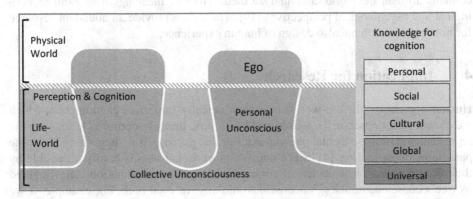

Fig. 2. A metaphorical mapping of the levels of knowledge and Hindu view of reality (adapted from Boeree [14])

Applying the same analogy with Jung's theory to our framework of human experience, a more thorough explanation can be drawn (see figure 2): the world above the water represents the physical world while the world under water refers to the life-world [5]. Human perception and cognition therefore appears to be the fine surface that connects between the air (the physical world) and the sea (the life-world). The water that surrounds us—as the society and the culture we live in—shapes our personal unconsciousness in an implicit way [15]. Besides the upper four levels of knowledge, the level of universal knowledge at the bottom links to the collective unconsciousness, which stands as the fundamental sea floor that we all connect with.

Continuing with the theory of the collective unconsciousness, Jung further developed the concept of archetypes [7]. Archetypes are defined as the components of the collective unconsciousness, which is an inborn tendency that cannot be consciously acquired to experience things in a certain way [13]. As the receptive fields of retina are not consciously perceived, but forms visual perception, archetypes, likened to another model of human, are psychic structures of a primordial origin, which are mostly inaccessible to consciousness, but determine the structure of our psyche [16]. Archetypes are very close analogies to instincts because the latter are impersonal, inherited traits that present and motivate human behavior long before any consciousness develops. Jung described archetypes as an unconscious psychic impulse, like instincts influence people as physical impulse toward actions [17]. A more extreme analogy would be describing archetypes as the structure of the psyche, which is similar to organs of the physical body [18]. By the same token, if our body functions as the 'hardware' of our perception, i.e. our physical organs, archetypes play as the role of 'software' that define our patterns of thoughts, emotions, and behaviors. Hence, symbols appear to be data, flowing between the physical world and the life-world.

Although archetypes are embedded in the deepest level in human unconsciousness, Jung found that archetypes are embodied as ancient motifs and predispositions to patterns of behavior that manifest symbolically as archetypal images in dreams, art, or cultural forms [7]. His followers continue this direction, collect archetypal symbolic contents all over the world, and analyze their symbolic meanings from both archeological and psychological perspectives [19]. These data provide an abundant resource for not only research but also design of human experience.

4   Implication for Research

Human experience (the life-world) is an ontologically-subjective phenomenon, which we cannot direct observe. To unfold this black box, the only option is to analyze the representation of these mental phenomena. For this purpose, it is suggested to seek the paradigms in psychology [4]. Since humans' unconsciousness is hardly accessible by their consciousness, it is unclear if some psychological representations are triggered by one's conscious thinking, unconscious thinking, or even both. For example, if we simply apply the 'memory-recall tasks' method: directly ask subjects to recall the semantic meaning of a symbol according to their own understanding. This approach is problematic for two reasons. First, semantic expression has limits in its nature, so that it might not be able to reflect complete symbolic meanings. As Jung states, symbolic meanings are abstract concepts that cannot be precisely described [7]. Second, memory-recall task is a conscious inference process for explicit memories (or declarative memories) [20, 21], which is supported by the personal level of knowledge instead of other knowledge that relate to unconsciousness. In contrast, implicit memories (or non-declarative memories) are unconscious and associative, which are suggested to apply association tasks in experiments [22].

Several studies have demonstrated the effectiveness of memory-association tasks in justification of the symbolic meanings for archetypal contents [23, 24]. This is also in accord with the mainstream of research into memories: the constructionist approach of memory recollection [25]. This approach regards memories as dynamic recollections instead of static records of something. Each recall task requires 'cues' that are is associated with fragments of memories of something. Those fragments of memories with strong connections with the cue would be easier to be cued. A similar paradigm is adopted in research on emotion, where researchers follow a stimuli-representation procedure. Although this procedure makes very few differences to traditional behaviorist methods, modern psychologists consider subjects' emotional responses as an indirect representation of their psychological phenomena instead of direct responses to the given stimuli. More importantly, researchers have found that emotions play the key role in strengthening the association between the fragment of memories and its cue [26]. This allows us to extend our framework in more details (see figure 3). In the context of our framework of human experience, some physical attributes in the physical world are identified as symbols according to the five levels of knowledge in the cognition process, and then are embodied as symbols in the life-world. Symbols function both as the *cue* that extracts the related memories and also the *stimuli* that elicit emotions out of subjects' life-world. These psychological phenomena aggregate as a new experience that emerges from the life-world. Each of new experiences represents the emergence of a new symbolic meaning. While an experience is embodied in the life-world, it is simultaneously influencing the knowledge for cognition. This reflects the concept of the hermeneutic circle [11], that humans change their way of thinking (knowledge for cognition as pre-understanding) while they are experiencing the world (human experience as understanding). The new experience again becomes memories in the life-world for future experience and recollection of memories.

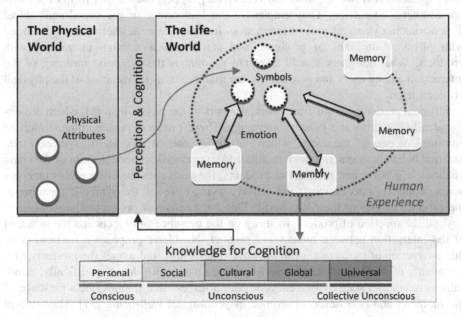

Fig. 3. Our advanced framework of how human experience is formed in the life-world

As the main focus of this framework is on the universal level of knowledge, i.e. archetypes, numbers of interesting research questions are raised for future work. First, how can we study archetypes? Since archetypes are hidden in the unconscious, the only way to study them is through their representation in different forms, such as stories, graphics, and even movies. Therefore, a starting point would be identifying archetypal contents as the materials that can be used for psychological experiments. Second, what is the correlation between archetypes and human experience? This research question actually involves two intertwined psychological phenomena: emotion and memory. Since these emotions and memories about archetype are all in the unconscious level, it suggests indirect approaches to capture these psychological phenomena, e.g. memory-association tasks instead of memory-recall task [23, 24], and physiological signals instead of self-reports of emotions [27].

5   Design for Aesthetic Experience

A more interesting topic to implication for design is how archetypal symbolic contents can be applied in design for aesthetic experience. Traditional product design mainly focuses on aesthetic experience, experience of meaning, and emotional experience in physical products [28]. With this definition, aesthetic experience relies on one's appreciation of the form and material, whereas the experience of meaning counts on the interpretation of the personal, social, cultural meanings of the products. In the end, emotional experience emerges as the overall result of the appraisal of these two experiences. However, Ross and Wensveen [29] propose another form of aesthetics: aesthetic interaction. They emphasize the importance of the social and ethical dimensions in dynamic forms of interaction. In which case, aesthetics is not bounded with physical attributes of products, and can manifest through interacting with products. What designers should take into account is the symbolic meaning of the interaction among users and products, rather than the intrinsic meaning of the physical products itself.

Physical products, in our framework, are part of the physical world, which are ontologically-objective and bear no meanings. These products then become stimuli of emotions or cues of memories, which initiate an internal process of experience and external behavior interacting with it. Apart from personal appreciation about the static qualities, e.g. form and material of products, the aesthetics experience also emerges when people are unconsciously yet actively trying to reveal the symbolic meaning of the product as part of their life-world. This perspective of product experience goes beyond the function of product, focusing on the presence of objects and the meaning of the interaction between human and product. Niedderer proposes a framework of this interaction of meaning making: mindful interaction, and names the products with the quality of meaning making as performative objects [30]. More specifically, mindfulness refers to a state of awareness or consciousness that implies one's presence of the moment, and is believed to promote psychological well-being [31]. The concept of performative objects addresses the product's consequences for human social interaction, raising awareness and reflection of oneself in the present. The ultimate goal of this framework is to enhance users' states of mindfulness through the mediating influence of products. According to our framework of human experience, mindful interaction demonstrates a kind of approach to transform physical attributes in physical world to symbols in the life-world, and with this interaction, users are *guided* to reflect the social phenomena behind the usage of the product. In other words, the attempt of mindful interaction is to bring the knowledge for cognition to a conscious level, allowing users to be aware of the experience that they are undergoing.

While Niedderer's framework focuses on social phenomena, we aim at leading users to a deeper level of their own experience, i.e. experience about archetypes. In this sense, archetypal symbolism provides us an opportunity to design a new form of aesthetic experience in a unconscious level. One typical expression of the experience about archetypal symbols might be Campbell's concept of the hero's journey [32]. Based on Jung's theory of archetypes, he identifies the basic structure of archetypal experience in all myths from different cultures in human history. This also sheds light on some study in user experience about using new products [33]. Metaphorical speaking, the storyline of hero's journey implements the construction of the life-world built by archetypal symbols. It seems promising to apply the storyline of the hero's journey as a new approach to achieve mindful interaction that leads users to achieve archetypal experiences.

6   Conclusion

Based on the theories of symbolic interactionism, phenomenology of perception, and archetypes, we introduce a new framework describing how human experience the world with symbols. In this framework, archetypes are the components of the deepest level of knowledge for cognition, the collective unconsciousness, which defines the basic structure of the life-world. This concept indicates a new direction of research on human experience. Furthermore, we suggest that archetypal symbolism can be a new resource of aesthetic experience design.

Acknowledgements. This work was supported in part by the Erasmus Mundus Joint Doctorate in Interactive and Cognitive Environments (ICE), which is funded by the EACEA Agency of the European Commission under EMJD ICE FPA n 2010-0012.

References

1. Manis, J.G., Meltzer, B.N.: Symbolic Interaction: A Reader in Social Psychology. Allyn and Bacon, Inc. (1978)
2. Kohler, A.: To think human out of the machine paradigm: Homo Ex Machina. Integrative Psychological & Behavioral Science 44, 39–57 (2010)
3. Varela, F.J., Thompson, E.T., Rosch, E.: The Embodied Mind: Cognitive Science and Human Experience. MIT Press (1992)
4. Barrett, L.F.: Emotions are real. Emotion 12, 413–429 (2012)
5. Husserl, E.: The Crisis of European Sciences and Transcendental Phenomenology: An Introduction to Phenomenological Philosophy. Northwestern University Press (1970)
6. Merleau-Ponty, M.: Phenomenology of Perception. Routledge (2002)
7. Jung, C.G.: Man and His Symbols. Doubleday, Garden City (1964)
8. White, L.A.: The symbol: The origin and basis of human behavior. Philosophy of Science 7, 451–463 (1940)
9. Sperber, D.: Rethinking Symbolism. Cambridge University Press (1975)
10. Scherer, K.R.: What are emotions? And how can they be measured? Social Science Information 44, 695–729 (2005)
11. Gadamer, H.-G.: Truth and Methods. Sheed & Ward Ltd. (1975)

12. Kooijmans, T., Rauterberg, M.: Cultural computing and the self concept: Towards uncons-cious metamorphosis. In: Ma, L., Rauterberg, M., Nakatsu, R. (eds.) ICEC 2007. LNCS, vol. 4740, pp. 171–181. Springer, Heidelberg (2007)
13. Jung, C.G.: The Archetypes and the Collective Unconscious. Princeton University Press, Princeton (1981)
14. Boeree, C.G.: Carl Jung, http://webspace.ship.edu/cgboer/jung.html
15. Wilson, T.D.: Knowing when to ask: Introspection and the adaptive unconscious. Journal of Consciousness Studies 10(10), 131–140 (2003)
16. Perlovsky, L.: Neural dynamic logic of consciousness: The knowledge instinct. In: Interna-tional Joint Conference on Neural Networks, IJCNN 2006, pp. 377–383. IEEE (2006)
17. Jung, C.: Instinct and the unconscious. The British Journal of Psychology 10, 15–23 (1919)
18. Jacobi, J.: The Psychology of C. G. Jung. Yale University Press (1973)
19. Ronnberg, A., Martin, K.: The Book of Symbols: Reflections on Archetypal Images. Tas-chen (2010)
20. Schacter, D.L.: Implicit memory: History and current status. Journal of Experimental Psy-chology: Learning, Memory, and Cognition 13, 501–518 (1987)
21. Squire, L.R.: Declarative and nondeclarative Memory: Multiple brain systems supporting learning and memory. Journal of Cognitive Neuroscience 4, 232–243 (1992)
22. Greenwald, A.G., Poehlman, T.A., Uhlmann, E.L., Banaji, M.R.: Understanding and using the Implicit Association Test: III. Meta-analysis of predictive validity. Journal of Personal-ity and Social Psychology 97, 17–41 (2009)
23. Bradshaw, S., Storm, L.: Archetypes, symbols and the apprehension of meaning. Interna-tional Journal of Jungian Studies, 1–23 (2012)
24. Rosen, D.H., Smith, S.M., Huston, H.L., Gonzalez, G.: Empirical study of associations be-tween symbols and their meanings: Evidence of collective unconscious (archetypal) mem-ory. Journal of Analytical Psychology 36, 211–228 (1991)
25. Van den Hoven, E., Eggen, B.: Informing augmented memory system design through au-tobiographical memory theory. Personal and Ubiquitous Computing 12, 433–443 (2007)
26. Szpunar, K.K., Addis, D.R., Schacter, D.L.: Memory for emotional simulations: Remem-bering a rosy future. Psychological Science 23, 24–29 (2012)
27. Ivonin, L., Chang, H.-M., Chen, W., Rauterberg, M.: Unconscious emotions: Quantifying and logging something we are not aware of. Personal and Ubiquitous Computing, 1–11 (2012)
28. Desmet, P., Hekkert, P.: Framework of product experience. International Journal of De-sign 1, 1–10 (2007)
29. Ross, P.R., Wensveen, S.A.G.: Designing behavior in interaction: Using aesthetic expe-rience as a mechanism for design. International Journal of Design 4, 3–13 (2010)
30. Niedderer, K.: Designing mindful interaction: The category of performative object. Design Issues 23, 3–17 (2007)
31. Brown, K.: The benefits of being present: Mindfulness and its role in psychological well-being. Journal of Personality and Social Psychology 84, 822–848 (2003)
32. Campbell, J.: The Hero with A Thousand Faces. Princeton University Press (1973)
33. McLoone, H.E.: Product archetype of personal computers as an expression of the collec-tive unconsciousness of people on their hero's journey. Proceedings of the Human Factors and Ergonomics Society Annual Meeting 54, 1771–1775 (2010)

A Prototyping and Evaluation Framework
for Interactive Ubiquitous Systems

Christine Keller, Romina Kühn, Anton Engelbrecht,
Mandy Korzetz, and Thomas Schlegel

TU Dresden - Junior Professorship in Software Engineering of Ubiquitous Systems
{christine.keller,romina.kuehn,mandy.korzetz,
thomas.schlegel}@tu-dresden.de,
anton.engelbrecht@mailbox.tu-dresden.de

Abstract. Ubiquitous systems often come with innovative design ideas and interaction concepts. To enhance and ensure the user's acceptance, it is necessary to test and evaluate those ideas in early design stages. In addition, early tests also validate the feasibility of those concepts. Rapid prototyping of ubiquitous systems enables researchers and practitioners to quickly test and implement new ideas, but is also necessary in iterative system development. We introduce a framework that supports rapid prototyping and evaluation of ubiquitous interactive systems using a modular approach, incorporating different interaction modes.

Keywords: Rapid Prototyping, Framework, Ubiquitous Systems, Interaction.

1 Introduction and Motivation

Ubiquitous computing aims at building intelligent environments, where computing devices of all sorts are pervasive but unobtrusive, as first envisioned by Mark Weiser [12]. A ubiquitous environment is supposed to support its users by providing easy information and computing access as well as usable interfaces. The key is *"Getting the computer out of the way"* [13]. Weiser's vision turned 20 in 2011 and although our computers are not out of the way yet, computing devices of all shapes and sizes become increasingly pervasive. However, most computing devices are standalone systems, lacking intelligent mechanisms to exchange data or incorporate context information, but also missing interaction concepts that ease the user's access to the system. Research for ubiquitous systems involves the design of innovative interaction concepts. It is necessary to test and evaluate those ideas in early design stages to avoid design errors. Prototypes are essential for developing and evaluating interaction concepts for ubiquitous environments. As Mark Weiser already stated 1993, *"the research method for ubiquitous computing is [...] the construction of working prototypes [...]"* [13]. Prototyping interactive ubiquitous systems facilitates the user-centered design process in ubiquitous computing and supports the development of systems that "get out of the way".

We developed a prototyping and evaluation framework for ubiquitous interactive systems, named *ProtUbique*. Our framework was designed and implemented to support rapid prototyping of interaction concepts for ubiquitous environments. It provides several components that implement different interaction channels to support a variety of

N. Streitz and C. Stephanidis (Eds.): DAPI/HCII 2013, LNCS 8028, pp. 215–224, 2013.

modalities. Our goal is to enable a prototyping engineer to rapidly assemble different interaction channels, to provide any level of background code and then to evaluate this prototype with user tests using the same framework. In the following paragraph, we will take a look on related work in the field of prototyping for ubiquitous systems. We will then present our prototyping tool for interactive systems and describe our realization. After that, we give an example of a prototype that was developed using ProtUbique and show, how the framework can be used. We conclude with the discussion of our framework and future work.

2 Related Work

A *prototype* is a partially realized system that serves as example of a planned system. It can be used to test implemented functionality, to assess design decisions or to evaluate system concepts. *Rapid prototyping* tools and frameworks allow software engineers and system designers to quickly assemble prototypes and are often used in iterative software development processes [7]. In order to design usable systems it is important to involve potential users in early stages of the development process, to evaluate design ideas and to improve the system concept [4], [2]. In the user-centered design process, prototyping is a key technique to evaluate and improve an interactive system [8]. Paper prototypes and the like can serve as a starting point for the requirements analysis [5]. However, it is also important to build technically mature prototypes, in order to evaluate and test ubiquitous interaction [6].

Several research efforts aim at supporting rapid prototyping for ubiquitous systems. The Context-Toolkit from Dey, Abowd and Salber is a distributed context-aquiring and handling toolkit [3]. The Context-Toolkit provides context-widgets, interpreters and aggregators to abstract, hide and reassemble sensor-data for context-aware applications. Because of its service-oriented architecture the different components can be implemented in various programming languages. The Toolkit supports rapid prototyping of context-aware ubiquitous systems, and although they focus on providing context-aware interaction, the implementation of the interaction itself is not supported, in contrast to our framework. More focused on prototyping interaction is the iStuff toolkit developed by Ballagas et al. [1]. It supports interaction on displays via physical tangible devices. The toolkit allows any physical object or device that has a wireless interface to be an input or output device by defining it as an *iStuff* component. An iStuff component then is connected to a central system. The toolkit supports multiple users, devices and applications and is therefore very adaptable to different scenarios and fields of application. The authors write, that *"event communication takes only a few lines of code"* in order to utilize iStuff [1]. They also provide some output devices, for example a vibrating device for haptic output, they call *iVibe*. However, the toolkit does not support other interaction techniques but tangible devices, whereas we focus on facilitating different interaction modalities.

The Distributed Wearable Augmented Reality Framework (DWARF) by Christian Sandor and Gudrun Klinker is a "software infrastructure that allows the rapid exchange of interaction styles" [11]. According to Sandor and Klinker there are currently three aspects of interaction of future human-computer interfaces: mobility, multichannel-communication and interactions embedded in the real world. DWARF adresses these three interaction-styles and is built of loosely coupled distributed components. It has a layered architecture that includes a hardware layer, which manages the sensors and recieves the input-data. This data is then processed and interpreted by an interaction-management layer. On top of that, a media-design-layer takes care of the output or routing of the data. The implementation and utilisation of interaction components however is more complex as our approach, where interaction channels are modified via graphical user interface.

The proximity toolkit by Marquardt et al. facilitates the creation of so-called proxemic-aware applications [9]. These are applications that use the distance and orientation towards entities to realize interaction, where enities can be people, digital devices and objects. Orientation, distance, motion, identity and location information between entities is captured via marker-tracking and cameras in an laboratory. These measures are provided to prototype engineers for usage in the implementation of interactions. The toolkit is also able to record and replay events that are generated by the tracked entities. The proximity toolkit provides a visual monitoring tool, that allows to observe and record the proxemic relationships of entities in three dimensional space. The architecture of the proximity toolkit separates sensing hardware from the processing layer. This way, different sensing technologies can be used. The layered architecture provides flexibility and extensibility, which is also supported by the plugin-concept that enables a prototyping engineer to use predefined templates for interactions to support rapid prototyping. The installation of cameras is fixed and therefore not portable. The proximity toolkit only provides one means of interaction based on the described relationships between entities, other interaction techniques are not planned. Our framework, in contrast, focuses on providing different interaction channels and on extensibility. Norrie and Murray-Smith show that the Microsoft Kinect sensor can simulate a proximity sensor for spacial interaction without the installation of special hardware [10]. Furthermore, the authors suggest additional sensor types that can be simulated using Microsoft Kinect data. Those are an accelerometer, a pose sensor, an occupancy sensor, a motion sensor, a light sensor and a sound meter. These sensors can then be used in prototypes for interactive ubiquitous systems. Their implemented tool simulates a proximity sensor by tracking the spatial position of the user's hand. The authors use it for a mobile application that utilizes the proximity data and displays useful information if the user points his mobile phone to different spots. Although the authors suggest the usage of kinect data for additional sensors and possible interactions, they did not implement these yet. Therefore, only one interaction technique is supported at the moment.

It is our opinion that toolkits or frameworks that support prototyping of interactive ubiquitous systems need to be highly flexible to support many different domains, since there are numerous fields of applications for ubiquitous systems. As multimodal interaction is very important for ubiquitous systems, they need to provide different means of interaction for the prototype. In the following sections we will therefore present our framework *ProtUbique*, that allows for rapid prototyping of interactive ubiquitous systems. It supports different interaction techniques and easy adaptation via graphical user interface. Its architecture is modular, encapsulating the different interaction channels and therefore facilitates the extension by additional interaction channels.

3   A Rapid Prototyping Framework for Ubiquitous Systems

We developed *ProtUbique*, a framework that facilitates the user-centered design of ubiquitous systems. It supports easy and rapid prototyping of interactive ubiquitous systems and also enables the evaluation of these prototypes. ProtUbique focuses on interaction prototypes and for this purpose provides an abstraction layer for the prototyping engineer that encapsulates different interaction channels for supporting a variety of modalities. The prototyping engineer therefore doesn't have to implement several interaction techniques but can use the readily implemented interaction components and easily plug them into his backend code, as displayed in figure 1. Because the backend code provides the program logic and is not restricted in any way, various prototypes for different interactive ubiquitous fields of application become possible.

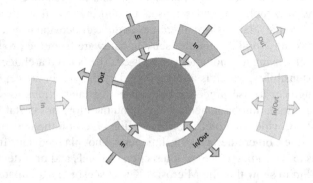

Fig. 1. Plugging together different implemented interaction channels for a new prototype

With our approach we are able to reduce the effort needed for programming. The user can quickly develop mixed or high-fidelity prototypes depending on the maturity of the backend code. The developed prototypes are then able to provide more or less functionality depending on the implemented backend code. In doing so several interaction techniques can be combined by using pre-implemented channels or by adding self-implemented channels to the framework.

Our goal is to facilitate the usage of different interaction channels without limiting the flexibility of their application. The interaction channels are therefore made available through a graphical user interface that allows customizing them. The interaction channels generate events that can be used to trigger responses to the specific interaction. These events have to be used in backend code. We intend to support as much customizing as possible through the graphical user interface. This way, prototyping engineers can concentrate on designing the prototype and providing backend code rather than implementing interaction techniques. In order to support the user-centered design of interactive ubiquitous systems, the ProtUbique framework also enables user tests. Prototypes that are realized within the ProtUbique framework can be evaluated within the framework itself. With the help of the framework interface user tests can be recorded and played back, showing all captured interactions. The following sections present our modular system architecture, the graphical user interface (GUI) and current implemented interaction channels in detail.

3.1 Architecture and Graphical User Interface

The first few interaction channels were implemented using the Microsoft Kinect sensor for the Xbox 360, which allows for various input modes. The ProtUbique framework is implemented in C#. We focused, however, on keeping the framework extensible and on allowing the easy development of additional interaction channels, as displayed in figure 2.

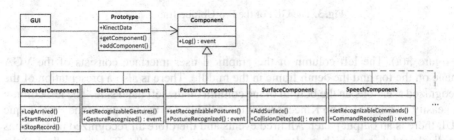

Fig. 2. The modular architecture of ProtUbique

Flexibility in ProtUbique is provided by the `Prototype` class. Its purpose is to mediate between the different hard- and software that realizes the interaction channels and the backend code that is provided by the user. An interaction channel can either provide output or input capabilities or both. An output component would consume data to deliver it to the user in the defined way, where an input component creates events whenever an interaction is recognized. The `Component` class represents general interaction channels. Individual channels can be realized as specializations of the `Component` class. If an implemented interaction channel should be applied in a certain prototype, the corresponding object is registered in the `Prototype` class, which then initializes the interaction channels and delegates resulting events to the backend code or delivers output data to output channels. A registered interaction channel can be tailored for the prototype it should be used for.

A prototype engineer must plug the events created by the interaction channels into his backend code, but apart from that should not have to write much additional code. This is why we decided to provide a **graphical user interface** (GUI) that facilitates the configuration of the selected interaction channels for a new prototype. The first step of creating a new prototype using ProtUbique is always the generation of a `Prototype` class and the registration of the used components. Each component then initializes a tab in the graphical user interface of ProtUbique, in which it can be configured. Since most of the implemented interaction channels use the Kinect sensor, we used its depth frame and VGA image to display the space that is used for the prototype, as shown

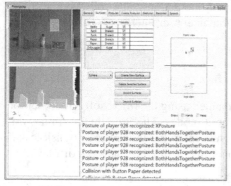
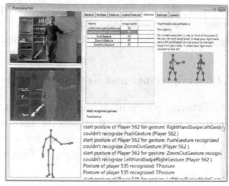

(a) Drawing interactive surfaces   (b) Using implemented gestures

Fig. 3. The GUI of the ProtUbique framework

in figure 3(a). The left column of the graphical user interface consists of the VGA image on the top and the depth frame in the middle. There is also a presentation of the recognized skeletons on the bottom of the column on the left hand side. The left column can easily be omitted, if no Kinect sensor is available. On the bottom of the ProtUbique GUI, there is an output panel. All fired events and therefore all recognized interactions are displayed there, which is also shown in figures 3 and 4(b). They also display the different configuration tabs of the interaction channels.

3.2 Implemented Interaction Channels

Up to now, we implemented postures, gestures, speech and interactive surfaces to support rapid prototyping of interactive and possibly multimodal ubiquitous systems. The `PostureComponent` can recognize designated **postures** of the skeleton detected by the Microsoft Kinect sensor. The Kinect is able to detect and distinguish 20 skeleton joints. We only use eleven of the skeleton joints for posture detection. A posture is defined using their relative positions. Constraints restrict the angle between two skeleton joints. The "Posture Creator" tab of the ProtUbique GUI provides a graphical tool for defining postures, as shown in figure 4(a). The skeleton joints that can be used for posture definition, are displayed on the left in the GUI. The skeleton can be edited by clicking on the nodes and dragging them into the required positions. The second page of the Posture Creator serves for editing constraints and angles between the different joints, as shown in figure 4(a). Constraints for postures helps distinguishing different postures from each other. A constraint is defined by selecting a base joint, displayed in red, and two leg joints, displayed in green. Base and leg joints form an angle. The constraint restricts this angle between the two leg and base joints and has a given tolerance, which translates into a minimum and maximum angle. The posture is then saved into an XML file, which can be loaded again at any time. The name given for the file is also the name for the posture. Using this name, the postures can be registered in the `Prototype` class. All registered and therefore available postures are then displayed in the "Posture" tab, where also the name of the last recognized posture is given, as shown in figure 4(b).

(a) Creating postures using the Posture Creator.

(b) Posture tab.

Fig. 4. Posture component: creating and customizing

The `SurfaceComponent` is used to create **interactive surfaces** (any polygons) or volumes (e.g. spheres) defined by their coordinates in space. Interactions are triggered by collisions of a body-joint with the defined surfaces using the Kinect depth sensor. A developer can use interactive surfaces to simulate buttons or interaction with fixed objects. The surfaces can be designed "around" the objects that are meant to be interactive. By touching these real-world objects and consequently interacting with the defined surface, the interaction with the object itself can be emulated. Interactive surfaces can be created by directly drawing them into the depth frame of the Kinect sensor, that is displayed on the left in the GUI. There are two drawing modes - a triangle mode that allows for creation of any kind of polygons, which are automatically split up into triangles. While in triangle mode, the user can click on the "Create New Surface" button and then mark the vertices of the polygon in the depth frame. A mouse click defines a vertex at the current x and y position. The depth information is taken directly from the depth information of the sensor. A right mouse click completes the definition of a new interactive polygon. The second mode is the sphere mode. By clicking into the depth frame, the center of a new interactive sphere is marked. A prompt allows to input the radius of the sphere. Each new interactive surface or sphere is given a name, that is also used to reference it in the underlying code. As shown in figure 3(a), the tab also shows a front view and a top view of the space that is captured by the Kinect sensor. The interactive surfaces are displayed there, in order to give a three dimensional impression. The detected skeletons can also be displayed in the front and top view. Interactive surfaces can be exported and saved to a file for reuse and import in other prototypes.

The detection of **gestures** is implemented in the `GestureComponent`. They are not so easy to define via graphical interfaces. Gestures consist of different postures that are performed in sequence. Variations in speed of the executed gesture as well as angles and movement during the transition between postures affect the precision of gesture recognition. The given tolerances have a strong influence on the precision of recognition and they differ for each gesture. Therefore, we decided to implement different gestures that are provided by ProtUbique. The gesture library can be extended by programming additional gesture recognition components and we hope that the future use of ProtUbique leads to the development of components that can be added to the library. Prototyping engineers that do not want to implement new gestures can use the predefined gestures from our library. Using the gesture tab of the GUI (3(b)), all registered gestures can be selected and a picture of the postures that form the start and end of one gesture is displayed as well as a textual description of the gesture.

By using the Windows Desktop **Speech** API from Microsoft, we also realized a `SpeechComponent`. Words and phrases can be defined as commands. The `Speech-Component` encapsulates the Windows Desktop Speech API and passes the events of recognized commands on to the `Prototype` class. A prototype engineer can add new words and phrases as commands by entering them on the speech tab of our ProtUbique GUI. The last word that was recognized is also displayed there for logging purposes.

To **evaluate** the prototypes created with our system, we additionally integrated a built-in recording-tool which is implemented as a specialized component, called `RecorderComponent`. It uses a camera and microphone to record audio and video data. In addition, the interactions that are recognized and fired events are also logged. In order to study the performance of test users, the prototyping or usability engineer can replay the recorded audio and video and also review the performed interactions. On the "Recorder" tab of the GUI it is possible to insert an ID to identify the current test user. This ID is then used to associate the recordings with the performed tests.

3.3   A Practical Example of How to Develop a Prototype Using ProtUbique

To test the functionality of ProtUbique, two developers, who were unfamiliar with our framework, developed a new prototype for a ubiquitous music player. To implement a new prototype there are only a few steps necessary. At first, a new ProtUbique project has to be created. It contains a Main class that initializes the different interaction components and instantiates the `Prototype` object. By instantiating `Prototype`, the prototype engineer can choose if the GUI, the Kinect sensor and the evaluation recorder should be enabled. The chosen interaction components are then added to the `Prototype` object. Once registered, the interaction components can be configured using the GUI, as described above. Afterwards, the events that are generated by ProtUbique and the used interaction components can be plugged into backend code, in order to trigger responses.

The music player's functions comprise a central storage of different types of music and the possibility to play this music. The player is controlled by gestures, surfaces, postures, and speech. The following functions were implemented by the developers: Associate different categories of music with objects through interactive surfaces, start and stop music, adjust volume up and down, forward and rewind, start and stop karaoke mode. The developers worked as a team because one person had to assemble the prototype and to program the backend code, while another person was necessary to test the behaviour of the implemented prototype and also to discuss their concept for the protoype. The developers were asked to assess their programming skills and experience with Microsoft Kinect and the Kinect SDK before starting the implementation. Both stated that they have middle-rated experience with the Microsoft Kinect sensor as interaction device and a lot of experience in programming in general. They rated their C# skills as little to moderate.This information was gathered to figure out whether users have to be experts for using the prototyping framework or not. It turned out that C# knowledge would be an asset but is not mandatory. This is actually due to the fact that the backend code and the processing of events proved difficult, given their moderate expertise using C#. The test programmers stated, that the ProtUbique framework was helpful implementing a prototype for a ubiquitous system. They also judged that ubiquitous prototyping supported by a framework is easy and fast in contrast to complex constructions that they figured would be needed if no framework is provided. Different interaction options are easy to integrate and development cycles are fast, too. Both developers evaluted the framework as usable, operable and easy to learn. In addition, the functions of the offered components were comprehensible. For applying gestures and postures they used the framework's GUI, which was considered suitable. Some suggestions for improvement were given by the developers, too: the realization of different grammars for `SpeechComponent`, allocation of templates, pre-assembled elements and patterns within the framework's GUI to speed up the prototyping and the support of composition by drag-and-drop. As our example shows, our modular concept seems to work and the facilitation of the prototyping process was highly appreciated.

4   Conclusions

In this paper we presented the ProtUbique framework, that facilitates rapid prototyping and evaluation of interactive ubiquitous systems. Since interactive ubiquitous systems come with innovative and for most users unfamiliar interaction concepts, they have to be designed involving users to ensure high usability. Therefore the ProtUbique framework is conceived to support the user-centered design process of ubiquitous systems.

It is extensible so that additional interaction channels can be easily implemented. With this functionality, rapid prototyping of ubiquitous interactive systems becomes easily feasible. A prototyping engineer however, can use the given interaction channels with minimal programming effort. He therefore can focus on providing detailed backend code or on conducting user studies and evaluating his ideas. For this purpose we provide a GUI that can be used to configure the different current implemented interaction channels as far as possible.

Our concept is not fully implemented yet, since there are no dedicated output components at the moment, e.g. a speech output channel. This is part of our future work on ProtUbique. In another iteration, we plan to further extend the available input interaction channels and also to implement new gestures by adding for example the Gesture Authoring Tool of Omek Beckon SDK[1]. So far, implementation of new interaction channels has proven to be easy and quick, due to the modular design. As interaction channels are separated from each other and implemented as individual components, the development of new components is straightforward. We would like to test the next

---

[1] http://www.omekinteractive.com/

version of ProtUbique with some participants, in order to evaluate the usability of the framework. The vision of our work is to evolve the ProtUbique framework from a tool-based rapid prototyping framework for ubiquitous systems into an integrated user interface and software engineering approach for multimodal ubiquitous systems, spanning the whole life-cycle of highly interactive ubiquitous systems.

Acknowledgements. We wish to thank Enrico Hinz, Josefine Zeipelt, Mirko Wolff, Nico Schertler, Philipp Sonnefeld and Ronald Graupner for the contributions made by their practical work.

References

1. Ballagas, R., Ringel, M., Stone, M., Borchers, J.: istuff: A physical user interface toolkit for ubiquitous computing environments. In: CHI 2003, pp. 537–544 (2003)
2. Bäumer, D., Bischofberger, W.R., Lichter, H., Züllighoven, H.: User interface prototyping - concepts, tools, and experience. In: Proceedings of the 18th International Conference on Software Engineering, ICSE 1996, pp. 532–541. IEEE Computer Society, Washington, DC (1996)
3. Dey, A.K., Abowd, G.D., Salber, D.: A Conceptual Framework and a Toolkit for Supporting the Rapid Prototyping of Context-Aware Applications. Human-Computer Interaction 16, 37–41 (2009)
4. Gould, J.D.: How to design usable systems. In: Handbook of Human-Computer Interaction (1988)
5. Kühn, R., Keller, C., Schlegel, T.: Von modellbasierten storyboards zu kontextsensitiven interaction-cases. i-com - Zeitschrift für Interaktive und Kooperative Medien 10(3), 12–18 (2011) (in German)
6. Liu, L., Khooshabeh, P.: Paper or interactive?: a study of prototyping techniques for ubiquitous computing environments. In: CHI 2003 Extended Abstracts on Human Factors in Computing Systems, CHI EA 2003, pp. 1030–1031. ACM, New York (2003)
7. Luqi: Software evolution through rapid prototyping. IEEE Computer 22, 13–25 (1989)
8. Maguire, M.: Methods to support human-centred design. International Journal of Human-Computer Studies 55(4), 587–634 (2001)
9. Marquardt, N., Diaz-Marino, R., Boring, S., Greenberg, S.: The proximity toolkit: Prototyping proxemic interactions in ubiquitous computing ecologies. In: UIST 2011 (2011)
10. Norrie, L., Murray-Smith, R.: Virtual sensors: Rapid prototyping of ubiquitous interaction with a mobile phone and a kinect. In: MobileHCI 2011 (2011)
11. Sandor, C., Klinker, G.: A rapid prototyping software infrastructure for user interfaces in ubiquitous augmented reality. Personal Ubiquitous Comput. 9, 169–185 (2005)
12. Weiser, M.: The computer for the 21st century. Scientific American 265, 94–104 (1991)
13. Weiser, M.: Some computer science issues in ubiquitous computing. Communications of the ACM 36(7), 75–84 (1993)

Parametric Ideation: Interactive Modeling of Cognitive Processes

Jörg Rainer Noennig and Sebastian Wiesenhütter

Juniorprofessorship for Knowledge Architecture, TU Dresden, Germany
`joerg.noennig@mailbox.tu-dresden.de`,
`sebastian.wiesenhuetter@tu-dresden.de`

Abstract. Our paper contributes to discourses on Computer Aided Thinking and introduces new techniques for the modeling of mental processes. The objective of our investigations is to support the description and creation of ideas through physical externalizations of cognition, and their subsequent translation into evolutionary algorithms. Through different types of tangible idea models derived from architectural design practice, we developed spatial representations of complex knowledge dynamics. As a central method we employed Parametric Design, a new way of spatial-architectural modeling.

Keywords: Computer Aided Thinking, Idea Creation, Parametric Design, Physical Modelling, Spatial representation.

1 Introduction

Architectural Intelligence. Architectural design as a form of human creativity may be one of the most complex ways of problem-solving, expressing itself by translating abstract concepts into spatial and embodied solutions. Thus it appears to be an interesting object of research for the fields of Artificial Intelligence and Cognitive Neurosciences, which endeavor in understanding intelligence, cognition and thinking. A recent turn in the intelligence discussion, the notion of "Embodiment" has indicated that our thought mechanisms are influenced to a great extent by the properties of our body - which sheds new light also on the procedures of architectural design as a form of creative intelligence in action. [1]

Architects use physical and spatial models as an externalization of their thought process. We argue that the properties of the models have influence on the thought process itself, and therefore want to investigate how they enhance the formation of concepts and the generation of new ideas. As the embodied, tangible nature of models equips them with distinct features, it appears meaningful to translate such analog models into digital representations.

Parametric Modeling. We will elaborate in this paper on how the concept of embodiment can be translated into computer-aided-thinking-processes. What are the benefits of parametric models, especially in terms of fast reconfigurations of knowledge spaces? To

N. Streitz and C. Stephanidis (Eds.): DAPI/HCII 2013, LNCS 8028, pp. 225–234, 2013.

what extent may the use of digital models enhance human creativity? These technical issues touch upon further aspects of epistemology: How can knowledge units act as agents within an embodied model? This leads to the adaptation of principles of evolutionary dynamics, as well as to representations of the environment as a setting in which knowledge processes take place. Basically we hold that the translation of abstract concepts into physical models, and further into digital representation may add valuable stimuli to creative thought processes of the "users" of such modeling.

Idea Engineering. Charles ·S. Peirce, the founder of Semiotics and thus a "co-inventor" of communication and information sciences, had asked more than a century ago: "How to make our ideas clear?" [2] The question is still at stake. Resting on many of Peirce´s concepts, information technology, knowledge management, innovation theory etc. have prospered in the meantime, but relatively little has been achieved on the task of idea clarification. Yet this question is at the center of the before mentioned fields: Without insight into the discovery, explication, and modeling of ideas there won´t be secure knowledge neither on innovation, communication nor education. Therefore, as a starting point, our paper takes up Peirce´s question again, and proposes an outline for idea engineering, or better: architecting of ideas.

In order to systematically model the process of ideation one may follow a Peircean "experimentalist method" too, assuming that knowledge is constituted through a process of scientific guessing (abduction), logical derivation of general models (deduction), and empirical verification by experiment (induction). Short speaking: mental achievements arise from experimental efforts, from re-making and re-modeling.

2   Abduction

State of the Art. Computer application has, without doubt, widely helped to support intellectual and scientific work. Before all it has helped to model the principles of natural, mechanical and informational sciences. In other words: the laws of nature and machines, thus ushering in a boost of technological development in the past decades. However, the immense capacities of computers have not yet solved the problem of thinking itself. Plainly: Although equipped with immense computing powers we still cannot sufficiently explain how ideas are being made and processed. We are in dire need of models to clarify to ourselves the life of ideas.

Discourses. Two more or less competing discourses have predominated the field in the past decades: 1) the application of reasoning machines in Artificial Intelligence, 2) computer imaging in Neurosciences. As it comes to the explanation of idea processes, certain fundamental restrictions mark the limitation of these approaches. On the one hand, computer imaging technologies in neurosciences do not refer to the semantics of thought processes. They rather look at the biophysical / biochemical activity of neural structures, yet they can hardly relate the "snapshots" of neural activities to the complex formation of concepts as happening in problem solving, ideation, or imagination.

On the other hand, from the highly differentiated systems of concept taxonomies, classifications, and logical operations as represented in semantic networks and AI procedures, convincing models on the appearance of new ideas could not be presented [4]. Heuristic "invention machines" (like the problem solving routines of TRIZ) do not grasp the dynamic "Eigenleben" of ideas, which is usually based on the very environment they are embedded in, which is continuous and cannot be broken down into distinct paths.

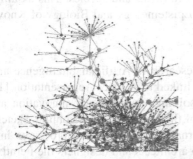

Fig. 1. Semantic Knowledge Representation (Source: Thintek)

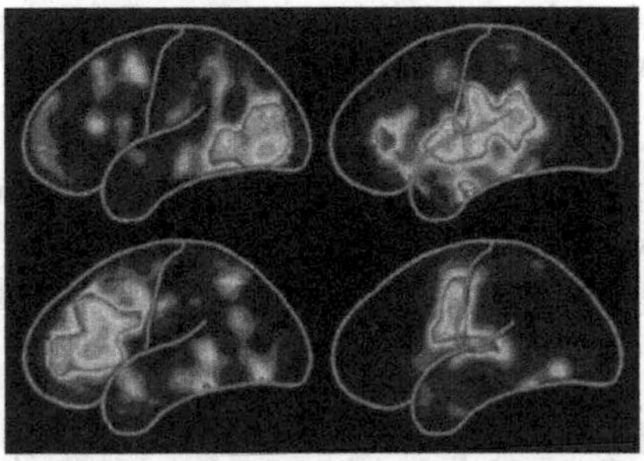

Fig. 2. Knowledge Representation by Neuroimaging (Source: TU Dresden)

Research Goal. Before mentioned question, however, is our primary interest and defines the goal of our investigation: *How to explain, and represent human knowledge processes in their making? How to dynamically model the development of thought?* Our approach, relating to the scope of the HCII conference, combines two arguments.

First, creative mental processes cannot only be represented by computing combinatorics, neither algorithmic nor self-organized. Abstract synthetic structures cannot describe the "invasion of the new", the "spark of invention". Logics are rarely creative. Idea processes need tangible, embodied interaction. Invention is based on problematic collisions with a complex environment, which the world of formal operations is not. Secondly, computers are not to be viewed as *creators or thinkers*, but shall be regarded as support actors in the dramas of scientific work. Computing is different from creative invention, it is massive conduct of logical operations. The core question then is how to relate this abstract logics to human ideation? How to relate computational power to the creative collisions of human bodies with the physical world?

Computer Aided Thinking. Since the 1990s, discourses on Computer Aided Thinking and Computer Aided Invention (CAI) have evolved which recognize the computer as supporting device also for creative intellectual processes. [3] Following this track, and in order to introduce a method for clarifying ideas by way of advanced modeling, we suggest to integrate two architectural techniques as conceptual extension:

- 3D description (spatial modeling)
- Parametric Design (computing environmental forces into shape).

These two means - if structured into a comprehensive method - may support the creation of ideas through physical externalizations of cognitive processes, and translate them into digital evolutionary algorithms. For this, our method employs three assumptions.

1st Assumption: Evolutionary Model. For the creative dynamics of idea generation ("Ideation") we propose an evolutionary approach. The repeated cycling of thoughts can be compared to iterative and mutative principle in evolution, which forms the generative machine for the development of new life forms and species. This assumption is informed by discourses on Evolutionary Epistemology and Biology of Knowledge [5][6].

2nd Assumption: Physical Representation. Research in Artificial Intelligence and Robotics has shown that cognitive processes are linked to physical representation [1]. We hold that creative activities like problem solving, invention, or innovation are strongly connected to "experimental" activities of the body, just as scribbling, sketching, or modeling. In other words, they are externalizations of mental processes into corresponding physical activity. For example, to architects and designers the iterative production of working models and prototypes is an essential part of their creative routine. Here, tangible objects and spatial descriptions are created as representatives of cognitive processes. With their invitation to immediate crafting and interaction, these objects and models enable a far better understanding of the problems at hand, and the uncovering of subsequent solution. Further, their physical composition allows an easy "grasp" and the re-structuring of their cognitive content. The latter, before all, directly feeds into the process of creating new ideas and concepts.

Environment as Condition. As stated above, environment must be regarded the trigger and source of creative invention and ideation. It is hence conditional to include environmental complexity into any model of idea making and processing. In this respect, environment can be either physical and psychological, spatial and social environment, and all combinations of such.

By Way of Body. There are multiple receptors, or sensors, for environmental factors in human cognition - yet almost all of them are bodily. An extensive discourse has formed on the way how the body shapes the way we think. Based on that tradition, our point is: To model ideational processes, a detour through the body is inevitable. There is no apt model of idea processing that does not include as a fundamental constituent a model, or representation, of the body. We may conclude: In order to stir up creativity, environmental information is to be bodily sensed as tangible information.

3rd Assumption: Tangible Heuristics and Algorithms. Above mentioned physical procedures on tangible objects and models may be interpreted as heuristic programs of ideation, problem solving etc. If well observed and formalized, such routines may be translated into computational representation. For the interaction with cognitive items in virtual space, parametric modeling tools like Rhinoceros / Grasshopper,

Evolutionary Solvers, Physics Engines (e.g. Kangaroo) present promising opportunities. They provide a wide range of flexibility combined with detailed control in the reconfiguration, and iteration, of thought spaces and their properties.

3   Deduction

Power of Architectural Modeling. Knowledge Architecture´s add-up to the theories of Computer Aided Thinking is, before all, insight into the nature of design processes. We understand "architecting" not only as the creation of houses and cities to be built, but also as a method of knowledge processing, an "epistemic modeling". Architecting is the attempt of bringing together diverse concepts in sound structure, an interactive engineering of complex ideas. We have systematically surveyed and observed the procedures of ideation and concept-development from sketch to building. Of major interest are the features of architectural modeling which bridge the gap between mental processing and physical manipulation, which rework a given context, or environment, into tangible explication of design concepts. In fact, it is a bundle of activities and procedures that may be summarized thus:

- Mind and matter: Simultaneous work on concepts and materials
- Hands-on: Bodily experience, manipulation, grafting
- Pragmatism: No idea without reference to some object
- Spatial: Working in three dimensions + x
- Repetition: Iterative re-making and re-modeling
- Experience: Establishing creative habits and implicit knowledge
- Heuristics: Partly design / goal oriented, partly self-organized

Fig. 3. The tangible intelligence of modeling and crafting

Idea Models. As a routine at TU Dresden´s Knowledge Architecture lab (which also hands out conventional architectural design tasks for buildings) students are asked to develop their design ideas via so-called idea models, that is: condensing their preliminary design concept into a symbolic, tangible icon. As it turned out, these handy models allow complex recognition, easy manipulation, and a quick assessment of design ideas. Certainly the further "clarification of idea" implies more iterative re-modeling. The first version never shows the design in full, yet the recognition of a projects theme becomes astonishingly lucid by this tool. However, the main deficit of this kind of idea modeling is its static character.

Fig. 4. Idea models for a building design (left), and for a brainstorm talk. The physical talk model (center) translates into digital semantic graph (right). (Source: TUD)

Dynamic Modeling. Based on above mentioned assumptions we propose a modeling framework for the dynamics of ideation that combines the features of physical embodiment on the one hand, and the capacities of computer on the other. At its very heart, this model is manipulative, bodily, and tangible. It rests to a large proportion on self-organization, but frequently shows goal-orientation too. In order to derive a first hypothetical models, we experimented with mechanisms showing the dynamics of growth and reproduction, with „natural phenomena" of transmitting information" (cell growth, barnacle mechanisms, bee and flower-principle, prey and predator interplay, copulation techniques, population growth).

Dynamic Knowledge Model. We established a simple physical mechanism which distinguishes two dynamic entities: The body - or bodies - of knowledge (red circles in the images below) in contrast to body of the unknown (black). In the course of development of ideas, islands of knowledge appear within the body of the unknown (Fig.5). Certainly these bodies of knowledge grow: discoveries are made, problems get solved. Whether the growing knowledge is of relevance and importance, is another question. This simple form of development applies to micro and macro levels similarly. On micro level it may be ideas that show up in talks or projects; on macro level it may be a depiction of the development of sciences which increasingly discovers and extends knowledge about nature and technology. [8]

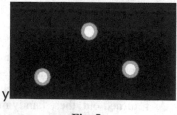

Fig. 5.

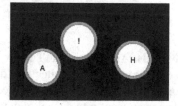

Fig. 6.

Knowledge growth raises the amount of interfaces / contact points to the area of unknown, i.e. uncertainty, open problems, unclarity. Uncertain too is the question whether the body of the unknown diminishes by the growth of knowledge. For example, the development of sciences and technology also create new problems; research is to discover new areas of the unknown. However, the more individual islands of knowledge, experience, insight etc. are being created, the more contact points, or interfaces, there are to the unknown (in Fig.6-7 the red perimeters extend).

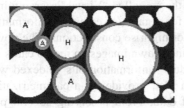
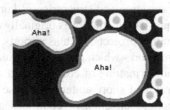

Fig. 7.   **Fig. 8.**

Further we suggest that advances of knowledge can be depicted by a) Increasing an existing area of knowledge, e.g. extending a doctrine (fig. 5-7), and b) Fusing multiple islands of knowledge into one, e.g. unifying theories or disciplines (Fig.8). In contrast to process (a), which is incremental in nature, the disruptive process (b) represents a genuine "Aha!" effect. It reduces uncertainty by reducing the interfaces to the unknown, by shrinking the perimeter while extending the area of the known (content). - This simple model with its two basic dynamics provides a blueprint for more complex procedures in "idea architecting".

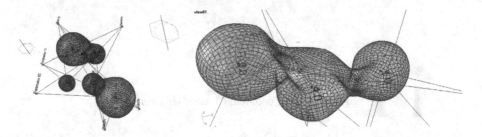

Fig. 9. Simulation of fusion process   **Fig. 10.** Minimizing surface as evolutionary goal

4   Induction

Applied Knowledge Modeling. In order to verify the above mentioned model, a series of experiments was carried out. In research seminars various options of physical modeling of knowledge processes were tested. Tangible models were developed for the processes of concept formation, conceptual evolution, cognitive self-organization, among others. Based on hands-on experiments with buildings blocks, fluids, or heaps of powders or grains, some of these models were eventually formalized into digital parametric description. By working with these very tangible matters, creative algorithms and "thought processes" were discovered and thereupon translated into computer algorithms through the architectural modeling package "McNeel

Rhinoceros", featuring a parametric model engine and a visual programming interface ("Grasshopper").

Idea Programming Process. In architecture and planning, an established method for the organisation and structuring of knowledge is the so-called "Visual Programming" technique. The method was originally developed for organizing extensive information for complex projects, such as airports, factories, or highrise constructions. The power of the method - which is mainly carried out by hand drawn images on memo cards - is the rigid formatting of complex data into individual "information bits" indexed with keywords and short sentences. These indices, in fact, provide for a parametrization and operationalization of enormous amounts of data. From observing several programming sessions (discussion panels, workshops) we developed a preliminary model of how to make idea clear, and how new concepts emerge. As it turned out, the procedure can also be used to propel ideation processes.

Particle Field. In a first step, a large number of particularized knowledge "bits" are assembled - thus creating a field condition, a cloud of knowledge units. (Fig. 11) In real programming sessions, this happens by collecting handwritten notes, sketches, memos. All elements are carefully indexed and presented on large panels. (Fig. 12)

Fig. 11. Field Condition: Cloud of information

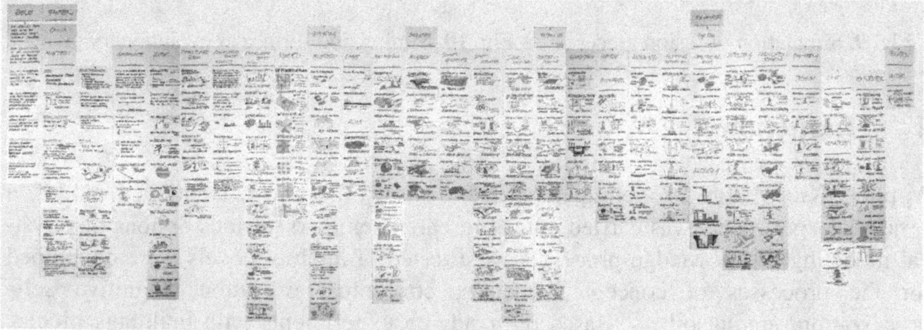

Fig. 12. Manual Programming Chart (Source: TUD Knowledge Architecture)

Mobilization. In a second step, the particles are dynamically set into action, the cloud of "information grain" starts moving, rotating, taking different stages of aggregation. The collection of data turns into an information swarm. - In real-world programming sessions, this is the part when all cards are being moved (sometimes be a number of people simultaneously) in order to search a definite placement, or order of arrangement.

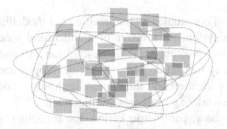

Fig. 13. Swarm Condition: Dynamic information

Anchorage. In contrast to a purely semantic clustering of cards according to their indexes - a process which resemble the "reasoning" of catalogues or search engines - we introduce certain new terms instead. This experimental move is supposed to form "common ground" for the assembled swarm of data, so-called "Test Centers". At this stage, it can be observed how the "intruders" function as anchorage points. If successful, they bring as many as possible of the floating elements to rest, and leave only few free floating. (Fig. 14) Their anchorage quality equals their capacity to match many cards without using the given indexes. In other words: they can include, combine, integrate formerly separate elements without referring to description already attached to them.

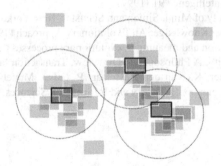

Fig. 14. Anchorage: New terms as gravity centers

If successful anchorage is achieved, new concepts can be stated as having emerged. This relates to the stage of "fusion" as represented in the generic model mentioned before (Fig. 8) - the emergence of new terms equals the merging of formerly unrelated fields, or units. - In real-world programming sessions this step happens when new "Header cards" are being introduced into the large collection of memo-cards.

This action, however, involves the completely re-arrangement of the set of data, which is given usually as chronological, or topical table charts. As regards the experimentally introduced new terms, they turn from "Headers" to "Centers of Gravity".

5   Conclusion

The insight and results of our studies on parametric idea modelling indicate the opportunities arising from a systematic transfer of architectural modelling techniques to knowledge representation. Not only for the description of epistemological concepts the proposed method may be useful. Purposefully developed and applied as a setting to generate impulses for ideation and innovation, it should be of interest in any field of knowledge intensive work (e.g. business intelligence).

As the experiments show, parametric knowledge modeling will hardly cope with capacities of human creativity. Rather it may stimulate creative thought by externalizing human thinking into tangible models, which in turn allow new idea manipulation. Thus the interaction of human mind and ideation algorithms may lead to a promising "ping-pong" relation, a cognitive partnership. Here parametric modeling takes the role of a "Proposal Engine".

References

1. Pfeifer, R., Bongard, J.C.: How the body shapes the way we think: a new view of intelligence. MIT Press, Cambridge (2007)
2. Peirce, C.S.: How To Make Our Ideas Clear. Popular Science Monthly, 286–302 (January 1878)
3. Sumi, Y., Hori, K., Ohsuga, S.: Computer-aided thinking by mapping text-objects into metric spaces. Artificial Intelligence 91 (1997)
4. Minsky, M.: The Society of Mind. Simon and Schuster, New York (1987)
5. Popper, K.R.: Objective Knowledge: An Evolutionary Approach (1972)
6. Harms, W.F.: Information and meaning in evolutionary processes (2004)
7. Rescher, N.: Complexity: A Philosophical Overview. Transaction Publishers (1998)
8. Scharnhorst, A., Börner, K., van den Besselaar, P. (eds.): Models of Science Dynamics: Encounters Between Complexity Theory and Information Sciences. Springer, Berlin (2012)

Requirements for Applying Simulation-Based Automated Usability Evaluation to Model-Based Adaptive User Interfaces for Smart Environments

Michael Quade, Andreas Rieger, and Sahin Albayrak

Technische Universität Berlin, DAI-Labor
Ernst-Reuter-Platz 7, 10587, Berlin
{michael.quade,andreas.rieger,sahin.albayrak}@dai-labor.de

Abstract. Users in smart environments benefit from context-aware applications that are able to adapt their user interfaces (UI) to specific situations. In the same way as the development of adaptive applications poses high demands on the designers, the evaluation of their usability also becomes more complex and time consuming because the context of use and different adaptation variants need to be considered. While automated usability evaluations cannot fully replace user tests in this domain, they can be applied to multiple adaptation variants at an early stage of development and thus reduce time and complexity. This paper presents general requirements for applying automated model-based usability evaluations that apply simulated user interaction as an approach to evaluate UIs of adaptive applications based on the underlying development models.

Keywords: automated usability evaluation, adaptive user interfaces, model-based UI development, smart environments.

1 Automated Usability Evaluation of Adaptive User Interfaces for Smart Environments - Benefits and Challenges

The main goal of smart environments is to assist users within their daily routines whether at work or at home. Smart environments are characterized by networked applications capable of coping with different situations that can be captured via integrated sensor systems. Usually, this is achieved with the help of adaptive applications that provide user interfaces (UI) which adapt to (predefined) situations within the observed context of use [7]. As a main challenge, adaptive applications need to present required information properly and tailored to the current users' needs and (dis-) abilities which is a complex task when dealing with many potential adaptations. Further, this high complexity also leads to problems in fully evaluating the usability of adaptive applications with user tests due to the state explosion problem [18]. Even though this would usually provide the best evaluation results, the required costs and time tend to become limiting factors for comprehensive user testing.

Understanding the formalization of interaction means and concepts of adaptive applications remains a main issue when evaluating usability. One way to address this

N. Streitz and C. Stephanidis (Eds.): DAPI/HCII 2013, LNCS 8028, pp. 235–244, 2013.

issue during development is integrating models of the application and models of the user as proposed by model-driven engineering and model-based usability evaluation. On the one hand, models of the application are able to formalize the design, express the underlying concepts and make them interpretable by machines [17]. On the other hand, user models are commonly used to describe users' physical and cognitive abilities [9] and to formalize different groups of users based on these attributes. Above all, the interconnection of both approaches can be utilized for providing adaptations to the UI and to evaluate the usability and accessibility for different groups of users. Especially for this purpose, automated usability evaluation (AUE) emerges as a paradigm allowing detailed and at the same time cheap testing of usability [6]. Most AUE approaches are using predictive analytical modeling and predictive simulation methods. Based on underlying psychological theories, concepts and models, these approaches have proved to correctly predict criteria relevant for judging an application's usability [6]; e.g. automated simulation of interaction paths, execution time predictions, cognitive load and learning time estimations.

However, there still exist main barriers to the adoption of AUE by the interaction design industry and specifically within the domain of smart environments. On the one hand, current AUE approaches require additional specific descriptions of the user, the UI and the tasks. In most cases, such descriptions of the UI and tasks do not exist or cannot be automatically derived from the final UI. For this reason, the required input (e.g. models) needs to be provided by the designers themselves, which is a time consuming and potentially error-prone task. On the other hand, most AUE approaches are hard to apply for complex tasks and more general usability evaluations. Further complicating is the fact that the context of use needs to be determined for an evaluation of adaptive applications, especially as it may change during interaction.

Initial work in the field of applying AUE to model-based UI development and adaptive user interfaces has been demonstrated. While [1] describes how usability evaluations in general can be applied to UIs stemming from a model-driven engineering process, an AUE was solely done on the code level and thereby lacking the benefits of using the development models which would reduce the effort. In [4] a model-based runtime framework for user interfaces is combined with a semi-automated workbench on the level of the final UI but does not involve the underlying development models and adaptation capabilities. Both approaches already address parts of combining model-based development with AUE but do not fully take advantage of the potential benefits or lack adaptivity capabilities.

In this paper, we examine the underlying basic requirements that have to be fulfilled for applying simulation-based automated usability evaluations on the same models that are already designed and implemented during the development process of adaptive applications within smart environments. At first, we start by narrowing the scope of applicable AUE methods to simulation-based approaches and lead over to specific requirements for such approaches during development of adaptive UIs in smart environments. Finally, we conclude this paper with a summary and give an outlook on our current and future work within this domain.

2   Why Apply Simulation-Based Automated Usability Evaluation to Adaptive User Interfaces?

As a matter of fact, different usability evaluation methods are suitable to predict and uncover different types of usability attributes. Hassenzahl et al. [5] distinguish these usability attributes into pragmatic and hedonic attributes. While the latter are mainly related to aspects of User Experience (UX); e.g. novelty and beauty of a design; they can usually only be provided with the help of extensive user tests and questionnaires. It is hard to predict hedonic attributes using AUE as these methods allow reasoning about human performance measurements mainly [6], which fall into the category of pragmatic attributes. Consequently, hedonic attributes should be out of scope when applying current AUE methods. However, quantitative and qualitative usability criteria can be applied when predicting pragmatic usability attributes; such as interaction execution time, number of required interaction steps and uncovering interaction errors by tracing the interaction path.

A simulation-based AUE method is essential in order to automate the interaction process and thereby gather a variety of different interaction paths by minimizing the effort involved. Especially designers of adaptive applications profit from such an approach, because they do not need to provide the interaction paths by hand for each possible adaptation of the UI and thereby tackle the state explosion problem. However, this does not exclude the possibility to provide a predefined interaction path in case a specific solution needs to be evaluated in more detail.

Simulation-based AUE approaches require specific input for conducting the evaluation process. This relies on the fact, that each targeted evaluation criteria, which defines how the outcome of the simulated interaction process is evaluated, can only be applied if the input information is available to the appropriate AUE method (Fig.1). Hence, this dependency between the chosen criteria for evaluation, the applicable simulation-based AUE approach and the required input-information is of high importance for the development and evaluation process.

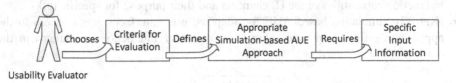

Usability Evaluator

Fig. 1. Appropriate input-information for the applied AUE method is required

3   Requirements and Benefits of Simulation-Based Automated Usability Evaluation for Adaptive User Interfaces

In this section we derive basic requirements for a simulation-based approach of AUE during development of adaptive user interfaces for smart environments. For this purpose we identify and provide detailed information about four basic factors:

– **Application factors**, such as UI information and interaction logic,
– **Context of use factors** that influence the interaction and the adaption process,
– **User factors** that are relevant for simulating user behavior, and
– **Task factors** (or a set of goals) which the simulated user tries to fulfill.

3.1   Application Factors

A formal description of the application needs to be available because simulation-based AUE rely on abstract interactions between user and application (models). As depicted in Fig. 2, information about the UI and its interaction logic is required and needs to be provided in a computer-processable way. For example, when applying GOMS-based usability evaluations [6] to graphical user interfaces, this usually comprehends all visible UI elements along the path of interaction and their specific attributes; e.g. type of the UI elements and their size and position on screen. Thus, the first basic requirement is:

- **(Req. 1)** Simulation-based AUE need to represent application-specific UI information for simulating their effect on the interaction process.

Further, for a simulation-based AUE it is essential to establish a connection between the UI elements and the task the user is currently performing in order to automatically simulate user interactions and the according system behavior. This implies that it has to be traceable what happens next if a specific UI element is activated; e.g. by clicking a button the next UI mask gets activated. Hence, this interconnection allows reasoning about the effects of using UI elements for a specific purpose within the current task. Current approaches for model-based UI development make use of executable UI and task models and thus are well-suited to provide this functionality; e.g. [14, 3]. This interconnection between UI and interaction concept builds the basis for the next requirements:

- **(Req. 2)** Simulation-based AUE for adaptive user interfaces requires access to interaction capabilities of the UI elements and their purpose for specific tasks.
- **(Req. 3)** Simulation-based AUE for adaptive user interfaces needs access to the application's follow-up states after simulated user interaction or changes in the context of use occurred.

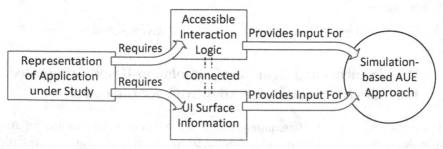

Fig. 2. The application's UI information and interaction logic serve as input for AUE methods

3.2   Context of Use Factors

In case of adaptive applications for smart environments, the system may actively take the initiative or respond to user input depending on the observed context of use. This is leading to a multitude of unique situations for which an appropriate system response needs to be ensured. Usually, an adaptation engine handles the analysis of these situations and applies appropriate adaptations. Thus, if an adaptation engine and a representation of the context of use, that can be edited and simulated, are available, simulation-based evaluation can be applied to extensively test possible interaction and adaptation paths in context-aware systems.

In general, the context of use [13] is distinguished into information about the *user environment*, the *computing environment* and the *physical environment* (see Fig. 3).

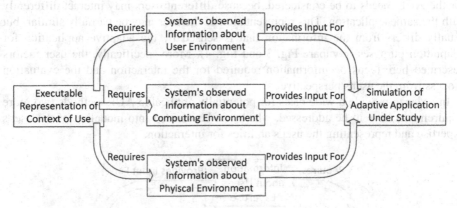

Fig. 3. The representation of the context of use needs to include the sensed information about the user, the computing environment and the physical environment in order to simulate unique situations to which the application under study can adapt to.

The information about the *user environment* includes all relevant information that can be sensed by the context-aware system via its sensor systems and internal representations via a user profile. Depending on the integrated sensor data, this may include the current location of the user and other people as well as historical and social data from a user profile. All of this information is required for the simulation-based interaction process in order to trigger required adaptations.

Information about the *computing environment* needs to include at least the relevant information about available interaction devices (for input and output); e.g. keyboard, mouse, touchscreen or display. Some AUE approaches require this information to be integrated into the information about the application under study because in some cases no sharp distinction can be made between software and hardware components. By providing this information further results can be expected from the AUE process, as e.g. GOMS-based approaches include extra time for switching between different interaction devices which might provide additional insights for the designer.

Information about the *physical environment* may include surrounding factors; e.g. acoustic or lighting conditions. In case of adaptive applications, the modeled surrounding factors need to include at least those which are sensed by the context-aware system and are source for potential adaptations; e.g. simulated movements and noise. Further side effects can be included if this data from the outside world is available to the usability evaluation. Consequently, we state the next requirement as following:

- **(Req. 4)** Simulation-based AUE for adaptive applications requires a representation of the context of use that can be edited and simulated to evaluation needs in order to create different situations to which the application can adapt to.

3.3   User Factors

Information about users, which is relevant for the simulated interaction and thus also for the AUE, needs to be considered, because different users may interact differently with the same application. This representation of the user may be partially similar, but usually differs from the information that is sensed by the adaptive application for adaptation purposes (compare Fig. 3 and Fig. 4). More specifically, the user factors described here focus on information required for the interaction and the evaluation process from the user's perspective.

In order to provide a wide basis for potentially applicable AUE methods two more requirements have to be addressed, which can be divided into modeling of the user's expertise and representing the user's abilities for interaction.

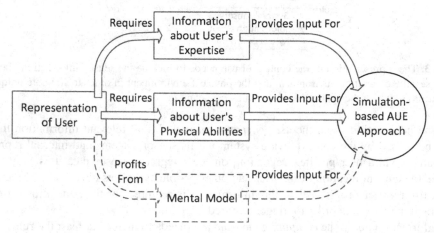

Fig. 4. The representation of the user requires information about the expertise and physical abilities for the evaluation process and profits from a mental model to reason about performed actions and their consequences to the application

On the one hand, users may differ in their expertise regarding the application and its UI, but also regarding the domain of the task. On the other hand, there exist adaptive applications that provide different user interfaces depending on the availability of this information. So basically, user expertise should be simulated in order to evaluate its effect on the interaction process on the user side and on the system side. However, most AUE methods expect that the user is an expert in the domain of the application and therefore optimal interaction paths are evaluated only. Just a few approaches model novice users, but then expect that the user has no knowledge of the domain at all; e.g. [15]. A main difference between modeling expert users and novice users is that in the latter case interaction problems due to a wrong understanding of the application can be accounted for. Unfortunately, errors due to a lack of experience with the application or domain are hard to predict. An exception is the simulation of browsing behavior, where category labels are evaluated based on semantic similarity between goal concepts and UI element labels; e.g. as in [15, 2]. On the other hand, known errors can also be modeled and their consequences can be evaluated using a simulation. This applies to cases, when e.g. the error type and its preconditions are known, but the design cannot easily be inspected manually for all adaptations due to complex adaptation rules; see e.g. [13]. A practical application of an AUE method is then to develop knowledge about error types and their precondition, either in a general way, or during the task analysis phase preceding the design of the actual application.

Another facade of the user's expertise is a mental model [10] which reflects beliefs about the application's behavior and the outside world. Such a mental model is especially useful when comparing the actual outcome of actions to the intended outcome and thus helps a user model to notice that an error occurred and may affect the following behavior; e.g. recovery strategies or canceling the interaction.

Finally, different users may have different preferences regarding interaction devices and techniques (e.g. using shortcuts) which should be accounted for as well when using simulation-based evaluation. These preferences could be included into the representation of the user (expertise) and then have an influence on the chosen actions during simulation. Thus, the fifth requirement reflects the user's expertise:

- **(Req. 5)** Simulation-based AUE for adaptive applications requires information about the user's expertise to account for individual behavior and profits from a mental model to account for expected and perceived results of actions.

Besides the user's expertise, further factors are required for a more beneficial combination of AUE and adaptive applications (see Fig. 4). An example gives the evaluation of GUIs for users with special needs and abilities, such as visual or motor impairments [8, 16]. This additional information allows to simulate different user groups and to respectively evaluate the effects of:

— different layout variants or adaptations in combination with information from the application's UI surface and interaction logic ; or
— different interaction devices and surrounding effects in combination with information from the context of use.

Consequently, AUE profits from a clear modeling of different user groups based on abilities, as it allows to reason about the effects of different adaptations based on the modeled abilities. We therefore state the sixth requirement as following:

- **(Req. 6)** Simulation-based AUE for adaptive applications requires a representation of the user's abilities to allow reasoning about their effects on the interaction process and the application's capabilities to cope with different users.

3.4   Task Factors

User interaction usually serves one or more specific goals which users try to achieve during interaction. Consequently, a description of the users' goals is also required in order to evaluate an application's usability.

Goals for interaction can be specified in form of a task which the user wants to perform. When conducting usability tests with real users, goals are usually predefined and the participants receive a description of the task to perform and (in most cases) a clear description when the goal is achieved. Like real user tests, automated usability evaluations based on simulated interaction require such predefined tasks.

If the task is to be used in simulations, the actions performed by the user to reach the goal state can be provided within the task description (Fig. 5). This would be similar to a step-by-step walkthrough which is applied by most predictive analytical modeling approaches. However, in case of some automated usability evaluations, these steps are not contained in the task description or it is not desired to have this information in advance; e.g. when evaluating novice users and their browsing behavior when looking for specific information (see e.g. [15]). Instead, the required steps have to be determined on the fly based on information describing how users would try to proceed; e.g. with the help of rules describing user behavior [12], available knowledge or further semantic information required to fulfill a task. Thus, as a final requirement regarding the task for simulation and evaluation we state:

- **(Req. 7)** Simulation-based AUE for adaptive applications requires a task description with information relevant for fulfilling the task, whether as a list of actions to perform or via an integrated solution approach.

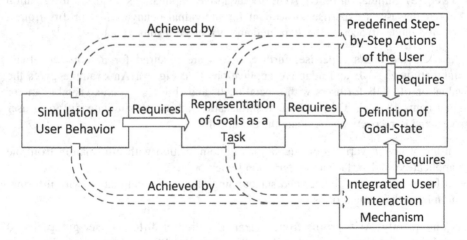

Fig. 5. The representation of the task for automated usability evaluations based on simulated user interaction requires a clear definition of the goal-state and all actions to perform or, if available, an integrated solution approach for simulating user interactions

4   Conclusion

In this paper we introduced seven generic requirements for applying simulation-based automated usability evaluations to adaptive user interfaces within the domain of smart environments. We have explained the necessity for each requirement and expected results if each of these requirements can be fulfilled.

A current state of implementation and exemplary evaluation results for such an approach that uses executable UI models stemming from a model-based runtime framework and a semi-automated usability workbench is described in [11]. Further, we are investigating the benefits of applying AUE to executable development models of adaptive user interfaces in more detail by conducting user tests within a testbed that provides a smart environment. By monitoring the effort involved and the gathered evaluation results from these user tests and comparing them to the effort and the results of the AUE conducted with the help of the development models we intend to give more insights on the benefits of the described approach in terms of saved time and ratio of uncovered usability issues.

References

1. Abrahão, S., Iborra, E., Vanderdonckt, J.: Usability evaluation of user interfaces generated with a model-driven architecture tool. In: Maturing Usability. Human-Computer Interaction Series, pp. 3–32. Springer, London (2008),
http://www.springerlink.com/content/t8861113t2764657/
2. Blackmon, M.H., Kitajima, M., Polson, P.G.: Tool for accurately predicting website navigation problems, non-problems, problem severity, and effectiveness of repairs. In: CHI 2005: Proceedings of the SIGCHI Conference on Human Factors in Computing Systems, pp. 31–40. ACM, New York (2005)
3. Blumendorf, M., Lehmann, G., Roscher, D., Albayrak, S.: Ubiquitous User Interfaces: Multimodal Adaptive Interaction for Smart Environments. In: Multimodality in Mobile Computing and Mobile Devices: Methods for Adaptable Usability, pp. 24–52. IGI-Global (2009)
4. Feuerstack, S., Blumendorf, M., Kern, M., Kruppa, M., Quade, M., Runge, M., Albayrak, S.: Automated usability evaluation during model-based interactive system development. In: Forbrig, P., Paternò, F. (eds.) HCSE/TAMODIA 2008. LNCS, vol. 5247, pp. 134–141. Springer, Heidelberg (2008)
5. Hassenzahl, M., Schöbel, M., Trautmann, T.: How motivational orientation influences the evaluation and choice of hedonic and pragmatic interactive products: The role of regulatory focus. Interacting with Computers 20(4-5), 473–479 (2008),
http://dx.doi.org/10.1016/j.intcom.2008.05.001
6. Ivory, M.Y., Hearst, M.A.: The state of the art in automating usability evaluation of user interfaces. ACM Comput. Surv. 33(4), 470–516 (2001)
7. Jameson, A.: Adaptive interfaces and agents. In: Sears, A., Jacko, J.A. (eds.) The Human-Computer Interaction Handbook: Fundamentals, Evolving Technologies and Emerging Applications, 2nd edn., pp. 433–458. CRC Press, Boca Raton (2008)
8. Keates, S., Clarkson, J., Robinson, P.: Investigating the applicability of user models for motion-impaired users. In: Proceedings of the Fourth International ACM Conference on Assistive Technologies, Assets 2000, pp. 129–136. ACM, New York (2000)

9. Kobsa, A.: Generic user modeling systems. User Modeling and User-Adapted Interaction 11(1-2), 49–63 (2001)
10. Norman, D.A.: Some Observations on Mental Models. In: Mental Models, pp. 7–14. Erlbaum, Hillsdale (1983)
11. Quade, M., Lehmann, G., Engelbrecht, K.P., Roscher, D., Albayrak, S.: Automated usability evaluation of model-based adaptive user interfaces for users with special and specific needs by simulating user interaction. In: Martín, E., Haya, P.A., Carro, R.M. (eds.) User Modeling and Adaptation for Daily Routines. Human-Computer Interaction Series, vol. 9, pp. 219–247. Springer, London (2013)
12. Ruß, A., Quade, M., Kruppa, M., Runge, M.: Rule-based approach for simulating age-related usability problems. In: Wichert, R., Eberhardt, B. (eds.) Ambient Assisted Living. Advanced Technologies and Societal Change, vol. 2, pp. 149–166. Springer, Heidelberg (2012)
13. Schilit, B., Adams, N., Want, R.: Context-aware computing applications. In: IEEE Workshop on Mobile Computing Systems and Applications, Santa Cruz, CA, US (1994)
14. Sottet, J.S., Calvary, G., Coutaz, J., Favre, J.M.: A Model-Driven Engineering Approach for the Usability of Plastic User Interfaces. In: Gulliksen, J., Harning, M.B., van der Veer, G.C., Wesson, J. (eds.) EIS 2007. LNCS, vol. 4940, pp. 140–157. Springer, Heidelberg (2008), http://dx.doi.org/10.1007/978-3-540-92698-6_9
15. Teo, L., John, B.E.: The evolution of a goal-directed exploration model: Effects of information scent and goback utility on successful exploration. Topics in Cognitive Science 3(1), 154–165 (2011)
16. Trewin, S., Pain, H.: Keyboard and mouse errors due to motor disabilities. Int. J. Hum.-Comput. Stud. 50(2), 109–144 (1999), http://dx.doi.org/10.1006/ijhc.1998.0238
17. Vanderdonckt, J., Guerrero-Garcia, J., González-Calleros, J.M.: A model-based approach for developing vectorial user interfaces. In: Proceedings of the LA-WEB 2009 (2009)
18. Goldsby, H.J., Cheng, B.H.C., Zhang, J.: AMOEBA-RT: Run-time verification of adaptive software. In: Giese, H. (ed.) MODELS 2008. LNCS, vol. 5002, pp. 212–224. Springer, Heidelberg (2008)

A User-Centered-Design Perspective on Systems to Support Co-located Design Collaboration

Javier Quevedo-Fenández, Derya Ozcelik-Buskermolen, and Jean-Bernard Martens

Dept. of Industrial Design, Eindhoven University of Technology. The Netherlands
{j.quevedo.fernandez,d.ozcelik.j.b.o.s.martens}@tue.nl

Abstract. This paper describes a contextmapping study that was conducted with designers from three companies to elicit design design-relevant insights into systems that can more optimally support co-located design collaboration. The study aim is to better understand the current and envisioned way of working of design professionals. The main results are a series of considerations regarding preferred ways to: 1) bring and share information in meetings, 2) document their outcome, 3) support multi-user interactions, 4) deal with social norms and protocols, 5) fit the exiting workflow, and 6) facilitate remote collaboration.

Keywords: Groupware, Human activity modeling and support, Ambient and Pervasive Interactions, CSCW, UCD.

1 Introduction

We study co-located collaboration in industrial design teams in order to increase our understanding of the context, people, and tasks, and with the goal to inform the design of interactive spaces that better support such practices. We elicit from such teams problems and issues that they regularly experience, and probe them to envision an alternative future in which the identified issues are resolved with the help on new (and speculative) support systems.

2 Background

Conducting design activities in teams is becoming increasingly popular due to the growing technological sophistication and complexity of new products. In fact, research has shown that in some cases team co-location can lead to higher productivity with shorter schedules [7, 8].

The emergence of novel hardware such as interactive displays, ambient sensors and digital pens at relatively low prices, together with advances in computer vision and speech recognition, are providing new opportunities to create previously unimaginable interactive spaces, including those to support co-located collaboration.

New technologies only provide new opportunities, and determining the specific requirements for systems that fit a particular community of practice is not a trivial

N. Streitz and C. Stephanidis (Eds.): DAPI/HCII 2013, LNCS 8028, pp. 245–254, 2013.

task. Scott and Wallace [9] argue that in order to design usable and effective systems, a clear understanding is required of common interactions between the users, accounting for social, cultural, activity based, temporal, ecological and motivational considerations.

3   Related Work

A number of relevant studies can be found in literature. Tang [6] carried out a series of observations on teams conducting group-drawing activities. He found out that hand gestures of participants are not only used to *mediate interaction*, such as negotiating turn-taking, but also to *express ideas* and to *convey information*. He observed that while creating and discussing drawings, much information is conveyed, some of which is not retained in the sketches that are the output of the session.

Bardram [1] describes collaborative work as a highly dynamic activity and suggests different levels of activities including *co-ordination*, *co-operation* and *co-construction*. He concludes that in order to be able to meaningfully support group activities, we must carefully examine the work activities at all three levels, and pay especially attention and support to the transitions between them.

Gutwin and Greenberg discuss the difference between designing systems for individual and group work [2]. According to these authors, individuals demand powerful ways to interact with the workspace, while the challenge for group work is to maintain awareness between the participants. They propose a series of techniques to minimize the tradeoffs between these two sets of requirements (i.e., provide multiple viewports, process feed through, include action indicators and view translations).

Amongst others, the aforementioned principles have been an inspiration for recently developed systems. The authors of such systems have also conducted different forms of user studies that revealed additional requirements. An example of such work is the *NiCe* discussion room from Haller et al. [3], for which its authors conducted an exploratory field study with a large steel company. A series of interviews and workshops were carried out for determining requirements in terms of business modeling, mock-up evaluation or requirement specification. Such studies led to new requirements such as: designing to support a *Diversity of Tasks,* to make *Use of Space and Accessiblity,* to *Foster the Creation of Shared Content,* or the *Integration of Individual and Shared Workspaces.* As part of the design of the WeSpace, a Shared Multi-Surface Collaboration System for data visualization, Wigdor et al [10] carried out a series of ethnographic studies to analyze the current practice of research-related group meetings of astrophysicists. These ethnographic studies lead to the following requirements: *Provide a Shareable Display, Allow the use of Personal Laptops, Maintain Interactivity of Existing Applications, Retain User Control Over Personal Data,* or *Provide a Record of the Meeting.* Some other systems have followed a more technology-push approach, as their aim was to solve technical challenges. An example of this latter approach is *Pictionaire,* where Hartmann et al. [4] created a collaborative system that integrates Physical and Digital artifacts by means of interaction techniques such as *Searching & Tagging, Physical-to-Digital Transitions, Remote Highlighting and Image Organization.*

Our approach differs slightly from the previous studies, mainly because the aim of our research was not to collect particular requirements, but instead to gain an improved insight into what motivates designers when conducting group activities, into the pitfalls they encounter, or their visions and aspirations for future systems.

4   Study Description

4.1   Subjects of the Study

Fifteen participants participated in our study; five from each of the three companies. These companies were active in very different application domains: document management and printing systems (Company A), food processing equipment (Company B) and automotive (Company C). Additional information on the background of the designers involved is provided in table 1.

Table 1. Number of participants for each of the domains of practice

Domain of Practice	Number of Participants
Product Designer	2
Interaction Designer	1
Usability Engineer	1
HMI Specialist	2
Sales representative	1
Mechanical Engineer	2
Mechanical R&D Designer	2
Visual Designer	1

4.2   Method of the Study

Contextmapping is a generative research method that actively involves users and stakeholders in the design process through a series of exercises. The primary goal is to understand their everyday life experiences and to gain tactic knowledge about the context of use [5]. Contextmapping can also provide access to people's visions, aspirations, fears and ideas about the future. We utilized this method in our study because we not only wanted to learn how designers hold co-located collaborative meetings, but also to understand their visions about the ideal way of conducting them in the future. Hence, we wanted insight in both current practices and future aspirations.

Phases of the Study. Our implementation of the Contextmapping method distinguished three phases. A first individual activity spanned approximately three weeks and required participants to fill in a cultural probe documenting different kinds of design-related meetings (sensitization). Secondly, two workshops carried out in the same day, one on eliciting existing problems during meetings, and a participatory design workshop on generating futuristic solutions.

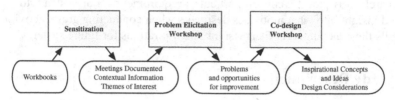

Fig. 1. Distinctive phases in the Contextmapping study, as well as created outcomes

Sensitization. The sensitization phase is used to prepare participants for a group session, by helping them *"remember past experiences, express their memories, opinions and dreams"* [5]. In order to promote this, participants were given a workbook to help them reflect on, document, and analyze their own context some time before the session. Our workbook asked them to describe occurrences of design-related face-to-face collaboration. In each entry participants were asked to write down the aim of the meeting, the people involved, a brief description of how the meeting went, describe what they liked or disliked about the meeting, and what they came and left with. Additionally they could attach a picture or a sketch.

The Workshops. The workshops were planned as a one-day activity involving all participants from all companies. The aim of the first workshop was to identify issues and concerns related to the current way of conducting co-located design-related meetings. The participants were divided in three groups, one per company, which created a series of storyboards that highlighted one or more problems or issues that reflected their current experience, which were subsequently discussed in a plenary meeting. The sensitizing workbooks were returned to the participants for inspiration.

In the second workshop each group was asked to create a product concept that addressed the issues raised in the stories. Participants were encouraged to make use of futuristic technologies, such as intelligent environments. To inspire them, participants were presented a video with extracts of futuristic concepts from science fiction movies. In addition, they were given the opportunity to experience three interactive working demos. The first was made by projecting an existing single-user tool (*Photoshop*) on a wall display and providing all participants with an individual input device (Bluetooth stylus) that they could use for turn-taking. The second demo was a large horizontal area for digital sketching that maintained a historical archive. The last demo used a horizontal 52 inch multi-touch table with stylus and finger input, with pictures that could be resized, rotated, scaled with the fingers, and sketched that could be created with the help of a stylus. The table could also receive pictures send wirelessly from a smartphone.

5   Results

5.1   Sensitization

A total of twelve workbook diaries were completed with an average of 5 reported meetings per workbook. We found the following themes of interest in the diaries:

Absence of Desired Material. During meetings, practitioners do not always have access to desired material, such as images, or videos. (S6) *"I would have liked more information instead of being dependent on what the others bring along"*. Even in cases when the relevant material was available in the meeting in the laptop of a participant, it is often too difficult and time consuming to share it publicly with the rest of the group. (S7) *"I dislike that it is difficult to share images on a computer, we lack a proper sharing tool"*. (S6) *"I would have liked to show the old website during the meeting which was only visible on my laptop"*. This lack of material may lead to making uneducated decisions. "(S1) *"I did not like worrying that wrong choices are made based on incorrect assumptions"*.

Creating Combining and Transforming Material. Often, material needs to be combined or transformed. (S7) "I would have liked a light way to create and visualize our ideas, being able to walk around it with the stakeholders and make easy adaptations, creating a preview of how it will look like". It happens that more than one participant wants to provide direct input for multiple participants to manipulate the material, rather than simply stare while others do it, which leads to loosing input and interest while waiting. (S14) "I disliked the fact that I could not physically interact, but only verbally … …I would have liked to be able to give input on the fly by shaping ideas" (S8) "I would have liked a quick drawing tool to be used by both". We also found that it is often hard to describe an idea involving dynamic behavior using only static sketches. We found that the current media that articulate design artifacts have limitations in the amount or kind of information that they can convey, and practitioners are in need of novel tools that allow them to quickly and easily express complex dynamic ideas in such settings. (S4) "I disliked that it was hard to express my ideas because I didn't have the proper medium to do so… I would have liked the availability of an interactive sketching tool "

Capturing and Documenting the Results. Currently, when a session is over, participants leave with a set of individual notes and sketches. Such notes are not shared between participants, and even if a person creates a summary or takes meeting minutes, some information is excluded, as it is restricted to those notes that were made, affected by personal perception of what was being said and done. (S8) *"I disliked that it was difficult to take all the information with you after the meeting"*(S2) *"I would like to avoid lots of papers which are later on not understandable and I would have liked a simple summary from everything that was discussed / sketched with comments"*.

Social. We found that some people tend to dominate, leaving too little time for others to provide input. (S2) *"I would like to avoid a decision without giving a fair chance to every opinion"*. Decision-making is a difficult aspect of meetings. It can take large amounts of time, and can create uncomfortable situations, like someone feeling emotionally offended. (S8) *"I'd like to avoid discussions that are not relevant, it's always the same people who comment and discussions that are going nowhere"*. It also happens that the focus of the meeting gets lost as a discussion heads off in other directions. Participants often realize too late that they may have lost valuable time. (S3) *"I like to avoid getting stuck in an accidentally though technically interesting topic"*.

5.2   Problem Elicitation Workshop

Company A described three stories. The first story concerned a co-design meeting where all parties involved are working closely together, but where the entire team needs to make a sudden shift, due to an external factor. Suddenly, additional unforeseen material needs to be consulted and the challenge is to quickly get acquainted with and adapt to a new situation.

The second story described a multidisciplinary meeting were participants have to reach a collective agreement with a potentially large impact on the final specifications of a design concerning large textual documents. Each member needs to know the details of his/her part of the design, but also needs to assess the interaction of their own part with the rest of the system. Such meetings pose frequent problems, as participants continuously get confused, and there are frequent clashes between proposed functionalities. Often, it is only some time after the agreement has been reached that individual participants realize that they have agreed on details that they were not fully aware of or had misinterpreted.

The third story talked about meetings where practitioners in the same field, usability engineers for instance, come together to align their graphics and interaction designs across different products. Participants frequently have different opinions on what the best solution might be, so there is a lack of shared interests and shared responsibility, but despite that they have to come up with a shared agreement. The main problem expressed is that as such meetings do not take place frequently, from meeting to meeting people slowly forget, and tend to personally reinterpret previous agreements, eventually leading to substantial differences in designs across projects.

Company B described a situation where two persons from different fields, in this case an engineer and a salesman, meet to discuss about a design for a client. The salesman has met previously with a client and has collected a request for a custom part. The salesman believes that the changes will be minimal, while the engineer thinks the opposite. The engineer tries to explain the magnitude of the consequences that derive from the required changes, but the salesman does not really understand, as he sees only the overall picture, which in his opinion does not appear to be so complicated. There is a lack of common understanding, there is a lack of material that can help them better reach such common understanding, and there are external factors that oblige them to come to an agreement quickly. The engineer feels forced to make a decision and commits to a plan of which he is not even sure if it is possible to implement, as he believes that a proof-of-concept prototype is needed for such a decision. As a side note, the participants who described this story were still arguing about a particular recent similar case.

The first story from Company C was about co-design meetings where designers of diverse backgrounds come together to work on, and further elaborate a concept (see Fig 2). These meetings happen because the deadline of the project is close and they do not have enough time to finish the standard distributed procedure. For this purpose, the two or three participants sit together behind a computer operated by one of them, the visual designer in their particular story. During the meeting there is an iterative process of discussion, refining and making changes to the design. The first problem expressed in the story is the inability to perform simultaneous interactions on the artifact. When a person that is not controlling the computer wants to propose a change, he / she has to rely on his verbal capabilities, as he / she can only talk but not act. There are continuous misinterpretations and confusions, followed by intense discussions on how things should look or behave, and a feeling of too much waiting for the other participants to carry out the changes in the artifact being discussed.

The second story talks about an evaluation meeting involving a multidisciplinary team of designers, engineers and management stakeholders. Normally they discuss over PowerPoint presentations, but in some cases the information they convey is insufficient, as ideally they should rely on simulations to reach an educated agreement.

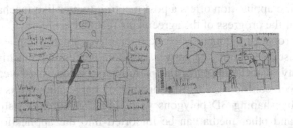

Fig. 2. Fragments of the Storyboard by Company C describing a co-design meeting where one of the participants regularly has to wait for the other to perform changes on the artifact

Cross Company Discussion. In general all of the problems were acknowledged and recognized by all companies, even those that were not present in their own story(s). This includes misunderstandings between people from the same or different disciplines, having different readings on the outcome of the sessions, forgetting and reinterpreting the decisions made, or suffering sudden unexpected changes in the agenda. Companies A and B do not conduct the kind of design meetings where two or more people work synchronously on a particular design case sharing the same computer. On the other hand they do experience similar limitations when conducting brainstorms or focus groups. However all companies expressed their skepticism of having tools that can enable simultaneous interactions, or that bring rapid replication and sharing of artifacts. The key issue in this respect is the emotional response from participants when experiencing a loose of control and ownership of their creations, or of their role in the process.

5.3   Group Design Workshop

For this workshop each company formed a group, and was asked to design a concept addressing some of the problems expressed in the storyboards. The groups were encouraged to make use of recent technological developments presented (see Phases of the Study), finishing with a group presentation and discussion.

Company A created an iPad application concept to support design meetings that provides a shared and a private area, and that is connected to personal and shared multimedia libraries. The documents can be loaded during a meeting on the private area of the application to visualize, interact with, or sketch on them and can be transferred to the shared area, which is common for all participating devices. The users can take private notes of the meeting that can be shared and donated to the archive, which also includes a history of all changes over the shared area. The devices can sense what is happening outside the screen, keeping track of how much time each person is participating or know which part of the agenda the meeting is currently at, and uses this information to intelligently moderate the meeting (i.e. suggest a dominant person to become less participative, or suggest to move to the next item of the agenda). The application offers an in-meeting secret messaging channel to coordinate thoughts, and remote users can participate in the meeting using a similar device. Finally, the application offers a post-meeting twitter like mechanism to update other members of the progress of the agreements reached.

Company B proposed a domain-specific interactive tabletop application for groups to create and discuss design alternatives of food processing machines, which can simulate a variety of different parts and parameters (speed, size, etc.), and can also intelligently detect conflicts such as collisions of parts. New parts can be created collaboratively by shaping 3D polygons with finger gestures. Existing 3D models, images, videos and other media can be imported into the application to build new parts. Finally, the system can connect to a similar system in a remote location where other participants can equally interact with all of the material.

Company C designed a multi-user application running on a vertical display and a tabletop. Designers approach it to combine their work, and make changes, visualizing the outcome in a virtual driving simulation context.   Users can import multiple types of CAD and graphic files and combine the material visually. It is possible to make changes on the fly, but the system must offer a mechanism to avoid conflicts in simultaneous interactions, to prevent the session from becoming chaotic. The application also tracks all changes and provides a historical view. At any moment the designs can be placed inside the cabin of a virtual vehicle to show different driving scenarios and conditions to help the stakeholders visualize and experience the designs under various conditions. Finally, the created concepts can be sent directly from the application to a real test driver in a vehicle, who is wearing a pair of magic goggles (augmented reality) and can provides immediate feedback on the concept.

Cross Company Discussion. Participants spoke about their concerns of having too many screens and devices to interact with, as it may lead people to loose attention and focus. It became apparent that future systems should offer some mechanisms to avoid this, (S8) "*Maybe the chairman can limit the activities to things that are only relevant for the meeting, and not your email*". Simultaneous editing may be interesting, but there are many concerns of how this can be properly supervised. (S11) "*When working together, how do we prevent that it becomes a big mess? I am more scared for getting some kind of clash*". Others feared the sense of lost responsibility and authorship of the content. (S9) "*I wouldn't like it if everyone is making changes to my design, that's my responsibility*".

The topic of remote collaboration was present in all of the designs. All companies saw this almost as a basic requirement, and remarked that one should not focus merely on the interactions around the table, but must keep remote access in mind, as it is part of the reality of their practice.

There was a general concern with privacy, especially for Company A. Even if the system is capable of capturing and storing everything they do, people will feel reluctant to interact if they do not feel as if they have sufficient control over their data. (S3) "*Some things you want to remember just for yourself for later on*".

6   Discussion

The study revealed a series of positive and negative considerations that are relevant to the design of interactive systems and spaces to support co-located design collaboration.

Designers often find it *difficult to access and share material* during meetings. This may turn into frustration or even become a problem as it may lead to making choices based on incorrect assumptions, or may require to postpone decisions. Similarly, designers often want to *create, combine or transform material in a collaborative way*, but they are unable to do so due to the (single-user) nature of the interfaces of existing tools. However, providing multi-user functionality is also looked upon with some skepticism. Designers generally do not want to lose ownership of their creations, and therefore do not necessarily have a positive attitude towards others altering their designs; some fear that allowing this may even lead to chaos. Designers are also concerned with how *social norms and protocols might be facilitated or enforced* by *meeting-ware*, and if this will respect the users privacy and will be based on their personality, cultural background, and particularities of the design situation. Design meetings most frequently do not consist of a single continuous activity, but instead of a *series of sub-activities that are carried out dynamically over time*. There is an expectation that systems may be designed just for a particular type of activity, or that they may constrain the users in switching from one activity to another. At the same time, such dynamic nature often makes it difficult to *communicate the outcome* of a collaborative session, as *capturing and documenting the results and interactions* is a cumbersome venture. Designers acknowledged that this area offers technology many opportunities for improvement. However, they also see it as a challenge, as the outcome is not always something that can be materialized into concrete artifacts, as on occasion it may be a more subjective quality such as a gut feeling or a mindset. Overall, there is a concern if new technologies will indeed *fit into the existing workflow and process*, meaning that one should not only consider what happens while they are being used, but what is required before and after doing so. We have also seen concerns regarding the *technological saturation and sophistication of the environments*. Designers identified the risk that more technology may distract individuals from the group tasks, it may lead participants to become immersed in individual activities, or the situation might become dominated by excessive interaction.

References

1. Bardram, J.: Designing for the dynamics of cooperative work activities. In: CSCW 1998: Proceedings of the 1998 ACM Conference on Computer Supported Cooperative Work, pp. 89–98 (1998)
2. Gutwin, C., Greenberg, S.: Design for individuals, design for groups: tradeoffs between power and workspace awareness. In: Proceedings of the 1998 ACM Conference on Computer Supported Cooperative Work (CSCW 1998). ACM, New York (1998)
3. Haller, M., Leitner, J., Seifried, T., Wallace, J.R., Scott, S.D., Richter, R., Brandl, P., Gokcezade, A., Hunter, S.: The NiCE Discussion Room: Integrating Paper and Digital Media to Support Co-Located Group Meetings. In: Proceedings of the SIGCHI Conference on Human Factors in Computing Systems (CHI 2010). ACM, New York (2010)
4. Hartmann, B., Ringel, M.M., Benko, H., Wilson, A.D.: Pictionaire: supporting collaborative design work by integrating physical and digital artifacts. In: Proceedings of the 2010 ACM Conference on Computer Supported Cooperative Work (CSCW 2010), pp. 421–424. ACM, New York (2010)
5. Sleeswijk Visser, F., Stappers, P.J., van der Lugt, R., Sanders. 2005. Contextmapping: Experiences from practice E.B.N 119-149. CoDesign (2005)
6. Tang, J.C.: Findings from observational studies of collaborative work. International Journal of Man-Machine Studies 34(2), 143–160 (1991) ISSN 0020-7373, 10.1016/0020-7373(91)90039-A
7. Teasley, S.D., Covi, L.A., Krishnan, M.S., Olson, J.S.: Rapid software development through team collocation. IEEE Transactions on Software Engineering 28(7), 671–683 (2002), doi:10.1109/TSE.2002.1019481
8. Teasley, S., Covi, L., Krishnan, M.S., Olson, J.S.: How does radical collocation help a team succeed? In: Proceedings of the 2000 ACM Conference on Computer Supported Cooperative Work (CSCW 2000), pp. 339–346. ACM, New York (2000)
9. Wallace, J.R., Scott, S.D.: Contextual design considerations for co-located, collaborative tables. In: 3rd IEEE International Workshop on Horizontal Interactive Human Computer Systems, TABLETOP 2008, pp. 57–64 (2008)
10. Wigdor, D., Jiang, H., Forlines, C., Borkin, M., Shen, C.: WeSpace: the design development and deployment of a walk-up and share multi-surface visual collaboration system. In: Proceedings of the SIGCHI Conference on Human Factors in Computing Systems (CHI 2009), pp. 1237–1246. ACM, New York (2009)

Design Considerations for Leveraging Over-familiar Items for Elderly Health Monitors

Edward Wang[1], Samantha Ipser[1], Patrick Little[1], Noah Duncan[1],
Benjamin Liu[1], and Shinsaku Nakamura[2]

[1] Harvey Mudd College, Department of Engineering, 301 Platt Blvd, Claremont, CA
{ywang,sipser,plittle,nduncan,beliu}@g.hmc.edu
[2] Kogakuin University, Department of Mechanical Engineering, 1-2-4-2 Nishishinjuku,
Shinjuku, Tokyo 163-8677, Japan
g109052@ns.kogakuin.ac.jp

Abstract. Japan is facing the phenomenon of an aging population. Elderly individuals in Japan are becoming increasingly isolated, with no one to look after him or her as the elderly individual's health deteriorates. To prevent this decline in elderly individuals, the Japanese government has been introducing various devices to monitor the health of elderly individuals. However, existing products in Japan do not fully address customer needs because they focus solely on functionality. As a result, elderly individuals that do not depend on monitoring may find the system too inconvenient. However, it is still important for elderly individuals in good health to be monitored to identify risks and prevent a decline in health. Therefore, health monitor designers must reduce the inconvenience to the user caused by systems that monitor elderly individuals.

Keywords: User Interface, Health Monitoring, Gernotechnology.

1 Introduction

The proportion of elderly individuals in Japan's population is growing rapidly [1]. The problem is compounded with elderly individuals becoming increasingly isolated. As individuals age, their health deteriorates, but elderly in Japan often have no one to take care of them [2]. Moreover, the Japanese government has also identified a gradual decline in mental health due to loneliness. Lack of contact with family and friends has a negative impact on the physical health of elderly individuals as mental stress takes its toll. This ultimately leads to a cyclic effect where the lack of family connection leads to mental stress that adversely affects physical health, leading to even more mental stress. To address these issues, the Japanese government has been introducing various ways to make sure the safety and health of elderly individuals are monitored. This provides capable and independent elderly individuals with the functionality of a caretaker, while also ensuring that they feel less mental stress because they are being watched over [3].

A key problem of existing health monitors for elderly individuals is that users are required to adjust his or her lifestyle to incorporate the new device into their daily

N. Streitz and C. Stephanidis (Eds.): DAPI/HCII 2013, LNCS 8028, pp. 255–261, 2013.

routines. The inconvenience not only makes it hard for users to remember to use the device, but also poses a problem with wide spread adoption. In addition, existing systems fail to address the mental deterioration of the elderly due to loneliness and lack of connection with their family.

To overcome the shortcomings of existing systems, which mainly address functionality, our group approached the problem from a user centric perspective. The project's main goal was to develop monitoring devices that non-intrusively integrate into a person's current lifestyle. To achieve this objective, our group's devices were designed with form factors that mimic items that an elderly individual would commonly use on a daily basis. A well-chosen form factor streamlines the process of health monitoring so that elderly individuals can have their well being measured and analyzed without learning a new interface. However, an invisible monitoring system does not address the mental stress of the user caused by loneliness and lack of connection. To address that issue, this project focused on development of devices that provide psychological reassurance or connection with his or her family.

This document will serve as a starting point for others interested in pursuing an extension to our implementation. Instead of focusing on the actual hardware implementations of this year long project, we will highlight the design space and thought process the group gathered in developing a prototype that demonstrates a health monitor that is both non-intrusive and promotes family connection.

2   Overview of Current Solution Space

Existing solutions are capable of monitoring the welfare of elderly individuals. However, the current solutions require a change in the lifestyle of the elderly user. The Japanese government, through regionally sponsored projects, has made various efforts in addressing this issue. Sponsored by the Niigata Prefecture, a company in Tokyo called IDUR designed the ABS1 continuous monitoring sensor package made to track different vital signs and activity data. The elderly would wear the ABS1 measurement device as a clip on their pants (Figure 1) [3]. On the other end of the spectrum, Paramatec designed the HN-301 is a central health measurement system at home that will take comprehensive data like a daily check up. To use the HN-301, the user will interact with the device once a day to get a measurement of heart rate, galvanic skin response (GSR), and blood pressure [4]. The SECOM Safety Call system is a check-up service that keeps track of the elderly through phone. The call system was introduced in Japan to address the issue of elderly loneliness. When an elderly feels unwell, he or she can notify the call center. The call services will contact the elderly and ask them about how they are doing and pay the elderly a visit when necessary. With the Safety Call System, the users self-evaluate their condition and determine whether it is appropriate to contact health officials. These services are often augmented by the use of connected health monitors that the elderly can use to measure his or her vitals to provide more information about their conditions during a call.

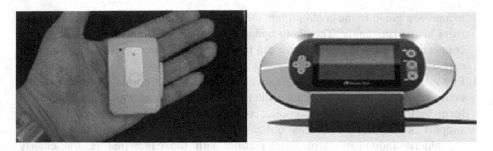

Fig. 1. Examples of health monitors being developed through local government projects. Left is the ABS1 and the right is the HN-301.

The main target of these devices is the elderly demographic that is still healthy enough to live independently but will benefit by being monitored for early signs of deterioration. These solutions require the user to actively adapt to the device or service. This is a flaw in the design, because elderly users who feel that they are healthy may have not have enough motivation to wear the ABS1 or pick up the HN-301, and may not relay health problems to the Safety Call System. Thus, while the functionality of the monitoring system exists, the user experience has prevented adoption in the Japanese market.

3   Proposed Solution

Instead of focusing on the monitoring functionality and finding ways to make the package of sensors as small as possible, the group focused on identifying interfaces that an elderly would already use on a daily basis. Leveraging an already familiar device removes the need for the user to adapt to the monitoring system. The established habits for interacting with the object also give an entry point for sensor choices and placement [5].

For this project, the group developed health-monitoring devices from several categories of form factors that the elderly user might interface with regularly. Each category was evaluated for its ability to enforce feelings of reassurance and connection in the user.

1. Wearable item: The current solution space exists primarily in this category. If the health monitor has a wearable form factor, a wider variety of data can be taken; however, this form factor is also very difficult to integrate into the user's lifestyle precisely because they interact with it the most. In our subsequent discussion on design considerations, we will be including this form factor to give a more complete comparison of the design space. However, this category of form factor was not the focus of this project and we did not produce a prototype of this variety, because it did not address the connectivity and psychological reassurance aspect of our project.
2. In-home Item: An item placed in the house, such as a television remote, electronic photo frame, or teacups, could take data regularly as the user interacts with it. For

example, a photo frame could prompt the user when there are new photos available from his or her family. The photo updates become a constant reminder of family connection. Meanwhile, the device can measure and transmit health data to remote caregivers.

3. Portable item: A portable item that an elderly user might normally carry outdoors could be used to take data not available to monitoring device with a stationary item form factor. A cane, for example, could provide physical and psychological support as the elderly individual utilizes it. The cane form factor would leverage the elderly individual's typical interaction with the cane; that is, the elderly individual would use it outdoors on walks. While the elderly is out of his or her home, the family member would be notified of the activity and can watch for any sudden changes that may need them to contact their parent. The reassurance that someone is looking out for the elderly user will further reduce the stress of leaving the house and encourage them to venture outdoors more frequently.

Because the monitoring system is intended to be easy to integrate into the user's lifestyle, the device must use the elderly user's typical interaction with the form factor as the basis for sensor selection and placement. Established habits can give a good guide to the frequency at which an object is used, how an object is used, and where an object makes contact with a person.

4   Device Interaction

4.1   Usage Frequency and Interaction Types

A high volume of information can be obtained by embedding sensors in items that the user would wear. This is the method that most have investigated, from instrumented clothing to watches. This type of device would be able to take data constantly as long as the user wears it. However, a user may prefer a specific style and not want to replace it with a different version despite added monitoring functionality. Additionally, because the device would be constantly used, it is more likely to experience wear and tear and would need to be very durable.

A cane with embedded sensors can act as a physical support while monitoring elderly users. A cane form factor would directly target the market that already uses and relies on canes for daily activities. For these users, the cane form factor would be easily adapted into their lifestyle. Because the use of a cane is typically outdoors, the form factor would be effective at monitoring the users when they leave the house. This is the form factor the group ultimately created a demo prototype, which measures ambient temperature and humidity, GPS, step count, fall detection, hand temperature, and heart rate (Figure 2).

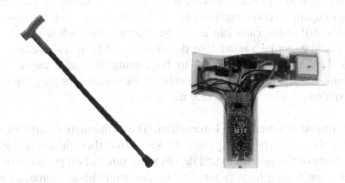

Fig. 2. Prototype as designed by the Harvey Mudd engineering team for the walking cane form factor. This initial prototype is capable of measuring ambient temperature and humidity, GPS, step count, fall detection, hand temperature, and heart rate.

Surveys conducted by the team show that most Japanese elderly individuals often watch television at home [6]. By incorporating sensors into a TV remote, the system can acquire health information and send it wirelessly to a data hub somewhere in the house while the elderly individual is using the remote. This method would gather heart rate and body temperature through sensors embedded in the remote that contact the skin when the remote is grasped. However, it would not be useful for determining body activity or location, since the remote will most likely be kept in one location. A person interacts with most objects at home infrequently and in short bursts. But usage is usually routine and can give access to the general activity level of a person. This form factor gravitates towards information that can be measured through the hand.

4.2   User Involvement

Taking into account the level of user involvement is crucial in providing a non-intrusive experience yet providing a sense of connection with the family. Mainly, the group looked at two aspect of involvement: Device power management and interaction encouragement.

Power Management. Power consumption of sensor devices is a topic of concern when designing a portable health monitor that will be used daily. Currently, the wearable devices such as the Fitbit employ ultra low power sensors such as MEMS accelerometers to monitor activity related to movement. The low power consumption allows these wearable devices to run for weeks on a single charge. However, for devices that employ active sensors such as the GPS on the cane, the power drain becomes significant. However, requiring the user to remember to plug in the device on a semi-daily basis will require the user to change their daily routine. This is particularly important for the idea of converting common items into health monitors. The act of charging a tea cup or a cane is definitely not a habit anyone has. More over, this makes the effectiveness of the health monitor dependent on the elderly to remember to charge the device. To address this issue, the group looked into different possibilities to again leverage common habits. For the canes, it is feasible to create a recharging stand that the cane can easily be dropped into when the elderly comes home. This could either be a standalone device or could be in a shape of a bucket that is commonly placed at the doorway to hold umbrellas and canes. Similarly, a television remote shaped monitor could rely on induction charging built into a tray that often exist on a coffee table to place remotes.

Intentional Encouragement for Interaction. These interaction aims to remind the elderly to use the device by giving them the sense that their family is watching over them. It is, however, important to still design these interaction points to be within the natural interaction for the form factor. For the electronic photo frame, an elderly will be prompted to interact with the photo frame through alerts that family members have uploaded new photos. The connection provided by new family pictures will act as motivation to interact with the health monitor. Similarly, if the elderly is at the doorway, the cane could give an audio reminder. This not only prompts the elderly to take the monitor along, but also creates just enough reminders that the cane is actively monitoring the elderly.

5   Discussion

There are many disadvantages to making health monitors out of common objects in a user's life. Most items used on a daily basis are used infrequently or for short periods. Each item provides limited health data based on the way the user typically interacts with it. For example, a picture frame can provide connectedness while periodically monitoring some basic health information such as heart rate and GSR, which tends to need the user to be stationary. However, the same picture frame cannot provide GPS location when the user goes for a walk, because the user is unlikely to interact with the frame in that manner.

Conversely, aside from the decrease in adoption barrier, the advantage of designing for different form factor is that one device does not need to record everything. This can reduce the design complexity significantly. Given a suite of devices, each device can record a short snippet of the user's daily state. Given enough of these interactions, a full picture of the senior's overall health can be produced. A suite of these devices may include a cup, television remote, chair, photo frame, and a walking aid. The cup can reveal water intake. Both the remote and the cup can opportunely record pulse and skin moisture level, which requires good skin contact. The combination of the chair and the remote can give an estimate of general activeness of the senior. The photo frame can act as both a central information hub that the other devices report and display the data collected and act as a portal to connect the elderly user with the rest of his or her family.

6   Conclusion

Designing health monitors from familiar items reduces the need to change the elderly user's already established life style. However, the creation of such a device requires significantly more understanding of user interactions. In order to create the walking cane implementation, the group had to understand not only how a user will generally hold the device, walk with the device, but even how the user will remember to take the device and put away the device. Most importantly, however, given a better understanding of the natural interaction with the device, it is also possible to find opportunities to introduce interaction points that will remind the elderly user that the health monitor is helping his or her family watch over them.

References

1. Statistics   Bureau   Handbook   –   Chapter   2   Population   (2011),
   http://www.stat.go.jp/english/data/handbook/c02cont.htm
2. Akiyama, et al.: Conference Proceeding at American Gerontology Conference: Health Deterioration of Male and Female Elderly (PowerPoint slides). Retrieved from personal contact with Yoichi Tao, Senior Director of SECOM (2008)
3. Sun, W., Watanabe, M., et al.: Factors associated with good self-rated health of non-disabled elderly living alone in Japan: a cross-sectional study. BMC Public Health 7, 297 (2007)
4. Mobile BioSensor ABS1 (in Japanese), http://www.idur.co.jp/sub/sensor-catalog.pdf
5. System for Support of Home Treatment (in Japanese), http://www.parama-tech.com/support/support_04.html
6. Morris, M., Lundell, J.: Ubiquitous Computing for Cognitive Decline: Findings from Intel's Proactive Health Research, Intel Corporation (2003)
7. Duncan, N., Ipser, S., Liu, B., Nakamura, S., Wang, E.: 2011-2012 Global Clinic: Non-Intrusive Monitoring System for Isolated Elderly (Archived in the official annual report for the Harvey Mudd College Clinic Program)

Part IV
Smart Cities

Portable Health Clinic: A Pervasive Way to Serve the Unreached Community for Preventive Healthcare

Ashir Ahmed[1], Sozo Inoue[2], Eiko Kai[1], Naoki Nakashima[3], and Yasunobu Nohara[3]

[1] Faculty of Information Science and Electrical Engineering, Kyushu University
744, Moto'oka, Nishi-ku, Fukuoka, Japan
{ashir,kai}@soc.ait.kyushu-u.ac.jp
[2] Faculty of Engineering, Kyushu Institute of Technology
1-1 Sensui-cho, Tobata-ku, Kita kyushu, Japan
sozo@mns.kyutech.ac.jp
[3] Kyushu University Hospital, 3-1-1, Maidashi, Higashi-ku, Fukuoka, Japan
{nnaoki,y-nohara}@info.med.kyushu-u.ac.jp

Abstract. One billion people (15% of the world population) are unreached in terms of accessing to quality healthcare service. Insufficient healthcare facilities and unavailability of medical experts in rural areas are the two major reasons that kept the people unreached to healthcare services. Recent penetration of mobile phone and the unmet demand to basic healthcare services, remote health consultancy over mobile phone became popular in developing countries. In this paper, we introduce two such representative initiatives from Bangladesh and discuss the technical challenges they face to serve a remote patient. To solve these issues, we have prototyped a portable health clinic box with necessary diagnostic tools, we call it a "portable clinic" and a software tool, "GramHealth" for archiving and searching patients' past health records. We carried out experiments in three remote villages and in two commercial organizations in Bangladesh by collaborating with local organization to observe the local adoption of the technology. We also monitored the usability of the portable clinic and verified the functionality of "GramHealth". We display the qualitative analysis of the results obtained from the experiment. GramHealth DB has a unique combination of structured, semi-structured and un-structured data which can be considered as BigData. We have partly analyzed the data manually to find common set of rules to build a better clinical decision support. The model of analyzing the GramHealth BigData is also presented.

Keywords: Portable Clinic, Personal Health Records (PHR), Remote Health Consultancy, BigData, CDSS (Clinical Decision Support System).

1 Introduction

There are 1 billion people are unreached in terms of accessing to quality healthcare service [1]. About four thousand children die of diarrhea in a day, one pregnant mother dies in every 90 seconds. This scenario can be dramatically changed if we can simply convey few simple medical tips to the target unreached community. Most of the unreached people are from rural areas in developing countries [2]. Healthcare

N. Streitz and C. Stephanidis (Eds.): DAPI/HCII 2013, LNCS 8028, pp. 265–274, 2013.
© Springer-Verlag Berlin Heidelberg 2013

service does not exist there for two major reasons: (1) Doctors do not want to stay in the village as they do not find their livelihood requirements fulfilled (2) Quality hospitals/clinics cannot sustain without stable income. Recently, mobile phone became available in each corner of rural areas. Health consultancy over mobile phone became popular in Bangladesh as an alternative solution. One such service holder receives 15000 calls per day for health consultancy [3]. Consultancy over mobile phones brought many benefits to the people especially to the remote female patients. Female patients can consult with a remote male doctor anonymously for discussing private diseases. People can call at any time of the day from anywhere in the country. A doctor can prescribe OTC (Over The Counter) medicine, can interpret clinical records and also can introduce a hospital or doctor near the patient's place. However, in order to diagnose a disease properly, doctors need to see the clinical records measured by diagnostic tools. Kyushu University in Japan and Grameen Communication's GCC (Global Communication Center) Project in Bangladesh have prototyped an affordable "portable clinic" [4] to be deployed in a community and to measure basic health data. The collected data will be made available at the doctor's side before the patient make a call. The "portable clinic" project started checking health data as a "health check up service" in the remote areas in Bangladesh. The health records were analyzed locally with a predefined logic and categorized them in four groups: green (healthy), yellow (caution), orange (affected), and red (emergent). Patients with orange and red have unusual clinical results and are selected to consult with the doctor over video conferencing tool to be equipped with the portable clinic.

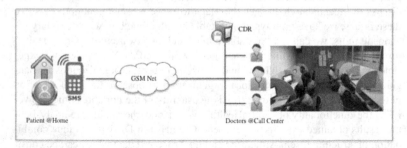

Fig. 1. A typical mobile based remote health consultancy system. A patient from home calls using a mobile phone. An urban doctor in a call center picks the call and provides health consultancy.

In this work, we introduce the current status of two representative remote health consultancy systems, case study results obtained from one of the health consultancy service providers in Section 2. We also describe the technical challenges. Section 3 describes the anatomy of our portable clinic and introduces a mechanism which can serve patients in a mass scale in rural community. GramHealth tool is also explained in this section which collects and archives personal health records. We have served 8690 patients and collected their health records to discover meaningful medical information. The results are discussed. Section 4 summarizes our work with future directions.

2   Remote Health Consultancy for the Unreached Community

Remote health consultancy in developing countries is applied quite differently than developed countries. Presence of mobile phone connectivity is higher than the Internet connectivity. Therefore, the patients in the remote areas use mobile phone for communicating a doctor. In a typical mobile phone based healthcare consultancy system, the doctor is located in an urban area in a call center. The doctor has a facility to receive phone calls, a computer based hospital database to support the patient. At the patient side, there is only a mobile phone. The patient calls to a hot-line number of a call center (Fig. 1). The call is usually routed to a doctor in a round-robin fashion. The consultancy has three major phases.

(a) Introduction phase: the doctor introduces him/herself, and then asks for patient basic information (name, age, sex, location etc.). Location is important to introduce a nearby hospital.
(b) Diagnosis phase: the patient explains the symptom and then the doctor interrogates the patient based on the symptoms to find out the cause of the symptom.
(c) Advice phase: the doctor then either prescribes medicine (over the counter medicine only because of the medical policy issue), or suggests a nearby hospital for further checkup and consultancy. An advanced healthcare service provider keeps the patient-doctor conversation records in a CDR (call details record) and uses special software tool to keep the patient profile details including the list of medicines prescribed.

We have gathered the patient-doctor conversation records archived in December 2009. We have found that there were more than 10,000 audio call records. We have clustered the records in 100 groups and randomly selected 400 audio records for our case study. There are a good number of female patients making calls (33%) by themselves. This is quite amazing to observe because a female patient is usually attended by the husband or parents. In many cases, they feel shy to share their private diseases with a male doctor. However, over a mobile phone, the female patients are less hesitant. This is an amazing advantage of remote consultancy over mobile phone. The following table [Table I] has the summary results of our observations. The detail explanations can be found in our previous work [8].

Table 1. Analysis of doctor-patient conversation in a call center

Observed Item	Results (n=400)
(a) Caller	Patient: 60%, Relatives: 40%
(b) Age distribution of the patient	0-10 years: 29%, 11-20 years: 15%
	21-30 years:24%, 31-40 years:17%
	41-50 years: 9%, 50+ years: 7 %
(c) Sex	Male: 67%, Female: 33%
(d) Location	Rural: 30%, Urban: 70%
(e) Call completion	Complete: 68%, Incomplete: 32%
(f) Time of call	Day (8:00-15:30): 57 %
	Evening (15:30-23:00): 18%
	Night (23:00-8:00): 25%

Table 1. (*continued*)

(g) Time occupancy of a single call	Introduction phase: 8%, Diagnosis phase: 27%, Advice phase: 67%
(h) Consultancy about	Disease related: 79%, Preventive healthcare related: 21%
(i) Type of advices	Prescribed medicine: 54% , Advice: 28%, Referred to specialist/hospital: 17%,
(j) Patients	Follow up: 17%, New: 83%
(k) Patients' satisfaction	Fully satisfied: 71%, unsatisfied: 21%, average: 8%
(l) Major diseases consulted	Gastro-intestinal: 22%, Respiratory: 17%, Reproductive:10%, skin: 10%

2.1   Technical Challenges

Although our study shows that 71% people are satisfied with the present mobile phone based consultancy service. There is however, a big room for improving the service by introducing simple additional functions into the present system without making any substantial changes in the infrastructure. In this section, we discuss the technical challenges followed by our ideas to address these issues.

1. Maintaining a patient ID: A patient ID is a key element to keep and maintain individual healthcare records. The present system does not offer a unique ID to their patients. A CDR keeps the mobile phone number of the caller, however there are cases when a patient calls from relatives' phone or uses a family-owned share phone. Therefore, the phone number cannot be a unique ID.
2. Disease diagnosis process: In the present system, there is no diagnostic tool at the patient side. The doctors are afraid of making inaccurate assumptions from the symptoms expressed by the caller. A physical measurement is necessary to better understand the degree of a symptom and to make a better clinical decision. Diagnostic tools for most of the common diseases are available in a nearby pharmacy. But there is no good way to transfer the data to the remote doctor.
3. Patient profile archive: The doctors at the call center are offered and trained to insert the patient profile during the conversation. Many doctors do not feel comfortable to use a computer during the conversation. Also it will take extra time to insert the patient profile keeping the patient on the phone which irritates the patient. As a result, the patient profile never gets sufficiently stored. Without past records, it is difficult to take care of the follow-up patients.
4. Patient's location: Currently the call center has to ask a series of questions to identify the geographical location of a patient. A doctor cannot accurately refer a patient to a hospital or to doctor if patient's location is not known. Recently Bangladesh Directorate General of Health Services (DGHS) provided a standard code for geo-location for every union (the smallest administrative unit) [http://app.dghs.gov.bd/bbscode/] in Bangladesh. However, the codes are not known to the villagers neither it is widely adopted in the country.

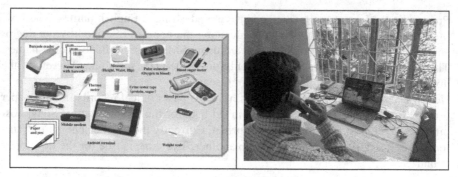

Fig. 2. (left) a prototype of the portable clinic with 12 basic diagnostic tools. (Right) a rural patient is consulting with a doctor by using mobile phone for voice and skype for video communication.

3.2   Experimental Environment

We carried out experiments in urban, sub-urban and rural areas in Bangladesh from September 2012 to January 2013. Our experiment environment consists of the following facilities: (a) a small call center in Dhaka (the capital city of Bangladesh) with two female and two male doctors, and one transcript writer (b) A portable clinic with 12 diagnostic tools (as in Fig. 2) (c) GramHealth software tool to obtain and maintain the patient health records (d) A portable clinic health check up team consisting two health assistants, 3 program assistants and one quality check officer. GramHealth does not automatically capture data from all the diagnostic tools, BAN supported tools automatically uploads measurement results through wireless; others are manually inserted into our GramHealth database through a user-friendly web interface (d) considering the network infrastructure facility in the village, we have developed a off-line version of GramHealth to store the obtained health profile locally and send to the central server when the sufficient network bandwidth is available.

In order to save time and cost, we designed a group checking methodology and introduced a triage to classify the patients by observing their health status and considering their level of emergency. There are four steps.

(a) **Registration**. A patient registers his/her vital information such as name, age, sex, location and disease complaints, if they have any. A data entry operator inputs the data into GramHealth DB. A patient ID is given to the patient.

(b) **Health Checkup**. A healthcare assistant takes the patient's physical check up (body temperature, weight, height, BMI, Waist, Hip, Blood test, Urine test etc.) and send the data to GramHealth server. Few diagnostic tools are equipped with wireless BAN (Body Area Network) to automatically send the measurement data to GramHealth DB. We have also developed a B-logic (Bangladesh Logic) to determine the risk satisfaction intro 4 grades, green (healthy), yellow (caution), orange (affected) and red (emergent) as depicted in Fig. 4. The "green" patients are given the health checkup results. The "yellow" marked patients are given a healthcare manual developed by us. The "orange" and "red" marked patients consults with a call center doctor.

(c) **Tele health consultancy**. As mentioned above, only "yellow" and "red" marked patients talk to the doctor for further investigations of their disease and explanation of their medical records. Tele health consultancy is over voice and video. The audio record is archived in GramHealth DB.

(d) **Prescription and Suggestion**. The doctor identifies the disease after checking the clinical data, discussing with the patient for their symptom analysis and his/her past health records, if any. The doctor then fills up the prescription and a technical assistant helps the doctor to insert the necessary information into the database.

In this experiment, we aim to (1) observe how the technical challenges mentioned in section 2.3 could be efficiently solved, (2) monitor whether the system can work with the compromised infrastructure- where unstable bandwidth and regular power-outage is common (3) Study the properties of GramHealth DB and find rules to feedback the CDSS system.

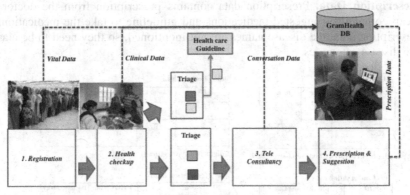

Fig. 3. Experimental environment with Portable Clinic and GramHealth systems and the 4 steps methodology to efficiently carry out group health check up in remote areas

3.3   Results and Discussion

We have checked up 8690 patients and accommodated the records in GramHealth DB. The experiment was carried out in two rural areas: Ekhlaspur in Chandpur district and Chhoygaon in Shariatpur distrcits. Total rural patients from rural areas were 2728 (31.28% of the total patients). We also carried out experiments for the women in a garment factory and for the daily laborers in a construction company totaling 2890 (33.3% of total patients). They are considered as sub-urban patients. 3032 patients from three different industries in urban area participated in our program.

We have developed necessary features in GramHealth to solve the issues described in Section 2.1. Our experiment confirmed that 5 of the 6 issues are functioning. We have not worked on the data portability issue yet. This will be a future work for us.

In one of our experimental areas in Ekhlaspur, there is no communication network. Our offline mode of GramHealth perfectly analyzed the data on the spot to classify them into four groups. Consulting with the doctor from the spot was not possible.

Properties of GramHealth DB: As depicted in Fig. 3, Gram Health DB collects data from four types of data from four different sources.

1. **Registration Data.** Registration data has personal data and inquiry data. Personal data (Name, Age, Sex, Address, Check-up date) is structured, but inquiry data (complain, symptom, family information and life style information) is Q&A text type and semi-structured.
2. **Check-Up Data.** Check-up data contains clinical measurement data. All data is structured and used for triage of patients, cohort analysis and comparison with past data. Triaged and colored sensor data items give us not only the value on each item for doctor but also some quantitative and educational information (crucial, risky, attention, healthy) for patients.
3. **Conversation Data.** Conversation data is captured by an audio recorder. These data are completely unstructured. In order to analyze these data, it is necessary to convert the data from speech to text. Unfortunately there is no efficient Bangla speech-to-text tool. At this stage, we have to manually listen to all the audio records and input the narration into the DB.
4. **Prescription Data.** Prescription data contains prescription from the doctor e.g. cheap complains, suggested medications and guideline to take the medications. In prescription data, the disease names are not mentioned, so they need to be classify into disease categories.

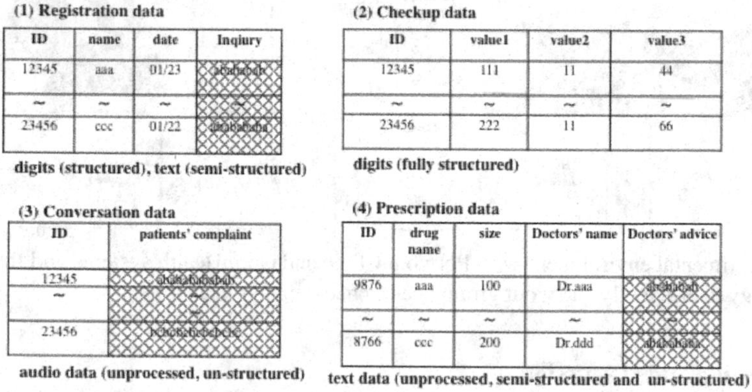

(1) Registration data

ID	name	date	Inqiury
12345	aaa	01/23	
~	~	~	
23456	ccc	01/22	

digits (structured), text (semi-structured)

(2) Checkup data

ID	value1	value2	value3
12345	111	11	44
~	~	~	~
23456	222	11	66

digits (fully structured)

(3) Conversation data

ID	patients' complaint
12345	
~	
23456	

audio data (unprocessed, un-structured)

(4) Prescription data

ID	drug name	size	Doctors' name	Doctors' advice
9876	aaa	100	Dr.aaa	
~	~	~	~	
8766	ccc	200	Dr.ddd	

text data (unprocessed, semi-structured and un-structured)

Fig. 4. Properties (variability) of GramHealth DB

As shown in Fig.4, GramHealth DB has heterogeneous types of data. In order to analyze GramHealth DB to discover meaningful medical information, we face two major issues: each data has different structure and is kept scattered; there is no connection between each silo of database. We have focused on health check-up data and prescription data and discovered few meaningful information. The information is under investigation and will be published elsewhere. The investigated items are- (1) Influence of clinical data on triage (2) Geographcal pattern in clinical data (3) Discovery of clinical diagnosis (disease name) from drug name (4) Disease pattern of patients (5) Influence on choosing drugs from doctors' preference (6) Tuning of triage (b-logic) (7) Relationship between prescribed drug name and clinical data and (8) Potential meaning in the inquiry data.

We came up with a model to analyze GramHealth BigData. Fig. 6 explaines the process. Firstly, we preprocess the GramHealth DB for easier analysis. Preprocess includes converting the audio data into text, shape the unstructured data into structured manner. This part needs further investigation. The processed data will be linked to produce meaning medical information. Once the data is ready, it will be fetched by the applications (CDSS, trending etc) to serve the patients and the doctors.

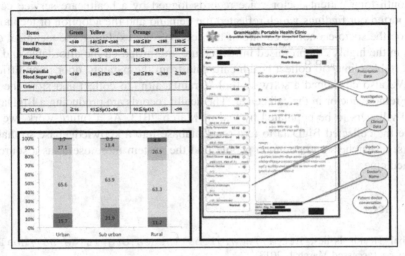

Fig. 5. (Left up): B-logic. Based on International Standards. This logic is applied to classify the patients in four groups. It is partially shown but full data is available in [8]. (Left bottom): after applying b-logic to 8690 patients. The bar graph shows the triage level in urban, sub-urban and rural areas. (Right): GramHealth prescription filled up by the doctor. The left side shows their health status for individual clinical results. The principal complain and investigation is mentioned on the top right area. The prescription, suggestions for health maintenance is also mentioned. Call center doctor's name is also recorded for the follow up consultancy in future.

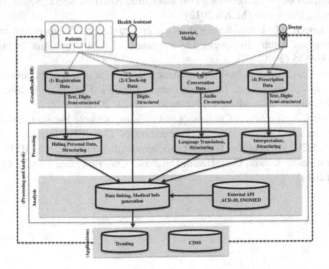

Fig. 6. GramHealth DB to produce useful medical information for the doctors and patients

4   Conclusion and Future Works

In this work, we introduced the technical anatomy of mobile phone based remote consultancy services in developing countries. We carried out a case study to analyze one-month long patient-doctor voice records logged by a healthcare service center. We reported our findings which reflected the demand and the adoption of technology based on the socio-economic culture of the country. We explained the technical challenges in the highly compromised infrastructure and proposed the affordable and usable "portable clinic" to collect health care data from the patients' door in an efficient way. We also developed a software tool "GramHealth" to collect and store the data for the remote doctor in the call center. The health records are producing a BigData of 10,000 villagers to be populated by end of March 2013. As a future work, we will analyze the collected BigData to turn our Database into a knowledgebase so that the patients, researchers and common people find the system more useful as a source of info-medicine.

References

1. Global Health Issues, http://www.globalissues.org/issue/587/health-issues (accessed March 1, 2013)
2. The Remote and Rural Steering Group.:Delivering for Remote and Rural Healthcare. The Scottish government, Edinburg (November 30, 2007)
3. Ahmed, A., Osugi, T.: ICT to change BOP: Case Study: Bangladesh. Shukosha, Fukuoka, pp.139–155 (September 2009)
4. Ahmed, A., Ishida, K., Okada, M., Yasuura, H.: Poor-Friendly Technology Initiative in Japan: Grameen Technology Lab. The Journal of Social Business 1(1) (January 2011)
5. Kato, S.: A Study on Implementing a Portable Clinic based on Social Needs. Undergraduate Thesis, Kyushu University (March 2012)
6. Nessa, A., Ameen, M., Ullah, S., Kwak, K.: Applicability of Telemedicine in Bangladesh: Current Status and Future Prospects. The International Arab Journal of Information Technology 7, 138–145 (2010)
7. Kai, E., Ahmed, A.: Remote health consultancy service for unreached community: amazing facts and technical challenges. In: Proceedings of the First MJIIT-JUC Joint Symposium, MJIIT, UTM, Kulalumpur, Malaysia, November 21-23 (2012)
8. Kai, E., Ahmed, A.: Technical Challenges in Providing Remote Health Consultancy Services for the Unreached Community. In: Proceeding of 27th IEEE International Conference (AINA), FINA-2013 Workshop, Barcelona, Spain (forthcoming, March 2013)
9. Kai, E.: An Investigation on GramHealth Database. Undergraduate Thesis, Kyushu University (March 2013)

Do Strollers in Town Needs Recommendation?: On Preferences of Recommender in Location-Based Services

Kenro Aihara

National Institute of Informatics
2-1-2 Hitotsubashi, Chiyoda-ku, Tokyo 101-8430, Japan
kenro.aihara@nii.ac.jp

Abstract. When we discuss about recommendation especially in Location-Based Services (LBS), we need to reveal whether users really want recommendations or not in fact while they are strolling in town, prior to evaluate each recommendation model.

In this paper, a Location-Based Service, called *nicotoco*, is shown. nicotoco is an iPhone-based LBS in Futako-tamagawa area, Tokyo, Japan and provides information about stores and events to users. In the experiment using nicotoco, recommendations may be preferred more than rankings which was made from access counts.

Keywords: context-aware computing, location-based service, behavioral cost.

1 Introduction

A lot of recommender systems have been proposed for strollers [8,3]. Almost all of them seem to be location-aware and assume that the nearer the provided information is located, the more useful it is for users. This assumption implies that the information that may be preferable for the user but located a little further away vanishes from the user because of a massive amount of information, such as micro blogs like tweets of Twitter. On the other hand, although a recommender system can filter out the information that is probably uninteresting to the user based on the collaborative filtering model that is broadly used in existing recommender systems on the Internet, the author supposes that the information that may be preferable to the user must depend on the user's situation and the collaborative filtering model is still naive, especially when the user is strolling around in town.

In addition, when we discuss about recommendation especially in Location-Based Services (LBS), we need to reveal whether users really want recommendations or not in fact while they are strolling in town, prior to evaluate each recommendation model.

N. Streitz and C. Stephanidis (Eds.): DAPI/HCII 2013, LNCS 8028, pp. 275–283, 2013.

2   Background

2.1   Location-Based Information Services

A lot of network services with location data are proposed, and some of them, such as foursquare[1], are getting popular. Usually location information is given as geographical coordinates, that is, latitude and longitude, a location identifier such as ID for facilities in geographical information services (GIS), or a postal address. Google has launched Google Places[2], which gathers place information from active participating networkers and delivers such information through Google's web site and API (application programmable interface). Google may try to grasp facts and information on activities in the real world where it has not enough information yet even though it seems to have become the omniscient giant in the cyber world. Google already captures some real world phenomena in its own materials. For example, it gathers landscape images with its own fleet of specially adapted cars for the Google Street View service[3]. However, the cost of capturing and digitizing facts and activities in the real world is generally very expensive if you try to obtain more than capturing photo images with geographical information. Although Google Places may be one of the reasonable solutions to gathering information in the real world, it's not guaranteed that it can grow into an effective and reliable source reflecting the real world.

Existing social information services, such as Facebook and Twitter, are expanding to attach location data to users' content.

2.2   Filtering Information for Strollers

In the field of recommender systems, collaborative filtering is one of the popular methods to judge whether information fits the user or not [6,5,2]. The collaborative filtering model is basically based on the assumption that similar users prefer the same information. However, when we consider recommending information to mobile users who are strolling in town, the author believes that the information must be selected further from a set of already filtered candidates in accordance with their situation because the input method and output devices of mobile terminals are highly restricted and also the number of candidates still has to be large even though they are already filtered.

2.3   Phenomena of Human's Preference

In the field of behavioral economics, the phenomena of time preference and temporal discounting are known, which refer to a decrease in the subjective value of a reward as the delay of its receipt increases [4]. People and other

---

[1] http://foursquare.com/
[2] http://www.google.com/places/
[3] http://www.google.com/streetview/

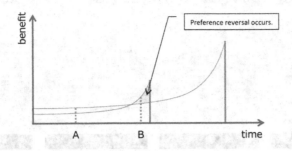

Fig. 1. Preference reversal phenomenon

animals discount future reward as a function of time. In addition, there is another remarkable phenomenon of preference reversal, which occurs when a subject places a lower selling price on the gamble that he/she chooses than on the other gamble in a pair [7]. Animal and human temporal discounting has been described better as hyperbolic functions than exponential ones in recent psychology (Figure 1).

This notion implies that humans prefer not always rational choices but sometimes irrational and impulsive ones, especially in stressful situations. The author proposed a recommendation model based on this notion for strollers in town[1].

3 Nicotoco: An LBS for Strollers

3.1 Service Description

"niconoto" is supplied since the end of November, 2011. The service is designed for strollers who visit Futako-tamagawa area, which is being redeveloped as a smart city in Tokyo and consists of complexes including shopping malls, supermarkets, offices, and residential areas around the Futako-tamagawa station. The service can be accessed both via web browser and via iPhone application. When visitors arrive in the service area and access the service, they can get information according to their location and their own user model that is learned from users' attributes and behavior logs.

Major functions of the service are as follows.

Top Page. When users access the top page of the service with web browser, the page gives general information including hot events, up-to-date tweets from stores, and recommended spots, such as stores.

If the user uses the iPhone application, three recommended spots are given (Figure 2(a)). Users also see more recommendations to tap "もっとみる" (means "see more") button at the bottom right on the screen. And also users can switch the list to the rankings of mostly accessed spots in recent days (Figure 2(b)) by tapping the medal icon on the top right.

(a)   Recommenda-   (b) Ranking   (c) Spot page   (d) Time line
tion

(e) Hot events   (f) Clipped spots   (g) QR scanner   (h) AR view

Fig. 2. Snapshot images of the nicotoco application

Spot Information. When a user selects one spot on the screen, the system shows an information including maps, coupons if available, tweets from the store (Figure 2(c)). Users can get further recommendation of spots the very next candidates to the spot by tapping "次いくとしたら" ("Where to Go Next?").

Time Line. The application gives two kinds of time lines: tweets (Figure 2(d)) and events (Figure 2(e)).

Clips. Users can clip spots and coupons when they see the correspondings page just like as bookmarking. Clipped spots and coupons can be reviewed in "クリップ" ("Clip") mode in the bottom menu (Figure 2(f)). In a typical scenario, users once check favorite spots in recommendations or rankings and then clip them. When they visit the spot and show the clipped coupon to get discount or corresponding service.

Spot Check-in with QR Code Markers. In addition to the basic functions above, the service deploys sticker markers at affiliates through the area. The

(a)   (b)

Fig. 3. QR Code Markers for Spot Check-in

marker shows the serivce logo and QR code, which is a popular two-dimensional code and it can be scanned and decoded by almost all of cell phones sold in Japan. When a user scans a code in nicotoco marker with one of standard QR readers, the information corresponding to the marker will be shown. If the store delivers coupons for the service customers, the user can get the coupon and the coupon is stored for recall when he/she uses. Figure 2(g) shows an image of scanner mode for QR in the application. Examples of QR code markers are shown in Figure 3.

The action of scanning the code is also regarded as "check-in" for the spot.

AR View. In the iPhone application, AR mode is equipped. In AR mode, icons of the spots that deliver coupons overlays onto the captured image of the iPhone camera in real time to search stores around the user (Figure 2(h)).

3.2   User Data

The nicotoco service collects user data as follows:

- attributes
  - gender
  - generation
  - zip code
- behavior logs

- access logs for selected spots
- check-ins for spots (readings of markers)
- locations (application only)

The nicotoco service collects users' demographic attributes at the first access, behavior logs including access logs to the service and their locations sensed with GPS and Wi-Fi signals when it is active and their location gets updated.

3.3   Process of Recommendation

Feature Value of Users. Users are characterized by vector of attributes and terms which occur in their own contents, such as tweets, and features of spots where they visited. That is, feature of each user will be updated by visiting spots.

Feature of user u at the current time c_{cur} is defined in Equation 1. $readmarker(u, s, t)$ denotes the log count of reading markers of spot s by user u at the time t.

$$\overrightarrow{user}(u, t_{cur}) = (gender, generation, \overrightarrow{visit}) \tag{1}$$

$$\overrightarrow{visit} = \sum_{s}^{S} \sum_{t \in ts}^{t_{cur}} (decay(t) \cdot readmarker(u, s, t) \cdot \overrightarrow{spot}(s, t_{cur}))$$

$$ts = timeslot(t)$$

$$decay(t) = exp(t - t_{cur}/C_t)$$

C_t denotes a constant of period for decay function. 12 time slots ts are provided: 12am-4am, 4am-10am, 10am-12pm, 12pm-3pm, 3pm-6pm, 6pm-9pm, and 9pm-12am of weekdays and weekends, respectively.

Feature Value of Spots. Spots are characterized by vector of terms which occur in their own descriptions and features of users who visited them, as well. That is, feature of each spot will be updated by users' visits. $\overrightarrow{desc}$ denotes feature value based on term frequency in descriptions on the spot.

$$\overrightarrow{spot}(s, t_{cur}) = (\overrightarrow{desc}, \overrightarrow{visited}) \tag{2}$$

$$\overrightarrow{visited} = \sum_{u}^{U} \sum_{t \in ts}^{t_{cur}} (decay(t) \cdot readmarker(u, s, t) \cdot \overrightarrow{user}(u, t_{cur}))$$

User's Commitment to Spots. The commitment of user u to spot s at time slot of the current time t_{cur} is given from behavior logs by Equation 3. α, β, γ are coefficients of linear combination.

$$cmt(u, s, ts) = \alpha \cdot vis(u, s, ts) + \beta \cdot acc(u, s, ts) + \gamma \cdot cpn(u, s, ts) \tag{3}$$

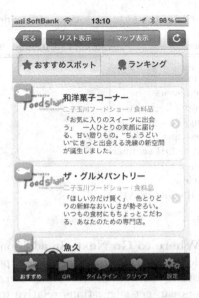

Fig. 4. List of Recommendation of the nicotoco application

$$vis(u, s, ts) = \sum_{t \in ts}^{t_{cur}} (decay(t) \cdot readmarker(u, s, t))$$

$$acc(u, s, ts) = \sum_{t \in ts}^{t_{cur}} (decay(t) \cdot accesspage(u, s, t))$$

$$cpn(u, s, ts) = \sum_{t \in ts}^{t_{cur}} (decay(t) \cdot accesscoupon(u, s, t))$$

Transitivity between Spots. Transitivity $tr(u, s_i, s_j, ts)$ from spot s_i to spot s_j of user u in time slot ts is calculated from occurrences of spot transitions within given interval in users' behavior logs.

Recommendation of Spots. By using $\overrightarrow{user}(u, t_{cur})$, $\overrightarrow{spot}(s, t_{cur})$, and $cmt(u, s, ts)$, relativity between user u and spot s in time slot ts are calculated in Equation 4.

$$score(u, s, ts) = C \cdot \cos(\overrightarrow{user}(u, t_{cur}), \overrightarrow{spot}(s, t_{cur}))$$
$$+(1 - C) \cdot cmt(u, s, ts) \tag{4}$$

Top k spots with higher relativity scores are given as recommendations as shown at top page (Figure 2(a)). In addition, more recommendation can be called (Figure 4).

Table 1. Statistics of the nicotoco service of iPhone application

type of action		number of unique users	number of actions
activate the application		243	935
get recommendation listing		324	1997
	picked spots	138	294
	"go next"	93	140
get ranking	listing	111	623
	picked spots	32	113
use Camera mode	activate QR scanner	46	130
	scanned QR	19	131
	AR view	80	209
	picked spots in AR	22	193

Recommendation of Where to Go Next. In addition to recommendations mentioned above, the nicotoco service gives another type of recommendation which aims to give suggestions where to go next when users visit a spot. In many usual recommenders, users can get suggestions relative to their favorites; that is, similar contents can be provided. For example, a user who likes cafe tends to get recommendations from cafes. The author, however, supposes that a user who just visited a cafe doesn't want recommendation of another cafe and may prefer somewhere favorite in another category. In nicotoco, such recommendations of where to go next are calculated by using transitivity between spots in addition to scores between user and spot (Equation 5). tr denotes transitivity from spot s_i to spot s_j. $score$ denotes recommendation score mentioned above.

$$nscore(u, s_{org}, s, ts) = C_n \cdot tr(u, s_{org}, s, ts)$$
$$+(1 - C_n) \cdot score(u, s, ts) \tag{5}$$

Top k recommended spots are shown when users tap "次いくとしたら" button as shown in Figure 2(c).

4   Statistics of the Service

Web-based service was launched at the end of November, 2011. 3,239 users are registered and 2,399 users accessed the service, as of the end of February, 2012. Male users are 803; female, 1,594; missing, 2.

For the iPhone application, it got ready to be downloaded from AppStore of Apple Inc. in February, 2012. The number of users is 357 (male is 192; female, 165). At first, 138 of 324 users (42.6%) picked recommended spots at least once. And also the number of unique users who used "Go Next" function is 93 (36.3%). The author believes that these results are able to support that recommendation function is potentially prefered in LBSs. In particular, the preference of "Go Next" relatively may be higher, considering the accessibility of the mode against normal recommendation listing.

In comparison with ranking, recommendation seems much preferred. This insight may be interesting because ranking is usually based on general popularity and users prefer personalized or "tailored" information more than such popularity. It may implies that users cannot be satisfied with "Like" count-based ranking.

5 Conclusions

The paper shows the service called nicotoco, which facilitates the model for recommendation. In results of statistics of the nicotoco service, the author believes that recommendation function can be preferred by strollers using LBSs.

The author continues to develop and provide these services. To evaluate the effectiveness of the model, experiments are being planned. Analysis of user behavior logs and the development of methods to capture users' situation including cognitive aspects are future issues.

Acknowledgments. The author thanks Tokyu Corporation and Kokusai Kogyo Co., Ltd. for their cooperation with this research. This work is partly supported by the Ministry of Economy, Trade and Industry of Japan.

References

1. Aihara, K., Koshiba, H., Takeda, H.: Behavioral cost-based recommendation model for wanderers in town. In: Jacko, J.A. (ed.) Human-Computer Interaction, Part III, HCII 2011. LNCS, vol. 6763, pp. 271–279. Springer, Heidelberg (2011)
2. Braak, P.T., Abdullah, N., Xu, Y.: Improving the performance of collaborative filtering recommender systems through user profile clustering. In: Proceedings of the 2009 IEEE/WIC/ACM International Joint Conference on Web Intelligence and Intelligent Agent Technology, vol. 3, pp. 147–150 (2009)
3. Ducheneaut, N., Partridge, K., Huang, Q., Price, B., Roberts, M., Chi, E.H., Bellotti, V., Begole, B.: Collaborative filtering is not enough? experiments with a mixed-model recommender for leisure activities. In: Houben, G.-J., McCalla, G., Pianesi, F., Zancanaro, M. (eds.) UMAP 2009. LNCS, vol. 5535, pp. 295–306. Springer, Heidelberg (2009)
4. Green, L., Fry, A.F., Myerson, J.: Discounting of delayed rewards: A life-span comparison. Psychological Science 5(1), 33–36 (1994)
5. Schafer, J.B., Frankowski, D., Herlocker, J., Sen, S.: Collaborative filtering recommender systems. In: Brusilovsky, P., Kobsa, A., Nejdl, W. (eds.) Adaptive Web 2007. LNCS, vol. 4321, pp. 291–324. Springer, Heidelberg (2007)
6. Su, X., Khoshgoftaar, T.M.: A survey of collaborative filtering techniques. Advances in Artificial Intelligence 2009, 1–19 (2009)
7. Tversky, A., Kahneman, D.: the framing of decisions and the psychology of choice. Science 211(4481), 453–458 (1981)
8. Zheng, V.W., Cao, B., Zheng, Y., Xie, X., Yang, Q.: Collaborative filtering meets mobile recommendation: A user-centered approach. In: Proceedings of the 24th AAAI Conference on Artificial Intelligence, pp. 236–241 (2010)

Empowering People through Mobile Devices
for Smarter Places

Federico Devigili, Daniele Magliocchetti, Giuseppe Conti, and Raffaele De Amicis

Fondazione Graphitech, Via Belenzani 12, 38122, Trento, Italy
{federico.devigili,daniele.magliocchetti,giuseppe.conti,
raffaele.de.amicis}@graphitech.it

Abstract. Increase in traffic volumes in urbanized areas of the world has caused a rise in congestion with negative consequences on safety, environment and quality of life of citizens. Only in Europe the cost of traffic congestion is 1% of the GDP, and this does not take into account the cost in terms of deaths caused by road network saturation. On top of this 30% of energy consumed by our population goes into public or private transport system. More than 55000Km of roads and railroads are monitored by webcams or vehicle counters. Some technologies to assess road network state and improve safety and quality of life of travelers already exists but many are limited to small networks or a particular public transport operator. Smart use and harmonization of available data on top of other real-time data acquisition methods can provide a better service to European citizens. Smart use of public transport possibilities can have a huge positive impact on traveling speed, quality and safety. In the last years availability of public transport real time data and the spread of smart mobile devices, allowed us to develop pervasive travel assistant applications for mobile phones. The project presented in this paper, i-Tour, shows how an IT solution for mobile phones can have sensible impact on personal mobility quality by promoting the use of mixed public-private transport. The application takes into account user preferences as well as real-time information on road conditions, weather and public transport network status. I-Tour also promotes a new approach to data collection based on a recommender system where the information provided by the whole user community enriches the trusted-knowledge common database with local up-to-date knowledge consisting of point of interest and real-time road network information. The client can adapt to user preferences to better meet user needs, young users may prefer using bikes or just walking while adults may prefer taking the car or public transports. At the same time some users need to always use the fastest mean of transport while other may prefer a more eco-friendly choice. Innovative user-friendly interfaces have been developed to create new interface metaphors; when a user search for a travel solution a set of possible routes will be given to the user on a graph showing not only each path but also the different meaning of transport, the quality of service, traffic conditions and waiting times of each route. The software also is potentially profitable since many areas of the client are adaptable to integrate ads or provide visibility to sponsored locations or commercial point of interests. The client provides 3 types of map visualization system, top-down 2D Map, full 3D map, and Augmented Reality visualization. To seamlessly switch between

N. Streitz and C. Stephanidis (Eds.): DAPI/HCII 2013, LNCS 8028, pp. 284–293, 2013.
© Springer-Verlag Berlin Heidelberg 2013

5. Prescription: Most of the medicines in Bangladesh have English names. The low-literate patients have difficulties to understand the names prescribed by the doctor and take a memo. Some providers started using SMS to send the medicine names. There is a policy that the doctor can only prescribe OTC medicine. Therefore, the doctors can treat only limited number of diseases.

6. Health Data Portability: Some patients have the past clinical records in hard paper format. It is difficult to read out the clinical data for the remote doctor. Some hospitals keep the past records in digital format. Currently there is no scheme to transfer the digital data from one hospital to another. The same is true for the developed countries.

3   Our Preventive and Pervasive Healthcare Approach

In this section, we describe our portable clinic concept and explain how to archive PHR of the villagers in an efficient way.

3.1   Portable Clinic and GramHealth to Efficiently Serve the Remote Patients

We considered "disease diagnosis issue" as the primary missing item in the current mobile phone based remote health-consultancy system and proposed an affordable, usable and sustainable concept "portable clinic" [5] to be added in the current initiative for preventive healthcare.

Portable Clinic: is a device equipped with essential diagnostic tools (for temperature, blood, blood pressure, ECG, urine, etc). The clinic is designed to be affordable (<US$300, this is an amount that village nurse can borrow from micro-finance institution such as Grameen Bank in Bangladesh) and can be carried by a village female health assistant. A prototype of the concept has already been developed and is in the field for our experiment (Fig. 2).

The portable clinic box will be owned and operated by a village health assistant. In an ideal situation, she will visit the patients' doorstep for regular and on-demand physical checkup. The personal health records will be stored in the local portable clinic as well as in the central GramHealth database.

GramHealth: is a software tool developed by our department considering the needs of the villagers. The call center doctor can access GramHealth through the Internet or have a copy of the database in their call center server. Upon receiving a call from a patient, the doctor now can find patient's previous record. This way, the doctor doesn't need to repeatedly ask questions about the patients' personal profile. The doctor's precious time is saved and also the cost burden of the patient will be less. It also provides a good mental impression to the patient when the doctor reads out patients' past records and asks follow up questions. A past record contains previous prescribed medicine and the doctor can easily ask the status for the follow-up patients.

different visualization methods an innovative system based on device orientation has been ideated. When the user keeps the device horizontal the client set the visualization to 2D map, when the device is kept vertical the device switch to augmented reality view; in between the map shows full 3D terrain visualization. Questionnaires responses shown that many solutions adopted were well appreciated by the users.

Keywords: Smart Cities, i-Tour, Ambient Intelligence, Personal Mobility Assistant.

1   Introduction

i-Tour has been thoughts as a platform that allows all the counterparts of multi-modal transportation system, included the end-users, to interact among them easily and share information on the same environment in order to improve services and citizens awareness about a better use of public transportation against private one with getting environmental benefits in the urban areas.

Being a personal travel assistant, which gives all the alternatives to route destinations for the end-user, this information can be delivered onto mobile personal devices;

i-Tour help people to get always organized and in time with public transportation thanks to its technology, one can access the service on the move and find all the better routes to get in time at the work or for leisure meeting friends;

i-Tour also give access to PC users through the internet asking route's indications in natural language: "get me to the closest shop that accepts my credit card where I can buy some food". 3D mapping is available, while users accept, they leave the office carrying with their own Smartphone that meanwhile automatically starts providing directions on how to get to the desired location;

The i-Tour community helps to maintain the system up to date with the latest information and/or changes in the routing thanks to the information provided by all the users. This service also gives in return the quantity of CO_2 reduction in the case of public transportation routing selected by the users.

The amount of CO_2 saved is commuted into points and an incentives scheme would be also based on rewarding mechanisms and/or mileage-like campaigns for public transportation, directly provided through the use of the such system as check-in check-out procedures for all the users.

2   Typical Scenario of i-Tour

Within a typical scenario the user interacts with the i-Tour client to retrieve routing information across a multimodal transport network. Unlike other navigation systems, in i-Tour suggested trips can be based on a combination of different transport modes such as bus, train, metro or have the user walking or cycling to get to a station. Routing information are adjusted according to real-time traffic information, information on quality of services as provided by the community of other users, or based on other real-time information such as weather conditions (e.g. the system would not recommend walking if rain is forecast).

The scenario set by the project requires that the system should be considered essentially as a pedestrian routing system, in an enlarged sense, i.e. providing specific directions targeted for instance to a user walking home as well as a user cycling to a station to catch a train or walking at a station to get on a connecting underground line. In short the focus will be on all the routing situations wherever the user will not be driving private vehicles.

The interface has been designed to ensure ubiquitous use of travelling services, whereas the users should be able to switch, at any time, from web to mobile client, yet retaining the same features, look and feel, and machine state in terms of data and information being managed.

This scenario has required developing client applications which could store and retrieve all the necessary information from the network. In fact all state-relevant information is stored in the cloud, with the user accessing this information through the Internet. For this reason the two i-Tour clients can be regarded as two access points to the functionalities provided, as service, at the server side through the i-Tour middleware.

The mobile clients makes use of all the latest sensing technologies available on the latest mobile devices to provide a more natural and ambient-aware experience leveraging on technologies including satellite receiver (e.g. GPS) and electronic compass, to identify the position of the device in space, accelerometers and gyroscopes, to understand movements of the devices, ambient light sensors, multi-touch screens, microphones, cameras etc.

The very nature of the system requires a scenario whereby the mobile device is always online, connected via 3D, UMTS or Wi-Fi in order to be able to access online information on routing, events of interests as well as other functionalities provided as a service to the i-Tour client (e.g. Natural Language Processing).

Additionally to the mobile client, i-Tour is developing a web client, as visible in (right), from which the user can access the same set of functionalities available to the mobile client. The goal set, when designing the interface of the web-client, was to provide a ubiquitous experience whereby the user, at any time, can migrate from mobile to web client yet having access to the same set of information.

The overall user experience and graphical language is consistent with the mobile interface, to minimise cognitive effort required to switch between web-based and mobile client and reduce learning time.

3   Related Works

The importance of creating interfaces capable to promote greener transportation has been highlighted in previous studies such as those carried on by Froehlich et al. (2009). The study revealed the complexity behind perception and selection of various transportation means. Promotion of greener transport means, leveraging on benefits of often healthier transportation patterns (e.g. walking or cycling) can be extremely effective. As shown in the study described by Froehlich et al. (2009) in fact 52% of interviewed users declared that they "would have been more likely to select bicycling or walking had they thought of health benefits (e.g., caloric expenditure) when making the travel decision". If these options are automatically computed and suggested to the final user accordingly with its preferences, we could expect that the probability of more sustainable travel solution choices will be higher.

With regard to the development of personal assistant for pedestrian, it must be noted that little attention has been paid by commercial applications to deliver routing other than for private vehicle. In particular very little attention has been paid to true pedestrian routing, as in fact most of the systems which offer pedestrian routing they do so essentially as an adaptation of car navigation, simply by loosening constraints set by driving on roads (one way streets etc.). Furthermore most portable car navigation system can be set to "pedestrian mode" however their interface does not take into account any specific requirement the new context may arise.

However it has been demonstrated that particular attention must be paid to cognitive aspects of the user when developing the routing and recommendation interface, particularly considering the so-called image schemata (Gaisbauer and Frank, 2008). This is a concept introduced in the late eighties, to define the conceptualization of the surrounding physical environment. Perceptive order is not just a rational and numerical problem, perception is not a picture of the outer world, it is the result of a selective mental process of organisation that involves the whole structure of the object.

If we steer away from car-based navigation systems, few dedicated cycling navigation systems are available from the market, either as adaptations of car navigation systems, such as TomTom Rider (http://www.tomtom.com/en_gb/products/bike-navigation/) or evolution of bike trip computers, essentially targeted to amateurs with a clear sport-oriented twist, such as Garmin Edge series (www.garmin.com). Their adaptation to specific requirements of bikers merely resides in an extended road network database which includes bike lanes and paths suitable for riding a bike, in the use of a larger buttons (e.g. to allow for easier interaction when wearing gloves), in the possibility to plot information on altimetry profiles or racing information. Instead little or no attention has been paid to providing different types of routing, for instance based on landmarks met along the street, on real-time information regarding availability of bikes at designated bike-sharing facilities, or least of all, integration with other transportation means.

With specific regard to multimodal routing interfaces, if we exclude web-based systems such as Google Transit (www.google.com/transit), which is practically an extension of a standard web-based routing system, and we focus on interfaces available for portable devices such as smartphones, very little is available from the market as well as from the research community.

A notable exception is CityAdvisor (http://www.cityadvisor.net/) an application for Windows Mobile 6.0 powered phones that provides routing over public transport network. The system allows routing over the public transport network based on indications and symbols of different network lines. The indications provided are essentially the ordered list of uni-modal journeys that the user has to take to reach destination, without providing any navigation on how to reach them nor on how to transit among different journey segments. Furthermore no advanced recommendation is available based on specific user preferences neither a mechanism based on updates is set in place.

When dealing with pedestrian routing several studies have proved the benefits of so-called landmark-based navigation if compared to turn-by-turn instructions as it provides a simpler navigation mechanism with constant contact with the surrounding scene. Landmark-based routing relies on directions given according to key points (landmarks) along the route. Usually routing by landmark is accompanied to use of images of the landmark, to help the user keep contact with the surrounding space. Additional graphics can be also used to superimpose arrows on top of images to better illustrate directions to take. One of the most relevant examples is described in (Hile et al., 2008) and (Hile et al., 2009). In this case, routing is ensured through use of geo-tagged images. The system renders on top of them directions (coloured arrow) identified around the path.

Especially for pedestrian routing, it has been demonstrated that traditional navigation based on distance and names of the streets is not effective whilst guiding a person through landmarks provides a much more effective navigation that improves confidence and trust (May et al., 2008).

4   The Ubiquitous Personal Travel Assistant

The mobile travel information system represents the heart of the i-Tour mobile client. Within standard personal navigation systems, routing is traditionally accessed through an interface where the user can type in an address of a place, or the name of a point of interest, and the system calculates the optimal route to reach the given location.

i-Tour instead starts from a completely different perspective. Although traditional navigation is still possible the system has been designed to ensure that routing is tightly integrated with the calendar(s) of the users. Calendars in fact are repositories of events and their corresponding locations that can be used, if properly described, to identify the daily activity of the user and the corresponding trips.

The user typically schedules events within their calendar at different times of the day, specifying the location. The system then uses this information to calculate the best route across the various locations where events are scheduled.

Most notably through the i-Tour interface the user can also define a list of activities by scheduling a time range to perform them without precisely defining neither their time nor their duration. This becomes particularly useful when the user has a certain degree of flexibility and does not require getting to a place by a given time. A typical example is the user willing to go shopping for 4 hours. In this case, the user can define a list of places (most probably shops) that he/she would like to visit without defining neither a precise time nor a precise order. These events, which are all defined within a single macro-activity called "shopping", scheduled from 12:00 to 16.00, can be then used by the system to calculate the optimal route, according to the user's travel preferences.

Overall Requirements. The i-Tour clients are both shown in Fig.1 The mobile client has been specifically designed for mobile Android-powered smartphones and tablets such as the recently released Galaxy Tab by Samsung. The requirements set by the project scenario imply that the client application must be capable to:

Manage events stored within one or more calendars.

Events can be created by learning from user's behaviours based on specific travel patterns by the users or other members of the social network.

The system is constantly tracking the user's position.

The system is online for most of the time.

The smartphone is fitted with a number of sensors, including accelerometers, gyroscopes, GPS, compass, light sensor, which are used to retrieve information on the user's movement as well as on the surrounding environment.

4.1   The Mobile Client Interface

As illustrated in Fig.1 (left) the home page of the mobile client provides access to high-level functionalities as well as to messages coming from the i-Tour service infrastructure. The interface, which graphically mimics a roundabout, is composed of a several areas. The central section is used as a dashboard for relevant alerts or messages. A set of icons, used to access the main functionalities, have been placed obliquely to improve selection when the device is being held with one hand only and the user interacts through their thumb. The interface can be mirrored for left-handed users. These icons are used to activate the main functions of the client, namely the calendar and scheduling of events and the map-based environment, the messages from the community of users, the recommendation system functionalities and finally the system settings and preference interface. The lower right corner of the screen is filled with the icon of an avatar which can be pressed, with a finger (e.g. the thumb), to activate speech recognition of natural language commands, whose interpreted message is shown in the balloon on top of the avatar's icon. The grey area at the bottom right of the screen is used to contain messages and alerts by the network services.

4.2   High-Level Map-Based Interaction

With i-Tour the user can check the forthcoming events, as scheduled in their agendas, based on their position over a map. This is accessible as a standard map-based environment (2D), as a 2.5 scene represented by a 2D map projected within a 3D space, as a 3D scene and last, but not least, as Augmented Reality scene. When the user is looking at the 2.5 or 3D visualization modes the system then adjusts the overall point of view so that the user can appreciate the relevant portion from a birds eye perspective. The map shows the portion of territory scaled to fit the locations of the forthcoming events.

If run on the mobile device, the system will automatically adjust the point of view of the scene, rendered as perspective image, to be aligned with the current position of the user and direction the device is being pointed at. In other words the image is aligned to make sure that the user can see on the screen the portion of the scene in front of them. This way when the user physically rotates around their position while holding the device, the system will ensure that the heading (the forward direction) of the virtual point of view of the scene on the screen is aligned with the user's heading direction in the real world.

By pressing the relevant icon the user can eventually switch to a full 3D view where the height of the terrain is rendered realistic manner. A smooth transition, showing the terrain deforming to reach the real orography, ensures a smooth interaction and pleasant user experience. During the transition all point of interests, as well as any other graphical element rendered on top of the map, including buildings, are moved upwards to the proper position in space, according to the 3D terrain information available.

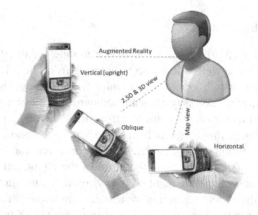

Fig. 1. The different position triggers different visualisation modes

Eventually the user can also turn on the Augmented Reality mode, where virtual information are projected on top of images captured by the camera fitted on the mobile device. This interface is particularly beneficial when the users need to explore information available in the nearby (for instance location corresponding to a number of close-by meeting in a given area) by simply pointing the device at the relevant position in space.

The user can switch between different views in a very simple manner, by simply holding the device at different angles (see Fig.2). If the device is held flat horizontal the system automatically moves the point of view to an azimuth map-like view (2D). A smooth transition ensures a user-friendly experience.

The system can also switch to Augmented Reality mode by holding it straight in front of the user. As soon as the system detects from the sensors that the device is nearly vertical it changes to Augmented Reality (AR) visualization mode. All the geometries representing the terrain and buildings fade away to leave room for the augmented scene, where information on events etc. are rendered on top of images from the surrounding scene as captured by the camera.

4.3   Graph-Based Route Selection

The route selection process relies on an interaction paradigm based on a graph-like structure. The graph has been developed to provide the user with an essential set of information required for the user to appreciate the best travel options as well as the state of the current trip.

There are various visualization modes that can be selected to identify the best route, specifically the graph can represent:

- Time to reach the final destination.
- Distance to reach the final destination.
- Emission (In terms of CO_2 or PM) generated to reach the final destination.
- Cost to destination.

The distance from the center of the graph can represent either the time required to get to the destination, the distance, the emission or the cost. When user switches within the different views, the graph adjusts automatically to account for the new configuration. When the user is interacting with the mobile i-Tour client he/she can switch between the various visualization modes by simply bending the device on the side.

Regardless of the visualization mode, the graph always shows the various alternatives available to reach the same destination. In other words all the leaf nodes (the terminating nodes) of the graph all represent the same destination. The various branches represent instead the different routes available to reach the final destination.

As soon as the user selects a segment, this is highlighted and when the user selects the segment additional information on that part of the travel is shown (e.g. bus number, expected delay etc.).

Each node of the graph reports the name of the corresponding station. The various graphical features of the graph are used to inform the user about relevant information on each travel option. The recommended travel option, i.e. the option providing fastest, most sustainable, shortest or cheapest solution (depending on the visualization mode), is highlighted by the corresponding branch of the graph being rendered with a thicker line. The recommended option is also highlighted with high contrast, will less favourable options are rendered with lower contrast.

Circles in the background highlight the top three options, providing the means to appreciate immediately the most interesting travel options for the users. An icon next to the three different routes clearly identifies the first three choices. A label next to the circle informs of the arrival time of the tree best options.

Additionally coloring is consistently employed to inform the user about quality of service. In particular the color of the arc inform the user weather the very journey leg will or will not be comfortable for instance due to the amount of passengers onboard that very vehicle or due to other factors that may influence the judgment of the user.

This information in fact summarizes the overall concept of quality of service resulting both from the information gathered by the system (e.g. information coming from sensors onboard a bus informing of the amount of passengers on a given vehicle), as well as information coming from the community of users through the recommender system (e.g. a bus may be badly rated because unclean).

The user can prune away undesired travelling options, by clicking on a read (delete) button next to each leaf node. The graph then automatically readjusts to maximize the readability. Since clicking on a relatively small icon on a small screen (as in the case of Smartphone) is not user friendly, especially when in a mobile context (e.g. while walking), the user can remove undelivered option by simply placing a finger onto the corresponding icon and by shaking the mobile device.

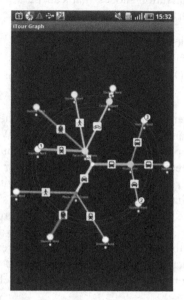

Fig. 2. Screenshot of the graph-based interface (PathGraph)

All the described graphical interfaces and interaction paradigms are the results of several sessions of internal development and experiments on a restricted number of users and are the most effective achieved so far. In the future, as soon as the first prototype of the system will be available, we have planned to extend and inspect more in depth the usability quality tests of our interfaces based on feedbacks provided by a wider set of daily users.

5   Conclusions and Further Developments

It has been demonstrated that standard turn-by-turn directions, traditionally effective to provide driving directions, are not best suited to pedestrian navigation, which is essentially the case of i-Tour where the user walks or uses public transport facilities. The use of landmarks to augment recommendations and navigation, which has been subject of extensive research, can be instead very beneficial to pedestrian routing as presented within section 4 "related works".

Since providing precise localization is often extremely complex, from the technical point of view, further works will explore the development of interface-based strategies to minimise the limitations of the lack of location information to deliver alternative strategies to routing, which do not require precise localization. One of the possible strategies which will be explored is to implement a properly balanced combination of traditional and landmark based routing.

At that point instructions could be formulated as a sequereference of images (with direction) that the user should move across as soon as they walk along the route. Given the fact that the system would be unaware of the actual position of the user speciall attention will have to be paid on how to ensure basic forms of localization in case a re-route request when satellite-based location is not available, for instance through automatic (trying to extract relevant features of the surrounding scene from images captured by the device) or by manually pointing their position within a map.

Acknowledgements. The research leading to these results has received funding from the European Community's Seventh Framework Programme (FP7/2007-2013) under the Grant Agreement n. 234239. This publication reflects the authors view, and the European Commission is not responsible for any use which may be made of the information contained therein.

References

1. Froehlich, J., Dillahunt, T., Klasnja, P., Mankoff, J., Consolvo, S., Beverly, H., James, A.L.: UbiGreen: investigating a mobile tool for tracking and supporting green transportation habits. In: Proceedings of the 27th International Conference on Human Factors in Computing Systems (CHI 2009), pp. 1043–1052. ACM, New York (2009), http://doi.acm.org/10.1145/1518701.1518861, doi:10.1145/1518701.1518861
2. Gaisbauer, C., Frank, A.U.: Wayfinding Model For Pedestrian Navigation. In: Proceedings of 11th AGILE International Conference on Geographic Information Science 2008, Girona, Spain (2009)
3. Hile, H., Grzeszczuk, R., Liu, A., Vedantham, R., Košecka, J., Borriello, G.: Landmark-Based Pedestrian Navigation with Enhanced Spatial Reasoning. In: Tokuda, H., Beigl, M., Friday, A., Brush, A.J.B., Tobe, Y. (eds.) Pervasive 2009. LNCS, vol. 5538, pp. 59–76. Springer, Heidelberg (2009), http://dx.doi.org/10.1007/978-3-642-01516-8_6, doi:10.1007/978-3-642-01516-8_6
4. Hile, H., Vedantham, R., Cuellar, G., Liu, A., Gelfand, N., Grzeszczuk, R., Borriello, G.: Landmark-based pedestrian navigation from collections of geotagged photos. In: Proceedings of the 7th International Conference on Mobile and Ubiquitous Multimedia (MUM 2008), pp. 145–152. ACM, New York (2009), http://doi.acm.org/10.1145/1543137.1543167, doi:10.1145/1543137.1543167
5. May, A.J., Ross, T., Bayer, S.H., Tarkiainen, M.J.: Pedestrian navigation aids: information requirements and design implications. Personal Ubiquitous Comput. 7(6), 331–338 (2003), http://dx.doi.org/10.1007/s00779-003-0248-5, doi:10.1007/s00779-003-0248-5
6. R.D.: Development of an open framework to provide intelligent multi-modal mobility services. In: REAL CORP 2011 Proceedings (May 2011), http://www.corp.at
7. Conti, G., De Amicis, R.: i-Tour - intelligent Transport system for Optimized URban trips

Experimental Study on Display of Energy-Related Information in Smart Homes Using Virtual Reality

Kodai Ito and Michiko Ohkura

Shibaura Institute of Technology, 3-7-5, Toyosu, Koto-ku, Tokyo,135-8548, Japan
{109009,ohkura}@shibaura-it.ac.jp

Abstract. Environmental pollution and electrical power shortages are serious issues, especially in Japan recently. Since private households are clearly constitute one of the main energy consumers today, positive effects on the environment can be expected if home energy consumption is reduced. Accordingly, our research purpose is to develop a prototype smart home that can offer "smart" quality of life, QOL, to its residents and reduce both CO_2 emissions and energy consumption. An important issue toward achieving this aim is how to show energy-related information to the home's residents.

As a first step, we perform a preliminary experiment on reducing the numbers of candidates of locations and contents of energy-related information. Next, we perform another experiment to clarify the locations and contents of energy-related information expected to be in demand for display in actual smart homes.

Keywords: Smart home, energy saving, user interface, information presentation.

1   Introduction

Environmental pollution and electric power shortages are serious issues, especially in Japan recently. Since private households are clearly constitute one of the main energy consumers today [1], positive effects on the environment can be expected if home energy consumption is reduced [2]. However, the deployment of automation technologies in the home offers several attractive benefits, among them most prominently increased energy (or even resource) efficiency, improved residential comfort, and the peace of mind of the residents. Accordingly, our research purpose is to develop a prototype smart home that can offer "smart" quality of life, QOL, to its residents and reduce both CO2 emissions and energy consumption. An important issue toward achieving this aim is how to show energy-related information to the home's residents. We conducted interviews and a questionnaire related to the QOL of smart home, and based on the results, we performed experiments to clarify where and how to display energy-related information in a smart home.

N. Streitz and C. Stephanidis (Eds.): DAPI/HCII 2013, LNCS 8028, pp. 294–301, 2013.
© Springer-Verlag Berlin Heidelberg 2013

2   Results of Interviews and a Questionnaire on QOL of Smart Homes

Our platform consists of two smart homes built in Saitama City in Japan [3]. A family consisting of a father, mother and daughter lives in one of them, and the other is open to visitors (Fig. 1). Based on the results of interviews with the family members and the results of a questionnaire given to the visitors, we found a strong demand to know energy-related information in real time.

Fig. 1. Photograph of smart home open to visitors

3   Preliminary Experiment

3.1   Method

A very important characteristic in a smart home is how easy it is for the residents to check energy-related information. Therefore, the locations and the contents of displayed information should be determined appropriately. However, there are very many possible candidates of such locations and contents. Therefore, we decided to perform a preliminary experiment to reduce the numbers of candidates and thus select the display locations and the contents of energy-related information for the next, main experiment. For the preliminary experiment, we created a virtual reality (VR) space modeled on the CAD data of the smart home open to visitors. The candidates of location are as follows:

1. TV monitor
2. Table in living room
3. Wall next to refrigerator
4. Wall in living room.

Participants were asked to choose at most eight of the following candidates of energy-related information for each location:

A. Amount of electricity generated by solar power
B. Amounts of electricity and heat generated by cogeneration
C. Amount of total electricity generated
D. Amount of commercial electric power consumed
E. Overall power consumption
F. Percentage of power consumption covered by home generation of electricity
G. Heating and lighting costs
H. Electric power-selling rate
I. Remaining home battery level
J. CO_2 emissions reductions
K. Temperature of hot-water supply system
L. Remaining EV car battery level

The VR space was projected to the screen, and the information displayed was changed based on the demands of the participants. Figure 2 shows examples of VR spaces, and Fig. 3 shows a system configuration. After finishing selection of the contents for all locations, the following questions were asked in our questionnaire:

- Do you need a display of each location?
- Are there any places that you want to display other than these candidates?
- Are there any contents that you want to display other than these candidates?

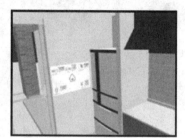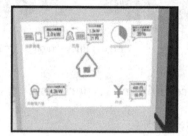

Fig. 2. Example of VR spaces

3.2   Results and Discussion

A preliminary experiment was performed using 12 staff members of our university as subjects.

Figure 3 shows results of preferences for locations of energy-related information. The table in the living room was judged unnecessary. Therefore, we employed the three locations other than the table in the living room.

Figure 4 shows the results for contents. Overall power consumption (E) was judged necessary at every location, but other selected contents varied from location to location. In particular, there was a large difference between Wall next to refrigerator and Wall in living room. This is because usually only the housewife looks at the Wall next to refrigerator. On the other hand, every person visiting this house often looks at

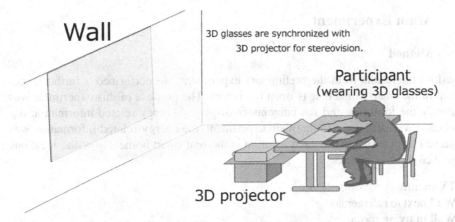

Fig. 3. System configuration of preliminary experiment

the Wall in living room. Therefore, we can conclude that necessary information differs depending on the place and that all candidates of information candidates necessary in some places. Accordingly, we employed all candidates of energy-related information in the next experiment.

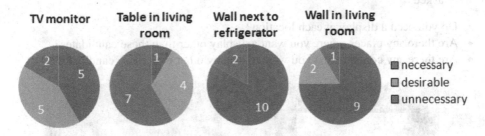

Fig. 4. Results for preferred locations of energy-related information

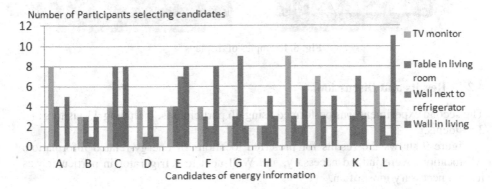

Fig. 5. Results of preferred contents of energy-related information

4   Main Experiment

4.1   Method

Based on the results from the preliminary experiment, we performed a further experiment in the smart home that is open to visitors. The purpose of this experiment was to clarify the locations and the contents of displayed energy-related information demanded in a smart home. In the main experiment, the energy-related information was displayed at or projected to each location in the real smart home. Now, the locations employed were as follows:

1. TV monitor
2. Wall next to refrigerator
3. Wall in living room.

We used the same twelve candidates of energy-related information content as in the preliminary experiment. The information displayed or projected was chosen by participants at each location. Participants could decide the position of the energy-related information at 1-4 or 5-9 in the layout. Figure 6 shows examples of displays, Fig. 7 shows the layout of a display, and Fig.8 shows a scene from the experiment.

After finishing the selection of contents for all location, the following questions were asked:

• Do you need a display at each location?
• Are there any places where you want a display other than these candidates?
• Are there any contents that you want to display other than these candidates?

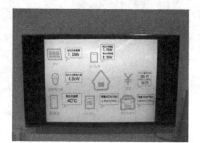

Fig. 6. Examples of displays

4.2   Results and Discussion

The second experiment was performed using 46 participants, including 43 visitors and 3 residents.

Figure 9 shows the results for preferred locations of energy-related information. All locations were judged necessary, and Wall next to refrigerator in particular was judged necessary most often.

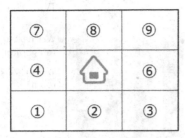

Fig. 7. Display layout

Fig. 8. Experimental scene

Figure 10 shows results for contents in this experiment as well as in the preliminary experiment. All energy-related information in this experiment was judged more important than in the preliminary experiment. This is because participants in this experiment observed the smart home in advance, which caused them to be more interested in energy information than the participants in the preliminary experiment. In addition, Overall power consumption (E), Percentage of power consumption covered by home generation of electricity (F), and Heating and lighting costs (G) were, in particular, judged necessary in this experiment. We found strong demand for the system to display the effects of energy savings.

Figure 11 shows the results for contents at each location. The numbers of participants who chose C, E, I and L were similar at the three locations. On the other hand, the numbers of participants who chose A and J tended to be less at the Wall next to refrigerator. This is because the monitor at the Wall next to refrigerator was smaller than that at the other locations. In addition, the number of participants who chose K was more at the Wall next to refrigerator, because this location is near the kitchen. Therefore, the energy-related information can be divided into two categories: necessary at all locations and necessary at specific locations.

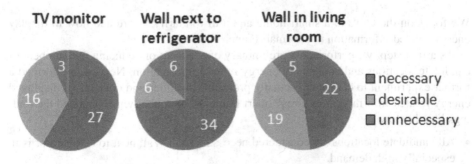

Fig. 9. Results for location of energy-related information

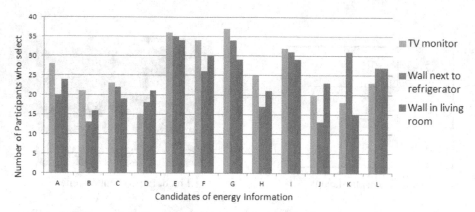

Fig. 10. Results for contents in main and preliminary experiments

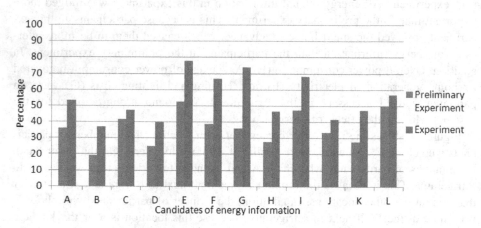

Fig. 11. Results for contents at each location

5   Conclusions

We focus on the QOL in a smart home and aim to clarify where and how to display energy-related information in the smart home.

As a first step, we performed a preliminary experiment on reducing the numbers of candidate locations and contents of energy-related information. Next, we performed a further experiment to clarify the actually preferred locations and contents of displayed energy-related information in a real smart home. Consequently, we obtained the findings listed below.

- All candidate locations are considered necessary, and Wall next to refrigerator is in especially high demand.
- All energy-related information is considered necessary, and the types of information that can give the user an actual feel for energy savings, such as Overall power consumption (E) and Heating and lighting costs (G), are in particular highly demanded.

- The desirable information is different depending on the location; for example, participants want to reduce the number of contents at the locations where the monitor is small, and they require the Temperature of the hot-water supply system (K) if the location is near the kitchen.

Acknowledgments. We express our gratitude to HONDA R&D and Saitama City Office for providing the smart homes for the experiment. In addition, we thank the staff and students of Saitama University and Shibaura Institute of Technology for their participation as volunteers in the experiments.

References

1. Bertoldi, P., Atanasiu, B.: Electricity Consumption and Efficiency Trends in European Union. Status Report, Institute for Energy, Joint Research Center - European Commission (2009)
2. Kofler, M.J., Reinisch, C., Kastner, W.: A semantic representation of energy-related information in future smart homes. Energy and Buildings 47, 169–179 (2012)
3. Honda "smart home" showcases off-the-grid energy solutions
4. http://www.gizmag.com/honda-demonstration-smart-home/22328/

A Precision Navigation System
for Public Transit Users

Masaki Ito, Satoru Fukuta, Takao Kawamura, and Kazanuri Sugahara

Graduate School of Engineering, Tottori University,
4-101 Koyamacho-Minami Tottori-shi, Tottori 680-8522, Japan
{masaki,s072041,kawamura,sugahara}@ike.tottori-u.ac.jp

Abstract. In this paper, we propose a context aware navigation for public transportation users. In the travel with public transportation, a user needs to switch several modality of moving such as walking, waiting at the station, and riding a vehicle. We developed a navigation system that automatically detect user's state how he/she is using public transportation, and then provide suitable information for each state. We developed the system as an Android application, and demonstrate its basic functionality in the field experiment with five examinees.

1 Introduction

Public transport is important infrastructure for modern society. The benefit of public transportation is not only for personal convenience, but also for society such as reduction of traffic jam, reduction of carbon dioxide. Therefore it is important to promote the use of public transportation for citizens including a person who normally uses a car. However, a person who seldom use public transportation or a stranger in the area faces great difficulties when he/she is trying to take a train or a bus. There are already many web services that provide information about public transportation such as timetables or an itinerary from the certain station to the destination. We have also developed and operating such kind of web service called "Busnet", where a user can plan a path on a public transportation network in Tottori Prefecture, Japan [1]. However, such web services are designed for a user who is planning to move a certain place, but does not guide a person who has exactly started to move to the destination.

We developed a navigation system for a smartphone that guide a passenger of public transportation in real-time. The system provides suitable information for a passenger in each situations of his/her travel just like a turn-by-turn navigation system that guides a driver. Comparing with the travel with a car which existing turn-by-turn navigation system support, travel with public transportation is much more complex, therefore we need to investigate the process of the travel with public transportation before designing the navigation system.

2 Information Technology for Public Transportation

With the recent development in information technologies, various IT services which do not necessarily have strong relation to the existing intelligent trans-

N. Streitz and C. Stephanidis (Eds.): DAPI/HCII 2013, LNCS 8028, pp. 302–308, 2013.

portation systems (ITS) for the users of public transportation is arising [2] [3] [4] [5]. Unlike existing ITS whose primary target is infrastructure such as managing road and operating trains and buses, arising services aim more gpassenger-centrich style in its feature. For example, Google provides gGoogle Transith which plans the trip between arbitrary two places including trains, buses and walking as a feature of Google Maps. A traveler searches for the best itinerary on the service, and move to the destination with the information.

Some researches point out that users feel less secure while the trip with railways or buses [6] [7], however, most existing IT services to support users of public transportation mainly focus on the planning process before the usage of buses or railways, and does not support on-board users to railways or route buses. In contrast there are rich support for car driver through automotive navigation system while traveling in this decade. One reason is that there are no reasonable device to support passenger of trains and buses, but a smartphone is changing the situation. The other reason is the process to travel with trains or buses is much complicated than the travel with a car. There are several research projects to support on-board traveler [8][9], but these products are still not in the practical use.

We studied the process to travel with public transportation, then we classified the process into the following three steps: walking, waiting and riding. Figure 1 illustrates the state diagram of the process. Firstly, a user walks to the bus stop or the station. Then he/she buys a ticket and wait for the vehicle. He/she takes the vehicle when the vehicle arrives at the station or the bus stop. In the vehicle, he/she stays until the vehicle arrives at the destination. After getting off the vehicle, he/she walks to the destination, or changes to another bus or train.

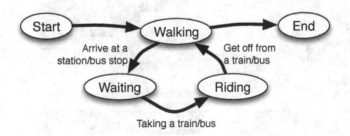

Fig. 1. State diagram in traveling with public transportation

3   A Precision Navigation System

Based on the study in the former section, we developed a context aware navigation system for public transport users that automatically switches three different modalities for navigation. We developed the navigation system as an application for an Android smartphone. The navigation system recognizes user's situation automatically with timetables and GPS, then provides suitable information for each step. As dividing a user's sequence of using public transport into three states and providing different information for each state, we accomplished a useful navigation system for public transport users.

3.1 Navigation for Walking

When a user is walking, a user needs information of his/her location, or map information around his/her location. Therefore the system provides a map and shows a route to the bus stop or the station where the user ride a vehicle. It also gives a turn-by-turn navigation to the station of the bus stop. Figure 2 illustrates the screenshot. In the upper part of the screen, it gives the information of the bus or the train he/she will ride. In the lower part of the screen, it provides a map with a route information and scenery around the bus stop or the station as a photograph in order to easily correlate direction with the surroundings of the user.

route to the bus stop   photo around the bus stop

Fig. 2. Navigation for walking to the bus stop

3.2 Navigation for Waiting for the Bus or the Train

While waiting for the bus or the train, a passenger needs to understand the system of the public transportation, and prepare for riding such as buying a ticket. Then he/she needs to go to the exact place to take the train or the bus such as a certain platform of the station. He/she may want to do something if there is enough time before the departure. The proposed navigation system gives guidance how to spend at the station or the bus stop with certain priority. Figure 3 illustrates the screenshot. The system countdown the departure time of the train in the lower part of the screen, or gives a detailed map around the station or the bus stops.

The system of public transportation is different even within the same country. For example, some route buses ask a user to pay when riding, but other route buses ask to pay when getting off. With the proposed system, a user is never confused by the difference of the system.

Countdown to the departure

Location of comming route buses

Fig. 3. Navigation while waiting for a bus or a train

3.3 Navigation for Riding a Bus/Train

After the user ride a vehicle, the navigation system shows a map and route to the destination. Figure 4 illustrates the screen. When a passenger is arriving at the destination, the system alerts the user to get off. If he/she must transfer to another bus or train, the system guides the transit after taking off the vehicle. A passenger tends to feel anxiety if he/she is taking the right train or bus. The navigation system reduces the anxiety, and enables prediction of arrival time.

4 Field Experiment

We conducted field experiment of the prototype system. Five examinees made a round-trip to the AEON shopping mall from the Tottori University campus with

Guidance of the bus route   Inform to push the bell

Fig. 4. Navigation for riding a bus or a train

the prototype system, and answered to the questionnaire after the travel. The trip is approximately 5 km including walking, riding a route bus and changing to another route bus at the bus stop. Table 1 is the detailed condition of the experiment.

Table 1. Field Experiment

Examinees	5 male (including students and a staff of bus company)
Devices	Google Galaxy Nexus for each examinee
To the AEON mall	54 min in total, 1 transfer, 6 min walk
From the AEON mall	36 min in total, 0 transfer, 14 min walk

4.1 Basic Functionality

The prototype system worked fine as we designed while the experiment. Since the frequency of the report of the vehicle location is one minute, detection of user's condition in the trip sometimes delays.

4.2 Result of the Questionnaire

Table 2 is the result of the questionnaire to the examinees. They are the scores of five grade evaluations and variances in each navigation and overall quality of the

Table 2. The Result of the Questionnaire

	Quality of the prototype	Easiness in inputting the destination	Navigation for walking	Navigation while waiting	Navigation while riding
Average	3.60	4.00	4.60	4.00	4.00
Variance	0.24	0.50	0.24	0.00	0.40

prototype system. Though there was a problem in the quality of the prototypes, many examinee were satisfied with the navigation method in each condition.

From the free description in the questionnaire, we found that the examinees especially satisfied with the location information of the route bus that he/she was taking. Supporting an on-board user is one of the most important essence in the proposed system. therefore we can say that the comment verify our initial hypothesis.

5 Summary

In this paper, we developed a precision navigation system for using public transport. It is difficult to guide a user of public transport, since a user needs different information in each stage of moving with public transport. The system divides process of the travel with public transportation into three states, and provides different guidance for a user in each state.

As a future work, it is needed to improve the recognition of user's state. There is various possible information to recognize user's state such as user's location, vehicle's location, delay of transport, arrival time at the transport, distance from user's location to next point. We are using only user's location and arrival time of public transport now. We will improve the recognition, and provide the system as a practical service in Tottori Prefecture.

Acknowledgements. This research is supported by Strategic Information and Communications R&D Promotion Programme (SCOPE), Ministry of Internal Affairs and Communications, Japan.

References

1. Kawamura, T., Sugahara, K.: Practical path planning system for bus network. IPSJ Journal 48(2), 780–790 (2007)
2. Giannopoulos, G.A.: The application of information and communication technologies in transport. European Journal of Operational Research 152(2), 302–320 (2004)
3. Camacho, T.D., Foth, M., Rakotonirainy, A.: Pervasive technology and public transport: Opportunities beyond telematics. Pervasive Computing 12, 18–25 (2013)
4. Arikawa, M., Konomi, S., Onishi, K.: NAVITIME: Supporting Pedestrian Navigation in the Real World. IEEE Pervasive Computing, 21–29 (2007)
5. Ferris, B., Watkins, K., Borning, A.: OneBusAway: Results from providing real-time arrival information for public transit. In: Proceedings of the 28th International Conference on Human Factors in Computing Systems, pp. 1807–1816. ACM (2010)

6. Lyons, G., Harman, R.: The uk public transport industry and provision of multi-modal traveller information. International Journal of Transport Management 1(1), 1–13 (2002)
7. Grotenhuis, J.W., Wiegmans, B.W., Rietveld, P.: The desired quality of integrated multimodal travel information in public transport: Customer needs for time and effort savings. Transport Policy 14(1), 27–38 (2007)
8. Zhang, L., Gupta, S.D., Li, J.Q., Zhou, K., Zhang, W.B.Z.: Path2go: Context-aware services for mobile real-time multimodal traveler information. In: 14th International IEEE Conference on Intelligent Transportation Systems (ITSC), pp. 174–179. IEEE (October 2011)
9. Carmien, S., Dawe, M., Fischer, G., Gorman, A., Kintsch, A., Sullivan, J., James, F.: Socio-technical environments supporting people with cognitive disabilities using public transportation. ACM Transactions on Computer-Human Interaction 12(2), 233–262 (2005)

Rapid Development of Civic Computing Services: Opportunities and Challenges

Shin'ichi Konomi[1], Kenta Shoji[2], and Wataru Ohno[2]

[1] Center for Spatial Information Science, The University of Tokyo,
Kashiwa, Chiba, 277-8568, Japan
[2] Department of Socio-Cultural Environmental Studies, The University of Tokyo,
Kashiwa, Chiba, 277-8563, Japan
`{konomi,wataru_ohno,nebosukesan}@csis.u-tokyo.ac.jp`

Abstract. Designing the right computing service for citizens can be extremely difficult without participatory and iterative service development processes. We discuss opportunities and challenges for quick, participatory service development by citizens, based on our experiences with two experimental context-aware services.

Keywords: civic computing, open-source hardware, data, collaboration.

1   Introduction

The ubiquity of computing and sensing technologies in everyday life is giving rise to a wide range of context-aware services for citizens, ranging from location-based social networking and navigation support to disaster information sharing and persuasive green-computing applications. Given the diversity of the target population and the complexity of the situations of use, the "one-size-fits-all" approach of providing a general service for everyone can limit the usefulness of the service significantly. To create useful context-aware civic computing services that suit different situations and needs, it is highly desirable to support citizen participation in the service development processes.

An important obstacle in enabling such participatory service development is the difficulty of handling context in civic computing systems. Although software architectures, such as Context Toolkit [1], can remedy some of the difficulty, context handling has other aspects besides software architectures, including hardware setup [2], data processing, and user experiences. In this context, we discuss a method to facilitate hardware setup by supporting exploration and contextualization of sensor data, and a strategy to facilitate data processing. The proposed method and strategy complements software architectures-based approach, thereby facilitating participation of people without the knowledge of programming, physical computing, or data processing/mining.

N. Streitz and C. Stephanidis (Eds.): DAPI/HCII 2013, LNCS 8028, pp. 309–315, 2013.

2   Developing Civic Computing Services

Civic computing provides digital services for various kinds of people who live in a city. Importantly, it can support citizens to cope with ill-defined social problems, and end-user development [3] based on citizen participation is a key approach in this context. In recent years, there is keen interest in such participatory approach as exemplified by the emergence of open-data hackathons and crowdsourcing projects.

To exploit open data as well as open source hardware components in a civic computing service, its development process can be understood a bit differently from traditional context-aware applications. As shown in Table 1, the development process can include Exploration (Step 2) as well as Setup (Step 3) to exploit hardware and data-source components, as well as the other steps that can be supported by appropriate software architectures (e.g., widget-based [1] or blackboard-based architectures).

Table 1. Steps for developing a civic computing service for sharing information about urban congestion

1. Specification	"Report congestion levels on trains using smart phones, sensors, and train-network data"
2. Exploration	Use sensors (CO_2, acceleration, etc.) to capture data on a train. Also, record congestion levels on the train manually. Create a model to transform sensor readings into a congestion level. Additionally, identify train-network data and explore ways to exploit them.
3. Setup	Connect a CO_2 sensor to a microcontroller and a wireless communication module, and integrate it with a physical object such as a bag.
4. Acquisition and delivery	Write software on a smart phone to obtain data from the CO_2 sensor, convert it to a congestion level, and upload it to a server along with the current location information.
5. Reception and action	Smart phone application receives data from the server and displays congestion levels on a map along with the train-network information.

3   Supporting the Use of Open-Source Hardware

This section introduces a prototype civic computing service for sharing congestion information, which we developed by using open-source hardware components. Our experience with this prototype service suggested the need to support exploration and contextualization of sensor data, which leads to a discussion on a general approach to supporting the use of open-source hardware.

3.1   A Congestion Sensing Service

Providing information about congestion in public spaces, including public transportation, can help citizens get around in a city without unnecessary stress. We therefore developed a prototype civic computing service that allows people to post congestion information using smart phones and/or open hardware-based sensors. As shown in Fig. 1, a CO_2 sensor and a battery are integrated with a bag, which forwards the data to a smart phone via a ZigBee-Bluetooth gateway. The smart phone estimates the congestion level based on the sensor reading and uploads it to a server along with the current location information.

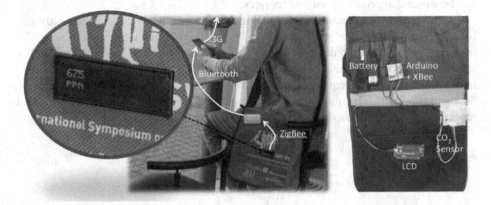

Fig. 1. Open hardware-based data capture environment for a congestion information service

3.2   Exploration of Sensor Data

To develop the congestion sensing service, we have explored the use of a CO_2 sensor, a pressure sensor, and an acceleration sensor. We expected that the CO_2 sensor could detect the increase of CO_2 concentration in a congested indoor space, and the other sensors could detect human posture (e.g., standing or sitting) that can be influenced by congestion. The result of this exploration suggested that we could use the CO_2 sensor only, whose measurements can be converted into estimated congestion levels relatively easily.

What we want to highlight here is the complicated work in this exploration process, which we cannot simply overlook in supporting the development of a civic computing service. As we are interested in providing the service for the users of a train network in Tokyo, we first obtained relevant information, such as the passenger capacity for different types of trains, from the railway company's website. We then developed simple data-logging devices using the sensors, and recorded various data in different congestion conditions, 11 times in total. We also counted the number of passengers in a train car for each data-recording sessions, and calculated actual congestion levels by dividing the number with the corresponding passenger capacity. Finally, we analyzed the data to discover the approximately linear relationship between the congestion levels and the CO_2 concentration.

3.3   Contextualization of Sensor Data

Past congestion information can become unreliable as people enter and leave the place of interest. For example, a congestion level reported by someone in a restaurant can become decreasingly reliable as people visit and leave the restaurant after the time of reporting. In this context, it can be useful to provide congestion information along with meta-information that indicates the reliability of the information. More generally, providing data along with relevant contextual information (e.g., reliability scores) can be a useful approach in various services.

In our prototype congestion information service, we devised an open hardware-based *"contextual sensor"* that can detect human flows in an entrance/exit area of a restaurant using an infrared sensor (see Fig. 2). It can be used to compute a reliability score of congestion information reported in the restaurant. Converting the sensor data into a reliability score requires a model that represents the correlation between the data and the score. This model was developed based on data recording sessions that resemble the ones we described in section 3.2.

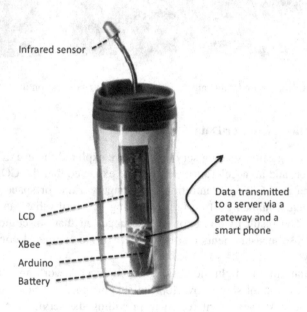

Infrared sensor

Data transmitted
to a server via a
gateway and a
smart phone

LCD

XBee

Arduino

Battery

Fig. 2. Prototype "contextual sensor"

3.4   Supporting Exploration and Contextualization

Clearly, it is a burdensome and time-consuming task to develop a civic computing service using open source hardware components, even though they are much easier to use than previous generations of ubiquitous sensing devices. That said, the following three approaches would minimize the burden to enable rapid prototyping, thereby facilitating participatory development by "expert amateurs" and other motivated citizens.

1. *Provision of a hardware toolkit*, which allow people to simply "plug in" and deploy different sensors without the knowledge of sensor network technologies. Such toolkit can be supported by web-based information sharing such as instructables.com.
2. *Support for crowdsourced data recording sessions*. Procedures for data recording sessions can be defined and shared so that a sufficient quantity of data can be collected quickly based on crowdsourcing.
3. *Support for sharing and reuse of data transformation models*. This can dramatically reduce the aforementioned burden since one could simply reuse an existing model.

4   Supporting the Use of Datasets

We now look into another prototype service, which exploits an existing dataset rather than sensor networks. The service recommends "nearby" restaurants based on a human-mobility dataset and the current location information. Deriving useful information for a civic computing service from a large-scale "general purpose" dataset can require multiple steps of costly data conversions, which could potentially discourage participatory development.

4.1   A Restaurant Recommendation Service

Existing location-based services that recommend restaurants simply based on Euclidean distances between the user and the restaurants do not consider other, more complex context of urban space, including patterns of transportation networks and human flows. We developed a prototype civic computing application that recommends restaurants in Tokyo, based on mobility patterns of crowds using the PFlow dataset [4]. Fig. 3 shows geographic areas that can be considered similar, based on people's mobility patterns in the dataset. As the service recommends restaurants based on this and other similar patterns, it can, for example, recommend a distant restaurant if it is located in a similar area that people at current location likely visit as well.

4.2   Data Processing

Deriving useful information for a civic computing service from a large-scale dataset such as PFlow can require multiple steps of data conversion.

Firstly, we divide the Tokyo region into small (1km x 1km) rectangular areas and find people who visit each area.   Secondly, we generate a network of the rectangular areas using a similarity measure that is based on people's co-presence in the areas. Thirdly, we obtain clusters of areas based on the network, and finally use the clusters to generate restaurant recommendations.

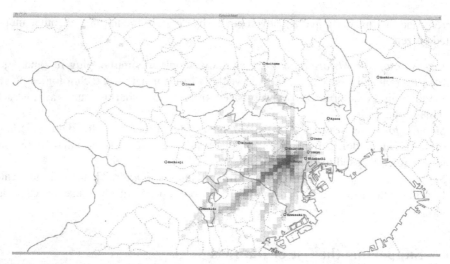

Fig. 3. Geographic areas that can be considered similar based on people's mobility patterns

4.3   Supporting Data Exploration and Processing

The data processing steps may appear somewhat simplistic. Nonetheless, it takes time (e.g., hours or days on a high-end desktop PC) to perform each step when the dataset is large. Moreover, each step requires the data processing person to determine several key parameters, including the size and shape of the rectangular areas, a threshold value for area-similarity judgment, and clustering parameters. The lengthy computation time inhibits casual modification and exploration of these parameters.

Here we suggest a couple strategies to cope with this issue:

4. *Publishing and sharing intermediate data conversion results.* It would be helpful to represent data conversion processes explicitly using a user-friendly (e.g., graphical) representations.
5. *Support for data exploration.* A tool for exploring the effects of different parameters using a small subset of the data would be extremely helpful.

5   Discussion and Conclusion

Our experiences with the prototypes suggested that the increasingly open sociotechnical environments (e.g., open source hardware, open data, open source, open access, etc.) create new opportunities to empower citizens in the development and use of civic computing services. We believe that effective support environment can be built based on the proposed methods and strategies, in order to address relevant challenges.

Acknowledgments. This research was supported by the Environmental Information project under the Green Network of Excellence (GRENE) program of MEXT, Japan.

References

1. Dey, A.K., Abowd, G.D., Salber, D.: A Conceptual Framework and a Toolkit for Supporting the Rapid Prototyping of Context-Aware Applications. Human-Computer Interaction 16(2-4), 97–166 (2001)
2. Beckmann, C., Consolvo, S., LaMarca, A.: Some assembly required: Supporting end-user sensor installation in domestic ubiquitous computing environments. In: Mynatt, E.D., Siio, I. (eds.) UbiComp 2004. LNCS, vol. 3205, pp. 107–124. Springer, Heidelberg (2004)
3. Fischer, G.: End-User Development and Meta-design: Foundations for Cultures of Participation. In: Pipek, V., Rosson, M.B., de Ruyter, B., Wulf, V. (eds.) IS-EUD 2009. LNCS, vol. 5435, pp. 3–14. Springer, Heidelberg (2009)
4. Sekimoto, Y., Shibasaki, R., Kanasugi, H., Usui, T., Shimazaki, Y.: PFlow: Reconstructiong People Flow Recycling Large-Scale Social Survey Data. IEEE Pervasive Computing 10(4), 27–35 (2011)

VIA - Visualizing Individual Actions to Develop a Sustainable Community Culture through Cycling

Benjamin Watson[1], David Berube[1], Nickolay Hristov[2], Carol Strohecker[2], Scott Betz[3], Louise Allen[3], Matthew Burczyk[4], Amber Howard[5], William Anthony McGee[6], Matthew Gymer[7], Daniel Cañas[8], and Mark Kirstner[9]

[1] North Carolina State University
{bwatson,dmberube}@ncsu.edu
[2] Center for Design Innovation, Univ. North Carolina
{nickolay.hristov,cs}@centerfordesigninnovation.org
[3] Winston-Salem State University
{betzs,allenl}@wssu.edu
[4] City of Winston-Salem
mattbk@cityofws.org
[5] New Kind
amber@newkind.com
[6] StokesCORE
wamcgee@gmail.com
[7] Novant Health
mgymer@novanthealth.org
[8] Wake Forest University
canas@wfu.edu
[9] Piedmont Together
markk@partnc.org

Abstract. Improving the sustainability of our society requires significant change in our collective behavior. But today, individuals in our society have no regular way of seeing that collective behavior, or how their own behavior compares to it. We are creating a research network that will study how new technologies such as mobiles and visualization can encourage individuals to change their behavior to improve sustainability. In Winston-Salem NC, network members will use new technologies to engage the community about its use of transportation—especially biking—and study how that communication affects sustainability awareness and behavior.

Keywords: sustainability, biking, mobiles, visualization, persuasion, measurement.

1 Introduction

Sustainability is connectivity: actions that are beneficial in the short term regularly have unseen economic, ecological and social impacts that harm us in the long term. Sustainability is also now in crisis: we are reaching natural limits, and are no longer

N. Streitz and C. Stephanidis (Eds.): DAPI/HCII 2013, LNCS 8028, pp. 316–325, 2013.

able to ignore those long term impacts. Mitigating this crisis will require behavioral change at both the individual and societal levels. Unfortunately, we often find it difficult to act toward achieving long-term goals, even when we are quite familiar with the benefits of such action.

Emerging mobile and visualization technologies may offer a solution. By improving connectivity in the web of sustainability, these technologies have the potential to:

- *Enable improved sustainability measurement.* For planners and researchers, mobile technologies such as GPS can provide crowdsourced "big" data measuring human sustainability behavior at an individual, nearly minute-by-minute level. For individual community members, mobile measurement can provide feedback on any improvement in their sustainable behavior, and enable comparison of their behavior to peer groups.
- *Enable improved sustainability action.* For planners and researchers, mobile measurement and resulting visualizations will provide prompt feedback on the effect of infrastructure improvements, incentives, and outreach efforts; to enable more effective investment and more relevant research. For individual community members, mobile wayfinding tools will make acting sustainably easier: individualized persuasive visualizations will motivate that action, and well-timed sustainability reminders will trigger that motivation.
- *Build cultures of community sustainability.* Community leaders communicate more directly and promptly with their constituents, and constituents with their leadership; researchers will study the effect of different communication campaigns on both awareness and behavior; and individual community members will be more tightly bound to communities by improved awareness.

Examining these possibilities will require a regionally-focused, broad collaboration across disciplinary, organizational and social boundaries. Our emerging VIA research network is just such a collaboration, centered around transportation and the growing biking movement in North Carolina.

The network will have three primary nodes associated with the triple bottom line of sustainability: ecology, economy and society[0]. Three teams of researchers from multiple disciplines will network to improve short distance transportation decision making. The methods and tools team is creating an ecology of mobile and visualization tools, used to measure and communicate about short-distance transportation behavior, especially bicycling. The tools will be field tested and instituted with the activities of the academic team, which functions as an iterative economy. The feedback will affect the next generation of method and tool development as well as guide our community institutions team in their visualization activities. This community institutions team will feed back to the academic and methods teams and provide assessment of activities and methods development, and interface through an extensive group of community supporters (CSs) to citizens. The goals of promoting a community of citizens for sustainability will be met through these networking exercises and activities.

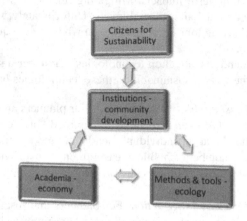

Fig. 1. The structure of the VIA research network

2   Prior Work

2.1   Community

Organizing the large number of motivations and barriers involved in short-distances transportation decision-making draws from a body of theory on effective communication of sustainability [2], taking into consideration cultural variables as well as individual responsibility. At the collective level, Pacanowsky and O'Donnell-Trujillo [3] observed more things happen in organizations than getting things done: they are not single-minded task-oriented communities; they are mini-cultures. Communication in this sense is more about creating a reality of the world consistent with strongly held beliefs and attitudes shared within the community and nurtured by the persuasive campaign. Using the metaphor of webs, also known as axiologies, organizational communication theory optimizes effect by building upon the existing panoply of beliefs and attitudes shared by a community and by tapping into these sensibilities and demonstrating significant and substantive linkage with the subject of the persuasive campaign, in this case sustainable transport decision-making, attracting and supporting individuals into a shared community by providing them with a coherent vision using concepts such as personal, effect, and cultural salience.

2.2   Sustainability

Bike transportation provides benefits to various measures of sustainability. The Triple Bottom Line approach is one measure of sustainability that includes multiple variable analyses. In this formulation sustainability is defined as an activity or process that contributes to economic, environmental and social welfare and persistence [4]. Multiple options for transportation within a city provide more access for those who live there and increases options for their travel. For this activity to be sustained and provide options into the future, transportation planners rely on accurate data collection and analysis to determine traffic patterns, usage and constraints. The lack of data around various transportation options limits the availability of these user groups to be accurately assessed. Many communities have undergone increased monitoring of bike transportation data in order to fill these gaps [5].

Biking contributes to environmental sustainability by decreasing fossil fuel consumption, thus generating an overall reduction of carbon in the environment. Increasing the mode share of all trips made by bicycling and walking could lead to fuel savings and reduce greenhouse gas emissions, the equivalent to replacing 19 million conventional cars with hybrids [6]. Biking also provides a great benefit for social welfare by creating more healthy transportation choices. Researchers compared the relationship between bicycling and walking travel and obesity in 14 countries, 50 U.S. states, and 47 U.S. cities, and found statistically significant negative relationships at all levels [7].

2.3   Technology

The mobile phone has become the most rapidly adopted technology in history [8]. The most recent PEW study showed that 83% of adults own a mobile phone, 42% of whom say that they own smartphones, meaning that 35% of all U.S. adults are now smartphone owners. There are now more than five-billion mobile phone subscriptions worldwide [10].

Mobile platforms are especially important to underrepresented populations. African-Americans talk on their cell phones an average of 1,300 minutes per month, more than twice the 647 minutes averaged by whites. Hispanics were next at 826 minutes per month, followed by Asians and Pacific Islanders at 692 minutes per month. Blacks and Hispanics were also the most likely to send and receive text messages, averaging 780 and 767 per month respectively [11].

Only 20 years ago, obtaining camera output required several days. Less than 15 years ago, civilians could not automatically locate themselves. Less than five years ago, speaking with a foreigner meant learning her language, or finding a human translator. Today all of that sensing functionality can be had by reaching into your pocket. Understandably, research and development in applications for these newly pervasive sensing capabilities has grown rapidly.

Fogg [12] was among the first to argue that technology should be used to persuade. Persuasive technology, he said, is any "interactive computing system designed to change people's attitudes or behaviors." Technology has several advantages over the traditional persuasive media, including its ability to simplify (e.g. Amazon's one-click purchasing) and recommend (e.g. Netflix). Fogg was particularly excited by the persuasive potential of mobile devices, with their convenient pervasiveness, ability to sense context, emotional importance to their users, and social connectedness [12].

With all this excitement about pervasive persuasion, it is not surprising that there has been a very recent explosion of research development applying mobiles to the problems of sustainability [13][14]. Moreover, given the complexity of sustainability problem, it is also no surprise that many of the same researchers have used visualization and sensing as they persuade [15][16].

3   Existing Regional Activity

3.1   Research and Education

In what follows, we provide only a sampling of current sustainability work in Winston-Salem and more broadly, North Carolina.

Scientific Visualization (SciViz)
This undergraduate Liberal Learning Seminar is situated at CDI and co-taught by WSSU faculty in art and science. Visiting contributors from other fields and nearby institutions augment their perspectives. The interdisciplinary seminar explores visual and human-computer interaction design processes through creative solutions to communicating about challenging scientific and visualization problems. Students from a variety of backgrounds learn content and techniques of visual art, the natural sciences and computer graphics by working together to design dynamic and interactive solutions for representing multimodal data. The approach is computer-intensive, experiential, and discursive. The students and their digital productions benefit from frequent display, discussion, and critique of work. Students keep track of their progress, showcase their work and reflect on their experience in the seminar using an individual, online blog. Weekly video-logs (vlogs) capture the dynamics of the class and provide another communication channel among peers and the faculty.

Data from the VIA network will become grist for visualization experiments incorporating themes of wellness, sustainability, connectedness, and comparisons of human behavior. Collaboration between SciViz and our Life on Two Wheels course (below) will give each group of students a deeper understanding of sustainability issues.

Life on Two Wheels (Lo2W)
Young people in college are creating new identities, trying different activities and expanding their minds far beyond what they learned at home. Increasingly independent, they may make both good and bad decisions. One of the most important choices concerns physical activity. A 2008 report by the National College Health Assessment team found that only 18% of college students are active most days a week and 23% of college students are not physically active on any days of the week [17]. Additional research confirms the physical and psychological benefits of physical activity and suggests that green exercise – that is, physical activity outdoors in nature – has a synergistic effect that provides mental and physical health benefits beyond exercise alone [18]. Further changes to lifestyle and awareness of how personal decisions impact one's community, environment, and the very lifespan of the planet can also be initiated during the college years.

Fig. 2. A pilot of the life on two wheels course, at Winston-Salem State

This course aims to determine whether a class focused on the benefits of riding can encourage positive thoughts and behavioral changes associated with physical activity and environmental awareness, as well as the factors that may influence and potentially increase the use of self-powered transportation modalities, including biking and walking. The Lo2W course has been successfully piloted at two local schools: at Salem College it was called Grassroots Biology, and at Winston-Salem State (WSSU) it is known as Life on Two Wheels: Exploring Human and Environmental Health through Cycling. Data collection is ongoing at WSSU. The research method involves measurements taken pre- and post-class, including physiological, psychological, and environmental assessments. Additionally, throughout the class, participants write reflections about the weekly lessons and activities. Allen analyzes these online blog entries throughout the semester.

RideTheWake
Developed by a team of undergraduate computer science students at Wake Forest University, RideTheWake is a web and mobile application that shows in real time the position of shuttle busses along the six WFU routes on campus and around W-S. The application responds to the most basic need of shuttle-users: where a bus is along its route and thus how long its users need to wait for it. The app has been in service for more than two years and is credited with increasing the adoption of the shuttle system by students and faculty.

Similar efforts are underway to develop tools for indicating the positions and patterns of route use by pedestrians and cyclists around the city, with the aim of promoting increased support for existing users and greater participation by new users.

One example is a crowd-sourced tool that facilitates communication between city officials and fellow citizens, by enabling designation of problems with safety and continuity in the city's existing alternative transportation network, as well as to recognition and appreciation of solutions to previously known problems. VIA expertise and infrastructure will facilitate the further development of such tools across the consortium of schools and cooperating organizations, to create support for pedestrian, bicycle, and shuttle-users moving freely and efficiently anywhere in the city. In particular, we envision using backend VIA functionality to disambiguate the use of busses and personal cars, to identify usage patterns, inform improvements and recognize more efficient adoption strategies.

4   Research Objectives

The VIA research collaboration network will bring these research and educational efforts together around three research goals, all exploiting mobile, visualization and communication technologies and methods.

4.1   New, Mobile-Based Sustainability Measures

As the EPA's report on sustainability measurement [19] makes clear, existing sustainability measures suffer from several shortcomings. One of our primary research goals is to develop new, mobile based measures of sustainability that have the potential to overcome these shortcomings, and study their effectiveness in planning, communication and community building. Exploiting the widespread use of smartphones and the rich set of sensors on each of these devices, we will, with the aid citizens:

- *Increase the temporal resolution of measurement:* many sustainability measures are only produced every 10 years with the census. Mobiles can provide daily and even minute-by-minute measures, permitting route tracking and inference of transportation modality.
- *Increase the spatial resolution of measurement:* census data is per-tract or per-block, while video can only sense fixed locations. With mobile GPS technology, resolution is 20-meters or less, at most any location. Measurement follows commuters wherever they go, with any modality.
- *Increase the accuracy of measurement:* much of existing sustainability measurement is self-reported. Mobile measurement need not rely on fallible human memory, or on the relatively sparse sampling of human measurement.
- *Reduce measurement cost:* crowdsourced mobile measurement does not require expensive sensor installation and maintenance, nor laborious human counting.

4.2   New Techniques for Sustainability Persuasion

As devices that are nearly always present and intensely personal, mobiles have unique potential as a platform for persuasion [12]. Today's most innovative companies such as Google, Apple and Facebook apparently believe this as well, and are in an intense battle for control of the mobile ad market. Our second research objective will examine mobiles as a medium for affecting sustainability behavior, rather than simply commercial behavior. With participant agreement, we will examine the effectiveness of persuasive messages delivered using:

- *Visualization:* emerging research shows the power of imagery as a persuasive medium [20]. We will use such imagery to deliver citizens their own data in a visually compelling form.
- *Gamification:* by introducing motivating elements from computer games, developers can affect human behavior [21]. We will introduce elements such as competition by allowing participants to compare their performance to peer groups.
- *Priming:* recent research shows that much of habitual human behavior is governed at an emotional level [22][23]. We will deliver well-timed, simple messages to citizens designed to trigger sustainable behavior.

4.3   Understand the Relationship of Community to Sustainability

For some Americans sustainability has little intrinsic meaning [24]. The public perceives sustainability in the context of the activities of those around them. They sense sustainability. Sustainability activities such as short-distances transportation decision making should privilege those activities with both a lighter carbon or consumption footprint and improved health and well-being. This demands a series of communication activities that improve understanding of benefits and represents the sustainable activities as opportunities. By exploring social capital and civic engagement through visualization [25] and developing open data sharing opportunities we can build and sustain a community culture that may be able to reinforce and perpetuate learned behaviors through supportive organizational communication [3]. This is the third research objective of the VIA network.

Acknowledgements. We send gratitude to the many community organizations in Winston-Salem and the Triad area who are providing assistance to the VIA effort.

References

1. Goethe Institute (2013), Sustainability – from principle to practice, http://www.goethe.de/ges/umw/dos/nac/den/en3106180.htm (accessed February 15, 2013)
2. Burgess, J., Harrison, C.M., Filius, P.: Environmental communication and the cultural politics of environmental citizenship. Environment and Planning A 30, 1445–1460 (1998)
3. Pacanowsky, M.E., O'Donnell-Trujillo, N.: Communication and organizational cultures. Western Journal of Speech Communication 46(2), 115–130 (1982)
4. Elkington, J.: Cannibals with Forks: the triple bottom line of 21st century business. New Society Press (1998)

5. Birk, M., Geller, R.: Bridging the Gaps: How the Quality and Quantity of a Connected Bikeway Network Correlates with Increasing Bicycle Use. Alta Planning + Design Publication (2005)
6. Gotschi, T., Mills, K.: Active Transportation for America. Rails-to-Trails Conservancy (2008)
7. Pucher, J., et al.: Walking and cycling to health: A comparative analysis of city, state, and international data. American Journal of Public Health 100(10) (October 2010)
8. Castells, M., Fernandez-Ardevol, M., Linchuanqiu, J., Sey, A.: Mobile Communication and Society: A Global Perspective (Information Revolution & Global Politics). The MIT Press (2006)
9. Smith, A.: Smartphone adoption and usage. PEW Internet and American Life Project, Washington (2011)
10. International Telecommunication Union. Global mobile cellular subscriptions, total and per 100 inhabitants (2000-2010), http://www.itu.int/ITU-D/ict/ statistics/material/excel/2010/Global_mobile_cellular_00-10.xls
11. Nagesh, G.: Minorities most active on mobile phones, http://thehill.com/ blogs/hillicon-valley/technology/115645-minorities-most-active-on-mobile-phones (August 24, 2010)
12. Fogg, B.J.: Increasing persuasion through mobility. In: Fogg, B.J., Eckles, D. (eds.) Mobile Persuasion: 20 Perspectives on the Future of Behavior Change. Mobile Persuasion (2007)
13. Disalvo, C., Sengers, P., BrynjarsdOttir, H.: Mapping the landscape of sustainable HCI. In: Proceedings of the 28th International Conference on Human Factors in Computing Systems, Atlanta, Georgia, USA, pp. 1975–1984. ACM, New York (2010)
14. Froehlich, J., Dillahunt, T., Klasnja, P., Mankoff, J., Consolvo, S., Harrison, B., Landay, J.A.: UbiGreen: investigating a mobile tool for tracking and supporting green transportation habits. In: Proceedings of the 27th International Conference on Human Factors in Computing Systems, Boston, MA, USA, pp. 1043–1052. ACM, New York (2009)
15. Pierce, J., Odom, W., Blevis, E.: Energy aware dwelling: a critical survey of interaction design for eco-visualizations. In: Proceedings of the 20th Australasian Conference on Computer-Human Interaction: Designing for Habitus and Habitat, Cairns, Australia, pp. 1–8. ACM, New York (2008)
16. Paulos, E., Honicky, R., Hooker, B.: Citizen science: Enabling participatory urbanism. In: Foth, M. (ed.) Handbook of Research on Urban Informatics: The Practice and Promise of Real-Time City. IGI Global, Hershey (2008)
17. Desai, M.N., Miller, W.C., Staples, B., Bravender, T.: Risk factors associated with overweight and obesity in college students. Journal of American College Health 57, 109–114 (2008)
18. Pretty, J., Peacock, J., Hine, R., Sellens, M., South, N., Griffin, M.: Green Exercise in the UK Countryside: Effects on Health and Psychological Well-Being, and Implications for Policy and Planning. Journal of Environmental Planning and Management 50(2), 211–231 (2007)
19. EPA, Guide to sustainable transportation performance measures (2011), http://www.epa.gov/smartgrowth/transpo_performance.htm (last accessed March 1, 2013)

20. Bateman, S., Mandryk, R.L., Gutwin, C., Genest, A., Mcdine, D., Brooks, C.: Useful junk?: the effects of visual embellishment on comprehension and memorability of charts. In: Proceedings of the 28th International Conference on Human Factors in Computing Systems, pp. 2573–2582. ACM (2010)
21. Bogost, I.: Persuasive games: The expressive power of videogames. The MIT Press (2007)
22. Howard, A.: Feedforward: A Mobile Design Strategy that Supports Emotive Learning for Preventive Health Practices and Enduring Lifestyle Change. NCSU dissertation (2011), http://www.lib.ncsu.edu/resolver/1840.16/7023 (last accessed on March 1, 2013)
23. Kahneman, D.: Thinking, fast and slow. Farrar, Straus and Giroux (2011)
24. Myers, G., Macnaghten: Rhetorics of environmental sustainability: Commonplaces and places. Environmental and Planning A 30(2), 333–353 (1996)
25. Katz, P.: The New Urbanism: Toward Architecture of Community. McGraw-Hill Professional, NY (1993) ISBN-13: 978-0070338890

A Novel Taxi Dispatch System for Smart City

Qingnan Zou, Guangtao Xue, Yuan Luo, Jiadi Yu, and Hongzi Zhu

Department of Computer Science & Engineering, Shanghai Jiao Tong University
{redsniper,gt_xue,yuanluo,jdyu,hongzi}@sjtu.edu.cn

Abstract. Taxis as a kind of public transit have been taken by citizens thousands of times every day in urban areas. However, it is economically inefficient for vacant taxis to randomly cruise around to seek for passengers. In this paper, we propose a dynamic taxi dispatch system for smart city which dispatches routes with high probability to encounter passengers for vacant taxis. In the system, a dynamic probabilistic model has been established, which considers the impact of time on passenger appearance and the effect of different vacant taxis traveling route on each other's pick-up probability. Specifically, a novel feedback system has been introduced in the system, which utilizes the information about where taxis pick up passengers to amend system probabilistic model. Moreover, extensive trace-driven simulations based on real digital map of Shanghai and historical data of over 2,000 taxis demonstrate the good performance of our system.

Keywords: taxi dispatch system, passenger probabilistic model, hot spot, feedback mechanism.

1 Introduction

As an important part of public transit, taking taxis are very popular among citizens' choices of traveling in the urban area. For example, according to an investigation in New York City [1], 41% respondents take a taxi every week and 25% of them take a taxi every day. Due to the huge demand of citizens, large amount of taxis are deployed in most metropolises such as Shanghai. Generally, in order to pick up passengers, drivers of vacant taxis often drive their vehicles along random routes or special routes based on their personal experience, which, however, due to the lack of passenger information, often ends up with not encountering any passengers. Thus, taxi drivers acquire decline of income because of the waste of time and energy in cruise. Moreover, the invalid cruise of vacant taxis also contributes to traffic jams in cities.

To help vacant taxi pick up passengers more efficiently and smart, however, is a challenging problem. First, it is difficult to gain the distribution of passengers since passengers can appear at any place and any time in the city. Second, despite knowing possible time and place where passengers may appear, designing a cruise route for a vacant taxi is still not trivial, which somehow can be reduced to a traveling salesman problem [2]. Third, since the number of passengers is limited,

N. Streitz and C. Stephanidis (Eds.): DAPI/HCII 2013, LNCS 8028, pp. 326–335, 2013.

different vacant taxies traveling on road can impact each other. For example, a vacant taxi heading for a place where passengers may appear will fail to meet passengers if another vacant taxi has arrived there earlier and pick up the only one passenger. Recently, some taxi schedule systems have been proposed to help vacant taxis pick up passengers more efficiently. Y. Ge et al. [2] introduced an algorithm for taxi dispatching called LCP, which however ignored neither the dynamics of passenger appearance nor the impact among different vacant taxis. An adaptive taxi dispatching system was proposed by K. Yamamoto [3], which simply takes passenger appearance for a fixed model.

In this paper, a novel taxi dispatch system is proposed to help vacant taxis pick up passengers more efficiently. Generally, the taxi dispatch scheme consists of two technical components. First, a dynamic model of passenger appearance is established in order to predict the appearance of passengers across the whole area. By clustering passenger appearance records from historical data into several clusters, places where passengers appear with high probability-**hot spots**-are found, around which the appearance of passengers within a short time is discovered to obey Poisson Process. In this way, the system can predict where and when passengers appear precisely. Second, an adaptive dispatch algorithm with feedback mechanism is proposed, which considers the impact among different taxis when designing routes for vacant taxis and introduces methods with pruning to search best routes for vacant taxis so that computing complexity declines. In order to enhance the accuracy of the system, a feedback mechanism is introduced, in which taxis report where they succeed to pick up passengers. The system is evaluated through extensive trace-driven simulation and results show that it can achieve performance.

- Discover that the appearance of passengers in a region within a short time obeys Poisson Process by analyzing massive historical records. This phenomenon is key to the system to establish an accurate model of passengers and predict the pick-up probability of vacant taxis precisely.
- Propose an online taxi dispatch system, which considers impact among different taxis while designing routes for vacant taxis and introduces a feedback mechanism to improve the accuracy of pick-up probability predicted by the system.
- Give a good method of pruning to reduce the computing complexity faced when designing routes for vacant taxis. In this way, our system can handle large scale vacant taxis in urban area, especially in metropolises.

The remainder of the paper is organized as follows. In Section 2, the related work in the literature is introduced. In Section 3, we present the problem definition and the system model. The design detail of our system is presented in Section 4. Section 5 describes the evaluation on the system and gives the result. We finally give a conclusion of our work in Section 6.

2   Related Work

As the GPS facilities is common in taxis, taxis dispatching system is attractive nowadays. D. Lee et al. [4] designed a taxi dispatch system based on current demands and traffic conditions, which, however, aims at reducing the waiting time of passengers but not consider much of taxi drivers' profit. S. Phithakkitnukoon et al. [5] proposed a method to predict vacant taxis on road, which, like [4], also only services passengers. The work in [2], [7], [8] and [9] all proposed taxi dispatch systems for taxi drivers so that they could pick up passengers more quickly and efficiently. But, they all missed the dynamics of passenger appearance and the impact among different taxis. J. Yuan et al. [6] introduced a taxi system which considered passenger appearance a dynamic process but ignored the impact among different taxis. An adaptive taxi dispatch system was proposed in [3], which also simplify the appearance of passengers as a fixed model.

Different from those systems, in our system, each design of routes for vacant taxis to pick up passengers is based on a dynamic model of passenger appearance and the impact of different taxis. Furthermore, a feedback mechanism is introduced in our system so that the system can be more accurate and adaptive.

3   System Model

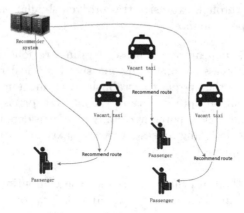

Fig. 1. System model

In this section, the model of our system and the problem solved by the system is presented. Generally, our system can be divided into two parts: a client integrated in taxis and an online dispatch server. In order to simplify the problem, it is assumed that all vacant taxis on road obey dispatching of the system. As shown in Fig. 1, when a taxi is vacant, it sends a request including its location information to the dispatch server. Then the server designs a route for the taxi according to historical data and routes designed for other vacant taxis, and sends it to the taxi. After that, the taxi will drive along the route until it encounters passengers. If the taxi fails to encounter any passengers until it drives to the end, it will send dispatch request to the server again, which however seldom happens in our system.

3.1   Metrics and Problem Formulation

In order to describe the problem clearly, some definitions are firstly given as follows.

Definition 1. Route. *A route is a limited sequence of consecutive roads.*

Definition 2. Hot spots. *Hot spots are special roads where passengers are more likely to appear than on other roads.*

The pick-up probability can be easily conceived of as the metric, which however is not always in accordance with the taxi drivers' profit. It is because what taxi drivers want is to pick up passengers while drives as short as possible. But high pick-up probability sometimes means long traveling distance. Since pick-up probability is not suit as metric in our system, we introduce the **expected traveling distance** as the metric, which represents the expected traveling distance before a vacant taxi can come across passengers.

Generally, there are several hot spots in urban area. An idea way to dispatch a vacant taxi is to design a route traveling all the hot spots with the lowest expected traveling distance, which however is very difficult. According to [2], even if passenger appearance is assumed to be with fixed probability, the problem can be reduced to a traveling salesman problem. It is more complex if a dynamic passenger appearance model is applied in the system since dynamic model is more complex than the fixed one.

In order to reduce the computing complexity of the problem, a traveling distance limit σ is set for designing routes in the system. Therefore, the problem becomes how to design a route through several hot spots with a limited distance for a vacant taxi so that the taxi has the lowest expected traveling distance when traveling along the route.

3.2   Passenger Appearance Model

From historical data, it is discovered that passenger appearance in a region spot within a short time obeys Poisson Process. Fig. 2(a) shows an example of passenger appearance number per minute in Xujiahui area, Shanghai from 14:00 to 17:00 every day during the period from 2007/02/20 to 2007/02/25. It is obvious that the curve in the figure is almost the same as the curve of Poisson distribution, which indicates passenger appearance obeys Poisson Process.

$$Pr[N(t_s - t_r) = k] = \frac{[\lambda(t_s - t_r)]^k}{k!}e^{-\lambda(t_s - t_r)}. \tag{1}$$

Since passenger appearance around a hot spot within a short time obeys Poisson Process, it can be presented by Eq. (1), where t_s is the start time, t_r is the end time, k is the number of passengers appeared during the period and λ is the eigenvalue of Poisson Process. **It should be noted that in the equation, "one passenger" represents a group of passengers taking the same taxi.** For the ith vacant taxi arriving at a hot spot, let

- t_i **denote the arriving time and** t_0 **denote the start time of Poisson Process;**
- A_i **represent that the** ith **taxi succeeds to pick up a passenger;**
- $Pr(A_i)$ **denote the probability of picking up a passenger around the hot spot for the taxi.**

Though the model of passenger appearance is known, it is still difficult to predict the pick-up probability i.e. $Pr(A_i)$. In order to simplify the problem, a function of two variables is introduced:

$$F(i,k) = \sum_{j=0}^{k+1} F(i-1,j)Pr[N(t_i - t_{i-1}) = k - j + 1]. \tag{2}$$

$F(i,k)$ denotes the probability that there are k passengers left around a hot spot after the ith arriving taxi leaves, which means there are $k+1$ passengers around the hot spot before the ith taxi arrives as Eq. (2) presents. It is obvious that Eq. (2) can be calculated iteration and the boundary iteration can be calculated intuitively. With Eq. (2), $Pr(A_i)$ can be easily calculated:

$$Pr(A_i) = 1 - Pr(\overline{A_i}) \\ = 1 - F(i-1,0)Pr[N(t_i - t_{i-1}) = 0]. \tag{3}$$

It should be noted that there is some difference on the boundary such as $i = 1$ or $k = 0$. But all these boundary situations can be derivate intuitively, and we do not present the details here due to room limit.

Considering the pick-up probability of the ith arriving taxi under the condition that the $(i-1)th$ taxi does not pick up any passengers i.e. $Pr(A_i|\overline{A}_{i-1})$. Since the $(i-1)th$ taxi fails to pick up any passengers, no passengers are left after the $(i-1)th$ taxi leaves i.e. $F(i-1,0) = 1$. Moreover, according to the features of Poisson Process, the event of passenger appearance from t_{i-1} to t_i is independent from that during other nonoverlapping period. Therefore, the conditional probability is:

$$Pr(A_i|\overline{A}_{i-1}) = 1 - Pr[N(t_i - t_{i-1}) = 0], \tag{4}$$

which can be used to update the passenger model in the system with feedbacks from taxis.

4   Design Details

In this section, the details of our taxi dispatch system will be exhibited. First, the contents about how the system finds hot spots and estimate eigenvalue of

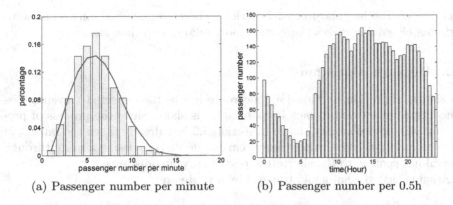

(a) Passenger number per minute   (b) Passenger number per 0.5h

Fig. 2. The feature of passenger appearance

Poisson Process at each hot spot according to historical records are presented; second, the dispatch algorithm i.e. how the system assign a route for each vacant taxi is shown; finally, the state buffer and feedback algorithm is demonstrated.

4.1 Analysing Historical Records

As defined in Definition 2, hot spot are special roads where passengers are more likely to appear. An intuitive thought is that there must be more passengers appearing around hot spots than in other places in historical records. Therefore, the system can divide historical passenger records into several clusters according to their clustering property in geographical location. Then, the geographical center of each hot spot can be treated as a hot spot. In our system, the K-means algorithm [11] is applied to cluster historical passenger records. Since the cluster number should be set before applying K-means algorithm, the system must choose a suitable cluster number for a region through test.

For each hot spot, the eigenvalue of Poisson Process should be ascertained in order to build passenger appearance model around it as presented in Eq. (1). However, the eigenvalue at a hot spot varies with time. Fig. 2(b) illustrates average passenger number per half hour across a day with one-month statistics retrieved from historical records in Xujiahui area, Shanghai. From the figure, it can be seen that passenger number varies much across a day due to most people's daily routine. However, the number does not change much during a short period like an hour, which gives the system a way to ascertain the eigenvalue during a short period without much deviation. In the system, a sliding window of which the length is set to be one hour is set to estimate the eigenvalue of a hot spot. For example, when the system needs to know the eigenvalue at time t, it counts passenger number from historical records in the time window $[t-30min, t+30min]$. Then the system uses the Maximum-likelihood Estimation (MLE) to estimate the eigenvalue during that period. Sliding window is better than dividing a day into several fixed periods because the second method is not accurate on the boundary of each period. Therefore, using sliding window to estimate eigenvalue makes the system more adaptive to time change.

4.2   Dispatch Algorithm

As shown in previous sections, a good route means the expected traveling distance for a vacant taxi to pick up passengers is short. Since the process of predicting pick-up probability shown in section 3.2 has already taken the impact of other taxis into account, what the system should do is to design a route through several hot spots with the shortest expected traveling distance.

Assume that the hot spots traveled by a route are:

$$\{S_1, S_2, ..., S_n\},$$

and the corresponding pick-up probabilities at each hot spot are:

$$\{P_1, P_2, ..., P_n\}.$$

Since the route is divided into n parts by the n hot spots, the corresponding distance of each part is:

$$\{D_1, D_2, ..., D_n\}.$$

In order to simplify the problem, the system uses the minimum distance got by Dijkstra algorithm [12] to represent the distance between two hot spots or the origin and a hot spot. Thus the expected traveling distance of the route is:

$$P_1 D_1 + (\sum_{i=1}^{n} D_i) \times \prod_{j=1}^{n} (1 - P_j) + \sum_{i=1}^{n-1} [P_{i+1} \times (\sum_{j=1}^{i+1} D_i) \times \prod_{k=1}^{i} (1 - P_i)]. \qquad (5)$$

Thus, the aim of designing route is to make Eq. (5) minimum.

As presented before, in order to reduce the computing complexity of designing a best route, a distance limit σ has been set. In the system, the branch and bound method is applied to searching solution space under the distance limit σ. With this method, the system can find the solution i.e. the best route quickly. The general steps of dispatch algorithm is presented in Algorithm. 1.

4.3   State Buffer and Feedback Mechanism

As presented before, the system needs the dispatch information, such as time and dispatch route, of previous vacant taxis to dispatch current vacant taxis. In the system, a linked table, which plays a role as state buffer, is established for each hot spot as shown in 1.

However, linked tables are enlarging with time in the system because the number of vacant taxis dispatched by the system is increasing, which brings large overheads in storing and computing. In order to solve this problem, a feedback

Algorithm 1. Dispatch algorithm

Input:
   Current GPS location of vacant taxi; Current time;
Output:
   A scheduled route;
   1: Match GPS location of vacant taxi with corresponding route in the digital map
      and calculate the distance (of the shortest route) to each hot spot;
   2: Build passenger model at each hot spot according to time and use branch and
      bound method to search for the best route for the vacant taxi under the distance
      limit σ.
   3: Once the best route is got by the last step, the predicted time of the taxi arriv-
      ing at each hot spot contained int the route is stored into the linked tables of
      corresponding hot spots.
   4: Send out the best route to the vacant taxi.

mechanism is introduced in the system. As Eq. (4) denotes, the conditional pick-up probability around a hot spot is independent from previous taxis if the last taxi does not pick up any passengers around the hot spot. Thus the system can remove information in a linked table of a hot spot before the time when a taxi reports it does not pick up passengers around the hot spot. Moreover, the feedback mechanism raises the precision of pick-up probability because it introduces the information in reality to amending the information retrieved from historical records.

5   Evaluation

In this section, we will show how we evaluate the system through trace-driven simulations and how the system performs under the evaluation. As presented before, the evaluation on the system is realized by trace-driven simulations. The simulation program is written by C# language under Visual Studio 2010 environment. The simulation is executed in a computer with I5 2400 CPU, 8 GB memory and 64bit Windows 7 Professional operating system. The training historical data and trace data are all collected around Xujiahui, Shanghai from ShanghaiGrid project [10]. The area where data is collected starts from 121.418409 to 121.463299 in longitude and from 31.181709 to 31.203882 in latitude with a length of 4.3 km and a width of 2.4 km. The data used as historical records is collected from 2007/1/31 to 2007/2/28 and the data used as trace is collected from 2007/3/1 to 2007/3/6.

5.1   The Impact of Hot Spot Number

In this simulation, we set the distance limit 5000 meters and change the number of hot spots from 4 to 10 to see the performance of the system i.e. the average distance traveled by vacant taxis before picking up passengers. The LCP system [2] is also realized in the simulation to be compared to our system.

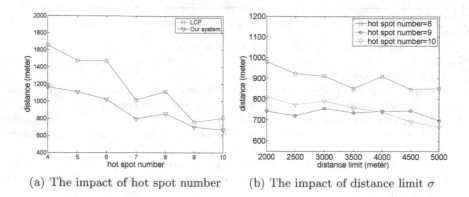

(a) The impact of hot spot number   (b) The impact of distance limit σ

Fig. 3. The result of evaluation

As Fig. 3(a) illustrates, the performance of both systems raises with the increase of hot spots number and our systems always precedes LCP. Though the gap is low when hot spot number is high, our system can reach the same performance with less hot spots, which means low computing overhead.

Since more hot spots means more precise passenger model around each hot spot, the performance of both systems raises with the increase of hot spot number. However, the performances improve when hot spot number is high is not as fast as that when hot spot number is low. This implies that for an area, high hot spot number does not always mean good as high hot spot not only brings performance improve but also high computing overhead.

5.2   The Impact of Distance Limit σ

In this simulation, we change the distance limit from 2000 meters to 5000 meters with 8, 9 and 10 hot spots to see its impact on system performance.

As Fig. 3(b) presents, the system performance improves a little with the increase of distance limit. However, the system improve caused by increase of distance limit is not as obvious as that caused by increase of hot spot number. Moreover, the average traveling distance is much shorter than the distance limit. This phenomenon implies that most vacant taxis pick up passengers at the first several hot spots. Therefore, for the evaluated area, the system can use a relatively short distance limit, which brings both good performance and low computing overhead.

6   Conclusion

This paper proposes a novel dynamic taxi dispatch system to dispatch route for vacant taxis to pick up passengers. In the system, a dynamic passenger appearance model is established according to historical records and an adaptive dispatch algorithm is introduced considering the impact of previous dispatched vacant taxis. Moreover, the dispatch algorithm is specially designed to reduce computing overhead. Furthermore, a feedback mechanism is introduced in the system to reducing computing and storing overhead and improving dispatch accuracy. Besides, a trace-driven simulation has been conducted to evaluate our system, of which the result shows our system has a good performance.

Acknowledgements. This research is supported by the National High Technology Research and Development Program (2011AA010502) and the National Natural Science Foundation of China (Grant Nos. 61170237).

References

1. Taxi of Tomorrow Survey Results. New York City Taxi and Limousine Commission (2011)
2. Ge, Y., Xiong, H., Tuzhilin, A., Xiao, K.: An energy-efficent mobile recommender system. In: Proc. KDD, pp. 899–908 (2010)
3. Yamamoto, K., Uesugi, K., Watanabe, T.: Adaptive routing of cruising taxis by mutual exchange of pathways. In: Lovrek, I., Howlett, R.J., Jain, L.C. (eds.) KES 2008, Part II. LNCS (LNAI), vol. 5178, pp. 559–566. Springer, Heidelberg (2008)
4. Lee, D., Wang, H., Cheu, R., Teo, S.: Taxi dispatch system based on current demands and real-time traffic conditions. Transportation Research Record: Journal of the Transportation Research Board 1882(-1), 193–200 (2004)
5. Phithakkitnukoon, S., Veloso, M., Bento, C., Biderman, A., Ratti, C.: Taxi-aware map: Identifying and predicting vacant taxis in the city. In: de Ruyter, B., Wichert, R., Keyson, D.V., Markopoulos, P., Streitz, N., Divitini, M., Georgantas, N., Mana Gomez, A. (eds.) AmI 2010. LNCS, vol. 6439, pp. 86–95. Springer, Heidelberg (2010)
6. Yuan, J., Zheng, Y., Zhang, L., Xie, X., Sun, G.: Where to find my next passenger. In: Proc. Ubicomp 2011, pp. 109–118 (2011)
7. Li, B., Zhang, D., Sun, L., Chen, C., Li, S., Qi, G., Yang, Q.: Hunting or waiting? Discovering passenger-finding strategies from a large-scale real-world taxi dataset. In: 2011 IEEE International Conference on Pervasive Computing and Communications Workshop (PERCOM Workshops), pp. 63–68 (2011)
8. Powell, J., Huang, Y., Bastani, F., Ji, M.: Towards reducing taxicab cruising time using spatio-temporal profitability maps. In: Proceedings of the 12th International Symposium on Adavances in Spatial and Temporal Databases, SSTD 2011 (2011)
9. Lee, J., Shin, I., Park, G.: Analysis of the passenger pick-up pattern for taxi location recommendation. In: International Conference on Networked Computing and Adavanced Information Management (2008)
10. Li, M., Wu, M.-Y., Li, Y., Cao, J., Huang, J., Deng, Q., Lin, X., Jiang, C., Tong, W., Gui, Y., Zhou, A., Wu, X., Jiang, S.: ShanghaiGrid: an Information Service Grid. Concurrency and Computation: Practice and Experience 18, 111–135 (2006)
11. Wagstaff, K., Cardie, C., Rogers, S.: SConstrained K-means clustering with background knowledge. In: International Conference on Machine Learning, ICML (2001)
12. Dijkstra, E.W.: A note on two problems in connection with graphs. Numerical Mathematics 1 (1959)

Part V

Multi-user, Group and Collaborative Interaction

MIDAS: A Software Framework for Accommodating Heterogeneous Interaction Devices for Cloud Applications

Euijai Ahn, Kangyoon Lim, and Gerard Jounghyun Kim

Digital Experience Laboratory
Korea University, Seoul, Korea
{saintpio,nandalky,gjkim}@korea.ac.kr

Abstract. Even though the computational power and storing capacities of mobile computing platforms have recently increased dramatically, so have the needs of mobile applications. With the advent of the cloud computing and wireless network technology, the mobile device finds itself as an ideal candidate as a multi-purpose interaction client device instead of as a standalone computing station. In the line of such a trend, we present a software framework (called MIDAS) that enables an application to lend itself to many different types of interaction methods (namely, sensing and display) and accommodate users with variant client devices without platform specific coding. The paper discusses the requirements and the design of the software architecture, and in addition, demonstrates its effectiveness with several case studies.

Keywords: Cloud based Interaction, Ubiquitous Interaction, Multimodal Interaction, Software Framework.

1 Introduction

Cloud computing, high speed wireless communication and smart phones have the potential to realize the true form of ubiquitous computing as conceptualized by Weiser nearly two decades ago [1]. The smart phone (as a broadband wireless communication device) based cloud computing allows the instant access of rich information and high quality service anywhere, and in addition, the smart phone (as a rich media device) can also serve as the medium through which the user interact efficiently and naturally. Thus we can easily imagine a future situation where users with variant smart phones (or hand-held devices with similar capabilities) accomplishing a given application task (e.g. shooting an opponent in a first person shooting game), but in different interactional forms (e.g. using the button, touchscreen, or voice). This may stem simply from the differences in the device processing, sensing and display capabilities (e.g. button-less device forcing the user to use the touchscreen) or simply from personal choice (e.g. preferring the use of button over touchscreen due to finger occlusion of the screen).

N. Streitz and C. Stephanidis (Eds.): DAPI/HCII 2013, LNCS 8028, pp. 339–348, 2013.

Traditionally, to accommodate a situation as described above, either separate client programs are developed for (or ported to) different devices (also because different devices often run on different system softwares and operating systems) enforcing a particular interface most suited for the given device, or a "large" client program is developed to cover all possible interaction possibilities. Practically, this has caused application services (cloud or local) to be compatible to only a small family or brand of devices and leaving no choices for the users in terms of interaction possibilities. Note that today's smart phones are not only increasingly equipped with various types of sensors, but can process computationally intensive recognition algorithms in real time (but only to a degree), not to mention meditate cloud based solutions. As such, user demands and expectations are higher with regards to the degree of interaction possibility.

In the line of such a need, we present a software framework, called MIDAS (Mixing and matching heterogeneous Interaction Devices to Applications and Services), that enables an application to lend itself to many different types of interaction methods (namely, sensing and display) and accommodate users with different client devices in a flexible manner (e.g. dispensing with the separate device dependent implementations). Through the proposed framework, the application server and interaction client device, upon connection, exchanges information regarding the generic interaction events (in the application) and the interaction methods/capabilities available in the client. Then the interaction events and the client interaction methods are mapped dynamically to allow the client to enact the application and receive output.

This paper is organized as follows. After comparing our work with other related research, the paper will first discuss the requirements and the design of the overall software architecture of MIDAS. Then in later sections, we demonstrate and present effectiveness of MIDAS with several use cases. Then we conclude the paper with a summary and directions for future work.

2   Related Work

The objective our work bears much similarity to concepts like migratory and plastic interfaces in the context of ubiquitous computing. Migratory interfaces are those that operate on changing operating platforms or interaction resources (e.g. a control panel interface for a whiteboard "migrating" and rendered on a connecting PDA). Plasticity further requires the migrating interface to preserve the usability as much as possible by adaptation to the specific operating platform (e.g. the control panel lay out changed according to the size of the PDA) [2]. Another early approach to realize multi-device interaction is the redirection technique [3][4] in which input events or content output may be sent to another collaborating/connected device. In all cases, separate platform specific implementations or compilation processes are needed.

For a more general and flexible migration and plasticity, several researchers have been working on a larger software framework or infrastructures. For example, Cameleon-RT and BEACH (as realized in the I-AM [5] and i-LAND [6]) are examples of such software architecture/infrastructures in which multiple interaction devices could be managed and interact with the given application in the most suited way. The middleware enables a "generically" described interactive application to build their own "view" for a given physical interaction platform. TERESA [7] is an authoring tool for "One Model, Many Interfaces" [8] type of applications. With the help of TERESA, different user interface codes can be conveniently generated from abstract user interface descriptions. However, these architectures serve to avoid separate implementations for different interaction devices at compile time. That is, only devices whose capabilities are known ahead of time can be accommodated.

Migratory or plastic architectures inevitably are distributed since the middleware components may reside among different "client" physical platforms [5]. In particular, the main application (possibly on the server or in the cloud) may be purely functional with its interface described generically or in abstract form to be interpreted and customized on the client side. One such approach is the SEESCOA component system [9] where abstract UI described in XML is interpreted to compose user interfaces at run time (by the adaptation/rendering components). Mark up languages for interactive web and cloud applications that describe UI objects, and interpreted and realized by different platform browsers, operate on similar principles [10][11]. Gilroy et al. has developed a client middleware that adapts application's "presentation styles" (expressed in an XML format specification document) most suited for a given device at run time. This way, the menus, form-fills, dialogue GUIs are adjusted and presented according to the device capabilities and thus high usability can be expected [12]. The X-Window system allows an application, through the X protocol, to interact with any device that runs the X server which handles the user interaction [13]. X server only supports the standard keyboard and mouse interface.

3 MIDAS Framework

3.1 Main Objectives

In this section, we describe the details of the software framework, called MIDAS (Mixing and matching heterogeneous Interaction Devices to Applications and Services), especially its main objectives and operating mechanism. First, we illustrate what we hope to achieve through MIDAS through a simple scenario.

Michael has a feature phone (on which the MIDAS interaction client software is installed). He goes to a movie theater. At the theater, there is a public display kiosk displaying previews of the feature movies. The kiosk has no external input devices, because it is designed to serve multiple people at once and the display needs to be protected from the public from possible abuse. So Michael uses his phone to connect to the application and interacts with the buttons to view specific movie information and selections for the movie and the seat. At the same time, Michelle comes along with her latest smart phone equipped with voice recognition software. She, too, connects to the same application and uses the touch screen and voice recognition to select the movie and seats. Michael goes to the nearby snack shop and notices a long waiting line. This time, he connects to the snack menu application using MIDAS, browses the choices, and makes an order, again using the buttons on his feature phone.

In this scenario, some of the important objectives of MIDAS are highlighted. One is the accommodation of different models of interaction devices dynamically (e.g. feature phone, smart phone, hand-held media devices, etc.). Different models of smart phones differ in the display sizes, types of sensors, and processing power and can affect how the user wants to interact with the application. The accommodation must be "dynamic" in the sense that the middleware should adapt to the different device capabilities at run time (at least to some degree). Another related but distinct objective is to allow different interaction methods. For example, in the above scenario, Michelle can choose to use the voice recognition or touch screen (or both) to interact with her latest smart phone. Finally, an important but less emphasized objective of MIDAS is the ability to coordinate interaction and share single application space among multiple users. MIDAS allows multiple users but the support for resource sharing and collaboration is only rudimentary.

The scenario also illustrates the larger context for which MIDAS is to be used for, that is, a ubiquitous computing environment in which there are dichotomous re-sources combined dynamically to enable a wholistic computational service and inter-action experience. The environment will contain high powered and fidelity computing, sensing and display resources (e.g. cloud, large location specific servers, high resolution display, sensor network) for things like processing large volume data and computationally intensive services for many users, while the individuals are expected to the lesser (e.g. mobile devices, wearable devices, hand-held media devices) mainly for interactional and personalization purpose.

3.2   Operating Mechanism and Architecture of MIDAS

Before presenting the overall architecture of MIDAS, we first go over the operating mechanism to help the readers understand the composition of MIDAS.

Server and Client Connection and Loading of MIDAS Modules. MIDAS, as a middleware to achieve the aforementioned objectives, is distributed among the servers and interaction clients. Aside from the MIDAS itself (running on the application server or client), there is a separate "Connection and Arbitration" server (dubbed "CAS" hereafter) that manages the connection between a number of available MIDAS-based applications (servers) and interaction devices. The application servers register themselves with the CAS to announce its existence and availability to the potential client devices. On the other hand, through the CAS, the MIDAS client devices can search for available MIDAS application servers that they can connect and interact to use. To reiterate, we are envisioning that there can be number of different cloud/ubiquitous applications available accessible with one's client interaction device. Once the client interaction device (i.e. user) chooses one of the registered available application service, it requests a connection to it through the TCP/IP.

In addition to this aforementioned role, the CAS also takes the role to relay the interaction capabilities of the connected server and client device. Both the server and client maintain a file describing its respective interaction capabilities. For instance, a particular version of a MIDAS server might be equipped to handle 10 different interaction methods, while the client device is only capable of two of them. The interaction methods acceptable to the application server and those that are available on the client are all described using an XML style "Interaction Resource" file, prior to the execution.

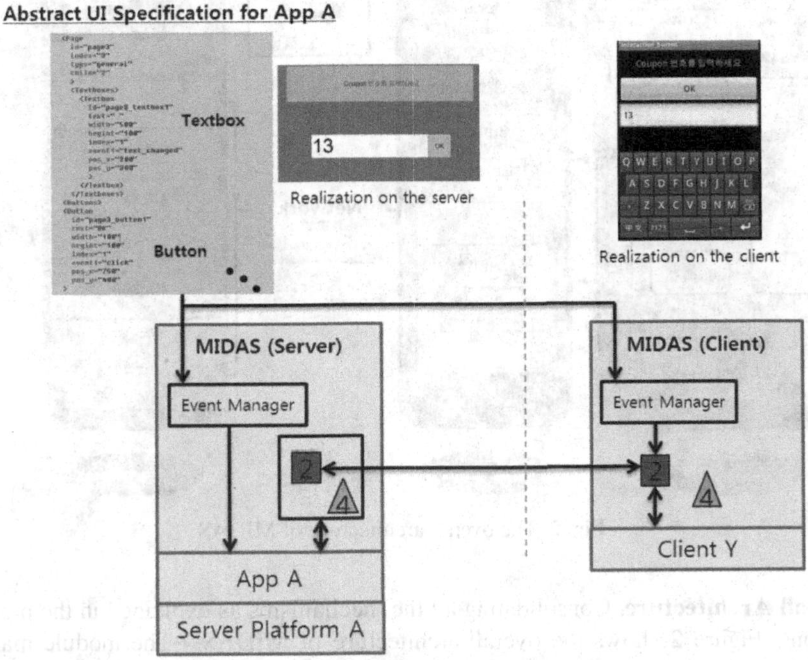

Fig. 1. Interpreting the application's user interface specification and sharing the event identification codes for mutual understanding between the server and client

User Interface Description and Management. Once the connection is established and proper modules all loaded, all possible "raw" client interaction events (e.g. touch screen click on a smart phone) must be mapped to the appropriate events in the application. In order to establish this mapping, an explicit application user interface description file is used. Figure 1 illustrates this process. An XML based user interface specification for the application is shared and interpreted by the server and client. UI objects are instantiated on the server and client (if necessary) by the "Event Manager" module on the respective side. These "Event Managers" (which are part of MIDAS server or client) are tailored for a given platform, and thus, the UI objects will have different look and feel accordingly (see Figure 1). During this step, the UI objects and the raw interaction events are assigned consistent indexed codes for identification on the either side. This way, any MIDAS client can be used as interaction device and no application specific modules are needed on the client side.

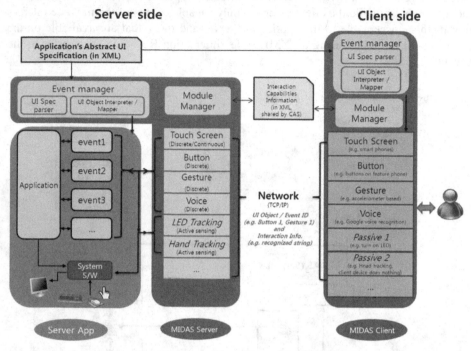

Fig. 2. The overall architecture of MIDAS

Overall Architecture. Consolidating all the mechanisms as explained in the previous sections, Figure 2 shows the overall architecture of MIDAS. The module manager on each side, load the proper MIDAS interaction information communication modules upon connection via CAS and by exchanging the mutual interaction capabilities (see previous subsection). The Event Managers on the respective sides also generate a consistent event mapping structure exchanged over the network so as for the application to invoke the right handler.

There are various MIDAS "modules" for different predefined types of interaction methods. They can be roughly classified into three groups: (1) discrete event type (e.g. button press, gesture recognition), (2) continuous input (e.g. cursor movement), (3) mixed type (e.g. text box with string input), (4) no-op (e.g. when the client device is used only as a physical target. For example, the touch screen on the client side would generate both "discrete" (e.g. button press) and "continuous" (e.g. finger location) events and data. The discrete events would be directly relayed to the application, while the continuous data can be "adjusted" or "filtered" and rather relayed to the server's system software to emulate mouse behavior.

4   Typical Use Cases

4.1   Replicating Server's User Interface on the (Multiple) Clients

One of the most typical uses of MIDAS would be to replicate the server application user interface (or interaction objects) on to the client device for private interaction. In order for this to happen, the user interface of the server application is first described declaratively (using the XML based UI configuration specification format) as already explained. In run time, the UI objects described in the UI configuration file, would be created (and displayed if e.g. a public display was available). The client, upon connecting to the server, will first load proper middleware modules (for mapping the client's various interaction events to those on the server side). Then the same UI configuration file received from the server is parsed and interpreted to be replicated on the client side. Replication of the server's UI components on the client side would ideally include an "adaptation" process for UI plasticity. Currently, MIDAS has only very limited such capability. Figure 1 shows an example with a simple application interface consisted of a text box, label and button replicated on the client device.

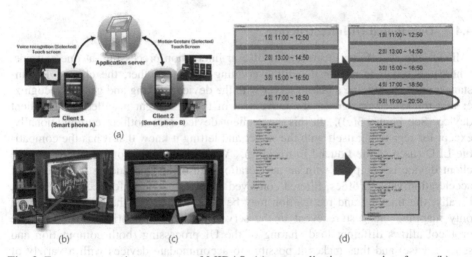

Fig. 3. Four representative use cases of MIDAS: (a) one application, many interfaces, (b) one client device connecting to many servers (e.g. coffee shop application (left), movie theater application (middle), subway application (right)), (c) user interaction processing distributed among the server and client (e.g. tracking by server, and touch processing by phone), (d) simple change of the user interface through modification of the UI specification file.

4.2   One Application, Many Interfaces

Extending to the first style of interaction, MIDAS naturally allows many modes of interaction according to the client's interaction capability. In the first example, the client device could have had both a touch screen or voice recognition capability to generate an event to select a menu item, and similarly so, for different clients who may possess different capabilities. When the client has more than one method available for generating a particular event, MIDAS first asks explicitly the user to select the method (e.g. touch screen or voice recognition). For instance, a client that can recognize 12 gestures might generate 12 events to the application events (e.g. Gesture 1 to App. Event 1, Gesture 2 to App. Event2 and so on). By default, the mapping is mechanical and arbitrary (e.g. in the implicit order of appearance in the UI specification file), but also user configurable through explicit specification in the XML UI specification file (See Figure 3(a)).

4.3   One Client Middleware, Many Applications

With MIDAS framework, the interaction client needs only the middleware (i.e. no application specific program) in order to connect and use any applications developed and running under the MIDAS server middleware. The same mapping mechanism and protocols are used for a client device to make input and receive output from a number of application servers as envisioned in the scenario described in Section 3.1 (see Figure 3(b)).

4.4   Distributed UI Infrastructure

MIDAS allows different distributions of user interaction processing, at one extreme, where the server is responsible for everything and at another, the client. For instance, one can imagine a public server with the device tracking and gesture recognizer that tracks and recognizes the movement of the LED light installed on the client device (See Figure 3(c)). In this case, client device does nothing computationally, except for registering itself with the server and letting it know that it has the compatible LED (used as the fiducial in tracking). We can suppose another case where the client device is equipped with an acceleration sensor and producing a sequence of acceleration value profiles, filtered conveyed to the application for recognition only. Finally, the tracking and recognition may be done entirely on the client device and only mapping the gesture event to the server. MIDAS's distributed and flexible protocol allows different load sharing of the UI processing (both computation and sensing wise) and thus makes it possible to accommodate devices with a variety of capabilities

4.5   Ease in the Application Development and Maintenance

Since MIDAS middleware separates the interaction "methods" (e.g. gesture recognition) and "events" (e.g. "Button 1" pressed) that are realized by the methods, the application development is much easier in that the developer needs not to worry about the various interaction methods available in different client device platforms (see Figure 3(d)). Since abstract user interface specification is used, in which UI object attribute information is included (to some extent), changing UI look and feel (e.g. GUI layout, fonts, sizes) is also possible without explicit recompilation.

5   Discussion and Conclusion

In this paper, we presented MIDAS, a user interface middleware (or server), that is designed to accommodate different client interaction devices for a given application. Migration and plasticity for multi-device interaction is needed because the computing service is again truly becoming centralized and ubiquitous (but transparently so, e.g. through the cloud), and on the other hand, the client devices are ever so diversifying in terms of their processing, sensing and display capabilities. In particular, the mobile clients will employ different interaction styles and input methods depending on the operating environment and conditions and application contexts [14]. MIDAS borrows several concepts such as abstract user interface interpretation, distributed event processing, and decoupling of interface methods and abstract application events.

MIDAS is an improvement to the latest approaches in migratory or plastic interface in mainly two ways. First, it focuses on supporting a variety of input methods. Prior approaches mostly have dealt with customizing application's output on different platforms. However, MIDAS can also be extended further to support more plasticity for platform output presentation as well. While output format customization would rely on conforming to certain adaptation rules (e.g. if screen size is reduced, reduce the button size in the same proportion), supporting a wide variety of and comprehensive input methods hinges on categorizing the input type, e.g. discrete event and data, continuous data, etc. and engineering a support structure that is as light and compact as possible.

Secondly, MIDAS is flexible in the distributed composition of UI processing. The paper has presented two typical examples, one in which the server senses and recognizes the user with the client essentially doing nothing computationally and another where, e.g. the voice is recognized on the client device (actually by connecting to yet another cloud server).

While MIDAS, as currently implemented, offers basic components for dynamically leveraging the environment and individual resources (i.e. computers, sensors, displays), it still falls short to be of complete. As already indicated, the output plasticity is either only ad-hoc or rudimentary at best. While multiple users can be supported, concurrency control is not possible yet. The scalability is in question; that is, architecturally, we would like to design a general purpose middleware to accommodate a comprehensive input methods rather than adding new MIDAS modules to each new interaction methods. As alluded above, the crux will be in generalizing different input methods according to their event and data types, and designing a general yet flexible software architecture. Despite its current shortcomings, we believe that the proposed framework is one way to realize the seamless computing environment of the future where processors, data, sensors, and displays are distributed ubiquitously in our everyday living environment.

Acknowledgement. The research described in this work was supported by the Korean Ministry of Knowledge Economy`s Strategic Technology Laboratory Program.

References

1. Weiser, M.: Hot topics-ubiquitous computing. Computer 26(10), 71–72 (1993)
2. Calvary, G., Thevenin, D.: A unifying reference framework for the development of plastic user interfaces. In: Nigay, L., Little, M.R. (eds.) EHCI 2001. LNCS, vol. 2254, pp. 173–192. Springer, Heidelberg (2001)
3. Elmqvist, N.: Distributed User Interfaces: State of the Art. In: Gallud, J.A., et al. (eds.) Distributed User Interfaces: Designing Interfaces for the Distributed Ecosystem. Human-Computer Interaction Series, pp. 1–12. Springer (2011)
4. Biehl, J.T., Bailey, B.P.: ARIS: an interface for application relocation in an interactive space. In: Graphics Interface 2004. Canadian Human-Computer Communications Society, pp. 107–116 (2004)
5. Balme, L., Demeure, A., Barralon, N., Calvary, G.: Cameleon-rt: A software architecture reference model for distributed, migratable, and plastic user interfaces. In: Markopoulos, P., Eggen, B., Aarts, E., Crowley, J.L. (eds.) EUSAI 2004. LNCS, vol. 3295, pp. 291–302. Springer, Heidelberg (2004)
6. Tandler, P.: Software infrastructure for ubiquitous computing environments: Supporting synchronous collaboration with heterogeneous devices. In: Abowd, G.D., Brumitt, B., Shafer, S. (eds.) UbiComp 2001. LNCS, vol. 2201, pp. 96–115. Springer, Heidelberg (2001)
7. Mori, G., Paterno, F., Santoro, C.: Design and development of multidevice user interfaces through multiple logical descriptions. IEEE Transactions on Software Engineering 30(8), 507–520 (2004)
8. Paterno, F., Santoro, C.: One model, many interfaces. In: Kolski, C., Vanderdonckt, J. (eds.) Computer-Aided Design of User Interfaces, vol. 3, pp. 143–154. Kluwer Academic Publishers (2002)
9. Luyten, K., Vandervelpen, C., Coninx, K.: Migratable user interface descriptions in component-based development. In: Forbrig, P., Limbourg, Q., Urban, B., Vanderdonckt, J. (eds.) DSV-IS 2002. LNCS, vol. 2545, pp. 44–58. Springer, Heidelberg (2002)
10. XHTML2 Working Group Home Page, http://www.w3.org/MarkUp
11. XAML Overview (WPF), http://msdn.microsoft.com/en-us/library/ms752059.aspx
12. Gilroy, S.W., Harrison, M.D.: Using interaction style to match the ubiquitous user interface to the device-to-hand. In: Feige, U., Roth, J. (eds.) DSV-IS 2004 and EHCI 2004. LNCS, vol. 3425, pp. 325–345. Springer, Heidelberg (2005)
13. X Window System, http://en.wikipedia.org/wiki/X_Window_System
14. Terrenghi, L., Lang, T., Lehner, B.: Elastic mobility: stretching interaction. In: 11th International Conference on Human-Computer Interaction with Mobile Devices and Services. ACM (2009)

Marker-Free Indoor Localization and Tracking of Multiple Users in Smart Environments Using a Camera-Based Approach

Andreas Braun[1], Tim Dutz[1], Michael Alekseew[2], Philipp Schillinger[2], and Alexander Marinc[1]

[1] Fraunhofer Institute for Computer Graphics Research IGD, Darmstadt, Germany
{andreas.braun,tim.dutz,alexander.marinc}@igd.fraunhofer.de
[2] Technische Universität Darmstadt, Darmstadt, Germany
{michael.alekseew,philipp.christian.
schillinger}@stud.tu-darmstadt.de

Abstract. In recent years, various indoor tracking and localization approaches for usage in conjunction with Pervasive Computing systems have been proposed. In a nutshell, three categories of localization methods can be identified, namely active marker-based solutions, passive marker-based solutions, and marker-free solutions. Both active and passive marker-based solutions require a person to carry some type of tagging item in order to function, which, for a multitude of reasons, makes them less favorable than marker-free solutions, which are capable of localizing persons without additional accessories. In this work, we present a marker-free, camera-based approach for use in typical indoor environments that has been designed for reliability and cost-effectiveness. We were able to successfully evaluate the system with two persons and initial tests promise the potential to increase the number of users that can be simultaneously tracked even further.

Keywords: Indoor localization, Computer Vision, Pervasive Computing.

1 Introduction

Reliably localizing and tracking multiple users in smart environments has evolved into one of the main challenges of this research area. The knowledge of the users' whereabouts is a central contextual information to an assistive system and oftentimes plays a pivotal role when such a system needs to decide, whether it is supposed to act; that is, whether it should influence the current state of its environment through its actuators. And although simple motion sensors can be used to provide for basic presence detection, much more sophisticated solutions are required for the concurrent localization of multiple people within the same area – or simply to distinguish between a person's pet, and herself.

In recent years, various indoor tracking and localization approaches for usage in conjunction with Ambient Intelligence systems have been proposed and there are even specific competitions with the intention of comparing the different methods'

N. Streitz and C. Stephanidis (Eds.): DAPI/HCII 2013, LNCS 8028, pp. 349–357, 2013.

performances against one another [1]. We can distinguish three different categories of localization methods, namely active marker-based solutions, passive marker-based solutions, and marker-free solutions. Both active and passive marker-based solutions require a person to carry some type of tagging item in order to function, which, for a multitude of reasons, makes them less favorable than marker-free solutions, which are capable of localizing persons independently of whether they are carrying additional accessories. Examples for approaches from this latter category include capacitive sensitive floors [2], using microphones for the detection of subtle noises caused by movement [3], and camera-based approaches [4]. The three main criteria that all of these localization solutions are judged on are the total costs for providing them for a specific area, such as a private apartment, their reliability, and the amount of persons that can be tracked and distinguished by them at a time.

In this work, we present a marker-free, camera-based approach for use in typical indoor environments, which allows the reliable localization of multiple persons. The system tested is able to successfully track two users in parallel.

2   Related Work

Detecting the presence and location of persons has been a research effort for many decades and as such, can now be achieved using a variety of technologies. Capacitive sensors use oscillating electric fields to measure the properties of an electric field, allowing the presence of a human body to be detected. Braun et al. have presented a system using electrodes laid out in a grid and hidden under floor covering to detect the location of one or more persons [2]. A similar system that integrates necessary electronics into a floor layer and communicates wirelessly to a central system has been presented by Lauterbach et al. [5]. Both systems furthermore allow the realization of additional use cases, such as intrusion detection and fall prevention.

Walking is creating a certain level of noise that can be picked up by microphones and used to infer the location of persons. Most of these systems use time-of-flight techniques; that is, calculating the distance of the source by measuring the time required for the signal to arrive at a specific location and triangulating its position [6]. While earlier system relied on speech to recognize sound sources [3], newer and more sensitive systems allow the detection of a person from the sound of the person's footsteps [7].

Another popular method is based on different radio frequency techniques, e.g., by measuring signal strength (RSSI) on different receivers and triangulate position [8] that require an active token to be worn. A newer approach is using tomography techniques to measure the signal attenuation by human bodies [9] and allows localization without wearing active tokens.

Finally, the method that our work is based on comes from the area of computer vision and uses different types of cameras [10], depending on visible light or infrared depth imaging [11]. Most systems use similar approaches that use background subtraction to detect movement in single images or time-series of images to infer the position of an object [4].

3   System Design

In this section, we describe the rationale that has been driving the development of our system with the specific requirements important in cost-effective personal localization solutions and how it has affected both the hardware architecture and software behind the system.

3.1   System Requirements

The system is based on a set of standard, off-the-shelf webcams and as such excels through its low cost factor – the hardware cost for an average living room should be less than fifty US$ (provided that a PC is already available). There are three main challenges associated to the design of such a system for smart environments:

- Scalability - it should be easy to attach additional cameras to the system and provide tools that allow setting position and orientation of the video devices within the environment
- Computational Feasibility - the algorithms used for person localization should be suitable for usage with low-resolution, low-bandwidth data, while still being able to reliably recognize moving persons
- Flexibility - the system should be able to distinguish between different persons and discard other moving objects, such as pets

The system we are using is set up using a simple configuration tool that models the environment and the extrinsic camera parameters by way of XML files. The video stream of each camera is analyzed for signs of movement and we register the results of each camera to the others. This allows the generation of three-dimensional data of moving objects and the inference of such an object's position within the environment. At least two cameras must capture the moving object for the method to work. In border cases, we use approximations and historical movement data to estimate the object's position. We are using simple metrics to distinguish between different persons, based on the color of their clothing and body volume.

3.2   Hardware Architecture

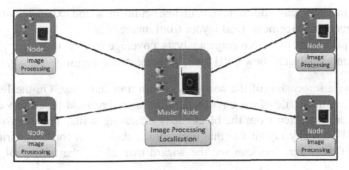

Fig. 1. Hardware architecture of the localization system

The system is comprised of various nodes made up of a single PC with various USB cameras attached. They are connected to each other using either a wired LAN connection (preferably), or WiFi. The cameras used should be controllable in terms of modifying their settings, such as automatic settings of white balance, gain, contrast and brightness. This allows offloading the image processing to the single systems and in consequence only higher-level features are sent through the network connections. This is reducing the required bandwidth and making this approach feasible for low-speed wireless networks. One of the nodes is acting as a master, analyzes the high-level data and provides the overall processing of the final localization. The overall architecture is shown in .

3.3   Data Processing

Fig. 2. Localization process

Our system is following a regular camera-based indoor localization process, as shown in **Fig.2**. Each individual system is processing the image of the camera using a motion detection algorithm. We use a custom variant of background subtraction that allows a fine-grained control of sample window, camera parameters and feature size, guaranteeing swift adaptation to different room geometries. In a second step, we extract features from the detected motion, in our case the center of gravity of each moving region and metrics about the detected regions, that allow us to identify persons in a future iteration. Only these features (and not the entire stream) are then sent over the network for further processing. Finally the master system is collecting all the features, combines it with its local representation of the environment and performs localization of the different persons.

A control software has been created that realizes all these steps. Furthermore, it provides various tools supporting this process. These tools include:

- Camera management: add/remove cameras, set intrinsic and extrinsic parameters
- Environment management: read layout from image files
- Camera placement tools: coverage analysis, coverage optimization
- Performance analysis: show CPU load, network status, logging

Fig.3. shows a screenshot of the software's main user interface. On the left, we can see the source image file of the environment. Using a threshold-based processing, the boundaries are extracted from the black areas indicating walls. The environment can be extracted from any layout file that uses similar dark areas for boundaries. On the right side of the figure, we can see the wizard that allows the adding of additional cameras.

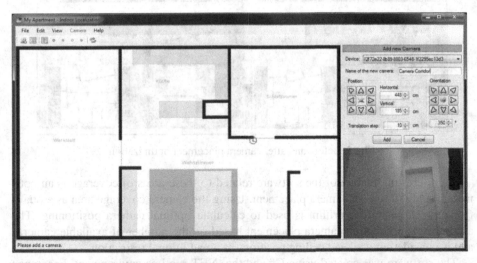

Fig. 3. Software's main view

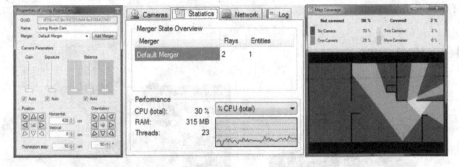

Fig. 4. Camera properties (left), Statistics (center), Coverage analysis (right)

The wizards of the software enable us to modify the position and orientation of cameras and check on the live camera stream. Once a camera is added, it is also possible to control the results of the image processing in a dedicated window and individually set post-processing parameters, such as white balance and color correction (**Fig.4.** - left). The statistics window as shown in **Fig.4** (center) gives an overview of available master nodes (mergers) and the load on all available CPU cores as well as the number of currently active threads. Finally, the coverage map shown **Fig.4** (right) displays by color, which areas of the environment are currently covered by cameras, and by how many (red indicates blind spots, orange areas are in the view of a single camera, yellow areas are surveyed by two cameras, and orange areas are covered by at least three cameras). We have found that, as a rule of thumb, a reliable localization is achieved for all yellow and green areas (areas covered by at least two cameras).

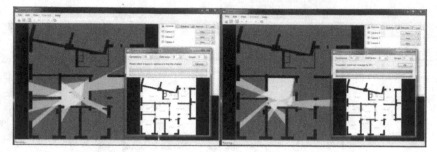

Fig. 5. Before and after camera placement optimization

An interesting feature of the software related to these areas of coverage is an optimization algorithm for camera placement. Using the camera coverage area as a quality metric, a genetic algorithm is used to calculate optimal camera positioning. The algorithm is optimizing camera placement based on the number of available cameras and is considering wall and ceiling positions as an additional restriction.

The software was created using C# and the .NET runtime environment. For image processing, we are using EmguCV[1], a .NET wrapper for OpenCV[2]. This is a comprehensive image processing and computer vision library, which already provides many of the methods required.

4   Prototype

Fig. 6. Playstation Eye camera out-of-the-box (left) and hanging upside-down in the custom-built stand (right)

---

[1] http://www.emgu.com
[2] http://opencv.org/

For our prototype set-up, we selected the Playstation Eye as the camera of our choice, because it is available at a low price and nevertheless allows the setting of parameters such as frames per second (FPS), deactivation of auto-white-balance and auto-contrast, as well as setting exposure and gain. Manually controlling these parameters is crucial in image processing applications and not a general feature available for all cheaper variety web cams. Additionally, we have designed a custom stand that allows the easy attachment of the cameras on walls, as shown **Fig.6**. While the system is easily scalable, for our initial tests we have used only two nodes, with two cameras attached to each of those (which results in a total of four cameras). This setup has proven to be sufficient for covering a large room (roughly 35 square meters). Both nodes were running our software on 64-bit multi-core processors (AMD Turion 64 and Intel Core i5). The cameras are running at 30 FPS and VGA resolution (640x480). The CPU load and amounts of threads used indicate that each node would be able to handle at least twice the number of cameras. RAM requirements have generally shown to be fairly low.

The system was installed in our institute's Living Lab, which consists of a combined living room and kitchen area, a bedroom and an office. For our evaluation, only the combined living room and kitchen area were considered. The area covered is approximately 35 square meters and is occupied by several large pieces of furniture (cupboards, desks, and the like). Therefore, a sophisticated camera placement is crucial in order to guarantee good coverage. The software tools as described were essential for finding optimal camera positions in this setting. As a next step, we intend to extend our prototype to all rooms of the Living Lab.

5   Evaluation

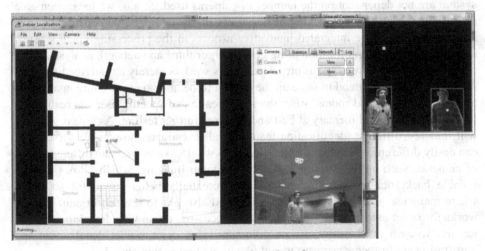

Fig. 7. The simultaneous detection of two persons

As indicated before, we have been able to successfully test our prototype system (software and hardware setup) for the simultaneous tracking of two persons, using four cameras to cover an average-sized living room. By using the camera placement optimization algorithm, we positioned the four cameras on different corners of the room and thus maximized the area covered by at least three devices. The screenshot one can see on Fig. 7 shows the software's main screen with the apartment's map on the left and one camera's viewing angle highlighted. The image stream of this selected camera can be seen on the lower right. The frame on the upper right shows the persons that are currently tracked by this camera (supported by the feeds delivered by the other three cameras). Making use of small markers on the floor, we have been able to verify that our system's distance estimation feature is already fairly precise for areas that are covered by at least three cameras (the estimation was rarely more than 30 cm off the mark). The processing power of the two medium-class PCs we used for handling the four camera's image streams proved to be more than capable for this and showed significant reserves. Based on this, we intend to build a new prototype system which will use only a single PC for handling four, six or maybe even eight cameras at once and which could then be used to monitor an entire small apartment.

6   Conclusion and Future Work

In this work, we have presented a system for the indoor localization of multiple persons. Based entirely on affordable hardware and open source software libraries, we created a reliable, scalable and versatile solution for tracking up to two users within a large indoor area. The hardware costs for the system itself are approximately $100 for four cameras, stands and cabling. Because multiple cameras can be attached to a single computer (mainly depending on its processing power), the overall costs of the system are not dependent on the number of cameras used. So far, we have been able to use our system for the tracking of two users in our equipped demonstration area. Additionally, we have integrated innovative aspects in the processing pipeline, such as camera coverage optimization using genetic algorithms and network analysis.

Nonetheless, the prototype as presented in this work is merely an intermediate step. As future work, we intend to scale up the system to be able to cover entire apartments and multiple separated rooms. Also, the identification of specific users as realized in its current state is rudimentary at best and requires further testing. As a next step, we will thus test different identification features and investigate, how many persons we can easily differentiate. In terms of hardware we would like to evaluate different types of cameras, such as the Microsoft Kinect for depth imaging, which allows a more reliable background subtraction and thus is potentially better suited for scenarios where many users are present. Finally, we would also like to test self-organizing networks for smart cameras that perform image processing on an included chip and send features to each other using wireless communication systems. Self-localization and registration are further aspects we would like to explore in this regard.

References

1. Chessa, S., Knauth, S.: Evaluating AAL Systems Through Competitive Benchmarking. Indoor Localization and Tracking. Springer, Heidelberg (2012)
2. Braun, A., Heggen, H., Wichert, R.: CapFloor – A Flexible Capacitive Indoor Localization System. In: Chessa, S., Knauth, S. (eds.) EvAAL 2011. CCIS, vol. 309, pp. 26–35. Springer, Heidelberg (2012)
3. Sturim, D.E., Brandstein, M.S., Silverman, H.F.: Tracking multiple talkers using microphone-array measurements. IEEE Comput. Soc. Press (1997)
4. Krumm, J., Harris, S., Meyers, B., Brumitt, B., Hale, M., Shafer, S.: Multi-camera multi-person tracking for EasyLiving. In: Proceedings Third IEEE International Workshop on Visual Surveillance, pp. 3–10. IEEE Comput. Soc. (2000)
5. Lauterbach, C., Steinhage, A.: SensFloor ® - A Large-area Sensor System Based on Printed Textiles Printed Electronics. In: Ambient Assisted Living Congress. VDE Verlag (2009)
6. Brandstein, M.S., Silverman, H.F.: A practical methodology for speech source localization with microphone arrays. Computer Speech Language 11, 91–126 (1997)
7. Guo, Y., Hazas, M.: Localising speech, footsteps and other sounds using resource-constrained devices. In: 10th International Conference on Information Processing in Sensor Networks (IPSN), pp. 330–341 (2011)
8. Balakrishnan, H.: The Cricket Indoor Location System. Doctoral Dissertation, Massachusetts Institute of Technology (2005)
9. Wilson, J., Patwari, N.: See-Through Walls: Motion Tracking Using Variance-Based Radio Tomography Networks. IEEE Transactions on Mobile Computing 10, 612–621 (2011)
10. Lopez de Ipina, D., Mendonça, P.R.S., Hopper, A.: TRIP: A Low-Cost Vision-Based Location System for Ubiquitous Computing. Personal and Ubiquitous Computing 6, 206–219 (2002)
11. Shotton, J., Fitzgibbon, A., Cook, M., Sharp, T., Finocchio, M., Moore, R., Kipman, A., Blake, A.: Real-time human pose recognition in parts from single depth images. In: CVPR 2011, pp. 1297–1304 (2011)

The Effects of Multimodal Mobile Communications on Cooperative Team Interactions Executing Distributed Tasks

Gregory M. Burnett[1], Andres Calvo[2], Victor Finomore[1], and Gregory Funke[1]

[1] Air Force Research Laboratory, 711 Human Performance Wing, WPAFB, OH
[2] Ball Aersopace, Fairborn, OH
{gregory.burnett,andres.calvo.ctr,victor.finomore,
gregory.funke}@wpafb.af.mil

Abstract. Mobile devices are rapidly becoming an indispensible part of our everyday life. Integrated with various embedded sensors and the ability to support on-the-move processing, mobile devices are being investigated as potential tools to support cooperative team interactions and distributed real-time decision making in both military and civilian applications. A driving interest is how a mobile device equipped with multimodal communication capabilities can contribute to the effectiveness and efficiency of real-time, task outcome and performance. In this paper, we investigate the effects of a prototype multimodal collaborative Android application on distributed collaborating partners jointly working on a physical task. The mobile application's implementation supports real-time data dissemination of an active workspace's perspective between distributed operators. The prototype application was demonstrated in a scenario where teammates utilize different features of the software to collaboratively assemble a complex structure. Results indicated significant improvements in completion times when users visually shared their perspectives and were able to utilize image annotation versus relying on verbal descriptors.

Keywords: Multimodal interfaces, mobile computing, remote collaboration.

1 Introduction

Today's global and on-the-move workforce relies heavily on digital, mobile communication technology and its expanding interconnected networks to effectively accomplish task. Although modern workers are connected to vast amounts of information though the internet and domain specific databases, they can still encounter scenarios and situations that are outside their expertise. Often workers are required to complete the tasks on their own accord or must wait for the arrival of an expert for additional assistance, both unfavorable in time sensitive situations.

Before the advent of mobile devices such as smartphones and tablets, obtaining remote guidance was limited to information relayed orally between a worker and a remote helper, usually transmitted using a radio or telephone. However, as noted by

N. Streitz and C. Stephanidis (Eds.): DAPI/HCII 2013, LNCS 8028, pp. 358–367, 2013.

Wickens, Vidulich, and Sandry-Garza (1984), communication of spatial information is often more effective through a visual, rather than verbal, medium. Consequently, a collaborative technology which affords users the ability to represent and transmit spatial information pictorially, may positively impact performance. Transmitting spatial information in the same modality may result in reduced uncertainty and misunderstanding concerning the content of a message, thereby allowing users to more accurately and succinctly convey information about current and projected future states. Our objectives were to design and implement a prototype multimodal mobile application for remote collaboration. We evaluated the effects of shared video and audio communication on cooperative team performance towards the completion of an abstract building task.

Clark and Brennan (1991) discuss that in order to effectively collaborate, distributed pairs need to have an interactive dialogue to gain mutual understanding and form a common ground. This concept of common grounding, or clarity of instructional directives, can be achieved through various modalities. Gergle et al. (2004) report that "communicative information can be provided in the form of linguistic utterances, visual feedback, gestures, acoustic signals, or a host of other sources; all of which play an important role in successful communication" (p. 487). Utilizing multiple sources of information through multiple modalities is more effective than relying on a single source, such as verbal communication, to arrive at a common ground (Wickens & McCarley, 2008). For situations where the environment or situation can change abruptly, the ability to leverage several modalities and sources of information to maintain shared common grounding or situation awareness between the distributed parties is critical for a successful outcome.

In this paper, we discuss the implementation and evaluation of a prototype multimodal mobile application seeking to facilitate remote collaboration. In sections 2 and 3, we discuss related work and discuss the multimodal communication features chosen for inclusion into our mobile application. The purpose of these features is to support efficient communication grounding between collaborating remote partners working towards the completion of a physical task. In section 4, we report the evaluation methodology and the results from an interactive demonstration of the mobile application, where teams cooperatively built complex models from building blocks. Finally, a discussion and future work section highlight how this research can be used to provide design and potential deployment of real-time decision making capabilities supporting distributed collaboration.

2   Related Work

Recent Computer Supported Cooperative Work (CSCW) research highlights several multimodal communication capabilities that show performance benefits when providing a shared perspective between Workers and remote Helpers. This is highlighted in a series of research efforts (e.g., Gergle et al., 2004; Fussell et al., 2000; Kirk et al., 2007; Kraut et al., 2002; Kuzuoka, 1992) that have leveraged streaming video with bi-directional audio between collaborating team members.

Kuzuoka's (1992) evaluation suggests that when Helpers are provided a shared perspective of the Worker's active focus, they have better situation awareness of the task and can provide improved guidance specific to the Worker's current needs. In addition, a shared perspective of the Worker's activities allows the Helper to monitor and assess the Worker's comprehension and accuracy (Kraut et al., 2002). Studies by Gergle (2005) and Fussell et al. (2000) suggest that the utility of sharing visual information positively affects the communication dialogue between Workers and Helper making the shared linguistic communication faster, less explicit, and more proactive then using audio alone during task completion.

Building upon sharing streaming video and bi-directional audio, the ability to share real-time markup annotations has been shown to improve cooperative performance on physical task completion (Kirk et al., 2007; Ou et al., 2003; Stevenson et al., 2008). Ou and colleagues' (2003) collaborative system DOVE (Drawing Over Video Environments), permitted remote Helpers to draw markup illustrations on shared video to assist in remote guidance. Their findings suggest that the utility of markup capability "significantly reduces performance time compared to camera alone." (p. 248). Kirk et al. (2007) and Stevenson et al. (2008) both describe systems that project remote gestures and markups on top of the Worker's workspace containing the physical task's objectives. Their research showed that task completion times were shorter and fewer mistakes were made when utilizing markup capabilities in conjunction with shared visual and auditory information.

A distinction that our current research makes from existing CSCW systems is the implementation of the various multimodal communication capabilities into the mobile domain. Specially, software development in the Android operating system supporting communication features executing on a mobile device thus enabling on-the-move, anytime, anywhere team collaboration. Based on previous work that demonstrated effective use of multimodal technology to foster distributed collaboration, we built and integrated custom software to enable, sharing video of the Worker's workspace, sharing full-duplex audio between users, and the support of markup annotation on captured still images in our prototype tool suite. The overarching goal of this research and development effort is to leverage multimodal mobile capabilities to establish and maintain shared awareness, provide precise guidance, and facilitate effective collaboration in a real-time, distributed task.

3   Implementation

We implemented the Worker's mobile application on a Samsung Galaxy Tablet running Android and the Helper's application on a personal computer running Windows 7. The mobile device's back-facing camera was used to capture a series of 800×600 images. Acquired images were then compressed into JPEG format, and transmitted to the remote Helper at an average rate of 30 frames per second. Our system also incorporates full-duplex audio communication. To transmit audio to the Worker, the Helper presses and holds a software button referred to as the push-to-talk button. Similarly, the Worker presses and holds a push-to-talk button to transmit audio. Initially, we considered transmitting audio continuously by default, but we decided to incorporate the push-to-talk buttons to lower network consumption. The system transmits both audio and video using the UDP network protocol.

The mobile application's interface displays the Worker's video on the left half of the screen. The Helper can capture images from the Worker's video, annotate them, and send them back to the Worker, where they are displayed on the right half of the screen. The Helper annotates images using drawing tools similar to Microsoft Paint. Every time the Helper draws on the image, the Worker sees the updates in real time. Figure 1 illustrates the process of capturing and annotating an image.

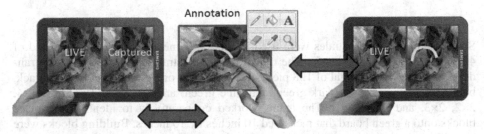

Fig. 1. The Helper captures an image from the Worker's video and annotates it to instruct the user on how to perform a task

4   Evaluation

To evaluate the effectiveness of the prototype mobile collaborative system two person teams had to work together to construct a multi-level, abstract structure with building blocks. The two people were separated from each other and had to utilize different features of the mobile collaborative system to build the structure. The Helper had a representation of the completed structure which they had to communicate to the Worker who physically assembled the blocks based on the Helper's guidance. This task was selected because of the high degree of communication and cooperation required between Worker and Helper to complete the task successfully. This type of task requires detailed collaboration for block identification, orientation alignment, and location placement. The mobile features investigated were Audio, Video with Markup, Video with Audio, and Video with Markup and Audio.

4.1   Participants

Volunteers for this study included 32 participants (17 men and 15 women) ranging in age from 23-30 (*M*=25) years. The participants teamed up in pairs of two, consisting of a Worker and a Helper, collaborating using various modalities to complete the building task. All participants had normal hearing and normal or corrected-to-normal vision

4.2   Experiment Design

A within-subject design, balanced using a Latin-square procedure was employed with the four levels of modality interface (Audio, Video with Markup, Video with Audio, and Video with Markup and Audio). All participants took part in a training session to familiarize themselves with the task and devices. The teams trained by collaboratively communicating with each other to construct one practice model per experimental condition. Teams were given the option for more practice trials; however, none of them felt the need for more. The four experimental conditions and building model configurations were randomized for each team.

4.3   Apparatus

Sixteen building block guides were used in the experiment. Each guide consisted of 46 pieces and had three levels. The model pieces illustrated in the guides were randomly selected from a total of 108 pieces that consisted of eight colors (orange, black, blue, red, yellow, brown, dark green, and lime green) and six sizes (1×2, 1×3, 1×4, 2×2, 2×3, and 2×4 studs). The teams worked cooperatively to identify and place blocks onto a green board that measured 10 inches by 10 inches. Building blocks were located in a pile next to the green board. Worker used a Samsung Galaxy Tablet running our developmental Android application to interact with the Helper through a Wi-Fi connection. The Galaxy Tablet was mounted on a stand above the green board to allow the participant to freely use their hands, as seen in Figure 2.

Fig. 2. Worker's Mobile Device Apparatus

The Helper was situated in front of a workstation, which was isolated from the experimental area. The Helper's workstation allowed them to communicate via voice and/or annotate images (depending on the trial condition) from the Worker's tablet to assist them in their task. The Helper's annotations consisted of free form shapes that were filled with selectable colors, as shown in Figure 3.

4.4   Procedure

The team, consisting of a Worker and a Helper, collaborated using various communication modalities to complete the building task. The modality interfaces

investigated

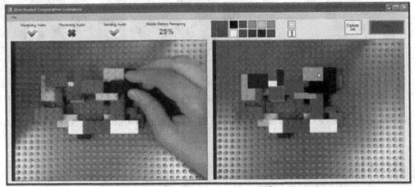

Worker's Live Workspace   Helper's Annotation

Fig. 3. Helper's Workstation

were Audio, Video with Markup, Video with Audio, and Video with Markup and Audio.

In the Audio condition, the Helper had to verbally describe the color, size, orientation, and placement of the building blocks to the Worker from the active build guide, shown in Figure 4 (a). The Helper's instructional dialogue describing the block and placement was not restricted in any manner, and it was left up to the teams to generate their unique shared common language used in the building process. The Video with Markup condition consisted of the Helper capturing a still picture of the Worker's live perspective from the mobile device's integrated camera. The still image could then be annotated in real-time on the Helper's workstation. The annotation process required the Helper to select the color used in the annotation, followed by clicking and holding the left mouse button down while dragging until the desired shape was created. Upon releasing the left mouse button, the markup annotation was fused with the still image and transmitted to the Worker, as shown in Figure 4 (b). The Helper could undo their annotation by selecting the right mouse button. The undo process could be applied five times to clear past annotations. If five corrections were not sufficient, the Helper could recapture a still image and apply fresh annotations. The Video with Audio condition consisted of the Helper monitoring the Worker's perspective while supplying verbal guidance to describe and place building blocks properly in the model. The Video with Markup and Audio condition combined the Audio and Video conditions so that the Helper and Worker were able to talk to each other as well as send annotated images. In each condition, team members were asked to complete the task as fast as possible without making any errors. Immediately following each condition, both the Helper and the Worker independently completed the NASA-Task Load Index (NASA-TLX, Hart & Staveland, 1988), a validated measure of perceived mental workload.

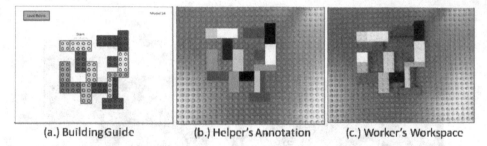

| (a.) Building Guide | (b.) Helper's Annotation | (c.) Worker's Workspace |

Fig. 4. Reference Guide, Helper's guidance to Worker, and Worker's execution of guidance

5   Results

Accuracy was measured by accurately placing the specific building block in the correct location as determined by the building guide. All teams in all four experimental conditions achieved accuracy of the building task of at least 98.3 %. Thus team performance was measured through completion time. Mean completion times for the four experimental conditions are presented in Figure 5.

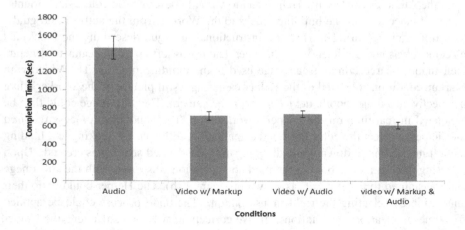

Fig. 5. Mean completion times for each of the four experimental conditions. Error bars are standard errors.

Data from Figure 5 was tested for statistical significance by means of a 4 (condition) within- subjects analysis of variance (ANOVA). A significant main effect was found for completion time across the four experimental conditions, $F(3, 42) = 34.2$, $p < .01$. Post hoc tests indicated that teams completed the building task significantly faster in the Video with Markup and Audio ($M = 625.0$ s) condition as compared to Video with Markup ($M = 735.1$ s) and Video with Audio ($M = 739.6$ s) which were not significantly different from each other, but were both faster than Audio alone ($M = 1490.3$ s).

Participants' mean perceived mental workload scores for each experimental condition for the Helper and the Worker are displayed in Figure 6.

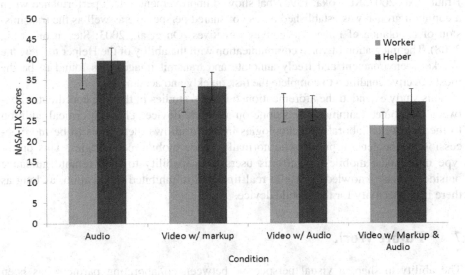

Fig. 6. Mean TLX for each of the four experimental conditions

A 2 (role) x 4 (condition) mixed ANOVA was completed on the NASA – TLX data in Figure 6. A statistically significant main effect was found for conditions, $F (3, 177) = 14.39$, $p < .01$. Post hoc tests indicated that participants rated the Audio ($M = 39.92$) as the most mentally demanding condition. Video with Markup and Audio ($M = 27.83$) and Video with Audio ($M = 29.31$) were not significantly different then each other but were less demanding then Video with Markup ($M = 33.23$). No other source of variance was found to be statistically significant, $p > .05$.

6   Discussion

This study evaluated the effectiveness of distributed teams working together to build an abstract structure out of building blocks with the use of a prototype multimodal mobile collaborative tool suite. The developed software allowed distributed teammates to verbally communicate, share video imagery, and send annotated picture messages to foster team collaboration. Our results indicated that the use of multimodal communications on a mobile device improved team performance when collaborating on their task. While all teams successfully completed the task with a high degree of accuracy there were significant differences in the complete times based on the functions available to the team. Teams performed the task quickest in the video with markup and audio condition and slowest in the audio only conditions. Both the Worker and the Helper rated the audio condition as the most mentally demanding condition.

The audio condition serves as a baseline condition to compare the additional features of the mobile prototype tool suite against since a majority of real-time coordination between distributed teammates is currently accomplished this way. This study replicated many of the earlier studies (Gergle et al., 2004; Fussell et al., 2000; Kirk et al., 2007; Kraut et al., 2002; Kuzuoka, 1992) that showed improvement in task performance when a common ground was established by use of shared perspective as well as the transmission of annotation of images to convey directives (Ou et al., 2003; Stevenson et al., 2008). The integration of voice communication with the ability of the Helper to view the Worker's environment and freely annotate and transmit images was found to be the most effective condition to complete the task quickly and accurately.

This study extended the aforementioned CSCW studies in that the coordination between distributed teammates was done on a mobile device. This is a critical addition to the field of collaborative technologies in that it allows these tools to be more accessible to the general public who normally utilize mobile technologies. This prototype multimodal mobile tool affords users the capability to seek remote guidance outside of one's knowledge base in real-time and uninhibited by location, as long as there is connectivity for the mobile device.

7   Future Work

The ability to share a visual perspective between collaborating partners has been shown to enhance cooperative performance. A limitation to the existing visual dissemination capability is that the Helper only receives visual information on what the Worker is currently focusing the mobile device's camera on and is constrained to the camera's field of view. This "soda straw" perspective can reduce the Helper's overall situation awareness and requires them to rely on the Worker to modify and/or expand awareness through camera movements or panning. Therefore, an extension to the visual capturing feature that would improve the Helper's ability to collaborate could be a virtual immersion in the Worker's scenario. This can be achieve through computer vision techniques that stitch a series of individual snap shots to form a 3D perspective similar to Google's Sphere, as depicted in Figure 7. The new perspective of the Worker's workspace can give the Helper the freedom to pan, zoom, etc. to obtain the necessary vantage view angle to provide better communication and guidance.

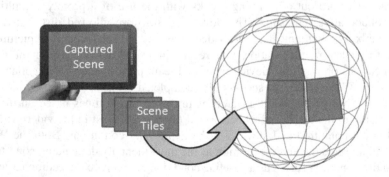

Fig. 7. Immersive 3D scene generated from a series of Worker's still images

References

1. Clark, H.H., Brennan, S.E.: Grounding in communication. In: Resnick, L.B., Levine, R.M., Teasley, S.D. (eds.) Perspectives on Socially Shared Cognition, pp. 127–149 (1991)
2. Fussel, S.R., Kraut, R.E., Siegel, J.: Coordination of communication: effects of shared visual context on collaborative work. In: Proceedings of CSCW 2000, pp. 21–30. ACM Press, NY (2000)
3. Gergle, D., Kraut, R.E., Fussell, S.R.: Action as language in a shared visual space. In: Proceedings of CSCW 2004, vol. 6(3), pp. 487–496. ACM Press, NY (2004)
4. Gergle, D.: The value of shared visual space for collaborative physical task. In: Proceedings of CHI 2005, pp. 1116–1117 (2005)
5. Hart, S.G., Staveland, L.E.: Development of NASA-TLX (task load index): results of empirical and theoretical research. In: Hancock, P.A., Meshkati, N. (eds.) Human Mental Workload, pp. 139–183. North-Holland, Amsterdam (1988)
6. Kirk, D., Rodden, T., Fraser, D.S.: Turn it this way: ground collaborative action with remote gestures. In: Proceedings of Computer Human Interaction (CHI): Distributed Interaction, San Jose, CA (2007)
7. Kraut, R.E., Darren, G., Fussell, S.R.: The use of visual information in shared visual co-presence. In: Proceedings of CSCW 2002, pp. 31–40 (2002)
8. Kuzuoka, H.: Spatial workspace collaboration: a sharedview video support system for remote collaboration capability. In: Proceedings of CHI 1992, pp. 533–540 (1992)
9. Ou, J., Fussell, S.R., Chen, X., Setlock, L.D., Yang, J.: Gestural communication over video stream: supporting multimodal interaction for remote collaborative physical tasks. In: International Conference on Multimodal Interfaces, pp. 242–249. ACM Press, Vancouver (2003)
10. Stevenson, D., Li, J., Smith, J., Hutchins, M.: A collaborative guidance case study. In: AUIC 2008, Wollongong, NSW, Australia, pp. 33–42 (2008)
11. Wickens, C.D., Vidulich, M., Sandry-Garza, D.: Principles of S-C-R compatibility with spatial and verbal tasks: The role of display-control location and voice-interactive display-control interfacing. Human Factors 26, 533–543 (1984)

Aesthetics and Design for Group Music Improvisation

Mathias Funk, Bart Hengeveld, Joep Frens, and Matthias Rauterberg

Department of Industrial Design, Eindhoven University of Technology,
Den Dolech 2, 5612AZ Eindhoven, The Netherlands
{m.funk,b.j.hengeveld,j.w.frens,g.w.m.rauterberg}@tue.nl

Abstract. Performing music as a group—improvised or from sheet music—is an intensive and immersive interaction activity that bears its own aesthetics. Players in such a setting are usually skilled in playing an instrument up to the level where they do not need to focus on the "operation" of the instrument, but can instead focus on higher-level feedback loops, e.g., between players in their section or the entire group. Novel technology can capitalize on these higher-level feedback loops through the creation of interactive musical instruments that stimulate playing in groups (collaborative music rather than parallel music). However, making this experience accessible to fresh or novice players involves two challenges: how to design (1) musical instruments for such a setting and experience, and (2) instrument support that extends the interaction between players to their instruments. This allows to interact not only via their instrument with other human players, but directly with other instruments, producing a much richer and more intertwined musical experience. The paper shows results from a class of design students and reports on the lessons learned.

Keywords: Design, Interaction design, System design, Music, Improvisation, Co-creation.

1 Introduction

Group music performance is one of the oldest interaction settings dating back thousands of years in human history. While the musical instruments have certainly changed over time, the actual interaction between players has remained a constant factor, resulting in a direct, immersive and expressive experience that is joyful not only to the musicians, but also to the audience. Our current time allows for the creation of novel musical instruments once more, with the advance of embedded and networked technology. These allow us to take on another approach to group music where the instruments themselves can take on a more active role, resulting in a new expressive aesthetics.

In the design of aesthetic musical experiences as we approach it in this paper, three important notions are explained as preliminaries: (1) *group improvisation* as the activity that has the main focus in this paper, (2) *extension of control* as a necessary ingredient to new ways of improvisation, and (3) *new musical instruments* as the means to

N. Streitz and C. Stephanidis (Eds.): DAPI/HCII 2013, LNCS 8028, pp. 368–377, 2013.

realize new musical improvisation experiences. These three are explained in the following.

1.1   Group Improvisation

In this paper, we focus on musical improvisation in group settings. In our view this activity involves multiple simultaneous feedback loops of musical expression [1] as shown in Figure 1. We see these loops as universal attributes of group music performance, whether played from sheet music (e.g., in a classical orchestra) or without (e.g., in a jazz quartet). We illustrate these loops first, before moving to the topic of group improvisation.

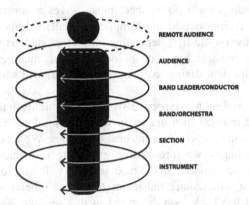

REMOTE AUDIENCE

AUDIENCE

BAND LEADER/CONDUCTOR

BAND/ORCHESTRA

SECTION

INSTRUMENT

Fig. 1. Different layers of feedback loops in musical performance

Firstly, no matter the musical setting or situation, a musician interacts with his musical instrument. The musician plays the instrument, which in turn generates a sound, to which the musician can respond (e.g., in intonation or expression). This feedback loop is at the core of playing music.

Secondly, in any setting involving musical interaction (e.g., multiple musicians together or a single musician and a play-along CDs) a musician can belong to a section. For example, a drummer and a bass player both belong to a rhythm section. All musicians within a section have to sound well together, which adds a feedback loop to the aforementioned one.

The *third* feedback loop originates when sections start belonging to a larger musical body. For example, a cellist (feedback loop one) in a classical orchestra belongs to the cello section (feedback loop two), but also to the string section (consisting of the first and second violins, violas, cellos and basses, feedback loop three). Moreover, the string section belongs to an even larger body: the orchestra.

To keep all these sections musically aligned, orchestras have a conductor who imposes his interpretation on the orchestra. This adds a *fourth* feedback loop. In jazz bands the role of the conductor often moves from musician to musician within a single piece of music.

The *fifth* feedback loop we identify is the one involving the audience: when the audience is enthusiastic typically musicians start performing better.

The *sixth* feedback loop we identify is less direct, but a feedback loop nonetheless: delayed feedback on your performance through sales, downloads, streams, Facebook likes, Tweets, etcetera. Clearly this feedback loop is of a different character than the previous five, but also one that may become more relevant in the near future.

As mentioned, we consider these feedback loops not unique for improvised group music, but pertaining to group music in general. What interests us in group improvisation though is the how the feedback loops are dependent on self-organization. Let us explain this.

Transcribed music has a clear organizing factor: the sheet music. Despite the openness for music interpretation or the relativity of tempi (*allegro ma non troppo*) or expressions (*crescendo poco a poco*) sheet music gives a common direction to all involved musicians. In improvised music much (not all) of this direction is absent; often music originates 'on the fly', depending on factors such as the group composition, the setting, the musical backgrounds of the group members, and more. This makes that a single musical design (e.g., a jazz standard) will sound differently each time.

From an interaction design perspective we find this highly interesting as it opens up a new domain of musical instruments in which technology-mediated, interactive musical instruments can lead to a new musical aesthetics. We elaborate on this in the next section. For example, we foresee that extending instrumental control among musicians (on which we elaborate in the next section) will lead to a different form of instrumentalism, as it will require musicians to accept other musicians to have an influence in the first feedback loop described in this section. As a consequence we anticipate that this will have repercussions on most of the other feedback loops, as shared control redefines the (self-) organizational structure between instrumentalists, sections etcetera. This will hopefully not only lead to a new aesthetics of instrumentalism alone, but also of group musicianship and of the resulting music.

1.2 Extending Control

In traditional group music settings, interaction happens usually non-verbal (to not disturb the music, or because one's voice would not carry over the music) using sign language, gestures, mimics, but mostly by listening to other instruments and watching other players play their instruments. Using this as an input, the players will adapt, for instance, volume, attenuation, and tempo of their own play–basically the application of multiple feedback loops as shown above. The connection between a player and other players' instruments is unidirectional in this process: the player can only perceive sound coming from another player's instrument, but not influence it–only indirectly, by influencing the other player. See Figure 2 (left side) for a visualization of this principle: players interact bi-directionally with their own instruments and with other players, and uni-directionally with other players' instruments.

What if a player could also influence the instruments of certain other players? As one can see from Figure 2 (right side), which shows a visualization of this new principle, the network of connections between players and instruments is denser and entirely bi-directional: players interact both with their own instruments, other players, and their instruments.

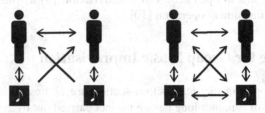

Fig. 2. Interaction modes in traditional music performance settings (left side) and in the proposed new setting (right side). Human players at the top interaction with each other, but also with their instruments denoted at the bottom of each figure.

This new interaction creates richer feedback loops, and necessarily adds to the complexity of the performance. In addition, this interaction mode changes how players perceive the setting of the performance: there is less a strong and exclusive bond between players and their own instruments. Instead, instruments become shared artifacts–same as the music has been already [2].

1.3   New Musical Instruments

Musical instruments have grown more sophisticated and nowadays allow for much richer expression. However, at the same time, the level of skills required to play state of the art musical instruments is higher than ever before. Some instruments cannot be played properly without years of (formal) training. Some instruments are too large or expensive to be owned and played by one's own will. Finally, nowadays frequent, ubiquitous, and high load music consumption has nurtured our tastes to a level where listening naïve musical expression or even just the sounds created by musical instruments are often not appreciated anymore–we simply do not enjoy the music we are able to create [3].

In the remainder of this paper, after showing related work, we will report on the process and outcomes of designing for group music improvisation, which is succeeded by important lessons learned. The paper concludes with a summary and an outlook on future steps of this line of design research.

2   Related Work

Although related work (interactive musical instruments designed specifically for group improvisation) is scarce, the history of interactive, electronic musical instruments in general is rich. Typically the Theremin and the Moog synthesizer are seen as pivotal milestones in this history, but recent work is superfluous and compelling. For example, Bevilacqua et al. explore digitally enhanced bow gestures in their "Augmented String Quartet" [4], IRCAM's MO project [5] offers a modular system allowing for the exploration of gestural interfaces for musical expressions, while other extend to mimics [6] or shift the interaction to collaborative objects [7], for instance, reacTable [8], which is a widely acclaimed interactive music tabletop. Another objective in this project was to open access to improvisation [9] as well as extending the control of musical instrument operation [10].

3   Designing for Group Music Improvisation

The challenges scoped in the introduction section are addressed in this section, describing the course of 5-month-long design project carried out by 20 Industrial Design undergraduate students. The project was initially framed as a system design project, but that alone would not properly capture the complexity: it is rather a setting, in which *multiple designers collaboratively design a multi-user system consisting of multiple (radically) different and unique devices acting individually and as a whole.* Designing for this new situation is easier said than done. A profound difficulty is that we seemingly cannot simply transfer our 'designing for interaction methods and tools' to this new paradigm. This has several reasons. Firstly, the systems we are aiming at are essentially too extensive and our targeted user-groups too heterogeneous to simply choose an approach (e.g., bottom-up or top-down) and start designing. Moreover, as designing for systems is relatively uncharted territory, we even don't know if these existing approaches apply or if we need an alternative hybrid approach [11]. Secondly, the interaction with systems appears to be different than with interactive standalone products as systems are more focused on facilitating opportunities for behavior rather than on disclosing functionalities.

The goal was a Group Music Improvisation System (GMIS) and students focused on different parts of the system, e.g. sound generation, sound modification, and technical infrastructure. We will first look at the process, how the designers approached the project and moved on to their own sub-projects, always with the GMIS in mind. Then, we will present the outcomes of this project, a number of instrument prototypes and the system as a whole.

3.1   Setup and Process

As described in the previous section we anticipated the requirement for a different design approach towards this project, for various reasons. To streamline the project as much as possible we stimulated all students to act as much as they could as a self-organizing system themselves, in order to have them co-shape the project and get grip on (musical) group dynamics. We organized weekly and bi-weekly coaching sessions, as well as regular jam sessions during which students could try out experiential mock-ups and prototypes of their designs together. In addition to these activities several workshops and invited talks were organized, for example involving a designer and maker of traditional musical instruments, and a composer and performer of contemporary electronic music.

All students were stimulated to design in iterative cycles of designing, building and evaluating models and experiential prototypes of different levels of detail, using a process known as the Reflective Transformative Design Process (RTDP, [12]), with which they were all well-acquainted. One of the fortes of this process is that it is highly flexible and not prescriptive; in other words it allowed for exploring hybrid systems design approaches.

3.2   Outcome

The outcomes of the design project were plenty, about 16 devices or installations from 20 students, some of which were working in groups of four. As already mentioned in the process section, self-organization happened–although quite late in the process–in the form of multiple dimensions (as depicted in Figure 3).

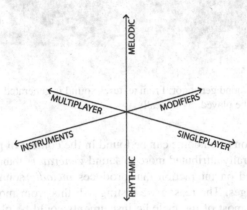

Fig. 3. Dimensions of outcomes as observed from the project: melodic–rhythmic (vertical), instruments–modifiers (left front to right back), multiplayer–single player (left back to right front).

Most importantly, the students divided into a large cluster creating music instruments, called *generators*, and another large cluster working on sound effects, called *modifiers*. The former mostly used tactile input captured by different kinds of sensors, mapped this to sound parameters, and finally emitted sound. The latter used, for instance, microphones and live sampling techniques to acquire sound input, which in turn could be processed and emitted again. Other modifiers used tangible interaction to shape the sound such as shown in Figure 4. The processing was determined by, again, tactile input. This dimension is shown in Figure 3as one horizontal axis, which is crossed by the other two important dimensions about users (multiplayer vs. single player) and about musical attributes (melodic vs. rhythmic).

As shown in the introduction, this design project had also the objective to extend control and likewise enrich the feedback loops in action during a performance. The mapping of user and instrument is important, and the outcome showed that both single user instruments as well as collaborative multi-user instruments were possible and could contribute to a diverse and rich performance.

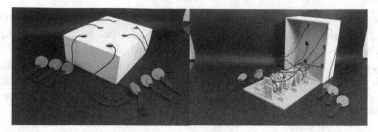

Fig. 4. Sound modifier, which uses tension on ropes attached to (or simply grabbed by) different players to modify sound. Ropes with same-colored handles have a mutual influence.

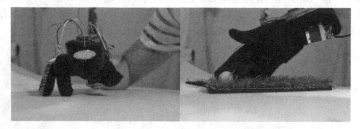

Fig. 5. Glove tangible sound generator. From textures sound is generated upon touch and stroking motions. Can even be played rhythmically.

The third dimension of outcome can be found in the content of produced sound and music, however naturally attributed more to sound *generators* than *modifiers*: some of the designers focused on interaction that produces *melodic* sound, aiming at pitch, tone, and tonal changes. The reason we distinguish this from more rhythmic instruments is that indeed most of the melodic instruments could be played with rhythmic accuracy and instead allowed players to work out aesthetic melodies or harmonics. The sounds produced by these instruments were, for instance, long tones, with slow transients and attack times, and long or undefined decays. Another example of focusing on the aesthetics of sounds was an instrument, with which the player could explore and play haptic textures of various materials (see Figure 5). On the other side of the spectrum, rhythmic instruments were usually very accurately playable, sometimes even purely acoustic instruments, sometimes relying on sampling and percussive sound generation.

4   Results

The results of this project can be seen from two angles: process and actual outcome. Both are worthwhile to report on and shed light on the overall task of designing for an aesthetic experience of interaction in a group performance.

The kind of design process students applied was no surprise, as they had learned and adopted a design process [12] that focuses on the individual designer with supplementary collaborative activities. This slowed them down in the first part of the design project. After a few weeks, we could however observe changing patterns: better communication and self-organization happened. Communication changed in terms of focus, from technology and prototyping, to what the students actually wanted to achieve in terms of music and experience. Self-organization at group level helped to focus on different aspects of the experience, such as sound generation and sound modification.

The *process* observed by us is very much characterized by rapid swings in terms of ideas, scopes, and technical foundations. As with any other explorative process, the swings are large in the beginning when most explorative action happens, and only over time processes stabilize until the point a narrow project is scoped and can be followed-through with minor changes. The problem arose when the design processes and swings of multiple designers were not synchronized and would not converge in the end. When reaching the final stage of the process, the processes should continue in parallel, which was what we had envisioned when setting up the design project. Unfortunately this could hardly be observed.

The *outcomes* of this design project were diverse and certainly product of a challenging process, however, the concepts and prototypes did not work as intended in a systematic way. We had aimed for truly connecting instruments and a lively jam session at the end, but the instruments did not work out that well due to (human) communication problems, which were pretty much unlike we have encountered before. Designing systems is a hard task, especially with multiple designers involved. The design students found it hard to focus on both micro and macro level, i.e. to design a musical instrument *individually*, and a system *together*. This required not only another perspective on design responsibility in the students, but also a certain acceptance of self-sacrifice: designing as a system demands individual designers to 'kill their darlings'—their part in the sum—for the sake of the whole. However, it is also clear that 16-20 different instruments, influencing each other would not only be a huge technical challenge, but also not produce the intended sonic results. A positive result from this design project is indeed that the designers interpreted the rules of the briefing such that also smaller, more effective teams were permitted. Thus, cluster of 2 to 4 designers emerged which jointly created instruments that could influence each other (at least conceptually) and that also produced sound complementary in pitch, tone, volume, rhythm, and texture—in short, a manageable experience both for the players and the audience.

5   Conclusions

Did this study reveal a new aesthetic experience of interaction in a group performance? Looking at the division we made in section 1.1 (aesthetics of instrumentalism, of group performance and of the resulting music) we have to conclude that we are not there yet: most of the results were similar to related work, which does not mean that this work is not aesthetic—on the contrary—but simply that we were looking for a novel aesthetics based on the effect of extended instrument control. The majority of resulting designs hinted at this, but not more than that, although we saw very interesting directions in force-fit combinations of modified acoustic instruments, fully digital instruments and (loop) modifiers. These seemed to generate an intriguing musical aesthetics, which is arguably not novel, but can be capitalized on in future studies.

We saw one prominent exception though. One of the students designed a very interesting set of instruments—one two-stringed tonal synthesizer and an augmented percussive instrument—in a 3D surround sound setting, where both instruments had their own behavior but were also open for one behavior modification by the other instrument. This meant that the percussive instrument could influence the pitch of the tonal instrument, and the tonal instrument the attack of the percussive instrument. The output of the tonal instrument was omnidirectional, but the percussive instrument moved around randomly in the 3D surround sound space, which added an intriguing additional feedback loop to those mentioned in Figure 1. Both instruments had a learning curve, which kept them interesting and challenging for the instrumentalists.

This set of instruments was used in two live, improvised performances by two of the design coaches, semi-professional musicians themselves (drummer and bassist). Their experience as traditional musicians helped un-steepening the learning curve of the instruments, but the diminished control over their instrument's musical contribution demanded a new musicianship: they were forced to search for their (individual and collaborative) aesthetic appreciation of their (individual and collaborative) music while performing. This made that the music itself played a more prominent role in directing the musicians, rather than the other way around.

As shown above in the results section, the design process taken by most of the students was not collaborative and converging enough to succeed. The students did not conceptualize via the aesthetics of interaction that a group music improvisation system should embody (including the sound and music it should product), but instead focused too much on actual instruments, technology and connectivity. In the coming iteration of this project, students need to be given more guidance and direction in the first part of their projects to gain the right momentum and understanding of the *differences* in this design process compared to design processes they have learned and applied in the past. This will be done by requiring all students to first think about the sound and music they would like their instruments to produce, instead of conceptualizing the instruments directly. These sound and interaction concepts will be documented and presented by means of video prototypes early in the design process.

The second aspect that needs revision is the technical infrastructure that supports the connectivity. In the coming iterations, all students can rely on a common infrastructure made of open-source building blocks that are not too challenging to program and still allow for the right amount of flexibility to design new instruments.

Acknowledgments. The authors would like to thank all students and coaches in the "Group Music Improvisation System" project that took place in the Out of Control theme at the Department of Industrial Design in Fall 2012. We thank Tom van 't Westeinde, Trieuvy Luu for allowing us to use their photographs. Special thanks to Vleer Doing for providing two new instruments and the infrastructure for influence.

References

1. Bahn, C., Hahn, T., Trueman, D.: Physicality and feedback: a focus on the body in the performance of electronic music. In: Proceedings of the International Computer Music Conference, pp. 44–51 (2001)
2. Nacsa, J., Barakova, E., Frens, J.: Sharing meaning and physical activity through a tangible interactive lighting object. In: Procedings of the Second Conference on Creativity and Innovation in Design - DESIRE 2011, pp. 227–230. ACM Press, New York (2011)
3. Bryan-Kinns, N., Healey, P.: Decay in Collaborative Music Making. In: Schnell, N., Bevilacqua, F. (eds.) Interfaces, pp. 114–117. ACM Press, New York (2006)
4. Bevilacqua, F., Baschet, F., Lemouton, S.: The Augmented String Quartet: Experiments and Gesture Following. Journal of New Music Research 41, 103–119 (2012)
5. Rasamimanana, N., Bevilacqua, F., Schnell, N., Guedy, F., Flety, E., Maestracci, C., Zamborlin, B., Frechin, J.-L., Petrevski, U.: Modular musical objects towards embodied control of digital music. In: Proceedings of the Fifth International Conference on Tangible, Embedded, and Embodied Interaction, pp. 9–12. ACM, New York (2011)
6. Funk, M., Kuwabara, K., Lyons, M.J.: Sonification of Facial Actions for Musical Expression. Design, 127–131 (2005)
7. Heinz, S., Modhrain, S.O.: Designing a shareable musical TUI. Technology 26, 339–342 (2010)
8. Jordà, S., Geiger, G., Alonso, M., Kaltenbrunner, M.: The reacTable: exploring the synergy between live music performance and tabletop tangible interfaces. In: Proceedings of the 1st International Conference on Tangible and Embedded Interaction, pp. 139–146. ACM, New York (2007)
9. Hsu, W.: Design issues in interaction modeling for free improvisation. In: Parkinson, C., D'Arcangelo, G., Singer, E. (eds.) Proceedings of the 7th International Conference on New Interfaces for Musical Expression - NIME 2007, p. 367. ACM Press, New York (2007)
10. Cappelen, B.: Expanding the role of the instrument. In: Proceedings of the International Conference on New Interfaces for Musical Expression, pp. 511–514 (2011)
11. Hengeveld, B.J.: Designing LinguaBytes: A Tangible Language Learning System for Non- or Hardly Speaking Toddlers (2011)
12. Hummels, C., Frens, J.: The reflective transformative design process. In: Proceedings of the 27th International Conference Extended Abstracts on Human Factors in Computing Systems CHI EA 2009, pp. 2655–2658 (2009)

Proxemic Interaction Applied to Public Screen in Lab

Huiliang Jin, Tao Xu, Bertrand David, and René Chalon

Université de Lyon, CNRS
Ecole Centrale de LYON, LIRIS, UMR5205
{huiliang.jin,tao.xu,bertrand.david,rene.chalon}@ec-lyon.fr

Abstract. Proxemics is the terminology used to describe spatial relationships among humans while communicating with each other. It could be interesting to apply the proxemics theory to the domain of human computer interaction, namely proxemic interaction. Computers, unlike people, find it hard to interpret instantly and precisely the user's nonverbal hints, such as body postures, movement, and distance. With the development of computer vision, these tasks can be performed with simple devices. In this paper, we build the abstract model for calculation in proxemic interaction, and further illustrate the prototype based on research life in the lab. We then describe evolution of the prototype through investigation of proxemic interaction. Finally, we ask users for their opinion via a preliminary user study and usability test. Our study shows that users are attracted by this kind of interaction, and especially by the application scenario in the lab with a large public screen.

Keywords: Proxemics, Proxemic interaction, Public screen, implicit interaction.

1   Introduction

Proxemics is a psychological concept, which is nonverbal terminology. It is defined as "the interrelated observations and theories of man's use of space as a specialized elaboration of culture". Edward T. Hall [4] identifies two overreaching categories, personal space and territory. He divides the space around a person into four categories - intimate, personal, social and public space, though these partitions could vary according to culture. It should be mentioned that proxemics rely not only on culture but on gender. Researchers found that men encroach frequently on a female's space, while the female is reluctant to "violate" a man's personal space [6]. In recent years, proxemics has been transplanted to artificial intelligence, ubiquitous computing and human computer interactions [2,3,5,7,8]. As a development of ubiquitous computing and computer vision, it is now possible to make computers measure the user's spatial relationship by means of a camera, passive markers or other technologies. Proxemic Interaction (PI) normally considers five factors: distance, orientation, movement, identity of entities, and location of feature [2]. Distance and movement imply the entity's (in this case the user's) intention of interaction. Orientation implies the user's focus of attention. Identity and location are useful contextual information. Location refers to layout of the fixed or semi-fixed features around the proxemics interaction

N. Streitz and C. Stephanidis (Eds.): DAPI/HCII 2013, LNCS 8028, pp. 378–387, 2013.

environment. We could explore many interesting interaction modes with single factor or multi-factor combinations, in particular with the application relating to a public screen [8], as a public screen could be deemed a "virtual" user rather than a passive machine. In this way, we could communicate with a public screen implicitly and naturally, just like we would communicate with another person, instead of explicitly and rigidly commanding "operation" of a machine. A public screen mounted in the public space of the lab (such as a coffee room) or bus shelter is a practical way of exploring PI usability. As there is a diversity of users with different genders, cultures and ages.

We first build the PI model based on a single detector. Then we describe the PI scenario with a public screen in a research lab, and present our prototypes. We end the paper with an analysis for usability tests and our proposal for future work.

2   User's Behavior Model

As aforementioned, PI needs to consider at least five factors. Among them, distance, orientation and movement are base sets to calculate user's proxemics relative to a public screen equipped with a detector. In this case, we abstract 3-dimensional coordinates (Fig. 1): (0, YC, 0) are the coordinates of the screen equipped with detector, YC is the detector height, and (XU, YU, ZU) are the user's coordinates, where YU is the user height. This abstraction is not fine-grained, as it abstracts both user and screen as points. Nevertheless, it is sufficient to calculate the three factors for the spatial relationship. If there is more than one user, we could also add them as points, and calculate their relative positions.

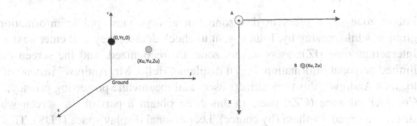

Fig. 1. PI coordinates

The user's movement in front of the screen is continuous. To track the user's movement, we change the user's coordinates from (X_U, Y_U, Z_U) to (X_U, Y_U, Z_U, T_U) where $\{T_U\}$ is the user's time point in one position.

For the same user, $\{Y_U\}$ does not change during interaction. It could be simplified as (X_U, Z_U, T_U): we pick up three points every 2 seconds, then obtain a vector $\overrightarrow{AB} = (X_U, Z_U)$, in which case $\|\overrightarrow{AB}\| = \sqrt{X_U^2 + Z_U^2}$ is the accurate distance of user to screen. Then, with time as one parameter, $\overrightarrow{AB_t} = (X_{Ut}, Z_{Ut}, t)$,

$$\|\overrightarrow{AB_x}\| = \sqrt{X_{Ux}^2 + Y_{Ux}^2}, \; x \in \{t, t+2, t+4\}$$

If $\|\overrightarrow{AB_{t+4}}\| - \|\overrightarrow{AB_{t+2}}\| > \mu$, $\|\overrightarrow{AB_{t+2}}\| - \|\overrightarrow{AB_t}\| > \mu$, the user is walking away from the screen, If $\|\overrightarrow{AB_t}\| - \|\overrightarrow{AB_{t+2}}\| > \mu$, $\|\overrightarrow{AB_{t+2}}\| - \|\overrightarrow{AB_{t+4}}\| > \mu$, the user is approaching. Where μ is a threshold, if it is a small value, PI will be more nimble, otherwise it will be more blunt. With this model, we could calculate the user's position instantly and predict the user's potential movements. However, we do not take orientation into account. For PI with a single screen, orientation is not always necessary.

3   Scenario of Proxemic Interaction on a Public Screen Deployed in a Research Lab

We build an application based on professional life in a research lab (Fig. 2). Just as in our lab, there is a diversity of users, with students from China and France, as well as many potential users from different countries as visitors.

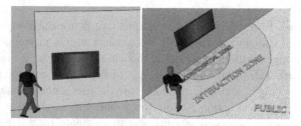

Fig. 2. A public screen in the lab

We divided the space in front of the screen into three partitions, as follows:

- Public zone (PZ): users in this zone can always view public information at a glimpse while passing by. If they want to check details, they will enter next zone;
- Interaction zone (IZ): users in this zone are recognized, and the screen displays limited personal information. E.g. it displays "Hello, Mr. Andrew" instead of "Hello, Jack Andrew": this trick attracts users and meanwhile protecting privacy;
- Confidential zone (CZ): users in this zone obtain a part of the screen which is strictly reserved for them (by choice), i.e. personal display space (PDS). This space displays personal information that the user authorizes to display, and the PDS moves along with the user in front of the screen.

This zone classification is not strict. If we are more concerned with privacy, we could add another zone between IZ and CZ, and vice versa. Except for the proximity features, the screen should also include some other features as follows:

- It is networked. Each member of the lab could update the personal contents via their own computers, and customize the personal information to be displayed.
- It is multi-partition. It could thus be used simultaneously by several users publicly and privately, as well as with simultaneous implicit and explicit interaction.
- It supports multi-person collaborative interaction. Users in CZ involved in collaboration work could easily exchange resources with one another.

Since the screen offers ambient and contextual awareness, we identified six questions to guide interaction design, known as 5W [1] 1H:

1. WHO, who engages in interaction?
2. WHEN, when does the user arrive? And how long does he stay?
3. WHERE, where is the user positioned near the screen?
4. WHAT, what does the user want?
5. WHY, why do users adopt that kind of behavior? Interpret user's activities.
6. HOW, How multi-user interact collaborative with each other? In fact, as we will consider interaction with mobile devices in the future, we need to clarify how users interact with or without mobile devices.

To study how to take the six factors into account, based on discussion in the lab and user study we identified five typical scenarios (Table 1)

Table 1. Scenario Classification

	Morning	Noon	Evening
Single User	1	2	3
Single User in CZ with Others waiting in IZ		4	
Multi-user collaborative interaction in CZ		5	

Scenario 1: a user named Jack ANDREW comes to the lab in the morning, and goes to take a coffee. When he enters the coffee room, he can see the general message from the screen hung on the wall, such as:

- Recent conference call for paper;
- Lab news, such as new publications, lectures or meetings;
- Technology news, related to the domain;
- Status of laboratory members, such as attendance status;
- New ideas shared by others for brainstorming.

Then, if he is interested by the new idea shared by another student, with his coffee, he steps into IZ. More details about each message will be displayed. Meanwhile the screen rapidly recognizes him, and pops up a banner at the bottom of the screen saying "Good Morning, Mr. ANDREW", along with some thumbnails of his personal messages, such as, "you have 7 new e-mails and 1 forthcoming conference".

If he just wants to check the new idea, then he waves this out by gestures, and raises his hand to select and browse details. One moment later, he finishes his coffee, and if he just walks away, the screen will return to the neutral state. Otherwise, if he thinks the idea is fairly interesting and wants to add some comments, then he steps further into the confidential zone.

Once he steps into CZ, a dialog box pops up to ask him whether he wants to be assigned a PDS. If he selects YES, all his personal information that he authorized will be displayed in PDS. Meanwhile, the other parts of the screen continue to be reserved for public information. If he chooses NO, some available operations menus arise surround the "idea" Textbox. He adds comments and sends it to the proposer. Afterwards, he turns back and leaves, and the screen resumes its neutral state.

Scenario 2: Jack comes back at noon, it is now lunch time. He doesn't want to eat in the university canteen today. He decides to eat outside with some friends. He walks directly to the screen IZ, after analyzing his personal tags, "I like sushi, and pasta", then compares with his history: for example, if he ate in an Italian restaurant last time, the screen displays the Japanese restaurant as priority, with the discount information. He could wave his hands to select. Then if he wants to check details, he could just step into CZ, and the details of the selected restaurant would be displayed. He could drag the details into his PDS, and then once he logs in his personal account with his mobile phone, he could view the details, such as the address and telephone number, without bothering to take a photo of the map, or noting anything down. He could invite others by dragging this information to their icons on the screen sidebar.

Scenario 3: Jack finishes his job and wants to leave at 6 pm, he comes back to the screen, and stands in IZ. According to the time, the system infers that he wants to leave for home. Then it checks his history: if he prefers to take the bus every day, it will display the time of the next bus in large text. If he has a car, then the screen will display the traffic information on the map instead of the bus. He does not need to enter the CZ, unless he wants to check the detailed bus timetable. Before leaving, he wants to make an appointment with a professor. So he steps into CZ and clicks the professor's icon, checking when he is available. He just needs to select one idle time, and the screen saves the appointment request automatically. He could also write some remarks and then send them. The professor can read the message once he is in the screen IZ, or he could check this by email as well.

Scenario 4: If Jack is in interaction in CZ, while other users are approaching and waiting in IZ, the size of the PDS assigned to Jack will be reduced to protect privacy, and also save more space for other people receiving messages.

Scenario 5: Multi-users refer to two or more users in CZ. With respect to the lab's practical situation, there are several possibilities according to user roles:

- Two visitors: they are not recognized, so the screen displays public info for them;
- Two members of the lab, who are not familiar friends. This could be inferred by the distance between them. As strangers tend to stand separately. The screen thus assigns two PDSs relatively far from each other in order to respect their privacy.
- Two members of the lab, who are friends. Contrary to the last situation, these two will stand close together, and thus have two PDSs displayed close to each other. Users could also select to merge their PDSs, for easy sharing of some contents.
- One member and one visitor: the screen just displays info related to the member, ranging from general to personal. The visitor will only see the public message.

4   Prototype Evolution of the PI Public Screen in the Lab

We have designed and developed two prototypes: one paper prototype and another low-fidelity PI public screen prototype.

1. PI paper prototype.

This kind of prototype is used to gather users' suggestions prior to development, and for primary usability tests. It is mainly aimed at UI which is displayed to users when they are in CZ. As shown in Figure 3, a is UI when two users who do not know each other stand in CZ simultaneously. On the contrary, b is UI for two users who are well acquainted. Their PDSs are merged for sharing. The UI layout is in large text and graphic. The sidebar contains a list of members in the lab: if they are in the lab, their image will be lightened, if not their image is grey. Urgent messages such as "CALL FOR PAPER" are highlighted in red.

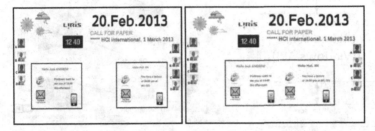

Fig. 3. Paper prototypes for the PI public screen (a b)

2. Double screen prototype.

We simulate two screens (left and right) installed in the airport or railroad station as information boards (Figure 4a). This prototype uses one camera to recognize the user's id, and by ARtoolkit markers to calculate user's distance and orientation to screen. Normally, the information board in the airport displays all the departure flights. Passengers need to run a detailed search to find their flight. In this prototype, when a user equipped with ARToolkit markers approaches this screen sufficiently close, it will only display his flight. And if he turns left, then the next screen located on the left will display the same information, and vice versa. If there are more than two users present, both screens display general flight information to protect privacy. We also designed another interface (Figure 4b).This is an overview of a user's agenda and a proximity bar, which indicates the user's distance from the screen.

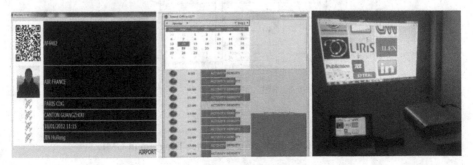

Fig. 4. Low fidelity prototype (from left to right a b c)

3. Single screen prototype.

Based on the first two prototypes, we found that ARToolkit markers are not ideal for detecting the user's position, as they are extremely sensitive to light conditions. Some testers are annoyed by the additional markers. Also, a two-screen prototype is not necessary for the lab for the time being. As a result, we have reduced the prototype to one screen (Fig 4c), optimized the framework, and designed a Web UI (Fig 5).

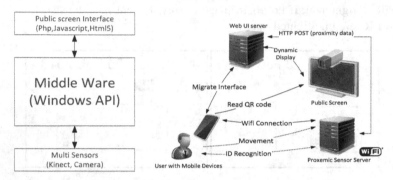

Fig. 5. Framework of the PI public screen (a b)

Figure 5a shows the overall structure of the prototype: we use two sensors, kinect for user position measurement, and camera for ID recognition by face. The Windows API is middleware which processes data acquired from sensors, and converts them to operation commands. Figure 5b shows workflows for single user interaction, mobile devices interact and backstage processing, distinguished by line pattern. UML sequence diagram of two users (correspondence to scenario 5) as illustrated in Figure 6.

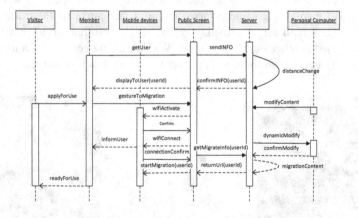

Fig. 6. Two users' interaction Sequence Diagram in UML

The prototype defines three interaction modalities by three aforementioned zones.

- Users in PZ could only see general information from the projected screen, and they will not be recognized.
- Users in IZ could be recognized if they are members of the lab, and both members and visitors could interact with the screen by gestures, up to 8 types. Authorized users operate the UI elements easily, as illustrated in figure 7. It should be noted that the same gestures made by users in different zones imply different operations, e.g. if users in CZ stretch out their arms, this implies zooming out the UI, while if users in IZ make the same gesture, this implies zooming in the UI. Also, if the user is editing a presentation file in a public screen (like PPT), if he moves backwards from IZ to PZ, the presentation will be automatically played, and the user could control the play sequence by waving his arm to the left or right. Then, if the user returns to the CZ, the presentation will exit the play mode, and allow the user to edit it manually.
- Users in CZ are allowed to interact directly with the screen. Users in this zone could acquire their PDSs. Also, the screen will return the user's personal contents to him. For this aspect, we do not develop a high-fidelity prototype. We combine the paper prototype and graphical Wizard-of -Oz prototyping to illustrate how it works.

Fig. 7. Proxemics gesture interaction in IZ

5   Usability Test and Results Analysis

Once the first stage of the prototype was developed, we organized usability tests. We invited 10 volunteers, 3 of which are engineering students from our school, 4 are Chinese PhD students in the HCI domain, and 1 is a student from another university who is learning French. 1 student is from another city in France, who is also a PhD student but in a very different field: she is invited to conduct a remote user study. The last student is a French PhD student from our lab. Age ranges from 20 to 29, with 6 men and 4 women.

Our test is not dedicated to test robustness of the low-fidelity prototype, but rather to test usability and novelty, as these generate useful feedback for further research. We designed three test steps as follows,

1. First, we explained the idea of PI to testers, and narrated the scenario: they are allowed to interrupt and ask questions, their questions are recorded.
2. Secondly, the user steps into IZ, and his/her ID is recognized. The system displays his/her name on the screen, after which the user is required to experience the PI by a simple game, i.e. via movement to control the cartoon character in the game, forward and backward. Then, the user is asked to browse the publication paper of the lab, and zoom in or out to change the size of the text, and adapt it for optimum comfort.
3. Lastly, the user stands in CZ, and interacts explicitly with the screen. While interaction with the touch screen is expected in the high-fidelity prototype, this is merely a primary usability test. Hence we merely ask the user to give commands, while the experimenter acting as a wizard simulates computer interaction with the paper prototype, and the UI shifts along with the user's movement in front of the screen. Additionally, we design an adaptive UI, allowing users to migrate UI to their device by reading QR code. Users could experience the UI migration from the public screen to their mobile devices.

On completion of the test, we asked the users to fill out a questionnaire. From Figure 8, we can conclude that our prototype is good at usability, as users are impressed by the PI: someone said "it's cool to control a computer from such a distance". And they also satisfied by the rapid response to their movement. However, they always complain about ID recognition, as it too easily recognizes them as another person. Also, when they try to migrate UI to their devices, the steps are somewhat tedious. Opinions vary as well: for example, one user said it's more convenient for their devices to connect to the public screen automatically with no code, while another user said he was worried about leaking his personal info by connecting to the public WiFi Hotspot even there is a code.

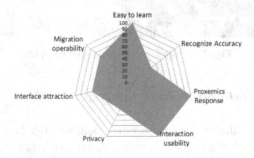

Fig. 8. Usability Test result

In addition to Figure 8, we also collected many useful suggestions from remote user studies and records during testing. We selected several suggestions as follows:

- Gestures should be natural: for example, some testers are not used to scrolling down the text using the "stretch out arm" gesture, as the feeling of rolling down something is more like waving hands down rather than raising the arm straight forward.

- The design needs to avoid maloperation: for example, when the user moves his/her hand trying to select an UI element, if his/her arm is across the center of the body, it could trigger another action by error.
- The prototype should offer some contents for entertainment, especially when the user comes in at noon or the evening, as he/she might be tired of work and just want to find something for relaxing from the screen.

6   Conclusion and Future Work

In this paper, we described Proxemic Interaction and built the user's behavior model, explaining how to analyze users' proxemic behavior while interacting with public screens. We propose that gender and emotion be considered as factors of PI study, as these are two key signs when people communicate with each other. We then apply the PI to the public screen, aiming at the research life in the lab. This is an attractive and practical topic, as well as a good means of exploring the application of this novel interaction. Through user studies and usability tests, we found that users are curious about this kind of interaction, and they made many useful suggestions. With respect to future work, we will consider possible ways of creating gender difference PIs and personalizing interaction modals to men and women, as well as PIs with consideration of emotion differences. By computer vision, to determine users' moods from their expression or even wear color, and finally design entire multi-user collaborative interaction modalities, along with development of high-fidelity prototype and usability tests.

References

1. Abowd, G.D., Mynatt, E.D.: Charting Past, Present, and Future Research in Ubiquitous Computing. ACM Transactions on Computer-Human Interaction (TOCHI) 7(1), 29–58 (2000)
2. Greenberg, S., Marquardt, N., Ballendat, T., Diaz-Marino, R., Wang, M.: Prox-emic Interactions: The New Ubicomp? Interactions 18(1), 42–50 (2011)
3. Harrison, C., Dey, A.K.: Lean and Zoom: Proximity-aware User Interface and Content Magnification. In: Proceedings of the Twenty-sixth Annual SIGCHI Conference on Human Factors in Computing Systems, pp. 507–510 (2008)
4. Hall, E.T.: The Hidden Dimension. Anchor Books (1966) ISBN 0-385-08476-5
5. Ju, W., Lee, B.A., Klemmer, S.R.: Range: Exploring Implicit Interaction Through Electronic Whiteboard Design. In: Proceedings of the 2008 ACM Conference on Computer Supported Cooperative Work, pp. 17–26 (2008)
6. Madden, S.J.: Proxemics and Gender: Where's the Spatial Gap. North Dakota Journal of Speech & Theatre 12, 41–46 (1999)
7. Marquardt, N., Greenberg, S.: Informing the Design of Proxemic Iteractions. IEEE Pervasive Computing 11(2), 14–23 (2012)
8. Vogel, D., Balakrishnan, R.: Interactive Public Ambient Displays: Transitioning from Implicit to Explicit, Public to Personal, Interaction with Multiple Users. In: Proceedings of the 17th Annual ACM Symposium on User Interface Software and Technology, UIST 2004, pp. 137–146. ACM, New York (2004)
9. Xu, T., Jin, H., David, B., Chalon, R., Zhou, Y.: A Context-aware Middleware for Interaction Devices Deployment in AmI. In: HCI International 2013, Las Vegas (2013)

Context-of-Interest Driven Trans-Space Convergence for Spatial Co-presence

Hyeongmook Lee, Taejin Ha, Seungtak Noh, and Woontack Woo

UVR Lab., Graduate School of Culture Technology, KAIST, S.Korea
{hmooklee,taejinha,stnoh,wwoo}@kaist.ac.kr

Abstract. In this paper, we propose a Trans-Space convergence system that exploits realistic 3D remote collaboration with spatial co-presence by using augmented reality technology. To experience it, we define two major enabling technologies: 1) Context-of-Interest (CoI) based Trans-Space registration and selective augmentation and 2) augmented object interaction for realistic collaboration. Through these technologies, a user wearing augmented reality (AR) glasses can naturally experience remote collaboration with spatial co-presence while moving in space. We implemented a prototype of the Trans-Space for a preliminary test experiencing spatial co-presence in an indoor environment. With an assumption that a common physical CoI is in each space, a distant mirror space can be conveniently linked with real user's mirror space and they are merged together as a Trans-Space. Through the proposed convergence system, a human's co-presence experience can be enlarged by selectively context sharing and effectively spatial interaction between remote mirror spaces. We expect this is applicable to AR-based time/space transcended smart applications, such as the next generation of experimental education, training, medical surgery, and entertainment.

Keywords: Context-of-Interest, Trans-Space, augmented reality, spatial co-presence.

1 Introduction

With the development of communications technology, a variety of systems is coming to experience real-time co-presence among people in remote places. The co-presence, which is a similar concept to sense of co-location, is defined as "feeling being together with other people" or "extent of being at the same place with others" in interaction through medium [1]. It can feel in a situation of real-time communication through human sensible elements. As for technically supporting this, the voice telephone is the representative real-time co-presence supporting system focusing communication of auditory sense. The video telephone and tele-conference system provide better immersiveness by delivering both auditory and visual sense on 2D display.

Using Virtual Reality (VR) and Augmented Reality (AR) techniques offers the great possibility of going through more realistic co-presence. It easily supports the enabling of 3D visualization and interaction, compared with the system that only

N. Streitz and C. Stephanidis (Eds.): DAPI/HCII 2013, LNCS 8028, pp. 388–395, 2013.

enables sitting or staring in front of a 2D display. It means that the spatial characteristic in co-presence is strengthened in remote communications. As state of the art, TeleHuman [2] is a VR system that provides non-verbal communication with a distant user using cylindrical display. It captures multi-view images of the user by using multiple RGB-D cameras for realistic viewing and visualizes a life-size 3D human model on the cylindrical display. Therefore, a user around the display is able to see the figure of the distant user at all viewpoints except up and down. In addition, MirageTable [3] is a projection based AR tabletop system using RGB-D cameras that allows one-to-one remote interaction. In real-time, it brings a small area that is covered by the same tabletop installation, including a remote user, and objects it on the table. For better user visual experience, the system provides rough user-head tracking using the user's glasses in-depth image and correcting 3D perspective views.

However, there are some limitations in existing co-presence supported systems using VR and AR technologies. Specifically, one is that cost and space demands for system construction are considerable, relative to the co-presence experience in implemented tele-communication systems. Furthermore, it is hard to provide realistic collaborative interaction maintaining spatial co-presence. These restrictions were found in the above-mentioned two recent systems. TeleHuman requires five PCs and ten RGB-D cameras for one-to-one video conferencing with 640 x 480-pixel quality on cylindrical display. IN addition, direct interaction between a real user around the display and a distant user on the display is impossible, whereas life-size rendering looks user-friendly. In the case of MirageTable, it enables the construction of the environment for experiencing co-presence with relatively less effort with a few devices, but it takes account of one-to-one user situations sharing objects on a small table. Therefore, it is necessary to cover the spatial co-presence considering the wider space and user movement for more realistic remote collaboration with multiple user support. In this paper, we suggest Context-of-Interest (CoI) driven Trans-Space convergence that coexist a real user and a remote user in each physical indoor space to physical identical space. Here, CoI is defined as an interested context about any information that characterizes a user situation. The situation is tightly coupled with relationships for the interaction between user, application, object, location, and so on [4]. The CoI driven Trans-Space convergence technology provides user-appropriated virtual information selectively to physical 3D space and supports realistic collaboration interaction experiencing spatial co-presence. To achieve this, we first suggest CoI based Trans-Space registration and selective augmentation for reducing the burden in implementation on tele-communication systems and filtering the less relevant information. Furthermore, based on spatial AR technology, we put on augmented object interaction methods for better remote collaboration.

This paper includes the following content: the Trans-Space convergence and phased approach are introduced in Section 2. In Section 3, the technical details of enabling technologies are explained. Section 4 introduces the initial implementation results of the Trans-Space convergence system. Finally, we conclude this paper in Section 5.

2   Trans-Space Convergence

The goal of Trans-Space convergence system is to support remote collaboration with co-presence, including social presence that allows users to overcome time/space restrictions and share information, knowledge, and mood. Conceptually, the Trans-Space, to transcend space, means a newly linked space across the remote spaces. It technically indicates an extended dual-space, which each corresponding mirrored space of each remote user is merged into a single space. Here, the dual-space is a set of real spaces where the user is and mirror space information included corresponding to the real space [5]. In dual-space, based on the referenced CoI (e.g. origin of space), it is necessary to coordinate localization between the CoIs in real space for tracking and the CoIs in mirror space for rendering.

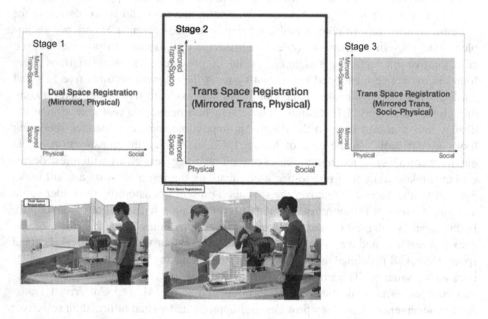

Fig. 1. Phased approach toward Trans-Space convergence

To achieve our Trans-space concept effectively, we planned a phase approach considering the scale of the registration space and manageable target CoI, as shown in Fig. 1. The objective of stage 1 is CoI-based, real-time, dual-space registration to robust under environmental changes. In this step, the main research is to enable robust real-time registration constructing a single space into a dual-space [6][7]. Based on this, the user is able to interact directly or indirectly with trackable and augmented CoIs in the space and visualizes virtual information stably on the space [8][9][10].

At stage 2, the goal is real-time, one-to-multi, semantic space convergence supporting spatial co-presence focused on this paper. From stage 1, we considered how to make a dual-space with a real space and the corresponding mirror space, so we know the agreement of different coordinates and the scale of two spaces. By using the key technology, we focused on realizing the trans-space convergence, in which multiple mirror spaces from remote distances come into single extended dual-space. Through the trans-space, a user in any position of registered real space is able to call remote people naturally and do collaborative interaction with them realistically. Beyond stage 2, CoI-based self-evolutionary Trans-Space convergence supported realistic collaboration among multiple users for stage 3. In this stage, we enlarge the manageable CoI to social factors, including user's sensitivity and emotion. This is the forward key to overcome time/space restriction and make co-presence more sociable.

3   Enabling Technologies

There are two key technologies to achieve CoI-driven Trans-Space convergence for spatial co-presence, as shown in Fig. 2. First is CoI-based Trans-Space registration and selective augmentation that allows users to overcome the restriction between heterogeneous spaces. Second, under the registered Trans-Space environment, augmented object interaction is meaningful and feasible for realistic collaboration.

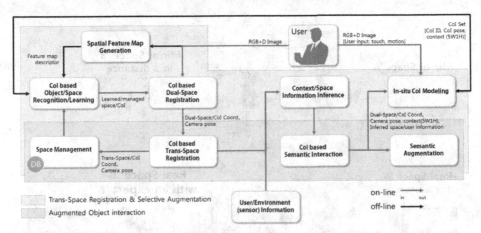

Fig. 2. An overall procedure for Trans-Space convergence (stage 2)

3.1   CoI Based Trans-Space Registration and Selective Augmentation

For real-time and robust Trans-Space registration, we need to figure out a novel spatial feature map that describes strong scene features by systematically exploiting color and depth information. Therefore, it overcomes troublesome vision issues, such as textureless, poor lighting conditions, multiple deformable moving objects, and heterogeneous image devices, in usage of color information only. By capturing and learning various contexts from space, the range of recognition, detection, and tracking is expanded to space domains from object domains. This helps reduce the redundancy for real-time processing so the system might cover wider areas containing lots of CoIs than existing stationary interaction areas (e.g. screen, table, etc.) and elevates users' movement. In addition, this semantic approach enables selective augmentation, focusing user-interested CoIs on all accessible CoIs.

Fig. 3 illustrates an overview of the registration and selective augmentation process for two real spaces with concept drawings. At first, there is a real space 'A' for normal users. The mirror space 'A' can be created by using dual-space registration beforehand and updated on real-time (we called this 'Mirroring'). Then every user who carries a camera and display in space 'A' might interact with tracked physical CoIs and annotated virtual CoIs. Equally, there is a real space 'B' for expert users to distant space. Different from space 'A', the user 'b' and trackable CoIs of the real space 'B' are monitored by the environmental camera system.

In this context, if there is a common physical CoI in both spaces 'A' and 'B', a user 'a' in space 'A' is ready to call the expert 'b' in distant space 'B' and the expert helps him on the spatial co-presence. According to collaborative situations, like teaching, training, or maintaining, Trans-Space is selectively converged with virtual CoIs by contextual requests and filter techniques. Because all of the CoIs do not need to account for visualization at a time, selective sharing of CoIs is required, reflecting user, environment, and event for maintaining real-time performance and effective collaboration.

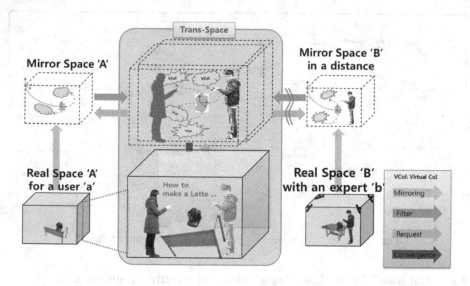

Fig. 3. CoI based Trans-Space registration with relation among real and mirror spaces

3.2   Augmented Object Interaction for Realistic Collaboration

Using Registered Trans-Space, the users between real and remote users enable 3D collaborative interaction. In case of the real users, they experience a seamless interaction with trackable physical CoIs or shared virtual CoIs. For this, we need real-time integrated coordinates management that localizes two independent coordinate systems, physical CoIs and virtual CoIs, to a Trans-Space coordinate system that has the same origin. With similar approaches, it is possible for real-time remote collaboration with distant space. Based on a common physical CoI, we are able to localize and augment distant CoIs, including remote users into real space. Therefore, stably shared CoIs on real-time 3D detection and tracking are easy to manipulate directly and indirectly with the modeled user's hand or sensor-rich mobile devices for realistic collaboration.

4   Implementation

We implemented a prototype of the Trans-Space convergence as a preliminary test in an indoor environment. With the assumption that a common physical CoI is in each space, its mirror world can be conveniently combined together. Specifically, our system captures an environment's images, including CoIs, with an HMD camera and computes image feature-maps for the CoIs in real time [11]. Then, local reference coordinates allocated on the CoI register the corresponding mirrored world and the other mirrored worlds from distant space for the Trans-Space convergence.

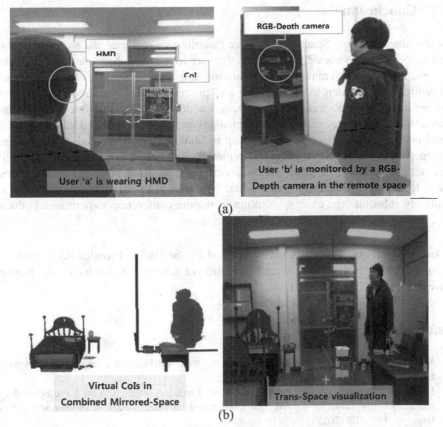

Fig. 4. Implementation of the trans-Space convergence: (a) our test-bed where two users are apart from each other; (b) virtual CoIs in the mirrored-space are registered in the Trans-Space.

Afterward, mirrored worlds are registered, and some of the virtual content can be shared and shown in an HMD view. In addition, humans in remote environments can be augmented by detecting and segmenting humans with a RGB-D depth camera, and then transmit texture data of the human to the mirrored world [12].

Considering the apparatus, a binocular video see-through HMD was used with 800 × 600 pixel resolution. A camera attached on the HMD captured 30 image frames per second with 640 × 480 pixel resolution. A RGB-Depth camera on the stand was used to detect and segment a remote user. A portable computer in the user's backpack executed CoIs based on mirror world registration, camera pose tracking, and visualization.

As a result, Fig. 4 (a) shows the test-bed. User 'a', who is wearing HMD in space 'A' can see the user 'b' captured from other space 'B'. Fig. 4 (b) shows the shared virtual CoIs, including live 3D models of user 'b' registered in the mirrored world and the HMD view of user 'a'.

5   Conclusion

We introduced a Trans-Space convergence that allows a real user and a remote user in each indoor space to coexist so they feel they are together in the same place. To enable this, a CoI-based Trans-Space registration and selective augmentation was used for reducing the burden in constructing and processing a tele-collaboration system. Toward a semantic AR, a novel feature map is addressed for real-time registration and management in complex environmental changes and massive spatial data. In addition, based on the spatial AR using feature map technology, an augmented object interaction method is introduced for realistic remote collaboration. The enabling technologies can be applicable to many AR collaborative applications. We expect the Trans-Space technology will enhance the spatial co-presence in most remote scenarios so positively substitute the existing solution in remote conference, experimental education, simulation, medical surgery, and entertainment.

Acknowledgments. This work was supported by the Global Frontier R&D Program on funded by the National Research Foundation of Korea grant funded by the Korean Government(MSIP) (NRF-2010-0029751).

References

1. Mason, R.: Using Communications Media in Open and Flexible Learning. Kogan page, London (1994)
2. Benko, H., Jota, R., Wilson, A.: MirageTable: Freehand Interaction on a Projected Augmented Reality Tabletop. In: SIGCHI Conference on Human Factors in Computing Systems, pp. 199–208 (2012)
3. Kim, K., Bolton, J., Girouard, A., Cooperstock, J., Vertegaal, R.: TeleHuman: Effects of 3D perspective on gaze and pose estimation with a life-size cylindrical telepresence pod. In: SIGCHI Conference on Human Factors in Computing Systems, pp. 2531–2540 (2012)

4. Oh, Y., Woo, W.: Linking Functionality for Ubiquitous Virtual Reality. In: 7th ISUVR, pp. 50–52 (2012)
5. Ha, T., Lee, H., Woo, W.: DigiLog Space: Real-time Dual Space Registration and Dynamic Information Visualization for 4D+ Augmented Reality. In: 7th ISUVR, pp. 22–25 (2012)
6. Ha, T., Woo, W.: ARWand for an Augmented World Builder. In: The IEEE Symposium on 3D User Interfaces (in press, 2013)
7. Kim, H., Reitmayr, G., Woo, W.: IMAF: In-situ Indoor Modeling and Annotation Framework on Mobile Phones. In: PUC (2012) (online published)
8. Kim, K., Lepetit, V., Woo, W.: Keyframe-based modeling and tracking of multiple 3D objects. In: ISMAR, pp. 193–198 (2010)
9. Park, Y., Lepetit, V., Woo, W.: Texture-Less Object Tracking with Online Training using An RGB-D Camera. In: ISMAR, pp. 121–126 (2011)
10. Kang, C., Woo, W.: ARMate: An Interactive AR Character Responding to Real Objects. Edutainment, 12–19 (2011)
11. Gil, K., Ha, T., Woo, W.: DigiLog Space Generator for Tele-collaboration in an Augmented Reality Environment. In: Schumaker, R. (ed.) VAMR/HCII 2013, Part I. LNCS, vol. 8021, pp. 343–350. Springer, Heidelberg (2013)
12. Kim, J., Ha, T., Woo, W., Shi, C.: Enhancing Social Presence in Augmented Reality-Based Telecommunication System. In: Schumaker, R. (ed.) VAMR/HCII 2013, Part I. LNCS, vol. 8021, pp. 359–367. Springer, Heidelberg (2013)

The New Communication Interface to Determine the Lifespan of Digital Information

Sooyeon Maeng and Bong-Gwan Jun

Graduate School of Culture Technology
Korea Advanced Institute of Science and Technology (KAIST)
373-1 Guseong-dong, Yuseong-gu, Daejeon 305-701, Republic of Korea
(secret-bless,junbg)@kaist.ac.kr

Abstract. In cyber space, freedom of self-expression prevails and millions of people enjoy the benefit of this right. Unfortunately, sometimes this privilege is taken for granted and what was written casually in the past remains permanently online and later becomes a label that marks one's identity. This enduring characteristic of online data stored in a form of digital information is known as digital eternity. In this paper, we will introduce a system which overcomes the limitations of digital eternity by using volatile messages that will leave no trace online. This system ensures freedom of expression and reduces regrets of past posting in online space. As a result, it was found that the digital eternity is a potential psychological threat which suppresses freedom of expression and the use of volatile messages reduces the burden and encourages greater degree of freedom.

Keywords: Social Network System, Digital Eternity, Digital Communication, Volatile Message, Communication Interface, Lifespan of Digital Information.

1 Introduction

Could there really be a Lifespan in digital information? If one publishes contents in the form of digital information in the online space, it would remain inside the online pages and servers until they are deleted. Even if the original postings are removed, the same contents are going to remain somewhere online as a result of copying, rewriting, sharing, retweeting and searching through bots. We refer to this concept as "Digital Eternity." Digital Eternity is an ongoing problem caused by outflow of personal information, invasion of privacy, suppression of freedom of expression, and strict self-censorship. For example, personal information or location data posted on a social network service (SNS) can easily be accessible by the public, and this can be wrongfully used. Furthermore, postings written in the past can have negative influence in the present. For example, one can either get in big trouble or even get fired by having posted his/her personal opinions or strong feelings related to certain subject that the company might view as inappropriate.

These kinds of stories have become social issues in the actuality, and people started to have psychological obstacles when dealing with online communication. When people communicate orally in an everyday life setting, we do take responsibility for

N. Streitz and C. Stephanidis (Eds.): DAPI/HCII 2013, LNCS 8028, pp. 396–404, 2013.

our own actions. However, in the online space, it is hard to determine the extent of someone's responsibility for that person's past postings because it is hard to determine and trace the contents that the person posted in the past and even that person cannot remember everything that he/she has posted.

The governmental regulation was the only way to solve this kind of problems. Companies around the world are forced to delete personal information, if people wish to do so, and that includes past postings. However, legal regulations have their own limits because they cannot cover all the areas. Each one of the cases is unique in its own ways, so it is difficult to generalize them. Therefore, a new communication platform is needed in order to fundamentally overcome the problems due to digital eternity.

In this study, volatile message interface provides people the flexibility to adjust the time of their postings by manually indicating the lifespan of their postings. Volatile message interface is a new communication interface which can be applied to the online space. People can set the lifespan (the period that the digital information remains in the online space) of their writing contents before they actually post them. By setting the lifespan of digital information in advance, people can take responsibility for up to that specific timeframe. After the pre-set time, the post will be deleted permanently from the server and the online space.

In this study, whether volatile message interface can reduce problems due to digital eternity has been verified.

2   Background

Digital eternity is an idea that the digital information entered through online cannot be erased permanently. Now, with rapid development of search engines, online contents can spread in the blink of an eye. Thus what one writes on a blog remains not just on the website but also appears on portals and other people's blogs who have forwarded the post. There are related researches concerning privacy problems regarding online profiles [1] and social suppression of 'fresh start' [2].

Defects of this digital eternity are amplified as a social network service (SNS) has turned into a space for self-expression in the cyber world. SNS is a web-based service that supports constructing individual profiles, sharing connections between people and interactions established upon those connections [3, 4]. Users of SNS like Facebook and Twitter expose their thoughts and daily lives to friends and strangers. It is possible to find out when and whereabouts of the person and what he or she is thinking only by following one's SNS posts [5, 6]. According to Acquisti and Gross [1, 7] who studied privacy problems regarding SNS, people are tremendously anxious about strangers discover where they live, what classes they are taking or what kind of relationships they have. Despite these worries, people do not stop expressing themselves on SNS.

Detriments of digital eternity are not just limited to privacy concerns. JF Blanchette [8] has commented that private information programmed through online not only causes privacy problems but it also takes away a second chance for those who want to start over. Digital eternity threatens the 'right to be forgotten.' Gandy [9] describes 'rights to be forgotten' as follows:

"[t]he right to be forgotten, to become anonymous, and to make a fresh start by destroying almost all personal information, is as intriguing as it is extreme. It should be possible to call for and to develop relationships in which identification is not required and in which records are not generated. For a variety of reasons, people have left home, changed their identities, and begun their lives again. If the purpose is non-fraudulent, is not an attempt to escape legitimate debts and responsibilities, then the formation of new identities is perfectly consistent with the notions of autonomy I have discussed." (Gandy 1993, p. 285)

Debates on obligation of 'rights to be forgotten' in online space is at a developmental stage and it is illuminated as the influence of SNS expands. There are instances that prove the need for 'rights to be forgotten' and to overcome digital eternity. Not long ago, there was a huge controversy over a Korean singer, Jay Park, who posted an unfavorable comment towards Koreans on MySpace in 2005. The comment was revealed by one netizen and was issued four years later when he gained fame after he debuted as a member of an idol group, 2PM. Although his writing was on par with any ordinary teenagers of his age, the public was outrageous and demanded his expulsion from the group. Because of the few lines written long ago perhaps with no intention to offense, Jay Park lost his job and had to leave Korea [10]. On May, 2001, one female Korean sports reporter committed a suicide once her postings on Twitter about her private love affairs and feelings were issued and drew negative attention from the public [11]. She removed her writing shortly after she posted it, but it was too late to take back what had been already retweeted, spread and lingered somewhere online. These incidents reflect that expressing one's thoughts or conversations with someone through SNS could be as threatening as publicly exposed personal information.

3   Methodology

We suggest a system called 'BunnyBurnit for Facebook' which uses a volatile message system that can overcome the limitations of digital eternity. This interface has been applied to social network services, which have a lot of privacy issues, in order to find out what kind of effects it might have on them. The problem with the SNS is that when people post on them, they tend to overlook the things that can happen to them in the future. They just post something on impulse quite often. As part of the experiment, a volatile message interface, as Facebook application, was released to the public. Then the major focus was on the postings that people wrote; whether they were dangerous to publish if they continuously remained in the online space.

3.1   BunnyBurnit for Facebook

BunnyBurnit for Facebook is a tool that can implement the existing communication system. It is a volatile message system which enables the sender to set the burn time of their digital messages. After the fixed amount of time programmed by the user, the message is burned out, erased and gone forever from the cyberspace. Application of this system to the social network service is the 'BunnyBurnit Facebook App'. By using this app, users can set the burn time of their posting from 1 second to 3 days and the countdown begins right from the time it is posted. The message itself and all relevant postings are erased after the set amount of time including the actions of other users – Share, Comment or Like it.

Fig. 1. Main page of 'BunnyBurnit for Facebook'

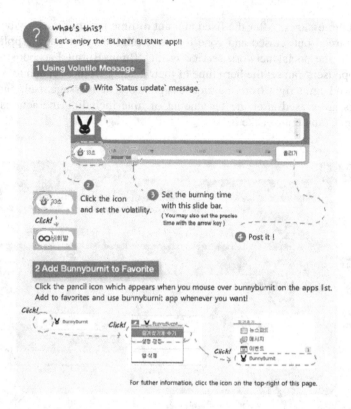

Fig. 2. How to use volatile message interface from the 'BunnyBurnit for Facebook'

3.2   Data Analysis

We have allowed the users to freely play with the 'BunnyBurnit for Facebook' application from October 3rd 2012 to January 3rd 2013. We examined the contents of the volatile messages to see how people used the volatile messages for what purpose. Then we matched the contents of the user postings to test whether volatile messages could overcome the digital eternity. According to Wang[12], people tend to regret posting about the issues regarding drinking, sex, religion and politics, work and colleagues, family, close friends, lies and secrets.

3.3   Interviews

We interviewed ten people who have used the 'BunnyBurnit for Facebook' application. The interview was conducted on January 18th, 2013, and the interviewees were active Facebook users in mid-twenties (6 male participants, 4 female participants). The interview questions included 'do you have any negative experience caused by your past SNS postings? What kind of posting was it?' and 'What do you think about setting a 'lifespan' upon your postings?

4   Results

The interview result below marked the interviewees as P# to protect their personal information. In the data analysis, we only show the contents of the data without specification of the participants.

4.1   Instances using volatile messages

There were total 467 people who used the 'BunnyBurnit for Facebook' application and among them, 268 were males and 199 were females. Total number of postings through the application was 1795. There were 29 non-volatile postings and 1666 volatile postings. The contents of the postings by using the volatile message interface are explained in the Table 1. The users tend to set their postings volatile when they wanted to talk about strictly private issues such as their sexuality, work stress and affairs. These volatile messages included postings such as 'I'm gay,' 'I won't let you get away with it, customers' or 'why have I dated with only bad guys?' Also, people used volatile messages to criticize or slander others, express strong emotional feelings or political stance.

Table 1. Instances using volatile messages

Issue	Number of Volatile messages
Drinking	8
Sex	39
Religion and Politics	104
Work and Colleagues	577
Family	12
Close friends	221
Lies and Secrets	523
Common	182

4.2   Necessity of 'Volatile Message System' and Participants Consent on Its Concept

The participants overall agreed with the idea that digital eternity hinders freedom of expression and communication and they had experienced anxiety because of that. Perceived danger on digital eternity varied widely from violation of privacy to simple emotional expression and conversation with acquaintances. Some participants confessed that they had experienced either direct or vicarious anxiety and been damaged by their writings in online space in the past. In fact, there were participants who attempted to erase their former writings online because they did not want to leave trails in cyber space and the potential negative repercussions the writings might cause in the future:

- "I'm worried about exchanging my personal information like a bank account. I think it would be easier for me to upload my information if it doesn't leave a trail." [P5]
- "There are instances I have to give my private information like my phone number or social security number but it's disturbing. I don't even leave my student account unless it has an anonymous feature. You can google it anyway. Actually, I don't even trust anonymous writing since it will remain somewhere." [P8]
- "It's uncomfortable to scribble things that other people can see. I write things privately so only I could have an access. It feels weird like I'm having a soliloquy." [P1]
- "There are people who reveal their political preferences on Facebook but it's discomforting that those comments remain. People who write about it are careless but I personally don't show any political preferences on Facebook." [P6]
- "There are cases you have to leave your email address when you share an 'illegal data.' Imagine long time later when someone googles my email address for a job interview and if my thread appears then... ouch!" [P4]
- "I sometimes jot down meaningless stuff on Facebook or Blogs and later when I read them again, they were too lame and embarrassing so I erased them. If my writings are volatile then there's no need to erase them. How convenient!" [P2]
- "I used to erase all the photos in my blog every year when I was in high school. I did not want other people to remember my past." [P9]
- "I have to be aware of what other people are thinking when I write things online so I think it's a good idea that my messages are volatile. There are times when I talk about people who are in the same space. One time I was working on a group project and it was quite painstaking so I tried to talk to my friends but since there were other group members so it was difficult to talk to my friend. I was too stressed out and I had to release it somewhere but I couldn't..." [P10]
- "Once I uploaded my family pictures on SNS and my wife asked me to delete them. There were instances when I posted other people's pictures and was asked to erase them." [P7]
- "From the infamous Jay Park incident I learned that I should not just write any things on SNS. One professor once said 'what you write without offense might haunt you back so be careful.' I totally agree with him." [P3]

4.3   Self-expression and Communication in 'BunnyBurnit for Facebook'

Furthermore, we wanted to know the users' psychological difference when using volatile and nonvolatile messages. In addition, we asked the participants to answer what they feel about the system how they would use 'BunnyBurnit for Facebook.':

- "There's definitely a psychological difference in writing volatile and nonvolatile messages. I could write without any burdens when using volatile messages." [P6]
- "It is essential when sending my bank account or social security number." [P2]

- "I think it could be used in inappropriate relationships or cheating on your boy-friend/girlfriend. Also it could be used in slandering and backstabbing others." [P3]
- "Important messages like an appointment should be remained. But situations like when friends are talking about going to a trip together, the procedure won't be necessary. If we could ignite all the words except the conclusion, it would be simpler and more meaningful." [P9]
- "Good thing about a telephone is that you have to pay attention to what the other is saying. With this system, people will pay more attention to the conversation since the words are volatile and the ignition time is not long." [P7]
- "This system is similar to a voice chat. Words spoken cannot be retrieved. I think it is similar to a verbal communication because of this characteristic." [P8]

5   Conclusion and Discussion

Cyberspace has provided the important communicative agora for free speech while at the same time this virtual place has also become the colosseum of conflicts over violating public privacy. Particularly, prevalence of digital eternity, the concept that contents once programmed online cannot be erased permanently, has begotten serious problems. Frequently, there have been incidents when public figures had gotten into trouble due to their online postings, comments and threads from the past. Ordinary people cannot be free from being targeted by this increasing fear of digital eternity. Company administrators admitted that they often trace the job applicants' online record and take it into consideration in the selection process because they believe online data reveals more genuine side of their applicants. Moreover, some people were fired from their job due to their supposedly private comments about their boss or the company.

In this paper, we wanted to show that people freely express themselves and communicate with others without the fear of their past online postings through the volatile message system. We applied this interface to Facebook to analyze the users' behaviors. As a result, by using this volatile message system, people posted more freely about the issues that they normally were afraid to talk openly about. The participants answered that they fear digital eternity and therefore were unwilling to express themselves freely because most of them have negative experiences regarding their past postings online. Through this experiment, we discovered a possibility that the volatile message can relieve the restraints on freedom of expression online caused by the remnants of their previous postings.

There are some limitations to this research. We could not examine the length of the lifespan and the relations between the contents and also we were unable to examine the degree of self-regulation in normal SNS postings. These issues need to be studied in the future research.

'Volatile Message System' can be used as a public arena for discussing controversial and delicate issues such as political disputes or social affairs. Also it could be used as descent protective device in a situation for exchanging private information like one's personal profile, bank account, and GPS. Moreover, online advertisements littering the websites can be reduced tremendously. In future research, it would be meaningful to apply 'Volatile Message System' in various situations to study human behavior and psychology.

Acknowledgments. Thanks to KAIST Graduate School of Culture Technology Communicative Interaction Lab members for their infinite support and encouragement.

References

1. Acquisti, A., Gross, R.: Imagined communities:awareness, information sharing and privacy protection on the Facebook. In: Danezis, G., Golle, P. (eds.) PET 2006. LNCS, vol. 4258, pp. 36–58. Springer, Heidelberg (2006)
2. Westin, A.F., Baker, M.A.: Data Banks in a Free Society. Quadrangle Books A. F. Westin, New York (1972); Social and Political Dimensions of Privacy. Journal of Social Issues 59(2), 431–453 (2003)
3. Boyd, D.M., Ellison, N.B.: Social Network Sites : Definition, History, and Scholarship. Journal of Computer-Mediated Communication 13, 210–230 (2007)
4. Boyd, D.: Friends, Friendsters, and My-Space Top 8 : Writing Community Into Being on Social Network Sites. First Monday 11(12) (2006)
5. Young, A.L., Quan-Haase, A.: Information revelation and internet privacy concerns on social network sites: a case study of Facebook. In: Proceedings of the 4th International Conference on Communities and Technologies (C&T), University Park, PA, USA, pp. 265–274 (June 2009)
6. Boyd, D., Heer, J.: Profiles as conversations: networked identity on Friendster. In: Proceedings of the Hawaii International Conference on System Sciences (HICSS-39), Persistent Conversation Track, Kauai, Hawaii, January 4-7 (2006)
7. Gross, R., Acquiti, A.: Information revelation and privacy in online social networks. In: Proceedings of the 2005 ACM Workshop on Privacy in the Electronic Society, Alexandria, VA, November 7. ACM Press, New York (2005)
8. Blanchette, J.F., Johnson, D.G.: Data Retention and the Panoptic Society: The Social Benefits of Forgetfulness. The Information Society 18(1), 33–45 (2002)
9. Gandy, O.H.: The Panoptic sort: A political economy of personal information. Westview Press, Boulder (1993)
10. From Wikipedia, http://en.wikipedia.org/wiki/Jay_Park#Myspace_Controversy
11. Anchorwoman Song Ji Sun commits suicide (May 23-30, 2011), http://www.allkpop.com/2011/05/anchorwoman-song-ji-sun-commits-suicide
12. Wang, Y., et al.: I regretted the minute I pressed share: A qualitative study of regrets on Facebook. In: Symposium on Usable Privacy and Security (2011)

Part VI

Smart Everyday Living and Working Environments

Application of Bio-inspired Metaheuristics to Guillotined Cutting Processes Optimize in an Glass Industry

Flavio Moreira da Costa, Tiago Vieira Carvalho, and Renato Jose Sassi

Industrial Engineering Postgraduation Program, Nove de Julho University – UNINOVE.
São Paulo, SP (Brasil)
flavio.costa@iduo.com.br, tiagovc@gmail.com, sassi@uninove.br

Abstract. Nowadays, sustainability is becoming a strong worry of our society. It can be defined as using resources to meet the needs of the present without compromising the ability of future generations to meet their own needs. An optimized cutting process minimizes the materials waste and is an important factor for production systems performance at glassworks industries, impacting directly in the products final cost formation and contributing for more environmentally sustainable products and production processes. Several studies have shown that combinations of bio-inspired meta-heuristics, more specifically, the Genetic Algorithms (GA) and Ant Colony Optimization (ACO) are efficient techniques to solving constraint satisfaction problems and combinatorial optimization problems. GA and ACO are bio-inspired meta-heuristics techniques suitable for random guided solutions in problems with large search spaces. GA are search methods inspired by the natural evolution theory, presenting good results in global searches. ACO is based on the attraction of ants by pheromone trails while searching for food and uses a feedback system that enables rapid convergence in good solutions. The results from the combination of these two techniques, when compared with the results from usual processes, are encouraging and have presented interesting solutions to the problem of optimizing guillotined cutting processes.

Keywords: Genetic Algorithms, Ant Colony Optimization, Guillotined Cutting, Glass Industry, Sustainability.

1   Introduction

The resource allocation problems have been a great impact factor on the industrial production systems performance and, due to practical applications potential to optimize industrial processes and the difficulties to obtain exact solutions, these problems category has been the subject of intense researches in the Operations Research (OR) and Artificial Intelligence (AI). The study of these problems provides a common basis for analysis and solution of other problems that belong to the same category [1, 3, 4, 7, 9, 11, 12] and, in this context, the bio-inspired metaheuristics techniques is being increasingly used in solving such problems.

N. Streitz and C. Stephanidis (Eds.): DAPI/HCII 2013, LNCS 8028, pp. 407–413, 2013.
© Springer-Verlag Berlin Heidelberg 2013

The guillotined cutting process is a complex combinatorial optimization problem, which consists in determining a cutting pattern of material pieces, so as to produce a set of smaller pieces, satisfying certain constraints. An optimized cutting process minimizes the materials waste and is an important factor for production systems performance at glassworks industries, impacting directly in the products final cost formation and contributing for more environmentally sustainable products and production processes. The Fig. 1 illustrates guillotined guillotine cutting process.

Consideration to the concept of sustainability is increasingly found in the management literature. It has been a subject with increasingly importance on scientific community, as the number of article written about it has grown considerable since the 1990's.

In addition, the companies 'environmental performance can be very important performance drivers to be measured in order to capture important information to be used to increase the competitive advantage. The findings of some researchers suggest that environmental criteria are increasingly important to develop sustainable business practices [5, 10].

Based in such factors, this paper approaches the application of bio-inspired meta-heuristics techniques, known as Genetic Algorithms and Ant Colony Optimization, to optimize guillotined cutting processes in a glass industry of Sao Paulo City, and thus contributing to making such processes more environmentally sustainable, through the material savings.

The applied approaches combines the search capabilities of these metaheuristics, aiming to minimize occurrences of local minima based solutions.

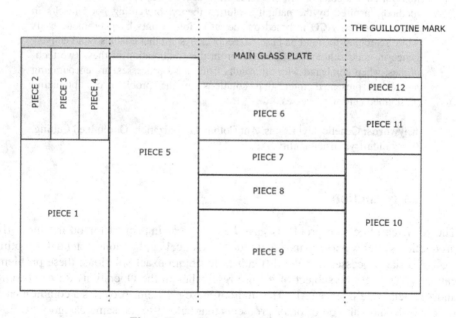

Fig. 1. The guillotined cutting process

Besides this introduction the paper is organized as follows: section 2 describes the bio-inspired metaheuristics used in this research, in section 3 we discuss the methodology, and section 4 dealing the results from this research and the conclusions.

2   The Bio-inspired Metaheuristics

The biologically inspired computing, or simply bio-inspired, is the research field that uses metaphors or theoretical models of biological systems in order to design computational tools or systems to solve complex problems. The results are algorithms or systems that have a similarity (often superficial) with phenomena or biological models studied [2].

The Genetic Algorithms and Ant Colony Optimization are bio-inspired metaheuristics techniques that, due to its efficiency in finding solutions in very large search spaces, is being increasingly applied to solve complex problems, especially combinatorial optimization problems.

2.1   Genetic Algorithms

Genetic Algorithms (GA) were first proposed by John Holland in the 60s and developed by him and his students during the subsequent years at the University of Michigan [8].

Holland presented the GA as an abstraction of evolution models in nature. Thus, GA are nondeterministic techniques for search and optimization, operating on a population of individuals (data structures that represent candidates for solving a problem) by applying selection mechanisms, crossover and mutation, generating new individuals every generation, they become more capable and therefore closest to the problem optimal solution. The GA is a robust and efficient method of searching for irregular, multidimensional and complex search spaces.

2.2   Ant Colony Optimization

The first Ant Algorithm was inspired by the observation of ant colonies that are able to find the shortest path between their nest and food sources [6].

The ants when foraging for food, randomly explore the environment around their nest in a seemingly disorganized. By walking this path, ants release a chemical substance called pheromone. At the same time, the ants are influenced by the presence of pheromones in the environment and has a probabilistic tendency to follow the direction in which the concentration of pheromones is increased.

The experiments with real ants demonstrated that indirect coordination between ants via pheromone trails produces a collective behavior of self-organization, where the shortest paths between their nest and food sources are gradually followed for other ants to enhance the trails pheromone on the best routes and eventually find the shortest path.

2.3   The Approach Used

For the experiments execution, was used a cooperative approach between Genetic Algorithms and Ant Colony Optimization, as can be seen in Fig. 2.

The processing occurs as follows:

- The GA processing was set at 500 generations;
- Every 50 GA generations the best chromosomes are used as ACO input;
- The ACO is executed 100 times;
- The best ACO are used as GA input.

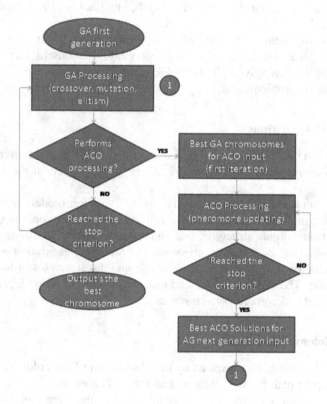

Fig. 2. Flow diagram showing, in simplified form, the GA and ACO metaheuristics combination

2.4   The Packing Algorithm

The Assessment of GA individuals and ACO solutions is performed with the aid of the packing algorithm called First Fit Decreasing Width Decreasing Height (FFDWDH).

The calculation consists in fit the pieces in master blade, simulating the cutting process and discovering the unused area (waste).

Steps for FFDWDH packing algorithm (the resulting arrangement can be seen in Fig.3):

- the pieces are sorted in decreasing order by width and height;
- then the pieces are allocated from left to right within vertical stripes (columns).

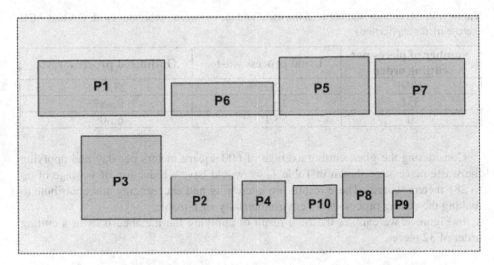

Fig. 3. Pieces sorted in decreasing order by width and height, when. (adapted from [11])

3   Methodology

The development of this paper is based on the study, revision and implementation of bio-inspired computing techniques for solving combinatorial optimization problems.

It was made a literature review of two-dimensional guillotine cutting processes derived from production systems in glass industry, as well as the options for combining GA and ACO.

To implement the GA and ACO bio-inspired metaheuristics are used the Java and Java Script programming languages.

Were performed several experiments using a data set of requests from a glass industry in São Paulo city. During these experiments, the results of application of bio-inspired metaheuristcs, GA and ACO, were compared with the results of usual cutting processes.

4   Results, Conclusion and Future Work

Several experiments were conducted with cutting orders provided by a real glass industry of São Paulo city.

During these experiments, were compared the waste resulting from the cutting of those requests in relation to the waste with application of optimization performed from the bio-inspired metaheusristics, GA and ACO.

The Table 1 shows the waste comparison between the usual and the optimized processes.

Table 1. Waste comparison between the usual and the optimized processes (with GA and ACO metaheuristcs application)

Number of pieces per cutting order	Usual process waste	Optimized process waste
1056	32.28%	27.83%
351	16.72%	9.48%
32	53.15%	6.30%

Considering the glass cutting average of 600 square meters per day and applying the waste percentage shown in Table 1, we would have a reduction of wastage of up to 281 meters square. These results are interesting and encouraging and contribute to making the cutting process more environmentally sustainable.

In Figure 4, we can see the final result of applying the metaheuristcs in a cutting order of 32 pieces.

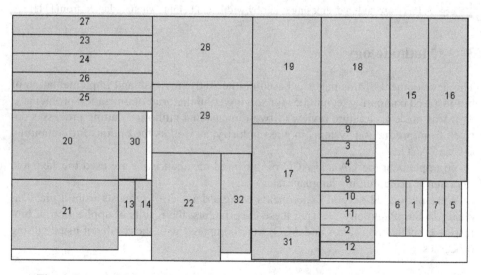

Fig. 4. Output of the metaheuristcs applied to a 32 pieces guillotine cutting problem

The purpose is to continue the research by changing the parameters and combination approaches of the GA and ACO and experimenting with other different bio-inspired metaheuristics like Bee Colony Algorithm.

References

1. Blum, C., Ibáñez, M.L.: The Industrial Electronics Handbook: Intelligent systems, 2nd. CRC Press (2011)
2. Castro, L.N., Zuben, F.J.V.: Recent Developments in Biologically Inspired Computing. Idea Group Publishing (2005)
3. Costa, F.M., Canto, N., Sassi, R.J.: Study of the Application of Genetic Algorithms in Optimization of Cutting Glass Sheets. In: Proceedings of the 9th IEEE/IAS International Conference on Industry Applications, Industry Applications (INDUSCON) 9th IEEE/IAS International Conference, São Paulo, vol. 1, pp. 1–3 (2010)
4. da Costa, F.M., Sassi, R.J.: Application of an hybrid bio-inspired meta-heuristic in the optimization of two-dimensional guillotine cutting in an glass industry. In: Yin, H., Costa, J.A.F., Barreto, G. (eds.) IDEAL 2012. LNCS, vol. 7435, pp. 802–809. Springer, Heidelberg (2012)
5. Cuthbertson, R., Piotrowicz, W.: Supply chain best practices – identification and categorisation of measures and benefits. International Journal of Productivity & Performance Management 57(5), 389–404 (2008)
6. Dorigo, M., Stützle, T.: Ant Colony Optimization. Bradford Book (2004)
7. Grosan, C., Abraham, A.: Hybrid Evolutionary Algorithms: Methodologies, Architectures, and Reviews. In: Grosan, C., Abraham, A., Ishibuchi, H. (eds.) Hybrid Evolutionary Algorithms. SCI, vol. 75, pp. 1–17. Springer, Heidelberg (2007)
8. Holland, J.H.: Adaptation in Natural and Artificial Systems. The University of Michigan Press, Ann Arbor (1975)
9. Hoseini, P., Shayesteh, M.G.: Hybrid Ant Colony Optimization, Genetic Algorithm, and Simulated Annealing for Image Contrast Enhancement. In: 2010 IEEE Congress on Evolutionary Computation (CEC), pp. 1–6 (2010)
10. Linton, J.D., Klassen, R., Jayaraman, V.: Sustainable supply chains: An introduction. Journal of Operations Management 25, 1075–1082 (2007)
11. Temponi, E.C.: Uma Proposta de Resolução do Problema de Corte Bidimensional via Abordagem Metaheurística, Dissertação de Mestrado. Diretoria de Pesquisa e Pós-Graduação, CEFET-MG (2007)
12. Zhang, D., Du, L.: Hybrid Ant Colony Optimization Based on Genetic Algorithm for Container Loading Problem. In: International Conference of Soft Computing and Pattern Recognition (SoCPaR), pp. 10–14 (2011)

Understanding Privacy and Trust Issues in a Classroom Affective Computing System Deployment

Shaundra Bryant Daily[1], Dante Meyers[2], Shelby Darnell[1],
Tania Roy[1], and Melva T. James[1]

[1] School of Computing, Human-Centered Computing Division, Clemson University, Clemson, South Carolina, USA
[2] Department of Psychology, Old Dominion University, Norfolk, Virginia, USA
{sdaily,sdarnell,taniar,melvaj}@clemson.edu
dmyer010@odu.edu

Abstract. Our research group is in the midst of working with teachers to co-design an affective computing system that uses physiological measures, gathered via wrist worn sensors, to understand how students are engaging with classroom instruction. Optimally, our goal is to find new ways of supporting empathetic practices in the classroom by providing teachers real-time (or reflective) feedback on student engagement. In parallel, with our work with teachers, we are working to pinpoint the privacy and trust issues that might be associated with this type of system. The objective of this paper is to present the results of a series of studies conducted to understand the challenges associated with introducing a pervasive affective computing system into classroom environments. While we focus on physiological sensors, the implications apply to other pervasive technologies as well.

Keywords: Affective Computing, Privacy, Adoption.

Introduction

Affective computing is "computing that relates to, arises from, or deliberately influences emotion." [1] As with any pervasive computing application, issues of privacy and trust for affective computing systems must be a part of the conversation from design to implementation. Reynolds & Picard [2] provide a framework for the evaluation of affective computing systems from a dimensional metaethical position and include privacy and trust, amongst other constructs, as a part of this analysis. Further, they evaluate systems in a small study based on this framework. Lane, et al. [3] raise important considerations as physiological sensing becomes more pervasive, including how to process data for best privacy, how to share data appropriately, unintended leakage of personal information, and who is responsible when collected data causes harm. Similarly, Ameen, et al. [4] caution that serious social unrest might arise if people fear being monitored. They suggest encrypting communications, keeping users anonymous unless completely necessary, and creating public awareness. These guidelines are a part of a larger literature about not only the importance of keeping these

N. Streitz and C. Stephanidis (Eds.): DAPI/HCII 2013, LNCS 8028, pp. 414–423, 2013.

data safe, but also ensuring that the system is able to overcome cultural, psychological, and other social barriers to adaptation and utilization. Although the focus of this paper is not the development of a pervasive affective computing system, we begin by describing our recent efforts here in order to provide the reader with the context.

It is imperative to support a teacher's ability to understand how he/she is connecting with his/her students in the classroom so he/she can adapt his/her pedagogical strategies to meet the needs of his/her diverse learners. Engagement, defined in the literature in a variety of ways, has been associated with student achievement, [5] positive classroom and school climate, [6] and effective instructional practices. [7] Engagement is a multidimensional construct with cognitive, behavioral, and affective dimensions. First, cognitive engagement is related to a student's investment in learning, seeking challenges, going beyond requirements, and self-regulation. [8] Cognitive engagement can be demonstrated by a student's mastery of the full meaning of material, taking the position of an expert rather than a novice. [9] Next, behavioral engagement is related to participation and involvement in activities. This includes observable behaviors such as positive conduct, persistence, effort, and attention. Lastly, affective engagement measures positive and negative reactions to stimuli including teachers, classmates, academics, or school. Positive emotional engagement supports student ties to institutions and is presumed to influence their willingness to work.

To date, much evaluation of each of these dimensions of engagement relies on self-report and other subjective, obtrusive, and inconsistent instruments. [10] The goal of our line of research is to contribute to the creation of a physiology-based, quantifiable, and unobtrusive technique for measuring the affective response associated with the dimensions of engagement with the goal of supporting teachers and students. The key measure in the affective computing system discussed in this paper relies upon wrist-worn sensors that measure electrodermal activity. In short, when sympathetic nervous system activity increases, sympathetic fibers that surround eccrine sweat glands modulate the production of sweat. The skin, in turn, momentarily becomes a better conductor of electricity (i.e., electrodermal activity). This electrodermal activity can be measured as conductance or resistance by different sensors. Here, we focus on skin conductance, for which sensors. [11] These sensors are placed on the fingers, the palm of the hand, or the wrists where there is a large concentration of sweat glands. [12] We have chosen to use the Q sensor to collect skin conductance, temperature, and motion data since this sensor can be worn outside of a laboratory setting (i.e., without being tethered to a computer) and since it is worn on the wrist like a watch, which might increase the possibility of it being unobtrusive to the student.

This sensor provides information about a person's level of arousal provided that other triggers of increased perspiration have been held constant (e.g., temperature). It will not provide any information as to the specific emotion that is being elicited unless other conscious emotion variables are collected. Further, numerous events such as pain, significant thoughts (not related to the current context), lying, exercise, individual changes in biochemistry, and motion artifacts can lead to changes in skin activity. Even with attribution and noise limitations, however, electrodermal activity is a useful measure that has been used in research focusing on stress and anxiety, [13] lie detection, [14] user interface evaluation, empathy, [15, 16] and game assessment. The final two are most relevant to the system under development in the classroom setting. By measuring skin conductance simultaneously from patients and therapists during a clinical session, Marci et al. [16] found that increased therapist empathy as perceived by the patient correlated with high concordance of skin conductance between the two. In other words, the more empathic the patient felt his/her therapist to be, the stronger the relationship between skin conductance measures. Next, Mandryk et al. [17] found that skin conductance was higher when playing a game against a friend rather than a computer and was correlated with subjective measures of "fun". Further, in a separate study, Mandryk et al. [18] found that a combination of physiological measures, which included skin conductance, were useful in evaluating the emotional response to entertainment technologies.

In order to support teachers in understanding how they are connecting with their students, our approach to this research incorporates two goals: First, we are co-developing, with teachers, principals, and district leaders, a user interface tool that allows a teacher to peruse this engagement data connected with video of his/her classroom activity. Second, we are conducting feasibility studies to understand the social, political, cultural, and psychological barriers to this pervasive affective computing system. The latter is the focus of the rest of this paper.

Methods

2.1   Study Context

In the midst of our participatory research with teachers, a blog post[1] was released about one author's opinion of the research. Unfortunately, the post was based on a mistake on a website connecting our efforts to empower teachers and students to understand engagement with another study trying to understand teacher effectiveness. The interpretation of this work in the blog post was, in effect, that the arousal levels of students would be utilized as a way to evaluate, and possibly fire, teachers. Even though the post, which generated hundreds of responses, was based on inaccurate information, the resulting perceptions of the project are valid and informative of the views people might develop about a pervasive affective computing system. Therefore, the post provided an opportunity, beyond the efforts in the participatory research with teachers, to examine the proposed affective computing system critically.

2.2   Data Sources

We have three main data sources: focus groups, online news articles, and social media sites. Our twenty-four participants in the focus groups have been divided into two cohorts: teachers and district administrators. The first cohort consists of ten sixth-through eighth-grade teachers and a principal from a middle school the Southeast who

---

[1] Our effort here is not to critique or refute this blog post. In an effort to focus on the privacy and trust topic of the paper and to avoid igniting further discussions of the blog post, we have purposefully chosen not name the author and source of the post.

teach English, science, social studies, and mathematics. All participants are White females with one to fourteen years of experience teaching who responded to a general request from their principal asking if they would be interested in participating in the study. They had no knowledge about the details of the study, so there should not have been a bias towards teachers who were more accepting of affective computing. The second group consists of various administrators from the school district including two principals, a professional development specialist, a responsiveness to instruction specialist, a high school instructor, a professor, and a project executive director.

Our focus groups were divided into three sessions held with each cohort. Consent forms were given to each group and participants were given the opportunity to opt out of participating. During the first session, we first introduced stakeholders to electrodermal activity as a measure, as well as the sensors for measurement. Next, we provided background for the goals of the project and familiarized ourselves with the ways in which they try and understand how their students are engaged in the classroom. We also asked questions related to the gaps they see inherent in their approach and how they could imagine improvement. In addition to field notes collected by a research assistant, we collected drawings from stakeholders to understand how an affective computing system might look. During the second session, we presented a paper-based prototype developed as a result of the previous discussion and asked for feedback and improvements. In an upcoming session, we will bring a tangible prototype to the stakeholders. During three different focus group sessions held thus far, two with the teacher cohort and one with the administrator cohort, field notes were generated from discussions.

The remainder of our sources consist of online news articles and social media sites (n = 522) containing articles written in response to a blog post reporting inaccurate information about the work. These sources were found using the Social Media Listening Center at Clemson, which uses Radian6 technology to filter relevant articles and posts dealing with the topic. Radian6 is a social media monitoring platform that gathers data, in part, from Facebook, Twitter, blogs, blog comments, message boards and online forums, news groups, podcasts, reviews on e-commerce sites, experience sharing sites, and mainstream news sites. In order to accomplish this task, a filter was created for terms in the initial blog post for a one-month time period that included the initial blog post.

2.3   Analysis

An initial analysis of the focus group and social media data consisted of computing percentages for positive, negative, and neutral sentiments. Data were coded by two raters as positive if the poster expressed clear agreement with the technology, discussed beneficial implications, or provided positive suggestions; coded as negative if the poster used profanity, totalitarian references, expressed anger, disgust, fear, or resentment; and neutral if remarks were indefinite (i.e., forwarded online article or no valenced opinion presented). Finally, an interrater reliability analysis was performed to determine agreement between raters.

Next, thematic analysis was utilized to generate themes from the focus group notes and online data. Thematic analysis is "an accessible and theoretically-flexible approach to analyzing qualitative data". [19] This method, widely used in psychology, calls for the demarcation of a qualitative data corpus into themes. Thematic analysis is valuable when attempting to understand a data corpus whose information is based on notes from study groups and blog posts with comments, in other words, data that were not collected under experimental conditions. All data were also analyzed using thematic analysis procedures which include building familiarity, generating codes, identifying features, finding, confirming, and defining themes for reporting. [19] The focus group and social media data presented separate themes after analysis and are explained in detail in the next sections.

Results

3.1   General Sentiments

Table 1 below depicts the positive, negative, and neutral sentiments found in the online news articles and other social media. The interrater reliability for the coders was found to be 78.7% with Cohen's Kappa = 0.55, indicating moderate agreement. [20]

Table 1. Results from analysis of positive, negative, and neutral sentiments

Groups	% Negative	% Positive	% Neutral
Focus Groups (n = 24)	2%	98%	0%
Articles & Social Media Coder A (n = 522)	31.4%	6.0%	62.6%
Articles & Social Media Coder B (n = 522)	25.5%	6.3%	68.1%

3.2   Social Media Themes

Theme One. Many of the authors and commenters believe that this project is just another effort to control aspects of citizen's private lives. The name "Big Brother" (a totalitarian dictator from George Orwell's novel entitled *Nineteen Eighty-Four*) [21] was commonly used. One author posted, "it is not too far of a stretch to assume that tracking bracelets could one day be used to weed out students or teachers that do not buy into…agenda[s]… By monitoring what is being taught and how students respond to it, Big Brother could theoretically read the human mind in real time, which has some fairly disturbing implications."

Theme Two. The second theme was that the technology was being used to *evaluate teacher performance*. Authors thought the technology would be used to evaluate teachers rather than help and empower the classrooms. One author posted, "Using students' emotional responses to various learning material as a metric of how well a teacher is performing is a flawed approach that could send many quality, veteran educators packing their bags." Another author posted, "A student's physical reaction to a classroom lesson soon could be used to judge how successful—or unsuccessful—an educator is in keeping students engaged." Lastly, an author suggested, "The student reactions recorded on the bracelets' sensors could be added to a host of more traditional teacher evaluation methods such as test grades, administrator observations, and student surveys."

Theme Three. Many believed that the technology would not be able to distinguish what is actually engaging a student. In other words, the technology would not work. One poster wrote, "In any case, even if a child is giving off highly engaged skin signals, how would the machines know whether he or she is deeply engaged in a beautiful daydream rather than 14th-century English literature?" Another author asked a similar question, "How would the bracelet tell if a student is responding to a teacher and not to something his friend whispers in his ear?" Authors and posters also cautioned at the fact that people can be deceptive. One poster maintained, "It's a fair point, but in terms of the GSR's actual effectiveness, there's one thing researchers should bear in mind: Children are very, very good at cheating."

3.3   Focus Group Themes

Theme One. The first of the focus group themes was *informative feedback*. Generally, the teachers and administrators expressed desires for the engagement pedometer to provide information that would help them adjust their lesson plans. One teacher insisted the technology should "Alert teachers of low levels of engagement, so teachers can monitor or re-engage students." Another said, "For lessons [the technology should tell] if the teachers consistently have low engagement or high engagement at specific points in the lessons." Some teachers wanted the information from the tool as a reflective feature while others wanted real-time information, or as one teacher stated, "Instruction intervention as class proceeds."

Theme Two. The second theme was the teachers having the option of using the pedometer to *view individuals or groups* within the class. One teacher asked to be able to "Target particular students upon request." Some teachers insisted that since class is not always individual work, this would be helpful. One teacher said, "Can each student's dots [points representing students] also have a number so we can track, if we move from individual to pair to group work?" Some teachers also expressed the desire to observe patterns and behaviors of students over time. One teacher suggested "A way to follow a particular student through lessons, class schedules, and four-week periods as a way of tracking progress/engagement."

Theme Three. The third theme was the desire to have *access to data immediately* for interpretation. Some teachers expressed that they wanted the data to come straight to different devices they have such as iPads or other mobile devices. One teacher maintained, "I would want data immediately to my PC or other device so I could access it to be able to adjust instruction and monitor students/groups." In relation to Theme

One, rather than having an alert for feedback, teachers want to interpret the data themselves. One teacher explained that it would be useful if "Each student [was] able to be monitored and the teacher [was] able to see live data to use immediately to be able to intervene and instruct in a different way to benefit all students."

Discussion

In this research, there is an obvious discrepancy between sentiments expressed between the two data sets. Most focus group participants found the idea amenable to use in classes and provided suggestions on the design of the tool. All the themes from the focus groups were about aspects they wanted in a tool to augment their own abilities to support students in their classrooms. Only once or twice were ideas expressed around who would be in control of the data and what the possible negative uses of this information were. This general positive sentiment, of course, can be attributed to how the information was presented to these groups. In the focus group sessions, we presented the technology, described its limitations (e.g., noise and attribution errors), discussed opportunities to opt into the research, and asked for teacher input. Although we asked for both feedback and concerns (i.e., should this be developed at all), this approach did not espouse the same number of negative reactions as the blog post.

The results confirm previous suggestions presented in the Introduction about privacy and trust of pervasive computing systems. First, public awareness of accurate information is crucial. Developers of pervasive affective computing systems must make sure that people understand the ins, outs, and limitations of what is being developed. The challenges associated with the interpretation of electrodermal activity are an important limitation that must be discussed when presenting the current system. Second, who has access to data and how they will be utilized is important. In this case, steps must be taken to prevent the technology from being used to evaluate the teacher. Rather, this system can be used by the teacher to help him/her understand better how students are responding to his/her pedagogical approach. The student, of course, cannot be forgotten in this picture. Although the technology has been framed for empowering the teacher, the system should not be used to evaluate the student either. Instead, it can be used to facilitate teachers' understanding of their impacts on students so they can be better supported. In addition, it can be used by the students to understand their own engagement. Finally, Ackerman [22] defines privacy as "the ability of an individual to control the terms under which their (sic) personal information is acquired and used". In order for systems to be respectful of teachers' and students' choices, opportunities must be provided to opt in, or out, at any moment. For our technology, teachers and students should have the choice about providing their engagement data to the system.

4.1   Limitations

The main limitations are the scope of analysis and biases. The scope of analysis limitation deals with the number of responses from the focus group compared to those from social media. Given the uniqueness of our research there exists no readily available information, in similitude to the notes taken during the focus group, other than what has been collected, from which to draw themes. The number of data points for the focus group is twenty-four, while the number of data points for social media is five hundred twenty-two. Another limitation is how each group was introduced to the topic. The focus group was introduced to the topic by researchers whose intentions are to build a tool to enable teachers to improve classroom experiences, while the social media group was introduced to the topic by a blog post that did not accurately represent the work. These disparate introductions impacted how the discussions proceeded. Finally, biases exist for interpretation of the sentiments. After performing the coding for the social media group, the two coders had moderate to substantial, instead of strong agreement. Even with definitions in place for the coding scheme, what we as researchers see as positivity and negativity can still differ.

Conclusions

From this research, we have public perception data from a real situation confirming that those interested in introducing pervasive technologies must fully describe a system's goals and possible limitations, they must emphasize respectful (e.g., opt in) opportunities to use the technology, and they have to provide intended users with choices about how, when, and where their data can and cannot be utilized. Kotter and Cohen [23] posit that "[p]eople change what they do less because they are given analysis that shifts their thinking than because they are shown a truth that influences their feelings." By providing a visualization that is informative, not evaluative, for teachers to understand how their classroom instruction is impacting their students (possibly, in unforeseen ways), we imagine that this type of influence is possible. Our continued understanding of privacy and trust issues generated by the research presented in this paper lays the groundwork for the realization of this vision.

References

1. Picard, R.W.: Affective Computing, 1st edn. The MIT Press, Boston (2000)
2. Reynolds, C., Picard, R.W.: Affective Sensors, Privacy and Ethical Contracts. In: Proceedings of the Conference on Human Factors in Computing Systems, Vienna, Austria, April 24-29, pp. 1103–1106. ACM, New York (2004)
3. Lane, N.D., Miluzzo, E., Lu, H.L.H., Peebles, D., Choudhury, T., Campbell, A.T.: A Survey of Mobile Phone Sensing. IEEE Communications Magazine (2010), http://ieeexplore.ieee.org/xpls/abs_all.jsp?arnumber=5560598 (retrieved)
4. Ameen, M.A., Liu, J., Kwak, K.: Security and Privacy Issues in Wireless Sensor Networks for Healthcare Applications. Journal of Medical Systems 36(1), 93–101 (2012), http://link.springer.com/article/10.1007%2Fs10916-010-9449-4?LI=true# (retrieved)

5. Appleton, J.J., Christenson, S.L., Furlong, M.J.: Student Engagement with School: Critical Conceptual and Methodological Issues of the Construct. Psychology in the Schools 45(5), 369–386 (2008)
6. Appleton, J.J., Christenson, S.L., Kim, D., Reschly, A.L.: Measuring Cognitive and Psychological Engagement: Validation of the Student Engagement Instrument. Journal of School Psychology 44(5), 427–445 (2006), doi:10.1016/j.jsp.2006.04.002.
7. Mant, J., Wilson, H., Coates, D.: The Effect of Increasing Conceptual Challenge in Primary Science Lessons on Pupils' Achievement and Engagement. International Journal of Science Education 29(14), 1707–1719 (2007), doi:10.1080/09500690701537973.
8. Fredricks, J.A., Blumenfeld, P.C., Paris, A.H.: School Engagement: Potential of the Concept, State of the Evidence. Review of Educational Research 74(1), 59–109 (2004), doi:10.3102/00346543074001059.
9. Yazzie-Mintz, E., McCormick, K.: Finding the Humanity in the Data: Understanding, Measuring, and Strengthening Student Engagement. In: Christenson, S.L., Reschly, A.L., Wylie, C. (eds.) Handbook of Research on Student Engagement, pp. 743–761. Springer (2012),
   http://www.springerlink.com/content/v53410867366517m/abstract/ (retrieved)
10. Fredricks, J.A., McColskey, W., Meli, J., Mordica, J., Montrosse, B., Mooney, K.: Measuring Student Engagement in Upper Elementary through High School: A Description of 21 Instruments (Issues & Answers Report, REL 2011–No. 098). U.S. Department of Education, Institute of Education Sciences, National Center for Education Evaluation and Regional Assistance, Regional Educational Laboratory Southeast, Washington, DC (2011)
11. Picard, R.W., Daily, S.B.: Evaluating Affective Interactions: Alternatives to Asking What Users Feel. In: CHI Workshop on Evaluating Affective Interfaces: Innovative Approaches, Portland, OR (April 2005)
12. Boucsein, W.: Electrodermal Activity. Plenum Press, New York (1992)
13. Fenz, W., Epstein, S.: Gradients of Physiological Arousal in Parachutists as a Function of an Approaching Jump. Psychosom. Med. 29(1), 33–51 (1967)
14. Podlesny, J.A., Raskin, D.C.: Physiological measures and the detection of deception. Psychological Bulletin 84(4), 782–799 (1977), doi:10.1037/0033-2909.84.4.782.
15. Marci, C., Orr, S.: The Effect of Emotional Distance on Psychophysiologic Concordance and Perceived Empathy Between Patient and Interviewer. Applied Psychophysiology and Biofeedback 31(2), 115–128 (2006), doi:10.1007/s10484-006-9008-4
16. Marci, C.D., Ham, J., Moran, E., Orr, S.P.: Physiologic Correlates of Perceived Therapist Empathy and Social-Emotional Process During Psychotherapy. Journal of Nervous and Mental Disease 195(2), 103–111 (2007)
17. Mandryk, R.L., Inkpen, K.M., Calvert, T.W.: Using Psychophysiological Techniques to Measure User Experience with Entertainment Technologies. Behaviour & Information Technology 25(2), 141–158 (2006), doi:10.1080/01449290500331156.
18. Mandryk, R.L., Atkins, M.S., Inkpen, K.M.: A continuous and objective evaluation of emotional experience with interactive play environments. In: Proceedings of the SIGCHI Conference on Human Factors in Computing Systems, CHI 2006, pp. 1027–1036. ACM, New York (2006b), doi:10.1145/1124772.1124926
19. Braun, V., Clarke, V.: Using Thematic Analysis in Psychology. Qualitative Research in Psychology 3(2), 77–101 (2006), doi:10.1191/1478088706qp063oa.

20. Rietveld, T., van Hout, R.: Statistical Techniques for the Study of Language and Language Behaviour. Mouton de Gruyter, Berlin (1993)
21. Orwell, G.: Penguin, London (1977,1984)
22. Culnan, M.J.: Protecting privacy online: is self-regulation working? J. Public Policy Market 19(1), 20–26 (2000)
23. Kotter, J.P., Cohen, D.S.: The Heart of Change: Real-Life Stories of How People Change Their Organizations. Harvard Business Press, Cambridge (2002)

An Approach to the Content-to-Content Interactivity in Performing Arts over Networks

Boncheol Goo

Graduate School of Culture Technology, KAIST, Daejeon, Republic of Korea
mgtech@kaist.ac.kr

Abstract. This paper discusses another potential dimension of interactivity in networked performance that enables the real time imagery of performer's impression and the continuous reaction of actors in different locations as if they were in the same stage. To realize this, an artist makes croquis of the scene immediately during the actual performance seeing the video received from far end site in real time via internet. Simultaneously, the captured video of the drawing croquis is transmitted back to the screen of the far end site. As a result, the content-to-content interactivity can form an sympathetic stage. To demonstrate its effectiveness, the author applied the concept to the Internet2 Distributed Interactive Multimedia Performance at NYU, US.

Keywords: networked performance, interactivity, communication.

1   Introduction

High-speed networks and those wide applications are recently getting popular. For example, within high-speed network-based application are such fields as tele surgery, weather observation, monitoring of cosmic radio, distance education, cultural exchange, and so on. One of cultural exchanges using internet is performing arts over networks. It has several synonyms of a distributed performance, a telematic performance, a cyber performance, and a networked performance, but all of them commonly have the meaning of sharing performing arts among multiple stages using networking techniques. To borrow Steve Dixon's phrase, "Telematic conjunctions enable real-time audiovisual collaboration between artists or performers both in the private context of process-based development work and rehearsals and in the public context of final performances." [3]

A networked performance can take various physical formations according to purpose of its producer or characteristics of intended performance content. It can be set up with diverse technical settings: bidirectional manner, server-operating star structure, or master-slave structure among peers. Regardless the form or topology employed, research on networked performances emphasize deriving interaction among the stages [1, 7].

Interactivity is generally classified into the three dimensions according to its subjects: human-to-computer, human-to-contents, and human-to-human [2, 4-6]. This

N. Streitz and C. Stephanidis (Eds.): DAPI/HCII 2013, LNCS 8028, pp. 424–429, 2013.

categorization also can be apply to the interactivity in a networked performance as a communication medium since a networked performance platform surely supports those three kinds of interaction. For examples, performers use computer systems to send or receive their video and audio (human-to-computer), performers watch and react to what the platform displays (human-to-content), and performers have interaction each other (human-to-human) through this kind of communication channel in most cases. Also, some of the examples can, not necessarily, apply to the reaction of audience. In this paper, this classification is used as a framework, or a theoretical lens, to examine the concept of interactivity in a networked performance.

2   The Positioning of Networked Performance

Media artists utilize network technology as a new media besides using it as a means for real time data transmission. When two areas meet, this case being technology and art, both areas should be able to complement one another. In this perspective, we should consider the technical and artistic positioning when dealing with networked performances. As shown in Fig. 1, the aim of networked performance is to expand the reach of artistic expression by effectively utilizing state-of-the-art media/network technology.

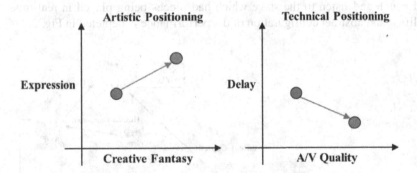

Fig. 1. The positioning of networked performance

2.1   Artistic Positioning

In an artistic perspective, a networked performance should increase the possibilities of realizing creative fantasy and give stronger impressions. However, if the total (network and system) delay makes exchanging feelings difficult, performers cannot be immersed in the networked performance, impressions of the audience drops, and the networked performance loses its vital power. Thus, it is essential to find out the content-to-content interactivity in networked performance.

2.2   Technical Positioning

On the technological side of the network, the media (audio/video) quality that is being transmitted is extremely important for realistic experience. However, increasing the definition of the video increases the data size and using compression technologies increases the latency as well as the complexity (and associated cost). As the total (network and system) delay becomes longer, no matter how high the quality may be, it becomes a hurdle for a networked performance that is based on sympathizing with one another in real-time. Therefore, the main issue in network technology needed in supporting networked performances is to increase the media quality while keeping the latency low. In this case, gigabit networks were used to guarantee high speed of the connections.

3   Approaches

A networked performance, named "Memory", was conducted in 2010. The performance consisted of ten pieces of modern dance, music, and media arts under the main theme of memory. It had three stages connected via high-speed networks to send and receive video and audio streams: KAIST in Republic of Korea, New York University, and University of Colorado Boulder in the United States of America. Each venue had its own stage, performers, staffs, and audience. Thus, audiences on three locations could watch and listen to the stage which had pieces being played in real-time. The simplified and abstract configuration of the performance is depicted in Fig. 2.

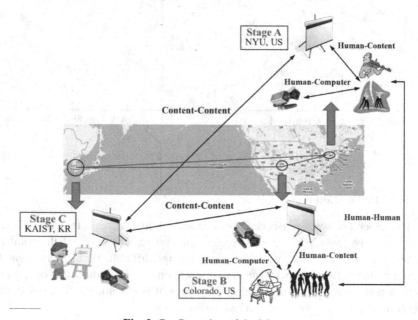

Fig. 2. Configuration of the Memory

3.1   Memory

Upon the basic configuration for a three-way networked performance, a unique experimental addition was made. As it appears in Fig. 2, a professional painter participated in the stage C. This was situated by the author in order to observe what non-traditional interactivity could be found in networked performance settings. In other words, unusual element of interactivity was introduced into the performance for the observation. The painter's role was watching the performance and drawing what he saw and felt into croquis. The painter produced several croquis which was impromptu and intuitive throughout the performance. For example, while dancers in stage A were dancing, the painter expressed his impressions and feelings from the dancing into a croquis and finished the work when the piece did. When musicians in stage B started to play the next piece, the painter began another croquis, in turn. The drawing processes and the results were also shared in real-time among the audiences on each screen of three sites via internet.

To sum up, the painter in stage C was drawing a piece being influenced by a dancer's motion and movement in stage A. The dance affected the color, stroke, shape he drew, and so on. Meanwhile, the drawing was displayed on screens in stage A to affect the improvised dance again. As a result, from the perspectives from audiences on three sites, as the thirds agents of the communication, they could observe that contents were influencing each other. As shown in the Fig. 3, the improvised drawings during the performance among three locations seem to have shown high level of content-to-content interactivity via the medium of networked performance platform. This means that the third participant to the communication, such as audience, could watch "interactive" contents in the performance.

Fig. 3. Screenshots of the performance

3.2   Conceptual Review

The interactivity in Memory can be summarized as follows. The medium for interaction was networked performance platform, which consists of transmission application, gigabit networks, screens, and so on. Interaction agents were the performers and the audiences on the three sites. Performers more actively exchanged their messages each other and the reactions from the audiences were relatively implicit. They could interact through telematics audio and video of the performers' movements, gestures, and plays. Following the aforementioned categorization [2, 4], the interactivity in Memory can be systematized in the same way. Showing up in front of the camera with some gestures and singing into microphones of performers were examples of human-to-computer interactivity. Audiences were passively participating in the interaction by watching the content via the platform. Watching performance of performers and audiences reflected human-to-contents interactivity, though there were generally little means to directly affect the content as reactions. Human-to-human interactivity was also observed when performers on two or more sites danced and played the music together through the networked performance platform. This category of interactivity also appears in interaction between performers and audiences.

4   Results and Discussion

The three existing dimensions: human-to-computer, human-to-contents, and human-to-human, however, couldn't embrace all aspects of the interactivity observed in the networked performance. Rather, the author was able to discover another sort of interactivity from the observation. In this paper, the finding is named as content-to-content interactivity and it is defined in communication with three or more agents as the extent to which un-predefined contents in messages bidirectionally influence each other from perspective of the third agent. This another potential dimension stems from the real time imagery of performer's impression and the continuous reaction of actors in different locations as if they were in the same stage.

5   Conclusion

The paper concludes by mentioning some of the further problems raised by this approach to the interactivity in performing arts over networks. The content-to-content interactivity has been newly observed as another potential dimension of interactivity from interactions in networked performance. The interactive communication is an important factor both in performing arts and social networking service. The areas of art and networking technology often dealt with networked performance, but there were little studies from the field of communication media or information systems. This paper included the discussion on one of significant concepts in networked performance, as a distinctive kind of communication media, which also exploits unusual form of communication. To greatly improve the interactivity of networked performance, it requires diverse challenges from artists, engineers, and producers as a novel kind of media, thus what, how, where, and who of the interaction in networked performances should be discussed further. Networked performance will be a form of entertainment in the near future's digital society, and a field in which cutting-edge technology and artistic direction are important.

Acknowledgements. This work has been supported by KISTI (Korea Institute of Science and Technology Information) in Republic of Korea. I would like to express my sincere thanks to Professor Gilbert, J.(New York University), Professor Kim, D.(Chungnam National University), and Professor Wohn, K.(Korea Advanced Institute of Science and Technology).

References

1. Bailey, H.: Ersatz dancing: negotiating the live and mediated in digital performance practice. International Journal of Performance Arts and Digital Media 3, 151–165 (2007)
2. Mcmillan, S.J.: The researchers and the concept: moving beyond a blind examination of interactivity. Journal of Interactive Advertising 5, 1–4 (2005)
3. Dixen, S.: Digital Performance: Telematics: Conjoining Remote Performances Spaces. The MIT Press, Cambridge (2007)
4. Mcmillan, S.J.: Exploring models of interactivity from multiple research traditions: users, documents, and systems. In: Lievrouw, L.A., Livingstone, S. (eds.) Handbook of New Media, London, pp. 162–182 (2002)
5. Jensen, J.F.: Interactivity: tracing a new concept in media and communication studies. Nordicom Review (19), 185–204 (1998)
6. Kiousis, S.: Interactivity: a concept explication. New Media & Society 4, 355–383 (2002)
7. Renaud, A., Carôt, A., Rebelo, P.: Networked music performance: state of art. In: 30th International Conference on Intelligent Audio Systems, Saariselkä, Finland (2007)

Attractiveness of an Interactive Public Art Installation

Jun Hu[1], Duy Le[1], Mathias Funk[1], Feng Wang[1,2], and Matthias Rauterberg[1]

[1] Department of Industrial Design, Eindhoven University of Technology, The Netherlands
[2] School of Digital Media, Jiangnan University, P.R. China
{j.hu,l.duy,m.funk,feng.wang,g.w.m.rauterberg}@tue.nl

Abstract. Interaction experiences with public art installations are becoming ubiquitous recently, however, interaction is usually unidirectional and the actual experience not very rich. This work reports on an interactive public art installation aiming at increasing the level of social connectedness among visitors, and the results of evaluating the attractiveness of the installation. By connecting visitors and computers physiologically, the installation has clear impact on social interaction and it also shows the attractiveness to people from aspects such as creativity, novelty, inviting and motivating. In this work we also found that the AttrakDiff instrument to be useful and convenient in evaluating the attractiveness of public art installations.

Keywords: Interactive Installation, Public Art, Attractiveness, Social Connectedness, Computers as Social Actors.

1 Introduction

The advances in science and technology bring the public digital arts from traditional media towards new media types often enabled by recent technological developments. The use, the language and the implications of the material itself are different from it being applied as a carrier for public digital arts. These new media types of public digital arts are in need of new carriers and new form languages for its progress and prosperity in the age of the new technologies, from traditional ones with static forms to new ones with dynamic and interactive forms [1].

Public interactive art installations are effective in addressing and engaging multiple people, and displays and projections are often used for these installations as output devices. While the use for advertisements, entertainment and promotion is quite farspread, the usual modus operandi of a single projection is to engage people as a single person in a 1:1 message. One of the drawbacks of this kind of installation is the limited interaction space for people "using" a public projection: messages are mostly unidirectional and there is a little that a person can actually do to be engaged in a richer interaction than consuming a simple information broadcast.

This work reports on the research aiming at using public art installations to address multiple (previously unconnected) people at the same time, increasing the level of social connectedness among them, and finally evaluating the attractiveness of the installation. The main challenge is to establish the public installation as a social actor – a socially acceptable participant in a social multi-user setting, in which the culture

N. Streitz and C. Stephanidis (Eds.): DAPI/HCII 2013, LNCS 8028, pp. 430–438, 2013.

would matter [2, 3]. Part of this research is also to investigate whether computers (controlling the public installation) can indeed act as social actors and improve social connectedness. "Social actor", in general ICT uses, was developed into a conceptualization model through a series of empirical studies. There are four dimensions in the conceptualization of a social actor: affiliations, environments, interactions, identities and temporalities [4].

In the field of HCI, computers are considered to be able to handle social tasks and tend to be treated like humans [5]. There is a growing community around public projection and large-scale installations, and social interaction of their users, which is picked up by user-dedicated devices such as RFID tags and mobile phones [6-8]. In the case of *Blobulous*, an interactive installation to be introduced in the next section, the large (possibly public) projection of abstract avatars is combined with bio signals, i.e., the heart rate, which other research also consider as a reliable and effective means of communication between people [9, 10]. With the system we explore the possibilities in utilizing related technologies to collect information from wearable objects for social interaction in public spaces [11].

2   Blobulous System

Blobulous is a novel interactive installation (see **Fig. 1** for example settings and **Fig. 2** for system overview) that interacts with participants through projected avatars in public spaces, which react to the participants' movement and body signals. Blobulous uses a large (possible public) projection to show abstract avatars, blobs of dots – therefore the name "Blobulous" – one for each participant and moving around slowly. The movement of the avatars is connected to the participant's movement in the space in front of the projection. The second mapping involved in the installation is from a participant's heart rate to the color of his or her avatar. The mapped colors range from blue (cold, low engagement) to red (warm, high engagement).

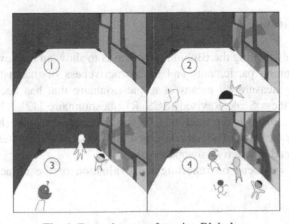

Fig. 1. Example space for using Blobulous

Fig. 2. Overview of system components

The Blobulous system consists of four parts:

1. Wireless heart rate sensors capture and send heart rate data from users to a central instance,
2. a central instance, including a receiver and a visual program, receives data from users and derives avatar behaviors represented as visuals on the projected screen,
3. a projector connected to the central instance, and
4. a Zigbee[1] network, which handles communication between sensors and the central instance.

3   Evaluation

The objective of evaluating the Blobulous system is to show an improvement of social connectedness among participants and the attractiveness of the installation. Social connectedness is measure by means of a questionnaire that has been derived from Social Connectedness Scale Revised (SCS_R) questionnaire [12]. The results about the social connectedness is reported in [13]. The experiment results showed a significant difference in the level of social connectedness between the two testing conditions (random avatars and interactive, mapped avatars).

In this paper we focus on reporting the evaluation of the attractiveness of the installation.

---

[1] http://www.zigbee.org/

3.1   Experiment Setup

In order to evaluate the attractiveness of the installation, it is better to include a group dynamics factor in the evaluation. 21 (14 male, 7 female) participants were recruited online and randomly divided into 7 groups according to their time preference. So, in most of the groups, participants did not know each other before the experiment. Users' backgrounds were distributed to Industrial Design (7), Electrical Engineering (4), Computer Science (3), Automotive/Logistics (3), Biomedical (2), Architecture (1), and Business (1).

Participants were asked to watch and explore the visuals projected on the wall (**Fig. 3**a) while wearing the sensor (**Fig. 3**b) and then have a short discussion about what they perceive from the visuals. Heart rate data was streaming automatically by the prototype while movement data was manually controlled via an Apple iPad using touchOSC [14] (Wizard of Oz) (**Fig. 3**c).

Fig. 3. Experiment room with a) projection screen, b) heart rate sensors, and c) central control

In the demo session, participants were explained details about the functionality of Blobulous and asked to come up with some ideas and try to demonstrate the ideas together with Blobulous. All sessions were recorded for later video analysis. The experiment room was prepared with a large projection onto the wall, an interaction space in front of the projection, and an experiment control area (depicted at the bottom of **Fig. 3**).

3.2   Instrument

AttrakDiff [15] is an instrument for measuring the attractiveness of interactive products. With the help of pairs of opposite adjectives, users (or potential users) can indicate their perception of the product. These adjective-pairs make a collation of the evaluation dimensions possible.

The following product dimensions are evaluated:

- Pragmatic Quality (PQ): Describe the usability of a product and indicates how successfully users are in achieving their goals using the product.
- Hedonic Quality – Stimulation (HQ-S): Mankind has an inherent need to develop and move forward. This dimension indicates to what extent the product can support those needs in terms of novel, interesting, and stimulation functions, contents, and interaction- and presentation styles.
- Hedonic Quality – Identity (HQ-I): Indicates to what extent the product allows the users to identify with it.
- Attractiveness (ATT): Describes a global value of the product based on the quality perception.

Hedonic and pragmatic qualities are independent of one another, and contribute equally to the rating of attractiveness.

3.3   Results

The map in **Fig. 4** was generated from the attrakdiff.de web service [15]. In this map, the values of hedonic quality are represented on the vertical axis (bottom = low value).

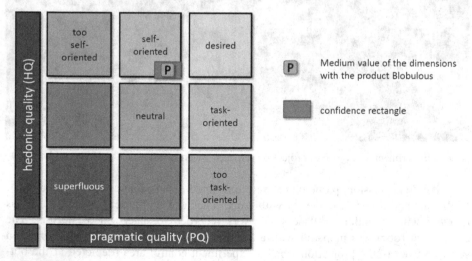

Fig. 4. Map with average values of the dimensions PQ and HQ and the confidence rectangle

The horizontal axis represents the value of the pragmatic quality (left = low value). Depending on the dimensions values the installation (called a product by AttrakDiff) will lie in one or more "character-regions". The installation was rated as fairly "self-oriented". However the value of pragmatic quality just reaches above the average values. Consequently, there is room for improvement in terms of usability. In terms of hedonic quality, the classification applies positively. The user is stimulated by the prototype; however the hedonic value is again just above average. So there is room for improvement in hedonic quality as well. The confidence rectangle is relatively small which shows the users are aware that they are evaluating a prototype, instead of a real product.

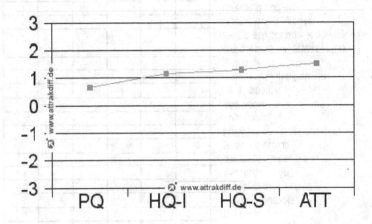

Fig. 5. Mean values of the four AttrakDiff dimensions for the prototype

Fig. 5 features a diagram of average values of the four dimensions PQ, HQ-I, HQ-S and ATT. With regard to HQ-I, the prototype is located in the above-average region. It provides the user with identification and thus meets ordinary standards. In order to bind the users more strongly to the concept, we must aim at improvement in the design. About HQ-S, the prototype is located in the above-average region and meets ordinary standards. In order to motivate and stimulate users even more intensely, we must aim at further improvement. The attractiveness value is located in the above-average region, which suggests the overall impression of the prototype is very attractive to the participants.

Fig. 6 presents the mean values of the word-pairs using in AttrakDiff questionnaire. Of particular interest are the extreme values. These show which characteristics are particularly well-received by the participants. For the Blobulous prototype it is clear that it is perceived as practical, manageable, integrating, bringing me closer, presentable, inventive, creative, innovative, captivating, challenging, novel, pleasant, attractive, likeable, inviting, appealing and motivating, while most of the word-pairs shows a tendency towards a positive experience.

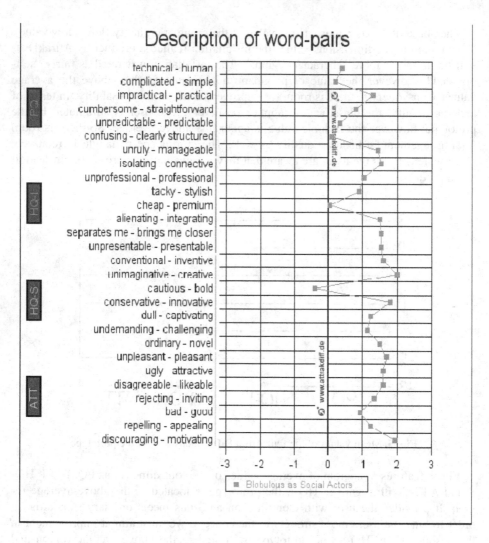

Fig. 6. Mean values of the AttrakDiff word pairs for the prototype

4   Conclusions and Future Work

The Blobulous installation was designed to act as a social actor, specifically to improve social connectedness between visitors. Blobulous draws great attention from users due to its colorful appearances and lively movements. It also raises social awareness between people while they are (acting) together. With those effects, Blobulous makes people talk about it, about each other and sometimes they try to understand Blobulous. By connecting people and computers physiologically, Blobulous has clear impact on social interaction and it also shows the attractiveness to people from aspects such as creativity, novelty, inviting and motivating.

In this work we also found that the AttrakDiff instrument to be useful and convenient in evaluating the attractiveness of public art installations.

The system needs to be further developed with the ability to act independently but not only mimicking to do so, which was a pragmatic design choice in this study. We are currently planning to bring the experience we had with Blobulous in a bigger public art installation project that will be carried out in Taicang, China. We are going to use multiple large LED displays and projections as part of a permanent public art installation, in combination with other art forms such as reliefs, lighting and metal work (see **Fig. 7**). The content of the displays and projects will be created by general public using social tools over social media[2].

It is clear that the current development in digital public arts involves a significant amount of new carriers in not only material, but also in technology, resulting new dynamic and interactive forms that require the artists to construct their work from a system view and with a good understanding of human-system interaction and related interface technologies.

Fig. 7. Interactive public art installation concept for Taicang, China

---

[2] http://youtu.be/m_Bjz1ekIdI

References

1. Wang, F., Hu, J., Rauterberg, M.: New Carriers, Media and Forms of Public Digital Arts. In: Culture and Computing, pp. 83–93. Springer, Heidelberg (2012)
2. Hu, J., Bartneck, C.: Culture Matters - a Study on Presence in an Interactive Movie. CyberPsychology and Behavior 11(5), 529–535 (2008)
3. Hu, J., et al.: ALICE's Adventures in Cultural Computing. International Journal of Arts and Technology 1(1), 102–118 (2008)
4. Lamb, R.: Alternative paths toward a social actor concept. In: Proceedings of the Twelfth Americas Conference on Information Systems. Citeseer (2006)
5. Reeves, B., Nass, C.I.: The media equation: How people treat computers, television, and new media like real people and places. Center for the Study of Language and Information, Cambridge University Press, Chicago, New York (1996)
6. Rogers, Y., Brignull, H.: Subtle ice-breaking: encouraging socializing and interaction around a large public display. In: Workshop on Public, Community. and Situated Displays (2002)
7. Rukzio, E., Wetzstein, S., Schmidt, A.: A Framework for Mobile Interactions with the Physical World. In: Proceedings of Wireless Personal Multimedia Communication, WPMC 2005 (2005)
8. Villar, N., et al.: Interacting with proactive public displays. Computers & Graphics 27(6), 849–857 (2003)
9. Cwir, D., et al.: Your heart makes my heart move: Cues of social connectedness cause shared emotions and physiological states among strangers. Journal of Experimental Social Psychology 47(3), 661–664 (2011)
10. Slovák, P., Janssen, J., Fitzpatrick, G.: Understanding heart rate sharing: towards unpacking physiosocial space. In: Proceedings of the 2012 ACM Annual Conference on Human Factors in Computing Systems. ACM (2012)
11. van der Vlist, B., et al.: Semantic Connections: Exploring and Manipulating Connections in Smart Spaces. In: 2010 IEEE Symposium on Computers and Communications (ISCC), pp. 1–4. IEEE, Riccione (2010)
12. Lee, R.M., Draper, M., Lee, S.: Social connectedness, dysfunctional interpersonal behaviors, and psychological distress: Testing a mediator model. Journal of Counseling Psychology 48(3), 310–318 (2001)
13. Le, D., Funk, M., Hu, J.: Blobulous: Computers As Social Actors. In: CHI 2013 workshop on Experiencing Interactivity in Public Spaces, EIPS, Paris (2013)
14. Helxer.net. TouchOSC (2012), http://hexler.net/software/touchosc
15. User Interface Design GmbH, AttrakDiff Tool to measure the perceived attractiveness of interactive products based on hedonic and pragmatic quality (2012), http://www.attrakdiff.de/en/Home/

Improving Motive-Based Search

Utilization of Vague Feelings and Ideas in the Process of Information Seeking

Mandy Keck[1], Martin Herrmann[1], Andreas Both[2],
Ricardo Gaertner[3], and Rainer Groh[1]

[1] Chair of Media Design, Technische Universität Dresden, 01062 Dresden, Germany
[2] Unister GmbH, Barfußgäßchen 11, 04109 Leipzig, Germany
[3] queo GmbH, Tharandter Str. 13, 01159 Dresden, Germany
{mandy.keck,martin.herrmann,rainer.groh}@tu-dresden.de,
andreas.both@unister-gmbh.de, r.gaertner@queo-group.com

Abstract. In complex search scenarios like planning a vacation or finding a suitable gift for a friend, the user usually does not know exactly what he is looking for at the beginning. However, this is the question that most search interfaces present as first step. In this paper, we discuss approaches for supporting the user in expressing a search query based on vague feelings and ideas. We therefore consider search interfaces on the syntactic, semantic and pragmatic level and discuss different mechanisms of these levels to support the first stages of the information seeking process.

Keywords: search interfaces, motive-based search, implicit interaction, context-aware systems, emotional interfaces.

1 Introduction

Complex search tasks such as looking for a suitable car, planning a vacation, or finding the perfect investment opportunity can last days or weeks and usually the user does not know exactly what he is looking for at the beginning. Unfortunately, most conventional web search interfaces require the user to transform a possibly vague information need into a specific search query [1]. These search systems are based on a bottom-up, system-driven approach that originated from a bibliographic paradigm. It is centred on collecting and classifying texts and devising search strategies for their retrieval, which describes the use of information from the system's perspective [2, 6]. But information seeking is an inherently complex human experience that includes a wide range of emotions and motivations beyond a particular problem or need. Consequently, search criteria are often based on emotional and desire-oriented decisions [3, 4]. There is an obvious gap between the system's traditional patterns of information provision and the user's natural process of information use: the system assumes certainty and order, whereas the problems of the user are characterized by uncertainty and confusion [5]. To get a better understanding of how people seek information and to describe the process of information search from the user's perspective, Carol Kuhlthau performed a series of studies and identified distinct phases and emotions

N. Streitz and C. Stephanidis (Eds.): DAPI/HCII 2013, LNCS 8028, pp. 439–448, 2013.

unique to each phase [6] (see Fig. 1). Particularly in the beginning stages, uncertainty and anxiety are an integral part of the process, followed by feelings of confusion, doubt and frustration in the exploration phase. The stage of exploration is often the most complex phase and involves actions such as locating information about the general topic, reading to become informed, and relating new information to what is already known to extend personal understanding. The formulation stage is the crucial turning point at which all the information explored thus far is expressed in a concrete, tangible requirement and the feelings change towards a sense of clarity. Although the first phases include the most complex tasks for the user, most search applications invest most of their effort in the collection and action phases [7] and the user is forced to express his vague ideas and feelings as a specific query which the system can understand.

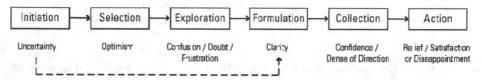

Fig. 1. The stages of the information seeking process and its distinct emotions [6]

Our goal is to investigate strategies and methods to support the first stages of the process of information search. In this paper, we focus on the stage of selection and exploration to lead the user from a feeling of uncertainty to clarity (see Fig. 1). Therefore, we concentrate on complex search tasks - we use the example of planning a vacation - in which the user is unsure of what he is looking for at the beginning. There is just a motive that specifies some general conditions and is influenced by emotions and interests of the user. Because this motive is the starting point of the search task, we call this type of task "motive-based" search.

2   Levels of an Information Retrieval System

Information retrieval systems operate on different levels depending on their ability to understand the user's needs. The three core levels described in Becker's IR Layer-Model [2] are defined as syntactic, semantic and pragmatic Level. These layers originate from linguistic and communication theory and can be subsumed under the large research area of semiotics [8].

2.1   Support on the Syntactic Level

Syntax operations represent the lowest form of semiotic user support. They are widely supported by popular search engines. Based on the contents of web pages, XML-descriptions and databases, the syntactic level enables the system to offer spelling corrections, query completion and many other search strategies described in [9] to improve the number of relevant hits and avoid empty results or deadlocks in the search process. The majority of these operations and moves still need explicit intervention by the user like choosing the most promising proposal or supplements for his query.

2.2   Support on the Semantic Level

The semantic model describes the meaning of signs and objects in form of hierarchies, whole-part relations and other meaningful linkages between concepts. Using these semantic models to provide the computer with a knowledge domain is a central idea of the Semantic Web [8]. With the help of web languages like RDF, DAML+OIL and OWL it is possible to create "machine understandable" knowledge by defining entities and their relations in subject-predicate-object triples [10]. The resulting Ontology Networks are a means of an intelligent and implicit user support and of the autonomous understanding of the domain and the goal of the user's actions. Lopez [11] identifies three different approaches to create a semantic engine: *The closed domain approach* supports only one previously selected domain (embodied by one or few linked ontologies). *Approaches restricted to the own semantic resources* like Wolfram Alpha[1] allow open domain requests relying on their own permanently updated dataset representing the knowledge of the world. *Open Linked Data search approaches* try to use the broadest information base by consulting different large knowledge sources like Freebase [2] or DBpedia[3].

2.3   Support on the Pragmatic Level

While the semantic level centres on the content [8] and its meaning for the computer, the pragmatic level is concerned with the context of the user's interaction with the machine. From the user's point of view, most of his information retrieval actions are basically on the pragmatic level [2]. He is trying to solve a specific task by combining his knowledge with the information presented by the search system. Therefore, the main challenge on this level is to present the most relevant information by considering the user's intentions. Since Computer and user don't share the same knowledge base it is important to observe and understand the context of the user [12].

The Pragmatic Web initiative addresses these issues by focussing on the user and his intention [8]. The goals of the initiative range from describing tools, practises and theories of why and how people use information [13] to improving the quality of collaborative, goal-oriented discourses in communities [14].

The Pragmatic Web cannot be seen as a separate web technology. Instead, it should be used as an additional input to enrich semantic technologies [15] to support and automate human to human knowledge exchange.

3   The Role of Context in Search Interfaces Design

When humans converse with other humans, they are able to incorporate implicit situational information like facial expressions and emotional dispositions of their conversational partner. In human-computer dialogue, the computer cannot take full advantage of the immediate situation of the user. By improving the computer's access

---

[1] http://www.wolframalpha.com/ (last access: 28.02.13)
[2] http://www.freebase.com/ (last access: 26.02.13)
[3] http://dbpedia.org/ (last access: 28.02.13)

to the context, the richness of communication in human-computer interaction can be increased [16, 17].

The context plays an important role in the research areas of embodied interaction and the design of search interfaces. This leads to a wide variety of definitions. Dourish claims that context can be manifold such as the tasks that the system is being used to perform, the reasons for which the tasks are being carried out, the settings within which the work is conducted, or other factors that surround the user and the system [17]. Schilit et al. define the main aspects of context as the computing environment such as devices and network capacity, the user environment such as location, collection of nearby people, social situation and the physical environment like lighting and noise level [19]. Abowd et al. define the context as "any information that can be used to characterize the situation of an entity. An entity is a person, place, or object that is considered relevant to the interaction between a user and an application, including the user and applications themselves."[16] Abowd et al. also distinguish between primary context types and secondary context. The primary context types such as location, identity, time and activity are used to characterize the situation of a particular entity. They can act as indices of other sources of contextual information and can help to find secondary context for the same entity, e.g. phone number or address to a given identity, as well as primary context for other related entities, e.g. other people in the same location [16].

Gathering contextual information to get a picture of the user's current task, problem or emotional disposition is a key for creating pragmatic and semantic support functions in information retrieval systems. Especially for a user who is entering a new and unfamiliar knowledge domain, context information could be used to adapt the interface, provide help or correct, specify and extend his inputs. An approach to the modeling of the user's context is to analyze interactions of the user. This includes explicit interactions such as direct and intentional clicks or touches, but also implicit interactions such as accidental movements, gestures and facial expressions. Since the visual analysis of the emotional disposition and spatial situation of the user is still a research issue, other clues could provide pieces of the context puzzle. Schmidt [18] and Davies [12] propose different sources of information like the location, time, duration, and technical aspects of the interaction, previous queries and parallel activities while searching, or the user's level of sophistication in language and tendency to spelling errors.

3.1   A Pragmatic Scenario

Tamani et al. propose a simple model to describe a pragmatic scenario with four types of collaborators [20] (see Fig. 2). The *Requestors* goal is to find web services providing solutions to his needs and problems. These services are made available by a large number of different *Providers*. The entity that matches the requirements of the requester with the services on the provider side is called *Broker Service*. To fulfill this task the broker needs to combine pragmatic and semantic functionality. It therefore needs access to contextual information on the requestor side as well as comprehensive meta information on the provider side. To make sense of the given information and resolve conflicts and ambiguities the broker should use machine readable ontologies and knowledge graphs of *Trusted Knowledge Bases (KB)*.

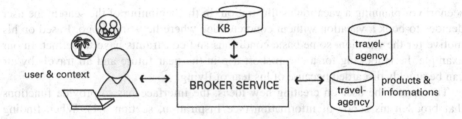

Fig. 2. A pragmatic scenario based on [20]

3.2   The Architecture of a Broker Service

Yuanchun et al. [21] refine the idea of the context sensitive Broker Service by adding a context layer to store personal, implicit, and explicit information about the user in a dedicated *Context Base*. The associated *Context Components* provide functions to acquire, manage, and distribute information about the user context. This covers detecting implicit and explicit context information by observing the input and sensors of the physical *Input Layer*, transferring them to the *Context Base* and offering an interface for the web service layer. The web service layer uses the preprocessed user information for Discovery and Collection of services that are likely to match the user's intentions. The *Service Composition Component* collects the service data and presents it to the user in a coherent and uniform way via the *Output Layer*.

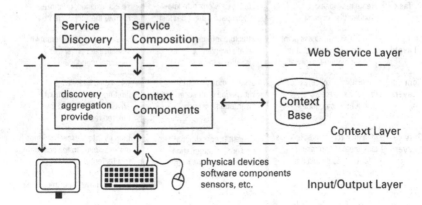

Fig. 3. Layered architecture of context services based on [21]

4   Supporting the Exploration Process

As shown in section 1, the initial stages of the search process need more support by the system and the user interface. Our goal is to develop a model with proposals on different layers for the interface designer to support the user in the exploration stage. Therefore, we distinguish different phases during the stage of exploration and, use the scenario of planning a vacation as illustration. In the beginning of the search, the user decides to book a vacation without concrete idea where he wants to go. Based on his motive for the vacation, some basic conditions and constraints have to be met. In our example, he is looking for a cheap short trip in the near future and all travels by air can be quickly discarded because of his fear of flying.

To support the user on creating new ideas, the interface has to provide functions that broaden his scope of information (see Inspiration, section 4.1). When finding some interesting topic, e.g. a trip to Paris, Rome or Madrid, the user's task is to read thematically relevant information, and to relate this information with previous knowledge in order to extend the personal understanding of the topic. The interface can support the user by offering functions to construct and organize his knowledge space (see Investigation, section 4.2). Subsequently, the user has to grasp the many possibilities of combining bits of information and different alternatives. The task of the interface is to help the user to narrow the scope and to create a focus (see Evaluation, section 4.3). These phases, illustrated in Fig. 4, cannot be seen as a sequential process; rather they describe different situations the user can be confronted with during the process of expressing his vague feelings and ideas as a concrete and tangible query.

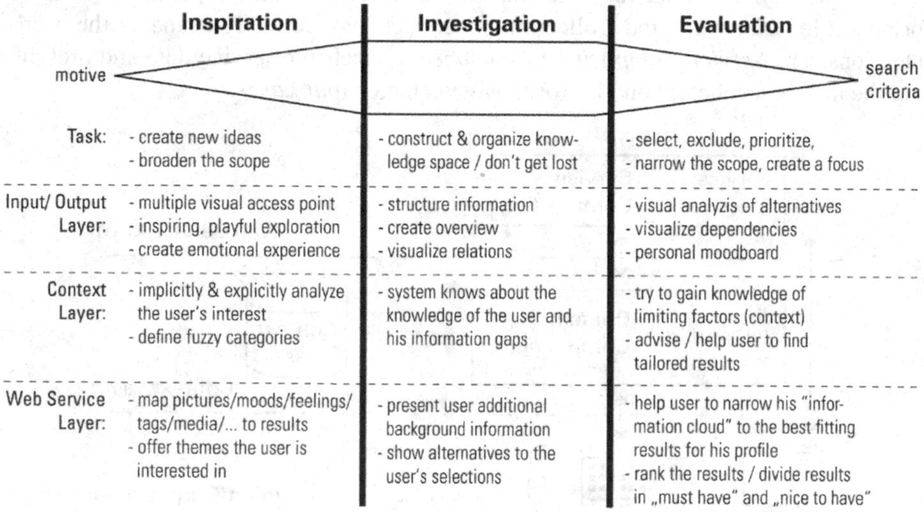

	Inspiration	Investigation	Evaluation
motive			search criteria
Task:	- create new ideas - broaden the scope	- construct & organize knowledge space / don't get lost	- select, exclude, prioritize, - narrow the scope, create a focus
Input/ Output Layer:	- multiple visual access point - inspiring, playful exploration - create emotional experience	- structure information - create overview - visualize relations	- visual analyzis of alternatives - visualize dependencies - personal moodboard
Context Layer:	- implicitly & explicitly analyze the user's interest - define fuzzy categories	- system knows about the knowledge of the user and his information gaps	- try to gain knowledge of limiting factors (context) - advise / help user to find tailored results
Web Service Layer:	- map pictures/moods/feelings/ tags/media/... to results - offer themes the user is interested in	- present user additional background information - show alternatives to the user's selections	- help user to narrow his "information cloud" to the best fitting results for his profile - rank the results / divide results in „must have" and „nice to have"

Fig. 4. Functions to support the exploration process

4.1   Inspiration

The motive of the user can depend on several factors such as a special reason for planning a vacation, e.g. relaxation, an activity like surfing or hiking, or a special place he wants to visit. For this reason, it is important to offer multiple access points to select the basic conditions and provide inspiration according to the user's needs.

Besides the collection of context information, the input/output layer displays the information to the user. To create an emotional experience, generate needs and stimulate desires, media like pictures, sounds, and movies can be used, e.g. mood boards in stylepark [22] or gettyImages Moodstream[4]. A playful interface is helpful as well, to increase curiosity, e.g. etsy.com, where the user can choose between different colour moods to explore the products (see Fig. 5, left).

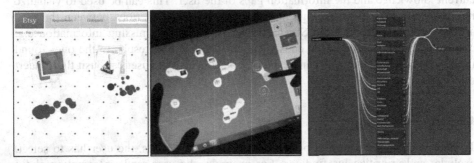

Fig. 5. Left: playful interaction on etsy.com, center: organizing collected items in BrainDump [23], right: visualized relations between included and excluded tags in DelViz [24]

The Context Layer is responsible for gathering information about the user and for analyzing where his interests lie. Therefore, context information can work with implicit information about the user, that is already known, or the device type, location, time etc. or the user can explicitly enter his interests, e.g. in form of selection of a theme or a questionnaire. For instance, the Moodstream of gettyImages offers different sliders describing tagged asset attributes, such as happy vs. sad, warm vs. cool, or nostalgic vs. contemporary, to gather explicit context information and match the pictures and sounds to this situation. Fuzzy Categories [26] can be helpful as well to describe vague ideas. The Context Layer has to deal with the challenge of generating fuzzy categories out of cultural, regional and individual preferences, e.g. "what does the colour red mean to the user?", "what is warm for the user?".

Finding suitable information according to the constructed context is the task of the Web Service Layer. It presents interesting articles concerning the user's interests or other people with similar interests and maps the selection, e.g. in form of a picture, sound or colour, of the user to relevant results.

4.2   Investigation

If the user is uncertain about the results gathered in the inspiration phase, e.g. a city he saw on a picture, he has to become informed about the topic, find relationships and create categories. In this phase, the user often has to handle a large amount of data and getting lost in this information space is highly probable.

---

[4] http://moodstream.gettyimages.com (last access: 26.02.13)

The interface can support the user in structuring his gathered information and visualize relations between his findings. The BrainDump system for example provides the functionality to create and manipulate visual images of his result set (see Fig. 5, center). The user can group collected items and annotate content during the search process, to visually memorize his findings [23]. In this case, the relations are made explicit. By using the capabilities of the Context Layer, the system keeps track of the current knowledge and the information gaps of the user. This can be used to visualize implicitly the state of knowledge in this topic and show relations between the read articles. The task of the Web Service Layer is to provide missing information e.g. climate and main season in the chosen country, and similar results to the ones found in the inspiration phase. This can be another place where the user can visit the concert of his favorite band.

4.3   Evaluation

To narrow down the scope of possibilities and create a focus, the user has to select, exclude, and prioritize his findings. For example, the user reads information about Paris and finds out that a concert of his favorite band is taking place there as well as in Rome, Madrid, and Berlin. Paris is easy to reach via train, but simultaneously with the concert the fashion-week takes place there, which leads to increased prices for accommodations in this time.

The task of the interface is to visualize the properties of his findings such as location, time, price, and activities and the dependencies between his constraints to support the user to compare the alternatives. For example, the search interface DelViz offers the selection and exclusion of different entities and the analysis of the relationships between these constraints using Bezier curves [24] (see Fig. 5, right). Another example is the Bohemian Bookshelf that uses interlinked visualizations to offer an efficient and analytical view on the properties of the result set [25]. The results that match the ideas of the user can be collected in a personal mood board as used in the Moodstream of gettyImages.

The Context Layer tries to gain knowledge of limiting factors, e.g. holiday times, religion, health issues, dislike, fears, and income of the user. With this kind of information, the system can advise against choosing Madrid by taking into account the user's fear of flying and the duration of travelling by car or train that would exceed a short trip. The Web Service Layer helps the user to narrow his "information cloud" down to the most fitting results for his profile and to rank his results, e.g. in likes/dislikes, must-have/nice-to-have.

5   Conclusions and Future Work

Search interface design in the area of embodied interaction has to address context as an important tool to adapt the interface to the user's needs. Recently many approaches have been developed that collect and provide contextual information through automated means, which removes the need for users to make all information explicit [16].

We introduced a scenario in the context of travel search that is supported on the syntactic, semantic, and pragmatic level and discussed requirements in different phases of exploration as well as the implicit use of context. We also emphasized the important role of visualization to support the user in finding (e.g. creating an emotional experience to inspire the user), structuring (e.g. visualize the state of knowledge) and analyzing (e.g. in visualize dependencies between the constraints of the user) huge amounts of data that the user has to deal with. Developing interfaces considering these levels and supporting the user in different stages of the search process to express his needs and to find suitable information is part of our future work.

Acknowledgments. This work has been supported by the European Union and the Free State Saxony through the European Regional Development Fund (ERDF). The research presented in this article has been conducted in cooperation of the Chair of Media Design -Technische Universität in Dresden, Unister GmbH from Leipzig and queo GmbH from Dresden, Germany. Thanks are due to Fred Funke, Annett Cibulka and Dana Henkens for their invaluable comments and support in this research.

References

1. Dörk, M., Williamson, C., Carpendale, S.: Navigating tomorrow's web: From searching and browsing to visual exploration. ACM Trans. Web 6(3), Article 13, 28 pages (2012)
2. Beckers, T., Fuhr, N.: Towards the Systematic Design of IR Systems Supporting Complex Search Tasks. In: Talk at the ECIR Workshop "Task Based and Aggregated Search" (TBAS), Barcelona, Spain (2012)
3. Dörk, M., Carpendale, S., Williamson, C.: The Information Flaneur: A Fresh Look at Information Seeking. In: CHI 2011: Proceedings of the SIGCHI Conference on Human Factors in Computing Systems, pp. 1215–1224. ACM (2011)
4. Baethies, S., Gaertner, C., Spanihel, S., Tsatsas, D.: Design of an Emotional Search in an Existing Product Platform. In: Proceedings of the IEEE/WIC/ACM International Conference on Web Intelligence, WI 2004, pp. 514–518, 20–24 (2004), http://www.stylepark.com
5. Kuhlthau, C.C.: The role of experience in the information search process of an early career information worker: Perceptions of uncertainty, complexity, construction, and sources. J. Am. Soc. Inf. Sci. 50, 399–412 (1999)
6. Kuhlthau, C.C.: Inside the Search Process: Information Seeking from the User's Perspective. Journal of the American Society for Information Science and Technology 42(5), 361–371 (1991)
7. Russell-Rose, T., Tate, T.: Designing the Search Experience: The Information Architecture of Discovery. Morgan Kaufmann (2012)
8. Di Maio, P.: The Missing Pragmatic Link in the Semantic Web, Business Intelligence Advisory Service Executive Update. Clutter Consortium 8(7) (2008)
9. Bates, M.J.: Information Search tactics. Journal of the American Society for Information Science 30(4) S. 205–S. 214
10. Mutton, P., Golbeck, J.: Visualization of semantic metadata and ontologies. In: Proceedings of the Seventh International Conference on Information Visualization, IV 2003, pp. S. 300–S. 305 (2003)

11. Lopez, V., Fernández, M., Motta, E., Stieler, N.: PowerAqua: Supporting users in querying and exploring the Semantic Web. Semantic Web 3(3), S. 249–S. 265 (2012)
12. Davies, C.: Finding and Knowing. Taylor & Francis (2007)
13. Paschke, A., Weigand, H.: The Pragmatic Web (and its many relations). In: 7th AIS SIGPRAG International Conference Session on Pragmatic Web, Monpellier (2012)
14. Schoop, et al.: The pragmatic Web: a manifesto. Communications of the ACM 49, S.75–S. 76 (2006)
15. de Moor, A.: What's up with the Pragmatic Web? Conversations in Context: A Twitter Case for Social Media Systems Design (2010), http://communitysense.wordpress.com/2010/09/14/whats-up-with-the-pragmatic-web/
16. Abowd, G.D., Dey, A.K.: Towards a Better Understanding of Context and Context-Awareness. In: Gellersen, H.-W. (ed.) HUC 1999. LNCS, vol. 1707, pp. 304–307. Springer, Heidelberg (1999)
17. Dourish, P.: Where The Action Is: The Foundations of Embodied Interaction. The MIT Press (2001)
18. Schmidt, A.: Implicit human computer interaction through context. Personal and Ubiquitous Computing 4(2), 191–199 (2000)
19. Schilit, B., Adams, N., Want, R.: Context-Aware Computing Applications. In: Proceedings of the 1994 First Workshop on Mobile Computing Systems and Applications (WMCSA 1994), pp. 85–90. IEEE Computer Society, Washington, DC (1994)
20. Tamani, E., Evripidou, P.: A Pragmatic and Pervasive Methodology to Web Service Discovery OTM Workshops (2006)
21. Yuanchun, L., Xianghong, Z.: A Personalized Service Oriented Pragmatic-Context Architecture and Supporting System. In: Seventh International Symposium on Instrumentation and Control Technology (2008)
22. Baethies, S., Gaertner, C., Spanihel, S., Tsatsas, D.: Design of an Emotional Search in an Existing Product Platform. In: Proceedings of the IEEE/WIC/ACM International Conference on Web Intelligence, WI 2004, pp. 514–518, 20–24 (2004), http://www.stylepark.com
23. Brade, M., Heseler, J., Groh, R.: An Interface for Visual Information-Gathering During Web Browsing Sessions: BrainDump. In: Proceedings of the Fourth International Conference on Advances in Computer-Human Interactions, Le Gosier - France, February 23-28, pp. S. 112–S. 119 (2011)
24. Keck, M., Kammer, D., Iwan, R., Taranko, S., Groh, R.: DelViz: Exploration of Tagged Information Visualizations. In: Informatik 2011 - Interaktion und Visualisierung im Daten-Web, Berlin (2011)
25. Thudt, A., Hinrichs, U., Carpendale, S.: The bohemian bookshelf: supporting serendipitous book discoveries through information visualization. In: Proceedings of the SIGCHI Conference on Human Factors in Computing Systems (CHI 2012), pp. 1461–1470. ACM Press, New York (2012)
26. Kianmehr, K., Koochakzadeh, N., Alhajj, R.: AskFuzzy: Attractive Visual Fuzzy Query Builder. In: IEEE 28th International Conference on Data Engineering (2012)

An Efficient Motion Graph Searching Algorithm
for Augmented Reality Characters

Sukwon Lee[1] and Sung-Hee Lee[1,2]

[1] Gwangju Institute of Science and Technology, Korea
[2] Korea Advanced Institute of Science and Technology, Korea
{sukwonlee,shl}@gist.ac.kr

Abstract. Realistic motion of virtual characters is a crucial factor for the reality and immersiveness of an AR application. Motion graph-based approach allows for generating infinitely many types of motions and may create remarkably realistic human motion from a limited set of motion data. In this paper, we present a method to efficiently search the motion graph using A* search algorithm in an AR environment. Specifically, we introduce three types of heuristic functions: the distance, previewed distance, and directional heuristic functions. The proposed heuristic functions reduce compute time significantly while not sacrificing the quality of motion. We demonstrate the effectiveness of our method by implementing an interactive AR application.

Keywords: Augmented reality, character animation, motion graph, A* search algorithm.

1 Introduction

A virtual character is an effective means to involve humans in the augmented reality (AR) environment; performing as a guide, tutor, actor, or even an adversary, virtual characters play a significant role to enrich a user's AR experiences while interacting with the user. Naturally, realistic motion of virtual characters is a crucial factor to increase the immersiveness of an AR application. The realism of motion depends on several aspects; for example, the visual realism (such as the smoothness of motion and non-penetration between a character and an environment), and the appropriateness of the motion regarding the context of interaction (such as accomplishing a user-specified goal) are both essential factors for the realism of a virtual character's motion.

The data-driven approach to generating character motions achieves remarkable visual realism by utilizing a database of the captured motion sequences of real humans. However, due to the limited size of the motion database, naïve data-driven approaches such as simple replay or minor editing of the captured motion sequences fail to create a wide variety of motions that are adaptive to the diverse, dynamic conditions of the AR environment.

Motion graph-based methods [1] overcomes this problem by allowing for generating infinitely many types of motions from a limited set of motion sequences through a

N. Streitz and C. Stephanidis (Eds.): DAPI/HCII 2013, LNCS 8028, pp. 449–458, 2013.

motion graph. The approaches mainly consist of two parts; one is constructing a motion graph, and the other searching for a proper motion sequence from motion graph. Motion graph is a data structure that encodes how a motion clip can make transitions to other motion clips. By traversing a motion graph, one can create a variety of motion sequences that can be reachable from a current motion clip.

In an AR environment, computational efficiency is critical since a virtual character must create motions in real time responsive to the dynamically changing environment. A main challenge of the motion graph-based approach in AR applications is thus to efficiently find a motion path that satisfies the goals and constraints. It is a difficult problem because, if a motion graph is too sparse,, it does not guarantee the existence of the transitions to satisfy the goals, and if it is too dense, it may take too long a time to find the optimal transitions.

In this paper, we present a method to efficiently search a motion graph in an AR environment. Specifically, we discretize the environment and apply A* search with a set of novel heuristic functions. We introduce three types of heuristic functions; that are, the *distance, previewed distance,* and *directional* heuristic functions. The proposed heuristic functions reduce compute time significantly while not sacrificing the quality of motion.

We demonstrate the performance of our method by implementing an interactive AR application in which a user specifies the start and end positions and orientations of a virtual character. The virtual character can then move toward the target point while avoiding obstacles and sit down on a sofa in a natural manner.

1.1   Related Work

Many AR works has studied AR agent for an interactive and user-friendly interface between computer and user. Barakonyi et al. [2] focused on how an AR character assists users for dealing with overwhelming information and widens user experiences. Holza et al. [3] and Chen et al. [4] embodied AR character into a simplified robot, enabling interaction with real objects for AR characters. Wagner et al. [5] and Kenji et al. [6] developed handheld AR applications that have the advantages of the portability in which AR agent can interact in a close range to the user. These studies focus on the functionality of an AR character as the medium that connects users with a computer system. In this paper, we deal with a motion planning problem of a virtual character in an AR environment.

Motion graph search algorithms have been studied extensively for finding a suitable motion sequence from a motion graph. Some approaches use the continuous path planning that is effective for synthesizing relatively short, single behavior motions when a good initial guess is provided. Lee et al. [7], Safonova et al. [8], and Sulejmanpašić et al. [9] developed methods to create a rather short sequence of motion that follows a rough path provided by the user. Since they plan the path only limited steps ahead, the performance may be significantly affected by the initial guess; For example, if the position of start state is far from the goal state, the initial facing direction points toward the far side, it may take infeasible computation time.

In contrast to the continuous path planning, the discrete path planning can handle longer motions that consist of multiple behaviors. In addition, the method does not require an initial guess because the search space is smaller and thus more extensive graph search is affordable. Our work uses a discrete path planning with A* search algorithm.

A* search algorithm has been applied to searching motion graphs in a discrete manner. Lau and Kuffner. [10] explored a behavior planning represented by finite-state machine (FSM) that defines the movement capabilities of a character. They used A* search for generating motions from FSM. Safonova et el. [11] represented the desired motion as an interpolation of weighted paths from a motion graph. The graph is carefully constructed to support interpolation and is pruned for efficient search. Our work is based on their method: We also prune the motion graph and search with A* algorithm to find the global optimum. The main difference is that they use only distance measurement for deciding the best next state while we define a novel heuristic function that uses the sum of three kinds of motion measurements.

2   Constructing Motion Graphs

The basic idea of motion graph is as follows: If motion frames are sorted in a different sequence than the stored one in a database, a character takes a different motion from an original motion. In this way one can generate infinitely many types of motions from motion data. However, rearranging motion sequences does not guarantee the realism unless the pose disparity between adjacent frames is sufficiently small. We can represent the disparity information as a directional graph, called motion graph, in which an edge corresponds to smooth transitions between frames in the motion database. For quantifying how smoothly a pose changes, we define the distance between two frames using the weighted sum of velocity differences of each joint.

$$D(i,j) = w_0 \|v_{p,i} - v_{p,j}\|^2 + \sum_{k=0}^{n} w_k \|v_{q_{k,i}} - v_{q_{k,j}}\|^2, \tag{1}$$

where $w_i \in \mathbb{R}$ is a weighting parameter that determines the importance of joints in terms of visual realism. The most influential joint has the highest weight value. $v_{p,i}$ is the linear velocity of the root at the i-th frame, and $v_{q_{k,i}}$ is the angular velocity of the k-th joint at the i-th frame. Specifically, the angular velocity is computed from the rotation matrix:

$$v_{q_{k,i}} = \log(R_{k,i}^T R_{k,i-1}), \tag{2}$$

where $R_{k,i} \in SO(3)$ is the rotation matrix of the k-th joint with respect to its parent joint. We can compute the distance $D(i,j)$ for every pair of frames.

2.1   Creating Transitions

If the distance $D(i,j)$ is less than a threshold determined by a user, we create an edge connecting the i-th and j-th frames. Determining the threshold value is related with choosing which is more important between the quality of motion transition and the connectivity of a graph. A lower threshold value increases transition quality, but decreases the connectivity of a motion graph, which deprives possible transitions to reach the goal state. In addition, poses in the same category tend to be connected easily while poses in different categories are harder to be connected. For example, a walking motion has periodic poses and could be connected with other walking motions on quite a low threshold value. In contrast, the density of transitions might be comparatively lower between walking and sitting motions. The low connectivity decreases the possibilities that one type of motion transits to the other, hindering creation of behavior-rich motions. Thus, the threshold value should be carefully chosen to keep balance between the acceptable quality and a rich connectivity.

3   Searching Motion Graph

Since every edge in a motion graph represents a piece of motion, graph walk corresponds to a motion generated by placing these pieces one after another. The remaining issue is to find proper motion pieces for making motion satisfy constraints. We use A* search algorithm for finding optimal motion through the motion graph.

A* search is to find the optimal path according to traveled cost and heuristic cost. Traveled cost measures the accumulated path cost from a start state to a current state, and A* searches for a solution that minimizes the traveled cost. Heuristic cost is measured by a problem-specific heuristic function that helps search algorithm examine states more likely to appear on solution path earlier than other states. To guarantee the optimality of the solution, the heuristic function must satisfy the triangle inequality and be admissible; for any pair s, s' where s' is a successor of s, $h(s) \leq c(s, s') + h(s')$ where $c(s, s')$ is a cost between s and s'. Additionally, $h(s)$ must not be lower than or equal to the distance from the state s to the goal. While these conditions guarantee the existence of an optimal solution path, it also means that A* must examine all the equally expected paths to find the optimal path. The weighted A* approach speeds up the search by relaxing the admissibility criterion by using an weighted heuristic, $h_{weighted}(s) = \epsilon h(s), \epsilon > 1$. Relaxing the criterion may cause a solution to fall into a sub-optimal result, a trade-off between the quality of the solution path and search time, but the resulting motion still looks quite natural because it consists of recorded data of human motion. To get problem-specific information about human motion, we design three types of heuristic functions; that are Distance, Previewed distance, and Directional heuristic functions.

Distance Heuristic Function $D(s)$: It measures how much distance remains for a virtual character to reach the goal position. At this point, the remaining distance is approximated by the remaining distance of the shortest path computed beforehand. To compute the shortest path, we discretize the environment into 2D cells and search for the shortest path using Dijkstra's algorithm on the cells. After a coarse 2D path is computed, we refine it by minimizing maximum acceleration and velocity.

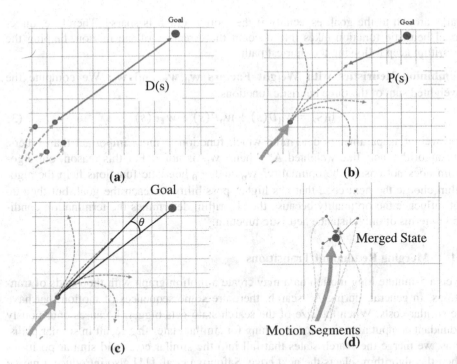

Fig. 1. (a) The distance heuristic function. The dashed line is candidates of the next edge. (b) The previewed distance heuristic function. The thick line is the current edge, and dashed line is the child edges (c) The directional heuristic function. (d) The nodes which fall into the same cell are merged into one red edge. The thick line is the merged edge.

Previewed Distance Heuristic Function P(s): Distance heuristic function cannot measure the possibility of the next type of motion when the next edge is selected. Because the type of current motion could transit to other types of motion that changes motion direction significantly, it is important to measure the possibility what type of motion is encountered after selecting one edge. Thus, we introduce new heuristic function using information which motion will be encountered. P heuristic function, named Previewed Distance, measures how much distance can be reduced when the edge s is taken as the next edge. The motion corresponding to the edge s has information where the motion will go at the next frame. If we preview several frames ahead instead one frame, P(s) can provide more accurate information what the remaining distance step becomes when s edge is selected in the next step.

Directional Heuristic Function $\theta(s)$: This function measures the difference between the direction of s and the direction of the shortest path. The direction of the edge can be computed by an imaginary line connecting the start and end points of the edge. In a similar way as the previewed distance, start and end points correspond to the start and end frames of the motion, respectively. Usually, when the goal position is given, human takes the shortest path instead of walking around. Since distance and previewed distance use only the distance measure, selected edge can give a path that walks around to the goal, especially if the motion graph is sparse. Therefore, directional heuristic function takes into account the direction of the motion, helping the algorithm keep following the shortest path.

Combining Heuristics with Weight Factors w_d, w_p, and w_t: We compute the weighted sum of the three heuristic functions.

$$h(s) = w_d D(s) + w_p P(s) + w_t \theta(s) \tag{3}$$

The weighting parameters determine which function is more important than others. Our algorithm acts like weighted A* when w_d is not 1. For this reason, our algorithm does not ensure the optimality. w_p and w_θ heuristic functions help the algorithm choose the next edge that has higher possibility to reach the goal, but they do not influence the optimality because the algorithm determines the termination condition in terms of only distance heuristic function.

3.1   Merging Redundant Transitions

Even a 5-minute long motion data may create a motion graph with thousands of transitions. In general, during A* search, there are some sequences of motion that have the similar costs. When the size of the search state gets bigger, it causes enormously redundant computation time for searching for similar states that result in similar paths. Thus, we merge the search states that fall into the similar costs and similar positions when the algorithm selects the next edge. Safonova et al. [11] also introduce a merge step, but they merge the redundant state in an offline step, in contrast to our merge step that works in on-line. In order to reserve transitions, we also merge the child states of the merged states. Fig. 1 (d) depicts the merge step. Blue small dots represent similar states, and dashed line is motion segment corresponds to motion graph edge. Whenever a set of child states reaches the same cell and direction, algorithm selects only one state, marked by a red dot, by minimizing the pose error among similar states. After selecting an optimal state, dashed lines (edges) are also merged into one thick edge.

4   Result

In this section, we describe experiments to validate the effectiveness of the proposed search algorithm for motion graphs.

4.1   Experimental Settings

We performed experiments in two different scenarios. In the first scenario, we set up a simple obstacle-free environment that includes only start and goal states. In the second scenario, the environment includes start and goal states, as well as an obstacle between the states. This example demonstrates that the algorithm can find an appropriate path while avoiding an obstacle. The environment has 1000×1000 cells, each of which has dimension of 0.5m ×0.5m, and has 16 directions. (Fig. 2)

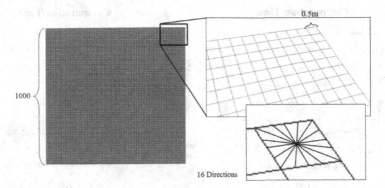

Fig. 2. The discretized environment has 1000×1000 cells. The size of cell is 0.5m $\times$0.5m, and each cell divided into 16 directions.

To construct a motion graph, we generated motion data of about 10-minute duration. The motion data consists of motions of walking in a straight line, stopping, turning, walking backwards, sitting and standing.

4.2 Simulation Results

In the two examples, we compared how much each heuristic function affects the result. We repeated the experiments as increasing the weighting factor. After the resulting path is computed, we measure the number of expands, the computation time, and the traveled cost. The graphs of the number of expansion and the computation time have the similar pattern because the computation time linearly increases according to the number of expansion of the edge in a graph. In addition, we measure the root mean square error (RMSE) of the resultant path with the optimal path that is acquired by A* algorithm without using a heuristic function.

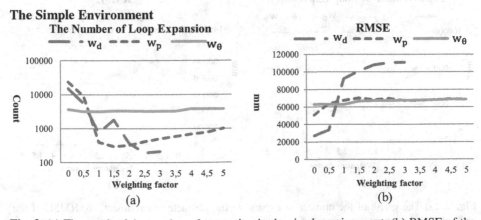

Fig. 3. (a) The graph of the number of expansion in the simple environment. (b) RMSE of the simple environment (in mm). (c), (d) The graph of the computational time according to weighting factor in the simple environment.

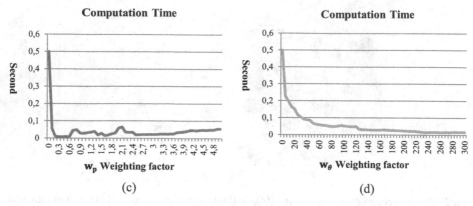

Fig. 3. (*continued*)

Fig. 3 (a) shows how much each weighting factor affects the number of expands. The expand number drastically decreases until w_p reaches 1.5 and increases after 1.5. The reason for this inflection is that higher weighting factor can cause redundant expand steps for reaching the optimal point. Since w_d is related with the optimality of the result path, RMSE is increased by w_d value as Fig. 3 (b). Fig. 3 (c) and (d) represent the computational time according to each weighting factor while w_d is set to 1. These graphs show our algorithm can reduce the computational time for searching motion graphs with holding the optimality.

The Obstacle Environment

In the obstacle example, the resulting graphs show the similar pattern with the simple environment. However, the error graph, RMSE, is affected by w_p factor because the optimal path is a curved line rather than a straight line.

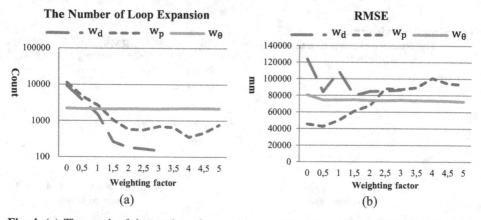

Fig. 4. (a) The graph of the number of expand in the obstacle environment. (b) RMSE of the obstacle environment (in mm). (c), (d) The graph of the computational time according to weighting factor in the obstacle environment.

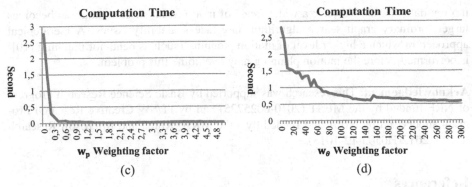

(c)   (d)

Fig. 4. (*continued*)

AR Application

Fig. 5. A virtual character walks toward user-specified positions in an AR environment

In this example, we apply our method to an AR environment that includes a chair and a sofa represented with 3D point clouds. The virtual character creates a smooth transition motions from the chair and sofa while achieving the desired pose specified on them.

5   Conclusion

In this paper, we dealt with a problem of searching motion graph using A* algorithm in AR application. One of the top priorities for motion graph-based method for AR applications is reducing computation time for searching an optimal path. To this end, we develop new heuristic functions capturing the characteristics of the human walking motion. The heuristic functions reduce computation time while not affecting the reality of the resulting motion. In addition, we developed a merging step that combines the redundant transitions of similar costs while the planner searches for the candidates.

In this work, we dealt with relatively small databases of 5 ~ 10 minute-long duration. With these databases, the character could create a small range of motions such as walking, sitting, and running. For the character to generate more various activities, motion database should have a wider range of motions. As motion database becomes larger, ordinary graph search algorithm may face scalability issues. A hierarchical approach in which a higher level of motion planning (such as behavior planning [10]) is performed before the motion planning may overcome this problem.

Acknowledgement. This research was supported by Basic Science Research Program of NRF funded by the MEST (2010-0025725) and by IT/SW Creative Research Program supervised by NIPA and funded by   the MKE, Korea and Microsoft Research (NIPA-2012-H0503-12-1013).

References

1. Kovar, L., Gleicher, M., Pighin, F.: Motion Graphs. J. ACM Transactions on Graphics 21(3), 473–482 (2002)
2. Barakonyi, I., Schmalstieg, D.: Ubiquitous Animated Agents for Augmented Reality. In: Proc. of IEEE and ACM International Symposium on Mixed and Augmented Reality 2006 (ISMAR 2006), Santa Barbara, CA, USA, pp. 145–154 (2006)
3. Holza, T., Campbella, A.G., O'Harea, G.M.P., Staffordb, J.W., Martinb, A., Dragonea, M.: MiRA—Mixed Reality Agents. J. Human-Computer Studies 69(4), 251–268 (2011)
4. Chen, I.Y.H., MacDonald, B., Wunsche, B.: Mixed Reality Simulation for Mobile Robots. In: IEEE International Conference on Robotics and Automation, ICRA 2009, pp. 232–237 (2009)
5. Wagner, D., Billinghurst, M., Schmalstieg, D.: How real should virtual characters be? In: Proceedings of the 2006 ACM SIGCHI International Conference on Advances in Computer Entertainment Technology, p. 57 (2006)
6. Kenji, M., Yasuyuki, S., Rieko, K.: The Weaved Reality: What Context-aware Interface Agents Bring About. In: Asian Conference on Computer Vision (ACCV 2000), Taipei (2000)
7. Lee, J., Chai, J., Reitsma, P.S.A., Hodgins, J.K., Pollard, N.S.: Interactive control of avatars animated with human motion data. ACM Transactions on Graphics (TOG) 21, 491–500 (2002)
8. Safonova, A., Hodgins, J.K., Pollard, N.S.: Synthesizing physically realistic human motion in low-dimensional, behavior-specific spaces. ACM Transactions on Graphics (TOG) 23, 514–521 (2004)
9. Sulejmanpašić, A., Popović, J.: Adaptation of performed ballistic motion. ACM Transactions on Graphics (TOG) 24(1), 165–179 (2005)
10. Lau, M., Kuffner, J.J.: Behavior planning for character animation. In: Proceedings of the 2005 ACM SIGGRAPH/Eurographics Symposium on Computer Animation, pp. 271–280 (2005)
11. Safonova, A., Hodgins, J.K.: Construction and optimal search of interpolated motion graphs. ACM Transactions on Graphics (TOG) 26, 106 (2007)

Intelligent Machine Space for Interacting with Human in Ubiquitous Virtual Reality

Youngho Lee[1], Young J. Ryoo[2], Jongmyung Choi[3], and Sungtae Moon[4]

[1] UVR Lab., Mokpo National University, Jeonnam, S.Korea
youngho@mokpo.ac.kr
[2] Intelligence Space Lab., Mokpo National University, Jeonnam, S.Korea
yjryoo@mokpo.ac.kr
[3] Department of Computer Engineering, Mokpo National University, Jeonnam, S.Korea
jmchoi@mokpo.ac.kr
[4] Future Convergence Technology Research Lab., Korea Aerospace Research Institute, S.Korea
stmoon@kari.re.kr

Abstract. Various computing paradigms such as ubiquitous computing, pervasive computing, ambient intelligence, and ubiquitous virtual reality have appeared. Now we should consider interaction between human and robots in ubiquitous virtual reality known as DigiLog space. In this paper, we propose intelligent machine space for human robot interaction in DigiLog space. For the human robot interaction in DigiLog space, a robot has to recognize the current situation and select proper behavior by itself. It has to receive information and context from DigiLog space and transfer current state of robot itself bidirectional way. Moreover, the robot has to accept user's commands and provide proactive services to users.

Keywords: human robot interaction, ubiquitous virtual reality, intelligent machine space.

1   Introduction

Recently various computing paradigms which are a concept of combining real and virtual world, such as ubiquitous computing, pervasive computing, ambient intelligence, and ubiquitous virtual reality have appeared to improve the quality of human life [1,2]. The paradigms are post-desktop model of human-computer interaction in which information processing has been thoroughly integrated into everyday objects and activities. Especially ubiquitous virtual reality supports expansion of human ability in real environment, like human in virtual environments with various technologies. Various sensors are installed in intelligent space such as smart home, smart office and smart car. The intelligent space acquires data from the sensors to understand situation and context and provides adaptive services or personalized services with human. Moreover ubiAgent and AR agent which have form of computer graphics have been developed [3,4,5]. These types of agents take a role of information guide. However it is lack of reality because it is not physical objects.

N. Streitz and C. Stephanidis (Eds.): DAPI/HCII 2013, LNCS 8028, pp. 459–465, 2013.
© Springer-Verlag Berlin Heidelberg 2013

Now we should consider how human and robots interact with each other in DigiLog space. Researches on robotics have a great effort to design and to implement various types of high performance robots [6,7]. Robots applying state-of-the-art technology such as ASIMO, HUBO have been developed [9,10] and robots such as a cleaning robot, AIBO are used in the daily life of human [14,15]. On the other hand some researchers on ubiquitous virtual reality proposed DigiLog space that combines physical world and its mirrored world to realize the 4D+ augmented reality [13]. In the DigiLog space, graphical agents could replace by physical robots and graphical agents and physical robots could exist in the same space. Now two research areas are fused, and it should be handled how to interact robots to coexist with humans in a smart environment.

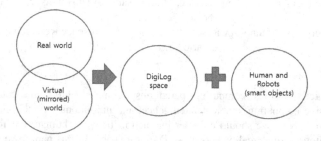

Fig. 1. Intelligent machine space with Digilog Space and Robots

In this paper, we propose intelligent machine space for human robot interaction in DigiLog space. DigiLog space is a place where virtual and real world are merged and where human and robots coexist (fig. 1). For the human robot interaction in DigiLog space, a robot has to recognize current situation and selects proper behavior by itself. It receives information and context from DigiLog space and transfer current state of robot itself bidirectional way. Finally the robot accepts the user's command and provides proactive service to a user.

This paper is organized as follows. In section2, DigiLog space and agent middleware in UVR is introduced. Intelligent machine space is proposed with several scenarios in section 3. We introduce a humanoid robot we are developing in section 4. Finally, the conclusions mentioned in section 5.

2   Related Works

2.1   Ubiquitous Virtual Reality and DigiLog Space

Ubiquitous virtual reality is a computing paradigm combining virtual reality with ubiquitous computing. Currently the ubiquitous virtual reality research aims at the development of novel computing paradigms for "holistic DigiLog life in smart space." 'Ubiquitous Virtual Reality' is called 'U-VR','Ubiquitous VR', or 'UVR', according to emphasizing viewpoint how to combine real and virtual world.

It was defined that "U-VR is a new paradigm combining virtual reality with ubiquitous computing. This can provide user with various applications according to the context of users or environments"[16]. In this definition, 'context' is one of important factor to combine virtual reality and ubiquitous computing. Later U-VR was defined as "A concept of creating ubiquitous VR environments which make VR pervasive into our daily lives and ubiquitous by allowing VR to meet a new infrastructure, i.e. ubiquitous computing". This is similar to the concept of cross reality [17].

Now, researchers on ubiquitous virtual reality began to study DigiLog space. DigiLog space is a result of combining physical world and its mirrored world (virtual world) for building the 4D+ augmented reality with the technology such as real-time dual-space registration and context of interest based information visualization [13]. It has following three properties: a plentiful 3D link between real and virtual space with additional information, an immersive five-sense augmentation in real world, and bidirectional interaction on the fly in linked dual spaces.

2.2   Agent Middleware in Ubiquitous Virtual Reality

UCAM stands for unified context aware application model. Early UCAM was evolution of middleware model ubiquitous computing researchers proposed such as the context toolkit. The UCAM connects sensors and applications by using a unified context in the form of Who (user identity), What (object identity), Where (location), When (time), Why (user intention/emotion) and How (user gesture), called 5W1H [18]. The UCAM applied to the sensors and applications in the ubiHome, a test bed for ubiComp-enabled home.

Later the UCAM has evolved in the three areas: ubi-UCAM, vr-UCAM, wear-UCAM. As ubi-UCAM is for ubiquitous computing environment (real world), vr-UCAM is for virtual environments and wear-UCAM is for human body area, that is wearable computing environments [19,20].

While people's attention has been focused on mobile computing, UCAM changed context-aware mobile augmented reality platform (CAMAR)[21,22]. CAMAR lets users interact with smart objects through a personalized control interface on a mobile AR device. Also, it supports enabling contents to be not only personalized but also shared selectively and interactively among user communities.   To realize CAMAR, CAMAR core platform was proposed. The architecture is mainly composed of two parts: context-aware framework for a mobile user (UCAM), and AR application toolkit using OpenScene Graph [23]. The architecture shows context-aware toolkit could help mobile AR application in order to enhance different levels of decision making process.

Initially CAMAR focused on the visualization methods and tracking algorithm for augmented reality, later it developed to AR agents [24]. In the ubiquitous virtual reality environment, AR agents adaptively perceive and attend to objects relevant to their goals. To enable AR agents to perceive their surroundings, the agents have to determine currently visible objects from the scene description of what virtual and physical objects are configured in the camera's viewing area.

To generalize the idea, context-aware cognitive agent architecture was proposed. The proposed agent architecture has a vertically layered two-pass agent architecture with three layers. The three layers are AR (augmented reality) layer, CA (context-aware) layer, and AI layer. This architecture enables ambient smart objects to interact with users in various ways of intelligence by exploiting context and AI techniques.

In summary, the UVR has been developed to provide a platform technology for complete DigiLog space, and agent technology for intelligent services and content. There has been much effort to merge virtual and real world with physical or contextual methods and to provide intelligent services or content in this environments. Now we need to consider not only software services in the form of invisible applications, AR agent but also visible physical objects in the form of embedded systems or robots.

3   Intelligent Machine Space in Ubiquitous Virtual Reality

In this section, we introduce intelligent machine space for human robot interaction in DigiLog space. DigiLog space is a place where merging real world with mirrored world. Here 'merging' means that matching real and mirrored world with 3D coordinates, context of interest (CoI), and bidirectional exchange of information between real and mirrored world. CoI is defined as a user's interesting context about any information that characterized the situation [13]. Mirrored world is a database for saving data and information of the real world. The mirrored world could be built by ubiquitous virtual reality infrastructure such as UCAM, CAMAR, etc. Therefore, the mirrored world is filled with contextual information.

Fig 2 shows robots and human in DigiLog space. Let R^4 and M^4 are real world and mirrored world including time dimension respectively. CoI_R and CoI_M are subsets of R^4 and M^4. R and H are space for representing a robot and human. Fig 3 shows interaction model for human robot in intelligent machine space. While real world and mirrored world can be surjective (not injective), CoIs could be a bijective mapping.

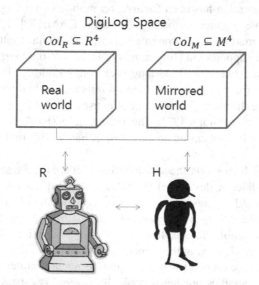

Fig. 2. Robot and human in intelligent machine space

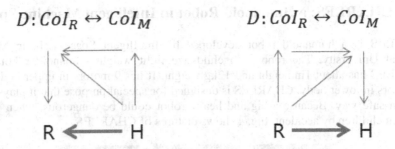

Fig. 3. Interaction model for Human and robot in intelligent machine space

For the human robot interaction in intelligent machine space, a robot has to recognize current situation and selects proper behavior by itself. A robot gathers data from sensors that it has and receives information from mirrored world. For instance, a robot would be able to identify positions in successive frames for object tracking, or to aggregate basic coordinate data and sensor values with clustering techniques into object regions. For the responsiveness, the robot would be able to generate behavior comparable to involuntary response directly from perceptual input, to generate behavior comparable to voluntary response by interpreting a local action, and to interpret the local action with respect to continuously updated information retrieved from perception, such as tracking data.

A robot should receive information and context from DigiLog space and transfer current state of robot bidirectional way. When a robot navigates in a building, it is hard to find current location of robot with only sensors attached itself because large scale indoor location tracking system is still not working perfectly. In this situation, the robot would receive proper clues to find current location from DigiLog space. The clue could be some textures for video tracking, Wi-Fi signal strength, ultra-sonic sound, etc. The robot compares the data from sensors attached itself with the data from DigiLog space to find out current position.

The robot has to accept the user's command and provide proactive service to a user. There are two types of user's command: direct response command and long-term goal command. Direct command means that a command from users which can be followed directly without special consideration or algorithm. For example, if the robot gets an order such as 'move this way' or 'turn around', then it could to it without any special approaches. If the robot gets an order such as 'go room 215 and find a document and bring it back to me', it has to solve many technical problems by itself. First it has to find a way form current position to room 215 and start to move. While it moving, if some obstacles appears (e.g. elevator is not working properly), the robot search the path again. After the robot arrives at the room 215, it has to find where the document is. Then the robot get back to a place where user stays currently (in case, user moves other place). This process is really hard work with only sensors robot has without information from DigiLog space.

4   CHARLES: a Humanoid Robot in Intelligent Machine Space

CHARLES is a humanoid robot developed by Intelligent Space Lab. in Mokpo National University. The robot is a child-size light weight humanoid robot. The CHARLES has about 1m height and 12kg weight. It has 9 motors in upper body and 12 motors in lower body. CHARLES is designed for special purpose that it plays with child in safe way. Because a big and heavy robot could be dangerous, when it fall down on children by accident. Fig. 4 shows pictures of CHARLES.

Fig. 4. CHARLES: a humanoid robot in intelligent machine space

5   Conclusion and Future Works

In this paper, we proposed intelligent machine space for human robot interaction in DigiLog space. For the human robot interaction in intelligent machine space, a robot has to recognize the current situation and select proper behavior by itself. A robot should receive information and context from DigiLog space and transfer current state of robot bidirectional way. Finally the robot has to accept user's commands and provide proactive service to users. We are developing CHARLES, a humanoid robot, for human robot interaction in intelligent machine space. We expect that CHARLES will provide users with proactive services.

References

1. Lee, Y., Oh, S., Shin, C., Woo, W.: Recent Trends in Ubiquitous Virtual Reality. In: International Symposium on Ubiquitous Virtual Reality, pp. 33–36 (2008)
2. Lee, Y., Oh, S., Shin, C., Woo, W.: Ubiquitous Virtual Reality and Its Key Dimension. In: International Workshop on Ubiquitous Virtual Reality, pp. 5–8 (2009)
3. Barakonyi, I., Weilguny, M., Psik, T., Schmalstieg, D.: Monkey Bridge: autonomous agents in augmented reality games. In: ACM SIGCHI International Conference on Advances in Computer Entertainment Technology, pp. 172–175. ACM (2005)
4. Barakonyi, I.: Ubiquitous Animated Agents for Augmented Reality. Institut für Softwaretechnik und Interaktive Systeme 188(2) (2006)
5. Oh, S., Woo, W.: ARGarden: Augmented Edutainment System with a Learning Companion. In: Pan, Z., Cheok, D.A.D., Müller, W., El Rhalibi, A. (eds.) Transactions on Edutainment I. LNCS, vol. 5080, pp. 40–50. Springer, Heidelberg (2008)
6. Goodrich, M.A., Schultz, A.C.: Human-Robot Interaction: A Survey Foundations and Trends. In: Human Computer Interaction, vol. 1, pp. 203–275. Now Publishers Inc. (2007)

7. Fong, T.W., Nourbakhsh, I., Dautenhahn, K.: A Survey of Socially Interactive Robots: Concepts, Design, and Applications. Robotics Institute (2002)
8. Sakagami, Y., Watanabe, R., Aoyama, C., Matsunaga, S., Higaki, N., Fujimura, K.: The intelligent ASIMO: system overview and integration. In: Proceedings of the 2002 IEEE/RSJ International Conference on Intelligent Robots and Systems (IROS 2002), vol. 3, pp. 2478–2483 (2002)
9. Mutlu, B., Osman, S., Forlizzi, J., Hodgins, J.K., Kiesler, S.B.: Perceptions of ASIMO: an exploration on co-operation and competition with humans and humanoid robots. In: 1st ACM SIGCHI/SIGART Conference on Human-Robot Interaction, HRI 2006, USA, March 2-3, pp. 351–352. ACM (2006)
10. Park, I.-W., Kim, J.-Y., Lee, J., Oh, J.-H.: Online Free Walking Trajectory Generation for Biped Humanoid Robot KHR-3(HUBO). In: ICRA, pp. 1231–1236 (2006)
11. Oh, J.-H., Hanson, D., Kim Null, W.-S., Han, I.-Y., Kim, J.-Y., Park, I.-W.: Design of Android type Humanoid Robot Albert HUBO. In: Proc. IEEE/RSJ Int. Conf. on Intelligent Robots and Systems, pp. 1428–1433 (2006)
12. Steels, L., Kaplan, F.: AIBO's first words: The social learning of language and meaning. Evolution of Communication 4, 3–32 (2001)
13. Ha, T., Lee, H., Woo, W.: DigiLog Space: Real-Time Dual Space Registration and Dynamic Information Visualization for 4D+ Augmented Reality. In: International Symposium on Ubiquitous Virtual Reality, pp. 22–25 (2012)
14. Sung, J.-Y., Grinter, R.E., Christensen, H.I.: "Pimp My Roomba": designing for personalization. In: CHI, pp. 193–196 (2009)
15. Sung, J.-Y., Grinter, R.E., Christensen, H.I.: Domestic Robot Ecology - An Initial Framework to Unpack Long-Term Acceptance of Robots at Home. I. J. Social Robotics 2, 417–429 (2010)
16. Jang, S., Kim, S., Woo, W.: When VR meets UbiComp. In: The Third Young Inverstigator's Forum in Virtual Reality (2005)
17. Lifton, J., Laibowitz, M., Harry, D., Gong, N.-W., Mittal, M., Paradiso, J.A.: Metaphor and Manifestation - Cross-Reality with Ubiquitous Sensor/Actuator Networks. IEEE Pervasive Computing 8, 24–33 (2009)
18. Jang, S., Woo, W.: ubi-UCAM: A Unified Context-Aware Application Model. In: CONTEXT, pp. 178–189 (2003)
19. Hong, D., Suh, Y., Choi, A., Rashid, U., Woo, W.: wear-UCAM: a toolkit for mobile user interactions in smart environments. In: Sha, E., Han, S.-K., Xu, C.-Z., Kim, M.-H., Yang, L.T., Xiao, B. (eds.) EUC 2006. LNCS, vol. 4096, pp. 1047–1057. Springer, Heidelberg (2006)
20. Lee, Y., Oh, S., Suh, Y., Jang, S., Woo, W.: Enhanced Framework for a Personalized User Interface based on a Unified Context-aware Application Model for Virtual Environments. IEICE Trans. Inf. & Syst. E90-D, 994–997 (2007)
21. Suh, Y., Park, Y., Yoon, H., Chang, Y., Woo, W.: Context-Aware Mobile AR System for Personalization, Selective Sharing, and Interaction of Contents in Ubiquitous Computing Environments. In: Jacko, J.A. (ed.) HCI 2007. LNCS, vol. 4551, pp. 966–974. Springer, Heidelberg (2007)
22. Oh, S., Woo, W.: CAMAR: Context-aware Mobile Augmented Reality in Smart Space. In: International Workshop on Ubiquiotus Virtual Reality, pp. 48–51 (2009)
23. Hong, D., Woo, W.: CAMAR Core Platform. In: ISUVR 2007, p. 260 (2007)
24. Oh, S., Gratch, J., Woo, W.: Explanatory Style for Socially Interactive Agents. In: Paiva, A.C.R., Prada, R., Picard, R.W. (eds.) ACII 2007. LNCS, vol. 4738, pp. 534–545. Springer, Heidelberg (2007)

The Association of In-world Avatar Investment with Expectations of Behavioral Change

Jacquelyn Ford Morie, Sin-Hwa Kang, and Eric Chance

Institute for Creative Technologies, University of Southern California
12015 Waterfront Drive, Playa Vista, CA 90094-2536, USA
{morie,kang,chance}@ict.usc.edu

Abstract. We explore whether watching the behavior of an avatar created by a user can affect that users' behavior in the actual world. This research aims to determine if we can achieve results similar to those obtained from an experimental design detailed in Study 3 of "Virtual Self-Modeling: The Effects of Vicarious Reinforcement and Identification on Exercise Behaviors" (Fox and Bailenson, 2009), but using avatars created by observers rather than experimenter-provided ones enhanced with a photographic likeness. Fox and Bailenson theorized that the behavioral change elicited stems from modeling the behavior of physically similar people as supported by social cognitive theory. In this study, we focused more on investigating whether people's own avatars' behavior would elicit behavioral change based on social-perception theory. Therefore, users observed their own avatars that were doing exercise or not regardless of any physical similarity between the avatars and their owners. The preliminary results showed there was a strong trend for users to engage in physical activities more when they watched their own avatars exercise, compared to observing their own avatars that did not exercise. The results also demonstrated that users with higher body mass index (BMI) engaged in physical activities more when they watched their own avatars with exercise behavior, compared to users with lower BMI. This study seeks to clarify whether or not the notions of psychological reflexivity and avatar ownership/investment are possible factors influencing avatar owners' behavioral outcomes.

Keywords: Avatar, virtual worlds, investment, VRE, self-perception theory.

1 Introduction

In the last decade there has been a progression from traditional immersive Virtual Reality Environment (VRE) applications towards inclusion of these techniques within persistent, socially connected Virtual Worlds (VWs). This change now permits what was formerly a complex, stand-alone system with costly equipment to become widely connected and accessible over the Internet by a potentially limitless audience. Beyond these differences, a major advancement separating VREs from VWs is the embodiment of the user in the form of a personalized avatar. Avatars are users' online self-representations through which they inhabit the virtual world and communicate with other beings. Users are typically able to customize their avatars and often make them

N. Streitz and C. Stephanidis (Eds.): DAPI/HCII 2013, LNCS 8028, pp. 466–473, 2013.

to project some aspect of their physical or internal self-image. Recent research is beginning to substantiate a deep connection that forms between the user and his or her avatar with repeated use [1,2,3].

We have been exploring affordances of avatars to determine what can be leveraged to create more effective applications delivered via VW platforms. We are especially interested in what they offer to health care applications, wherein the avatar, as a personal expression of self, can make visible potentially useful cues about a person's psychological state. Inhabitants of virtual worlds take great care to form an avatar representation that relates to themselves in important ways. This may be a physical similarity, as much as can be achieved with the toolset provided by the virtual world designers, or it may be a projection of an internal state the person perceives is a more truthful representation of self than what nature has provided.

This research study aims to determine if we can achieve results similar to those obtained from an experimental design detailed in Study 3 of "Virtual Self-Modeling: The Effects of Vicarious Reinforcement and Identification on Exercise Behaviors" by Fox and Bailenson [4], but using avatars created by participants rather than experimenter-provided virtual humans enhanced with the photographic likeness of the user. Fox and Bailenson theorized that the behavioral change they found stems from modeling the behavior of physically similar people as supported by social cognitive theory. The results of their study demonstrated that when people observe a virtual representation of self (VRS) exercising, they are more likely to report an increase in subsequent exercise behavior than those who view their VRS loitering.

1.1   Theoretical Background: Self-perception Theory

This study design was based on self-perception theory, which asserts that an altered self-representation can affect people's behavior by basing their own beliefs and attitudes on a third person perspective of themselves [7,8]. This indicates that one could alter one's own behavior and change beliefs or attitudes based on watching one's self presented via an avatar. Johnson and Downing [9] found that people who wore a costume representing a Ku Klux Klan group increased the amount of electric shock more than people wearing a nurse's uniform when they played a role of a teacher and were asked to deliver the shock to a learner who made mistakes. Yee and colleagues [8] report that people can achieve self-perception through role-play, such as a virtual setting with an avatar. This environment lends itself more easily to this kind of objective behavioral self-perception since role-playing by a user's own avatar would decrease any deliberate manipulation of behavior in his/her role-playing in the real world offline. Wolfendale [10] addresses an attached perspective as a means to explore how people associate with their own avatars. She argues that attachment to other beings allows people to create their identity through constructing relationships with others. She specifically describes that attachment to an avatar is not a drastically different concept from attachment to others in the real world offline because "avatar attachment is expressive of self-identity and is a means of communication with others – communication that takes place in a setting of shared values and expectations" [10].

Based on these findings, we speculate that people's behavior could be affected by watching their own avatar performing a deliberately designed behavior. For instance, regarding the Proteus Effect, Yee [11] argues (but doesn't prove) that people would engage in their usual workout more if they are represented using a physically fit avatar for themselves, compared to an average-looking avatar. The Proteus Effect provides a basis for people's behavioral change as a result of their avatars' appearance. We extend this concept to observe people's behavioral changes regarding avatars they themselves had created and therefore had some perceived investment in, whether or not they were physically similar to their offline self.

1.2   Research Problems and Questions

We found contradictory findings in previous work. Some researchers [4] assert physical similarity between a user and his/her own avatar is required to elicit the user's behavioral change. Other researchers [5,6] argue that a physically dissimilar avatar might work to provoke a user's behavioral alteration. Based on previous findings, we believe that the mechanism of behavioral change is unclear as to whether it results from a personal recognition factor or if a feeling of ownership/investment of the avatar is at play. In this study, we explore whether or not the notions of psychological reflexivity and avatar ownership/investment are possible factors influencing the behavioral outcomes. Users in our study observed avatars that they had created using their own desktop monitor (their usual way of participating in the virtual world). In the original study [4], authors also suggest to explore the influence of VRSs in other types of virtual worlds than immersive virtual environments, such as desktop settings. In the study, users experienced virtual reality using a virtual reality head-mounted stereo display, or HMD, but participants in our study were situated within a full online virtual world that was displayed on a desk-top computer monitor.

In this study, we specifically investigated whether people's experience with their personal avatars' behavior could alter their own behavior in the offline world, as was found with the Fox and Bailenson study [4] which used photo-graphically textured avatars as VRS. We further explored how users' BMI and the length of their ownership of their avatar are associated with the amount of their engagement in physical activities after watching their own avatars within the virtual world that were doing exercise or not.

2   Study Design

The experimental design[1] was a 2 between-subjects experiment: own avatar with exercise behavior (participant's personal avatar running on a treadmill) and own avatar without exercise behavior (participant's personal avatar loitering) (see images in Fig. 1). Using a between-subjects design, participants observed an avatar in the virtual world of Second Life for 5 minutes 20 seconds in one of the experimental conditions.

---

[1] The experimental design in this paper was part of a more extensive design involving three conditions.

As in the original study, the nature of the experiment was masked, and visual attention kept on the avatar, by a visual distractor task wherein a sequence of 20 numbers flashed over the avatar for later recall. Twenty four hours after the experiment, participants were emailed a link to a survey. The main dependent variable was a physical activity scale. Before starting a main interaction with avatars, subjects filled out a general demographic survey that included questions on personality characteristics. Participants were compensated using a virtual currency in Second Life.

Participants. One hundred and forty three participants (own avatar with exercise behavior: 97, own avatar without exercise behavior: 46; 72% women, 28% men; average 37 years old) were recruited from Second Life through the posting of flyers in various user groups. Participants were told they could invite their friends to participate as well.

Measurements. Avatar age (i.e. "How long have you used this avatar?") and BMI (Body Mass Index) were assessed as explanatory variables including general demographic information in a pre-questionnaire before an actual interaction. In a post-questionnaire, the number of hours for users' engagement in their physical activities using PPAQ (Paffenbarger Physical Activity Questionnaire, [12]) was measured as a dependent variable. The questionnaire has nine items and the sample items include "Sleep, rest" and "Standing, washing dishes or cooking, driving a car or truck."

 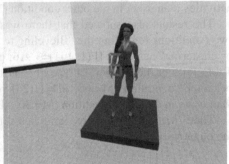

(b) Condition 1: Own avatar with exercise behavior   (a) Condition 2: Own avatar without exercise behavior

Fig. 1. Two experimental conditions

3   Preliminary Results

We first ran a MANOVA (Multivariate Analysis of Variance) to investigate users' own avatars' activity type in owners' behavioral changes. The independent variable was the two types of condition: own avatar with exercise behavior and own avatar without exercise behavior. The dependent variables were the amounts of users' nine physical activities. Preliminary analyses were conducted to ensure no violation of the assumptions of normality, linearity, univariate and multivariate outliers, homogeneity of variance-covariance matrices, and multicollinearity. We further ran a Pearson's

Correlation to find the associations of users' BMI and own avatar age with the amount of their physical activities. Preliminary assumption testing was performed to check for normality, linearity and homoscedasticity, with no serious violations observed. The average of BMI was 27 for the "own avatar with exercise behavior" condition and 32 for the "own avatar without exercise behavior" condition. The average avatar age was 2.8 years for the "own avatar with exercise behavior" condition and 3.2 years for the own avatar without exercise behavior" condition. In this preliminary data analysis, we wanted to find the specific types of physical activities users performed more after their participation in the study, so we did not run a Factor Analysis to combine the original items of the physical activities into a smaller number of factors. Other analyses of the associations between other variables are currently in progress.

3.1   Results of MANOVA Analysis

The results showed that there was a moderately significant difference between two conditions regarding the "Sitting quietly, watching television, listening to music, or reading" activities [$F(1, 141)=3.823$; $p=.053$; Wilks' Lambda$=.878$; $\eta^2=.026$ (see Table 1)]. For these sedentary type of activities, users in the "own avatar without exercise behavior" condition (M=3.78, SD=2.788) reported higher amount of their activities than users in the other condition (M=2.92, SD=2.308).

The results also showed that there was a strong tendency of difference between two conditions regarding the "Bicycling to work for pleasure, brisk walking, painting or plastering" activities [$F(1, 141)=3.916$; $p=.050$; Wilks' Lambda$=.878$; $\eta^2=.027$ (see Table 1)]. For these vigorous type of activities, users in the "own avatar with exercise behavior" condition (M=.65, SD=1.128) reported greater amount of their activities than users in the other condition (M=.30, SD=.511).

There was no statistically significant difference between two conditions regarding the other activities.

3.2   Results of Correlations Analysis

We did not discover statistically significant results of correlations between the avatar age and other variables. However, we found statistically significant results of positive associations between BMI and two physical activities.

In the "own avatar with exercise behavior" condition, the results showed that users with a higher BMI did "standing, washing dishes or cooking, driving a car or truck" activities more than users with a lower BMI after observing their own avatars running on a treadmill [$r=.220$, n=97, p=.030] (see Table 2 (a)).

In the "own avatar without exercise behavior" condition, the results demonstrated that users with a higher BMI did "sleep, rest" activities more than users with a lower BMI after watching their own avatars loitering [$r=.346$, n=46, p=.019] (see Table 2 (b)). There were no statistically significant associations between BMI and the other activities.

Table 1. MANOVA results with the independent variable (own avatars' activity type) and dependent variables (the hours users engaged in their physical activities)

	Own avatar with exercise behavior		Own avatar without exercise behavior		F	η^2	P
	μ	SD	μ	SD			
Sitting quietly, watching television, listening to music, or reading	2.92	2.308	3.78	2.788	3.823	.026	.053
Bicycling to work for pleasure, brisk walking, painting or plastering	.65	1.128	.30	.511	3.916	.027	.050

Table 2. Pearson's Correlation Coefficients between Avatar age, BMI, and the amount of physical activities (the hours users engaged in their physical activities)

(a) Condition 1: Own avatar with exercise behavior

	Avatar age	BMI	Sleep, rest	Standing, washing dishes or cooking, driving a car or truck
Avatar age	1	.036 (p=.724)	.033 (p=.746)	.096 (p=.350)
BMI	.036 (p=.724)	1	-.076 (p=.457)	.220* (p=.030)
Sleep, rest	.033 (p=.746)	-.076 (p=.457)	1	-.239* (p=.018)
Standing, washing dishes or cooking, driving a car or truck	.096 (p=.350)	.220* (p=.030)	-.239* (p=.018)	1

(b) Condition 2: Own avatar without exercise behavior

	Avatar age	BMI	Sleep, rest	Standing, washing dishes or cooking, driving a car or truck
Avatar age	1	-.127 (p=.402)	-.007 (p=.961)	-.222 (p=.138)
BMI	-.127 (p=.402)	1	.346* (p=.019)	-.129 (p=.394)
Sleep, rest	-.007 (p=.961)	.346* (p=.019)	1	-.243 (p=.104)
Standing, washing dishes or cooking, driving a car or truck	-.222 (p=.138)	-.129 (p=.394)	-.243 (p=.104)	1

4   Conclusions and Implications

The outcome of our study indicates that users' own behavior is affected after observing their avatars' behavior. There is a strong tendency that users engage in physical activities more when they watched their own avatars that did exercise, compared to observing their own avatars that did not. This might be explained by avatar owners' attachment to their avatars, which may increase the likelihood that they will perceive their avatars as themselves in virtual worlds online. We further observed that there were significant correlations between users' BMI and the amount of their physical activities after watching their avatars' exercise behavior. This outcome suggests that overweight users may be encouraged to engage in more physical exercise in the real world after observing their avatars' exercise behavior. However, there were no significant associations between the length of users' avatar ownership and the quantity of their physical activities. This implies that avatar creation matters regardless of how long the owner has been using it.

Our findings are supported by self-perception theory that asserts people's behavior can be altered by observing their own behavior with a third person perspective. Fox and Bailenson [4] also point out that this effect may possibly be the result of users being reminded of good memories associated with exercise that inspired them, or perhaps guilt from neglecting a healthy exercise regimen that motivates them after seeing their avatar exercise. However, that explanation would not account for the increase in rest for the own avatar without exercise condition.

We argue that the outcome of our study indicates a potential for avatars in a desktop setting to be used within a health care application regarding physical exercise similar to that mentioned by Fox and Bailenson [4], who envision a program that motivates employees to work out in the gym during lunch and subsequently see a visual reward of some sort through the avatar after logging a history of their exercise routine.

We anticipate that data from this study will help clarify whether or not the psychological relationship between the avatar and its owner should be further investigated as a factor influencing the results of behavioral changes elicited by avatar use.

References

1. Jensen, S.S.: Actors and their Use of Avatars as Personal Mediators. MedieKuture 25(47), 29–44 (2009)
2. Vasalou, A., Joinson, A.N.: Me, myself and I: The role of interactional context on self-presentation through avatars. Computers in Human Behavior 25(2), 510–520 (2009)
3. Fox, J.: Avatars for Health Behavior Change. In: Noar, S.M., Harrington, N.G. (eds.) eHealth Applications. Routledge (2012)
4. Fox, J., Bailenson, J.N.: Virtual self-modeling: The effects of vicarious reinforcement and identification on exercise behaviors. Media Psychology 12, 1–25 (2009)
5. Yee, N., Bailenson, J.: The Proteus effect: The effect of transformed self-representation on behavior. Human Communication Research 33(3), 271–290 (2007)

6. Jin, S.A.A.: "I Feel More Connected to the Physically Ideal Mini Me than the Mirror-Image Mini Me": Theoretical Implications of the "Malleable Self" for Speculations on the Effects of Avatar Creation on Avatar–Self Connection in Wii. Cyberpsychology, Behavior, and Social Networking 13(5), 567–570 (2010)
7. Bem, D.: Self perception theory. In: Berkowitz, L. (ed.) Advances in Experimental Social Psychology, vol. 6, pp. 2–57. Academic Press, New York (1972)
8. Yee, N., Bailenson, J.N., Ducheneaut, N.: The Proteus Effect: Implications of transformed digital self-representation on online and offline behavior. Communication Research 36(2), 285–312 (2009)
9. Johnson, R.D., Downing, L.L.: Deindividuation and valence of cues: Effects on prosocial and anti-social behavior. Journal of Personality and Social Psychology 37, 1532–1538 (1979)
10. Wolfendale, J.: My avatar, my self: Virtual harm and attachment. Ethics and Information Technology 9(2), 111–119 (2007)
11. Yee, N.: The Proteus Effect, Health Games Research: Advancing Effectiveness of Interactive Games for Health (2009), http://www.healthgamesresearch.org/our-publications/research-briefs/the-proteus-effect (retrieved)
12. Paffenbarger Jr., R.S., Wing, A.L., Hyde, R.T.: Physical activity as an index of heart attack risk in college alumni. American Journal of Epidemiology 108, 161–175 (1978)

Atmospheres and Socio-spatial Patterns: Designing Hyperspaces for Knowledge Work

Jörg Rainer Noennig[1] and Lars Schlenker[2]

[1] TU Dresden, Department of Architecture, Junior Professorship of Knowledge Architecture,
Dresden, Germany
joerg.noennig@mailbox.tu-dresden.de
[2] TU Dresden, Media Centre/Centre for Continuing Education, Dresden, Germany
lars.schlenker@tu-dresden.de

Abstract. The paper focuses on the importance of socio-spatial patterns and atmospheric qualities for knowledge work in real and virtual environments. On the background of research in the fields of Knowledge Architecture, Online Worlds and Environmental Design we show the interdependence between architectural design and human-computer interaction. The paper presents a design approach for "hyper-spaces" that fuses the qualities and opportunities of both realms into defined design-patterns.

Keywords: Atmosphere, Socio-Spatial Patterns, Knowledge Work, Architecture, Environmental Design, Virtual Worlds.

1   Introduction

In processes of knowledge work like learning, researching, or innovating, interactive communication is commonly regarded a central factor for success. Yet, communication is a complex environmental mechanism that goes beyond the technical transmission of information between humans and machines. Our point is that interactive communication is strongly determined by physical, psychological, and social context. We therefore advocate additional modes of ambient communication - communication that transfers information and activity via social structure, via spatial design, as well as through the "atmospheric" conditions arising from the combination of both.

In this paper, specifically, we want to line out the importance of socio-spatial patterns and the impact of atmospheric qualities on interaction in learning environments. We will show the interdependence and mutual relation between these two factors.

As it comes to knowledge workers, research teams, or learning groups, communication is not only to link communities in physical proximity. More than ever, communication has to bridge between separated people, institutions and locations, sometimes over large geographical or organizational distance. For this, a central question is how to combine the advantages of near-physical contact and face-to-face communication with the demands of far-distance interaction. In order to support the creation of high performance work-environments with this capacity, the paper puts

N. Streitz and C. Stephanidis (Eds.): DAPI/HCII 2013, LNCS 8028, pp. 474–483, 2013.

forward an integrated approach that combines design sciences and behavioral sciences into a new form of "environmental conditioning". As its very endeavor, the paper fuses research from the fields of Knowledge Architecture and Human Interaction Design into the concept of "hyperspaces for knowledge work". The concept regards "Atmosphere" and "Socio-Spatial Pattern" as key success factors for successful knowledge workplaces. Employing this insight for physical and for virtual environments, as well as for their combination, a wide range of applications can be found in the context of work place design, in educational settings, and in R&D planning.

2   Atmosphere as Cognitive Primer for Knowledge Work

2.1   Environmental Factors for Cognition

The diffuse nature of cognitive processes makes it difficult to identify success factors for intellectual achievements. However, besides neurological and psychological determinants, environmental factors have emerged as a new focus both on macro and micro scale [2], [5]. The way a classroom is set up on micro-scale, or how a technology cluster is organized in a larger region, directly impacts on the knowledge performance of the respective place and its users. Still there are few investigations about the relation of intellectual performance and environmental conditions, that is: the social, psychological and physical conditions of knowledge creation.

Experiments and surveys have shown that besides the "hardware" of physical environments also a number of "soft factors" has to be recognized as essentially contributing to knowledge processes. To a wide extent, such soft factors may be organizational and administrative items, however a large part of them is atmospheric in nature. Common terms like "ambience", "climate", or "mood" indicate such vague yet highly determining kinds of environment. Good ideas are "in the air" and inventions come "out of the blue". Generally, one easily recognizes a "creative atmosphere", "a relaxing mood", or "a climate of fear". That is due to the very powers of atmospheres as a collective shared experience - which renders it a high-potential media for knowledge work too, for knowledge work itself turning into a complex group- and networking matter.

Atmospheric qualities are understood not only by individuals who emotionally respond within seconds, but also by large groups, or societies, who manage to quickly establish a common sense. As can be observed in music or sports events, atmosphere immediately tells and transmits even across large crowds. This distinguishes atmospheres from the "hardware" configuration of cities, buildings, or spaces: the latter may well control societies and their physical behavior, but they lose power when it comes to impacting on individuals mind (Fig.1). Individuals detach themselves from physically defined / defining environment by simply changing place, yet detaching oneself from an atmosphere, from a mood, or an environmental climate is far more difficult. It stays attached not only with the very location, but also with the persons who recognized it.

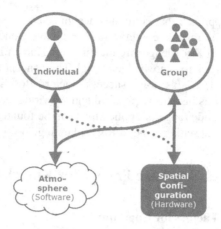

Fig. 1. Different impact of environment: Strong "atmospheric control" upon individuals and groups; weak "spatial control" on individuals (yet strong upon collectives)

2.2   Designing Atmospheres

Atmospheres play a decisive role in environments for learning and researching, yet they are almost impossible to design. Being commonly recognized as a chief environmental impact, they slip off the design and planning agendas though. Atmospheres appear to be sensitive items with far too complex dynamics as to cope with them with static schemes. Still, there is a dire need for atmosphere design, for approaches that address this kind of soft conditioning for knowledge work spaces.

Diverse philosophical and sociological inquiries have clarified that "atmosphere" is a field condition that arises from dynamic interaction - the interaction of people with people ("Milieu"), as well as from the interaction of people with things ("Ritual"), and even activity between and around things ("Aura"). For our case, these constellations may be re-interpreted as the relations of knowledge workers and their work ethics with their physical and social work environment.

2.3   Creative Microspaces

It may be difficult, if not impossible, to design atmosphere in large. On micro-scale, however, there is reliable experience and insight on how to condition atmospheres for learning and research, for creativity and innovation. Hence, the very focus of this paper is on microspaces, on places that allow face-to-face interaction among small groups, or teams. Thus a knowledge microspace may be defined as a place of limited extension, dedicated to creative production, innovation, and learning. The place is determined by specific hardware, software, and atmosphere. Here, "Hardware" may be understood as spatial division, furniture, surface material e.g. "Software" may be understood as administrative and organizational structures, communication processes, and / or control mechanisms. These architectural and managerial terms are relatively easy to describe and to design. However, "Atmosphere" as an ambient quality arising from the interplay of social and spatial structure, is more difficult to describe and define. In order to conceptualize this third core measure, we have especially investigated Garage laboratories and Coworking spaces. These microspaces may be surprisingly far from conventional knowledge work environments, nonetheless they are of immense interest because of their outstanding intellectual and creative performance. Their configuration of hardware, software and atmosphere provides a setting which enables and empowers outstanding intellectual achievements. In other words: they feature a high "knowledge performance" which can be described as the ratio of intellectual output, or cognitive activity, in relation to spatial efforts (e.g. size, equipment, construction costs). Commonly, the power of such microspaces is due to their ambience, to a strong atmospheric definition which emerges as a result of spatial-organizational setup and the mental "operation systems" of its users.

Example 1: Garage Lab. Garage labs have become a myth as an environment of maximum entrepreneurial creativity. On the one hand, this can be explained by socio-spatial configuration: small work teams, high physical proximity, real-time interaction and intense communication. On the other hand, and as decisive as well, psychological and atmospheric determinants enable the very "Garage creativity": detachment, seclusion, un-observedness, and a sense of low value environment. The combination of these factors generates a start-up spirit of experimentalism and challenge, a sense of alertness, activity, and motivation. Widely independent from environmental constraints, this clandestine setting is the very location for what economists call "Radical" or "Disruptive Innovation" (Fig. 2).

Fig. 2. Radical Innovators: Google in their startup garage at Menlo Park (Source: Abondance.com)

Example 2: Coworking Spaces. As a new trend worldwide, Coworking spaces are collective workplaces that attempt to translate the knowledge performance of garage environments to a more public and formal setting. Besides its formal architectural definition - which takes stylistic reference to the studio-environment of the creative class, a specific kind of atmosphere is being cultivated and enhanced. As a means of environmental enrichment, exchange and interaction are to be displayed, creativity to be demonstrated. Dictated by fast changing project work and team re-configuration, sociability and community spirit have become requisite conditions for the 21st century creative class - which is to be supported by adequate environments. (Fig.3).

Fig. 3. Creative atmosphere in Coworking Space (Source: Neonworx)

2.4   Online Games: Multi User Virtual Environments

Besides places of immediate physical interaction like Garage Labs or Coworking Spaces, online games and virtual worlds are increasingly gaining importance as places for social interaction and exchange. Especially so-called Multi User Virtual Environments (MUVIs) are used for communication and collaboration in learning and knowledge work. As a socially oriented variation, MUVIs have developed from online games; they differ from other online communication environments by their idea that - in addition to the persistence of an internal virtual world - also scenes from the real world are involved, creating thus a reference to architectural forms and typologies.

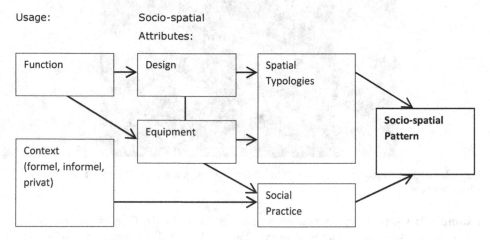

Fig. 4. Contents of Socio-spatial patterns of real-built environments (Source: [6], p.22)

Whereas spaces, as a part of a micro-context, signal the common presence of participants, their atmosphere indicates the social conditions of joint interaction. The commitment to a space-typology and to related socio-spatial patterns represents a contextualization of interaction based on well-known social rules. Socio-spatial patterns produce a recognizable form. They include specific spatial-typologies as well as instructions for action in terms of their social practice (Fig.7). Further, they also induce spatial atmospheres which in turn associate with psychological factors like acceptance, motivation, or inspiration. By this chain of effect, socio-spatial patterns influence the social climate and thus the work attitude of users.

Better Face-to-Face? Interaction takes place on the basis of verbal and non-verbal communication and includes a high degree of socio-emotional information. In contrast, computer-based interaction is an exchange of persons who are not assembled at the same time in one location or room. Measured in terms of the high social contextualization of face-to-face conversations, computer-mediated interaction is as impersonal as its perception of another person is limited. It therefore leads to problems such as a reduced social presence of the participants and a limitation of a commonly shared knowledge background.

Example: 3D Online Worlds. Since a few years, 3D online worlds are available via local client and broadband internet connection, thereby giving path for bringing the third dimension into virtual environments. Despite their artificiality and lack of tactile qualities, online worlds very directly appeal to experiences and strategies of dealing with designed environments and associated spatial information and knowledge. Their affordances are completely legible only against the background of their social connotations.

Users and creators of online worlds design specific spaces and places for the social interaction of communities or social units. These buildings and spaces not only have metaphorical significance; they are symbols of social organization too. Their socio-spatial features and affordances relate to everyday spatial practices and form a basis for a common understanding, thereby influencing the success of social activities in online environments. Just as atmospheres, also spatial-typological references help to create an interaction background that can be read and accepted by all users (Fig. 4). This provides the chance for alternative social constructions, even social re-engineering: In online worlds it is easy to experiment with changing teams, projects, and spatial configurations. Architecture, as a deliberately designed, semantic and visible structure of the room, would be a symbol of social arrangement with the aim to enable space-related activities. Described as social spaces in online worlds and virtual environments they provide a framework of certain possibilities for action [1].

3D is more Atmospheric. Certainly, 3D representations open up more opportunities to adjust and tune atmospheric qualities. Thus, in turn, enables the psychological pre-conditioning as is necessary for high performance knowledge work (emotions, motivation, and thus impact on learning success. In our investigations, 3D spaces are seen to be more inspirational ("Never seen before!") and easy-to-adjust ("Change wall pattern!"). In regard to contemporary developments in interactive design (emotion sensing, smart environments, ubiquity etc.) it may be claimed that space not only tunes emotions, but space itself becomes emotional, sensitive, and responsive (Fig. 5). Then, space cannot be seen as a tool to enact power and control over people, but rather as a participator on its own, an actor within creative communities. Then, architectural design in online worlds and interactive digital environments turn into active players, supporting social contextualization of online communication and collaboration processes [6].

Fig. 5. Informal atmosphere in the Virtual World Second Life (Source: [6], p.IX)

2.5   Conclusion

Users of real and virtual environments select and use specific spatial settings for their interaction with other people. They prefer defined socio-spatial typologies as a means of socialization, and specific atmosphere as a means of mental conditioning. For highly interactive work and communication processes, knowledge workers depend on environments conditioned to a low-threshold of social participation and comfortable and informal atmosphere. There is a dire need for approaches that integrate appropriate soft qualities into comprehensive architectural planning and environmental design. As the term "design" seems not very applicable to the qualities at stake, new means and measures for a dynamic "conditioning" of atmospheric environments must be established. Before all, they may be found in the field of Environmental psychology and behavioral studies.

The benefits of adequate atmospheric conditioning in the context of knowledge work can be easily described: knowledge workers get primed for intellectual challenge, for creative activity, for sharing and cooperation. As environmental psychology holds, this can be suggested by certain environmental settings. Spaces and environments can be purposefully emotionalized, charged with semantics and with sentiments. The "sciences" of marketing and propaganda have developed powerful means for this purpose already. As shopping lanes and supermarkets can be purposefully set to trigger a mood of consumption, knowledge workplaces may be set for intellectual production as well. Stages, bars, and hotels explicitly show how ambience and atmosphere can be created. The mechanisms that induce certain social behavior thereupon are unclear, but powerful. That much can be said: Through conditioning suitable atmospheres social climate may emerge.

3   Research Design: Design Research

Transdisciplinary Approach. As a crossboundary endeavor, our research links design science and behavioral sciences, specifically: the fields of architectural and human-computer interaction design on the one hand and environmental and social psychology on the other. Within this combination, the emerging field of Knowledge Architecture investigates the correlation of spatial configuration, social interaction, and knowledge processes. Thus far, the importance of built environments for knowledge generation has been confirmed by investigations in the field of innovation management and creativity studies [4]. Digital communication systems and virtual environments in turn offer spaces explicitly designed for interaction processes and mutual exchange. Media design provides effective means to apply such insight to larger communication networks and information processes. The sociability of game designs gives an overview of the organization and structure of online communities. Users of virtual worlds and online games can be engaged with generating different types of spaces for social interaction. These spaces may consist of textual or iconic information, three-dimensional items or complex buildings like in a real-world environment. Visitors may not only perceive these objects, but even interact with them. Virtual spaces can offer options for activities just like real-life environments.

Priming by Design. Environmental and social psychology explains how people are get "programmed" by physical and social context ("priming"). Various means and measures were tested to track the cognitive performance of humans in certain spatial configurations and their dependence on factors like environmental perception or awareness. There is strong evidence that cognitive performance of knowledge workers - which widely depends on soft factors like motivation, inspiration, and cooperation mindset - can be influenced by spatial environments [3]. Physical or digital, they are strong atmospheric triggers for the necessary mental setup. So far investigations were carried out either in physical or digital contexts, and only rarely related to cognitive performance. Hence our assumption is that combined cyber-physical environments ("Hyperspaces") whose emergence seems an inevitable future development, will heavily influence the performance of knowledge workers, be them in education, R&D, or administration. We have looked for exemplary models and design procedures - and found telling references.

3.1   Stage Design

Apparently the most promising microspaces for knowledge work are stages. Spatial settings in computer games and virtual worlds can be regarded a form of stage sets too. A stage is to establish ad hoc atmosphere and creative activity. It is an "atmospheric device" for stimulating defined moods and sceneries. Over the centuries, stage set and stage design have developed detailed routines for the application of shape, color, light, perspective, sound etc. Thus a stage enacts multiple powers to evoke atmosphere. At least three distinct modes of affect can be distinguished. Firstly, a stage set works as an image to look at. For the observers in the ranks, a stage is to create an image, or a visual atmosphere. But viewer and scenery are separated: the stage presents a picture to be seen from a distance. Secondly, especially for the actors, the stage is an inclusive environment, a space container. The actors act within a scenery; they are immersed in a virtual space. Thirdly, the stage is an experimental laboratory for the enactment of a process of social interaction. "Staging" means in its broadest sense: Making place for human activity, and defining a point of view for its observation. The stage is an experimental playground for social interaction (drama), and atmosphere (scenery).

Fig. 6. Neutral stage for ad hoc atmosphere (Oskar Schlemmer)

In order to fulfill these different modes of atmosphere, the space as it is must be without specified qualities. A stage without drama is uncanny. A scenery without atmosphere dead. A good stage therefore appears as a rich neuter, physically empty, full of virtual stories and settings. Exactly this quality makes the stage a prototypical creative workplace. As a social workshop, laboratory, and showroom in one, it is a blueprint for high performance knowledge work spaces. A virtual environment that hints at the potential power of online knowledgescapes.

4   Outlook: Towards Hyperspace

People work, learn, and interact in real and virtual spaces alike. Whereas spaces of the built environment are medially determined and perceived, medial environments are spatially determined. Interaction similarly takes place in virtual and physical spaces, thus embedding itself in a "hyper-environment". We hold that only an approach that conceptually integrates virtual and real-built environments will be able to respond to the current demands of knowledge work. Despite being increasingly based on communication media, knowledge work environments ought to employ the immediate power of "natural" spatial interaction, of direct personal and social contact, and of atmospheric conditioning. They may translate such features into digital settings, and explore uncommon new ways of interacting with, and tuning-in to spaces. In the digital architectural environments, the mental images and ambiences as evoked by the setting turn into eminent design items. Looking at the creation of atmosphere in stage design e.g. as well as in digital media (computer game design) valuable hints can be gained on 1) how atmospheric environments may be purposefully created, 2) how they influence, impact and determine their varity of users. Studies have shown that especially atmospheric settings decide upon attitude and performance of the involved communication partners [6], [2].

We plead for common design patterns in the creation of real and virtual environments. Atmosphere shall be seen as a prime design objective in physical as well as in online architectures. The conditioning of social, psychological, and intellectual climate instead of designing configurations of things and objects appears to be a powerful approach. It introduces new creative procedures as well as new targets to design. It puts emphasis on items that seemed unrelated to design work hitherto but have emerged as key features in the recent past (human behavior and recognition). We have to extend our notion of communication. Besides the established modes of information logistics and data exchange, the diffuse yet complex media of space, environment and context come into play. They usher in a new type of ambient communication.

References

1. Adamus, T., Nattland, A., Schlenker, L.: Second Life as a social environment. In: Hebbel-Seeger, A., Reiners, A., Schäffer, T. (eds.) Synthetic Worlds: Emerging Technologies in Education and Economics, vol. 33. Springer, Heidelberg (2013)
2. Brenn, S., Krzywinski, N., Noennig, J.R.: Creative Microspaces. In: Proceedings of IFKAD 2012 (2012)
3. Gosling, S.D., et al.: A Room with a Clue: Personal Judgements Based on Offices and Bedrooms. Journal of Personality and Social Psychology 82(3) (2002)
4. Katz, R.: Managing Creativity and Innovation. Harvard Business School Press, Boston (2003)
5. Noennig, J.R., Brenn, S., Hadelich, V.: Urban Atmospherics. In: Proceedings of IFKAD 2012 (2012)
6. Schlenker, L.: Soziale Kontextualisierung von symbolischen Lern- und Arbeitsräumen am Beispiel des dreidimensionalen Multi User Virtual Environment Second Life. Dissertation. Universität Duisburg-Essen (2012)

Smart Technology in the Field of Interior Design

Ela Tekkaya Poursani

College of Architecture, UTSA
501 W. César E. Chávez Boulevard
San Antonio, Texas, 78207
ela.poursani@utsa.edu

Abstract. This paper has two main objectives. The first objective is to present a set of design projects of interior design students focused on distributed, ambient and ubiquitous interactions. In this context, student works are analyzed under a theoretical framework. The second objective is to introduce the field of interior design as one of the forthcoming parties in smart technology implications. Interior design is a multi-faceted profession in which creative and technical solutions are applied to achieve a built interior environment. These solutions involve functionality, enhancement of the quality of life and the culture of the occupants and aesthetics. Interior design includes a scope of services to protect and enhance the health, life safety and welfare of the public. The paper analyzes and discusses nine design projects of the Topics Studio at the Interior Design Program, College of Architecture, University of Texas at San Antonio. In the 2012 Spring Semester, interior design students have applied an intense research pairing healthcare design strategies and smart technologies to two self-directed design thesis projects: A residence for Alzheimer's Disease patient, and a healthcare clinic for medical professionals who treat patients including Alzheimer's Disease. Projects are designed through the research and hypothetical application of remote control technologies, automation technologies, monitoring technologies, prompting / reminding technologies and prediction technologies. Physical and cognitive impairments, ADL limitations of older adults and patients, difficulties faced by family members and caregivers and clinical interventions in community health are considered not only from the interior design standpoint but also through technological advances. Results of this paper discuss how advanced technology is used as a design element by interior design students and merged with patient, caregiver and physician needs triad of healthcare projects. Perspectives on the studio experience are emphasized for future integrated design and practices of smart technology and interior design.

Keywords: Interior Design, Smart Technology, Smart Home, Smart Clinic, Ubiquitous Computing, Healthcare Design, Alzheimer's Disease, Aging in Place.

1   Introduction: Interior Design Profession

National Council for Interior Design Qualification defines Interior Design as a multi-faceted profession which achieves built interior environments and performs through

N. Streitz and C. Stephanidis (Eds.): DAPI/HCII 2013, LNCS 8028, pp. 484–494, 2013.
© Springer-Verlag Berlin Heidelberg 2013

creative and technical solutions. These solutions involve functionality, enhancement of the quality of life and culture of the occupants and aesthetics. Interior design includes a scope of services to protect and enhance the health, life safety and welfare of the public.[1] It is considered a discipline concerned with examining the interaction between human beings and their environments and the study of the fabrication of material goods, a subset of architecture, construction and planning.[2] Knowledge areas for the potential contribution of interior design are Human Environment Needs, Interior Construction, Codes and Regulations, Products and Materials, Design Theory and Process, Communication, and Professional Practice.[3]

There are 358 interior design programs in the U.S. and 172 are accredited by the Council for Interior Design Accreditation. [4] The most recent data shows 26,400 students enrolled in the accredited interior design programs. [5] In interior design education, studio-based curriculum integrates theoretical, technical, and professional topics to foster creative problem solving. Similar to an undergraduate education in Computer Sciences, problem solving ability, technical knowledge and practical skills are provided in interior design programs. Again, similar to Computer Sciences, these form a foundation for lifelong learning and prepare students for employment in industry.[6]

According to the American Society of Interior Designers, interior design holds a relatively small segment of the entire building industry, but its impact is immense. From homes to schools or hospitals, 'interior design directs and influences the look, the feel, the quality and the functionality of the interior environments we move in every day.'[7] In the U.S., people spend approximately 90% of their time indoors.[8]

---

[1] Definition of Interior Design, National Council for Interior Design Qualification, Viewed 21 February 2013, < http://www.ncidq.org/aboutus/aboutinteriordesign/definitionofinteriordesign.aspx>

[2] Career Index of Interior Design, EducationNews.org, Viewed 22 February 2013, <http://www.educationnews.org/career-index/interior-design-schools/>

[3] Denise A. Guerin and Caren S. Martin, *The Interior Design Profession's Body of Knowledge and Its Relationship to People's Health, Safety, and Welfare* (University of Minnesota, September 2010), 202, Viewed 22 February 2013, <http://www.ncidq.org/AboutUs/AboutNCIDQ/News/InteriorDesignBodyofKnowledgeReleased.aspx>

[4] Career Index'.

[5] Guerin, *'Body of Knowledge'*, 128.

[6] B.S. in Interior Design, UTSA College of Architecture, Viewed 22 February 2013, <http://architecture.utsa.edu/academic-programs/interior-design/b.s.-in-interior-design/>. And, Undergraduate Education, Department of Computer Sciences, UTSA, Viewed 22 February 2013, <http://www.cs.utsa.edu/undergrad/>

[7] Interior Design Industry-Overview to *State of the Industry*, American Society of Interior Designers (Washington: 2012), 4.

[8] The Business Case for Green Building (U.S. Green Building Council, 27 July 2012), Viewed 22 February 2013, <http://new.usgbc.org/articles/business-case-green-building>

A professional interior design practitioner, qualified by means of education, experience and examination, performs a scope of services.[9] In 2011, there were approximately 58,000 employed and self-employed interior designers and an estimated 12,100 interior design firms in the U.S. Most interior designers are generalists who work on more than one type of design project a year. Residential (76%) and office design (52 %) are the most commonly practiced specialties. Hospitality design (47%) runs a distant third, followed by health care (41%).[10] A seminal industry research report issued by six leading interior design organizations -ASID, CIDA, IDC, IDEC, IIDA and NCIDQ- underlines a growing body of evidence that supports the positive impact of interior design especially on public health, safety and welfare.[11]

The latest U.S. Census shows senior citizens are increasing faster than younger people, making the nation's median age older. The aging of the baby boom population (born between 1946-1964), along with stabilizing birth rates and longer life expectancy, contributes to the increase in median age.[12] This increase will potentially lead to increased demand for healthcare facilities and designers. Environmental needs of an aging population and designing specifically for the elderly are emerging responses to the oncoming age wave and elder design (geriatric care-by-design) is becoming increasingly more important for interior designers. Aging population is expected to influence the dynamics of the healthcare market. How, when, and where medical care is delivered significantly impacts the design and re-design of the existing homes to accommodate the physical challenges that come with age[13]. As increasing numbers of people desire to 'age in place', this may result in a corresponding increase in renovations to existing homes.[14]

2   Topics Studio:
Pairing Healthcare Design and Smart Technologies

In Spring 2012, senior interior design students of the University of Texas at San Antonio College of Architecture applied an intense research pairing healthcare design strategies and smart technologies to two self-directed design studio projects: A Residence for Alzheimer's Disease Patient, and A Healthcare Facility. Alzheimer's disease is a growing threat in the U.S.[15] One in eight older Americans has Alzheimer's disease. In the U.S., it is

---

[9] 'Definition of Interior Design'.

[10] *State of the Industry*, American Society of Interior Designers (Washington: 2012), 19.

[11] Guerin, *'Body of Knowledge'*, 130.

[12] Lindsay M. Howden and Julie A. Meyer, Age and Sex Composition, 2010 Census Briefs (United States Census Bureau, 2011), 2, Viewed 22 February 2013,
<http://www.census.gov/prod/cen2010/briefs/c2010br-03.pdf>.

[13] Cindy Coleman, and Katie Sosnowchik, *Interior Design Trends and Implications* (Council for Interior Design Accreditation, 2006), 5-51, Viewed 22 February 2013,
<http://dlpotts.iweb.bsu.edu/arch263/310files/
310-reading2-trends.pdf>

[14] Ibid., 11.

[15] Alex Wayne, 'U.S. to Boost Funding for Alzheimer's Research by $50 Million This Year', in *Bloomberg News*, 7 February 2012, <http://www.bloomberg.com/news/
2012-02-07/u-s-to-boost-funding-for-alzheimer-s-research-by-
50-million.html>

the sixth-leading cause of death. Over 15 million Americans provide unpaid care for a person with Alzheimer's or other dementias. Payments for care are estimated to be $200 Billion in 2012.[16] The numbers will escalate rapidly in coming years as the baby boom generation ages. CEO of the Alzheimer's Association calls the disease 'the public health crisis of this century.'[17]

IDE Topics Studio was grounded on the concepts of Alzheimer's Disease, Aging in Place and Ubiquitous Healthcare. Aging in place, the option to grow old in one's home instead of institutional healthcare facilities, has led the students to smart technologies. Older adults, especially Alzheimer's Disease patients, stand to benefit tremendously from smart home technology. In the Smart Home project, Aging in Place was supported with the development of technologies and resources that network patients, caregivers, and medical personnel. Home automation systems, ubiquitous computing technologies and health monitoring were considered to be the means to establish these connections.

The semester study has addressed the new trend of 'technology-based personal health system' to move from hospital-based health system to home and community-based health promotion. Within this system, basically, smart home has functioned as the 'sender' and smart clinic as the 'receiver'. Students, as designers, experienced both ends of the system. The studio offered an opportunity to exclusively access to experts with real-world experience. In Spring 2012, physicians, scientists, academicians, and practitioners from various institutions have provided evidence-based information and shared their knowledge, experience and perspective with students.[18] One of the collaborators, UTSA Computer and Electrical Engineering Department, has facilitated valuable hands-on information on human-computer interaction.

3   Research on Smart Technology

Human computer interaction is highly important in the day-to-day tasks performed by interior designers.[19] As a means of production, exploration, research and communication, computer has integrated to the practice and education of interior design. Technology is natural; and, computer and networking technologies are considered mainstream in the

---

[16] 2012 Alzheimer's Disease Facts and Figures, Alzheimer's Association, *Alzheimer's & Dementia* 8 (2012), 15-27, Viewed 22 February 2013, <http://www.alz.org/downloads/facts_figures_2012.pdf>

[17] Julie Steenhuysen, 'Obama Boosts Funds for Alzheimer's Research', *Reuters*, 7 February 2012, Viewed 22 February 2012, <http://www.reuters.com/article/2012/02/07/us-alzheimers-idUSTRE8161FQ20120207>

[18] Topics Studio collaborators are Department of Geriatrics, Gerontology and Palliative Medicine, UTHSCSA; Department of Family and Community Medicine, UTHSCSA; Audie L. Murphy VA Hospital, STVHCS; Department of Computer and Electrical Engineering, UTSA; College of Sciences, UTSA; Air Force Village Foundation Freedom House Alzheimer's Care & Research Center; WestEast Design Group LLC; Alamo Architects; Overland Partners; Lucifer Lighting Company; Alex Caragonne and Margie Shackelford.

[19] Melinda Lyon, Shiretta Ownbey, and Mihyun Kang, 'Interior Designers' Perceptions of the Influence of Technology on Workplace Performance', in *International Journal of Instructional Technology & Distance Learning* (2009), Viewed 22 February 2012, <http://www.itdl.org/journal/jan_09/article07.htm>

field.[20] Correspondingly, smart technology is a growing practice. Within the scope of interior design, categories of Smart Technology include smart homes, buildings and structures, materials, appliances, environmental technologies, energy technologies and smart pervasive-ubiquitous computing. Healthcare design interventions enlarge this list with smart healthcare products, gadgets and study areas such as Ubiquitous Healthcare (Ubi-Care, UHealth) and Telehealth.

In Spring 2012, students have developed a deeper understanding of distributed, ambient and ubiquitous interactions.[21] Ambient intelligence is characterized as a set of paradigms including tangible interaction, augmented reality, mixed reality, and ubiquitous computing which are sensitive, adoptive, and responsive to the presence of people. Ubiquitous computing is defined as 'access to any information source anywhere any time'. Projects included alternative definitions for smart technology categories. At concept statements, smart technology was underlined as a means to withstand time (P#3);[22] ubiquitous healthcare was emphasized to save money, time of medical staff and provide rapid medical care (P#6); or, the use of smart technology in connecting the clinic to the surrounding neighborhoods was highlighted as providing patients medical assistance at their homes (P#8). Students have demonstrated an understanding of the different levels of application of technology to building systems.

IDE Topics Studio focused on the hypothetical application of state-of-the-art and high-performance technologies. Cost effectiveness in technologies set a secondary goal and the use of prototypes was permitted. Students researched home applications of advanced technology under three topics: Case studies, organizations, and industry/vendor. As observed during the industry/vendors research, students processed technical information much easier. Marketing language of technology stood closer to them than the academic language. However, students were caught up with the term 'architecture'. Though both address spatiality, the term architecture has different scopes for interior design and computer sciences. In computer sciences, it refers to a diagram showing the linkage of devices and mechanisms. In interiors it means 'the shell', an enclosed space to fill in with design.

A study of smart home components and technical structures provided guidance in applying technology to studio projects. Students researched smart technology through technical aspects (e.g. location tracking technologies, sensor application, installation), functional aspects (e.g. activity centers for sensor placement, way finding, security), and social aspects (e.g. social performance levels of older people, acceptance of smart technology). Also, as a current trend in design professions, sustainability was scrutinized through adaptive control of the environment or eco-friendly products (e.g. Stryker sustainable solutions, LDI solutions). Healthcare aspect of the projects required a focus on medical concerns in aging, medical technology, materials, furniture, devices, active and passive alarm systems, remote support for care staff, family and care givers. At the Smart

---

[20] Andrew J. Milne, 'Designing Blended Learning Space to the Student Experience', in *Learning Spaces* (Educause, 2006), 9, Viewed 22 February 2013,
<http://net.educause.edu/ir/library/pdf/PUB7102k.pdf>

[21] Text books of the course: Diane Cook, *Smart Environments: Technology, Protocols and Applications* (New York: Wiley, 2004); William C. Mann, ed., *Smart Technology for Aging, Disability, And Independence, The State of the Science* (New York: Wiley, 2005).

[22] Nine student projects are analyzed in the paper. Student projects are annotated with numbers (P#3 for Project 3).

Clinic Project, students were interested in white goods (functional) than brown goods (leisure). The research on healthcare gadgets provided students the features of design. Smart gadgets in student researches spanned from IR-RFID badge or speech recognition programs for transition to electronic medical records (EMRs), to clinical dashboard systems. Some students approached to smart technology solely through mobile technology: 'Everything in medicine is going mobile'. Mobile technology was underlined as bringing the patient's bedside to the physician's smart phone or tablet computer (P#7).

4   Smart Technology as a Selection

Making selection is a key facet of interior design and it is closely tailored to the education and practice of the profession. In Topics Studio, the scope of selections was expanded from typical equipment, furniture, fixture, system, material and color to smart technology. The research phase supported design not only as a body of knowledge but also by providing an array of choices of technology. Students made informed decisions among a range of remote control, automation, monitoring, and prompting/reminding technologies. Selections were made for assemblies (wall, floor, ceiling), spaces, features (FF&E), systems (MEP, HVAC, security and fire safety), environmental factors (day lighting, sun exposure) and for user needs of healthcare design. Those selections were detailed through specifications and schedules. For comparison purposes, cost estimates were prepared.

Key elements of intelligent environment implementations were sensors and networks. Among the gadgets and technologies selected, probably the most popular one was sensors. Interior design students loved sensors and creating sensor-augmented environments. At the projects, sensors were everywhere from shoes for tracking location, to picture displays, showers or even pets. The understanding of sensor types and devices/applets was an important step for students in applying ubiquitous computing to programmatic needs and spatial design. Pervasiveness of technology was applied to space basically through sensors and wireless technologies.

Not in the first generation hardwired pervasive space prototypes, students were interested in wireless technology. Elimination of the need to have a cable or wire between devices meant flexibility for them. Ability to transform any existing building through wireless technology was seen as an opportunity for innovative design. Regarding infrastructure, projects included information on area networks. Among three layers of cables and four network families that are currently used to support smart home, two types of small area wireless technology for homes were mentioned in student projects: Bluetooth & WiFi and Hybrid network (powerline + other cables + wireless components (WLAN)).

5   Smart Technology as a Design Element

As stated above, projects were developed at the intersection of three fields: Healthcare + Technology + Interior Design. Healthcare defined the specific needs of users and spaces; smart technology provided technical tools for design resolutions; and, conceptual, contextual and critical thinking layers of interior design were utilized to articulate healthcare needs and technological products and applications.

In interior design, concept means a generic idea that shapes the space. In Topics Studio, projects were envisioned through various design ideas that rendered technology. For instance, P#2 was evolved around a children's book: The Giving Tree, written and illustrated by Shel Silverstein. Students approached the smart home project as in the story: The smart house itself was the giving tree; it cared for its occupants and gave them everything it could. Creative thinking through smart technology was also applied at P#1. Designers envisioned one single wall which contained all smart technology features and applications that the program necessitated. Unfortunately, this preliminary idea wasn't kept at the development phase and the project ended up having the wall in addition to a medical room, medical office, IT closet and a smart office, all serving for the same purpose.

In general, at the smart home project, concepts were developed through invisible technology and through visible technology at the smart clinic. Students created ambient intelligence environments mostly through walls and objects. Surface applications provided interior design students a variety of design opportunities with various materials. In Spring 2012, almost every project included a smart wall, mostly interactive or with embedded tablets. As they did sensors, students loved smart walls and surface applications; the idea of treating floor or countertop surface similar to a wall was meant folding the dimensions of space. Though, this analytical approach to smart technology was not furthered in the development phase. Only few projects included the study of system detailing and most projects demonstrated a lack of construction detailing in smart technology.

Students defined the needs of Alzheimer's patient and sought for assistance from technology accordingly. Open space plan, way finding, wandering, forgetfulness, falls, and disorientation were specifically taken into consideration in space planning. Smart technology was applied to ease the activities of daily living of patients and care givers. Projects were designed with mail alert systems, smart fridge with self-ordering function, light path for night time bathroom trips, smart blinds, vital monitoring sensored chairs and many other technological features.

Advanced technology was utilized for the programmatic needs of the healthcare facility. Students placed an emphasis on monitoring technologies in clinic design. Popular gadgets were self-check in kiosks, body detection walls and vital monitoring or BMI calculating sensored chairs. Public health profile of San Antonio was taken into consideration through diabetes, especially child diabetes. Interactive play wall, persuasive games for kindergarten children for healthy dietary behaviors, smart lunch tray (context awareness + interactive media persuasion) were some of the prompting technologies used by the students. Population demographics were reflected to design interventions. Electronic reference tools such as MediBabble was used for non-English speaking patients of San Antonio. At consultation rooms, quality of healthcare was assured by an array of sensors for detecting whether the sanitizer dispenser was used before seeing the patient or by monitoring steps of medical staff while taking care of patient.

Advanced technology generated new usages thus new spaces and spatial relationships at the planning and programming of the projects. Most of the projects included an IT Room to the residential and clinic programs. P#2, for instance, utilized the laundry as the server space. IT functions were housed at closets, rooms, or smart offices. Projects revealed 3-D articulation of technology through perspectives, sections and interior elevations.

6   Discussion of Results:
Smart Technology in the Field of Interior Design

One of the central issues of smart technology is whether innovations should be introduced through 'technology push' or through 'market pull'. A 'technology push' describes a situation where an emerging technology provides the driving force for an innovative product and problem solution in the market place. On the other hand, the term 'market pull' implies that the product or process innovation has its origins in the customer needs.[23] Despite the chicken-egg analogy frequently articulated to define the symbiotic relationship of the drives, there is a gap between technology push and market pull.

Interior design has the potentials to fill the gap between the technology push and consumer pull in building industry. In building industry, technology and market can be paraphrased as 'technology and application'. Interior designers can take a more active role in bridging the gap between 'technology and application', in other words, 'product and user'. These potentials arise from the practices of the profession for the reason that Interior Design;

> . Serves human needs,
> . Works closely with human,
> . Actively involves in health, life safety and welfare of the public,
> . Applies expertise to a wide range of building types,
> . Partakes in building industry
> . Closely follows the market,
> . Constantly updates knowledge on systems, materials and products,
> . Performs through a process of selection-making,
> . Targets creation and implementation, and,
> . Designs and re-designs existing buildings which are in large numbers and
> in need of update or reuse.

Interior design is moving forward than seeing smart technology as a trend. Within the prospect of a move from technology push to consumer pull, interior design will find more theoretical and practical groundings as a collaborator. Accordingly, a common language between interior design and the field of smart technology is needed for future joint intellectual and practical efforts.

UTSA Topics Studio experience in Spring 2012 brings up the following perspectives for an integrated design-build intervention of smart technology and interior design;

-      Technology through Usage: The work of interior designers is informed by knowledge of behavioral science and human factors.[24] Consideration of the relationship between human activities and built environment is essential in interior design. Introducing, branding or marketing smart technologies through functional usage –or, use, the act or manner of using- will enlarge the circle of interior design engagement.

-      Technology through Storytelling: Interior designers have the ability to integrate the art of design with the social sciences concerning the interaction of people and their

---

[23] Cornelius Herstatt, 'Management of 'Technology Push' Development Projects', in *Int. J. Technology Management* (Inderscience Enterprises: 2004), 21.

[24] Standard 3, *Council for Interior Design Accreditation Professional Standards* (2011), Reviewed 22 February 2013,
<http://accredit-id.org/professional-standards>

environment. Storytelling, a method of social sciences, conveys ideas in a narrative form. Topics Studio experience showed that technology is vividly grasped through stories, such as in the Microsoft EasyLiving Project. Students have utilized stories to bring smart technology contents to design. Storytelling provides rich opportunities for interior design to understand the use and application of technology.

- Technology through Flexibility & Transformability: In interior design, transformability is characterized by the capacity of adding or removing units or components. Transformable structures can open and close, change form, function, condition, nature, or change color. Flexible properties of space are fluidity, versatility, convertibility, scaleability, and modifiability.[25] In computer sciences, flexibility refers to interoperability. In interior design, flexibility and transformability leads not only to multi-functionality but also to creativity. Consideration of smart technologies in various ways of applications leaves room for creative design. In this sense, interior design recognizes smart technology as a design open to re-design and reads it through its capabilities for creativity and transformability.

- Technology through Implementation: Concepts, principles, and theories of interior design pertain to building methods, materials, and systems. Interior construction and building systems are produced through competent contract documents including coordinated drawings, schedules, and specifications appropriate to project size and scope and sufficiently extensive to show how design solutions and interior construction are related. Articulation of smart technologies to interior design manifests itself mainly through the practice of the profession. Construction, system detailing and specifications play an important role in putting technologies into practice. From early conceptual and selection making phases to implementation, interior design will benefit from basic construction guidelines of smart technologies. Technical guidelines on how to integrate advanced technology into building systems –or, into budgeting with cost estimates- will contribute to the body of knowledge of the profession and bring opportunities for active collaborations of interior designers.

Ela Tekkaya Poursani teaches interior design and architecture at the College of Architecture, UTSA. Her current research interests include healthcare and smart technology.

References

2012 Alzheimer's Disease Facts and Figures. Alzheimer's Association. Alzheimer's & Dementia 8 (2012),
    http://www.alz.org/downloads/facts_figures_2012.pdf

—B.S. in Interior Design. UTSA College of Architecture,
    http://architecture.utsa.edu/academic-programs/interior-design/b.s.-in-interior-design/

---

[25] Torin Monahan, 'Flexible Space & Built Pedagogy: Emerging IT Embodiments, in *Inventio* (2002), Viewed 22 February 2013,
    <http://www.torinmonahan.com/papers/Inventio.html>

—Career Index of Interior Design. EducationNews.org,
http://www.educationnews.org/career-index/interior-design-schools/

Coleman, C., Sosnowchik, K.: Interior Design Trends and Implications. Council for Interior Design Accreditation (2006),
http://dlpotts.iweb.bsu.edu/arch263/310files/310-reading2-trends.pdf

Cook, D.: Smart Environments: Technology, Protocols and Applications. Wiley, New York (2004)

—Council for Interior Design Accreditation Professional Standards: 2011,
http://accredit-id.org/professional-standards

—Definition of Interior Design. National Council for Interior Design Qualification,
http://www.ncidq.org/aboutus/aboutinteriordesign/definitiono finteriordesign.aspx

Herstatt, C.: Management of 'Technology Push' Development Projects. Int. J. Technology Management. Inderscience Enterprises (2004)

Howden, L.M., Meyer, J.A.: Age and Sex Composition, Census Briefs. United States Census Bureau (2010), http://www.census.gov/prod/cen2010/briefs/c2010br-03.pdf

Guerin, D.A., Martin, C.S.: The Interior Design Profession's Body of Knowledge and Its Relationship to People's Health, Safety, and Welfare. University of Minnesota (2010)

—Interior Design Industry: Overview. State of the Industry. American Society of Interior Designers. Washington (2012)

Lyon, M., Ownbey, S., Kang, M.: 'Interior Designers' Perceptions of the Influence of Technology on Workplace Performance. International Journal of Instructional Technology & Distance Learning (2009),
http://www.itdl.org/journal/jan_09/article07.htm

Mann, W.C. (ed.): Smart Technology for Aging, Disability, and Independence, the State of the Science. Wiley, New York (2005)

Milne, A.J.: Designing Blended Learning Space to the Student Experience. Learning Spaces. Educause (2006),
http://net.educause.edu/ir/library/pdf/PUB7102k.pdf

Monahan, T.: Flexible Space & Built Pedagogy: Emerging IT Embodiments. Inventio (2002),
http://www.torinmonahan.com/papers/Inventio.html

Steenhuysen, J.: Obama Boosts Funds for Alzheimer's Research. Reuters (February 7, 2012), http://www.reuters.com/article/2012/02/07/us-alzheimers-idUSTRE8161FQ20120207

—The Business Case for Green Building. U.S. Green Building Council (2012), http://new.usgbc.org/articles/business-case-green-building

—Undergraduate Education. Department of Computer Sciences, UTSA, http://www.cs.utsa.edu/undergrad/

Wayne, A.: U.S. to Boost Funding for Alzheimer's Research by $50 Million This Year. Bloomberg News (2012), http://www.bloomberg.com/news/2012-02-07/u-s-to-boost-funding-for-alzheimer-s-research-by-50-million.html

SmartAssist:
Open Infrastructure and Platform for AAL Services

Peter Rothenpieler, Darren Carlson, and Andreas Schrader

Institute of Telematics, University of Lübeck, Germany
{rothenpieler,carlson,schrader}@itm.uni-luebeck.de

Abstract. In this paper we present the open health monitoring platform Smart-Assist, which combines flexible in-home and mobile sensing features with a comprehensive social network that is designed to enhance communication between caretakers, caregivers and the community. SmartAssist supports the integration of new sensor types, algorithms, and mobile components through an integrated platform, which consists of an in-home sensor network; a web based service portal; and an extensible infrastructure for mobile devices. Through the adoption of open standards (Android, OSGi, OpenSocial, etc.), the system addresses issues of data protection and privacy, while simultaneously providing support for third-party extensions and context-aware services. In this paper, we will present the individual building blocks of the SmartAssist Platform as well as some illustrative example services.

Keywords: AAL, OpenSocial, Android, OSGi, Sensor Network.

1 Introduction

Worldwide, life expectancy has been constantly growing for many years. This fortunate development also creates challenging demands on the organisation of daily life for elderly people and will impose significant financial and organisational challenges for the healthcare systems of our societies. Ambient Assisted Living (AAL) approaches these challenges by providing technical solutions. Unfortunately, very often AAL is focused on high-tech infrastructure (sensors, ambient intelligence and actors) in order to replace human activities with (semi-)automated technical services (e.g., observation, activity tracking, automated food ordering). This view focuses on the negative aspects of growing life expectancy, like loss of cognitive and physical means. Although the negative aspects of the growing life expectancy are often overemphasized, this trend represents a very positive development, leading to increasing demands by the elderly population for support mechanisms that enable an autonomous, active and fulfilling lifestyle.

AAL should therefore also focus on the positive aspects of growing life spans and strengthen the existing private and professional networks and infrastructures, reducing the burden of caregivers and increasing the autonomy of caretakers at the same time, while preserving the immense skills and experiences of the group of elderly people for our society. Especially, AAL could be used to extend the autonomous life time in the elderly person's own household and delay or even prevent the transition to a nursing home. This goal can only be reached by a coordinated and supported action of many

N. Streitz and C. Stephanidis (Eds.): DAPI/HCII 2013, LNCS 8028, pp. 495–504, 2013.
© Springer-Verlag Berlin Heidelberg 2013

peers (which we call patrons) of the social network, including relatives, friends, neighbours, service providers, nursing staff, doctors and emergency rescue services. In addition, urban and Internet-based social communities could deliver valuable assistance.

Many projects in the AAL research community focus on certain aspects of service provisioning and develop dedicated solutions for those. Examples are robots for cognitive and emotional stimulation of lonely or dement people [14][1]; silver games for motivation of physical exercises [2]; dedicated and rather sophisticated sensor solutions for certain aspects, e.g., fall detection [10]; or comprehensive infrastructure projects for developing ambient intelligence environments, e.g., smart homes [9]. Unfortunately, most of these approaches are not compatible, require a certain amount of technical infrastructure and maintenance and do usually fulfill only service aspects, that have been planned within the scope of the respective projects. Some projects try to consider ambient parameters and context information in their decision strategies and service adaptation [3,1]. There are also first attempts to deal with the interoperability challenges of AAL infrastructures by creating middleware and reference architectures with standardized protocols[2].

In our approach, we try to integrate low complexity installation, on-demand software provisioning and context-awareness in an open flexible architecture. Third-party providers as the main experts in their respective domain are supported to develop and integrate specific and yet interoperable services in a holistic approach. The core concept of SmartAssist is to provide context information to the patrons, to provide health monitoring and context information for the user. We realise a few prototypical example services within the framework and allow third-party providers to add domain specific services. SmartAssist combines technical infrastructure at home, a web based service portal and mobile infrastructure to support users seamlessly at home and on the move. In this paper we will focus on the service integration, describe a few implemented services and outline potential opportunities and scenarios for third-party service providers. The SmartAssist project is supported by the German Federal Ministry of Education and Research (BMBF) under the ID 16KT0942.

2   Project

In SmartAssist, we focus on the social network of the user, comprising personal patrons. Patrons assist the user in her autonomous life. This includes normal daily-life activities, like communication (relatives), sports (friends), shopping (neighbours), household maintenance (crafts services); and more exceptional situations of illness (doctor), rehabilitation (nursing service) or even emergency (ambulance). The user and her patrons are all registered members of the SmartAssist social network. Each member of the network creates a dedicated profile on the server using a web-based service portal (see section 3.2). User input for the elderly and her patrons consists of personal data (name, age, address, illnesses, preferences, contact info, security and privacy settings, etc.) Beside the manually entered profile information, automatically derived status information is acquired using sensor input in order to support context-aware service optimisation (see

---

[1] http://www.parorobots.com/
[2] http://www.universaal.org/

section 3.1). The sensor data is filtered and aggregated using dedicated data processing algorithms hosted by the SmartAssist server. The algorithmically derived aggregated health status in combination with edited profile information of the user can be shared with patrons in order to realize context-aware services.

Inside the profile, each member can specify her role as service consumer or provider. SmartAssist does not restrict the scope of the services and supports dynamic extension of the network and the offered services using respective APIs (see section 3.2). Service providers can act as domain experts (e.g., taxi services, food delivery services, Internet pharmacies) and offer dedicated support on the platform. Of course, the elderly user can also act as a service provider to other members of the network (e.g., offering homework supervision for school kids; or book reading sessions for local institutions), therefore enhancing Quality-Of-Life and providing a valuable contribution to society.

Members of the network can agree on relations (e.g., friendship or service contracts), exchange status information and messages, and register for specific services (including detailed configuration of data access and service process flows). Registered patrons (e.g., doctors, nurses, relatives) can use the platform to monitor the condition of the elderly (e.g., telediagnosis and electronic health records), and trigger context-sensitive communication (e.g., telemedical services). For example, if no coffee machine usage is detected over the course of a day, the neighbour might receive an SMS suggesting to knock at the door to check the status. External third-party providers can use the system to offer health or lifestyle services to the users (e.g., automatically scheduled taxi transport for dialysis sessions based on calendar entries of the customer). We will outline potential usage of this paradigm in section 4.

3   Infrastructure

The SmartAssist platform infrastructure consists of the following components for realising context-aware support for this social network: an in-home sensor network; a central data server; a web based service portal; and a mobile infrastructure.

3.1   In-home Sensor Network

The sensor network consists of unobtrusive, easy-to-install, self-configuring wireless sensor nodes, which are distributed inside the user's home. Sensors include pushbuttons (opening and closing of furniture doors), motion detectors (user passing door frames), water sensors (water consumption in sinks), electricity sensors (power consumption of household devices), temperature sensors (opening and closing of windows) and more. Sensor nodes support the IEEE 802.15.4 standard and connect automatically to a base station in the home. The base station is responsible for data collection from each sensor, filtering and/or aggregating sensor values, and uploading the data to the SmartAssist Server using either phone or modem networks.

It is important to note that SmartAssist explicitly does not rely on invasive health monitoring and does not foresee the usage of cameras or microphones. Instead, very general household data is sensed. On the SmartAssist server, dedicated signal processing algorithms are provided, which allow for automatically detecting gradual changes of the user's health status based on slow variation of typical activity patterns. An example might be "80% less water consumption than average during this week". The methods include, but are not limited to, statistical analysis, Gaussian modelling and highly developed Markov model. By combining the sensor data in an abstract, context-based and adaptive model, the system learns the normal case by the first measurements, and is able to detect new events that are used to trigger respective actions. Details of these algorithms are outside the scope of this paper and will be presented in a following publication.

For storage, processing and provisioning of these data, sophisticated means have to be established in order to protect the data and to ensure data privacy. In cooperation with the center for data protection in Kiel, Germany (ULD)[3], we have analysed the necessary processes and considered respective means in the design of the infrastructure. Users can manage their own sensors, transparently observe the data collection and specify their access control and privacy settings in detail using the OAuth-Protocol[4] (for more details see also [12] and [11]).

3.2 Service Portal

The Service portal is based on the Content Management System Drupal in combination with Apache Shindig[5], which is an implementation of the OpenSocial[6] standard. A REST-based web service interface offers external access to user profile and sensor data within the registered social network. OpenSocial gadgets are used to integrate external services into the portal. Technically, an OpenSocial gadget is an XML file containing information about the web service, such as name, author, description, as well as the service application itself using HTML, CSS and JavaScript. The service, which is implemented using such an XML file, is interpreted, rendered into the web-interface of the Service Portal and presented to the user for interaction. The services can access the user's data using JavaScript interfaces, potentially including sensor values and sending messages to registered patrons of the user. The OpenSocial standard is used in many common social network implementations, including XING, MySpace and iGoogle as well as the large German social networks VZ-Networks(meinVZ[7], studiVZ, and schülerVZ).

3.3 Mobile Platform

To support seamless context-aware services in mobile activities outside the household, we developed a mobile infrastructure called Dynamix [6], targeting Google's Android platform. Through Dynamix, users can employ any Android smartphone or tablet to access and control their SmartAssist home network, interact with the web service portal and run health related Android apps that integrate SmartAssist portal and sensor data

---

[3] https//www.datenschutzzentrum.de/
[4] http://oauth.net/
[5] http://shindig.apache.org/
[6] http://www.opensocial.org/
[7] http://www.meinVZ.net/

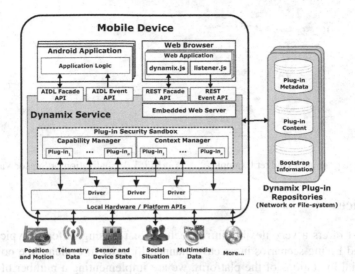

Fig. 1. Overview of the Dynamix Framework

information. In addition, Dynamix is using phone based sensors in order to add further mobile health monitoring functionality and to act as a mobile sensor for SmartAssist. The foundation of the Dynamix approach is an extensible middleware framework as shown in Fig. 1, which runs as a background service on a user's device, modelling context information from the environment using the device itself as a sensing, processing and communications platform [8]. Context modelling is performed by a tailored set of plug-ins, which are packaged as OSGi Bundles and provisioned to the device over-the-air (OTA) during runtime. Context plug-ins are used to insulate app developers from the complexities of context modelling, which often involve specialized domain knowledge.

We evaluated the framework's abstractions by creating eight example context plug-ins, which ranged in complexity from simple extensions of existing Android sensor services (e.g., geolocation, orientation, WIFI radio signal detection) to relatively complex aggregated context types (e.g., ambient sound level, step detection and step force calculation), and also integrated externally developed proprietary and open-source projects (e.g., ZXing barcode scanner[9]). Dynamix can also be used to extend the collection of sensor types by adding existing medical devices or services. We have added dedicated Dynamix plug-ins to support WLAN-based weight monitoring (using the Withings Scale[10]); heart rate, step count, and speed information from a Zephyr HxM physiological monitoring belt[11] connected over Bluetooth; blood pressure information; face detection using open source APIs; and many more. Dynamix apps can access the SmartAssist profile and sensor data on the server using a dedicated SmartAssist plug-in, which raises respective events, in case updates are available.

---

[8] http://ambientdynamix.org/

[9] https://code.google.com/p/zxing/

[10] http://www.withings.com/en/scales/

[11] http://www.zephyr-technology.com/products/

Fig. 2. Integration of Gadget Examples   **Fig. 3.** Visualization of Sensor Values

4   Services

SmartAssist offers a very flexible infrastructure for realising different typical Ambient Assisted Living scenarios in an easy manner. In order to evaluate the possibilities and potential limitations of the platform, we are implementing a number of example services. In this section, we will outline the current state of development and give an outlook of future planned and possible services.

4.1   Integrated Services

In order to test the appropriateness of the server-based interfaces and APIs, we successfully integrated a number of existing OpenSocial gadgets into the SmartAssist Service Portal, taken from the top ten list of iGoogle Gadgets (weather forecasts, TV programs, Sudoku puzzles, German Bundesliga soccer tables and joke-of-the-day). Although this test showed the correctness of the interfaces and provided some useful hints for designing the user interfaces, these integrated services do not use the context data of the SmartAssist platform. To show the potential of the SmartAssist Platform, we developed additional OpenSocial Gadgets that use the user's profile data. Some of these gadgets include a pharmacy and a delivery service finder, which use the user's zip code and street address; a BMI (body mass index) calculator, which uses the height and weight of the user; and a horoscope service, which uses the birthday of the user as depicted in Figure 2. We also included a birthday reminder, which shows a list of all upcoming birthdays of the user's friends and patrons.

In addition, we developed a set of visualisation gadgets for the data from the sensors which have been linked to the user. This allows for ambient awareness of the user's activities and health status record. Figure 3 shows an example of two of the sensors of the user "Andreas". The first one shows the temperature and humidity, which are changing over time, e.g., caused by the opening and closing of windows. The visualization from the second room shows the data collected by a passive infrared motion sensor.

4.2   Mobile Services

To simulate the process of third-party mobile service integration, we are currently developing additional dedicated healthcare service Apps for the Dynamix platform with the help of Master and Bachelor students:

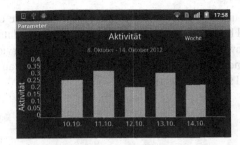

Fig. 4. Visualization of the the amount and distribution of the users activity over several days [5]

- *SmartAssist Cockpit:* As a general awareness system for the user, we have developed mobile access to the SmartAssist service. This includes the visualisation of the SmartAssist user profile data and a track record of the sensor values and aggregations. The user is able to access her data, subscribe and configure services and to manage her social network as depicted in Figure 4. For this service, an additional Dynamix plugin was developed, which uses the accelerometer and gyroscope sensors of the mobile device to detect activity patterns (i.e. sitting, standing, walking, stair climbing, biking) using feature extraction and classifiers. The user is supported to choose a set of health sensor parameters and is motivated to continue measurements by an integrated gamification approach, allowing for specifying individual goals.
- *Medication Reminder:* The increasing number of concurrently taken medicines in combination with age-related limitations in vision and retentiveness, can make proper medication scheduling and handling more difficult. The medication reminder system [8] can help to overcome some of the limitations. It includes a personalised planning tool; dedicated views and interfaces for patients, nurses and doctors; a record track of taken doses; information about certain medicines (e.g.; spoken patient information sheet based on barcode scanning); and many more. Different views for users, doctors and peers support group-based support of compliance by the patient's network of registered patrons.

This list will be continually expanded over time and we are targeting a large integrated set of stationary and mobile health services within the SmartAssist platform. In particular, we are focussing on the integration of existing services and the interoperation with other AAL infrastructures and standards.

If stationary and mobile services are combined, more advanced scenarios can be supported by SmartAssist. An example is a smart weight control services that can use the wireless scale in the household, can also automatically connect to the wireless scale at the next pharmacy visit, and present and exchange the weight history with other members of the weekly diet club. Another example might be a smart emergency pharmacy finder, which queries the user's preferences and health prescription from the electronic health record service, tracks the user's current geo-position, queries the database of overnight pharmacies nearby and offers a respective navigation support including real-time bus schedule and/or automatic taxi ordering. The service might also inform the pharmacy in advance about the need for a certain prescription, lowering the waiting time before receiving the medicine. These kinds of scenarios are only possible due to the easy exchange and hierarchical access methods for context data in the SmartAssist framework. In the following section, we describe a smart sport service (developed in our institute) as a more concrete example of how health sensor data can be used to motivate mobility and increased social connections.

5   BikeWars

One of the core features of the SmartAssist platform is the early detection of a degrading health status by monitoring slow variations in the activity pattern of the user. The goal is to maintain independence and autonomy as long as possible. Towards this goal, sport is recognized as an important means to stay fit and healthy. Sport activities also help to create and maintain social contacts, gain new personal and social skills, relieve stress and to experience a healthy and fulfilled life [4] [13] [16]. Unfortunately, elderly or ill people often suffer from limitations in mobility and performance, often preventing them from joint sportive activities with peers. Therefore and to show the potential of the SmartAssist platform, we have developed a social exercise game, called BikeWars, to help motivate increased sport activities. BikeWars belongs to the field of Serious Games or Exergames [15], often called Silver Gaming in the context of AAL. The use of training bikes in the field of AAL has e.g., been proposed in [7], where it is used for controlling a videogame (i.e. moving the game character by cycling faster or slower). BikeWars uses the data available through SmartAssist to adapt to the user by changing the difficulty depending on the social data of the user and the gathered sensor data from the in-home sensor network. By implementing BikeWars, we demonstrate how external developers can use the SmartAssist platform to build their own AAL applications.

5.1   Game Setup

BikeWars is a multiplayer application using the SmartAssist health sensor values to improve training results and increase enjoyment during exercise. In BikeWars two or more bikers train together in a virtual bike race using home training bikes that are connected to their respective SmartAssist infrastructure at home. To start the game, bikers agree on the level of difficulty and a certain racing track. During the race, the bikes measure the cycling speed while the break is controlled by the BikeWars system in accordance to the user's current position on the chosen track (i.e. if they are driving uphill or downhill). BikeWars uses a USB-enabled ergotrainer from the company Tacx[12], which allows to monitor the power, speed and pedalling frequency and to control the resistance through an electromagnetic brake during the course of the exercise.

In addition to the indoor scenario, BikeWars will also enable users to use the application outdoors, taking advantage of GPS for location, altitude and speed tracking. This provides the user with the possibility to record his own tracks, which can be shared with other users, or used for training at home (e.g., when it's rainy outside or in winter); however, this feature will be primarily used to allow real-time races (or bike trips)

---

[12] http://www.tacx.com/

between indoor seniors and outdoor patrons. This will allow seniors to partake in a bike trip with adapted difficulty, the possibility of taking a break when needed and avoid being exposed to potential allergens.

5.2 Using SmartAssist Profile and Race Data

Through accessing the user's sensor values and profile data in the SmartAssist Server, the difficulty of the racing conditions can be automatically adapted to match the competing users and their environments. For example, the social data in the user profile can be used to adapt the level of difficulty to the age, weight, height and other body parameters of the racer (e.g., prostheses). Also, the sensor values (e.g., temperature, humidity) of the racing room can be considered as well. In addition, health sensors on the body of the racer (e.g., heart rate monitor) can be used to measure the current fitness of the racer. By using all of these values, BikeWars is able to adjust the level of difficulty accordingly in an individualized manner in order to increase the fairness and equality during the game experience. Untrained players have a change to win, and experienced players are provided more interesting and challenging race conditions. Of course, the players could override these settings as well, allowing for personally adjusting the training target (e.g., a certain heart rate or calorie consumption) and avoiding unhealthy training situations.

The data gathered for the competing users during each individual race can be used as an indication of their physical fitness or individual training progress, and can further be incorporated into the analysis of the user's activity patterns and health. In addition to the analysis of the data through SmartAssist, the data can also be displayed in the Service Portal to give the user long-term feedback on his training results and provide comparisons to the results family, friends and neighbours. Social rankings use the same mechanisms as the race to adapt the training results to the user's profile data, environmental conditions and relative improvements, which increases fairness and makes the long-term BikeWars experience more challenging and motivating.

6   Conclusion and Future Work

We are currently equipping about 50 single households in the city of Lübeck with SmartAssist sensors and infrastructure. In addition, a second group of 50 patients with equal age and gender distribution have been selected as a comparison group. Over the course of 12 months, we plan intensive measurements and algorithmic tests on the health data. An accompanying medical evaluation will compare both populations and analyse potential benefits of the system. Evaluations are based on both medical and social terms. Medical terms include the Geriatric Basis Assessment, Barthel-Index, Mini-Mental-Status (MMSE), Geriatric Depression Scale (GDS), etc. Social terms include questionnaires evaluating quality-of-life (e.g., using SF36). In addition, we are evaluating the number of raised alarms of the patron groups and the necessary ambulant and stationary medical treatments. Finally, to promote continual evolution of our approach, we are inviting third-party service providers to integrate and contextualise their existing applications and services or to jointly build innovative new ambient assisted living scenarios using SmartAssist.

References

1. Chapko, A., Feodoroff, B., Werth, D., Loos, P.: A personalized and context-aware mobile assistance system for cardiovascular prevention and rehabilitation. In: 6. Deutscher AAL Kongress, Berlin, Germany (January 2013)
2. Seewald, B., John, M., Senger, J., Belbachir, A.N.: Silvergame – A project aimed at social integration and multimedia interaction for the elderly. e&I Magazine (September 2010), http://www.silvergame.eu
3. Franz, B., Buchmayr, M., Schuler, A.: Werner Kurschl: Context-Enriched Personal Health Monitoring. In: 6. Deutscher AAL Kongress, Berlin, Germany (January 2013)
4. Broek, Cavallo, Wehrmann: AALIANCE Ambient Assisted Living Roadmap. Ambient Intelligence and Smart Environments 6 (March 2010)
5. Burmeister, D.: Aktivitätserkennung für Ambient Health Monitoring. Master's thesis, University of Lübeck, Germany (January 2013)
6. Darren Carlson, A.S.: Dynamix: An Open Plug-and-Play Context Framework for Android. In: Proceedings of the 3rd International Conference on the Internet of Things (IoT 2012), Wuxi, China (October 2012)
7. Göbel, S., Hardy, S., Steinmetz, R., Cha, J., Saddik, A.: Serious Games zur Prävention und Rehabilitation. In: 4. Deutscher AAL Kongress, Berlin, Germany (2011)
8. Kaluza, M.: Medication Support System. Master's thesis, University of Lübeck, Germany (December 2011)
9. Alam, M.R., Reaz, M.B.I., Ali, M.A.M.: A Review of Smart Homes—Past, Present, and Future. IEEE Transactions on Systems, Man, and Cybernetics, Part C: Applications and Reviews 42 (November 2012)
10. Noury, N., Fleury, A., Rumeau, P., Bourke, A.K., Laighin, G., Rialle, V., Lundy, J.E.: Fall detection – Principles and Methods. In: Proceedings of the 29th Annual International Conference of the IEEE EMBS Cité Internationale, Lyon, France (August 2007)
11. Rothenpieler, P., Becker, C., Fischer, S.: Privacy concerns in a remote monitoring and social networking platform for assisted living. In: Sixth International PrimeLife/IFIP Summer School on Privacy and Identity Management for Emerging Internet Applications throughout a Person's Lifetime, Helsingborg, Sweden (2010)
12. Rothenpieler, P., Zwingelberg, H., Carlson, D., Schrader, A., Fischer, S.: Datenschutz im AAL Service System SmartAssist. In: 4. Deutscher AAL Kongress, Berlin, Germany (2010)
13. Koch-Institut, R. (ed.): Lebensführung und Sport. Beiträge zur Gesundheitsberichterstattung des Bundes (2008)
14. Bemelmanns, R., Gelderblom, G.J., Jonker, P., de Witte, L.: Socially Assistive Robots in Elderly Care: A Systematic Review into Effects and Effectiveness. Journal of the American Medical Directors Association 13(2), 114–120 (2012)
15. Pigford, T., Andrews, W.: Feasibility and Benefit of Using the Nintendo Wii Fit for Balance Rehabilitation in an Elderly Patient Experiencing Recurrent Falls. Journal of Student Physical Therapy Research 2(1) (2010)
16. US Department of Health and Human Services: of Health and Human Services: Physical activity and health: A report of the Surgeon General (1996)

Design and Evaluation of a Nonverbal Communication Platform between Assistive Robots and their Users

Anthony L. Threatt[1], Keith Evan Green [1,2], Johnell O. Brooks[3],
Jessica Merino[2], Ian D. Walker[2], and Paul Yanik[2]

[1] School of Architecture,
[2] Department of Electrical and Computer Engineering
[3] Department of Automotive Engineering,
Clemson University, Clemson, SC 29632 USA
{anthont,kegreen,jobrook,jmerino,iwalker,pyanik}@clemson.edu

Abstract. Inevitably, assistive robotics will become integral to the everyday lives of a human population that is increasingly mobile, older, urban-centric and networked. *How will we communicate with such robots, and how will they communicate with us?* We make the case for a relatively ``artificial" mode of nonverbal human-robot communication [NVC] to avoid unnecessary distraction for people, busily conducting their lives via human-human, natural communication. We propose that this NVC be conveyed by familiar lights and sounds, and elaborate here early experiments with our NVC platform in a rehabilitation hospital. Our NVC platform was perceived by medical staff as a desirable and expedient communication mode for human-robot interaction [HRI] in clinical settings, suggesting great promise for our mode of human-robot communication for this and other applications and environments involving intimate HRI.

Keywords: assistive robotics, nonverbal communication, human factors, human-centered design.

1 Introduction

The overwhelming demands on healthcare delivery, alone, will compel the adoption of assistive robotics as integral to the everyday lives of a human population that is increasingly mobile, older, urban-centric and networked. We consequently envision a future *ecosystem* comprised of assistive robots of *wide-ranging functionality* --- not only the highly-functioning humanoid but also the ubiquitous Roomba. Across this ecosystem, *how will we communicate with such robots, and how will they communicate with us?*

Towards a response, we build upon our lab's research developing an Assistive Robotic Table [ART] [1-4] and make the case for a relatively ``artificial" mode of *nonverbal human-robot communication* [NVC] to avoid unnecessary distraction for people, busily conducting their lives via human-human, natural communication. In this way, robotic artifacts, living and working with us and for us, do not run the risk of demeaning what it means to be human. We propose that this NVC be conveyed by

N. Streitz and C. Stephanidis (Eds.): DAPI/HCII 2013, LNCS 8028, pp. 505–513, 2013.
© Springer-Verlag Berlin Heidelberg 2013

familiar Audio-Visual means: lights and sounds. Informed by an understanding of cognitive, perceptual processes, our NVC platform affords a communicative dialogue that conveys the purpose of accomplishing tasks. The employment of learning algorithms will offer both user and robot the capacity to interrupt the dialogue and modify utterances. A user-friendly tablet interface allows for the addition of new utterances to the platform. Our hypothesis: *that our NVC platform will be perceived as a desirable and expedient communication mode for HRI, proving to be particularly effective in clinical settings, and promising to be apt and productive in intimate HRI applications at home, as well as in spacecraft and other extreme environments.*

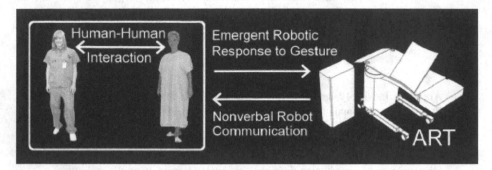

Fig. 1. Proposed Human Robot Interaction

2   NVC: Theory and Related Work in NVC

With respect to human-machine communication, research has suggested that people tend to react adversely to robots issuing commands to them in spoken language or dictating the terms of their interaction in spoken language [5-7]; instead, people have been shown to be relatively more receptive to non-verbal communication emanating from robots [5, 7, 8]. But whatever side one takes in the human-machine communication debate, nonverbal communication has received much more attention from investigators working with humanoid or zoomorphic robots [9-12] (e.g., where the robot is communicating in the manner of, respectively, a human being and household pet) than with investigators employing robots that are not humanoid or zoomorphic. It has been shown that people can easily interpret the meaning of nonverbal utterances (see [12-13] for overviews of this literature). As well, people who are ill or in pain tend to reduce their level of verbal communication, making more use of nonverbal communication [14]. It is noteworthy, as well, that the nonverbal communication of American Sign Language is reportedly more effective ``than spoken English because of the linearity of spoken language" [15]. Collectively, these findings and observations further underscore the need for, and desirability and promise of, a novel NVC-approach like ours to HRI for robots of wide-ranging appearances and behaviors.

Closer to our own investigations reported here, the related research employing non-humanoid, non-zoomorphic robots conveying nonverbally has been limited to human-robot communication that remains uni-directional: participants in previous studies do not communicate with the robot(s) but instead, assume the role of *the recipients* of the robot's utterances (e.g., [8, 16-18]). In our research trajectory, beginning with the experiments presented in this paper, *we envision a bi-directional "communication loop" and add to the aforementioned investigations:* larger sample sizes, focus groups with assessments employing not only interviews and questionnaires but also tablet interfaces for direct user-modifications, EEG headsets for measuring user satisfaction, and NVC evaluation within the real-world situation of a rehabilitation hospital where the stakeholders --- clinicians, post-stroke patients, and their intimates --- can advance it. ``There has been little research,'' of the kind proposed here, situated ``in the wild'' and ``focused on bi-directional human-robot communication employing models of nonverbal communications as both input and output'' [19] (Fig. 1).

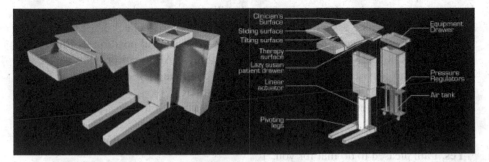

Fig. 2. Assistive Robotic Table (ART)

3   Experiment Overview

In our investigation, we designed and evaluated several alternative modes of nonverbal, robot communication towards establishing an effective NVC loop (as conceptualized in Fig. 1) --- one that is efficient, expedient, user-extendable and user-customizable. For this and future experiments, we embed our developing NVC platform in a real-world context, the Roger C. Peace Rehabilitation Hospital of the Greenville Hospital System University Medical Center, where medical clinician's and their post-stroke patients determine its effectiveness. Soliciting user-input over the course of our research will allow the NVC platform to ``evolve,'' and ensures utility for a broad range of users.

The robot we employ for this investigation is a novel one developed in our lab: the Assistive Robotic Table [ART] presented in figure 2. The result of participatory design and evaluation with clinicians, including doctors, nurses, occupational therapists, physical therapists, and speech therapists, at the Roger C. Peace Rehabilitation Hospital (hereon identified as ``RCP''), ART is comprised of a cantilevered, over-bed table. The robotic table has two degrees of freedom: it raises and lowers from its base and has a tilting work surface. At the extreme tip of the table surface is a continuum-robotic surface supporting post-stroke patient therapy, actuated by twelve pneumatic muscles (with, theoretically, infinite degrees of freedom).

In our study, clinicians were told that they would evaluate a non-verbal communication platform consisting of lights and sounds. The clinicians were told that the sounds were designed for specific actions that ART would perform. The lighting or display type (individual LEDs or LED screen) would also communicate what actions ART would perform. As these are the first steps in the development of our NVC, the following scenario helps define the character and vision of our NVC as integrated into ART.

4   Scenario

Joanne, a post- stroke patient, is rehabilitating at RCP. Next to Joanne is ART, a robotic table that assists Joanne in her rehabilitation. Joanne's sister, Amy, enters Joanne's room. Joanne asks Amy to borrow her computer to check her email. To accommodate the computer, Joanne would like ART to raise and position its flip tray for her. Joanne still feels a little unsteady holding things; ART can provide the needed support for this activity. While Joanne and Amy continue their exchange, the following nonverbal dialogue occurs between Joanne and ART:

Joanne: [Gestures ART to kindly rise and tilt, as if to say, ``ART, please rise and tilt for me."]

ART:[Displays **two quick light flashes** and a **beep beep** sound , as if to say, ``Yes, I am pleased to do that for you."]

All the while, Joanne and Amy are chatting, catching up on recent news in their lives and the world. A few moments later:

Joanne: [Gestures for ART to raise, but ART does not comprehend at first].

ART: [Displays **blinking lights** and a sound that, if written, might be **ant ant**, as if to say, ``Hmmm, I don't know what you are asking of me. I am puzzled."]

Joanne: [Makes the gesture once more in a way that ART comprehends, learns from, and responds with the correct behavior.]

{\itshape To reinforce ART's actions},

Joanne: [Runs her hand along ART's sensors at the perimeter of the table, in what appears to be a ``pet" to convey, ``Thank you."]

ART: [Displays **gradient on/off light pattern** and a **purrr** sound, as if to say, ``I understand that I performed the task correctly!"]

ART communicates with Joanne nonverbally; consequently, ART neither competes for Joanne's attention nor detracts from Joanne and Amy's intimate conversation. As an intelligent machine, ART operates at a level that lies between an application-specific robot and a humanoid.

5   Method

5.1   Participants

Volunteers for this study consisted of research team members and clinicians at RCP. Eight members of the research team participated in the pre-study activities.   Thirteen subject-matter experts --- all clinicians including doctors, occupational, physical, speech therapists, and environmental service technicians --- participated in the research study. Given the small sample size, descriptive statistics were assessed (i.e., no statistical validity could be determined). In the interest of protecting the privacy of this small, exploratory sample population and based upon the conditions of the approval for this study-design by the *hospital's* institutional review board, demographic data are not presented here.

5.2   Procedure

To develop the NVC, eight members of the research team, who were not subject-matter experts, participated in brainstorming activities to provide a list of twenty actions by which the NVC could be matched to ART (e.g., *up, down, forward, back, correct action, something is in the way, I don't understand*). The lab members then met in small groups to generate potential sound and lighting sequences to describe the actions. Regarding which sounds and lights were best matched to a given action, there was consistency, both within the groups (e.g., by a group discussion) and between the groups (e.g., after all the focus groups were conducted, each team member completed a survey about his or her sound and lighting contribution). This information served as the beginning for the research sessions. Each focus group session was conducted in less than sixty minutes. The survey was completed in less than sixty minutes.

Data for this descriptive study were collected through structured interviews and recorded on a personal computer. Approval from the appropriate institutional review boards was obtained prior to data collection. Clinicians at RCP were interviewed in focus groups of 3-5 over three days. Each clinician had participated in previous research sessions for ART, were familiar with the research efforts, reviewed the study's informational letter, and had given consent to participate. The clinicians were told the purpose of the study was to evaluate lights and sounds, two features to be added to ART, as each related to patient-clinician communication with an assistive robot. Each session had one research moderator and a note-taker for every two participants. The clinicians sat across from the research moderator at a long table with the note-taker beside the volunteer. Audio speakers to play the sounds were placed on the table in front of the clinicians equidistant from each other and the clinicians.

Two feedback methodologies were used: open-ended response and a forced-choice methodology. Open-ended questions were used to determine clinician preferences for NVC in healthcare environments. The forced choice methodology required the clinicians to verbally select their preference from a choice of *A, B, or Neither* after each sound played (two sounds for each of the 20 ART actions). Similarly, the clinicians chose between two lighting prototype designs (individual LEDs or LED screen) that were presented. The clinicians were told that the lighting would display information regarding the 20 ART actions. Finally, on a sheet of paper showing three architectural-drawn views of ART, each clinician marked where he or she thought the light communication displays should be located (Fig. 4) and verbally answered how he or she would customize the display. Each focus group took less than sixty minutes.

6   Results

Figure 3 shows the percentage preferences of the clinicians for the 20 sounds tested. More than two-thirds (66%) of the clinicians had to select the sound for it to be evaluated as a preferred sound. Interestingly, a specific *Can't Do* sound was chosen by all clinicians in the study. The clinicians maintained a majority preference for the *Reprimand* (92%), *Something in the way* (84%), and *Confirm request* (76%) sounds.

> 66% agreement	< 66% agreement
Can't Do (A)	Down
Reprimand (A)	Stop
Something in the way (B)	Pet
Confirm Request (B)	*Swipe*
Go (N)	Come
Bend out (N)	Emergency
Bend in (N)	I'm thinking
	Select
	Tilt Forward
	Tilt Back
	Do not understand request
	Up
	Drag

Fig. 3. Clinician Agreement on Sounds

Of the seven sounds that had a preferred choice, three sounds (*Go, Bend Out, Bend In*) had a preference for *Neither* sound. The *Bend Out* and *Bend In* sounds relate to an added therapy surface feature (see figure 2) that will be used by clinicians to help expedite stroke patient recovery. Overall, the clinicians did not feel that a sound was required for these movements because clinicians would be interacting with the patient during these sessions. Because the *Go* sound is an important feature designed for the mobility of ART, it will be retested and evaluated in a session with an interactive prototype to ensure that the sound is not required. The remaining sounds that did not have majority preference will also be retested in a future research session with an interactive prototype.

Figure 4 shows the clinicians' location preferences for selected lighting display prototypes as a ``heat map". Four participants chose an LED screen, six participants chose the individual LEDs, and three participants chose both displays. The green color represents the individual LEDs, and the blue color represents a LED screen. The color shade variations describe the number of participants who placed the lighting type in the same location. From this data, we can see a trend for the lighting displays. The individual LEDs were drawn on the edges of ART, while the LED screens were drawn primarily on ART's table top surface. Clinicians' preferences for customization of the lights included the brightness of the LEDs and the colors displayed, primarily red, green, yellow. However, one participant noted that red and green should not be used due to patients who are color blind.

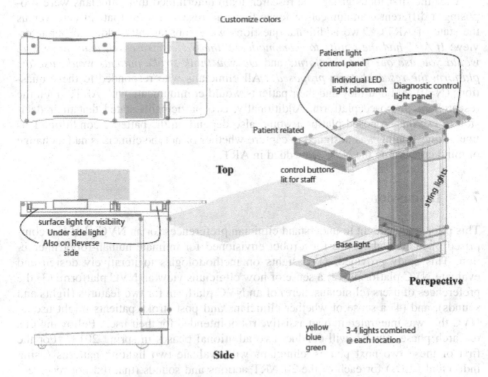

Fig. 4. Clinician Lighting Location Heatmap

At the beginning of each study session, clinicians were asked the following: *If ART had the ability to communicate, would the clinicians communicate with ART?*. The clinicians unanimously agreed that they would like to communicate with ART. Clinicians then answered 12 open-ended questions regarding what types of information are appropriate in the healthcare setting, how the information should be communicated, and the interaction with stroke patients. Finally, clinicians were asked again if they would communicate with ART. Again, 100% of the clinicians said that they would like to communicate with this assistive robot.

Interestingly, the clinicians proposed a different nonverbal communication focus than the research team; the clinicians proposed patient care terminology instead of "the state of ART" terminology (e.g., up, down, emergency) proposed by the research team. A content analysis, developed by frequency analysis, showed that 10 clinicians preferred that ART communicate orientation information (e.g., day, date, time, schedule, nurse's name) to the patients. Eleven clinicians stated that they would program ART to give the patients clinical reminders (e.g., bed safety, fall safety, therapy assistance) to assist in patient care. Despite no overwhelming majority, clinicians also stated that they would like ART to increase their ability to care for the patient by ART communicating to the clinician the patient's vital signs, if the patient attempted to get out of bed, and if the patient attempted to perform their therapy homework.

After the first focus group, the research team determined that clinicians were proposing a different communication focus than the research team (patient care versus the state of ART). Two additional questions were subsequently added to our interview: *If ART had the ability to `communicate' the way the research team proposed, would you use our NVC platform?* and *Do you think stroke patients would use the platform the research team proposed?*. All clinicians who responded to these questions (N=9) said that they and their patients would communicate with ART, given the researchers' proposed platform. Additionally, two participants stated that their decision to use our proposed platform would also depend on the patient's condition. This line of questioning was designed to capture whether or not the clinicians had a change of mind concerning the NVC embedded in ART.

7   Discussion

This pilot study sought to understand clinician preferences for an NVC platform comprised of lights and sounds for a robot envisioned for intimate human-robot interaction. This study provided: (1) insights on methodologies to iteratively design and evaluate NVC platforms, (2) a sense of how clinicians view an NVC platform, (3) the preferences of users (clinicians, here) of an NVC platform for two features (lights and sounds), and (4) a sense of whether clinicians and post-stroke patients might use an NVC that was integrated into an assistive robot intended for their use. Following this research phase, our lab will conduct two additional phases in spring 2013. For the first of these two next phases, clinicians will evaluate two lighting patterns (using individual LEDs) for each of the 20 ART actions and sounds (that did not receive a majority preference for specific ART actions) with the working ART prototype. In the last of the anticipated research phases, clinicians will evaluate a refined list of lighting patterns and sounds embedded within our final ART prototype.

In NVC research, researchers should consider both clinician and patient input, ambient monitoring, the ability of the NVC platform to ``understand" (i.e., learn of) its users, and the ability of an assistive robot like ART to convey information. NVC platforms must be integral with the robot, developed to accept multiple sources of input, act on the data given, and present data back to the user. More broadly, a dynamic NVC like ours may improve job performance of caregivers and increase patient satisfaction.

Acknowledgment. This research was supported by the U.S. National Science Foundation under award IISSHB-116075.

References

1. Merino, J., Threatt, A.L., Walker, I.D., Green, K.E.: Forward kinematic model for continuum robotic surfaces. In: 2012 IEEE/RSJ International Conference on Intelligent Robots and Systems, Vilamoura, Algarve, Portugal (October 2012)
2. Threatt, A.L., Merino, J., Green, K.E., Walker, I.D., Brooks, J.O., et al.: A vision of the patient room as an architectural robotic ecosystem. In: 2012 IEEE/RSJ International Conference on Intelligent Robots and Systems, Vilamoura, Algarve, Portugal (October 2012)

3. Yanik, P., Manganelli, J., Merino, J., Threatt, T., Brooks, J.O., Green, K.E., Walker, I.D.: Use of kinect depth data and growing neural gas for gesture based robot control. In: PervaSense2012, the 4th International Workshop for Situation Recognition and Medical Data Analysis in Pervasive Health Environments, San Diego, California, May 21, pp. 283–290 (2012)

4. Green, K.E., Walker, I.D., Brooks, J.O., Logan Jr., W.C.: Comfortable: A robotic environment for aging in place. In: HRI 2009, La Jolla, California, USA, March 11-13 (2009)

5. Dautenhahn, K.: Socially intelligent robots: dimensions of human-robot interaction. Philosophical Transactions of the Royal Society of London - Series B: Biological Sciences 362(1480), 679–704 (2007)

6. Mutlu, B., Bartneck, C., Ham, J., Evers, V., Kanda, T. (eds.): ICSR 2011. LNCS, vol. 7072. Springer, Heidelberg (2011)

7. Syrdal, D.S., Dautenhahn, K., Koay, K.L., Walters, M.L.: The negative attitudes towards robots scale and reactions to robot behaviour in a live human-robot interaction study. In: Proceedings on New Frontiers in Human-Robot Interaction, AISB 2009 Convention, pp. 109–115 (2009)

8. Komatsu, T.: Audio subtle expressions affecting user's perceptions. In: Proceedings of 2006 International Conference on Intelligent User Interface, San Diego, pp. 306–308 (2006)

9. Breazeal, C., Siegel, M., Berlin, M., Gray, J., Grupen, R., Deegan, P., Weber, J., Narendren, K., McBean, J.: Mobile, dexterous, social robots for mobile manipulation and human-robot interaction. In: SIGGRAPH 2008: ACM SIGGRAPH 2008 New Tech Demos, New York (2008)

10. Cassell, J.: A Framework for Gesture Generation and Interpretation. In: Computer Vision in Human-Machine Interaction, Cambridge University Press, Cambridge (1998)

11. Lallee, S., Lemaignan, S., Lenz, A., Melhuish, C., Natale, L., Skachek, S., van Der Tanz, T., Warneken, F., Dominey, P.: Towards a platform-independent cooperative human-robot interaction system: I. perception. In: IROS, Taipei (2010)

12. Rossini, N.: Reinterpreting Gesture as Language. Language "in Action". IOS Press, Amsterdam (2012)

13. Read, R., Belpaeme, T.: Interpreting non-linguistic utterances by robots: studying the influence of physical appearance. In: Proceedings of AFFINE 2010, the 3rd International Workshop on Affective Interaction in Natural Environments, Firenze, Italy, pp. 65–70 (October 29, 2010)

14. The journal of pain of the american pain society: "pain in non-verbal elderly largely undetected by family caregivers"

15. Quenqua, D.: Pushing science's limits in sign language lexicon (December 4, 2012)

16. Matsumoto, N., Fujii, H., Goan, M., Okada, M.: Minimal design strategy for embodied communication agents. In: The 14th IEEE International Workshop on Robot-Human Interaction, Nashville, pp. 335–340 (2005)

17. Okada, M., Sakamoto, S., Suzuki, N.: Muu: Artificial creatures as an embodied interface. In: Proceedings of 27th International Conference on Computer Graphics and Interactive Techniques (SIGGRAPH 2000), New Orleans, p. 91 (July 2000)

18. Yamada, S., Komatsu, T.: Designing Simple and Effective Expressions of Robot's Primitive Minds to a Human. In: Human-Robot Interaction. Itech, Vienna (2007)

19. Burtt, B.: Star Wars: Galactic Phrase Book and Travel Guide. The Ballantine Publishing Group, New York (2001)

Author Index